Y0-DLI-754

Digest of Motor Laws

Summary of laws and regulations governing the
operation of passenger cars in the United States,
its Territories, and the Provinces of Canada.

For information concerning the availability of this publication
contact your AAA club or:

AAA Government Relations

607 14th Street, NW, Suite 200

Washington, DC 20005

202-942-2050

Copyright AAA 2006
ISBN: 1-59508-158-5
ISBN 13: 978-1-59508-158-2

Special thanks to the Insurance Institute for Highway Safety
for information related to automated enforcement and electric personal
assistive mobility devices.

Table of Contents

UNITED STATES

Alabama	1	Montana	216
Alaska	7	Nebraska	227
Arizona	12	Nevada	235
Arkansas	19	New Hampshire	246
California	26	New Jersey	255
Colorado	35	New Mexico	264
Connecticut	42	New York	272
Delaware	49	North Carolina	282
District of Columbia	55	North Dakota	293
Florida	62	Ohio	301
Georgia	71	Oklahoma	310
Hawaii	80	Oregon	321
Idaho	89	Pennsylvania	331
Illinois	97	Rhode Island	341
Indiana	105	South Carolina	350
Iowa	113	South Dakota	360
Kansas	125	Tennessee	369
Kentucky	134	Texas	377
Louisiana	141	Utah	388
Maine	151	Vermont	399
Maryland	159	Virginia	407
Massachusetts	170	Washington	415
Michigan	178	West Virginia	427
Minnesota	187	Wisconsin	437
Mississippi	197	Wyoming	446
Missouri	207		

U.S. TERRITORIES

American Samoa 454	Puerto Rico 467
Guam 459	Virgin Islands 474

PROVINCES OF CANADA

Alberta 482	Nova Scotia 533
British Columbia 491	Ontario 541
Manitoba 500	Prince Edward Island 550
New Brunswick 509	Québec 556
Newfoundland and Labrador 517	Saskatchewan 566
Northwest Territories 526	Yukon Territory 573

APPENDIX

General Information 582

Foreign Driver's License/Registration 587

State Insurance Commission Offices 590

Accident Report Filing 593

Alcohol Laws Chart 596

Automated Enforcement Chart 604

Distracted Driving Chart 614
(Hand-held Cell Phone Ban, Teen Driver Ban, Distracted/Negligent Driving, Study/Data Collection, State Preemption, School Bus Driver Ban)

Driver's License Laws Chart 618
(Graduated Licensing, Older Drivers, Vision Requirements, Social Security Number on License, Duration in Years/Expiration Date, Non-Resident Violator Compact)

Electric Personal Assistive Mobility Devices 626

Gas Tax Chart 632

Motor Vehicle Registration Chart 634
(No-Fault Insurance, Transfer of Plates, Plate Color Scheme, Vehicle Inspection, Onboard Diagnostics (OBD))

Occupant Protection Chart 642
(Child Restraint Laws, Safety Belt Use Laws, Standard Enforcement)

Other Traffic Laws Chart 646
(Headlight Use, Studded Tires, Hazard Light Usage, Tire Chains, Accident Reports, Radar Detectors)

State Safety Chart 650
(Aggressive Driving, Riding Between Lanes on a Motorcycle, Speed Limits, Left Foot Braking, Left Lane Restrictions, Turning, Helmets)

Title & Registration Fees Chart 656

Towing Chart 668

Since 1902, AAA has represented the interests of its members on Capitol Hill and in state legislatures. AAA was actually founded as an advocacy organization to improve the quality and safety of our roadways. Today, AAA supports a vast array of traffic safety measures, including legislation to protect novice drivers, curtail drunk driving, and promote the use of child restraints. Our commitment to providing safety, security, and peace of mind to our members is unwavering.

In 2006, AAA will continue to emphasize child passenger safety, distracted driving, drunk driving countermeasures, senior mobility, and teen driver safety. For more information about these initiatives, contact your local AAA club.

Digest of Motor Laws

The Digest of Motor Laws is prepared from information compiled from state statutes and regulations as well as submissions from local and state jurisdictions to AAA. Information relating to motor vehicle laws of the 50 states, territories, and the provinces of Canada is classified under those major topics covering general interest subjects on private passenger vehicles. Limited coverage of laws governing commercial vehicles is included. Some special laws relating to motorcycles and mopeds have been included.

The information contained in this book reflects state statutes as of November 2005. While AAA makes every effort to provide accurate and complete information, AAA makes no warranty, expressed or implied, and assumes no legal liability or responsibility for the accuracy or completeness of any information contained herein.

Section descriptions are contained in the Appendix, General Information section. Also included for your quick reference in the Appendix are charts pertaining to alcohol laws, automated enforcement laws, driver's licensing laws, electric personal assistive mobility devices, gas taxes, motor vehicle registration, occupant protection, title and registration fees and information, towing regulations, and various state safety and traffic laws.

ALABAMA

Contact Information

Alabama Department of Revenue (ADOR)
Motor Vehicle Division
50 North Ripley Street
Montgomery, AL 36132-7123

(334) 242-9000
www.ador.state.al.us

Alabama Department of Public Safety (DPS)
Highway Patrol Division
301 South Ripley Street
Montgomery, AL 36104-4425

(334) 242-4128
www.dps.state.al.us

Alabama Department of Transportation (ADOT)
1409 Coliseum Boulevard
Montgomery, AL 36110

(334) 242-6358
www.dot.state.al.us

Vehicle Title

Application: Application is made to ADOR for 1975 and all subsequent year motor vehicles.

- All applications contain certification from designated agent verifying (1) physical inspection of vehicle; (2) accuracy of vehicle identification number and descriptive data; and (3) identification of person signing application.
- Application for certificate of title must contain (1) owner's name, current residence, and mailing address; (2) description of vehicle; (3) date of purchase; (4) name and address of person vehicle acquired from; and (5) lienholder information, if relevant. For first certificates other than for new vehicles, must contain either copy of notarized bill of sale or certified copies of license tags and tax receipts from previous 2 years, in lieu of manufacturer statement of origin.
- If vehicle purchased from dealer, must contain (1) name and address of lienholder; (2) date of security agreement; and (3) signature of dealer and owner.
- If application for new vehicle, must contain manufacturer's statement of origin.
- If application refers to vehicle registered in another state or country, application must contain certificate of title issued by state or country, and information reasonably required to establish ownership.

Transfer of Ownership: If owner transfers interest in vehicle, except by creation of security interest, may execute assignment and warranty of title at time of vehicle delivery.

- If dealer buys car to resell and obtains certificate of title within 15 days of vehicle delivery, must execute assignment and warranty of title upon vehicle transfer to another person, unless transfer by security interest.
- If owner interest is terminated or vehicle sold under security agreement by lienholder, application must contain last certificate of title, assignment of title, and affidavit certifying that vehicle is repossessed and that interest lawfully terminated or sold pursuant to security agreement.

Mobile Homes: Application is made to ADOR for 1990 and all subsequent year mobile homes and travel trailers.

- If mobile home is affixed to real property, and ownership of mobile home and real property is identical, owner may obtain cancellation of title to mobile home provid-

ed (1) mobile home title; (2) certified copy of deed or conveyance instruments of real property; (3) affidavit certifying ownership interests; and (4) lien release forms are sent to ADOR.
- 1990 and subsequent year mobile homes and travel trailers subject to certificate of title; utility trailers not exceeding 16 feet in length, excluding the tongue and the hitch and with not more than one axle exempt, beginning January 1, 2004.

Vehicle Registration

Application: Upon acquiring motor vehicle, registration with probate judge or county official must occur within 20 calendar days from purchase date.

Non-Residents: Non-residents must register vehicle in Alabama within 30 days from date of entry, or expiration of previous tag, whichever comes first. Must have title application; certificate of title; or certification from the previous state that titles were not issued in that year. Then previous state registration must be produced. Vehicles must be inspected by the state unless owner is a college student or in the military. Vehicle must be in state.

Registration Type: Staggered — first letter of individual's last name determines month of registration.
- If last name begins with A or D, registration is in January; if B=February; if C or E=March; if F, G, or N=April; if H or O=May; if M or I=June; if P or L=July; if J, K, or R=August; if Q, S, or T=September; if U, V, W, X, Y, or Z=October.
- License plate expires on last day of month preceding month assigned for registration of vehicle.
- Truck, mobile home, and commercial and fleet vehicle registration is in October and November; IRP vehicles registered in an assigned month.

Safety Inspection: City may provide for inspection of motor vehicles operated on its streets, alleys, or highways.

License Plates

Disbursement: License plates for automobiles and pickup trucks with 2 axles and a gross weight not greater than 12,000 lbs. are valid for 5 years.
- During 5 year license period, tabs, stamps, or devices as determined by ADOR must be affixed to the vehicle to indicate expiration.
- Person changing county residence must purchase new license plate upon expiration of previous license plate or at return of old license plate.
- All plates shall be treated with reflective material.
- License plates must be placed at rear of vehicle.
- Distinctive license plate and placard provided for handicapped individual if medical proof submitted.

Transfer of Plates: When motor vehicle is sold or otherwise disposed of, license plate must be removed and may be transferred to a newly acquired vehicle of same class if transfer fees and other regular fees and taxes due on vehicle are paid.

Driver's Licenses

Examination: All persons applying for original driver's license must take a written, oral, vision (20/40 acuity required), and driving examination.

- If individual passes exam, certificate provided to judge of probate or license commissioner in county with application for license; certificate and application forwarded to Director of Public Safety.

Graduated Drivers Licensing: State has a system of graduated licensing for teen drivers.

- At 15, teens are eligible for a learner's/instruction permit.
- Teens must hold the permit for at least 6 months and accumulate at least 30 hours of supervised driving.
- At 16, teens are eligible for an intermediate license. Intermediate license holders are restricted from driving between Midnight and 6:00 a.m.
- At 17 and with 6 months of driving experience with no violations, teens are eligible for an unrestricted license.

Issuance/Application: Driver's license is required before driving motor vehicle in state.

- New residents must obtain driver's license within 30 days of establishing residence.
- License shall contain licensee's assigned number, color photograph, name, birth date, address, personal description, and signature.
- At issuance, oath administered and color photograph taken by judge of probate or license commissioner.
- License shall not be issued to habitual drug or alcohol user.
- A person 16 years of age or older, having met all state requirements, is eligible to obtain a driver's license pursuant to conditions of the graduated driver license law.
- A person 16 years of age or older may apply for a learner's permit for a 4-year period that permits the driver to operate a motor vehicle so long as a licensed driver is occupying the seat beside the driver.
- A person older than 15 but under 16 years of age may obtain a permit license for a 4-year period to operate a motor vehicle when a parent or legal guardian is occupying the seat beside the driver.
- All licenses are good for 4 years, except for CDL permit, which is good for 1 year.

Renewal: Renewal license issued after the expiration of original license does not require examination.

- After original license expires, subsequent renewals are required 4 years from the expiration date of the original license, regardless of when the preceding license is issued. Exception: CDL permits are not renewable.
- Renewal notice mailed to each licensee 30 days after expiration date of license, if not yet renewed.
- Grace period of 60 days granted after the expiration of license for purpose of renewal, and license is valid during this period.
- Renewal of license may occur from 30 days prior to expiration to 3 years after date; afterwards, applicant required to take and pass examination.
- Any valid driver license in possession of a person on active duty with the armed forces, their dependents, or any person temporarily out of Alabama at license renewal time may be eligible to renew by mail with submission of proper documents. Upon return to the state, the licensee should apply for a duplicate license with photo at the office of the probate judge or license commissioner.

AL

- A valid home state license of military personnel and their dependents is honored while based in state.

Types of Licenses: Class A, B, C, D, M, V licenses valid for 4 years. CDL permit valid for 1 year.

- Class A is valid for driver with combination of vehicles with Gross Vehicle Weight Rating (GVWR) of greater than 26,001 lbs., if vehicle is towing an excess of 10,000 lbs.
- Class B is valid for single vehicle with GVWR of 26,001 lbs. or more, and vehicle is not towing an excess of 10,000 lbs.
- Class C is valid for single vehicle with GVWR of less than 26,001 lbs. or vehicle towing another vehicle that has a GVWR that does not exceed 10,000 lbs., which includes vehicles designed to carry 16 or more passengers with the driver, and vehicles used to transport hazardous materials.
- Class M is valid for motorcycle and motor-driven cycles.
- Class V is valid for motorized watercraft.

Traffic Rules

Alcohol Laws: By operating vehicle, a person is presumed to have consented to chemical tests of blood, breath, or urine. Open containers are not permitted. Meets TEA-21 requirements.

- Illegal per se BAC level is 0.08.
- BAC level for people under 21 is .02.
- BAC level for commercial drivers is .04.

Emergency Radio/Cellular: Emergency phone number is 911 or *HP (*47).

- Citizen band radio channel 9 is monitored in some areas for emergency calls.

Headsets: Wearing of radio headsets while operating a motor vehicle is permitted.

Occupant Restraints: Front seat occupants are required to wear seat belts when the vehicle is in motion.

- Child passenger restraints are required for children under 4 years of age if the motor vehicle registered in state; children 4 and 5 must be in seat belts or child restraints in front and back seats.
- Violation of occupant restraint laws is a primary offense.
- Riding in the back of an unenclosed pickup truck is permitted.

Railroad Crossing: Driver shall keep to the right half of highway at railroad crossing unless area is obstructed or impassable.

- School buses, vehicles carrying explosives, and buses or trucks carrying passengers must stop at all railroad crossings.

School Buses: Upon meeting or overtaking in either direction a school bus receiving or discharging children, or a church bus receiving or discharging passengers, driver must stop and not proceed until bus resumes movement or visual signals are no longer actuated.

Vehicle Equipment & Rules

Bumper Height: Modification of original vehicle bumper height is permitted.

Glass/Window Tinting: Tinting of front windshield glass to reduce light transmission is not permitted.

- For side windows or rear windshield, glass tinting that reduces light transmission to less than 32% or increases light reflectance to more than 20% is not permitted.

Telematics: No television screen shall be located in front of driver's seat or in a way to obstruct driver's field of vision.

Windshield Stickers: No person may operate motor vehicle with sign, poster, or other non-transparent material that obstructs visibility.

Motorcycles & Mopeds

Equipment: Motor-driven cycle includes every motorcycle that, when equipped, weighs less than 200 lbs., motor scooters, and bicycles with a motor attached.
- Motor-driven cycle shall have brakes adequate to control movement and stopping of vehicle.
- Motorcycle carrying passengers, except in sidecar or enclosed cab, shall have footrests for passenger.
- No person shall operate motorcycle with handlebars more than 15 inches in height above seat.
- Protective headgear and shoes required for motorcycle operators and passengers.
- No parent or legal guardian of juvenile shall knowingly permit or allow juvenile to operate or ride motorcycle without protective headgear or shoes.

Licenses: A driver's license issued pursuant to state law suffices to operate a motor-driven cycle.
- A person 14 years of age or older may obtain an operator's permit for motor-driven cycle and must register with the Director of Public Safety.

Mopeds: Registration and license plate are required.
- Minimum age to ride a moped is 14.
- The following safety equipment is required: headlamp, taillamp, stop lamp, side and rear reflectors, brakes, mirrors, horn, muffler, helmet, and shoes.

Passenger Car Trailers

Brakes: Independent braking system required over 3,000 lbs.

Dimensions: Total length: not specified; trailer length: 40 feet (includes bumpers); width: 96 inches (102 inches allowed on designated roads); height: 13.6 feet.

Hitch/Signals: Drawbar or connection between vehicles must not exceed 15 feet in length; a red flag, other signal, or cloth not less than 12 inches in length and width must be used.

Lighting: Trailer, semitrailer, pole trailer, or vehicle drawn by another vehicle must be equipped with at least one taillamp on rear that emits red light from a distance of 500 feet and the lamp height must be no more than 60 inches but not less than 20 inches.
- Trailer, semitrailer, or pole trailer with a gross weight of 3,000 lbs. or less must have two reflectors on the rear with one placed on each side.
- If load or trailer obscures stop light view of towing vehicle, stop light must be placed on towed vehicle.

Mirrors: Rearview mirrors required on both sides.

AL

Speed Limits: Must be reasonable and proper.

Other Provisions: Riding in towed trailer not permitted.
- House trailers more than 40 feet long or 8 feet wide excluded without state permit.
- Maximum of one boat or general utility trailer may be towed behind passenger or pleasure vehicles.

Miscellaneous Provisions

Bail Bonds: Maximum amount not to exceed sum of $300.

Liability Laws: State has security-type law applicable in event of accident causing property damage in excess of $250 or personal injury or death. Minimum required coverage is $20,000 for bodily injury or death of 1 person in 1 accident; $40,000 for 2 or more persons in any 1 accident; and $10,000 for injury or destruction of property in 1 accident.
- State has non-resident service of process law and guest suit law.

Weigh Stations: An officer may require the measuring or weighing of truck or trailer.
- Measurement may be conducted by portable or stationary scales.
- Officer may order truck or trailer to stationary scales if within a distance of 5 miles.

Fees & Taxes

Table 1: Title & Registration Fees

Vehicle Type	Title Fee	Registration Fee
Motor Vehicle	$18.00	$23.00 + issuance fee (may differ by county)
Mobile Home	$18.00	$24.00-$96.00 + issuance fee (may differ by county)
Utility or Travel Trailers	$18.00	$12.00-$15.00
Full or Semitrailers of more than 10,000 lbs.	$18.00	$12.00-$15.00
Non-Commercial Trailer less than 6,000 lbs.	$18.00	$12.00
Motorcycles	$18.00	$23.00 + issuance fee
Mopeds	$18.00	$16.25
Duplicate Registration		$3.00
Duplicate Plate	$2.00	

Table 2: License Fees

License Class	Fee	Driving Test Fees
A	$53.00	$25.00
B	$43.00	$25.00
C	$23.00	$25.00
D	$23.00	$5.00
Learner's Permit	$23.00	$5.00 (cash) written test fee
Duplicate Fee	$18.00	
Motorcycle	$23.00	$5.00
School Bus	$23.00	$25.00

Table 3: Vehicle Taxes

Tax	Rate
Gasoline Tax; (Diesel)	$0.18/gallon; ($0.19/gallon)
State Sales Tax	2%

Table 4: Miscellaneous Fees

Fee	Amount	Payable Upon
Air Quality Fee	N/A	N/A
Delinquent Registration / Transfer Fee	$10.00 + interest	Registration
Non-Resident Daily Commuter Fee	N/A	N/A
Special Plates Fee	$50.00	
Special Plates Transfer Fee	$1.25 + local fees	

ALASKA

Contact Information

Division of Motor Vehicles (DMV)
3300 B Fairbanks Street
Anchorage, AK 99503

(907) 269-5559
www.state.ak.us/dmv/

Alaska State Troopers, Department of Public Safety
5700 East Tudor Road
Anchorage, AK 99507

(907) 269-5976
www.dps.state.ak.us

Alaska Department of Transportation, Office of the Commissioner
3132 Channel Drive
Juneau, AK 99801-7898

(907) 465-3900
www.dot.state.ak.us/

Vehicle Title

Application: Application is made to the DMV, and must contain the signature of the vehicle owner and previous owner's certificate of title or manufacturer's statement of origin.

Transfer of Ownership: For any vehicle less than 10 years old, the transferor must include an odometer statement.

Vehicle Registration

Application: A registration application can be made at any local office of the DMV, and an applicant must show proof of insurance and a vehicle title.

Non-Residents: Non-residents must register their vehicles in Alaska within 60 days, and must surrender out-of-state title.

- Non-residents accepting employment in the state must register their vehicles within 10 days of commencing work.

Registration Type: Registration is biennial.

AK

Emissions Inspection: Emissions inspections are done every 2 years, but only in designated areas of the state. Currently, only Fairbanks and Anchorage require the inspections.

Safety Inspection: State troopers may inspect vehicles at roadside when there is reasonable cause to believe vehicle is unsafe.

License Plates

Disbursement: Two plates are required on vehicles. Plates before 1997 will have blue on yellow/gold; plates beginning in 1997 will celebrate the Gold Rush Centennial, and will be black on blue sky, with white mountains and trail climbers.
- License plates are reflectorized.
- Plates are validated biennially with a sticker that is placed on the rear license plate.
- Disability plates are available upon application and a medical certificate.

Transfer of Plates: License plates remain with the car upon transfer, unless they are specialty plates.

Driver's Licenses

Examination: For an original license, applicants must pass a written exam, vision test (20/40 vision acuity required), and driving test.

Graduated Licensing: State has a system of graduated licensing for teen drivers.
- At 14, teens are eligible for a learner's permit. During this stage, teens must be supervised by a parent or guardian at all times.
- At 16, teens are eligible for a provisional license. Provisional license holders are restricted from driving between 1:00 a.m. and 5:00 a.m. and transporting passengers under age 21, with the exception of family members.
- In this stage, provisional license holders must accumulate 40 hours of supervised driving during the permit stage—including 10 hours in "progressively challenging circumstances" such as inclement weather and nighttime conditions.
- Teens are eligible for a full unrestricted license after 6 months if they have not been convicted of a violation of a traffic law or at age 18.

Issuance/Application: Drug or alcohol motor vehicle offenses can cause postponement of new driver's license eligibility.
- License is valid for 5 years, and expires on the birthday of the licensee.
- Non-residents have 90 days before they are required to apply for an Alaskan license.
- A photo is required on driver's licenses, except in special circumstances.
- Individuals on active duty military orders stationed in Alaska that choose to remain a resident of another state are not required to obtain a license in Alaska. This applies only to active duty personnel and not to dependents. Military dependents are required to surrender their out-of-state license and obtain a license in Alaska.
- Licenses do not normally include social security numbers.

Renewal: Renewal by mail is allowed.
- Non-commercial driver's licenses for military personnel are valid for 90 days after discharge or return to the State of Alaska, whichever occurs first. License remains valid as long as resident remains on active duty.

Types of Licenses: Commercial:

- Class A: combination of a motor vehicle and one or more other vehicles with a Gross Vehicle Weight Rating (GVWR) greater than 26,000 lbs.; where GVWR of vehicle(s) being towed is less than 10,000 lbs.
- Class B: a motor vehicle with a GVWR of greater than 26,000 lbs., or a motor vehicle greater than 26,000 lbs. that is towing a vehicle of less than 10,000 lbs.
- Class C: a motor vehicle or a combination of a motor vehicle and one or more other vehicles with a GVWR of greater than 26,000 lbs. where the GVWR of the towing vehicle is less than 26,000 lbs.; or a vehicle not described in Class A or B and is either designed to transport more than 15 passengers or transports hazardous materials.

Non-commercial:
- Class D: for automobiles other than commercial vehicles or motorcycles.
- Class M1: for motorcycles.
- Class M2: for motor-driven cycles and motorized bicycles.
- Class IP: instruction permit for Class D.
- Class IM: instruction permit for Class M1 or M2.

Traffic Rules

Alcoholic Beverage Container: Alaska has an implied consent law.
- Open containers are not permitted.
- Does not meet TEA-21 requirements.
- Illegal per se BAC level is .08.
- BAC level for people under 21 is .00.
- BAC level for commercial drivers is .04.

Bicycles: Operators of bicycles must obey the motor vehicle laws.
- Cyclists must ride with traffic.
- There is no helmet requirement for cyclists.

Emergency Radio/Cellular: The emergency phone number is either 911 or *273.

Headsets: Wearing an audio headset is not permitted while operating a motor vehicle.
- Headsets are allowed when used and designed to help the driver's hearing ability.

Lane Restrictions: There are no left lane restrictions on divided highways.

Occupant Restraints: All passengers age 16 and up must wear seat belts while vehicle is being operated.
- All passengers under the age of 4 need to be in a child safety seat.
- All passengers between the ages of 4-16 need either a seat belt or safety seat.
- Violation of the seat belt law is a secondary offense, however violation of the child restraint law is a primary offense.
- Riding in the back of a pickup truck bed is permitted.

Railroad Crossing: All vehicles are required to stop when warning signs indicate to stop.
- School buses and vehicles carrying fuel or hazardous material are required to stop at all railroad crossings.

School Buses: Vehicles must stop for buses when loading or unloading passengers.
- Vehicles are not required to stop if on the opposite side of a divided highway.
- School buses are to be painted National School Bus Chrome Yellow.

Vehicle Equipment & Rules

Bumper Height: Modifications of original vehicle bumper height is permitted. Maximum height 24 inches up to 4,500 lbs. GVWR; 26 inches for 4,501 to 7,500 lbs. GVWR; and 28 inches for 7,501 to 10,000 lbs. GVWR.

Glass/Window Tinting: The front windshield can have tinting applied, but only on the top 5 inches of the window.
- Side windows must have 70% light transmittance.
- Rear windows must have 40% light transmittance.
- Mirrored tints are not allowed.

Telematics: A television screen may not be installed where the viewer or screen is visible from the driver's seat.
- Television-type equipment is allowed for navigational devices such as GPS or Loran.

Windshield Stickers: Stickers cannot obstruct the view of the driver.

Motorcycles & Mopeds

Equipment: Glasses, goggles, or a windscreen is required.
- Reflectorized helmets are required for operators age 17 and under and for passengers of all ages.
- Left and right rearview mirrors are required.
- Passenger seat and footrests are required if carrying passengers.
- A license plate is required.
- Daytime headlights must be on while the motorcycle is in operation.
- Helmet speakers are prohibited.
- Taillights are required.

Licenses: Licenses are required for operators at least 16 years old.
- Learner's permits are available for those age 14, but they must ride under the supervision of a licensed motorcycle operator at least 19 years old.
- Operators under age 18 are required to have a 6-month instruction permit.
- A license is required for mopeds. Drivers must be 14 years old, and the bikes can have a maximum engine size of 50 cc.

Riding Between Lanes: Riding between lanes is prohibited.

Mopeds: Minimum age for driver's license is 14. Helmets are required.

Passenger Car Trailers

Brakes: An independent braking system is required when gross weight exceeds 5,000 lbs.
- A breakaway system capable of applying all required brakes in the event of a separation from the towing vehicle is required.

Dimensions: Total length: 75 feet (includes bumpers); trailer length: 40 feet (includes bumpers); width: 102 inches; height: 14 feet.

Hitch: A vehicle towed upon a street or highway must be coupled to the towing vehicle by means of a safety chain, chains, cable, or other equivalent device, in addition to the regular hitch or coupling.

AK

- The additional connecting safety devices must be connected to both the towing and towed vehicles and to the drawbar or other rigid connecting device so as to prevent the device from dropping to the ground in the event of a failure.
- The additional safety devices must be of sufficient strength to retain control of the towed vehicle in the event of failure.

Lighting: The following lights are required on trailers: taillights, brake lights, license plate lights, turn signals, 2 clearance lights, 2 side markers, and 2 reflectors.

Mirrors: Two mirrors are required on a towing vehicle: the left side mirror is required, and 1 mirror may be an interior mirror.

Speed Limits: The maximum speed while towing a mobile home is 45 mph.

Special Provisions: Riding in a house trailer while it is being towed is prohibited.

- Riding in the back of a pickup or camper is permitted.

Miscellaneous Provisions

Liability Laws: Mandatory insurance law applies to all accidents involving death, injury, or more than $501 damage to property of any 1 person.

Minimum financial responsibility limits:
- $50,000 due to bodily injury or death of 1 person in 1 accident.
- $100,000 due to bodily injury or death of 2 or more persons in 1 accident.
- $25,000 due to injury to or destruction of property of others in 1 accident.
- Alaska has a non-resident service of process law.

Weigh Stations: Trucks over 10,000 lbs. GVWR are required to stop.

Fees & Taxes

Table 1: Title & Registration Fees

Vehicle Type	Title Fee	Registration Fee
Automobiles	$5.00	$100.00, once every 2 years
Pickup Truck or Van Not Exceeding 10,000 lbs.	$5.00	$78.00, once every 2 years
Motorcycle or Motor-Driven Cycle	$5.00	$38.00, once every 2 years
Trailer Not Used or Maintained for a Commercial Purpose		$10.00, once every 2 years
Commercial Trailer		$10.00 permanent registration
Duplicates	$5.00	$2.00

Table 2: License Fees

License Class	Fee	Driving Test Fees
A	$100.00	$25.00
B	$100.00	$25.00
C	$100.00	$25.00
D	$15.00	$15.00
Motorcycle License	$20.00	$15.00
Instruction Permit	$15.00	
Duplicate License Fee	$15.00	
Temporary License Fee	$5.00	
Renewal by Mail	extra $1.00	

Table 3: Vehicle Taxes

Tax	Rate
Motor Vehicle Registration Tax	Biennial tax, for passenger cars and trucks, begins at $121 for the 1st year, and declines to $16 for the 8th and subsequent years; for motorcycles and trailers, the range goes from $17 to $4
Personal Property Tax	None
State Sales Tax	None
Gasoline Tax; (Diesel)	$0.08/gallon; ($0.08/gallon)

Table 4: Miscellaneous Fees

Tax	Amount	Payable Upon
Registration and Plate Reinstatement Fee	$50.00	Reinstatement of registration and suspended plates due to cancellation or non-renewal of liability insurance policy
Emission Control Inspection Fee	$2.00	Only in designated parts of the state, payable at inspection
Historic Vehicle Fee	$10.00	Initial registration
Special Registration Fee	$30.00-$50.00	Biennially
Special Plates Fee	$50.00-$150.00	Disbursement of plate
Disabled Plates Fee	$0	
Duplicate Plates	$5.00	Application

ARIZONA

Contact Information

Motor Vehicle Division (MVD)
P.O. Box 2100
Phoenix, AZ 85001-2100

(602) 255-0072
www.azdot.gov/mvd

Department of Public Safety
Highway Patrol Division
P.O. Box 6638
Phoenix, AZ 85005

(602) 223-2000
www.dps.state.az.us

Arizona Department of Transportation (ADOT)
206 South 17th Avenue
Phoenix, AZ 85007

(602) 712-7227
www.azdot.gov

Vehicle Title

Application: Application is made to ADOT within 15 days of purchase or transfer of vehicle.

- Transferee must sign application.
- If vehicle previously registered, application must contain odometer mileage disclosure statement.
- If a new vehicle, must contain certificate from manufacturer showing date of sale

to dealer, name of dealer, description of vehicle, statement certifying vehicle was new when sold.
- Applicants that appear in person may be required to take a vision-screening test.
- No certificate of title is required for mopeds.

Transfer of Ownership: Transferor must deliver an odometer mileage disclosure statement unless the vehicle is 10 years old or older or the vehicle has a gross vehicle weight of 16,000 lbs. or more.

- If vehicle is registered, the registration expires and the owner shall transfer the license plates to the department or an authorized third party or submit affidavit of license plate destruction within 30 days of transfer of title.
- If transfer is by operation of law, transferee has 30 days to apply for new title.

Mobile Homes: Must be titled with department unless the mobile home is permanently affixed.

- A mobile home consisting of 2 or more separate sections must have a title for each section.

Vehicle Registration

Application: Application is made to ADOT and must include name and residence of owner, date of sale if a new vehicle, vehicle description, and certificate of title.

- Registration cards issued by the department must be carried in the vehicle at all times.
- A vehicle belonging to a person must be registered in the county where the person maintains a permanent and actual residence.
- Registration may be done via mail, internet, in person, or by an authorized third party.

Non-Residents: A resident is defined as a person that remains in the state for an aggregate period of 7 months or more during a calendar year; a person that engages in work other than seasonal or temporary work; a person that places children in public school without paying non-resident tuition; a person that declares residency in the state for purposes of state rates of tuition or licensing fees; or a company that maintains a main office in the state.

- It is illegal for a person to operate a motor vehicle unless it has been properly registered for the current year in the state or county in which the person is a resident.

Registration Type: Biennial Registration — vehicles not otherwise disqualified may be registered biennially; newly licensed or leased vehicles will be automatically selected for biennial registration.

- **Staggered Registration** — not applicable to vehicles exempt from registration, government vehicles, non-commercial trailers, seasonal agricultural vehicles, mopeds, or vehicles subject to alternative registration.
- If effective date of registration falls between the 1st and the 15th day of the month, annual registration expires on the 15th day of the month 12 months later; biennial registration expires 24 months later.
- If effective date of registration falls between the 16th and last day of the month, annual registration expires on the last day of the month 12 months later; biennial registration expires 24 months later.
- Renewal registration must be submitted no later than the day the prior registration expires.

Emissions Inspection: Emissions inspection is required prior to registration and restrictions vary according to Area A and B.
- Area A includes townships in Maricopa, Yavapai, and Pinal counties; Area B includes select townships in Pima county.
- Vehicles manufactured in or before 1966 are exempt from inspection.
- Vehicles in Area B and manufactured in or before 1980, other than diesel-powered vehicles, must pass the curb idle test condition; vehicles in Area B and manufactured in or after 1981, other than diesel-powered vehicles, must pass the curb idle test condition and the loaded test condition. Exempts collectible vehicles and motorcycles from emission inspections in Area B.
- Vehicles in Area A and manufactured in or after 1981 with a Gross Vehicle Weight (GVW) rating of 8,500 lbs. or less, other than diesel vehicles, must pass a transient loaded test or an on-board diagnostic test; all other vehicles in Area A, except diesel vehicles, must pass a steady state loaded test and a curb idle emissions test.
- Repair and maintenance costs not to exceed $500 in Area A and $300 in Area B.

Safety Inspection: If at any time there is reasonable cause to believe a vehicle is unsafe or improperly equipped, officers and employees of the Department of Public Safety may stop and require a vehicle be submitted to inspection.

License Plates

Disbursement: The department shall issue one plate per vehicle registered.
- Every plate shall be coated with reflective material.
- Mutilated or illegible license plates shall be returned to the department for replacement plates.
- New or replacement plates may be received via mail.
- Special plates for disabled drivers are available upon application.

Transfer of Plates: The owner of a vehicle shall retain the vehicle's license plates when the owner transfers the vehicle to another person.
- The department may assign the plates to a new vehicle of the owner if the new vehicle is of the same type and the owner pays the appropriate transfer fees.
- If the vehicle is not of the same type, the owner must surrender the plates to the department or submit an affidavit of license plate destruction.
- An owner who transfers, submits, or destroys plates is entitled to a credit for the unexpired portion of the fees and taxes paid.

Driver's Licenses

Examination: Examinations are conducted by ADOT or approved third parties, or waived upon documentation of successful completion of a driver education course approved by MVD.
- Examination includes eyesight test (20/40 visual acuity required), written test, roadside demonstration test, and medical questionnaire.
- ADOT retains discretion to require a licensee to submit to re-examination upon giving at least 5 days' notice.

Graduated Drivers Licensing: State has a system of graduated licensing for teen drivers.
- At 15 years and 7 months, teens are eligible for a learner's permit.
- During this stage, teens may not drive unsupervised.

- Teens must hold the permit for at least 5 months and complete a driver education course or have a custodial parent or guardian certify in writing that the applicant has completed at least 25 hours (5 at night) of supervised driving practice, before being eligible for a full license.

Issuance/Application: Persons with conventionally corrected vision must wear corrective lenses at all times while driving.
- Application for license and driver's license must contain a photo image of the applicant.
- License exemptions exist for military personnel and non-residents duly licensed in other states or foreign countries.
- Social security number on license is optional.
- The MVD may not accept another state license as a primary source of identification if it is issued by another state that does not require a driver licensed in that state be lawfully present in the U.S. under federal law.

Renewal: Upon issuance, a driver's license is valid until the applicant's 65th birthday and is renewable thereafter for successive 5-year periods.
- Any valid driver's license issued to a person on active duty is effective without requirement for renewal until 6 months after the date of the person's discharge from the service.

Types of Licenses: Classes A, B, C, D, G, and M.
- Classes A - D permit operation of motor vehicles based on GVW rating and must be renewed every five years.
- Class G is valid for operation of a single motor vehicle with a GVW rating of 26,000 lbs. or less.
- Class M is valid for operation of a motorcycle or moped; class M license can be endorsed on a valid class A, B, C, D, or G license.

Traffic Rules

Alcohol Laws: Operation of a motor vehicle gives implied consent to a test of blood, breath, urine, or other bodily substance for determining blood-alcohol content. Open containers are not permitted. Meets TEA-21 requirements.
- Illegal per se BAC level is .08.
- BAC level for people under 21 is .00.

Cellular Telephone Use: School bus drivers are prohibited from talking on a cell phone and driving, except in emergencies.

Emergency Radio/Cellular: The emergency phone number is 911.
- Citizen band radio channel 9 is monitored for emergency calls in some counties.

Headsets: Licensees of child care facilities must ensure that an individual who uses a motor vehicle to transport enrolled children does not use audio headphones while the car is in motion.
- School bus drivers may not wear headsets whenever the bus is in motion.

Occupant Restraints: The operator of a motor vehicle is charged with requiring all passengers under the age of 16 to be properly restrained and any child under the age of 5 to be properly secured in a child passenger restraint system, otherwise each front seat passenger is held responsible to wear a seat belt.

- Violation of the seat belt law is a secondary offense, however violation of the child restraint law is a primary offense.
- Riding in a pickup truck bed is permitted.

Railroad Crossing: Drivers are not required to stop unless a signal indicates the approach of a train.
- Motor vehicles carrying passengers for hire, school buses, and vehicles containing explosive or flammable materials must stop at all crossings except those in business or residential districts, or where a police officer or signal directs traffic to proceed.

School Buses: Drivers must stop when buses are stopped and displaying alternately flashing signals except when the school bus is on a different roadway or controlled access highway or stopped in a loading zone where pedestrians are not permitted to enter the roadway.

Vehicle Equipment & Rules

Bumper Height: Modification of original vehicle bumper is permitted.

Glass/Window Tinting: Application or installation of a substance or material that alters the color or reduces the light transmittance is permissible for a luminous reflection of 35% or less.

Telematics: It is illegal to drive a motor vehicle equipped with a television screen or any other means of receiving a television broadcast that is located at any point forward of the back of the driver's seat or is visible directly or indirectly to the driver while operating the vehicle.

Windshield Stickers: Windshield stickers are prohibited if driver's view is obstructed.

Motorcycles & Mopeds

Equipment: All motorcycle operators under 18 years of age must wear a protective helmet; all operators must wear protective glasses, goggles, or a transparent face shield unless the motorcycle is equipped with a transparent windshield.
- A rearview mirror, seat for the operator and passengers, and footrests for both operator and passengers are required; handrails for passengers are required.
- Handlebars cannot be above the height of the operator's shoulders.
- License plates shall be displayed on the back of a motorcycle.
- Headlamp modulators are permitted.

Noise Limits: Specific motorcycle noise limits, based on motorcycle model year and rate of speed, are in effect.

Mopeds: Registration and driver's license are required.
- Minimum age to ride a moped is 16.
- The following safety equipment is required: headlight, horn, brakes, muffler, tail light, license plate light, and rearview mirror.

Passenger Car Trailers

Registration: A non-commercial trailer with a gross vehicle weight of 6,000 lbs. or less receives a permanent trailer registration. Travel trailers or tent trailers do not qualify.

Brakes: Independent brake systems are required when the gross weight is 3,000 lbs. or more.

Dimensions: Total length: 65 feet (includes bumpers); trailer length: 40 feet (includes bumpers); width: 96 inches (total width of 102 inches is allowed on certain roads); height: 13.6 feet.
- May pull 2 units if the middle unit has a 5th wheel and brakes and has a weight equal to or greater than the rear unit; the rear unit is 3,000 lbs. or more and is equipped with brakes.

Hitch: Devices used for towing shall not exceed 15 feet from one vehicle to the other.

Lighting: Trailers with a GVW of more than 3,000 lbs. must be equipped with 1 clearance lamp on each side of the front of the vehicle, 2 side marker lamps on each side of the vehicle, 2 reflectors on each side, 2 clearance lamps on the rear, 2 reflectors on the rear, and 1 stoplight on the rear.

Mirrors: Vehicles with trailers that obstruct driver's rear view must be equipped with mirrors that reflect at least 200 feet of the roadway.

Speed Limits: Vehicles towing trailers or semitrailers may not exceed a rate of speed that causes lateral sway.

Towing: Devices used for towing shall not exceed 15 feet from one vehicle to the other.
- If a chain, rope, or cable is being used, a white flag or cloth at least 12 inches square must be displayed on the device itself.

Miscellaneous Provisions

Bail Bonds: Mandatory recognition of AAA Arrest Bond Certificates recognized up to maximum $300 amount.

Border Inspections: Agricultural inspections required for all commercial vehicles.

Liability Laws: Minimum $15,000 financial responsibility for any 1 person in 1 accident, $30,000 for any 2 people in 1 accident; $10,000 for property destruction in any 1 accident.
- State has non-resident service of process law. Does not have guest suit law.

Parking Restrictions: Vehicles parked on roadways with curbs must be parked with right-hand wheels parallel to and within 18 inches of the curb.
- It is illegal to park on a crosswalk, within 15 feet of a fire hydrant, within 20 feet of a crosswalk at an intersection, within 30 feet of approach to any flashing beacon, within 50 feet of the nearest rail of a railroad crossing, within 20 feet of the driveway of a fire station, on a bridge or in a highway tunnel.

Weigh Stations: Any commodity shipped into the state is subject to inspection for agricultural pests.
- Gross weight fees apply to trailers and semitrailers with GVW of 10,000 lbs. or less; motor vehicles or vehicle combination if used primarily for transporting passengers for compensation; a hearse or ambulance or similar vehicle used in conduct of a mortician's business.
- Gross weight fees do not apply to station wagons, pickup trucks, or trailers with a GVW of 6,000 lbs. or less if not used in furtherance of commercial activity.

Fees & Taxes

Table 1: Title & Registration Fees

Vehicle Type	Title Fee	Registration Fee
Motor Vehicle	$4.00	$8.00* ($8.25 in Metro Tucson and Phoenix)
Mobile Home	$7.00 per singles section	
Trailers of 10,000 lbs. or less	$4.00	$245.00
Trailers of more than 10,000 lbs.	$4.00	$145.00 for trailers under 6 years old and $90.00 for trailers at least 6 years old previously registered in another state*
Non-Commercial Trailer less than 6,000 lbs.	$4.00	$20.00 initial; $5.00 renewal
Motorcycles	$4.00	$9.00
Mopeds	N/A	$9.50
Duplicates	$4.00	$4.00

* Plus a $1.50 air quality fee and vehicle license tax.

Table 2: License Fees

License Class	Fee	Driving Test Fees
A	$25.00	$25.00
B	$25.00	$25.00
C	$12.50	$15.50
D, G, M (age 16-39)	$25.00	
D, G, M (age 40-44)	$20.00	
D, G, M (age 45-49)	$15.00	
D, G, M (age 50 or older)	$10.00	
Duplicate License Fees	$4.00	
Endorsements	$10.00 (motorcycles = $7.00)	

Table 3: Vehicle Taxes

Tax	Rate
Air Quality Fee	$1.00 - payable upon registration
Emissions Inspection*	Area A = $25.00 Area B = $9.00
License Tax	based on each $100.00 of vehicle value with a maximum of $2.95 per $100.00; vehicle value decreases 16.25% every 12 months
Gasoline Tax; (Diesel)	$0.18/gallon; ($0.18/gallon)
Non-Resident Daily Commuter Fee	$8.00 - upon filing application
State Sales Tax	5.6% of value less trade-in
Use Fuel Tax	$0.18 per gallon for light class (less than 26,000 lbs. GVW) vehicles $0.26 per gallon for use class (more than 26,000 lbs. GVW) vehicles

* For vehicles over 5 years old (effective 06/30/06).

Table 4: Miscellaneous Fees

Fee	Amount	Payable Upon
Delinquent Registration/ Transfer Fee	$8.00 first month; $4.00 each additional month, not to exceed $100.00	failure to timely register or file transfer
Registration and Plate Reinstatement Fee	$50.00	upon reinstatement of registration and suspended plates due to cancellation or non-renewal of liability insurance policy
Special Plates Fee	$25.00	issue / annual renewal
Special Plates Transfer Fee	$12.00	transfer
License Plate Replacement Fee	$5.00	new issued plates
Gross Weight Fees	$4.00 commercial registration fee plus weight fee ranging from $7.50 for vehicles up to 8,000 lbs. GVW of 75,001 to 80,000	at time of application for registration

ARKANSAS

Contact Information

Office of Motor Vehicles
Department of Finance and Administration
P.O. Box 1272
Little Rock, AR 72203

(501) 682-4630
www.state.ar.us/dfa/motorvehicle

Arkansas State Police
Headquarters
#1 State Police Plaza Drive
Little Rock, AR 72209

(501) 618-8000
www.asp.state.ar.us

Arkansas State Highway & Transportation Department
10324 Interstate 30
Little Rock, AR 72211

(501) 569-2612
www.ahtd.state.ar.us

Vehicle Title

Application: Application is made to the Office of Motor Vehicles for all motor vehicles and shall include a description of the vehicle, a vehicle identification number, and a list of all liens or encumbrances on the vehicle. For new vehicles, an applicant must provide a certificate of origin, and if purchased from a dealer, the application should also include a statement by the dealer or a bill of sale showing any lien retained by the dealer.

- Vehicle titles are permanent. There is no need to renew a title.
- An owner of a mobile home may license the home with the Office of Motor Vehicles.

Transfer of Ownership: The owner shall endorse an assignment and warranty of title upon the certificate of title for the vehicle and shall deliver the certificate of title to the purchaser or transferee at the time of delivery of the vehicle.

- The transferee of any new or used vehicle required to be registered shall do so within 30 days.
- The transferee shall at the time of application present the assigned certificate of title prior to obtaining the new title.
- An odometer reading is required.

Vehicle Registration

Application: Application is made to the Office of Motor Vehicles and shall include the owner's name, bona fide residence, and mailing address, as well as a description of the vehicle.

- Registration cards must be carried in the vehicle at all times and shall be displayed upon demand to a police officer or any officer or employee of the Office of Motor Vehicles; a photocopy of the license is deemed in compliance.
- Within 30 days of becoming a resident, an owner shall obtain a motor vehicle registration; nonresidents physically present in Arkansas for 6 months shall also obtain motor vehicle registration.
- Applications for vehicles under 10 years old must include odometer mileage disclosure statement.
- Applicants may register in person or by mail in the county of residency.
- Vehicle owners are required to show a certificate of origin on the vehicle.
- Proof of insurance is required for new and renewing applications.

Non-Residents: Persons are considered residents of Arkansas if they reside in the state for any period exceeding 6 months in a calendar year, or if domiciled in Arkansas for any period of time. Non-residents with temporary worker's or visitor's permit must register vehicle within 10 days of entering state. Permit is valid for 90 days.

Registration Type: Staggered.

Emissions Inspection: None required.

Safety Inspection: Safety Inspection is not required, but an officer can stop a vehicle for a safety inspection if he believes that the vehicle is unsafe to operate. The officer can issue a safety citation, and the vehicle must be repaired.

License Plates

Disbursement: From January 1, 1998, no plate shall be issued or renewed without satisfactory proof of insurance.

- Upon registration, the owner of every vehicle shall receive a permanent license.
- Every plate shall be reflectorized and shall have imprinted a multicolor reflectorized graphic design or logo that will promote tourism and improve public relations in and out of Arkansas.
- No identical plates shall be issued for more than 1 vehicle.
- Special personalized plates are available for an additional $25.00 fee.
- Special license plates are available for disabled drivers, but must have doctor's certification of disability.
- Owners of permanent license plates may renew their registrations in person or by mail at a county revenue office, or by fax within 45 days of the date of expiration.
- Plates must have sticker bearing expiration date.

- An applicant may renew license plates in the county where he resides in person or by mail to the revenue collector.

Transfer of Plates: An owner may transfer plates from one vehicle to another for a fee of $10.

Driver's Licenses

Examination: Original license requires a written or oral examination, driving test, and vision test.

- Renewal applications and applications by licensed new residents require only a vision test.
- The minimum visual acuity for an unrestricted license is 20/40.

Graduated Drivers Licensing: State has a system of graduated licensing for teen drivers. At 14, teens who have passed the knowledge and vision tests are eligible for an instruction/learner's permit.

- Permit holders may only drive when accompanied by a licensed driver, 18 years of age or older, who has at least 1 year of driving experience and is occupying a seat beside the driver, except in the event the permittee is operating a motorcycle.
- Teens must hold the permit for at least 6 months before being eligible for an intermediate license.
- At 16, teens are eligible for an intermediate license if they have been crash- and conviction-free for at least 6 months.
- Intermediate license holders are prohibited from transporting passengers who are unrestrained.
- The intermediate license will automatically expire when the driver reaches age 18, provided that the driver has been free of a serious accident and conviction of a serious traffic violation for at least 1 year prior to his or her 18th birthday.
- Drivers with an intermediate license may operate a vehicle only when all vehicle occupants are wearing passenger restraints.

Issuance/Application: A learner's permit is required for 30 days prior to a first license application, unless under age 18. For drivers under 18, the learner's permit is required for 6 months.

- Drivers under age 18 are also required to show receipt of a high school diploma, or, if the driver is still a student, he must have at least a "C" average and regular attendance.
- New drivers can have eligibility postponed due to alcohol/drug offenses.
- New residents must obtain license within 30 days of becoming a resident.
- License issued with an assigned 9-digit number. Social security number does not appear on the license.
- The license must be carried whenever operating a vehicle.
- License includes color photograph.
- Requires proof of citizenship, social security account number or verification of a person's legal status to receive a driver's license.

Renewal: Licenses are valid for 4 years, expire on the licensee's date of birth, and are obtainable only at County Revenue Offices.

- Military personnel on active duty out of the state and their dependents may renew their driver's licenses by mail.

- Military personnel on active duty may be granted an extension of expiration for a driver's license not to exceed 30 days after the applicant's first tour of duty, or release from active duty, whichever occurs first.

Types of Licenses:

Commercial:
- Class A: Combination vehicles, Gross Vehicle Weight Rating (GVWR) over 26,000 lbs., towing trailer over 10,000 lbs.
- Class B: Single or Combination vehicles, GVWR over 26,000 lbs., towing trailer under 10,000 lbs.
- Class C: Vehicle under 26,000 lbs., transporting hazardous materials or carrying 16+ passengers.

Non-Commercial:
- Class D for Automobiles; Class M for Motorcycle; Class MD for Motor-driven cycle.

Traffic Rules

Alcohol Laws: Arkansas has an implied consent law. Open containers are permitted.
- Illegal per se BAC is .08.
- BAC level for people under 21 is .02.
- BAC level for commercial drivers is .04.

Cellular Phones: School bus drivers are prohibited from using cell phones while driving, except in emergencies and while parked.

Emergency Radio/Cellular: Citizen band radio channel 9 is monitored for emergency calls in some counties.
- Emergency phone number is 911.

Headsets: There is no law prohibiting the use of headsets while operating a motor vehicle.

Occupant Restraints: Each driver and front passenger is required to wear a seat belt.
- All occupants must wear a seat belt when the vehicle is being operated by a driver with an intermediate license.
- Children less than 6 years old and under 60 lbs. shall be restrained in a child passenger safety seat.
- Children who are 6 years old or weigh over 60 lbs. must be restrained in a seat belt until they are 15.
- Violation of the seat belt law is a secondary offense, however violation of the child restraint law is a primary offense.
- Riding in back of an unenclosed pickup truck is not permitted, except employees on duty.

Railroad Crossing: Vehicles are not required to stop unless directed by warning signals or when train is approaching.
- Buses transporting passengers and vehicles transporting hazardous waste must stop.

School Buses: School buses must be painted "national school bus chrome."
- Vehicles must stop for school bus loading or unloading, unless on a separate roadway of a highway divided by 20-foot strip.

Vehicle Equipment & Rules

Bumper Height: Modification of original vehicle bumper height is permitted.

Glass Tinting: Tinting may not extend more than 5 inches from the top of the windshield.

- On all model 1994 and later vehicles, side may use a tint that allows at least 25% net light transmission.
- On all model 1994 and later vehicles, the rearmost window may be covered with after-market tint that allows at least 10% net light transmission.
- All vehicles with after-market tints must have a label with the name and phone number of the company that installed the tint on the front glass immediately to the driver's left.

Towing: Special permit is required if towed vehicle is not registered. Proof of ownership is required. Drawbar is required (maximum length 15 feet). Reciprocity is granted.

Windshield Stickers: It is unlawful to have any substance other than a rear-view mirror or required decals attached to the windshield at any point more than 4 1/2 inches above the bottom of the windshield, if it obstructs the operator's view.

Motorcycles & Mopeds

Equipment: Driver is required to display lighted lamps at all times though, between sunrise and sunset, may operate either a continuous or pulsating beam.

- Every motorcycle shall have either 1 or 2 headlights; a red rear light; and at least one reflector.
- Goggles or face shield is required.
- Safety helmet is required for riders under 21.
- One rearview mirror is required.
- Passenger seat and footrests is required if carrying passenger.

Licenses: Licenses are required for motorcycles:

- Minimum age is 16.
- Written and road tests are required.
- Ages 14-16 may use motor-driven cycle (between 50 cc-250 cc).
- Title and registration are required.
- Registration is not required.
- Certificate is issued by state police.
- Minimum age is 10 for up to 50 cc engines.

Mopeds: The following equipment is required:

- 1-2 headlights; red rear reflector; and red rear light.

Passenger Car Trailers

Brakes: Every trailer or semitrailer with a gross weight of 3,000 lbs. or more shall be equipped with brakes adequate to control the movement of and to stop and to hold such vehicle; and the brakes should automatically apply in the event of an accidental break-away.

- Every new trailer or semitrailer weighing at least 1,500 lbs. shall come equipped with brakes on all wheels.

Dimensions: Total length: 65 feet; trailer length: 53.5 feet; width: 102 inches; height: 13.6 feet.

Hitch: Connection must be sufficiently strong to pull all weight towed.
- Safety chain is required.
- 12-inch flag or cloth required on connections consisting only of chains, ropes, or cables.

Lighting: Taillights are required; brake lights are required if towing vehicle's brake light is obscured; license plate lights are required.
- Turn signals are not required unless width is greater than 80 inches.
- Reflectors on each side of vehicle are required.

Speed Limits: Speed limits are 70 mph on rural roads; 65 mph on suburban freeways; 55 mph on urban freeways; or as posted.
- 45 mph is maximum when towing house trailer.

Other Provisions: Riding in towed trailer is prohibited.
- Camping in rest areas is permitted.
- May tow more than one boat or general utility trailer.

Miscellaneous Provisions

Bail Bonds: Automobile clubs may issue bond cards not to exceed $200.

Liability Laws: Security-type law is applicable in event of accident causing property damage in excess of $1,000 or personal injury or death.

Minimum financial responsibility limits are the following:
- $25,000 for bodily injury or death of 1 person in 1 accident.
- $50,000 for bodily injury or death of 2 or more persons in 1 accident.
- $25,000 for injury to or destruction of property of others in 1 accident.
- State has "add-on" no-fault insurance law.
- Sale is mandatory, but purchase is optional.
- Benefits, medical, and hospital, $5,000.
- Wage loss, 70%; up to $140/week (8-day waiting period, maximum 52 weeks).
- Essential services up to $70/week (8-day waiting period, maximum 52 weeks).
- Accidental death, $5,000.

Inspection/Weigh Station: The following vehicles must stop: (1) agricultural vehicles; (2) passenger or specialty vehicles, whether single or in combination (towing a trailer) with GVWR of 10,000 lbs. or more; (3) commercial trucks with GVWR of 10,000 lbs. or more.

Fees & Taxes

Table 1: Title & Registration Fees

Vehicle Type	Title Fee	Registration Fee
Automobiles	$5.00	$17.00 for cars 3,000 lbs. or less, $25.00 for cars 3,001-4,500 lbs., and $30.00 for cars over 4,500 lbs.
Trucks rated under 1 nominal ton and Vans having nominal tonnage of 3/4 ton or less	$5.00	$21.00
Passenger Car Trailers pulled by passenger cars, 1/2, 3/4, and 1-ton pickups for private use		$21.00 for 3 years; after January 1, 2002, $36.00 for a permanent registration
Motorcycles 0-250 cc engine displacement	$5.00	$3.25
Motorcycles 251cc+ engine displacement	$5.00	$6.50
Mobile Home	$7.00 per single section	$26.00/year
Transfer of plates to new owner		$10.00
Transfer of plates to new automobile		$1.00
Duplicates	$4.00	$4.00

Table 2: License Fees

License Class	Fee	Driving Test Fees
A	$42.00	$5.00
B	$42.00	$5.00
C	$42.00	$5.00
D	$20.00	$5.00
Motorcycle License	$12.00/$5.00 for existing licensed drivers	$5.00
Moped License	$2.00	$5.00
Duplicate License Fee	$5.00	
Endorsements	$10.00 (motorcycles = $7.00)	

Table 3: Vehicle Taxes

Tax	Rate
Gasoline Tax; (Diesel)	$0.215/gallon; ($0.225/gallon)
License Tax	based on each $100.00 of vehicle value with a maximum of $2.95 per $100.00 vehicle value decreases 16.25% every 12 months
Personal Property Tax	varies by county
State Sales Tax	4.625% on new and used vehicle purchases of at least $2,500.00; tax imposed on price of vehicle minus net trade-in

Table 4: Miscellaneous Fees

Fee	Amount	Payable Upon
Registration and Plate Reinstatement Fee	$50.00	upon reinstatement of registration and suspended plates due to cancellation or non-renewal of liability insurance policy
Special Plates Fee	$5.00 - $25.00	issue/annual renewal

AR

CALIFORNIA

Contact Information

Department of Motor Vehicles (DMV)
Headquarters Building
2415 First Avenue
Sacramento, CA 95818

(916) 657-6940
www.dmv.ca.gov

Highway Patrol Headquarters
2555 First Avenue
Sacramento, CA 95818

(916) 657-7261
www.chp.ca.gov

Department of Transportation (DOT)
1120 N Street
Sacramento, CA 95814

(916) 654-5266
www.dot.ca.gov

Vehicle Title

Application: Certificate of ownership is issued by the DMV upon registration of vehicle.

- The DMV may issue a title to a non-registered vehicle so long as the vehicle has not been driven, moved, or left standing on a highway and will not be driven or moved.
- The vehicle title is valid until suspended, revoked, or canceled by the DMV or upon a transfer of interest in the vehicle.

Transfer of Ownership: An effective transfer requires endorsement and delivery of certificate of ownership by transferor to transferee and delivery by transferee of the certificate to the DMV, with proper transfer fee and application for transfer of registration, within 10 days of receipt by the transferee.

- Transfer may also be effected when an owner, within 5 calendar days of transfer or sale, provides notice to the DMV of such transfer or sale including the name and address of the owner and the transferee, a description of the vehicle, and the mileage at the time of sale or transfer.
- Prior to, or at the time of sale or transfer, the owner must provide the transferee with a valid certificate of compliance stating that the vehicle meets state air pollution control standards.

Mobile Homes: Mobile homes that are not installed on a foundation system are subject to annual registration.

Vehicle Registration

Application: Application for original or renewal registration for vehicles and motorcycles is made to the DMV.

- Application for initial registration or transfer of registration must be accompanied with a valid certificate of compliance with state air pollution control measures.
- Registration card (or facsimile) issued upon registration must be carried with the vehicle and must be presented upon demand to any peace officer.
- DMV may suspend, cancel, or revoke registration of a vehicle when notified by an

insurance company that coverage has been canceled and when sufficient notice to insured has been given by the insurance company. DMV must give the owner at least 45 days' notice of intent to suspend, cancel, or revoke registration.
- DMV will not accept application for registration if the vehicle is not in the state unless the DMV is satisfied, at the time all documents and fees are submitted, that the vehicle will be registered to a resident of California.
- DMV must refuse original, renewal, or transfer of registration if the application contains a false or fraudulent statement, fees have not been paid, the vehicle has failed emissions standards, evidence of financial responsibility has not been provided, or applicable use tax has not been paid.
- DMV must refuse renewal registration for delinquent parking violations or failure to pay a lawfully imposed fine, penalty, or bail.
- DMV will waive all registration renewal late payment penalties on a vehicle which is registered to a member of the armed forces reserve or National Guard who is called to active service or active duty out of the state.

Non-Residents: A non-resident vehicle must be registered in California if the vehicle is based in California or primarily used in California; a vehicle is considered to be primarily used in California if it is operated or located in the state for a greater amount of time than it is located or operated in any other jurisdiction.

- A non-resident vehicle may be operated in California without registering the vehicle in California provided that the vehicle is registered in another jurisdiction.
- A non-resident vehicle becomes subject to registration 20 days after gainful employment is accepted or residency is established, at which time application for registration must be made.
- Non-resident military personnel or spouses may operate their vehicles in California with their valid home state license plates or until the plates issued by the foreign state where they were last stationed expire. They may renew the vehicle registration in their home state before the end of the registration period or register the vehicle in California.

Registration Type: Application for renewal registration must be accompanied by evidence of compliance with California financial responsibility laws—unless electronically reported to the DMV by insurer.

- Application for renewal may not be made more than 60 days prior to expiration of current registration and must be made not later than midnight on the day of expiration.
- Registration expires at midnight on the last day shown on the registration card.
- A vehicle with expired registration may be operated on highways so long as timely application for renewal registration has been filed and the old registration remains on/with the vehicle.
- The penalty for delinquent renewal is $10 if the fee is 10 days late or less, $15 if the fee is more than 10 days and as many as 30 days late, $30 if the fee is more than 30 days late and as much as 1 year late, $50 if the fee is more than 1 year and as much as 2 years late, and $100 if the fee is over 2 years late.
- 2 tabs issued by the DMV must be displayed on the rear license plate, 1 indicating the year of expiration and the other indicating the month of expiration, except vehicles over 10,000 lbs. Gross Vehicle Weight (GVW) rating that must display tabs on the front license plate.
- Trailer coaches must be registered annually.

- Commencing December 31, 2001, owners of trailers may apply for a permanent trailer identification plate, which shall not expire.
- Upon sale or transfer of a trailer, the permanent identification plate remains with the trailer.

Emissions Inspection: Smog inspections are required for all vehicles except diesel powered vehicles, motorcycles, or those vehicles manufactured prior to the 1976 model year. Vehicles registered in areas subject to the biennial smog certification program are required to submit evidence of a smog certification every other renewal period.

- Vehicles that are 6 model years old or less are exempt from the biennial smog requirements for registration renewal. Evidence of a current smog certification must be provided by the seller except when transfer occurs between a spouse, sibling, child, parent, grandparent, or grandchild.
- Smog certifications are good for 90 days from the date of inspection. The inspection is not required on a transfer if a biennial smog certification was submitted to DMV within 90 days prior to the vehicle transfer date.
- Smog inspections are required in the following counties: Alameda, Butte, Colusa, Contra Costa, Fresno, Glenn, Kern, Kings, Los Angeles, Madera, Marin, Merced, Montery, Napa, Nevada, Orange, Sacramento, San Benito, San Fransisco, San Joaquin, San Luis Obispo, San Mateo, Santa Barbara, Santa Clara, Santa Cruz, Shasta, Solano, Stanislaus, Sutter, Tehama, Tulare, Ventura, Yolo, and Yuba.
- These are 6 other counties that require smog certifications within certain zip codes only. These counties are El Dorado, Placer, Riverside, San Bernardino, San Diego, and Sonoma.

License Plates

Disbursement: The DMV issues 2 reflectorized license plates per motor vehicle registered, except for motorcycles, and 1 license plate for all other vehicles (trailers, semi-trailers, etc.) required to be registered.

- When 2 plates are issued, 1 must be displayed on the front, the other on the rear; when only 1 is issued it must be displayed on the rear of the vehicle.
- Special plates are issued for historic vehicles, current or retired members of the Legislature, street rods, diplomats, disabled persons, members of the media, qualifying tax exempt organizations, various current and retired public employees, and special organizations.
- License plates must be illuminated so as to be visible from a distance of 50 feet.
- Special license plates or placards for disabled drivers are available upon application with medical certificate to DMV.

Transfer of Plates: Transfer of specialized plates to another vehicle is permitted provided proper transfer fees are included.

- Regular plates remain with vehicle upon transfer or sale.

Driver's Licenses

Examination: Written exam includes knowledge of motor vehicle laws, English language proficiency, and traffic signs and signals recognition.

- Roadside test is mandatory but may be waived if the applicant submits a license

held by another jurisdiction and the DMV is able to verify there are no holds or impediments on the license.
- Roadside examination officers may refuse to administer the exam if applicant is unable to provide proof of financial responsibility.
- Applicants for a provisional license who fail the written exam must wait 1 week before re-taking the exam; those who fail the driving exam must wait 2 weeks before re-taking.
- Hearing and vision tests are also administered; visual acuity may not be 20/200 or worse when wearing corrective lenses.
- Application for Class A or B license shall also include a report of medical examination of an applicant given not more than 2 years prior to the date of the application.

Graduated Drivers Licensing: State has a system of graduated licensing for teen drivers. At 15 1/2, teens are eligible for a state issued learner's permit. During this stage, teens may only drive when supervised by a parent, guardian, or licensed driver at least 25 years old.
- Teens 15 1/2 to 17 1/2 must be simultaneously enrolled or have passed a driver education course to be eligible for a learner's permit. Teens must hold the permit for at least 6 months and accumulate at least 50 hours (10 at night) of parental/guardian certified driving experience. Teens must also complete 6 hours of professional driving.
- At 16, teens are eligible for an intermediate license. During the first year of the intermediate license stage teens may not drive between the hours of 11:00 pm and 5:00 am, and teens may not transport any passengers under 20 unless they are supervised by a driver at least 25 years old.
- Teens are eligible for an unrestricted license at age 18.
- Exception allows a class C restricted license to enlistees in the California National Guard.

Issuance/Application: Application for license must be made not more than 10 days after establishing residence.
- Application must contain a legible print of the applicant's thumb or finger and applicant's social security number. Social security number does not appear on license.
- DMV must require all applicants to provide proof of legal presence in the U.S.
- Prior to issuing or renewing a license, the DMV must check the applicant's record for traffic violations, accidents, failure to appear in court, or reports indicating incapacity to drive.
- All licenses must bear an engraved picture or photograph of the licensee.
- License is issued with a magnetic strip containing driver information.
- License applicants that do not take driver education must wait until age 18 for a license. They are not required to go through the intermediate license stage.
- A non-commercial Class B license or endorsement must be obtained in order to operate a motor home of over 40 feet in length. Persons licensed to drive motor homes must submit medical information verifying minimal health requirements upon initial license application and every 2 years thereafter.

Renewal: All original licenses expire on the 5th birthday of the applicant following the date of the application for license and are renewable for successive 5-year periods.

- License renewal must be done in person, but may be done by mail if licensee is not probationary and the licensee's records for the 2 years preceding renewal show no violation of specified traffic laws, a point count of not more than 1, no refusal to submit to a chemical test, and no suspension of the license.
- Licenses of out of state active military personnel are valid beyond their normal expiration date. Active military personnel with expired licenses must carry a DL 236 card with their licenses. Extended licenses are good for 30 days after return to California.
- Spouse and/or dependents of military personnel may apply for a renewal of their license by calling DMV or requesting a no-fee 1-year extension by writing to the DMV.

Types of Licenses: Class A: Any combination of vehicles, if any vehicle being towed has a GVW rating of more than 10,000 lbs.; any vehicle towing more than 1 vehicle; any trailer bus; any vehicle under Class B or Class C.

- Class B: Any single vehicle with a GVW rating of more than 26,000 lbs.; any single vehicle with 3 or more axles, except any single 3-axle vehicle weighing less than 6,000 lbs.; any bus except a trailer bus; any farm labor vehicle; any 3 or more axle vehicle or vehicle with a GVW rating of more 26,000 lbs. towing another vehicle with a GVW rating of 10,000 lbs. or less; any motor home over 40 feet in length; any vehicle covered under Class C.
- Class C: Any 2-axle vehicle with a GVW rating of 26,000 lbs. or less, including when such vehicle is towing a trailer with a GVW rating of 10,000 lbs. or less; any 3-axle vehicle weighing 6,000 lbs. or less; any 2-axle vehicle weighing 4,000 lbs. or more unladen when towing a trailer not exceeding 10,000 lbs. GVW rating; any motor home of 40 feet in length or less, or vehicle towing another vehicle with a GVW rating of 10,000 lbs. or less.
- Class M1: Any 2-wheel motorcycle or motor-driven cycle; Class M1 endorsements may be included on Class A, B, or C licenses upon completion of the exam.
- Class M2: Any motorized bicycle or moped; Class M2 endorsements may be included on Class A, B, or C licenses upon completion of the exam.
- DMV may accept a certificate of competence in lieu of the driving exam for Class A or B applications so long as applicant has first qualified for a Class C license, and for Class M1 applications, if approved by law enforcement. A certificate of satisfactory completion of a novice motorcyclist training program may be submitted in lieu of driving test for Class M1 or M2 applications.

Traffic Rules

Alcohol Laws: Operation of a motor vehicle gives implied consent to a test of blood, breath, urine, or other bodily substance for determining blood-alcohol content.

- Open containers are not permitted. Meets the requirements of TEA-21.
- Illegal per se BAC level is .08.
- BAC level for people under 21 is .01.
- BAC for commercial drivers is .04.

Cellular Telephone Use: School bus drivers are prohibited from using cell phones while driving, except in emergencies.

Emergency Radio/Cellular: The emergency telephone number is *911.
- The citizen band radio channel 9 is also monitored for emergency calls.
- Interference with emergency communications over a citizen's band radio frequency is a crime.

Headsets: Operation of a motor vehicle or bicycle while wearing headsets or earplugs in both ears is not permitted.

Occupant Restraints: The driver and passengers 16 years of age and older must wear a safety belt at all times.
- Children under the age of 1 year or less than 20 lbs. must be in a rear-facing seat in a rear seat if the front air bag is active.
- Children under the age of 6 or weighing less than 60 lbs. must be restrained in a child passenger restraint system in the rear seat, if available. Children weighing more than 40 lbs. may be belted without a booster seat if they are seated in the rear seat of a vehicle not equipped with lap/shoulder belts.
- Children between the ages of 6 and 16, who weigh more than 60 pounds, must be restrained by a safety belt or a child passenger restraint system.
- Violation of the occupant protection laws is a primary offense.
- It is unlawful to transport a person or to ride in the back of a pickup truck unless the person in the back is secured with a restraint system. Additional gaps in coverage apply; see Occupant Protection Chart.

Railroad Crossing: Buses carrying passengers, motortrucks transporting employees, school buses, and vehicles carrying flammable materials, farm labor vehicles carrying passengers, commercial motor vehicles carrying chlorine, commercial motor vehicles requiring markings or placards according to federal regulations, cargo tank motor vehicles transporting a commodity that at time of loading had a temperature above its flashpoint, and cargo tankers whether loaded or empty must stop less than 50 feet but more than 15 feet from the nearest rail before proceeding, unless otherwise directed by a traffic officer or traffic control device.
- All other vehicles need only stop when directed to do so by traffic signal or traffic officer.

School Buses: Vehicles must stop upon meeting, from either direction, a school bus that is stopped for loading or unloading children that displays flashing red light signals and a stop signal arm, unless the school bus is on the opposite roadway of a divided highway.

Vehicle Equipment & Rules

Bumper Height: Modification of original vehicle bumper height is permitted, but limitations exist on maximum ground-to-frame measurements.

Glass/Window Tinting: Window tinting is permitted only for the side windows to the rear of the driver; rear windows may be tinted but only if the vehicle has outside mirrors on both sides that provide 200 feet of visibility; the uppermost portion of the windshield may also be tinted.

Mudguards/Mudflaps: Any motor vehicle with 3 or more wheels, or any trailer or semi-trailer must be equipped with mudguards if the body of the vehicle does not provide adequate protection against spray or splash of water or mud to the rear of the vehicle; trailers and semitrailers weighing less than 1,500 lbs. or vehicles made before January 1, 1971, and weighing less than 1,500 lbs. are not required to have mudguards.

Telematics: It is unlawful to drive a motor vehicle equipped with a television receiver, a video monitor, or a televison or video screen, or any other similar means of usually displaying a television broadcast if the receiver is located in the vehicle at any point forward of the back of the driver's seat.

Windshield Stickers: Stickers are permitted if stickers are 7-inch square or less and placed in the lower left corner of the windshield.

Motorcycles & Mopeds

Equipment: After 1973, motorcycles must be equipped with lamp-type turn signal systems.
- Headlamp modulators are permitted but may not be used during darkness.
- After 1978, motorcycles must be equipped with at least 1 and not more than 2 headlamps that turn on automatically when the engine is started and remain lighted while the engine is running.
- Motorcycles must have at least 1 mirror located so as to give the driver a view of at least 200 feet to the rear of the vehicle.
- Prohibits a seat position too high for a motorcyclist's feet to reach the ground while driving.
- All riders and passengers must wear a safety helmet.

Licenses: Motorcycles may be operated by holders of instruction permits who are at least 15 years and 6 months old and have completed both an approved driver education course and a driver training course, or by holders of instruction permits who are at least 17 years and 6 months old. Motorcycles may not be operated by either instruction permit holder after dark or on freeways and may not carry passengers.
- Class M1 or M2 licenses shall not be issued to persons under 21 unless they provide evidence of completion of an approved motorcycle safety training program.

Noise Limits: A noise limit of 92 decibels applies to any motorcycle manufactured before 1970.
- A noise limit of 88 decibels applies to motorcycles manufactured after 1969 and before 1973; 86 decibels applies to motorcycles manufactured after 1972 and before 1975; 83 decibels applies to motorcycles manufactured after 1974 and before 1986; 80 decibels applies to motorcycles manufactured after 1985.

Mopeds: Class M2 license is not required for mopeds or motorized bicycles that cannot reach speeds over 20 mph.

Passenger Car Trailers

Brakes: Every trailer and semitrailer manufactured after 1940 with a GVW of 6,000 lbs. or more and operated at a speed of 20 mph or more must be equipped with brakes; trailers and semitrailers built after 1966 and with a GVW of 3,000 lbs. or more must have brakes on at least 2 wheels; every trailer or semitrailer built after 1982 and equipped with air brakes must be equipped with brakes on all wheels.

- Every trailer coach or camp trailer with a GVW of 1,500 lbs. or more must be equipped with brakes on at least 2 wheels.

Dimensions: Total length: 65 feet (includes bumpers); trailer length: 40 feet (includes bumpers); width: 102 inches (a trailer may exceed the maximum width established if an appurtenance less than 6 inches is added to the side of the vehicle); height: 14 feet.

Hitch: Fifth wheel mechanisms and adapters must be equipped with a manual release locking device.

Lighting: The combination of vehicles towing a trailer coach or camp trailer must be equipped with a lamp-type turn signal system.

- Trailers and semitrailers 80 or more inches in width and manufactured after January 1, 1969, must be equipped with a lamp-type turn signal system.
- Any vehicle 80 or more inches in width must contain at least 1 amber clearance lamp on each side and at least 1 red clearance lamp on each side, as well as at least 2 amber and 2 red side-marker lamps on each side, and must carry at least 3 red emergency reflectors.
- Every vehicle at the end of a combination of 2 vehicles must have at least 2 tail lights; trailers manufactured after July 23, 1973 and less than 30 inches wide may be equipped with 1 tail lamp.

Mirrors: A motor vehicle towing a vehicle or trailer must be equipped with mirrors on both the left and right side which provide a view of at least 200 feet of the highway.

Speed Limits: Maximum speed for any vehicle towing another vehicle is 55 mph.

Miscellaneous Provisions

Border Inspections: Vehicles engaged in the shipment of agricultural commodities must stop for inspection when entering the state.

Liability Laws: Financial responsibility is required of every driver and owner of a motor vehicle at all times. Low cost auto policies are available in Los Angeles and San Francisco counties and effective April 2006 in Alameda, Fresno, Orange, Riverside, San Bernardino and San Diego counties for qualified low income pensions.

- Drivers without proof of financial responsibility are punishable by a fine of not less than $100 to not more than $200 for a first conviction, $200–$500 for subsequent convictions. State has non-resident service of process law. Guest may sue driver.
- Every driver and every owner of a motor vehicle must carry evidence of financial responsibility in their motor vehicle at all times and be ready to present such evidence at the demand of a peace officer; failure to comply carries a minimum $100 but not more than $200 fine for the 1st infraction and a minimum $200 but not more than $500 fine for any subsequent infraction within 3 years of the 1st.
- Minimum liability insurance coverage must be at least $15,000 for bodily injury or death of each person as a result of any 1 accident and $30,000 for bodily or injury or death of all persons as a result of any 1 accident and at least $5,000 for damage to property as a result of any 1 accident.

Helmets: Operators and passengers under 18 of non-motorized scooters, skateboards, and in-line skates must wear helmets.

Fees & Taxes

Table 1: Title & Registration Fees

Vehicle Type	Fee Amount
All Vehicles	$31.00 - original or renewal registration
Motorcycles	$31.00 plus $1.00 supplement (payable on original registration only)
New Vehicles Purchased Outside of California	$31.00 plus $15.00 service fee
Vehicles Previously Registered Outside of California	$31.00 plus $15.00 service fee
Commercial Vehicles	$31.00 plus the following fees
With 2 or Fewer Axles and up to 10,000 lbs. GVW	$8.00 - $360.00
With 3 or More Axles and up to 10,000 lbs. GVW	$43.00 - $539.00
With a GVW of between 10,001 to 45,000 lbs.	$257.00 - $837.00
With a GVW of between 45,001 to 80,000 lbs.	$948.00 - $1,700.00
Single Trip Permits	$15.00
New Trailers (not to exceed 5 consecutive days)	$35.00
Commercial Vehicles (not to exceed 4 consecutive days)	$45.00
Certificate of Ownership Issued Without Registration	$15.00
Duplicate Certificate of Ownership or Registration Card	$7.00
Transfer of Title or Registration	$15.00

Table 2: License Fees

License Class	Fee
A - Commercial	$57.00 original 4-year license, $64.00 original 5-year license
	$27.00 4-year renewal, $34.00 5-year renewal
B - Commercial	$57.00 original 4-year license, $64.00 original 5-year license
	$27.00 4-year renewal, $34.00 5-year renewal
C - Commercial	$30.00 original or renewal 4-year license
	$34.00 original or renewal 5-year license
C	$24.00 original, $24.00 renewal
M1	$24.00 original, $24.00 renewal
M2	$24.00 original, $24.00 renewal
Duplicate License Fees	$19.00
Endorsements	$15.00
Retake Driver's Test	$5.00 for original or renewal

Table 3: Vehicle Taxes

Tax	Rate
Gasoline Tax; (Diesel)	$0.18/gallon of fuel; ($0.18/gallon); plus 7-8% sales tax
Sales Tax	7% - 8.25% - on new and used cars

Table 4: Miscellaneous Fees

Fee	Amount	Payable Upon
Air Quality Fee (District)	$1.00 - $4.00 depending on district	registration
Air Quality Fee (State) For the first 6 years on new vehicles	$12.00	registration
Abandoned Vehicle Abatement	$1.00	registration
Highway Patrol Staffing	$6.00	registration
Highway Emergencies	$1.00	registration
Anti-Theft Deterrence	$1.00	registration
Fingerprint Identification System	$1.00	registration
Permanent Trailer Identification Plate Program	$20.00	initial registration
	$10.00	renewal registration
	$7.00	substitute plates
Duplicate License Plates	$7.00	application for new plates
Specialized Plates	$10.00 - $35.00 depending on type	application for special plates
License Plate Reflectorization Fee	$1.00	registration
Emission Non-Compliance Fees	up to $500	at next registration renewal
Non-License ID Card	$20.00 (except free for seniors)	application
Vehicle License Fee	65% of market value	registration

COLORADO

Contact Information

Department of Revenue (DOR)
Motor Vehicle Business Group
1881 Pierce Street
Lakewood, CO 80214

(303) 205-5600
www.mv.state.co.us/mv.html

State Police
Headquarters
700 Kipling Street
Denver, CO 80215

(303) 239-4500
www.csp.state.co.us/

Department of Transportation (DOT)
Office of Public Information
4201 E. Arkansas Avenue
Denver, CO 80222

(800) 999-4997
www.dot.state.co.us

Vehicle Title

Application: Application is made to the DOR.
- All information contained on title application is required to be verified by a physical inspection by an agent of the DOR. Information includes: vehicle identification number; the vehicle's make, model, type, year of manufacture; type of fuel used and the odometer reading.

- On a form provided by the DOR the applicant must also provide: owner's name and address, the applicant's source of title as well as any mortgages or liens which exist on vehicle.
- Application shall be verified by a statement signed by the applicant. The statement shall contain a written declaration that all information in the application is made under the penalties of perjury.

Transfer of Ownership: If a person other than a dealer sells or wishes to transfer their vehicle, the individual shall execute a formal transfer of vehicle. This transfer shall be affirmed by a statement signed by the person whose name is currently on the certificate of title of said vehicle.

- Within 45 days, the purchaser or transferee shall present certificate with application for a new certificate of title to the DOR.

Mobile Homes: Certificates of title on mobile homes shall be signed by the director of the DOR. The title shall contain: the manufacturer and model of the mobile home, the date on which the home was first sold to the initial owner, a serial number, and a description of the home for identification purposes.

Vehicle Registration

Application: Every owner of a motor vehicle or trailer shall within 45 days of purchase obtain a registration.

- Motor vehicles are to be registered periodically. Vehicles may be registered for a 12-month interval or a 2-year interval.
- Application shall be in writing and signed by the owner.
- The application shall include: applicant's name, the name and correct address of owner, and a description of the vehicle. The description of the vehicle includes: the vehicle identification number, make, model, type, year of manufacture, body color, type of fuel used, and odometer reading.

Non-Residents: Non-resident must register vehicle within 30 days of becoming a resident or becoming gainfully employed in the state.

- Non-resident military personnel on duty may retain the current vehicle registration from another state.

Emissions Inspection: Emissions testing of gas- and diesel-powered vehicles is required when registering, re-registering, or selling vehicles in the following counties known as the Enhanced Areas: Adams, Arapahoe, Boulder, Denver, Douglas, El Paso, and Jefferson. Testing is also required in Weld, Larimer, and Pitkin counties, known as the Basic Area.

- In the enhanced emissions program areas, no motor vehicle that is required to be registered shall be sold or registered for the first time without a certificate of emissions compliance, or registered unless such vehicle passed a clean screen test.

Safety Inspection: Uniformed police officers at any time, upon reasonable cause, may require the driver of a vehicle to stop and submit vehicle and its equipment to an inspection.

License Plates

Disbursement: License plates are distributed with registration of vehicle. Two plates are ordinarily issued.

- Every license plate shall expire on the last day of the month at the end of each 12-month period.
- Special license plates for disabled drivers are available upon application with medical certificate and Colorado identification on driver's license to clerk and recorder of county in which the applicant resides, except in Denver where obtained from the Denver Motor Vehicle Department.

Transfer of Plates: If vehicle is bought or sold there is no transfer of plates between the two different owners.
- Tags may be transferred between vehicles of the same owner, after paying a $1 transfer fee and submitting the appropriate paperwork.

Driver's Licenses — CO

Examination: Required for every applicant of a driver's or a minor's license.
- Includes vision (a minimum of 20/40 acuity required), written, and behind-the-wheel tests.

Graduated Drivers Licensing: State has a system of graduated licensing for teen drivers. The learner's permit eligibility is based on age and driver's education.
- At 15, teens may drive with a learner's permit if they are enrolled in driver education, completed a 30-hour classroom and 6-hour behind-the-wheel course, and are supervised by a parent, guardian, or driver instructor.
- A driver who holds a permit is prohibited from using a cell phone (secondarily enforced).
- At 15 1/2 teens may drive with a learner's permit if they are supervised by a licensed driver 21 or older and completed a 4-hour defensive driving course.
- At 16, teens may start to drive with a learner's permit, if they choose not to enroll in any formal driver's education course.
- Teens must hold the learner's permit for at least 1 year and parents/guardians must certify that the teen has accumulated at least 50 hours of supervised driving time (with 10 hours at night).
- Teens can be eligible for an intermediate license between 16 and 17.
- During this stage, teens may not drive any motor vehicle between the hours of 12 midnight and 5 a.m. unless accompanied by a parent, or other responsible adult or unless driving to or from the person's place of employment to his or her residence or vice versa. If driving to or from the teen's place of employment, the individual shall have a statement signed by his or her employer or parent.
- Teens with an intermediate license for less than 6 months are restricted from transporting a passenger under 21 and teens with an intermediate license for less than 1 year are restricted from transporting more than 1 person under 21 (secondarily enforced).
- Teens are eligible for an unrestricted license at age 17.

Issuance/Application: Driver's license is required before driving a motor vehicle in the state.
- Driver shall have his or her license in immediate possession when operating a motor vehicle.
- Non-residents are exempt from license requirement if they have in their possession a valid driver's license from their state of residence.
- Licenses shall include the licensee's photograph, distinguishing number (may be social security number), full name, date of birth, residence, brief description, type or class of vehicles that licensee may drive, any restrictions, expiration date, offi-

cial seal, and licensee's signature.
- No person under the age of 18 shall operate a motor vehicle used to transport explosives or inflammable material or any motor vehicle used as a school bus for the transportation of pupils to or from school. No person under the age of 18 shall drive a motor vehicle used as a commercial, private, or common carrier of personal property unless such person is certified to drive such vehicle.
- Applicants that submit, as proof of age or identity, a driver's license or identification card issued by a state that issues licenses and identification cards to people not lawfully in the United States must submit additional proof of age and identity.

Renewal: Driver's license expires every 5 years on date of birth.
- Eye test required on renewal.
- A driver's license can be issued by electronic means to those drivers at least 21 years and under 61 years of age, if the applicant can attest to having an eye exam within 3 years of the application.
- If license has been suspended during the period of that license, written test is also required.
- Military personnel and their dependents are entitled to one 3-year extension. This extension is free of charge.

Traffic Rules

Alcohol Laws: Any person who drives a motor vehicle in the state shall be required to submit to and to cooperate in the completing of tests to determine the person's blood alcohol level.
- Open containers are permitted. Some cities have ordinances prohibiting open containers. If found guilty of DUI or of driving with excessive alcohol content, there is a mandatory surrender of license.
- Illegal per se BAC level is .08.
- BAC level for people under 21 is .02.
- BAC level for commercial drivers is .04.

Emergency Radio/Cellular: The citizen band radio channel 9 is monitored for emergency calls in some areas.
- Emergency number is 911 or *CSP (*277).

Headsets: Wearing earphones while operating a motor vehicle is prohibited.

Occupant Protection: Every driver of and every front seat passenger in a motor vehicle shall wear a seat belt while the motor vehicle is being operated.
- Violation of seat belt law is a secondary offense.
- A child under the age of 1 and who weighs less than 20 lbs. shall be properly restrained in a rear-facing child restraint system. If the child is 1 until 4 years, and weighs at least 20 lbs. but less than 40 lbs., he shall be properly restrained in a forward-facing child restraint system. Violation of this provision is a primary offense.
- Children aged 4 and 5 and under 55" tall must use a booster seat or belt positioning device unless the vehicle transporting a child only has a two point lap belt only system, then the child may be restrained with a lap belt. Violations of these provisions are secondarily enforced.
- Children over 6 years or at least 55" tall must wear seat belts. Violation of this provision is a secondary offense.

- Riding in a pickup truck bed is not permitted unless a person is seated in an enclosed cargo area.

Railroad Crossing: Any driver of a motor vehicle approaching a railroad crossing sign shall slow down to a reasonable speed.

- If required to stop, driver shall stop at the marked stop line. If there is no line, driver shall stop no less than 15 feet nor more than 50 feet from the railroad crossing.
- The driver of a school bus, or the driver of any vehicle carrying hazardous materials is required to stop vehicle, listen, and look before proceeding across railroad tracks.

School Buses: Upon meeting or overtaking from either direction a school bus that has stopped, a motor vehicle driver must stop before reaching the bus and not proceed until the visual signal lights are no longer being used.

Vehicle Equipment & Rules

Bumper Height: Modification of original vehicle bumper height is permitted.

Glass/Window Tinting: The windshield shall allow no less than 70% light transmission.

- The windows to the side of the driver may be tinted to allow a minimum of 27% light transmittance.
- The windows to the rear of the driver, including the rear window, may be tinted less than 27%. However, if such windows allow less than 27% light transmittance, then the front side windows and the windshield shall allow 70% light transmittance.

Windshield Stickers: Stickers may be affixed to the top most portion of the windshield if the bottom edge of the material extends no more than 4 inches from the top of the windshield down, the material is not red or amber in color, the material does not reflect sunlight or headlight glare into the eyes of any other drivers and the material is not metallic or mirrored in appearance.

Motorcycles & Mopeds

Equipment: Every motorized bicycle shall be equipped with a lamp on the front, which shall emit a white light visible from a distance of at least 500 feet from the front, and a red reflector in the rear.

- Any motorcycle carrying a passenger, other than in a sidecar or enclosed cab, shall be equipped with footrests for such passengers.
- Any driver or passenger on a motorcycle or motor-driven cycle on any public highway shall wear goggles or eyeglasses with lenses made of safety glass or plastic.

Licenses: Any operator of a motorized bicycle shall possess a valid driver's license.

Noise Limits: Motorcycles manufactured on or after July 1, 1971 and before January 1, 1973 may not exceed a noise level of 88 decibels measured at a distance of 50 feet from the center of the lane of travel.

- Motorcycles manufactured on or after January 1, 1973 may not exceed a noise level of 86 decibels measured at a distance of 50 feet from the center of the lane of travel.

- These noise restrictions are not applicable for vehicles designed exclusively for racing purposes.

Mopeds: Registration is required.
- Minimum age is 16.
- The following safety equipment is required: headlight, horn, brakes, red rear reflector, and rear-view mirror.

Passenger Car Trailers

Brakes: Every trailer or semitrailer of a gross weight of 3,000 lbs. or more shall be equipped with brakes adequate to control the movement of and to stop and hold such vehicle. Brakes shall also be designed and connected that in case of an accidental breakaway of the towed vehicle, the brakes shall automatically apply.

Dimensions: Total length: 70 feet; trailer length: not specified; width: 102 inches (allows outside width to exceed 102 inches if excess is due to an appurtenance); height: 14.6 feet.

Hitch: Safety chain required. No limitations on hitch except the connections between vehicles must be of sufficient strength to pull all weight being towed.

Lighting: Every trailer shall be equipped with at least one taillamp mounted in the rear. Lamp shall emit red light plainly visible from a distance of 500 feet from the rear. Taillamps shall be located at a height of not more than 72 inches nor less than 20 inches.

Mirrors: Every motor vehicle shall be equipped with a mirror or mirrors so located as to reflect to the driver a free and unobstructed view of the highway for a distance of at least 200 feet.

Speed Limits: Same as passenger cars.

Miscellaneous Provisions

Bail Bonds: County sheriff policy determines recognition of AAA arrest bond certificates up to $200, with specified exceptions.

Liability Laws: Colorado has a no-fault insurance law. Sale and purchase mandatory. Motorists required to carry evidence of insurance at all times. Benefits: medical expenses $50,000, rehabilitation $50,000, loss of income up to $400/week for 52 weeks, death $1,000. General damages: threshold, $2,500 medical and rehabilitation expenses, or permanent disfigurement, permanent disability, dismemberment, loss of earnings for more than 52 weeks.
- Security-type law applicable in event of accident causing property damage or personal injury or death; $100 minimum in judgments for property, otherwise any amount. Minimum financial responsibility limits: $25,000/$50,000/$15,000.

Parking Restrictions: Cities, counties, and towns shall regulate and enforce all parking restrictions.

Weigh Stations: Every owner or operator of a motor vehicle having a manufacturer's gross vehicle weight rating or gross combination weight rating of over 26,000 lbs. shall secure a valid clearance from an office of the DOR, from an officer of the Colorado State Patrol, or from a port of entry weigh station before operating such vehicle or combination of vehicles in the state.

Fees & Taxes

Table 1: Title & Registration Fees

Vehicle Type	Title Fee	Registration Fee
Motor Vehicle	$7.20	$10.00 for cars up to 2,000 lbs. + $0.20 extra per 100 lbs. to 4,500 lbs. 4,500 lbs. or more $17.50 + $0.60 each additional 100 lbs.
Trailers of 2,000 lbs. or less	$6.25	
Trailers of more than 2,000 lbs.	$9.65	
Motorcycles	$6.50	$2.25
Mopeds		$5.00
Duplicate Registration		$2.20
Duplicate Plate	$5.00	
Duplicate Title	$7.50	

Table 2: License Fees

License Class	Fee
Driver's License age 16-21 valid until 20 days after 21st birthday	$15.60
Driver's License age 21-60 valid for 10 years	$15.60
Driver's License age 61+ valid for 5 years	$8.10
Commercial License Fee	$25.60
Duplicate Fee	1st: $5.00 2 or more: $10.00
Motorcycle Endorsement	$16.00

Table 3: Vehicle Taxes

Tax	Rate
Ownership Tax	1st year of vehicle ownership: 2.10% of value
	2nd year of vehicle ownership: 1.50% of value
	3rd year of vehicle ownership: 1.20% of value
	4th year of vehicle ownership: 0.90% of value
	5-9 years of vehicle ownership: 0.45% of value
	10 or more years of vehicle ownership: $3.00
State Sales Tax	3%; localities may impose more
Gasoline Tax; (Diesel)	$0.22/gallon; ($0.205/gallon)

Table 4: Miscellaneous Fees

Fee	Amount	Payable Upon
Emissions Test Fee	$22.00 to $24.25 based on locality	test
Special Plates Fee	varies	
Plates Transfer Fee	$2.00	transfer
License Plate Replacement Fee	$5.00	

CO

CONNECTICUT

Contact Information

Department of Motor Vehicles (DMV)
60 State Street (860) 263-5700
Wethersfield, CT 06161 www.ct.gov/dmv/site/default.asp

Connecticut State Police
1111 Country Club Road (860) 685-8000
Middletown, CT 06457-9294 www.state.ct.us/dps/csp.htm

Connecticut Department of Transportation
2800 Berlin Turnpike (860) 594-3000
Newington, CT 06131-7546 www.dot.state.ct.us

Vehicle Title

Application: Application is made to the DMV and shall contain a description of the vehicle, including make, model, Vehicle Information Number (VIN), number of cylinders, type of body, and odometer statement.

- Vehicle titles are permanent, and need not be renewed.
- Title applications shall also contain the name and address from whom the vehicle was purchased, as well as the names and addresses of all lienholders.
- Title applications may be mailed.

Transfer of Ownership: At the time of transfer of a vehicle, the transferor shall execute an assignment and warranty of title to the transferee, showing the name and address of the transferee, and the transferor shall deliver such title to the transferee or commissioner.

- A lienholder shall, at the request of the owner or transferee, deliver the certificate to the transferee or the commissioner.

Vehicle Registration

Application: Application is made to the commissioner of the DMV, and shall include a current automobile insurance identification card or a copy of the card.

- Registrations must be renewed biannually.
- An odometer statement is required at the time of registration.
- Vehicles over 10 years old may not, at the discretion of the commissioner, be registered unless it has passed a safety inspection.
- Applications for registration of a vehicle by a minor shall not be accepted unless the minor provides proof of financial responsibility and a signature from a spouse, or from parents/guardian if not married.
- Registrations expire upon transfer of ownership. The new owner must re-apply.

Non-Residents: Drivers have 60 days from the date of moving into Connecticut to register a vehicle.

- Military personnel stationed in state may operate vehicle with out-of-state license plates.

Registration Type: The certificate of registration and any automobile insurance identification card shall be carried in the motor vehicle at all times when it is being operated on a public highway.

- The commissioner may issue to each registered owner of a motor vehicle an identification card that contains electronically encrypted information concerning the vehicle description, VIN, and registration and title history of the vehicle. The card shall be carried in the vehicle.

Emissions Inspection: All 1968 model year and later vehicles are required to have an effective air pollution control device.

- All vehicles except those listed below shall be inspected biannually to ensure that air pollution control equipment complies with the exhaust emissions standards defined by the Commissioner of Environmental Protection and approved by the U.S. EPA.
- The following vehicles are exempt: those with a Gross Vehicle Weight (GVW) of more than 10,000 lbs.; electric-powered vehicles; motorized bicycles; motorcycles; vehicles with temporary registration; vehicles manufactured at least 25 years ago; new vehicles at the time of registration; vehicles not designed primarily for vehicle use; and antique, rare, or special interest motor vehicles.
- Beginning July 1, 2002, vehicles with a model year of 1999 or later will be exempt from the emissions inspection for the first 4 years.
- Prior to July 1, 2002, new vehicles are exempt for 1 year.
- The commissioner may issue a sticker that shows the expiration date of the inspection on both sides, and an expiration date for exempt vehicles.
- Inspections may be made at authorized dealer and repair locations.
- Used motor vehicles registered in Connecticut from out-of-state are required to pass emission testing and VIN verification before they can be registered.

Safety Inspection: Cars at least 10 years old must pass a safety examination upon being sold or transferred.

License Plates

Disbursement: Two license plates are required, and the rear plate shall have a sticker denoting the expiration date of the registration.

- Each plate issued by the state shall be reflectorized and shall bear the words "Constitution State" and "Connecticut."
- Special plates for disabled persons are available upon application with medical certificate to any DMV branch office.

Transfer of Plates: All plates remain the property of the state and shall be returned to the commissioner's office within 10 days of the sale of the vehicle.

Driver's Licenses

Examination: Prior to receiving an initial driver's license, an applicant must pass a vision test with minimum visual acuity of 20/40, a written examination of the rules of the road, and a driving test.

Graduated Drivers Licensing: State has a system of graduated licensing for teen drivers. At 16, teens are eligible for a learner's permit. During this stage teens may only drive when accompanied by a parent or guardian. Teens must hold the permit for at least 6 months (4 months if a teen is enrolled in driver education) and complete 20 hours of certified driving before being eligible for an unrestricted license. Intermediate license holders are restricted from driving with passengers for the first 3 months (family members exempt) and from driving from midnight to 5 a.m. Teens are eligible for an unrestricted license at 17 years.

- Prohibits teens with learner's permits and provisional licenses from using a cell phone while driving.

Issuance/Application: No motor vehicle operator's license shall be issued until the applicant signs and files the application under oath, has proven that he or she is at least 16 years old and has proven that he or she has sufficient knowledge of the mechanism of the motor vehicle to ensure safe operation and satisfactory knowledge of the rules of the road.

- An operator's license shall contain a picture of the licensee.
- License does not usually include a social security number.
- For operators under the age of 21, a license shall contain the date of the licensee's 21st birthday.
- Applicants may be fingerprinted.
- Military personnel and dependents assigned to Connecticut do not have to obtain a Connecticut license.
- Non-citizens are required to provide proof of legal status in the United States.

Renewal: Driver's licenses are valid for 4 or 6 years and expire on the operator's birthday.

- On or after July 1, 2005 vision screenings are required at the first renewal, and then at every other renewal.
- A licensed driver age 65 and over may renew a license for either 2 or 4 years.
- Military personnel may renew a license by mail.

Types of Licenses: Class 1: Any non-commercial motor vehicle.

- Class 2: Any non-commercial motor vehicle, including a combination of motor vehicle and trailer or trailing unit used exclusively for camping or any other recreational purpose.

Commercial Licenses (must be renewed every four years):

- Class A: Any combination of vehicles with GVW of 26,000 lbs. or more, where the towing vehicle is in excess of 10,000 lbs.
- Class B: Any combination of vehicles with GVW of 26,000 lbs. or more; or any vehicle towing a vehicle less than 10,000 lbs.
- Class C: Any single commercial vehicle with a GVW of less than 26,000 lbs., or any vehicle towing a vehicle less than 10,000 lbs. that is designed to carry at least 16 passengers; or vehicles carrying hazardous materials.

Traffic Rules

Alcohol Laws: State has an implied consent law.

- Illegal per se BAC level is .08.
- BAC level for people under 21 is .02.

Emergency Radio/Cellular: Citizen band radio channel 9 is not normally monitored for emergency calls. Emergency cell phone number is 911.

Cellular Telephone Use: No person shall use a hand-held phone while driving.

- School bus drivers are prohibited from using a cell phone while driving except in emergencies.

Headsets: Wearing radio headsets while operating a motor vehicle is prohibited.

Occupant Restraints: All persons in the front seats of a motor vehicle must wear a seat belt while the vehicle is in operation.
- Any passenger under the age of 7 and weighing less than 60 pounds must be restrained in a child restraint system.
- Children 7 and older and 60 or more pounds must be secured by a safety belt or child restraint system.
- Violation of the occupant protection laws is a primary offense.
- It is unlawful to operate a pickup truck with any child under the age of 16 riding in the truck bed unless the child is wearing a properly adjusted and fastened seat belt or for parades, farming operations, and hayrides (August through December).

Railroad Crossing: Commercial vehicles transporting passengers, school buses, and operators of vehicles carrying hazardous materials must stop at railroad crossings.
- All vehicles must stop when signs or warning signals require it.

School Buses: Vehicles must stop for school buses loading or unloading. Vehicles from the opposite direction on a parkway or divided highway need not stop.

Vehicle Equipment & Rules

Bumper Height: Modification of original vehicle bumper height is permitted, up to 4 inches from manufacturer's original height for passenger vehicle, up to 30 inches above roadway for commercial vehicle.

Glass/Window Tinting: The side and rear windows shall have a light transmittance of at least 32%.
- The front window may have tinting only from the top of the window to a point 29 inches above the top of the driver's seat.
- All vehicles with tinted windows shall have a window sticker legible from the outside of the vehicle that indicates the sticker registration number and a certification of compliance with the tinting laws.

Telematics: No television screen or other device of a similar nature, except a video display unit used for instrumentation purposes, shall be installed in any position where it may be visible to the driver or may interfere with the safe operation of the vehicle.

Windshield Stickers: Signs, stickers, or other materials may be displayed in a 7 inch square location in the lower corner of the windshield farthest removed from the driver, or in a 5 inch square location in the lower corner of the windshield nearest the driver.

Motorcycles & Mopeds

Equipment: All motorcycles must have at least 1 brake, and those manufactured after 1973 must have brakes on both the front and rear wheels.
- Every motorcycle must have either 1 or 2 headlamps.
- All headlamps must be of sufficient intensity to reveal a person or vehicle at a distance of at least 100 feet when the motorcycle is operating below 25 mph, at least 200 feet between 25-35 mph, and 300 feet when traveling 35 mph or more.
- Every motorcycle must have at least 1 taillamp and 1 rear stop lamp.
- Every motorcycle must have at least 1 red rear reflector.

- A person operating a motorcycle shall not carry another person unless the motorcycle has a seat designed for 2 persons or there is a second seat firmly attached to the rear or side of the operator's seat.
- All motorcycle operators must either have a safety shield installed on the motorcycle, a helmet shield, or wear safety goggles.
- All motorcycle operators under age 18 must wear a protective helmet.

Licenses: Applicants are eligible for a learner's permit at age 16, after passing a vision test and written test.

- Applicants for motorcycle licenses between the ages of 16 and 18 must have the consent of a parent, guardian, or spouse, proof that they have completed a full course of motor vehicle operation that included at least 6 hours of on-the-road instruction, and a novice motorcycle training course.
- All applicants who have not had a Connecticut license in the previous 2 years must pass a vision test, written test, and an on-the-road examination.

Noise Limits: Maximum noise level when vehicle is traveling 35 mph or less in soft site: 72 decibels.

- Maximum noise level when vehicle is traveling 35 mph or less in hard site: 74 decibels.
- Maximum noise level when vehicle is traveling over 35 mph in soft site: 79 decibels.
- Maximum noise level when vehicle is traveling over 35 mph in hard site: 81 decibels.[1]

Passenger Car Trailers

Brakes: Each trailer or semitrailer having a GVW of 3,000 lbs. or more shall be equipped with a braking system operating on all wheels.

- The braking system shall be adequate to control the movement of the trailer safely and to hold the trailer stationary.
- All trailers over 8,000 lbs. shall be capable of braking by foot or hand.

Dimensions: Total length: 60 feet; trailer length: not specified; width: 102 inches (excludes appurtenances); height: 13.6 feet.

Hitch: Every camp trailer is required to be attached by a hitch and shall be coupled to the frame of the towing vehicle by means of a safety chain, chains, cables, or equivalent device which shall be of sufficient strength to control the trailer in event of failure of the regular hitch or coupling.

Lighting: Every trailer shall be equipped with at least 2 taillamps mounted on the rear that emit a red light plainly visible from at least 1,000 feet.

- Every trailer shall be equipped with at least 2 red rear reflectors.
- Every trailer shall be equipped with at least 2 red rear stop lamps.
- Trailers 80 inches or more in width shall also have 2 front clearance lamps, 2 rear clearance lamps, 3 identification lamps mounted as close as possible to the vertical centerline, and 2 side marker lamps on each side, 1 at the front and 1 at the rear.
- Trailers 80 inches or more in width shall also have 2 reflectors on each side.
- Trailers with an overall length of 30 feet or more shall have 1 amber side marker lamp on each side and 1 amber lamp showing the center point of the trailer length-wise.

[1] Soft site means a testing site covered with grass or other ground cover, while a hard site means a test site covered with concrete, asphalt, gravel, or other hard compound.

Mirrors: Every motor vehicle used for towing a house trailer must be equipped with a mirror located so as to give the operator a clear reflected view of the highway directly to the rear on a line parallel to the side of the body of the vehicle.

Passenger Restrictions: No person shall occupy a house trailer while it is being moved upon a public highway.

Speed Limits: 55 mph where posted. Some areas 65 mph where posted.

Miscellaneous Provisions

Bail Bonds: Recognition of AAA arrest bond certificate up to $1,000-$5,000 with specified exceptions.

Liability Laws: Compulsory liability insurance.
- No owner of any motor vehicle may operate the vehicle without automobile insurance.
- Minimum insurance coverage: $20,000 for injury to 1 person, $40,000 for injuries to more than 1 person, and $10,000 for damage to property.
- Motorcycles are required to maintain the same levels of insurance.
- State has non-resident service of process law; does not have guest suit law.

Weigh Stations: All commercial motor vehicles are required to stop.

Fees & Taxes

Table 1: Title & Registration Fees

Vehicle Type	Title Fee	Registration Fee
Motor Vehicle	$25.00	$70.00 every 2 years + $4.00 renewal fee
Motor Vehicle with Special Request Plates	$25.00	$65.00 in addition to regular fee; $15.00 for other special edition plates
Campers	$25.00	$62.00 every 2 years + $4.00 renewal fee
Trailers Used Exclusively for Recreational Purposes	$25.00	$18.00 every 2 years + $4.00 renewal fee
Other Trailers or Semitrailers Not Drawn by Truck Trailer up to 20,000 GVW	$25.00	$1.15 for every 100 lbs., with a minimum fee of $39.00
Non-Commercial Trailer less than 6,000 lbs.	$25.00	$70.00 every 2 years + $4.00 renewal fee
Motorcycles	$25.00	$36.00 every 2 years + $4.00 renewal fee
Registration for Seniors (Age 65+)	$25.00	Can register for 1 or 2 years: $35.00 for 1 year, $75.00 for 2
Duplicates	$25.00	$5.00

Table 2: License Fees

License Class	Fee	Driving Test Fees
Commercial Class A	$66.00 (renewal)	$56.00-$71.00 ($40.00 for driving test, $16.00 for knowledge test, $5.00 each for endorsement to license; test for air-brake restriction removal; and combination vehicle test)
Commercial Class B	$66.00 (renewal)	$56.00-$71.00 ($40.00 for driving test, $16.00 for knowledge test, $5.00 each for endorsement to license; test for air-brake restriction removal; and combination vehicle test)
Commercial Class C	$66.00 (renewal)	$56.00-$71.00 ($40.00 for driving test, $16.00 for knowledge test, $5.00 each for endorsement to license; test for air-brake restriction removal; and combination vehicle test)
Non-Commercial Class 1	$1.00/month, up to $4.00/6 months + $3.50 fee	$40.00
Non-Commercial Class 2	$1.00/month, up to $4.00/6 months + $3.50 fee	$40.00
Renewal of Motor Vehicle License	$44.00 for 4 years	$40.00
Motorcycle License	$37.00	
Renewal of Motorcycle License	$37.00	
Learner's Permit	$18.00	
Motorcycle Learner's Permit	$5.50	
First Duplicate License	$30.00	
Second Duplicate License	$30.00	
Additional Duplicates	$30.00	
Endorsements	$12.00/year	

Table 3: Vehicle Taxes

Tax	Rate
State Sales Tax	6%, credit allowed for trade-in value
Gasoline Tax; (Diesel)	$0.25/gallon; ($0.26/gallon)
Use Fuel Tax	6%

Table 4: Miscellaneous Fees

Fee	Amount	Payable Upon
Security Interest Noted on Title	$10.00 each	application
Assignment of Security Interest on Title	$3.50	application
Emissions Inspection	$20.00 for 2 years	testing
Special Plates Fee	$50.00-$70.00 1-time fee	application
License Plate Replacement Fee	$11.00	application

DELAWARE

Contact Information

Division of Motor Vehicles (DMV)
P.O. Box 698
Dover, DE 19903

(302) 744-2510
www.dmv.de.gov

Delaware State Police
P.O. Box 430
Dover, DE 19901

(302) 739-5901
www.delawarepublicsafety.com/index.cfm

Delaware Department of Transportation Headquarters
800 Bay Road
P.O. Box 778
Dover, DE 19903

(302) 760-2080
www.deldot.net

Vehicle Title

Application: The purchaser of a motor vehicle shall make an application for a new certificate of title immediately following the purchase and no later than 30 days after the purchase of the vehicle.

- Every application for an original certificate of title shall be made upon the application form furnished or approved by the DOT and shall contain a full description of the motor vehicle including the name of the maker, the vehicle serial number, any distinguishing marks, whether the vehicle is new or used, and a statement of any liens or encumbrances upon the vehicle.

Transfer of Ownership: Upon transfer of ownership, the buyer must surrender to the DMV the seller's endorsed certificate of ownership.

Mobile Homes: Every owner of a mobile home shall apply to the DMV for a placement permit for each mobile home he or she owns within 60 days after the mobile home is acquired or moved into this state, whichever is sooner.

Vehicle Registration

Application: The DOT shall not register or renew the registration of any motor vehicle unless and until the owner makes an application for, and is granted an official certificate of title for the vehicle.

- Every owner of a motor vehicle or trailer, within 60 days after taking up residence in the state, shall apply to the DOT and obtain the registration for the vehicle.
- An application for the registration of a motor vehicle shall contain the name and address of the owner, and a description of the vehicle including the make, model, type of body, the serial number of the vehicle, and whether it is new or used.

Non-Residents: A vehicle which has been registered in the state, country, or other place of which the owner is a resident, and which at all times has displayed license plates issued for any such vehicle in the place of residence of the owner, may be operated without registering the vehicle or paying any fees to the state.

- The DOT shall allow registration of motor vehicles owned by individuals who are

not residents of Delaware upon presentation of an affidavit by the applicant, on a form approved by the DOT, swearing or affirming that the vehicle is principally garaged in Delaware and that the applicant is the owner of at least 1 other vehicle which is registered and insured in the state of the applicant's residence.
- The DOT shall allow the registration of trailers for individuals who are not residents of the state if the individual provides documented proof of ownership of a residence in Delaware and signs a declaration indicating that the trailer will remain in Delaware at all times.

Registration Type: The DMV mails registration renewal notices to each vehicle owner on record approximately 90 days before a vehicle's registration expiration date. Vehicle registrations may be renewed up to 90 days prior to their expiration date.

Emissions Inspection: Emissions inspection is required for all vehicles manufactured from 1968 to motor vehicles manufactured in the past 5 model years.

Safety Inspection: Before the DOT registers or renews the registration of a vehicle, such vehicle shall be inspected by the DOT and determined to be safe and fit for operation and found equipped according to the law.
- The DOT may waive all inspection requirements of vehicles no older than the last 5 model years.
- At any time any authorized agent of the DOT or any police officer may, upon reasonable cause, require the owner or operator of a vehicle to stop and submit such vehicle and the equipment for a safety inspection.

License Plates

Disbursement: The number and registration plates shall be the property of the state and shall be furnished by the DOT for each registered motor vehicle without additional cost to the owner.
- The DOT shall furnish 1 numbered plate for each vehicle registered.
- Handicapped license plates may be issued only if applicant submits proof satisfactory to the DOT.

Transfer of Plates: The license plate remains with the car upon transfer of title if new owner is a Delaware resident. If vehicle is sold to a new owner outside the state of Delaware, the plate must be returned to the DMV.

Driver's Licenses

Examination: Applicants must pass a knowledge exam, a vision screening (20/40 visual acuity required), and a driving test for an original license.
- A vision screening is required every 5 years upon renewal of license.

Graduated Drivers Licensing: State has a system of graduated licensing for teen drivers.
- Individuals who are 15 years and 10 months are eligible for a learner's permit. Permit holders may not drive unsupervised or while using a cell phone.
- To be eligible for an intermediate license, teens must be at least 16 years and 4 months old and have held a permit for at least 6 months.
- Intermediate license holders may not drive unsupervised between the hours of 10:00 p.m. and 6:00 a.m. and may not transport more than 2 passengers.

- To be eligible for an unrestricted license teens must be at least 16 years and 10 months and have held the intermediate license for at least 6 months.
- Driver education is required for all license applicants under 18.

Issuance/Application: An application for driver's license must include the name and address of the applicant; the applicant's color photograph; a physical description of the applicant; the applicant's signature; the date of birth; the name of the state; the date of issue of the license; and the expiration date of the license.

- For an original license, a written test, eye screening, and driving test are required.
- Non-citizens must provide immigration and naturalization documents when applying for a license.
- Social security number on license is optional.

Renewal: Driver's licenses are in effect for a period of 5 years.

- When an application for a license renewal is made, the driver must surrender the expired license, fill out an application, and pass an eye-screening test.
- Military personnel, their dependents, and students may renew licenses by calling (302) 744-2506 or by mail. See www.dmv.de.gov.
- Members in the military service and their dependents are not required to acquire Delaware driver licenses and vehicle registrations until 60 days after separation from the service.

Types of Licenses: Driver Education Learner Permit: Authorizes the holder to operate the same vehicles as a Class D license while taking an approved driver education course.

- Class D Operator's License: Authorizes license holders to operate any vehicle with a Gross Weight Rating (GWR) of less than 26,001 lbs., and cannot be designed to transport more than 15 passengers, or carry hazardous material.
- CDL Class A: Any combination of vehicles with a GWR of 26,001 lbs. or more, provided that the GWR of the vehicle(s) being towed is in excess of 10,000 lbs.
- CDL Class B: Any single vehicle with a GWR of 26,001 lbs. or more.
- CDL Class C: Any single vehicle with a GWR of less than 26,001 lbs.
- Endorsements and Restrictions: H — authorizes driver to carry hazardous materials; L — restricts the driver to vehicles not equipped with airbrakes; T — authorizes driving double and triple trailers; P — authorizes driving vehicle carrying passengers; N — authorizes driving tank vehicles; and X — combines both H and N endorsements.

Traffic Rules

Alcohol Laws: State has implied consent. The state's open container law does not meet TEA-21 requirements.

- Illegal per se BAC level is .08.
- BAC level for people under 21 is .02.

Cellular Phones: School bus drivers are prohibited from using cell phones while driving, except in emergencies and while parked.

Emergency Radio/Cellular: The emergency phone number is 911 or #77.

- Citizen band radio channel 9 is monitored for emergency calls.

Headsets: Wearing of radio headsets while operating a motor vehicle is permitted.

Occupant Restraints: The driver of a motor vehicle and each passenger who is 16 years of age or older shall wear a properly adjusted and fastened seat belt.

- Children under 7 that weigh less than 60 lbs. must be properly restrained in a child safety seat or booster seat that meets federal motor vehicle safety standards appropriate for the child's weight and height.
- Children who become 4 years old before 1/1/03 will not be required to be in a child restraint system; they must wear a seat belt.
- Children age 7 to 16 or weighing 60 lbs. or more must be properly secured in a seat belt, or booster seat, whichever is appropriate for the child's weight and height. Applies to all seating positions.
- No child who is 65 inches or under in height or who is under the age of 12 years shall occupy the front passenger seat of any vehicle equipped with a passenger-side airbag that has not been deliberately rendered inoperable.
- Violation of the occupant protection laws is a primary offense.
- Riding in pick-up truck beds is permitted.

Railroad Crossing: Whenever any person driving a vehicle approaches a railroad grade crossing, drawbridge, or automatic signal system controlling the flow of traffic, the driver of such vehicle shall stop within 50 feet but not less than 15 feet from the nearest rail of such railroad, and shall not proceed until the driver can do so safely.

School Buses: When a school bus is stopped on the roadway or shoulder and is displaying flashing lamps, the driver of any vehicle approaching the school bus from the front or from the rear shall stop before passing the bus and remain stopped until such bus begins to move or no longer has the red stop lamps activated. On roadway or roadways with 4 or more lanes, the driver approaching from the front shall not stop.

Vehicle Equipment & Rules

Bumper Height: No passenger vehicle or station wagon shall be registered or operated upon any highway of the state if the bumper height exceeds 22 inches from the ground to the bottom of the bumper.

Glass/Window Tinting: No person shall operate any motor vehicle on any public highway, which does not conspicuously display a certificate by the manufacturer of any "after manufacture" tinting material, stating that the tinting material meets the requirements of Federal Motor Vehicle Safety Standard 205.

Windshield Stickers: No person shall drive upon the highways of this state with any sign, poster, or other non-transparent material upon the front windshield, or side or rear window of the vehicle other than a certificate or other paper required to be displayed by law.

Motorcycles & Mopeds

Equipment: A person operating a motorcycle shall ride only on the permanent and regular seat.

- If the motorcycle is designed for passengers, it must be equipped with passenger footrests.
- Every person 18 years and under operating a motorcycle shall have a safety helmet and wear an eye protection approved by the DOT.

- Every motorcycle shall be equipped with at least 1 and not more than 2 headlamps.

Licenses: No person shall operate a motorcycle without being properly licensed, having passed an examination testing the person's ability to operate such a vehicle safely, or without completing the Motorcycle Rider Education Program as implemented by the DOT.

Noise Limits: No person shall drive a motorcycle on a public roadway unless the motorcycle is equipped with a muffler to prevent excessive or unusual noise.

Mopeds: Mopeds shall not be operated upon interstate highways.
- No person shall operate a moped without having been licensed as an operator of a motor vehicle; minimum age is 15 years, 10 months.
- Regulations applicable to bicycles shall apply whenever a moped is operated upon any public road.
- Mopeds shall be registered for a 3-year period.
- Driving on interstate or limited access highways is not permitted.
- The following safety equipment is required: helmet, headlamp, side and rear reflectors, brakes, mirror, and muffler.

Passenger Car Trailers

Registration: The owner of a trailer may elect to register it for a 2-year period.

Brakes: Every motor vehicle when operated on a highway shall be equipped with brakes adequate to control the movement, and to stop and hold such vehicle and any trailer attached thereto, including 2 separate means of applying the brakes.

Dimensions: Total length: 65 feet; trailer length: 40 feet; width: 102 inches; height: 13.6 feet.

Hitch: Safety chain is recommended.

Lighting: Every trailer shall be equipped with at least 1 taillamp, mounted on the rear, which when lighted emits a red light plainly visible from a distance of 500 feet to the rear.

Mirrors: All motor vehicles shall be equipped with a mirror placed so that the driver may readily ascertain the presence of any vehicle traveling in the same direction and overtaking the driver's vehicle.

Speed Limits: No trailer carrying a gross weight of load in combination with a vehicle in excess of 4,000 lbs. shall be operated at a speed over 10 mph unless equipped with suitable brakes controlled by the operator of the towing vehicle.

Towing: No vehicle shall be driven upon any highway pulling more than 1 other vehicle.
- The drawbar or other connection between any vehicle and the vehicle it is towing shall not exceed 15 feet in length.
- If the connection between 2 vehicles, 1 towing the other, consists of a chain, rope, or cable, there shall be a red flag or other cloth not less than 12 inches square attached to the connection.

Other Provisions: It shall be unlawful to ride in a house trailer being towed by another vehicle.

Miscellaneous Provisions

Bail Bond: Mandatory recognition of AAA club guaranteed arrest bond certificates up to $200, except for misdemeanors or felonies.

Liability Law: State has security-type law. All vehicles registered in the state are required to have the minimum liability insurance coverage of $15,000 for any 1 person injured in an accident; $30,000 for all persons injured in any 1 accident; or $10,000 for the property damage which may be done by any 1 accident.

- State has add-on, no-fault insurance law. Sale mandatory. Benefits, $15,000 per person, $30,000 per accident; covers medical, loss of income, loss of services, and funeral ($3,000 limit).
- No limit on tort actions except benefits received cannot be used as evidence in suits for general damages. Non-residents are covered as pedestrians or guest passengers in insured vehicles.
- State has non-resident service of process law.

Weigh Stations: The Secretary of the DPS may adopt such regulations and procedures as may be necessary for law enforcement weighing purposes.

Fees & Taxes

Table 1: Title & Registration Fees

Vehicle Type	Title Fee	Registration Fee
Motor Vehicle	if no lien: $15.00	6 months: $11.00
	with lien: $25.00	1-5 years: $20.00 per year
Trailers of 1,000 lbs. or less		$10.00
Trailers of 1,001-2,000 lbs.		$12.00
Trailers of 2,001-5,000 lbs.		$20.00
Trailers over 5,000 lbs.		$20.00 + $16.80 per each additional 1,000 lbs.
Motorcycles	if no lien: $15.00	$10.00 per year
	if lien: $25.00	
Mopeds		$5.00 for 3 years
Duplicate Registration		$2.00 for card
		$1.00 for sticker
Duplicate Plate		$6.00 plain plate
		$10.00 special plates
Duplicate Title	$15.00	

Table 2: License Fees

License Class	Fee
Driver's License	$12.50
Late Renewal Fee	$1.15
Change of Name	$1.15
Commercial License Fee	$30.00
Duplicate Fee	$5.00
Motorcycle Endorsement	$8.00

Table 3: Vehicle Taxes

Tax	Rate
Document Fee	2.75% of purchase price of vehicle or NADA book value, whichever is higher
State Sales Tax	no sales tax
Gasoline Tax; (Diesel)	$0.23/gallon; ($0.22/gallon)

Table 4: Miscellaneous Fees

Fee	Amount	Payable Upon
Emissions Test Fee	no fee	
Delinquent Registration/ Transfer Fee	$10.00	renewal of registration
Special Plates Fee	$10.00 - $50.00	application for plate
Plates Transfer Fee	$10.00	transfer of plates
License Plate Replacement Fee	$6.00	application for replacement plates

DISTRICT OF COLUMBIA

Contact Information

Department of Motor Vehicles (DMV)
301 C Street, NW, Room 1018
Washington, DC 20001

(202) 727-5000
www.dmv.washingtondc.gov/main.shtm

Metropolitan Police Department
John A. Wilson Building
1350 Pennsylvania Avenue, NW
Washington, DC 20004

(202) 727-1000
http://mpdc.dc.gov/

District Department of Transportation
2000 14th Street, NW, 6th Floor
Washington, DC 20009

(202) 673-6813
www.ddot.dc.gov/main.shtm

Vehicle Title

Application: Every application shall contain the owner's full name, address, driver's license number, date of birth, description of vehicle (including make, model, year, type of body, VIN, weight, and whether new or used), odometer statement, date of purchase, and from whom it was purchased.

- A certificate of title is valid for the life of the vehicle, as long as the title is held by the owner to whom the title is assigned.
- If a certificate of title is lost, stolen, or destroyed, a vehicle owner shall make an application for a duplicate title.

Transfer of Ownership: An owner has 4 days after selling a vehicle to execute and deliver an assignment and warranty of title to the transferee.

Vehicle Registration

Application: The application shall contain the name of the applicant's insurance company, the policy number, the applicant's signature, and other things the DMV may require.
- Applicants can request 1 or 2-year registrations.
- Applicants must secure the title to a vehicle prior to registering it.
- Upon completion of the application, the applicant shall receive 1 registration card and 2 registration plates.

Non-Residents: Non-residents may operate a vehicle in the District for 30 continuous days before registering and can extend that period for an additional 180 days by paying a fee.
- Non-residents may also purchase a reciprocity sticker that allows that person to operate a vehicle in the District for 180 days. A non-resident may only purchase 1 such sticker per year.
- Military personnel may maintain registration in home state.

Registration Type: Class A: Non-commercial passenger vehicle.
- Class B: Commercial vehicle, tractor, and passenger-carrying vehicle for hire having a seating capacity of at least 8 passengers.
- Class C: Trailers.
- Class D: Motorcycle.
- Class E: Motorized Bicycle.
- Class F: Historic Motor Vehicle.

Safety and Emissions Inspection: All motor vehicles and trailers are to be inspected biennially.
- Vehicles that fail inspection will receive a rejection sticker and will be permitted to use the vehicle for 20 days in order to have the necessary repairs made to bring the vehicle into compliance.
- The inspection sticker shall be placed in the lower right-hand corner of the windshield.
- To comply with emissions standards, failing vehicle owners must make at least $450 in repairs before receiving conditional approval.

License Plates

Disbursement: License plates shall be disbursed at the time of registration.
- All vehicles other than motorcycles and trailers shall have 2 license plates, 1 on the front and 1 on the rear of the vehicle.
- Registration validation stickers shall be displayed on the plates, with the month sticker applied to the lower left corner and the year sticker in the lower right.
- Personalized license plates are available for a fee.
- Plates and special windshield I.D. cards for disabled drivers are available from the DMV.

Transfer of Plates: A transferor must remove the license plates from the vehicle at the time of transfer, and has 5 days to return them to the DMV.
- A registrant who wishes to transfer license plates from 1 vehicle to another must apply for a transfer within 5 days of acquiring the new vehicle.
- License plates may not be transferred from 1 owner to another.
- Personalized plates may be transferred for a fee, but only to a surviving spouse,

from a joint ownership of a vehicle to a sole ownership, and from a sole ownership to a joint ownership.

Driver's Licenses

Examination: A driving test, vision test (20/40 visual acuity required), and written knowledge test are required for an initial driver's license.

- Drivers previously licensed to drive in another jurisdiction may skip the driving test unless they have failed the District's driving test within 6 months or are at least 75 years of age.
- Applicants at least 75 years of age are limited to 3 examinations within a year.
- Applicants for a learner's permit must pass the vision and written tests.
- An applicant must have a visual acuity of at least 20/40 in one eye, and no worse than 20/70 in the other eye, with or without corrective lenses.

Graduated Drivers Licensing: The District has a system of graduated licensing for teen drivers.

- At 16, teens are eligible for a learner's permit. During this stage, teens must be supervised by a parent or guardian at all times.
- In this stage, novice drivers may not drive between the hours of 9:00 p.m. to 6:00 a.m. and must accumulate at least 50 hours (10 at night) of supervised driving that is certified by a parent or guardian.
- After holding the learner's permit for 6 months teen drivers are eligible for an intermediate license.
- For the first 6 months, intermediate license holders may not carry any passengers (except drivers 21 and older and family members). Thereafter, drivers may transport no more than 2 passengers under 21 (except family members).
- Passenger restrictions are lifted after 1 year.
- Intermediate license holders may not drive from 11:00 p.m. to 6:00 a.m., Sunday through Thursday from September through June and midnight to 6:00 a.m. July through August.
- Teens are eligible for a full, unrestricted license at 18.
- In the District, all license applicants must hold a learner's permit for 6 months, regardless of age.

Issuance/Application: Each application shall include the applicant's full name, date of birth, sex, social security number, address, and brief physical description of the applicant.

- Applicants for a learner's permit or driver's license must display a birth certificate and social security card or other documentary evidence of the date of birth and social security number of the applicant, but an applicant for a renewal license or an applicant with a valid out-of-state license need only show a social security card.
- Applicants under the age of 18 must have consent from a parent or guardian.
- Each license shall include the licensee's full name, address, social security number, date of birth, physical description, expiration date, a distinguishing number assigned to the licensee, and a signature of the licensee.
- Each license will also contain an imprinted photograph of the licensee, with a profile of the licensee if under 21 years of age, and a frontal photograph if the licensee is 21 years of age.

Renewal: The initial term of a driver's license issued after September 1, 2001 and the

next renewal date of licenses issued prior to September 1, 2000 shall expire on the licensee's birth date occurring in the 5th year of the license term.
- Any subsequent renewals may be renewed for up to a 5-year period ending on the licensee's birth date.
- Each person applying for a renewal must pass a vision test.
- For every other renewal, an applicant may renew by mail, so long as he or she certifies that he or she meets the visual requirements, and that there has been no change in his or her physical condition.
- Licensees who have reached the age of 70 have the following renewal requirements: at age 70 or the nearest renewal date thereafter, the applicant shall complete the eye test and may be required to pass the reaction test, and must show a physician's certification that the applicant is physically and mentally competent to operate a motor vehicle; at age 75 or the nearest renewal date thereafter, the applicant may also be required to pass the written test.

Types of Licenses: Commercial Licenses:
- Class A: Any combination of vehicles with a Gross Vehicle Weight Rating (GVWR) greater than 26,000 lbs.; where the GVWR of the vehicle being towed is in excess of 10,000 lbs., or is a semitrailer or trailer with 2 or more axles.
- Class B: Any single vehicle with a GVWR greater than 26,000 lbs. and any such vehicle towing a vehicle not in excess of 10,000 lbs. GVWR.
- Class C: Any single vehicle with a GVWR of 26,000 lbs. or less, or any such vehicle towing a vehicle with a GVWR not exceeding 10,000 lbs. GVWR.

Non-Commercial Licenses:
- Class D: All non-commercial motor vehicles, except those in Class M.
- Class M: Motorcycles.
- Class N: Mopeds and motor-driven cycles.

Traffic Rules

Alcohol Laws: The District has an implied consent law. All operators consent to give 2 samples for alcohol presence.
- Open containers are prohibited. Meets TEA-21 requirements.
- Illegal per se BAC level is .08.
- Drivers under the age of 21 may not have any measurable amount of alcohol in their system.
- BAC for commercial operators is .04.

Cellular Telephone Use: The use of a hand-held cell phone while driving is prohibited. Driver's with learner's permits and school bus drivers are prohibited from using cell phones of any type while driving. Distracted driving in general, which is defined as inattentive driving while operating a motor vehicle, is prohibited.

Emergency Radio/Cellular: Emergency cell number is 727-6161. Citizen band radio channel 9 is monitored for emergency calls.

Occupant Restraints: The driver and all passengers in a motor vehicle shall wear a properly adjusted and fastened seat belt while the vehicle is in operation. This includes motor vehicles for hire. Signs are to be placed in motor vehicles for hire which state that there is a $50 penalty for noncompliance. In passenger cars for hire

the passenger, not the driver of the vehicle, is ticketed for being in non-compliance.
- Children less than 8 years of age must be properly restrained in a child safety seat.
- Children between the ages of 8 and 16 must be properly restrained in a child safety seat or by a seat belt.
- Violation of the occupant protection laws is a primary offense.
- Riding in the bed of a pickup truck is prohibited, except for employees on duty.

Railroad Crossing: All drivers must stop between 15 and 50 feet of a railroad crossing before safely crossing it, in any of the following circumstances:
- A clearly visible electric or mechanical signal gives warning of an approaching train,
- A crossing gate is lowered or human flagman gives a signal of an approaching train,
- A train approaching within 1,500 feet emits an audible signal and is an immediate hazard, or
- An approaching train is plainly visible and in hazardous proximity to the crossing.

School Buses: A driver of any vehicle shall stop the vehicle at least 15 feet from a school bus when its warning light is flashing, unless the vehicle is on the other side of a divided median.
- All school buses shall be painted national school bus chrome.

Vehicle Equipment & Rules

Bumper Height: Modification of original bumper height is permitted.

Glass/Window Tinting: All vehicles other than minivans must have the following light transmittance:
- The front windshield and the front side windows: 70% light transmittance.
- The rear windshield and the rear side windows: 50% light transmittance.

All minivans must have the following light transmittance:
- The front windshield and the front side windows: 55% light transmittance.
- The rear windshield and the rear side windows: 35% light transmittance.
- No tint on the windshield may come down lower than 5 inches from the top.

Telematics: No television equipment shall be installed in or on any motor vehicle in a location where the reception would be visible to the operator of the vehicle.

Windshield Stickers: Signs, posters, or other non-transparent materials may not be placed on any window unless authorized by the District.

Motorcycles & Mopeds

Equipment: Motorcycles must have 1 or 2 headlamps.
- Motorcycles must have 1 taillamp and 1 stop lamp.
- Motorcycles must have 1 red rear reflector.
- Brakes are required on both wheels.
- Passengers may not ride on a motorcycle unless there is a seat designed for 2 people, or another seat, along with footrests and handgrips, is firmly attached to the rear or side of the motorcycle.
- A helmet is required on each person operating or riding on a motorcycle.

- No person shall operate a motorcycle unless he or she wears goggles or a face shield.

Licenses: Applicants for a motorcycle license must fulfill the same requirements as applicants for motor vehicles.
- Motorcycle operators are not subject to the minimum insurance liability requirements.
- The types of licenses are Class M: Motorcycle; Class N: Moped.

Noise Limits: The maximum noise level for a motorcycle is 83 decibels.

Mopeds: Registration required.
- Minimum age to ride a moped is 16.

Mopeds must have a headlamp that meets the following requirements:
- At speeds less than 25 mph, the headlamp must be visible for 100 feet.
- At speeds between 25-35 mph, the headlamp must be visible for 200 feet.
- At speeds of at least 35 mph, the headlamp must be visible for 300 feet.
- The following safety equipment is required: headlight, taillight, stop light, license plate light, ignition lock, horn, brakes, muffler, chain guard, and rearview mirror.

DC

Passenger Car Trailers

Registration: All trailers are to be registered, and the procedures are the same as for other motor vehicles.

Brakes: Brakes shall be placed on all wheels, except for trailers not exceeding 3,000 lbs., so long as the total weight on and including the wheels of the trailer does not exceed 40% of the GVW of the towing vehicle, and the combination of vehicles can meet the state stopping requirements.
- Each trailer in excess of 3,000 lbs. shall be equipped with brakes acting on all wheels that will be applied automatically and promptly, and remain applied for at least 15 minutes upon breakaway from the towing vehicle.
- There shall be a manually controlled device for applying and releasing the brakes that is readily operable by a person seated in the driving seat.

Dimensions: Total length: 85 feet; trailer length: 60 feet; width: not available; height: 13.6 feet.

Hitch: Any time a vehicle is being towed by use of a hitch, safety chains shall also be used to secure the vehicles.

Lighting: Trailers have the same headlamp and taillamp requirements as other motor vehicles.
- Each trailer 3,000 lbs. or less must have 2 rear reflectors, and if the towing vehicle's stop light is obscured, 2 stop lights.
- Each trailer or semitrailer exceeding 3,000 lbs. must have 2 front clearance lamps, 2 side marker lamps on each side, 2 rear clearance lamps, 2 reflectors, and 2 stop lights.
- Each pole trailer exceeding 3,000 lbs. must have 1 side marker lamp and 1 clearance lamp on each side, and 2 reflectors on the rear.

Mirrors: Must see 200 feet to rear.

Miscellaneous Provisions

Bail Bonds: Mandatory recognition of AAA arrest bond certificates up to $200 with specified exemptions.

Liability Laws: Compulsory motor vehicle insurance.

- The minimum insurance coverage required is $25,000 for injury to any 1 person, $50,000 for injury to more than 1 person, and $10,000 for personal property damage.
- The District has a non-resident service of process law, which allows a person to serve papers against a non-resident with the District for any action that arises out of the non-resident's use of a vehicle while in the District.

Parking Restrictions: No person shall park a vehicle in a roadway other than parallel with the edge of the roadway headed in the direction of lawful traffic movement.

- A vehicle shall be parked within 12 inches of the curb.
- Vehicles shall not be parked on a roadway to advertise for sale.
- Parking is prohibited at all of the following: within an intersection; on a crosswalk; upon any bridges, viaducts, freeways, highway tunnels, ramps leading to and from each, medians, safety zones, and traffic islands.

DC

Fees & Taxes

Table 1: Title & Registration Fees

Vehicle Type	Title Fee*	Registration Fee*
Motor Vehicle Below 3,500 lbs.	$26.00	$72.00
Motor Vehicle 3,500 lbs.	$26.00	$115.00
Trailers	$26.00	$50.00 to $550.00, depending on weight
Motorcycles	$26.00	$52.00
Mopeds		$10.00
Reciprocity Stickers for Vehicles not Housed in the District		$25.00, valid for 180 days
Reciprocity Stickers for Vehicles Housed in the District		$250.00, valid for 180 days
Duplicates	$26.00	$7.00

*Some fees provided by the DC DMV.

Table 2: License Fees

License Class	Fee	Driving Test Fees
Commercial Licenses	$117.00	
Renewal of Commercial License	$117.00	
Duplicate Commercial License	$13.00	
Required DC License for Commercial Drivers	$30.00	
First Time Non-commercial Licenses	$39.00	$10.00
Renewal of Motor Vehicle License	$52.00	
Motorcycle License	$30.00	$10.00
Renewal of Motorcycle License	$30.00	
Learner's Permit and Provisional Driver's License	$20.00	$10.00
Duplicate Learner's Permit	$7.00	
Motorcycle Learner's Permit	$15.00	
Duplicate Licenses	$5.00	

Table 3: Vehicle Taxes

Tax	Rate
Excise Tax on Vehicles below 3,500 lbs.	6%
Excise Tax on Vehicles 3,500 lbs. and above	7%
Gasoline Tax; (Diesel)	$0.20/gallon; ($0.20/gallon)
Sales Tax	9%

Table 4: Miscellaneous Fees

Fee	Amount	Payable Upon
Inspection	$25.00	testing
Residential Parking Permit	$15.00	application
Lien Recordation	$20.00	application
Personalized Plates Fee	$52.00	application
Transfer of Personalized Plates	$26.00	application
License Plate Replacement Fee	$10.00	application

FLORIDA

FL

Contact Information

Department of Highway Safety and Motor Vehicles (DMV)
Neil Kirkman Building
2900 Apalachee Parkway
Tallahassee, FL 32399-0500

(850) 922-9000
www.hsmv.state.fl.us

Florida Highway Patrol
Neil Kirkman Building
2900 Apalachee Parkway
Tallahassee, FL 32399

(850) 487-3139
www.fhp.state.fl.us

Florida Department of Transportation
605 Suwannee Street
Tallahassee, FL 32399-0450

(850) 414-4100
www.dot.state.fl.us

Vehicle Title

Application: Application for a certificate of title shall be made upon a form prescribed by the DMV and shall include the applicant's full name, date of birth, sex, personal identification number, and the license plate number of the vehicle to be titled.

- The application shall also indicate if the motor vehicle is to be used as a taxicab, police vehicle, or if it is a rebuilt vehicle.
- If a certificate of title has not previously been issued for a motor vehicle or mobile home, the application shall be accompanied by a proper bill of sale, a sworn statement of ownership, or a duly certified copy thereof, or a certificate of title. A sworn affidavit from the seller and purchaser must verify that the vehicle identification number shown on the affidavit is identical to the vehicle identification number shown on the motor vehicle. If such affidavit is not prepared, the application may be accompanied by an appropriate DMV form indicating that a physical examination

has been made by a law enforcement official, a licensed motor vehicle dealer, or a notary public and that the vehicle identification number shown on the form is identical to the vehicle identification number on the motor vehicle.
- If the vehicle is a used car, a sworn affidavit from the owner is necessary to verify that the odometer reading shown on the affidavit is identical to the odometer reading shown on the motor vehicle at the time that the application for title is made.
- The application for a certificate of title for a motor vehicle or mobile home previously titled or registered outside of Florida shall show on its face such fact and shall indicate the time and place of the last issuance of certificate of title or registration.

Transfer of Ownership: No person shall sell or otherwise dispose of a motor vehicle or mobile home without delivering to the purchaser or transferee a certificate of title indicating the name of the purchaser.
- Upon transfer or reassignment of a certificate of title to a used motor vehicle, the transferor shall complete the odometer disclosure statement provided on the title. The transferee shall acknowledge the disclosure by signing and printing his or her own name in the spaces provided.
- Each lien, mortgage, or encumbrance on a motor vehicle or mobile home title in Florida shall be noted upon the face of the Florida certificate of title.

Mobile Homes: Under Florida law, mobile homes are to be registered using the same process as a motor vehicle.

Vehicle Registration

Application: Every owner of a motor vehicle, which is operated or driven on the public roads, shall register the vehicle.
- The owner of any motor vehicle or mobile home may file an application for renewal of registration with the county tax collector, at any time during the 3 months preceding the date of the expiration of the registration period.

Non-Residents: Registration is not required for non-residents if the vehicle is registered or licensed under the laws of some other state or foreign country, except:
- In every case in which a non-resident accepts employment or engages in any trade, profession, or occupation in this state or enters his or her children to be educated in the public schools, a non-resident shall within 10 days after the commencement of employment or education, register his or her motor vehicle.
- Any person who is enrolled as a student in a college or university is not required to register his or her vehicle in Florida if it is registered in another jurisdiction.
- Vehicles owned by military personnel stationed in state may be operated on home state registration.

Registration Type: For a motor vehicle subject to registration, the registration period begins the 1st day of the birth month of the owner and ends the last day of the month immediately preceding the owner's birth month in the succeeding year.

Safety Inspection: Any police officer may at any time, upon reasonable cause to believe that a vehicle is unsafe or not equipped as required by law, or that its equipment is not in proper adjustment or repair, require the driver of the vehicle to stop and submit the vehicle to an inspection.

License Plates

Disbursement: Upon the receipt of an initial application for registration, the DMV shall assign a motor vehicle a license plate bearing the registration license number.

- License plates are valid for 5 years and when issued will be issued with validation stickers indicating the expiration month and year. The plates will expire on the last day of the owner's birth month. At the end of 5 years, upon renewal, the plates shall be replaced.

Transfer of Plates: The registration license plate and certificate of registration shall be issued to, and remain in the name of, the owner of the vehicle registered and may be transferred by the owner from the vehicle for which the registration license plate was issued to any vehicle which the owner may acquire within the same classification.

- Upon a sale, trade, transfer, or other disposition of a motor vehicle, the owner shall remove the registration license plate and either return it to the DMV or transfer it to a replacement motor vehicle.

Driver's Licenses

Examination: For an applicant for a Class D or a Class E driver's license, the required examination shall include a test of the applicant's eyesight (20/40 visual acuity required) given by the driver's license examiner designated by the DDL or by a licensed ophthalmologist or optometrist and a test of the applicant's hearing given by the driver's license examiner or a licensed physician.

- The examination shall also include a test of the applicant's ability to read and understand highway signs regulating, warning, and directing traffic; his or her knowledge of the traffic laws, including the laws regulating driving under the influence of alcohol. Testing shall also include an actual demonstration of the ability to exercise ordinary and reasonable control in the operation of a motor vehicle.
- The DDL may waive the knowledge, endorsement, and skills tests for an applicant from another state or a province of Canada who surrenders a valid driver's license from that state or province.
- The examination for an applicant of a commercial driver's license shall include the following: tests of the applicant's eyesight, hearing, ability to read and understand highway signs and traffic rules of the state. Tests will also include a skill test specifically designed for the class of commercial license being applied for as well as an examination of the applicant's ability to perform an inspection of his or her vehicle.

Graduated Drivers Licensing: State has a system of graduated licensing for teen drivers. At 15, teens are eligible for a learner's permit.

- Permit holders may only drive during the day (after 3 months teens can drive until 10 p.m.) with a licensed driver 21 years or older. Permit holders must also accumulate at least 50 hours (10 at night) of parental/guardian certified driving.
- At 16, teens who have held the permit for at least 12 months without a traffic conviction are eligible for an intermediate license.
- Intermediate license holders who are 16 may not drive unsupervised between 11 p.m. and 6 a.m. At 17, intermediate license holders may not drive unsupervised between the hours of 1:00 a.m. and 5:00 a.m.
- At 18, teens are eligible for an unrestricted license.

Issuance/Application: Each application for a driver's license shall be made in a format designated by the DDL and sworn to or affirmed by the applicant as to the truth of the statements made in the application.

- Each application shall include the following information regarding the applicant: full name, digital photo (full face), gender, social security number, residence and mailing address, a brief description of the individual, proof of birth date, proof of identity, legal presence in the U.S., whether the applicant has previously been licensed to drive, and, if so when and by what state. Each application shall also include a consent to release driving record information.
- Social security number not required on license.
- The DMV may not issue a driver's license to a person who has never been issued a driver's license in any jurisdiction until he or she successfully completes the traffic law and substance abuse class.
- The expiration date of a non-citizen's driver's license is linked to the expiration date of that person's visa.

Renewal: Driver's licenses are valid for a period of 6 years and expire at midnight on the licensee's birthday, which next occurs on or after the 6th anniversary of the date of issue.

- An applicant applying for a renewal issuance or renewal extension shall be issued a driver's license or renewal extension sticker which is valid for 4 years except that a driver whose driving record reflects no convictions for the preceding 3 years shall be issued a license renewal extension sticker which is valid for 6 years.
- Drivers who have not had any moving violation convictions for the last 3 years preceding renewal and whose driving privilege in Florida has not been revoked, disqualified, or suspended at any time during the 7 years preceding renewal, are only required to have tested their eyesight and hearing upon renewal. Those drivers who have had moving violation convictions in the last 3 years or who have had their license suspended during the 7 years preceding renewal are required to, in addition to the eyesight and hearing tests, pass a test of their ability to read and understand highway signs.
- Active duty members of the armed forces and their dependents (spouses, children, and step-children under 21 living in the same household) stationed out of state may request a license extension. The license extension card keeps class D and E licenses valid until 90 days after discharge from military service. Extension card must be kept with driver's license and presented with your military ID. The extension card is only available to military personnel who are stationed outside Florida and have a license which expired after July 1, 1995. Members of the military may renew their motor vehicle or motor home registration without penalty, if the service member was on active duty more than 35 miles away from home.

Types of Licenses: Class D: Holder can operate a truck or tractor between 8,000-26,001 lbs. Gross Weight Rating (GWR) or a vehicle that is more than 80 inches wide.

- Class E: Holder can operate a vehicle that is less than 8,000 lbs.
- Motorcycle Endorsement: "MTCY ALSO" or "MTCY ONLY."
- Commercial Class A: Holder can operate a vehicle with a GWR of 26,001 or more, only if the tow is greater than 10,000 lbs.
- Commercial Class B: Holder can operate any single vehicle with a GWR of 26,001 lbs. that is towing less than 10,000 lbs.

- Commercial Class C: Holder can operate a vehicle with a GWR of less than 26,001 lbs.

Traffic Rules

Alcohol Laws: Any person who accepts the privilege of operating a motor vehicle in Florida is deemed to have given his or her consent to submit to an approved chemical or physical test, if the person is lawfully arrested for any offense allegedly committed while the person was driving or was in actual physical control of a motor vehicle.

- Open containers are not permitted. Meets TEA-21 requirements.
- Illegal per se BAC level is .08.
- BAC level for people under 21 is .02.

Cellular Telephone Use: Use of a cellular phone with a headset is permitted while driving if sound is provided through one ear and allows surrounding sounds to be heard with other ear. Localities are prohibited from regulating the use of commercial mobile radio services including cell phones.

Emergency Cellular: Emergency cell *FHP or *347.

Headsets: No person shall operate a vehicle while wearing a headset, headphone, or other listening device, other than a hearing aid or instrument for the improvement of defective human hearing.

Occupant Restraints: It is unlawful for any person to operate a motor vehicle unless the driver and all front seat passengers 18 years and older are restrained by a safety belt. All passengers under the age of 18 must be restrained by a safety belt or by a child restraint device (primary enforcement).

- Every operator of a motor vehicle shall, if the child is 5 years old or younger, provide for the protection of the child using a child restraint device or a seat belt. For children 3 years and under, such restraint device must be a separate carrier or a vehicle manufacturer's integrated child seat. For children ages 4 through 5 a seat belt, a separate carrier, or an integrated child seat may be used.
- Violation of the seat belt law is a secondary offense, however violation of the child restraint law is a primary offense.
- Riding in pickup truck beds is not permitted, except employees on duty.

Railroad Crossing: Any person driving a vehicle and approaching a railroad-highway grade crossing shall stop within 50 feet but not less than 15 feet from the nearest rail of such railroad and shall not proceed until he or she can do so safely when a highway sign is indicating that a train is approaching or when the driver can hear or see an approaching train.

School Buses: Any person using, operating, or driving a vehicle on or over the roads or highways of this state shall, upon approaching any school bus, which displays a stop signal, bring such vehicle to a full stop while the bus is stopped, and the vehicle shall not pass the school bus until the signal has been withdrawn.

Vehicle Equipment & Rules

Bumper Height: Motor vehicles with a net weight of less than 2,500 lbs. shall have a maximum front bumper height of 22 inches and a maximum rear bumper height of 22 inches.

- Motor vehicles with a net weight of between 2,500 lbs. and 3,500 lbs. shall have a maximum front bumper height of 24 inches and a maximum rear bumper height of 26 inches.
- Motor vehicles with a net weight of 3,500 lbs. or more shall have a maximum front bumper height of 27 inches and a maximum rear bumper height of 29 inches.

Glass/Window Tinting: A person shall not operate any motor vehicle on which the vehicle's side windows have been tinted with a material that has a total solar reflectance of visible light of not more than 25% and a light transmittance of at least 28% in the visible light range.

- A person shall not operate any motor vehicle on which the windows behind the driver have been tinted with a screening material consisting of film that has a total solar reflectance of not more than 35% and a light transmittance of less than 15% in the visible light range.
- A person shall not operate any motor vehicle on which the windows behind the driver have been tinted with a perforated screening material which has a total reflectance of visible light of more than 35% and a light transmittance of less than 30%.
- A person shall not operate any motor vehicle on which the windows behind the driver have been tinted by louvered materials that reduce the driver visibility by more than 50%.
- The DMV shall issue a medical exemption certificate to persons who are afflicted with Lupus or similar medical conditions, which require a limited exposure to light. This certificate shall entitle the person to whom the certificate is issued to have screening material on the windows of his/her car which may be a violation of Glass/Window Tinting laws above.

Telematics: No motor vehicle operated on the highways shall be equipped with television-type receiving equipment so located that the viewer or screen is visible from the driver's seat.

Windshield Stickers: No person shall drive any motor vehicle with any sign, poster, or other non-transparent material upon the front windshield, sidewings, or side or rear windows of such vehicle which materially obstructs, obscures, or impairs the driver's clear view of the highway or any intersecting highway.

Motorcycles & Mopeds

Equipment: Every motorcycle shall have brakes capable of developing a brake force that is not less than 43.5% of its gross weight, decelerating to a stop from not more than 20 mph and not less than 14 feet per second, and stopping from a speed of 20 mph in not more than 30 feet. These requirements are based on a surface that is substantially level and is a dry, hard, smooth surface free from loose material.

- Every motorcycle shall be equipped with at least 1 and not more than 2 headlamps.
- Every motorcycle shall carry on the rear, either as part of the taillamp or separately at least 1 red reflector.
- Every motorcycle shall have at least 1 taillamp which shall be located at a height of not more than 72 inches and not less than 20 inches measured from the ground.
- Either a taillamp or a separate lamp shall be so constructed and placed as to illuminate with a white light the rear registration plate and render it clearly legible from

- a distance of 50 feet from the rear.
- Any person who operates a motorcycle on the public streets shall, while so engaged, have the headlight or headlights of the motorcycle turned on.
- Any motorcycle carrying a passenger, other than in a sidecar or enclosed cab, shall be equipped with footrests for such passenger.
- No person shall operate any motorcycle with handlebars that are higher than the top of the shoulders of the person operating the motorcycle.
- A person may not operate or ride upon a motorcycle unless the person is properly wearing protective headgear unless the operator is 21 years of age or older and is covered by an insurance policy providing at least $10,000 in medical benefits for injuries incurred as a result of a crash while operating or riding on a motorcycle.
- A person may not operate a motorcycle unless the person is wearing an eye-protective device over his or her eyes of a type approved by the DMV.
- A person operating a motorcycle shall ride only upon the permanent and regular seat attached and shall not carry any other person unless the motorcycle is specifically designed to carry more than 1 person.

Licenses: The examination for a motorcycle license endorsement tests the applicant's knowledge of the operation of a motorcycle and of any traffic laws specifically relating to motorcycles. Examination also includes an actual demonstration of the applicant's ability to exercise ordinary and reasonable control in the operation of a motorcycle.

- Every 1st-time applicant for licensure to operate a motorcycle who is under 21 years of age must provide proof of completion of a motorcycle safety course.

Mopeds: A person under 16 years of age may not operate or ride upon a moped unless the person is properly wearing protective headgear.

- A person under 16 years old may not operate a motorcycle that has a motor with more than 150 cc displacement.
- A person operating a moped at less than the normal speed of traffic shall ride as close as practicable to the right-hand curb or edge of the roadway unless passing another vehicle proceeding in the same direction or preparing for a left turn.
- No person shall propel a moped upon and along a sidewalk while the motor is operating.

Passenger Car Trailers

Brakes: Every such vehicle and combination of vehicles shall be equipped with service brakes adequate to control the movement of and to stop and hold such vehicle under all conditions of loading, and on any grade incident to its operation.

- Every vehicle shall be equipped with brakes acting on all wheels except trailers, semitrailers, or pole trailers of a gross weight not exceeding 3,000 lbs., provided that the total weight on and including the wheels of the trailer or trailers shall not exceed 40 percent of the gross weight of the towing vehicle when connected to the trailer or trailers; and the combination of vehicles, consisting of the towing vehicle and its total towed load, is capable of complying with the performance requirements of the law.
- Pole trailers with a gross weight in excess of 3,000 lbs. manufactured prior to January 1, 1972, need not be equipped with brakes.
- Every towing vehicle, when used to tow another vehicle equipped with air-controlled brakes, in other than driveway or tow-away operations, shall be equipped with 2 means for emergency application of the trailer brakes.

Dimensions: Total length: 65 feet (excludes safety devices approved by the state); trailer length: 40 feet (excludes safety devices approved by the state); width: 102 inches (excludes mirrors and safety devices); height: 13.6 feet.

Hitch: When a vehicle is towing a trailer or semitrailer by means of a hitch to the rear of the vehicle, there shall be attached in addition thereto safety chains, cables, or other safety devices.

Lighting: Every motor vehicle shall be equipped with at least 2 taillamps mounted on the rear, which, when lighted emit a red light plainly visible from a distance of 1,000 feet to the rear.

Mirrors: Every vehicle, operated singly or when towing any other vehicle, shall be equipped with a mirror so located as to reflect to the driver's view of the highway for a distance of at least 200 feet to the rear of the motor vehicle.

Passenger Restrictions: No person or persons shall occupy a house trailer while it is being moved upon a public street or highway.

Speed Limits: Unless otherwise posted, 30 mph in business and residential districts, and 55 mph at any time at all other locations. Turnpike and other designated highways 65 mph, except where posted 70 mph (minimum speed 50 mph).

Towing: When 1 vehicle is towing another, the drawbar or other connection shall be of sufficient strength to pull all weight towed.
- The drawbar connection shall not exceed 15 feet from 1 vehicle to the other.
- When 1 vehicle is towing another and the connection consists of a chain, rope, or cable, there shall be displayed upon such connection a white flag or cloth not less than 12 inches square.

Miscellaneous Provisions

Bail Bonds: Mandatory recognition of AAA arrest bond certificates up to $1,000 with specified exceptions. May vary within 67 counties.

Liability Laws: No fault law requires anyone who owns or has registered a motor vehicle with 4 or more wheels (excluding taxis and limos), that has been in the state for at least 90 days of the past 365 to have the following coverage. All drivers are required to have insurance policies of at least $10,000 for an individual's bodily injury; $20,000 for injury to multiple persons; $10,000 for property damage; and a $30,000 minimum per accident.

Weigh Stations: The following vehicles must stop: (1) agricultural, motor vehicles (including trailers) which are or could be used in the production, manufacture, storage, sale, or transportation of any food product or any agricultural, horticultural or live stock product, except private passenger automobiles with no trailer in tow, travel trailers, camping trailers, and motor homes; (2) any commercial vehicle (a) with a GWR of 10,000 lbs. or more, (b) designed to transport more than 10 passengers, or (c) used to transport hazardous materials.

Fees & Taxes

Table 1: Title Fees

Vehicle Type	Title Fee
New Vehicle, Never Titled Before	$31.25
Vehicle Previously Titled in Florida	$29.25
Vehicle Previously Titled in Another State	$33.25
Lien Recording	$2.00 + title fee
Mopeds	no title required
Duplicate Title	$10.00
Fast Title Service	$7.00

Table 2: Registration Fees

Vehicle Type	Registration Fee
Initial Registration of Motor Vehicle	$100.00
Motor Vehicle under 2,500 lbs.	$27.60
Motor Vehicle 2,500-3,499 lbs.	$35.60
Motor Vehicle 3,500 lbs. or more	$45.60
Trailers of 500 lbs. or less	$16.60
Trailers of over 500 lbs.	$21.60
Motorcycles	$24.10
Mopeds	$19.10
Duplicate Registration	$2.50
Duplicate Plate	$10.00

Table 3: License Fees

License Class	Fee
Driver's License (D&E)	$20.00
Learner's Permit	$20.00
Class D & E Renewal	$15.00
Commercial License Fee	$50.00
Late Renewal Fee	$1.00
Change of Name	$10.00
Duplicate Fee	$29.25
Motorcycle Endorsement	$5.00

Table 4: Vehicle Taxes

Tax	Rate
Service Fee if processed at a tax office rather than the DMV	$5.25
State Use Tax	6%
Gasoline Tax; (Diesel)	$0.141/gallon; ($0.267/gallon)

Table 5: Miscellaneous Fees

Tax	Amount	Payable Upon
Fast Service Title	$7.00	application for title
Special Plates Fee	$15.00-$25.00	application for plates
Plates Transfer Fee	$4.50	transfer of plates
License Plate Replacement Fee	$10.00	replacement of plate

GEORGIA

Contact Information

Department of Driver Services (DDS)
2206 East View Parkway
P.O. Box 80447
Conyers, GA 30013

(678) 413-8400
www.dds.ga.gov

Georgia State Patrol
2100 Roswell Road
Marietta, GA 30062

(770) 528-3251
www.state.ga.us/gsp

Georgia Department of Transportation
No. 2 Capitol Square, S.W.
Atlanta, GA 30334

(404) 656-5267
www.dot.state.ga.us/

Department of Revenue
Property Tax Division
4245 International Parkway, Suite A
Hapeville, GA 30354-3918

(404) 968-0707
www2.state.ga.us/Departments/DOR/

Georgia's Clean Air Force
GCAF Waiver Center
Franklin Square Office Park
2141 Kingston Court, Suite 106
Marietta, GA 30067

1 (800) 449-2471
www.cleanairforce.com

Vehicle Title

Application: An application for the first certificate of title in the state must be submitted to the DDS or the county tag agent within 90 days from the date of purchase.

- The application must contain (1) the name, residence, and mailing address of the owner; (2) a description of the vehicle; (3) the date of purchase; and (4) the name and address of the person from whom the vehicle was acquired and the existence or non-existence of any liens on the vehicle.
- If the vehicle was purchased from a dealer, the dealer is required to submit the application.
- If the application is for a vehicle last previously registered in another state, the certificate of title issued by the other state or county must be included with the application. If the applicant is the last previously registered owner in such state, the application need not contain the name and address of the person from whom the vehicle was acquired.

Transfer of Ownership: The transferor must enter on the certificate of title the mileage shown on the odometer at the time the transferor assigns the vehicle unless the vehicle is more than 10 model years old or the vehicle has a Gross Vehicle Weight Rating (GVWR) of more than 16,000 lbs.

- The transferor must, at the time of delivery, execute an assignment and warranty of title to the transferee in the space provided on the certificate of title.

- If the transfer is by operation of law, the transferee has 30 days to apply for new title.
- Requires proof of the payment of the sales and use tax as a precondition to titling motor vehicles.

Mobile Homes: Owners of manufactured homes are required to obtain a motor vehicle certificate of title.

- The purchaser of a manufactured home must submit a certificate stating that all ad valorem taxes assessed against the manufactured home have been paid.

Vehicle Registration

Application: All applications are made to the tag agent of the county wherein the applicant's vehicle is required to be returned for ad valorem taxation.

- The application must include the name, place of residence, and address of the applicant; a description of the vehicle; from whom, where, and when the vehicle was purchased; and the total amount of liens with the name and address of the lienholder.
- Initial applications for registration must contain satisfactory proof of ownership.
- No application shall be accepted and no certificate of registration shall be issued to any motor vehicle which was not manufactured to comply with federal emission and safety standards applicable to new motor vehicles.

Non-Residents: A person must register his or her motor vehicle within 30 days of becoming a resident of the state.

- A non-resident owner must register his or her vehicle if temporarily residing in Georgia longer than 30 days.
- Military personnel who are stationed in Georgia but are not residents of Georgia are not required to obtain Georgia automobile license plates if they have valid license tags from the resident state.

Registration Type: Every owner of a motor vehicle, including a motorcycle, and every owner of a trailer must, during the owner's registration period in each year, register the vehicle and obtain a license to operate it for the 12-month period until the person's next registration period.

- For individuals, the registration period is the 30-day period ending at midnight on the birthday of the owner whose surname first appears on the certificate of title except in counties authorized by a local act to have a 4-month staggered period. For businesses and organizations, registration periods are staggered throughout the calendar year depending on the first letter of the entity's name.
- A purchaser or transferee must register a motor vehicle within 30 days of acquiring the vehicle. This registration is valid until the person's next registration period.

Emissions Inspection: An annual emissions inspection is required prior to registration in covered counties. The covered counties are Cherokee, Clayton, Cobb, Coweta, DeKalb, Douglas, Fayette, Forsyth, Fulton, Gwinnett, Henry, Paulding, and Rockdale. All covered vehicles must have a current passing Certificate of Emission Inspection or a waiver to obtain a vehicle registration each year.

- The inspection requirement applies to all 1975 and newer model year light duty vehicles, all 1975 and newer model year light duty trucks with a GVWR of 8,500 lbs. or less, and vehicles operated for 60 days or more per year on federal installations located in whole or in part in the covered counties.
- Vehicles which are capable of being operated on both gasoline and any alternate

fuel are covered by the inspection requirements, and must be tested on gasoline.
- New vehicles are exempt from testing until the test year 2 years following the model year of the vehicle. Effective January 1, 2001, new vehicles are exempt from testing until the test year 3 years following the model year of the vehicle.
- A vehicle that is driven less than 5,000 miles per year, is 10 years old or older, and is owned or currently registered by a person 65 years or older is exempt from inspection.
- A vehicle that is an antique or collector car or truck 25 years old or older is exempt from inspection.
- A vehicle that fails reinspection despite appropriate repairs meeting or exceeding $627 will be granted a waiver. This amount increases each year by the Consumer Price Index.

Safety Inspection: No person may drive or move on any highway any motor vehicle or trailer unless the equipment is in good working order and adjustment as required by law and the vehicle is in a safe mechanical condition that will not endanger the driver, other occupant, or any person on the highway.
- Any law enforcement officer may conduct an inspection of any vehicle suspected of being operated in an unsafe condition.

License Plates

Disbursement: License plates and revalidation decals are issued only upon applications made to the local tag agent.
- The owners of new or unregistered vehicles are allowed 7 business days after the date of purchase to purchase a tag and/or renewal decal.
- License plates and revalidation decals may be purchased by mail.
- Metal license plates issued on or after January 1, 1997 are used for a period of 5 years, and a revalidation decal is issued in those years in which a metal plate is not issued.
- Defaced or illegible plates or renewal decals must be turned in at the time the replacement tag and/or renewal decal is issued. If replacement tags or decals were obtained for lost or stolen tags or decals, the original tags or decals must be immediately turned in to the Internal Administration Unit (IAU) of the DOR.
- All passenger cars, including station wagons and other utility vehicles, including motorcycles, motor scooters, and buses, must display the license plate assigned to it on the rear of the vehicle.
- All trucks and trailers must, where practical, display the license plate on the rear of the vehicle. However, if the truck or trailer routinely engages in activities wherein it is inevitable that a license plate attached to the rear would be defaced, destroyed, or lost, the plate may be attached to the front.
- Every motor vehicle must at all times have the license plate assigned to it firmly attached in such a manner that it will not swing and that it will be plainly visible. It is the duty of the operator to keep the license plate legible at all times. No license plate may be covered with any material unless the material is colorless and transparent.
- Applicants for a disabled persons license plate must submit to the county tax commissioner or tax collector a certificate from a doctor certifying that the applicant has permanently lost the use of a leg or both legs, or an arm or both arms, or any

combination thereof, or is so severely disabled as to be unable to move without the aid of crutches or a wheelchair.

Transfer of Plates: If a person ceases to own the vehicle for which an annual or 5-year license plate and revalidation decals were issued, the owner may apply to have the plates assigned to a new vehicle of the same class as the original vehicle.

- The transferee of a motor vehicle may not use the license plate and renewal decal assigned to that vehicle unless the transferor also assigns the plate and decal to the transferee.
- When the registered owner of a jointly owned vehicle is deceased, the license plate issued for the vehicle may be transferred to the surviving owner's name, provided that the surviving owner acquires a new certificate of title.
- The local tag agent can transfer or assign renewal decals and license plates for all license plates which they maintain in inventory. All other transfers must be mailed directly to the IAU of the DOR.
- All tags and renewal decals are transferable to a new owner except dealer tags, amateur radio operator tags, handicapped veteran tags, national guard tags, disabled veterans tags, citizens' band radio tags, special prestige tags, foreign consuls tags, commanders of patriotic organizations tags, legislative tags, and other special tags.

Driver's Licenses

Examination: The DDS examines every applicant for a driver's license.

- Applicants 18 years of age or older with a valid and current license issued by another state of the United States or the District of Columbia who surrender their previous licenses to obtain a Georgia license are only required to take an eyesight test (20/40 visual acuity required).
- All other applicants are required to take both a written and on-the-road driving test as well as an eyesight test.
- An applicant that fails the driving test the first time must wait until the next day to retake the test. After the second failure, the applicant must wait 5 working days to retake the test. After the third or subsequent failures, the applicant must wait 30 days to retake the test.

Graduated Drivers Licensing: State has a system of graduated licensing for teen drivers.

- Novice drivers at least 15 years of age may apply to the DDS for an instruction/learner's permit to operate a non-commercial Class C vehicle. While driving, the permit holder must be accompanied by a person at least 21 years of age with a Class C license. Novice drivers must hold the permit for at least 12 months and pass a road test before being eligible for an intermediate license.
- Teens at least 17 years of age may apply for an intermediate license. Intermediate license holders may not drive between midnight and 6:00 a.m. — no exceptions. For the first 6 months of the intermediate license, novice drivers are prohibited from transporting any non-family members under 21. Thereafter, intermediate license holders are prohibited from transporting more than 1 passenger who is a non-family member under 21. Intermediate license holders must accumulate 40 hours (6 at night) of supervised driving certified by a parent or guardian.
- Teens are eligible for a full unrestricted license at age 18 as long as they have had

no major traffic convictions in the last 12 months.
- The intermediate license requirements apply to all applicants for an unrestricted license.
- Drivers may only move from one stage of licensing to the next if he or she has completed 12 consecutive months without a conviction for one or more of the following: DUI, eluding a police officer, drag racing, reckless driving, hit and run, and any moving violation for which 4 or more points are assessed.

Issuance/Application: The applicant is required to state whether his or her driver's license has ever been revoked or suspended in any jurisdictions and whether he or she has any previous convictions for violation of motor vehicle laws. All applicants will be screened through the National Driver's Registry, and if they are found to be in suspension, revocation, or cancellation in their former licensing jurisdiction, then their Georgia driver's license will be subsequently suspended, revoked, or cancelled and they could be punished for the commission of a misdemeanor.

- An applicant for an initial Georgia driver's license must supply a birth certificate, certified copy of court records for adoption or a name or sex change, certified naturalization documentation, immigration card, or valid passport. A color photograph is required on all new licenses.
- All applicants must provide valid documentation of U.S. citizenship or legal authorization from the U.S. Immigration and Naturalization Service.
- All applicants must provide proof that they reside in Georgia and provide a valid Georgia address. The following items are acceptable proof: (1) a utility bill, bank statement, or rental contract or receipt with a valid Georgia address; (2) employer verification; or (3) Georgia license issued to parent, guardian, or spouse.
- A marriage license, social security card, previous year income tax return, current insurance policy, current automobile registration receipt, or voter registration card are acceptable proof of identity to obtain a replacement Georgia driver's license.
- Applicants and licensees have 60 days to notify the DDS of a change of name or address.
- License exemptions exist for military personnel, their spouses, and children and for non-residents who have a valid license issued by their home state. Military personnel on active duty may drive on an expired license for 6 months after returning to the state.
- Persons under 18 years of age who have dropped out of school or been suspended or expelled may be denied a license.
- A person must be 18 years of age to receive a Class A, B, or C license.
- Social security number on license is optional.

Renewal: Every driver's license will expire on the licensee's birthday in the 5th year following the issuance of such license. Every person applying for a renewal must successfully complete an eyesight exam.

- Requires drivers 64 and older to have an eye examination at the time of renewal.
- Licenses are renewable 150 days prior to expiration.
- Active-duty military and full-time students (or dependent of same) living out-of-state may obtain a non-photo renewal of their Georgia driver's license by mail.

Types of Licenses: Classes A & B: Vehicles with a GVWR of 26,001 lbs. or more.

- Class C: Any single vehicle with a GVWR not in excess of 26,000 lbs. or any such vehicle towing a vehicle with a GVWR not in excess of 10,000 lbs. and any self-

propelled or towed vehicle that is equipped to serve as temporary living quarters for recreational, camping, or travel purposes and is used solely as a family or personal conveyance.
- Class D: Provisional license applicable to non-commercial Class C vehicles for which an applicant desires a driver's license but is not presently licensed to drive.
- Class P: Instructional/learner's permit applicable to all types of vehicles for which an applicant desires a driver's license but is not presently licensed to drive. This permit is applicable to all drivers 15 years of age and older.

Traffic Rules

Alcohol Laws: State has implied consent law (implied consent applies only to motor vehicles).
- Open containers are not permitted. Meets TEA-21 requirements.
- Illegal per se BAC level is .08.
- BAC level for people under 21 is .02.

Cellular Telephone Use: The proper use of a radio, citizen band radio, or mobile telephone is permitted as long as a driver exercises due care in operating a motor vehicle on the highways of the state and does not engage in any actions which distract him or her from the safe operation of the vehicle.
- The emergency phone number is 911 or *GSP (*477).

Headsets: No person may operate a motor vehicle while wearing a headset or headphone which would impair that person's ability to hear, nor may any person wear any device which impairs such person's vision.

Occupant Restraints: Each occupant of the front seat of a passenger vehicle shall wear a seat belt when the vehicle is in motion.
- Safety belts are required for all minors ages 6 through 17 in all seats.
- Children 5 years of age or younger are required to be restrained in a system installed and being used in accordance with the manufacturer's directions while the vehicle is in motion.
- Violations of the occupant protection laws are a primary offense.
- It is unlawful for anyone under the age of 18 to ride as a passenger in the uncovered bed of a pickup truck on any interstate highway in the state.

Railroad Crossing: A driver must stop within 50 feet but not less than 15 feet from the nearest rail of a railroad when: (1) a clearly visible device gives warning of the immediate approach of a train; (2) a crossing gate is lowered or a human flagman signals the approach of a train; or (3) an approaching train is plainly visible and is in hazardous proximity to the crossing.
- Motor vehicles carrying passengers for hire, school buses, and vehicles containing hazardous substances, explosive substances, or flammable liquids must stop at all railroad crossings and look and listen in both directions.

School Buses: The driver of a vehicle meeting or overtaking from either direction any school bus stopped on the highway shall stop before reaching the bus when the visual signals indicating that traffic should stop are in operation.
- The driver of a vehicle upon a divided highway need not stop upon meeting a passing school bus which is on a different roadway, or upon a controlled access highway

when the school bus is stopped in a loading zone where pedestrians are not permitted to cross the roadway.

Vehicle Equipment & Rules

Bumper Height: Modification of original vehicle bumper height or altering suspension system is illegal if altered more than 2 inches above or below factory recommendations.

Glass/Window Tinting: Front windshields may not have material or glazing applied or affixed to reduce light transmission.

- Material and glazing may not be applied or affixed to the rear windshield or the side or door windows so that light transmission is reduced to less than 32%, plus or minus 3%, or light reflectance increased to more than 20%.
- The glass tinting restrictions do not apply to any vehicle not registered in the state.
- The restrictions do not apply to the rear and side windows, except those windows to the right and left of the driver, of any multipurpose passenger vehicle, school bus, bus for public transportation, church or other nonprofit organization van, limousine owned or leased by a public or private entity, any vehicles with windows that were tinted before factory delivery or are permitted by federal law or regulation.

Windshield Stickers: No person may drive any motor vehicle with any sign, poster, or other non-transparent material upon the front windshield, side windows, or rear windows of such vehicle which obstructs the driver's clear view of the highway or any intersecting highway.

Motorcycles & Mopeds

Equipment: A person may wear a headset or headphone for communication purposes while operating a motorcycle.

- No person may operate or ride upon a motorcycle unless he or she is wearing protective headgear that complies with standards established by the Commissioner of Motor Vehicle Safety.
- No person may operate or ride upon a motorcycle that is not equipped with a windshield unless he or she is wearing an eye protective device that complies with standards established by the Commissioner of Motor Vehicle Safety.
- Any motorcycle carrying a passenger, other than in a sidecar or enclosed cab, must be equipped with footrests for such passenger.
- Motorcycle handlebars cannot be more than 15 inches in height above that portion of the seat occupied by the operator. Motorcycles cannot be equipped with a backrest more commonly known as a sissy bar that is designed in such a way as to create a sharp point at its apex.
- A person must ride a motorcycle only upon the permanent and regular seat; and the operator must not carry any other person unless the motorcycle is designed to carry more than 1 person.

Licenses: Operators of motorcycles, motor-driven cycles, and 3-wheeled motorcycles must have a Class M driver's license.

- A person must be 16 years of age to receive a Class M license.
- Motorcycle license applicants who have successfully completed the DPS-sponsored beginner rider education and training course will only be required to pass an eye examination.

Mopeds: Mopeds are exempt from registration and title requirements.
- Every person operating a moped has all the rights and is subject to all the duties applicable to the driver of any other vehicle except that the operator of a moped is not required to comply with requirements relating to headlights, taillights, windshields, and eye-protective devices.
- No person under 15 years of age may operate a moped or an electric-assisted bicycle upon the public roads and highways. No person may operate a moped upon the public roads and highways of this state unless he or she has in his or her possession a valid driver's license, instructional permit, or limited permit issued to him or her. All classes of licenses, instructional permits, or limited permits issued are valid for the purposes of operating mopeds upon the public roads and highways of this state. No license or permit is required for the operation of an electric-assisted bicycle.
- No person may operate or ride as a passenger upon a moped unless he or she is wearing protective headgear that complies with standards established by the Commissioner of Motor Vehicle Safety.

Passenger Car Trailers

Brakes: Every trailer of 3,000 lbs. GVWR or more must be equipped with brakes on all wheels.

Dimensions: Total length: 60 feet (excludes safety and energy conservation devices); trailer length: not specified; width: 102 inches (allowed on certain roads); height: 13.6 feet.

Hitch: Safety chain required.

Lighting: Every trailer and pole trailer must be equipped with 2 taillights located at a height of not more than 60 inches nor less than 20 inches and that emit a plainly visible red light from a distance of 500 feet to the rear.

Mirrors: Every motor vehicle which is so loaded as to obstruct the driver's view through the rear of the vehicle must be equipped with a mirror so located as to reflect to the driver a view of the highway for a distance of at least 200 feet to the rear of the vehicle.

Speed Limits: 55 mph/30 mph in urban or residential district.

Towing: No driver of a motor vehicle may allow a person or persons to occupy a towed house trailer while it is being towed by a motor vehicle upon a public highway.

Miscellaneous Provisions

Bail Bonds: Mandatory recognition of AAA arrest bond certificates up to $1,000 with specified exceptions. State law also permits surrender of driver's license in lieu of bond for Georgia drivers only.

Liability Laws: Compulsory liability insurance law. Owners of motor vehicles must certify by affirmation evidence of liability insurance at the time they apply for registration. Insurance coverage must be submitted electronically by insurance companies to the DMVS. Exceptions: (1) vehicles covered under a commercial vehicle policy may continue to use an insurance card; (2) if a policy was provided in the last 30 days a written binder agreement is sufficient; (3) a rental car agreement provides proof of insurance; and (4) if a driver can prove that he or she bought the car within the last 20 days then a written declaration of coverage for another motor vehicle is good proof of insurance.

- Drivers must keep proof of minimum insurance coverage in vehicle. The requirement does not apply to the owner of any vehicle for which records or the database at DMVS indicates that coverage is effective.
- All motor vehicle insurance policies issued in the state must provide coverage for damage for liability on account of accidents of not less than $15,000 because of bodily injury or death of 1 person in any 1 accident, to a limit of not less than $30,000 because of bodily injury or death to 2 or more persons in any 1 accident, and $10,000 because of injury to or destruction of property of others in any 1 accident.
- State has non-resident service process of law and limit on liability to injured guests.

Weigh Stations: The following vehicles must stop: (1) agricultural vehicles; (2) passenger or specialty vehicles, either single or in combination (towing a trailer) with GVWR of 10,000 lbs. or more; and (3) commercial trucks with GVWR of 10,000 lbs. or more.

Fees & Taxes

Table 1: Title & Registration Fees

Vehicle Type	Title Fee	Registration Fee
Passenger Motor Vehicles	$18.00	$20.00
Private Trucks less than 14,000 lbs.	$18.00	$20.00
Farm Trucks	$18.00	$20.00
Farm Trailers including but not limited to Livestock Trailers	no title required	$12.00
Non-Commercial House Trailers and Auto Trailers	$18.00	$12.00
Boat Trailers and Pole Trailers	no title required	$12.00
Motorcycles	$18.00	$20.00
Mopeds	no title required	no registration required
Replacement	$8.00	$1.00

Table 2: License Fees

License Class	Fee
Purchase of License Plates and Revalidation Decals by Mail	$1.00
License Plate Transfer from Vehicle to Vehicle	$5.00
License Plate Transfer from Owner to Owner with Transfer of Vehicle	$1.00
Replacement of Tags or Decals	$8.00
Personalized Prestige Plates	$25.00
Instruction Permit for Classes A, B, C, D, and M Driver's Licenses	$10.00
Classes A, B, C, and M Driver's Licenses	$15.00
Class D Provisional License	$10.00
Replacement	$5.00

Table 3: Vehicle Taxes

Tax	Rate
Personal Property Tax	Annually the state revenue commissioner prepares and publishes a manual of motor vehicle assessments for the various types of motor vehicle property in Georgia. The motor vehicles value is determined as an average of current fair market value and current wholesale value
State Sales Tax	4% of retail price (additional 1% Rapid Transit Tax in DeKalb and Fulton Counties) or 1% local option tax in certain jurisdictions
Gasoline Tax; (Diesel)	$0.075/gallon; ($0.075/gallon) + 4% sales tax

Table 4: Miscellaneous Fees

Tax	Amount
Emissions Inspection	not less than $10.00; no more than $25.00
Delinquent Registration / Transfer Fee	25% of registration fee, plus $1.00

HAWAII

Contact Information

Hawaii's motor vehicle laws are governed at the state level and are also regulated at the individual county level by the county directors of finance.

Division of Motor Vehicles and Licensing
City and County of Honolulu
1455 S. Beretania Street (808) 523-4100
Honolulu, HI 96814

Department of Motor Vehicles
County of Maui
1580 Kaahumanu Avenue (808) 270-7363
Wailuku, HI 96793

Department of Finance, Division of Treasury
County of Kauai
4444 Rice Street (808) 241-6577
Lihue, HI 96766

Motor Vehicle Licensing and Registration
County of Hawaii
Aupuni Center
101 Pauahi Street, Suite 5 (808) 961-8351
Hilo, HI 96720 www.hawaii-county.com/forms/mvrforms.html

Hawaii Department of Transportation
Aliiaimoku Building
869 Punchbowl Street (808) 587-2150
Honolulu, HI 96813 www.state.hi.us/dot/

Vehicle Title

Application: Upon registration of a vehicle, the county director of finance issues a certificate of registration and a certificate of ownership.

- A certificate of ownership does not need to be renewed each year and remains valid until replaced by a new certificate of ownership or cancelled by the director of finance.

Transfer of Ownership: Within 30 days of a transfer of ownership, the transferee must forward the certificate of ownership to the county director of finance, after both the transferor and transferee have signed the certificate in the appropriate space for transfers.

- Upon receipt of the certificate of ownership, the director of finance issues a new certificate of registration and a new certificate of ownership.
- Within 10 days of a transfer of ownership, the transferor must give notice, on an official form, to the director of finance of such transfer indicating the date of transfer, the names and addresses of the transferor and transferee and a description of the vehicle; failure to comply with this rule carries a fine of not more than $100.

Vehicle Registration

Application: The application for registration is made to the director of finance for the county where the vehicle is to be operated and must contain the name, occupation, and address of the owner, a description of the vehicle, and the type of fuel it uses.

- Upon registration of a vehicle, the director of finance issues a certificate of registration and a certificate of ownership.
- If the address or name of the registered owner of a vehicle is changed from that stated on the application or the certificate of registration, the registered owner must notify the appropriate county finance director, in writing, within 30 days of the change; when the name of the registered owner is changed, along with the notification of such change, the registered owner must submit the certificate of ownership, the current certificate of registration, and proof of the change of name.
- An application for registration will not be accepted unless the vehicle is to be operated in the county of application at the time of application, but an application for a vehicle that is not within the state will be accepted provided the vehicle is currently registered in the state and the application is accompanied by the name and local address of the applicant, a description of the vehicle, a copy of the bill of sale, and a written statement signed by the applicant stating that the use tax will be paid within 60 days of arrival of the vehicle in the state.
- If a vehicle is moved to another county and is to be operated in that county, the existing registration will remain valid until it expires, at which time the owner must apply for registration to the finance director of the county in which the vehicle is located, whether or not the owner is domiciled or has his principal place of business in that county.
- A new unlicensed vehicle that is not within the state may be registered when the application is accompanied by a written certificate signed by the seller stating the name and address of the seller, the purchaser, and a description of the vehicle.

Non-Residents: Within 30 days of operating a vehicle that has been registered in another state or country, the owner must apply to the director of finance for an out-of-state vehicle registration permit.

HI

- Upon receipt of an out-of-state permit, the director of finance issues the owner of an out-of-state vehicle a distinctive registration certificate and an emblem indicating the date of expiration of the permit which must be affixed to the rear bumper of the vehicle, or rear fender of a motorcycle.
- A certificate of registration issued for out-of-state vehicles is valid for the unexpired portion of the registration period in accordance with the law of the other jurisdiction.
- Military personnel on active duty in Hawaii may maintain home state vehicle registration.

Registration Type: The certificate of registration must be kept in the registered vehicle at all times and must be presented at the request of a peace officer.

- All certificates of registration expire at midnight on December 31 of each year and must be renewed annually before April 1 of each year with such renewal taking effect as of January 1 of each year; however, the individual counties may employ a staggered system of registration.

Safety Inspection: Any police officer of any county may require the owner of a vehicle to submit the vehicle for inspection.

- All vehicles having a Gross Vehicle Weight Rating (GVWR) of 10,000 lbs. or less must obtain a certificate of inspection prior to the issuance of registration, and all such vehicles must be certified every 12 months.
- Vehicles with a GVWR of more than 10,000 lbs., as well as taxicabs, buses, and ambulances must obtain a certificate of inspection prior to the issuance of registration, and must be certified every 6 months.
- Stickers indicating issuance of a certificate of inspection must be affixed to the vehicle.
- Operation of a vehicle that has not been granted a certificate of inspection carries a fine of not more than $100.

License Plates

Disbursement: Two plates are issued by the director of finance upon original registration; motorcycles and trailers receive only 1 plate.

- Special plates are issued for consuls and official representatives of foreign governments at no charge.
- Special plates are also authorized for owners of an amateur radio station license and for disabled persons.
- Regulation plates must be surrendered to the county civil defense agency upon receipt of special plates.
- Special plates are issued for antique motor vehicles and are used in lieu of standard plates.

Transfer of Plates: An owner of a vehicle may request, and the director has discretion to permit, the transfer of license plates from an old vehicle to a new vehicle acquired by the owner.

- Upon the transfer of ownership of a vehicle or upon the expiration or revocation of an amateur radio station license, a holder of special plates must surrender them to the administrator of the county civil defense agency.

Driver's Licenses

Examination: A driver's license examination includes a test of the applicant's eyesight (20/40 visual acuity required) and any further physical examination the examiner of drivers finds necessary to determine the applicant's fitness to operate a vehicle, a written exam demonstrating ability to understand highway signs and rules of the road, and a roadside examination.

- Every applicant under 18 years old must provide proof of completion of an approved driver education program and a behind-the-wheel training course.
- An applicant that is at least 16 years old, but not more than 17 years old will not be examined by the examiner of drivers unless the applicant has held a valid instruction permit for at least 90 days.
- The examination for an instruction permit does not include a roadside test.
- An applicant who fails the knowledge or practical test must wait 1 week before re-taking the exam.

Graduated Drivers Licensing: State has a system of graduated licensing for teen drivers.

- At age 15 and 6 months, teens are eligible for a learner's permit and must hold it for at least 6 months.
- At age 16, teens are eligible for an intermediate license. During this stage, teens are restricted from driving from 11:00 p.m. to 5:00 a.m. (exceptions include driving to and from work or school-authorized activities). Transportation of more than 1 passenger under age 18 who is not a family member also is prohibited during this stage.
- Teens who have held a provisional license for 6 months and are at least 17 years of age can apply for an unrestricted license.

Issuance/Application: A license will not be issued to any person whose license has been suspended or revoked, or has within 2 years been convicted of driving under the influence of alcohol or drugs.

- Learner's permit may be issued to a person who is at least 15 years old; such permits are valid for 1 year and require the holder to operate a vehicle, other than a motorcycle, only when a licensed driver at least 18 years old accompanies the permit holder in the vehicle.
- A driver's license may be issued to a person who is at least 16 years old, but less than 18 years old, but such persons must provide proof that they have completed an approved driver education program and a behind-the-wheel training course.
- An application by any person under 18 years of age for a driver's license or instruction permit must be signed by the applicant's father and mother, the custodial parent or guardian(s), or any responsible individual who is willing to assume obligation for negligence or misconduct of the minor applicant; whichever individual(s) signs for the applicant will be held jointly and severally liable for any negligence or misconduct by the minor applicant when driving a motor vehicle.
- All applicants must produce a valid motor vehicle or liability insurance identification card; the examiner of drivers will not issue a license without such liability card.
- An application for a driver's license or temporary permit must include such information as necessary to allow the examiner of drivers to register the applicant with the United States Selective Service System; failure to include such information will cause the examiner of drivers to refuse to issue a license or permit.
- A license must include a color photograph. License does not include social security number.

- Allows a person who does not have a social security number to receive a driver's license if they have a Social Security Administration letter stating that the applicant is ineligible to obtain a social security number; and either show a government issued photo identification document or other identification documents deemed as acceptable by the DMV Director.
- If the holder of a license changes residence or his or her name, the licensee must notify the examiner of drivers, in writing, of the person's old and new addresses, or former and new name, within 30 days of the change; failure to comply with these rules carries a fine of not more than $25.

Renewal: Licenses expire on the first birthday of the licensee not less than 6 years after the license was issued, unless the licensee is 15 to 17 years old, in which case the license will expire on the first birthday of the licensee not less than 4 years after the license was issued, or if the licensee is 72 years old or older the license expires 2 years after the date of issuance. An application for renewal may not be made more than 6 months prior to expiration of a license, and an application for renewal that is made more than 90 days after expiration of an old license will be treated as an application for a new license and the applicant will be examined as such.

- A license holder seeking renewal must apply in person before the examiner of drivers but is not required to undergo re-examination of the person's driving skills.
- No driver's license will be renewed until the applicant has passed the vision test.
- Application for renewal may be made by mail if the licensee holds a category (1), (2), or (3) license and is temporarily absent from the state when the license expires. The licensee must submit a statement from a licensed physician not more than 6 months prior to the date of expiration of the license indicating the applicant meets the necessary physical requirements to operate a vehicle and the licensee must also include a notarized statement certifying he or she is a resident of the state and does not hold a valid license from any other jurisdiction.
- Active duty military personnel are exempt from renewal requirements until 30 days after separation from the military or return to the state.

Types of Licenses: Licenses are issued according to 4 categories:
- Category (1) permits operation of a motor scooter.
- Category (2) permits operation of a motorcycle or a motor scooter.
- Category (3) permits operation of passenger cars of any GVWR, buses designed to carry 15 or fewer passengers, and trucks or vans with a GVWR of 15,000 lbs. or less.
- Category (4) permits operation of any category (3) vehicle and any truck having a GVWR of between 15,001 and 26,000 lbs.

Traffic Rules

Alcohol Laws: Operation of a motor vehicle carries with it the implied consent to have the driver's blood, breath, or urine tested for the presence of alcohol or drugs. Open containers are not permitted. Meets TEA-21 requirements.
- Illegal per se BAC level is .08.
- BAC level for people under 21 is .02.

Emergency Radio/Cellular: Emergency cell phone number is 911 or *273.
- Citizen band radio channel (9) is not monitored for emergency calls.

Headsets: Wearing of radio headsets while operating a motor vehicle is permitted.

Occupant Restraints: It is unlawful to operate a motor vehicle unless the driver and any front seat passengers 17 and older are restrained by a seat belt. All passengers in the front or back seats of the vehicle between the ages of 4 and 17 must be restrained by a seat belt. Children under 4 years of age must be restrained in a child passenger restraint system.

- Violation of the occupant protection laws is a primary offense.
- It is unlawful to operate a pickup truck with passengers in the bed of the truck unless there is no seating available in the cab. However, the passengers must be seated on the floor and the side racks must be securely fastened and the tailgate securely closed.
- Riding in a pickup truck bed is prohibited, unless there are no available seats in the cab. Additional gaps in coverage apply; see Occupant Protection Chart.

Railroad Crossing: Vehicles approaching a railroad crossing must stop within 55 feet but not less than 15 feet from the nearest rail when a signal device indicates the immediate approach of a train, a crossing gate is lowered or a flagman signals stop, a train within 1,500 feet signals that it is approaching, or is in hazardous proximity to the crossing.

School Buses: Whenever a school bus is stopped on a roadway and its visual signals are activated, the driver of every motor vehicle on the same roadway, in either direction, must stop not less than 20 feet from the school bus and may proceed only when the school bus resumes motion and the visual signals are turned off. This rule does not apply when a bus is traveling on a different or divided roadway.

Vehicle Equipment & Rules

Bumper Height: The maximum bumper height for passenger vehicles is 22 inches for both the front and rear bumpers; the maximum height for vehicles with a GVWR of 4,500 lbs. and under is 29 inches for both the front and rear bumpers; the maximum bumper height for vehicles with a GVWR of 4,501 to 7,500 lbs. is 33 inches for both the front and rear bumpers; and the maximum height for vehicles with a GVWR of 7,501 to 10,000 lbs. is 35 inches for both the front and rear bumpers.

Glass/Window Tinting: It is unlawful for any person to operate a motor vehicle if the glazing material on any windows or windshield, excepting the top edge of the windshield, does not meet the requirements of Federal Motor Vehicle Safety Standard 205.

Windshield Stickers: Signs or stickers displayed in a 7-inch square in the lower corner of the windshield farthest removed from the driver, or signs or stickers displayed in a 5-inch square in the lower corner of the windshield nearest the driver are permissible.

Motorcycles & Mopeds

Equipment: Operators and passengers on motorcycles must wear safety glasses, goggles, or a face shield, unless the motorcycle is equipped with a windscreen.

- No person less than 18 years of age may operate or ride as a passenger on a motorcycle unless the person wears a safety helmet.
- It is unlawful for any motorcycle or motor scooter driver to carry as a passenger a person under the age of 7 years; violation of this rule carries a fine of not more than $200.

- Every motorcycle or motor scooter must have at least 1 lighted headlight which must be in use from 30 minutes after sunset until 30 minutes before sunrise, and must be powerful enough to reveal a person, vehicle, or substantial object at least 200 feet ahead.
- Every motorcycle or motor scooter must have at least 1 lighted, red taillight which must be in use from 30 minutes after sunset until 30 minutes before sunrise and must be powerful enough so as to be visible from a distance of 200 feet to the rear.
- If carrying a passenger, a motorcycle must be equipped with footrests, unless the passenger is riding in a sidecar.

Licenses: A temporary instruction permit may be obtained at age 15 1/2 but holders of temporary permits may not operate a motorcycle or motor scooter during the hours of darkness or carry any passengers.

- The temporary instruction permit for a motorcycle may not be renewed more than once.
- The roadside examination for a motorcycle license may be waived if the applicant has completed the approved motorcycle education course.

Noise Limits: All motorcycles and mopeds must be equipped with a muffler designed to limit excessive or unusual noise, and it is unlawful to modify a muffler in order to amplify the noise emitted by the motor.

Mopeds: No person may drive a moped unless the person possesses a valid driver's license of any type issued by the state, or the person is at least 18 years old and holds a valid license from another jurisdiction.

- No person under the age of 15 may drive a moped and it is unlawful to carry anybody other than the driver upon a moped.
- Every person riding a moped on a roadway enjoys all the rights and is responsible for all the duties of the driver of a vehicle.
- Unless otherwise determined by individual counties and posted upon a roadway, a moped must use a bicycle lane wherever one exists.
- A moped may not be driven at a speed greater than 35 mph.
- From 30 minutes after sunset until 30 minutes before sunrise and whenever visibility is such as it is difficult to see persons and vehicles clearly at a distance of 200 feet, a moped must display a lighted headlamp and taillamp.
- A moped must be permanently registered.
- The transfer of ownership of a moped requires the signature of both the transferor and transferee on the certificate of registration, and the transferee must forward the signed certificate to the county director of finance within 30 days.

Passenger Car Trailers

Registration: Upon registration of a trailer, a certificate of registration is issued by the county director of finance, but a certificate of ownership is not issued for trailers.

Brakes: Independent braking system required where gross weight exceeds 3,000 lbs.

Dimensions: Total length: 65 feet; trailer length: 40 feet; width: 108 inches; height: 14 feet.

Hitch: Ball hitch either mounted on bumper or secured to frame is acceptable; safety chain is required.

Lighting: Trailers must be equipped with a light on the extreme width of each side such that the light shall be in use 30 minutes after sunset and 30 minutes before sunrise and shall be visible from all directions at a distance of 200 feet.

Other Provisions: It is unlawful to occupy a trailer designed as temporary or permanent abode while such trailer is being moved on a public highway.

- Maximum of 1 boat or general utility trailer may be towed behind passenger or pleasure vehicles.

Miscellaneous Provisions

Liability Laws: It is unlawful to operate a motor vehicle, motorcycle, or motor scooter unless it is insured at all times.

- The minimum liability policy coverage is $20,000 per person with an aggregate limit of $40,000 per accident and $10,000 for all damages to or destruction of property.
- A valid motor vehicle or liability insurance identification card must be in the possession of the driver of a vehicle at all times and must be presented when requested by a peace officer.
- State does not have non-resident service of process law, but non-residents may be served when in state; does not have guest suit law.

Weigh/Inspection Stations: Trucks over 10,000 lbs. GVWR must stop.

Fees & Taxes

Table 1: Title & Registration Fees

Title & Registration Fees	Fee Amount
All Vehicles (except new vehicles and official vehicles) State Fee	$25.00 plus applicable weight tax
Honolulu City and County*	$10.00 plus $1.25 per pound
Maui County*	$6.00 plus $0.75 per pound
Hawaii County*	$4.00 plus $0.50 per pound
Kauai County*	$1.25 per pound
Registration Tag / Emblem Fee	$0.50
Honolulu City and County*	$16.00 flat fee
Maui County*	10% of registration fee
Hawaii County*	10% of registration fee
Kauai County*	20% of county registration fee plus 20% of state registration fee
Duplicate Registration Certificates	
Honolulu City and County*	no fee
Maui County*	$10.00
Hawaii County*	$2.00
Kauai County*	$3.00
Title Transfer Fees	
Honolulu City and County*	$10.00
Maui County*	$10.00
Hawaii County*	$2.00
Kauai County*	$3.00
Bicycle / Moped Permanent Registration Fee	$15.00
Non-Resident Registration Fee	$5.00

*Indicates information provided directly from county offices.

Table 2: License Fees

Category 1-4 Driver's License	Fee
1-Year License	
Maui County*	$3.00
2-Year License	
All Counties*	$6.00
4-Year License	
Kauai County*	$6.00
All Other Counties*	$12.00
6-Year License	
Kauai County*	$12.00
All Other Counties*	$18.00
State-Imposed Fee	$5.00 for each 30-day period, or fraction thereof, after the initial 90-day grace period.
County Fees	
County Fees - All Counties*	same amount as for original license
Duplicate License	
Kauai County*	$6.00
All Other Counties*	$5.00
Learner's Permit	
Honolulu City and County*	$5.00
Maui County*	$10.00
Hawaii County*	$10.00
Kauai County*	$4.00

*Indicates information provided directly from county offices.

Table 3: Vehicle Taxes

Tax	Rate
Vehicle Weight Tax (new vehicles exempted)	$0.75 per lb. for every vehicle up to 4,000 lbs. net weight
	$1.00 per lb. for every vehicle between 4,000 and 7,000 lbs. net weight
	$1.25 per lb. for every vehicle between 7,000 and 10,000 lbs. net weight
	$150 flat rate for every vehicle over 10,000 lbs. net weight
Use Tax	4% of the value of all personal property imported into the state
Gasoline Tax; (Diesel)	$0.16/gallon; ($0.16/gallon)

Table 4: Miscellaneous Fees

Tax	Amount	Payable Upon
Highway Beautification and Abandoned Vehicle Abatement	$2.00 - $5.00 depending on which county	initial and subsequent registration
Duplicate Bicycle and Moped Tags	$2.00	application
Duplicate Certificate of Registration for Bicycle and Moped	$5.00	application
Untimely Bicycle/Moped Transfer of Ownership	$10.00 plus $5.00 registration fee	registration
Untimely Trailer Transfer of Ownership	$50.00 plus registration fee	registration
Untimely Passenger Car Transfer of Ownership	$50.00 plus registration fee	registration
License Plate Reassignment Fee	$5.00	upon request of reassignment
Antique Motor Vehicle Plates	$10.00	registration
Special Plates	$25.00	initial application and each subsequent registration

IDAHO

Contact Information

Idaho Division of Motor Vehicles (DMV)
3311 W. State Street
P.O. Box 7129
Boise, ID 83707-1129

(208) 334-8606
www.itd.idaho.gov/dmv/index.htm

Idaho State Police (ISP)
P.O. Box 700
Meridian, ID 83680-0700

(208) 884-7000
www.isp.state.id.us/

Idaho Transportation Department (ITD)
3311 W. State Street
P.O. Box 7129
Boise, ID 83707-1129

(208) 334-8000
www.itd.idaho.gov

Vehicle Title

Application: All applications must be made to the county assessor and contain a full description of the vehicle including make, identification number, odometer reading at the time of sale or transfer, and whether the vehicle is new or used, together with a statement of the title and any liens, and the name and address of the person to receive the title.

- If this is the 1st certificate of title, the application must be accompanied by a bill of sale or certified copy of the bill of sale, or certificate of title, and the bill of sale or evidence of ownership from the state in which the vehicle is being bought. A vehicle identification number inspection must also be completed.

- If the vehicle is being purchased from a dealer, the application must be accompanied by a manufacturer's certificate of origin or manufacturer's statement of origin. The certificate or statement of origin must contain the year of manufacture or model year, manufacturer's vehicle identification number, name of the manufacturer, number of cylinders, general description, and type or model.
- All vehicles that require registration are also required to be titled. Additionally, all-terrain vehicles, motorcycles, snowmobiles, and manufactured homes are also required to be titled.

Transfer of Ownership: A vehicle may not be sold or disposed of without handing over the title to the buyer.

- In all cases of vehicle transfer, applications for certificate of title must be filed within 30 calendar days after delivery of the vehicle.

Vehicle Registration

Application: All applications for registration of motor vehicles should be made to a county assessor. Applications for registration of motor homes should also be made to the county assessor.

- All applications for registration must be signed by the owner and contain an address of residence and a brief description of the vehicle that includes the name of the maker, type of fuel used, and identification number. If the application is for a new vehicle, it should also contain the date of sale by the manufacturer or dealer.

Non-Residents: New residents who will be operating motor vehicles must obtain an Idaho license after establishing residency even if they hold a valid unexpired driver's license from another state. This can occur before 90 days but residency is considered established after living 90 continuous days in Idaho (30 days for Commercial Driver's licenses).

- Military personnel stationed in state may maintain out-of-state registration.

Registration Type: Vehicle registration renewal is to be done annually or in the same registration period manner as the original registration and with payment of the required fee.

- There is an option for biennial registration with a fee that is double the current annual registration fee.

Emissions Inspection: Emissions inspections are determined by local ordinance. Required in Ada County.

License Plates

Disbursement: Personalized license plates are available and must have numbers, letters, or any combination thereof with no more than 7 characters.

- Special license plates may be issued but must utilize the same red, white, and blue background as the standard issue of license plates. The word Idaho must be on every plate but identification of county and inscription of "Scenic Idaho" may be omitted. No slogans infringing on trademarks of the state are permitted, unless otherwise provided.
- Special license plates and cards are issued for persons with disabilities. The license plate must be the same size and color as other license plates and display

the international accessible symbol. The license plate must also display the registration number of the vehicle. An application for special license plates or cards must be made to the DMV and include written certification by a licensed physician verifying the applicant's impairment qualifies as a disability.
- Two license plates are issued except in the case of a motorcycle, all-terrain vehicle, or vehicles displaying year of manufacture, old timer, classic car, or street rod license plates. License plates are to be displayed on both the front and rear or rear only if given 1 plate. All license plates are to be displayed for the current registration year with an annual registration sticker on each license plate.

Transfer of Plates: License plates remain the property of the original owner and do not transfer from person to person. The owner may put them on another vehicle upon registration of that vehicle.

Driver's Licenses

Examination: Every person applying for an instruction permit, seasonal driver's license, driver's license, or motorcycle endorsement must have an examination consisting of an eyesight test and the ability to read and understand highway signs.
- Drivers not previously licensed are also required to take a driving test.
- A minimum of 20/40 visual acuity in at least one eye, with or without corrective glasses, is required.
- A driving test can also be administered to anyone else at the discretion of the examiner.
- Written examination testing knowledge of state traffic laws may also be administered.
- An applicant for a motorcycle endorsement may also be tested on safe motorcycle operating practices and traffic laws relating to motorcycles.

Graduated Drivers Licensing: State has a system of graduated licensing for teen drivers. At 14 and 6 months, teens are eligible for an instruction/learner's permit.
- During the permit phase, teens may not drive unsupervised and must accumulate at least 50 (10 at night) hours of parental/guardian certified driving.
- Teens must hold the permit for at least 4 months.
- At 15, teens are eligible for an intermediate supervised instruction permit. These permit holders are prohibited from driving unsupervised from sunset to sunrise, except when accompanied in the front seat by a licensed driver 21 years or older. No other occupant may be in the front seat at this time.
- Teens are eligible for an unrestricted license at 16.
- Idaho has 3 classes of permits: a training instruction permit for persons 14 and 6 months old taking driver education; a supervised instruction permit for persons under 17 who have completed driver's education, but not the 50 hours; and for persons 17 and older without either driver education or supervised driving.

Issuance/Application: A driver's license is required prior to driving in the state.
- Licenses shall not be issued to persons under 18 years of age not enrolled in school, not having received a waiver, or not having satisfactorily completed school.
- Driver's licenses will contain a distinguishing number (not social security number), full name, date of birth, Idaho residence address, sex, weight, height, eye color, hair color, color photograph, dates of issuance and expiration, license class, endorsements, restrictions, and the applicant's signature.

Renewal: All driver's licenses for persons 21 years of age and over are renewable on or before expiration with application, payment of fee, and satisfactory completion of the required eye examination.

- For persons 21 and over, the license shall expire on the licensee's birthday 4 years after issuance. A person between the ages of 21 and 62 may opt to have their license expire on their birthday 4 or 8 years after issuance.
- For persons under 18 years of age, the license shall expire 5 days after the licensee's 18th birthday.
- For persons between the ages of 18 and 21 years, the license shall expire 5 days after the licensee's 21st birthday.
- No knowledge test is required for driver's license renewal.
- Active duty or a dependent of military personnel in the U.S. armed forces may apply for a license extension of up to 4 years. The extension will expire 60 days from the date of discharge from active military duty or the expiration date on the extension card, whichever comes first.
- After this time, military personnel with valid military driver's licenses are not required to take the written examination and skills tests for renewal of an Idaho driver's license if the Idaho driver's license has expired while on active duty.

Types of Licenses: Class A: Combination vehicles with a Gross Combination Weight Rating (GCWR) of 26,001 lbs. or more, provided the Gross Vehicle Weight Rating (GVWR) of the vehicle(s) being towed is greater than 10,000 lbs. A driver with a Class A license may, with the proper endorsements, operate vehicles requiring a Class B, C, or D license.

- Class B: Single vehicles with a GVWR of 26,001 lbs. or more, or any such vehicle towing a vehicle 10,000 lbs. GVWR or less. A driver with a Class B license may, with the proper endorsements, operate vehicles requiring a Class C or D license.
- Class C: Vehicles with a GVWR or GCWR less than 26,001 lbs. Class C is strictly for vehicles designed to carry 16 or more people (including the driver), or carry hazardous materials requiring the vehicle to display placards. A driver with a Class C license may also operate vehicles requiring a Class D license.
- Class D: Allows the holder to drive motor vehicles on Idaho roads. Class D vehicles include vehicles under 26,000 lbs. GVWR and not placarded for hazardous materials nor designed to carry 16 or more people, including the driver; taxis; limousines; military vehicles; recreational vehicles; farm vehicles not used for hire and if driven within 150 miles of the farm; and fire fighting and emergency equipment.
- M: Motorcycle endorsement.
- Seasonal Class B or C: Commercial license not to exceed 180 days in a 12-month period, valid within a 150-mile radius of the place of business or farm being serviced. Valid only in conjunction with a current Idaho Class D driver's license.

Traffic Rules

Alcohol Laws: Idaho has an implied consent law.

- Open containers are not permitted. Meets TEA-21 requirements.
- Illegal per se BAC level is .08.
- BAC level for people under 21 is .02.
- BAC level for commercial drivers is .04.

Emergency Radio/Cellular: Emergency phone number is 911 or * 477 from a cellular phone.

Occupant Restraints: Any occupant of a vehicle shall wear a seat belt at all times when the vehicle is moving.

- Any child under the age of 7 years shall be transported in a child safety seat that meets federal requirements.
- Violation of the seat belt law is a secondary offense, however violation of the child restraint law is a primary offense.
- Riding in pickup truck beds is permitted.

Railroad Crossing: Whenever a person driving a vehicle approaches a railroad crossing and there is a signal indicating an approaching train, the driver must stop within 50 feet, but not less than 15 feet, from the nearest rail of the railroad and must not proceed until he or she can do so safely. It is unlawful to drive through, around, or under any crossing gate or barrier while the gate or barrier is closed or is being opened or closed.

- A school bus must come to a complete stop before crossing any railroad track.

School Buses: Upon meeting or overtaking a school bus in either direction, a driver must stop and not proceed until the bus resumes movement or visual signals are no longer functioning. Oncoming traffic is not required to stop on a highway of more than 3 lanes even if visual signals are functioning.

Vehicle Equipment & Rules

Bumper Height: Maximum bumper heights are determined by vehicle class and the GVWR. As such, the maximum heights are:

- Passenger cars, front: 22 inches; rear: 22 inches.
- Trucks and multipurpose vehicles, front: 24 inches; rear: 26 inches.
- Vehicles from 4,501 to 7,500 lbs. GVWR, front: 27 inches; rear: 29 inches.
- Vehicles from 7,501 to 10,000 lbs. GVWR, front: 28 inches; rear: 30 inches.
- 4-wheel drive or dual-wheel vehicles with a 10,000 lbs. or less GVWR, front: 30 inches; rear: 31 inches.

Glass/Window Tinting: The front windshield can have tinting applied, but only on the top 6 inches of the window.

- The front side vents, front side windows to the immediate left and right of the driver and rear window may have a light transmission not less than 35%.
- The side windows to the rear of the driver may have a light transmission of not less than 20%.

Windshield Stickers: Signs, posters, or other non-transparent materials that could obstruct the driver's view are illegal.

Motorcycles & Mopeds

Equipment: A helmet of a type and quality equal to or better than the standards established for helmets by the director of the ITD must be worn by operators or passengers under 18 years of age.

- Motorcycles are required to have at least 1 and not more than 2 headlamps.
- A motorcycle may be equipped with either single-beam or multiple-beam lighting, provided that it be of sufficient intensity to reveal a person or vehicle not less than

100 feet away when the motorcycle is traveling at a speed less than 25 mph, or at a distance of not less than 200 feet when the motorcycle is traveling at a speed of 25 mph or more, or at a distance of 300 feet when the motorcycle is traveling at a speed of 35 mph or more.
- Every motorcycle must have 1 red reflector on the rear. The reflector must be visible at night from all distances within 350 feet to 100 feet from the vehicle when seen by the upper beams of another vehicle's headlamps.
- Every motorcycle must be equipped with at least 1 stop lamp but is not required to have mechanical or electrical turn signals.
- To lawfully carry a passenger, a motorcycle must be equipped with footrests specifically designed for said passenger.

Licenses: No person under 21 years of age may apply for or obtain a motorcycle license endorsement without successful completion of a motorcycle rider training course.
- Any person who applies for a motorcycle endorsement may be required to pass the motorcycle skills test.

Noise Limits: Modification of an exhaust system to increase the noise of the vehicle is prohibited.

Mopeds: Minimum age for a license is the same as for motorcycles.
- Helmet is required for people under 18.
- Internal combustion engine shall not exceed 50 cc.

Passenger Car Trailers

Registration: Utility trailers that weigh less than 2,000 lbs. when empty must be registered but are not required to be titled.

Brakes: Trailers with an unladen weight of 1,500 lbs. must have an independent braking system, and a breakaway system capable of applying the brakes in the event of a separation from the towing vehicle is required.

Dimensions: Total length: 75 feet (includes bumpers); trailer length: 48 feet (includes bumpers); width: 102 inches (the width excludes devices or appurtenances related to safe or efficient operation of the vehicle); height: 14 feet.

Hitch: Hitch must be secured to frame; no safety chain required.

Lighting: Every trailer, semitrailer, pole trailer, or any other drawn vehicle at the end of a train of vehicles must have 1 rear taillamp, which when lit will emit a red light plainly visible from a distance of 500 feet to the rear.
- Every trailer, semitrailer, or pole trailer weighing 3,000 lbs. gross or less must have 2 reflectors on the rear, 1 on each side, and 2 reflectors on the front, 1 on each side.
- Any trailer that blocks the stoplight of the towing vehicle, whether loaded or unloaded, must also have 1 stoplight.

Mirrors: Left- and right-side mirrors are required if a driver's view straight to the rear is obstructed.

Speed Limits: Same as passenger cars.

Towing: Passenger or pleasure vehicles may tow 2 units behind them.

Miscellaneous Provisions

Bail Bonds: Mandatory recognition of AAA arrest bond certificate up to $500, with specified exceptions.

Liability Laws: State has security-type law applicable in event of accident causing property damage in excess of $500 or personal injury or death; no judgment minimum. Applicant must certify that vehicle is covered by automobile liability insurance at the time of registration. Certificate of liability insurance must be carried in vehicle or on person.

- State has non-resident service of process law. Guest suit law has been declared unconstitutional. Release of liability statements must be completed by the owner of a motor vehicle upon sale of the vehicle to another party. The statements are to be mailed to the Department of Transportation along with a $2 filing fee.
- Minimum required coverage is $25,000 for bodily injury or death of 1 person in 1 accident; $50,000 for 2 or more persons in 1 accident; $15,000 for injury or destruction of property in 1 accident.
- A motor vehicle owner may choose to post an indemnity bond in lieu of a liability insurance policy. The bond must guarantee payment of no less than $50,000 for any 1 accident, of which $15,000 is for property damage, for each vehicle registered, up to a maximum of $120,000 for 5 or more registered vehicles.

Weigh Stations: 10 fixed ports of entry, 10 roving units.

Fees & Taxes

Table 1: Title & Registration Fees

Vehicle Type	Title Fee	Registration Fee
Passenger Cars and Motorhomes	$8.00	$24.00 - $48.00* (depending on vehicle age and county of residence)
Mobile Home	$8.00	$24.00 - $48.00
Motorcycles and All-Terrain Vehicles	$8.00	$9.00* (except Ada County where the fee is $19.25)
Non-Commercial Trailer more than 8,001 lbs. and less than 16,000 lbs.		$15.00 (registration fee) $48.00 (operating fee)
Recreational Vehicle Annual License		$8.50 for the first $1,000 or less of market value and an additional $5.00 for each additional $1,000 or less of market value
School Bus		$24.00
Utility Trailer		$5.00 1-year registration $20.00 5-year registration $30.00 10-year registration
Duplicate Plate	$3.00	$8.00; $23.00 for "RUSH DUPLICATE"
Duplicate Title	$4.00	

* Vehicles registered in Ada County also pay a $10 - $20 Ada County Highway District Fee.

Table 2: License Fees

License Class	Fee	Driving Test Fees
A	$28.50 4-year license (over 21 years old); $17.50 3-year license (18-21 year olds); $11.50 1-year license (20 years old)	$3.00 written test $55.00 skills test
B	$28.50 4-year license (over 21 years old); $17.50 3-year license (18-21 year olds); $11.50 1-year license (20 years old)	$3.00 written test $55.00 skills test
C	$28.50 4-year license (over 21 years old); $17.50 3-year license (18-21 year olds); $11.50 1-year license (20 years old)	$3.00 written test $55.00 skills test
License Classification Change (Upgrade)	$15.50	
D	$24.50 4-year license/renewal; $45.00 8-year license; $17.50 3-year license (under age 18); $17.50 3-year license (18-21 year olds)	$3.00 written test $3.50 road test
Instruction Permit	$11.50	$3.00 written test $15.00 skills test
Duplicate Fee	$11.50	
Motorcycle Endorsement	$11.50	$3.00 written test $5.00 skills test

Table 3: Vehicle Taxes

Tax	Rate
Gasoline Tax; (Diesel)	$0.25/gallon; ($0.25/gallon)
State Sales Tax on Vehicles	6% of purchase price (minus trade-in if purchased from a licensed dealer)

ID

Table 4: Miscellaneous Fees

Fee	Amount
Transfer Fee	$5.00
Special Plates Fee	$25.00 - $35.00 initial fee $15.00 - $25.00 renewal
License Plate Replacement Fee	$3.00

ILLINOIS

Contact Information

Driver's Services Department (DSD)
2701 South Dirksen Parkway	(217) 782-6212
Springfield, IL 62723	www.sos.state.il.us/services/services_motorists.html

Vehicle Services Department (VSD)
501 South 2nd Street, Room 312	(217) 785-3000
Springfield, IL 62756	www.sos.state.il.us/services/services_motorists.html

Illinois State Police
401 Armory Building	(217) 782-2841
Springfield, IL 62706	www.state.il.us/isp/isphpagen.html

Illinois Department of Transportation (IDOT)
2300 South Dirksen Parkway	(217) 782-7820
Springfield, IL 62764	www.dot.state.il.us/

Vehicle Title

Application: The application for vehicle title is made to the Secretary of State and must include a description of the vehicle, date of purchase, odometer reading, and, if applicable, the name and address of the person from whom the vehicle was acquired and any lienholders.

- If the vehicle was purchased from a dealer, the dealer must promptly mail and deliver the application to the Secretary of State.
- The applicant must furnish proof of payment for all applicable taxes.
- The Secretary of State shall refuse issuance of a certificate of title if any required fee is not paid or if he has reasonable grounds to believe that the applicant is not the owner of the vehicle; the application contains a false or fraudulent statement; the applicant fails to furnish required information or documents or any additional information the Secretary of State reasonably requires; or the applicant has not paid to the Secretary of State any fees or taxes due under this Act.

Transfer of Ownership: Transferor must give the transferee an assignment and warranty of title at the time of the delivery of the vehicle in the space provided on the certificate of title and mail the certificate and assignment to the transferee or the Secretary of State.

- Transferee must within 20 days after the delivery of the assigned title, execute the application for a new certificate and mail or deliver it to the Secretary of State.
- Whenever the owner of a registered vehicle transfers or assigns his title, or interest thereto, the registration of such vehicle shall expire and the owner shall not be entitled to any refund of the registration fee.
- When the transferee of a vehicle is a dealer who holds it for resale and lawfully operates it under dealers' number plates or when the transferee does not drive such vehicle or permit it to be driven upon the highways, such transferee shall not be required to obtain a new registration of said vehicle.

Mobile Homes: Mobile homes must be titled and include a description of the home.

- The owner of a mobile home not located in a mobile home park shall, within 30 days after initial placement of such mobile home in any county and within 30 days after movement of such mobile home to a new location, file with the county assessor, supervisor of assessment, or township assessor, as the case may be, a mobile home registration.
- The registration must show the name and address of the owner and every occupant of the mobile home, the location of the mobile home, the year of manufacture, and the square feet of floor space contained in such mobile home together with the date that the mobile home became inhabited, was initially placed in the county, or was moved to a new location. Such registration shall also include the license number of such mobile home and of the towing vehicle, if there be any, and the state issuing such licenses.

Vehicle Registration

Application: Application is made to the Secretary of State upon the appropriate forms furnished by the Secretary of State and must bear the signature, name and address of the owner, a description of the vehicle, information relating to the required insurance coverage of the vehicle, and such further information as may reasonably be required by the Secretary to enable him to determine whether the vehicle is lawfully entitled to registration.

- Registration stickers must be displayed at all times and firmly attached to the license plate of the motor vehicle in such a manner that it cannot be removed without being destroyed.
- Notice of change of address or name must be made within 10 days to the Secretary of State.

Non-Residents: Non-residents may operate vehicles not registered in the state so long as such vehicles have at all times duly registered in, and displayed upon it, a valid registration card and registration plate or plates issued for such vehicle in the place of residence of such owner and is issued and maintains in such vehicle a valid Illinois reciprocity permit as required by the Secretary of State, and provided like privileges are afforded to residents of this state by the state of residence of such owner.

- Every non-resident including any foreign corporation carrying on business within Illinois and owning and regularly operating in such business any motor vehicle, trailer, or semitrailer within this state in intrastate commerce, shall be required to register each such vehicle and pay the same fees as is required with reference to like vehicles owned by Illinois residents.

Registration Type: Registration must be renewed annually for all normal passenger vehicles. When registered on a calendar year basis commencing January 1st, expiration shall be on the 31st day of December or at such other date as may be selected at the discretion of the Secretary of State; however, registrations of apportionable vehicles, motorcycles, motor-driven cycles, and pedalcycles shall commence on the first day of April and shall expire March 31st of the following calendar year.

- New residents have until 30 days after establishing residency to secure registration, provided the vehicle is properly registered in another jurisdiction.
- Application for renewal of a vehicle registration shall be made by the owner not later than December 1st of each year, upon proper application and by payment of the registration fee and tax for such vehicle.

- Registration plates issued for motor vehicles are valid for an indefinite term of not less than 1 year.
- Registration plates issued as 2-year plates may be issued as multi-year plates at the discretion of the Secretary of State.

Emissions Inspection: Dependent upon year of vehicle. Annual testing required for vehicle owners in Cook, Dupage, parts of Kane, Lake Madison, St. Clair, Will, Kendall, Monroe, and McHenry counties.

Safety Inspection: Vehicles over 8,000 lbs. or designed to carry 10 or more passengers must submit to a safety inspection and secure a certificate of safety furnished by DOT.

License Plates

Disbursement: Plates issued for a motor vehicle other than a motorcycle, trailer, truck, or bus must display 2 license plates, 1 on the front and 1 on the rear, and be securely fastened in a horizontal position to the vehicle for which it is issued so as to prevent the plate from swinging and at a height of not less than 12 inches from the ground, measuring from the bottom of such plate.

- Special license plates for disabled drivers are available upon application, with medical certificate, to the Secretary of State.

Transfer of Plates: Registration expires on transfer by owner and no refunds on registration fees are allowed.

- The transferor must remove plates and stickers and either forward them to the Secretary of State or have them assigned to another vehicle upon payment of fees.
- When any person who has been issued vanity or personalized license plates sells, trades, or otherwise releases the ownership of the vehicle, he or she shall immediately report the transfer of such plates to an acquired motor vehicle and pay the transfer fee or shall, upon the request of the Secretary, immediately return such plates to the Secretary of State.

Driver's Licenses

Examination: Examinations are required for applicants for a driver's license or permit that have not been previously licensed as a driver under the laws of Illinois or any other state or country, or any applicant for renewal of such driver's license or permit when such license or permit has been expired for more than 1 year.

- Applicants must successfully complete a vision screening, written examination, and driving examination.
- An applicant who is required to take a vision screening must obtain a binocular (both eyes) acuity reading of 20/40 or better before being issued a driver's license without vision restrictions. If an applicant utilizes corrective eyeglasses, contact lenses, or a combination thereof in order to obtain an acceptable acuity reading, a driver's license issued to this applicant shall be restricted to operating a motor vehicle while using the corrective lenses.
- Drivers must be reexamined at least once every 8 years unless they possess a driving record devoid of any convictions of traffic violations or evidence of committing an offense for which mandatory revocation would be required.

Graduated Drivers Licensing: State has a system of graduated licensing for teen drivers. At 15, teens enrolled in driver education are eligible for an instruction/learn-

er's permit. Permit holders may only drive when supervised.
- During the permit stage, all vehicle occupants under age 18 must wear safety belts.
- Teens who are at least 16 and have held a permit for at least 3 months and accumulated at least 25 hours of behind-the-wheel practice time certified by a parent or guardian are eligible for an initial/intermediate license.
- Prohibits drivers with an instruction permit or graduated license from using a cell phone while driving.
- Initial/intermediate license holders are prohibited from driving unsupervised from 11:00 p.m. to 6:00 a.m. Sunday-Friday and midnight to 6:00 a.m. Friday and Saturday. All occupants in a vehicle operated by a driver under 18 must wear a seat belt. For the first 6 months of an intermediate permit, no more than one person younger than 20 may be a passenger in the car (family members exempt).
- Teens may receive an unrestricted license at age 17.

Issuance/Application: Applicants must be at least 18 years of age to apply for a license but minors enrolled in a driver education program may acquire an instructional permit after 15 years of age. An Illinois driver's license must be applied for within 90 days of establishing residence.
- Applications shall be made upon a form furnished by the Secretary of State. The proper fee shall accompany every application and payment of such fee shall entitle the applicant to not more than 3 attempts to pass the examination within a period of 1 year after the date of application. After the third attempt, a subsequent attempt will require another fee.
- Every application shall state the name, social security number, zip code, date of birth, sex, and residence address of the applicant; briefly describe the applicant; state whether the applicant has theretofore been licensed as a driver, and, if so, when and by what state or country and whether any such license has ever been cancelled, suspended, revoked, or refused, and, if so, the date and reason for such cancellation, suspension, revocation, or refusal; include an affirmation by the applicant that all information set forth is true and correct; and bear the applicant's signature. Applicants will be requested to prove name, date of birth, and social security number and verify residency and signature.
- Notice of change of address or name must be made within 10 days to the Secretary of State.
- License normally includes a color photograph. Social security number does not appear on license.
- An Illinois driver's license must be applied for within 90 days of establishing residence.
- Prohibits a new resident from getting a driver's license if their privileges are revoked in another state.

Renewal: For new applicants aged 21 to 80, the expiration date is 4 years from the applicant's next day of birth. For renewal applicants, the expiration date is 4 years from the present expiration date. Drivers between the ages of 81 to 86 will be issued a 2-year license and drivers aged 87 and older will be issued a 1-year license.
- The Secretary of State shall, 30 days prior to the expiration of a driver's license, forward to each person whose license is to expire a notification of the expiration of said license, which may be presented at the time of renewal.
- Each original or renewal driver's license issued to a licensee under 21 years of age shall expire 3 months after the licensee's 21st birthday.
- Active duty military and dependents may have the expiration of their driver's licens-

es deferred for up to 45 days after discharge or reassignment to a military base in the state. A military deferral certificate must be carried with the expired license.

Types of Licenses: Class A: Any combination of vehicles with a Gross Combination Weight Rating (GCWR) of 26,001 lbs. or more, provided the GVWR of the vehicle(s) being towed is in excess of 10,000 lbs.

- Class B: Any single vehicle with a Gross Vehicle Weight Rating (GVWR) of 26,001 lbs. or more, or any such vehicle towing a vehicle not in excess of 10,000 lbs. GVWR.
- Class C: Any single vehicle with a GVWR of 16,001 lbs. or more but less than 26,001 lbs. GVWR, or any such vehicle towing a vehicle not in excess of 10,000 lbs. GVWR or any vehicle less than 26,001 lbs. GVWR designed to transport 16 or more people including the driver or used in the transportation of hazardous materials which requires the vehicle to be placarded.
- Class D: Any single vehicle with a GVWR of 16,000 lbs. or less that is not designed to transport 16 or more people or not used in the transportation of hazardous materials which would require such vehicle to be placarded.
- Class L: Any motor-driven cycle (mopeds).
- Class M: Any motorcycle.

Traffic Rules

Alcohol Laws: Any driver is deemed to have given implied consent to any alcohol or drug test administered by a police officer.

- Open containers are not permitted. Meets TEA-21 requirements.
- Illegal per se BAC level is .08.
- BAC level for people under 21 is .00.

Cellular Telephone Use: School bus drivers are prohibited from talking on a cell phone and driving, except in emergencies. Hand-held cellular phones are prohibited in Chicago.

Emergency Radio/Cellular: Citizen band radio channel 9 is monitored for emergency calls. Emergency cell number is *999 or 911.

Headsets: It is illegal for a driver to wear headset receivers while driving, except that intercom helmets on motorcycles are allowed as are cellular phone earpieces and single-sided headsets.

Occupant Restraints: The driver and front seat passengers are required to use seat belts.

- If the driver is under age 19, all passengers under 18 must be restrained in all seats.
- When transporting a child under 8 years of age the child shall be properly secured in a child restraint system. A child 8 years of age or older but under the age of 16 must be placed in either a child restraint system or a seat belt. Children weighing more than 40 lbs. may be transported in the back seat of a vehicle with only a lap belt if the back seat is not equipped with a lap and shoulder belt.
- Violation of the occupant protection laws is a primary offense.
- Riding in pickup truck beds is permitted.

Railroad Crossing: Drivers are required to stop between 15 and 50 feet of the nearest rail of a railroad crossing when a signal indicates the approach of a train, or an approaching train is plainly visible.

- All drivers of vehicles for hire carrying passengers, buses, or vehicles carrying hazardous materials must stop between 15 and 50 feet of the nearest rail before proceeding.

School Buses: Drivers in either direction must stop for any school bus receiving or discharging students and may not proceed until the school bus resumes motion or the driver is signaled to proceed by the school bus driver.

Vehicle Equipment & Rules

Bumper Height: The maximum bumper height on all motor vehicles except multipurpose passenger vehicles is 28 inches for the front bumper and 30 inches for the rear bumper, measured from the road surface.

Glass/Window Tinting: Any glass tinting on the front and side windows is prohibited, except when accompanied by a certification by a licensed physician stating that the driver's medical condition would require it.

- A nonreflective tinted film may be used along the uppermost portion of the windshield if such material does not extend more than 6 inches down from the top of the windshield.
- The use of nonreflective, smoked or tinted glass, nonreflective film, perforated window screen, or other decorative window application on windows to the rear of the driver's seat is permitted, except that any motor vehicle with a window to the rear of the driver's seat treated in this manner must be equipped with a side mirror on each side of the motor vehicle.

Telematics: It is illegal for any vehicle to be equipped with a television receiver, video monitor or video screen that is operating or located at any point visible to the driver.

Windshield Stickers: No person shall drive a motor vehicle with any sign, poster, window application, reflective material, nonreflective material or tinted film upon the front windshield, sidewings or side windows immediately adjacent to each side of the driver.

Motorcycles & Mopeds

Equipment: A person operating a motorcycle shall ride only upon the permanent and regular attached seat and such operator shall not carry any other person nor shall any other person ride on a motorcycle unless such motorcycle is designed for that purpose.

- Any motorcycle carrying a passenger, other than in a sidecar or enclosed cab, must be equipped with footrests for such passenger.
- No person shall operate any motorcycle with handlebars higher than the height of the shoulders of the operator when seated on the motorcycle.
- Every driver and passenger must be protected by glasses, goggles, or a transparent shield.
- Motorcycles and motor-driven cycles need not be equipped with electric turn signals.

Licenses: Licenses will not be issued to any person under the age of 18 as an operator of a motorcycle unless the person has completed a motorcycle training course approved by IDOT and the required Secretary of State's motorcycle driver's examination.

- A 12-month instruction permit for a motor-driven cycle or motorcycle may be issued to a person 18 years of age or more, which entitles the holder to drive upon the highways during daylight under the direct supervision of a licensed motor-driven cycle operator or motorcycle operator with the same or greater classification, who is 21 years of age or older and who has at least 1 year of driving experience.

Noise Limits: It is illegal to modify the exhaust system of any motor vehicle in a manner that will amplify or increase the noise of such vehicle.

Mopeds: Every owner of a moped purchased new on and after January 1, 1980 shall make application to the Secretary of State for a certificate of title.

- Registrations of mopeds commence on the 1st day of April and expire March 31st of the following calendar year.
- Every moped, when in use at nighttime, shall be equipped with a lamp on the front which shall emit a white light visible from a distance of at least 500 feet to the front, and with a red reflector on the rear which shall be visible from all distances from 100 to 600 feet to the rear; a lamp emitting a red light visible from a distance of 500 feet to the rear may be used in addition to the red reflector.
- A person operating a moped shall ride only upon the permanent and regular attached seat and such operator shall not carry any other person nor shall any other person ride on a moped unless such moped is designed for that purpose.
- Every driver and passenger must be protected by glasses, goggles, or a transparent shield.

Passenger Car Trailers

Title/Registration: The application for certificate of title must include the square footage of the vehicle based upon the outside dimensions of the house trailer excluding the length of the tongue and hitch, and, if a new vehicle, the date of the first sale of the vehicle. Trailers are subject to the same registration requirements as motor vehicles.

Brakes: Every trailer or semitrailer of a gross weight of over 3,000 lbs. must be equipped with brakes when operated upon a highway. Such brakes must be so designed and connected that in case of an accidental breakaway of a towed vehicle over 5,000 lbs., the brakes are automatically applied.

Dimensions: Total length: 65 feet (excludes safety and energy conservation devices); trailer length: 60 feet (includes bumpers); width: 96 inches (102 inches allowed on designated roads); height: 13.6 feet.

Hitch: Safety chains are required in addition to regular coupling device (drawbar). Trailers of 3,000 to 5,000 lbs. are required to have brakes on only one wheel on each side. Trailers over 5,000 lbs. must be equipped with brakes on all wheels and must have automatic breakaway application.

Lighting: Every trailer and semitrailer shall be equipped with an electric turn signal device which indicates the intention of the driver to turn to the right or to the left in the form of flashing red or amber lights located at the rear of the vehicle on the side toward which the turn is to be made, and mounted on the same level and as widely spaced laterally as practicable.

- Every trailer and semitrailer having a gross weight of 3,000 lbs. or less including the weight of the trailer and maximum load, shall be equipped with 2 red reflectors located on the rear of the body of such trailer, not more than 12 inches from the lower left-hand and lower right-hand corners, and which will be visible when hit by headlight beams 300 feet away at night.

Mirrors: Mirrors must give a view of 200 feet to rear.

Speed Limits: The maximum speed limit for trucks, buses, and passenger cars towing trailers, house trailers, and campers is 55 mph on all tollways.

Miscellaneous Provisions

Bail Bonds: The mandatory recognition of AAA arrest bond certificates is up to $300, with specified exceptions.

Liability Laws: Has security-type law applicable in event of accident causing damage to property of 1 person in excess of $500 or personal injury or death; no judgment minimum. Proof of financial responsibility is required at all times. There is a fine for driving without such proof.

- A minimum policy of $20,000 is required for bodily injury or death to any 1 person in 1 accident; a minimum of $40,000 for any 2 or more people in 1 accident; and a minimum of $15,000 for injury to or destruction of property of others in 1 accident.
- State has non-resident service of process law and guest suit law (applicable to hitchhikers only).

Weigh Stations: A police officer may pull over any vehicle suspected of exceeding weight limits.

Fees & Taxes

Table 1: Title & Registration Fees

Vehicle Type	Title Fee*	Registration Fee*
Motor Vehicles	$65.00	$78.00 (year) $39.00 (half-year)
Motor Homes	$65.00	
B-truck (Gross Weight 8,000 lbs. or less)	$65.00	$78.00
Vehicles of More than 8,000 lbs.	$65.00	$10.00
Non-Commercial Trailer less than 3,000 lbs.	$0	$19.00
Motorcycle	$65.00	$38.00 (year) $19.00 (half-year)
Mopeds	$65.00	$38.00 (year) $19.00 (half-year)
Duplicate Registration		$3.00 (cards) $20.00 (stickers)
Duplicate Plate		$26.00 (1) $29.00 (2)
Duplicate Title	$65.00	

Table 2: License Fees

License Type	Fee*
Original	$10.00
Renewal	$10.00
Drivers aged 69-80	$5.00
Drivers aged 81-86	$2.00
Drivers aged 87 and older	free
Drivers aged 18-20 renewal	$5.00
Learner's Permit	$20.00
Duplicate/Corrected Fee	$10.00
Commercial	$60.00
Motorcycle Endorsement	$5.00
School Bus Permit	$4.00

*Some fees provided by the Illinois Driver Services Dept.

Table 3: Vehicle Taxes

Tax	Rate
Vehicle Use Tax	If vehicle price is under $15,000.00, the range is $25.00-$390.00 depending on model year. If vehicle price is over $15,000.00, the range is $750.00-$1,500.00 depending on price bracket. The tax on motorcycles and mopeds is $25.00.
Gasoline Tax; (Diesel)	$0.19/gallon; ($0.215/gallon)
State Sales Tax	6.25%, counties may impose an additional 1%

Table 4: Miscellaneous Fees

Fee	Amount
Registration and Plate Reinstatement Fee	$30.00
Special Plates Fee*	$78.00-$91.00
Special Plates Transfer Fee	$15.00
License Plate Replacement Fee	$6.00 (1) $9.00 (2)

* Annual fee of $13.00 in addition to regular renewal fee for vanity plates each year thereafter.

INDIANA

Contact Information

Bureau of Motor Vehicles (Bureau)
Indiana Government Center North
100 North Senate, Room N440
Indianapolis, IN 46204

(317) 233-6000
www.in.gov/bmv/

Indiana State Police
Indiana Government Center North
100 North Senate
Indianapolis, IN 46204

(317) 232-8250
www.in.gov/isp/

Indiana Department of Transportation
100 North Senate Avenue, Room IGCN 755
Indianapolis, IN 46204

(317) 232-5533
www.in.gov/dot/

Vehicle Title

Application: The Bureau may issue a certificate of title when a vehicle is registered.

- A person applying for a certificate of title must submit an application provided by the Bureau. This application asks for a full description of the vehicle, a statement of the person's title and of the existence of any liens or encumbrances on the vehicle, and any other information that the Bureau might require.
- If a certificate of title was previously issued for the vehicle in Indiana, then the application for certificate of title must be accompanied by the previously issued certificate of title. If that certificate of title does not exist, then the application must be accompanied by the manufacturer's certificate of origin.
- If a certificate of title was not previously issued for the vehicle in Indiana, the application for the certificate must be accompanied by the certificate of title issued for the vehicle from another state. If that state does not have a certificate of title law,

a sworn bill of sale or dealer's invoice fully describing the vehicle and the most recent registration receipt issued for the vehicle must accompany the application.
- The Bureau will deliver a certificate of title to the person who owns the vehicle if no lien or encumbrances appear on the certificate of title.
- A certificate of title is required for all mobile homes.

Transfer of Ownership: An effective transfer of title requires filling out, endorsing, and delivering the certificate of title by the transferor to the transferee and delivering the certificate to the Bureau, with proper transfer and application fees.
- Generally, the certificate of title must be given to the transferee at the time of sale. If not, the title can be given to the transferee within 21 days of the sale if the transferor meets all of the following conditions: (1) the seller or transferor is a vehicle dealer licensed by the state; (2) the vehicle dealer is unable to deliver title; (3) the dealer believes he or she will be able to deliver the title without a lien within 21 days; (4) the vehicle dealer provides the transferee with an affidavit; and, (5) the transferee has made all initial agreed-upon vehicle payments.

Vehicle Registration

Application: Application for registration should be made at the Bureau of motor vehicles in the county where the resident lives. The application will request the following: (1) name, residence, and mailing address of the person who owns the vehicle; and (2) a description of the vehicle including the vehicle manufacturer, the vehicle identification number, the type of body of the vehicle, the model year of the vehicle, and anything else the Bureau determines is necessary.
- A person must show proof of title and proof of insurance.
- An Indiana resident that is an active member of the armed forces assigned outside of Indiana is not required to register, pay excise tax, or pay property tax on his or her vehicles while he or she is absent from the state if that person has registered the vehicle in Indiana in any previous calendar year.

Non-Residents: Non-residents must register their vehicles within 60 days of becoming residents of Indiana. Non-residents must show proof of the date on which they became residents.
- The only exception to this rule is if the vehicle is properly registered in another jurisdiction in which the non-resident is a resident. This exception only applies if Indiana residents are also granted registration exemptions in the non-resident's home jurisdiction.
- Military personnel on active duty in Indiana may maintain vehicle registration from another state. Indiana military personnel on duty out of state may receive Indiana vehicle registration upon request.

Registration Type: Passenger car registration expires on a staggered basis each month from January through October according to the last name of the person who registered the car.
- If a vehicle that is required to be registered is operated on the highways and not registered in a timely manner, the Bureau will collect any and all registration fees that would have been collected if the vehicle had been properly registered.

Emissions Inspection: Requirements vary from county to county.

Safety Inspection: The police have the authority to check a vehicle to determine whether it is safe.

- The police can check the following: the vehicle's brakes; headlights; taillights; brake lights; clearance lights; turn signals; the vehicle's steering and suspension; the vehicle's exhaust systems; the vehicle's body in general; and the vehicle's tires.
- If the inspection reveals that a vehicle meets the previously mentioned safety requirements, the inspecting officer shall issue to the owner of the vehicle a certificate stating that the vehicle was inspected and that it met the safety requirements.

License Plates

Disbursement: When registration is completed, the Bureau will provide the registrant with a license plate, renewal tag, or other indication of registration.

- Special plates for disabled drivers are available upon application, with affidavit of disability, to Bureau of Motor Vehicles.

Transfer of Plates: Unexpired license plates can be transferred when a motor vehicle, trailer, semitrailer, recreational vehicle, or motor home that is currently registered in Indiana is transferred to another person as long as the vehicle from which the license plate is transferred is the same type of vehicle, and the vehicle has not been operated in Indiana for more than 31 days after the date of acquisition of the vehicle. The person that is registering the new vehicle must prove ownership by having either the manufacturer's certificate of origin, the assigned certificate of title, or a notarized bill of sale.

Driver's Licenses

Examination: All examinations will include an eyesight test, a testing of the ability of the applicant to read and understand highway signs, a knowledge of Indiana traffic laws, a testing of the ability of the applicant to exercise reasonable control in the vehicle, and any physical or mental examination the Bureau sees fit, if necessary.

- The Bureau will waive the demonstration portion of the exam for any person who has passed a driver education class and road test given by an approved commercial driver training school or a high school driver education program.
- The state requires that both eyes have 20/40 visual acuity or better for an unrestricted license.

Graduated Drivers Licensing: State has a system of graduated licensing for teen drivers.

- A learner's permit may be issued at 15 years of age if the applicant is enrolled in an approved driver education course.
- The permit must be held for 2 months before receiving an intermediate license, which restricts the driver from driving between 1 a.m. and 5 a.m. on Fridays and Saturdays and after 11 p.m. Sundays through Thursdays. A driver with an intermediate license is also restricted from having teen passengers for the first 3 months of this intermediate phase. An unrestricted license can be obtained at age 18.
- This permit allows a holder to operate a motor vehicle while the holder is participating in an approved driver education course, and accompanied by a certified driver education instructor while practicing driving.

- If the learner's permit applicant is school age, and either habitually misses class, is under suspension for a second time during the same school year, is under expulsion from school, or withdrawn from school for reasons other than proven financial hardship, then the applicant is not eligible to receive his or her learner's permit until 18 years of age.

Issuance/Application: If a learner's permit has been validated and the holder is younger than 18 years of age, the permit holder may drive if the front seat passenger's seat is occupied by a parent, guardian, or stepparent who holds a valid operator's, chauffeur's, or public passenger chauffeur's license.

- The application of an individual younger than 18 years must be signed and affirmed by a parent having custody of the minor applicant, or by a guardian having custody of the minor applicant. If neither parent lives in Indiana and there is no guardian, then any adult willing to assume this responsibility can do so.
- A chauffeur's license may be issued to an individual who is 18 years of age, if that individual has operated a motor vehicle for more than 1 year, makes proper application on the Bureau's form, passes the examination and tests required for issuance of a chauffeur's license, and pays the fees prescribed by the Bureau.
- A commercial driver's license for transportation of individuals may be issued if an individual is at least 21 years of age and has at least 1 year of driving experience as a licensed driver.
- A public passenger chauffeur's license can be issued at 21 years of age. A taxicab license can be issued for driving a taxicab. Additionally, the applicant must have at least 1 year of driving experience as a licensed driver.
- License includes a color photograph, a signature, and a state assigned number. Social security number may be added upon request.

Renewal: The application for renewal must be filed within 6 months of the license's expiration date.

- All individuals must provide verification of social security number and 2 proof of residency documents upon application for renewal.
- An individual who applies for a license renewal must pass an eye exam.
- If an applicant is under 21 years of age and has 6 active points on his or her license, he or she must also pass a written examination.
- License expires after 4 years on date of birth for people 18-74; 3 years on date of birth for people 75 and older.
- If an active military person has an Indiana driver's license, it does not expire until 90 days after his/her discharge from the military. As far as their family is concerned, their licenses do expire. They can renew by mail with a "photo exempt" license. Military families are the ONLY Indiana motorists who have the privilege of renewing by mail.

Types of Licenses: Driver's license classes include: (1) operator's license; (2) chauffeur's license; (3) public passenger chauffeur's license; (4) motorcycle license; (5) learner's permit; and (6) commercial license.

Traffic Rules

Alcohol Laws: The state's open container law meets TEA-21 requirements.

- Illegal per se BAC level is .08.
- BAC level for people under 21 is .02.

Emergency Radio/Cellular: Emergency phone number is 911.
- Citizen band radio channel 9 is randomly monitored for emergency calls.

Headsets: Wearing of headsets while operating a motor vehicle is permitted.

Occupant Restraints: Seat belts are required for the driver and all front seat passengers while the vehicle is in motion.
- Children under the age of 4 must be properly restrained in a child restraint system.
- Children age 4 through 7 must be in a booster seat.
- Children under 8 must be restrained in an adult belt if it is reasonably determined that they cannot fit in a child restraint system.
- Children between the ages of 8 and 16 must be properly fastened in a seat belt, or properly restrained in a child restraint system in all seating positions of all vehicles.
- Violation of the occupant protection laws is a primary offense.
- Riding in pick-up truck beds is permitted over age 16.

Railroad Crossing: Passenger vehicles, buses carrying passengers, motortrucks carrying employees, school buses, and vehicles carrying flammable material must stop between 15 and 50 feet from the nearest railroad tracks before proceeding, unless directed to do otherwise by a traffic signal or traffic officer.

School Buses: Vehicles must stop upon meeting, from either direction, a school bus that is stopped for loading or unloading children and displays or has recently displayed a stop signal arm. This rule does not apply if the bus is on the opposite roadway of a divided highway.

Vehicle Equipment & Rules

Bumper Height: A passenger vehicle that was originally equipped with a standard bumper must have a bumper when operated on a highway. The height of the bumper cannot be more than 3 inches from the original manufactured bumper height.

Glass/Window Tinting: A person may not drive a motor vehicle with any tinted windows that obstruct the driver's clear view of the highway or intersecting highway. A person may not drive a motor vehicle with any tinted windows that prevent the ability of people outside the vehicle to recognize the people inside the vehicle. The exceptions to this rule are tinted windows installed by the manufacturer that are in compliance with federal law, and windows that are tinted for medical reasons. Windows tinted for medical reasons require a physician's or optometrist's certification that must be carried in the car at all times. This certification must be updated annually.

Telematics: A person may not own or operate a motor vehicle that has a television set installed in a manner that allows the person driving the vehicle to see the television set.

Windshield Stickers: Stickers can be placed on the windshield if the stickers are 4 square inches or less and placed on the bottom of the passenger's side of the windshield.

Motorcycles & Mopeds

Equipment: Helmets and eye protection are required for all persons under the age of 18.
- A motorcycle operated on the roads of Indiana must be equipped with handlebars that are not higher than 15 inches above the driver's seat.

- Additionally, the motorcycle must have good working front and rear brakes, and be equipped with lights and reflectors meeting the standards of the U.S. Department of Transportation.
- Motorcycles that were manufactured before January 1, 1956, are not required to be equipped with headlights and other light devices if they are not operated when these lights are necessary for safety.

Licenses: The operator of a motorcycle may have either a temporary motorcycle learner's permit, a motorcycle learner's permit, a regular motorcycle operator's license, or a regular driver's license, chauffeur's license, or public passenger chauffeur's license with a motorcycle endorsement.

- A temporary motorcycle learner's permit can be issued to a person that is at least 15 years of age that passes a written test. This person must also be enrolled in an approved motorcycle driver education course. However, the motorcycle can only be driven during daylight, with a helmet, with no passengers and under the direct supervision of a licensed motorcycle operator who is at least 18 years old.
- A motorcycle learner's permit can be issued to an individual that holds a valid operator's, chauffeur's, or public passenger chauffeur's license and passes a written examination. A learner's permit allows the driver to drive on the highway for a period of 1 year as long as the driver wears a helmet, does not carry passengers, and only operates the motorcycle during daylight.
- A motorcycle license or a motorcycle license endorsement can be issued if the operator completes one of the following: (1) an approved motorcycle driver education and training course and passes the exam; (2) satisfactorily completes the written test, has a motorcycle learner's permit for at least 30 days, and completes the operational test; or (3) has a current motorcycle operator endorsement or license from any other jurisdiction and successfully completes the written test.
- A motorcycle operator's license cannot be issued to a person younger than 16 and 1 month of age.

Noise Limits: Any motorcycle must either be equipped with a muffler or any other device that prevents noise pollution. This device must be in good working condition.

Mopeds: Registration is not required.
- Minimum age to ride a moped is 15.
- Persons under 18 must wear protective headgear and goggles.

Passenger Car Trailers

Registration: A semitrailer used on the highway must be registered with the Bureau. It can be registered either annually, every 5 years, or permanently.

- A trailer or pop-up camper pulled on the highway must be registered with the Bureau on an annual basis. Upon registration, a license plate and registration card will be issued.

Brakes: A trailer or semitrailer that weighs at least 3,000 lbs. must be equipped with brakes adequate to control the movement of and to stop and to hold the towing vehicle and trailer or semitrailer.

- These brakes must be designed so that the driver of the towing vehicle can apply the brakes from the towing vehicle itself and adequately stop both the towing vehicle and the trailer or semitrailer.

Dimensions: Total length: 65 feet; trailer length: not specified; width: 102 inches; height: 13.6 feet.

Hitch: Double safety chain required for all trailers; type of hitch not specified.

Lighting: A motor vehicle, trailer, semitrailer, or any other vehicle that is pulled at the end of another vehicle must be equipped with at least one rear-mounted red taillight. This taillight must be plainly visible from a distance of 500 feet away. This vehicle must also be equipped with 2 or more rear-mounted white taillights. These taillights must be mounted between 20 inches and 72 inches from the ground. A separate white light must be placed on the vehicle so that it illuminates the rear plate and makes it clearly visible from a distance of 50 feet. All of these taillights must be properly wired so that when the headlights are illuminated, these lights are also illuminated.

Mirrors: A motor vehicle that is constructed or loaded in a manner that obstructs the driver's rear view must be equipped with a mirror located in place where it is able to reflect the driver's view of the highway for a distance of at least 200 feet.

Towing: The maximum length of 2 or more vehicles together, including any cargo is 60 feet. The maximum length for 3 or more vehicles together, including a load, is 65 feet. The maximum load size in length is 3 feet beyond the front and 4 feet beyond the rear.

Miscellaneous Provisions

Bail Bonds: Mandatory recognition of AAA and other accepted motor club arrest bond certificates up to $500, with specified exceptions.

Liability Laws: Every driver and every owner of a motor vehicle must have evidence of continuous financial responsibility. Failure to comply can result in the suspension of the person's current driver's license or vehicle registration or both.

- The required minimum amounts of financial responsibility are $25,000 for bodily injury to or the death of 1 individual, $50,000 for bodily injury to or the death of 2 or more individuals in any 1 accident, and $10,000 for damage to property in 1 accident.

Parking Restrictions: It is unlawful to park or stop on a highway when it is feasible to stop or park off of the highway, unless a vehicle is disabled to such a degree that it is impossible to avoid stopping and temporarily leaving the vehicle on the roadway.

- A driver may not stop or park a vehicle on a sidewalk; in front of a public or private driveway; within an intersection; within 15 feet of a fire hydrant; on a crosswalk; within 20 feet of a crosswalk at an intersection; between a safety zone and the adjacent curb or within 30 feet of points on the curb immediately opposite the end of a safety zone, unless the traffic authority indicates a different length by signs or markings; within 50 feet of the nearest rail of a railroad crossing; within 20 feet of the driveway entrance to a fire station and on the side of a street opposite the entrance to a fire station, in a fire lane, within 75 feet of the entrance; along side or opposite a street excavation or obstruction if stopping or parking would obstruct traffic; upon a bridge or other elevated structure upon a highway; within a tunnel; or any place where official signs prohibit stopping.
- Except where angle parking is allowed, a person must parallel park within 12 inches of the right-hand curb.
- State has non-resident service of process law.

Inspection/Weigh Stations: All trucks with a Gross Vehicle Weight Rating of 10,000 lbs. or more must stop.

Fees & Taxes

Table 1: Title & Registration Fees

Vehicle Type	Title Fee	Registration Fee
All Passengers Cars	$15.00	$20.75
Trucks of 7,000 lbs. or less	$15.00	$29.75
Trucks of 9,000 lbs. or less	$15.00	$49.75
Trucks of 11,000 lbs. or less	$15.00	$84.75
Trucks between 11,001 lbs. and 66,000 lbs.	$15.00	fees range from $144.75 to $867.75
Trucks over 66,000 lbs.	$15.00	$965.75
Trailers of 3,000 lbs. or less	$15.00	$16.75
Trailers of 5,000 lbs. or less	$15.00	$25.75
Trailers of 7,000 lbs. or less	$15.00	$31.75
Trailers of 9,000 lbs. or less	$15.00	$36.75
Trailers of 12,000 lbs. or less	$15.00	$79.75
Trailers between 12,001 lbs. and 22,000 lbs.	$15.00	fees range from $119.75 to $179.75
Trailers over 22,000 lbs.	$15.00	$239.75
Semitrailer 1 Year	$15.00	$41.75
Semitrailer 5 Year Cycle		
1st Year		$77.75
2nd Year		$63.75
3rd Year		$49.75
4th Year, 5th Year		$41.75
Semitrailer Permanent	$15.00	$82.75
Annual Renewal Fee		$10.75
Motorcycles	$15.00	N/A

Table 2: License Fees

License Class	Fee	Driving Test Fees
Learner's Permit	$9.00	
Motorcycle Learner's Permit	$9.00	$5.00
Operator License 4-Year	$14.00	
Operator License 3-Year (Over age 75)	$12.00	
Motorcycle License 4-Year	$14.00	$5.00
Chauffeur License	$18.00	
Public Passenger Chauffeur License	$14.00	
Duplicate – Amendments (Oper., Chauf & P.P. Chauf)	$10.00	
Motorcycle Endorsement (Oper., Chauf & P.P. Chauf)	$10.00	
Motorcycle Endorsement (P.P. Chauf)	$8.00	
Commercial Driver's License	$30.00	
Amended Driver's License	$20.00	
Commercial Driver's License Learner's Permit	$16.00	
Amended Commercial Driver's License Learner's Permit	$10.00	

IN

Table 3: Vehicle Taxes

Tax	Rate
State Excise Tax	Determined based on MSRP of vehicle when new.
State Sales Tax	5% on new and used vehicles
Gasoline Tax; (Diesel)	$0.18/gallon; ($0.16/gallon)

Table 4: Miscellaneous Fees

Tax	Amount	Payable Upon
License Plate Transfer	$10.75	
Motorcycle Plate	$25.75	registration
Recreational Vehicle Plate	$29.75	registration
Antique Motor Vehicle Plate	$20.75	request
90-Day Temporary Plate	$79.75	request
Duplicate Plate	$9.00	request
Replacement Plate	$9.00	request
Personalized Plate Application	$48.00	request
Disabled Parking Placard		request
Temporary	$5.00	
Permanent 1st 2	free	
Speed Title Service	$25.00	request
Delinquent Title Fee	$21.00	request
Handling and Processing Fee for Licensing Plate	$1.50	request
Duplicate/Corrected Registration Fee	$6.00	request

IOWA

Contact Information

Iowa Motor Vehicle Division (MVD)
Park Fair Mall, 100 Euclid Avenue
P.O. Box 9204
Des Moines, IA 50306-9204

(515) 237-3110
www.dot.state.ia.us/mvd/ovs/index.htm

Iowa State Patrol
Wallace State Office Building
Des Moines, IA 50319-0044

(515) 281-5824
www.state.ia.us/government/dps/isp/

Iowa Department of Transportation
800 Lincoln Way
Ames, IA 50010

(515) 239-1101
www.dot.state.ia.us

IA

Vehicle Title

Application: All motor vehicles, trailers, and motor homes, if driven upon the highways, must be registered and titled, except for public school buses and mobile or manufactured homes.

- Private school buses are required to be titled.

- Non-travel trailers with an empty weight of 2,000 lbs. or less are exempt from title requirements.
- Applications for registration and certificates of title are made to the county treasurer in the county of the owner or lessee's residence.
- The application for registration and certificate of title requires the owner's name, social security or passport number, driver's license number, date of birth, bona fide residence, mailing address, vehicle description, statement of liens, and amount of use tax to be paid.
- The application must be signed in ink.
- The last issued certificate of title must be submitted with the application for a new certificate of title for a used vehicle.
- If a certificate of title is lost or destroyed, the owner or lienholder must apply for a certified copy of the original certificate of title. There is a 5-day waiting period unless the applicant surrenders the original to the MVD or the county treasurer. The application must be signed by the lienholder if there is a lien.

Transfer of Ownership: Upon the transfer of any registered vehicle, the owner must endorse an assignment and warranty of title upon the certificate of title for the vehicle with a statement of all liens and encumbrances. The owner must deliver the certificate of title to the purchaser or transferee at the time of delivering the vehicle. The owner must indicate the name of the county in which the vehicle was last registered and the registration expiration date.

- The transferee within 30 calendar days after purchase or transfer must apply for and obtain from the county treasurer of purchaser's residence a new registration and a new certificate of title.
- The applicant will be required to pay a delinquent fee from the 1st day the registration fee was due prorated to the month of application for the new title.
- When a vehicle is sold outside of the state for purposes other than for junk, the seller must detach the registration plates and indicate on the reverse of the registration card the name and address of the out-of-state purchaser or transferee over the seller's signature. The seller must surrender the registration plates and registration card to the county treasurer, unless the registration plates are properly attached to another vehicle.
- The transferor of a used motor vehicle must provide the transferee with a damage disclosure statement before a new certificate of title will be issued. The new certificate of title and registration receipt shall state whether a prior owner had disclosed that the vehicle was damaged to the extent that it was a wrecked or salvage vehicle.
- The transferor of a motor vehicle less than 10 model years old must furnish an odometer statement that is in compliance with federal law and regulations. This odometer statement must be furnished with the application for a new certificate of title. The statement must reflect whether the mileage is "actual," "not actual," or "exceeds mechanical limits."

Mobile Homes: The owner of a mobile home must submit a tax clearance form to show that no taxes are owed prior to obtaining the title.

- A mobile home or manufactured home that is located outside a mobile home park is converted to real property by being placed on a permanent foundation. It will then be assessed for real estate taxes. The assessor will note the conversion on the face of the certificate of title and deliver it to the county treasurer for cancellation.
- When a mobile home is reconverted from real property by adding a vehicular frame, the owner may apply to the county treasurer for a certificate of title.

Vehicle Registration

Application: A vehicle is registered for the "registration year," which is the period of 12 consecutive months beginning on the 1st day of the month following the month of the birth of the owner of the vehicle. A vehicle registered for the 1st time in the state will be registered for the remaining unexpired months of the registration year, and the registration fee will be prorated. The county treasurer may adjust the renewal and expiration date when deemed necessary for administrative efficiency.

- A vehicle may be operated without registration plates for 45 days after the date of delivery from a dealer with a "registration applied for" card.
- A vehicle's registration card must be carried at all times in the vehicle.
- Application for renewal of a vehicle registration may be made on or after the 1st day of the month of expiration or registration and up to and including the last day of the month following the month of expiration of registration. The county treasurer will refuse to renew the registration if the treasurer knows that the applicant has a delinquent account, charge, fee, loan, taxes, or other indebtedness owed to or being collected by the state.
- A vehicle owner who moves out of state can receive a refund on their registration fees by returning their vehicle plates and proving that they are registered in another state.
- Delinquencies begin and penalties accrue the 1st of the month following the purchase of a new vehicle, and 30 days following the date a vehicle is brought into the state.
- The owner of the vehicle must inform the county treasurer of the county where the vehicle is registered of a change of address, change of name, or change of fuel type within 10 days.
- The registration fee is computed on the month of purchase of a new vehicle, except that the registration fee on a new vehicle acquired outside the state is based on the month that the vehicle was brought into Iowa.
- The registration fee for a vehicle from another state or country becomes due in the month that the vehicle is sold or transferred to an Iowa resident or the month that a non-resident owner establishes Iowa residency or accepts employment of 90 days' duration or longer.
- If a vehicle is in storage and the registration is not delinquent, the owner may surrender the registration plates to the county treasurer and will not be obligated to register the vehicle while it remains in storage.

Non-Residents: If a non-resident owner or operator of a vehicle is employed within the state or carries on business within the state, the owner must register the vehicle, pay the same fees for registration, and maintain the same financial liability coverage as required for residents of the state. However, these requirements do not apply to a person commuting from the person's residence in another state or whose employment is seasonal or temporary, not exceeding 90 days.

- Any non-resident owner of a private passenger motor vehicle, not required to register their vehicle in the state, may operate the vehicle in the state if the vehicle is duly registered in, and displays valid registration plates issued for the vehicle in the owner's state of residence.
- Non-resident members of the armed services are not required to register their vehicle in Iowa if the vehicle is properly registered in the person's state of residence.

Registration Type: Multipurpose vehicles (SUVs and vans) are defined as motor vehicles designed to carry not more than 10 people, and constructed either on a truck chassis or with special features for occasional off-road operation. Model year 1992 and older multipurpose vehicles are classified differently than other passenger vehicles for the purpose of determining registration fees.

- A Class A motor home has a driver's compartment and an entire body equipped with temporary living quarters. Class A motor homes also include passenger carrying buses that have been registered at least 5 times as a motor truck and which have been converted to provide temporary living quarters.
- A Class B motor home is a completed van-type vehicle which has been converted or constructed to provide temporary living quarters.
- A Class C motor home is an incomplete vehicle upon which is permanently attached a body designed to provide temporary living quarters.

Safety Inspection: Peace officers may stop and inspect a vehicle if the officer has reasonable cause to believe it is a danger to other motorists or lacks required equipment.

License Plates

Disbursement: After receiving the registration and title application accompanied by the appropriate fee, the county treasurer will issue 1 license plate for a motorcycle, motorized bicycle, or trailer, and 2 license plates for every other motor vehicle. The registration plates, including special plates, are assigned to the owner of the vehicle.

- A person who acquires a vehicle which is currently registered or from a dealer's inventory may operate the vehicle without plates for 30 days if ownership evidence is carried in the vehicle.
- A person who acquires a vehicle which is currently registered or from a dealer's inventory and who has possession of plates may operate the vehicle for 45 days if ownership evidence is carried in the vehicle.
- The registration plate for a motorcycle, motorized bicycle, or trailer must be displayed on the rear of the vehicle.
- Annual validation stickers are issued after payment of registration fees for each set of plates. The stickers are to be displayed on the lower left corner of the registration plates, except for motorcycles and small trailer plates, where the stickers are to be displayed on the upper left corner of the plate.
- Three-year or permanent registration plates are issued for trailers. Payments for permanent plates may be made at 5-year intervals or on an annual basis.
- Special License Plates are available for persons with disabilities.

Transfer of Plates: When the owner of a registered vehicle transfers or assigns ownership of the vehicle to another person, the owner must remove the plates from the vehicle. The owner must then either forward the plates to the county treasurer where the vehicle is registered or have the plates assigned to another vehicle within 30 days after transfer, upon payment of the required fees.

Driver's Licenses

Examination: The MVD may examine every new applicant for a driver's license or any person holding a valid driver's license when the MVD has reason to believe that the person may be physically or mentally incompetent to operate a motor vehicle, or whose driving record appears to the MVD to justify the examination. The examination will include a vision test (20/40 visual acuity is required in at least one eye), knowledge test, and driving skills test.

- An applicant for a new or renewed driver's license may submit a vision report signed by a licensed vision specialist in lieu of the vision test.

Graduated Drivers Licensing: State has a system of graduated licensing for teen drivers. At 14, teens are eligible for an instruction/learner's permit.

- Permit holders may not drive unsupervised.
- Permit holders must accumulate at least 20 (4 at night) hours of parental/guardian certified driving hours.
- At 16, teens who have held a permit for at least 6 months, have completed driver education, and have passed driving, written, and vision tests are eligible for an intermediate license.
- Intermediate license holders may not drive unsupervised between the hours of 12:30 a.m. and 5:00 a.m.
- Teens must also accumulate an additional 10 hours of parental/guardian supervised driving in the intermediate stage.
- At 17, teens who (1) have held an intermediate license or a comparable license from another state for at least 12 months; (2) have been accident- and conviction-free for at least 12 months; (3) have not had their license suspended or revoked; (4) have permission from a parent or guardian; and (5) present an affidavit by a parent/guardian attesting to the applicant's driving experience are eligible for an unrestricted license.
- Persons who were convicted of a moving violation or involved in a traffic accident while holding an instruction permit or intermediate license are subject to a remedial driver improvement action or suspension of the permit or intermediate license. A person possessing an instruction permit when he or she was convicted of a moving violation or involved in an accident must remain free of moving violations and not be involved in an accident for 6 months before he or she may be issued an intermediate license.

Issuance/Application: A non-resident is not required to hold an Iowa driver's license if the person is in compliance with the driver's license requirements of the person's home state or country.

- All applications must include the applicant's full name, signature, current mailing address, current residential address, date of birth, and physical description including sex, height, and eye color. Licensees must notify the MVD of changes of address within 30 days. Applicants must surrender all other driver's licenses and nonoperator's identification cards, certify that the applicant has no other driver's licenses, and certify that the applicant is not currently subject to suspension, revocation, or cancellation of any driver's license or has committed an offense likely to result in suspension, revocation, or cancellation of any driver's license.
- An applicant must submit one primary and one secondary document as proof of age and identity. Acceptable primary documents include: photo driver's license; photo I.D. card; birth certificate issued in the U.S. or Canada; approved INS documents; court order containing full name, date of birth, and court seal; military I.D. card; valid passport issued by the U.S. or Canada; I.D. card issued by the Canadian Dept. of Indian Affairs; and approved Iowa Department of Corrections documents.
- Acceptable secondary documents includes any primary document; Bureau of Indian Affairs or Indian Treaty Card; photo driver's license that has been expired for more than 1 year; court order that does not contain applicant's date of birth; foreign birth certificate translated by approved translator; military discharge or separation papers; military dependent I.D. card; health insurance card; IRS or state tax form;

marriage license or certificate; medical records from a doctor or hospital; gun permit; pilot's license; school record or transcript; social security card; Canadian social insurance card; photo student I.D.; vehicle certificate of title; voter registration card; prison release document; and parent or guardian affidavit.
- Driver education is required for an intermediate license if applicant is under 18.
- License normally includes a color photograph.
- Applicants for licenses and I.D. cards must show proof of Iowa residency.
- License and I.D. card expiration dates of non-citizens match the expiration date of the person's visa.
- License number is an assigned number. Social security number will only be used if requested.

Renewal: Except as otherwise provided, a driver's license, other than an instruction permit, expires at the option of the licensee, 2 or 4 years from the licensee's birthday in the year of issuance if the licensee is between 17 years 11 months and 70 years on the date of issuance of the license. If the licensee is under the age of 17 years 11 months or over the age of 70, the license is effective for 2 years from the licensee's birthday in the year of issuance.
- A person has 60 days to renew his or her license after the expiration date.
- Applicants with vision or other physical restrictions may be required to renew their license every 2 years.
- A vision test or vision report signed by a licensed vision specialist is required.
- The expiration date for persons who enter military service while holding a valid Iowa driver's license is 6 months after separation from active duty.
- The licenses of active duty military personnel may be extended until 6 months after separation from the military. Active duty military personnel must obtain a military service extension. A 5-year extension is available for military personnel and their families.

Types of Licenses: Restricted: Persons between 16 and 18 years of age who are not in attendance at school or attend a school where a driver's education course is not offered may be issued a restricted license for travel to and from work if necessary for the person to maintain the person's present employment.
- Special Instruction Permit: A person with a physical disability, who is not suffering from a convulsive disorder and who can provide a favorable medical report, may obtain a special instruction permit if the person's license renewal was denied for failure to pass a required examination or because the MVD believed that the person would not be able to operate a motor vehicle safely by reason of physical or mental disability.
- The MVD may issue a temporary permit to an applicant while the MVD is completing an investigation to determine all facts relative to applicant's privilege to receive a driver's license. The permit will be invalid and must be returned to the MVD when the applicant's license is either issued or denied.

Classification of licenses:
- Classes A and B: Commercial driver's licenses for vehicles with a Gross Combination Weight Rating (GCWR) of 26,001 lbs. or more.
- Class C: Commercial and non-commercial; valid for the operation of some combinations of vehicles with a GCWR of more than 26,000 lbs.; any combination of vehicles with a GCWR of 26,000 lbs. or less excluding motorcycles, farm vehicles, fire vehicles, and motor homes solely for personal or family use.

- Class D: Chauffeur license excluding motorcycles.
- Class M: Motorcycle license.

Traffic Rules

Alcohol Laws: A person who operates a motor vehicle in this state under circumstances which give reasonable grounds to believe that the person has been operating a motor vehicle while intoxicated is deemed to have given consent to the withdrawal of specimens of the person's blood, breath, or urine and to a chemical test or tests of the specimens for the purpose of determining the alcohol concentration or presence of a controlled substance or other drugs.

- Open containers are not permitted. Meets the requirements of TEA-21.
- Illegal per se BAC level is .08.
- Persons under the age of 21 may not operate a motor vehicle while having an alcohol concentration of .02 or more.

Emergency Radio/Cellular: Citizen band radio channel 9 is also monitored for emergency calls. Emergency cell number is 1-800-525-5555, 911 or *55.

Headsets: Wearing radio headsets while operating a motor vehicle is permitted.

Occupant Restraints: The driver and front seat occupants of a motor vehicle over 6 years of age must wear a properly adjusted and fastened seat belt.

- Infants through age 1 and under 20 pounds must be restrained in a rear-facing safety seat.
- Children under 6 years of age must be restrained in a safety or booster seat.
- Children ages 6 through 10 years of age must be restrained in a seat belt or booster seat.
- Riding in the beds of pickup trucks is permitted.
- Violation of the occupant protection laws is a primary offense.

Railroad Crossing: All vehicles must stop within 50 feet but not less than 15 feet of a railroad crossing when warning of the immediate approach of a train is given by automatic signal, crossing gates, a flag person, or otherwise. The vehicle must stop, remain standing, and not traverse the crossing when a crossing gate is lowered or when a human flagman continues to give a signal of the approach or passage of a train.

- The driver of any vehicle approaching a railroad grade crossing across which traffic is regulated by a stop sign, a railroad sign directing traffic to stop, or an official traffic control signal displaying a flashing red or steady circular red-colored light must stop prior to crossing the railroad at the first opportunity at either the clearly marked stop line or at a point near the crossing where the driver has a clear view of the approaching railroad traffic.
- Vehicles carrying passengers for hire, school buses, and vehicles carrying hazardous material are required to stop at all railroad crossings and look and listen in both directions for an approaching train, and for signals indicating an approaching train, and must not proceed until the driver can do so safely. This rule does not apply if the crossing is designated "exempt" because the tracks have been partially removed on either side of the roadway.

School Buses: The driver of a vehicle, including the driver of a vehicle operating on a private road or driveway, when meeting a school bus with flashing amber warning lamps must slow to not more than 20 mph and not pass the bus, and must bring the vehicle to a complete stop when the school bus stops and the stop signal arm is extended. The vehicle must remain stopped until the stop signal arm is retracted after which time the driver may proceed with due caution.

- The driver of a vehicle upon a highway with two or more lanes in each direction need not stop upon meeting a school bus which is traveling in the opposite direction even though the school bus is stopped.

Vehicle Equipment & Rules

Bumper Height: Modification of bumper height is permitted.

Glass/Window Tinting: No person may operate a motor vehicle with a windshield, a side window to the immediate right or left of the driver, or a sidewing forward of the driver that has less than 70% transparency unless the person suffers from a severe light-sensitive condition documented by a licensed physician.

Windshield Stickers: Permitted if driver's view is not obstructed.

Motorcycles & Motorized Bicycles

Equipment: A person must not operate or ride a motorcycle on the highways with another person on the motorcycle unless the motorcycle is designed to carry more than one person. The additional passenger may ride upon the permanent and regular seat if designed for two persons, or upon another seat firmly attached to the motorcycle at the rear of the operator. The motorcycle must be equipped with footrests for the passenger unless the passenger is riding in a sidecar or enclosed cab. The motorcycle operator must not carry any person nor may any other person ride in a position that will interfere with the operation or control of the motorcycle or the view of the operator.

- A person operating a motorcycle or motorized bicycle must ride only upon the vehicle's permanent and regular attached seat. Every person riding upon the vehicle must be sitting astride the seat, facing forward with one leg on either side of the vehicle.
- The operator of a motorcycle or motorized bicycle must not carry any package, bundle, or other article that prevents the operator from keeping both hands on the handlebars.
- Every motorcycle and motorized bicycle must be equipped with at least 1 and not more than 2 headlamps.
- Every motorcycle and motorized bicycle must be equipped with at least 1 brake, which may be operated by hand or foot.

Licenses: Class M driver's licenses are issued for the operation of a motorcycle.

- Applicants under the age of 18 for a motorcycle driver's license must successfully complete a motorcycle education course.

Motorized Bicycles: Motorized bicycles are required to be registered if the MVD believes that a particular model or vehicle is capable of speeds exceeding 30 mph. Registration plates issued for motorcycles are to be issued also for motorized bicycles.

- The MVD may issue a license valid only for the operation of a motorized bicycle to a person 14 years of age or older who has passed a vision test and written knowledge

test. Fourteen- and fifteen-year-olds are also required to successfully complete a motorized bicycle education course. The license is valid only for a period not to exceed 2 years from the licensee's birthday in the year of issuance.
- A person operating a motorized bicycle on the highways must not carry any other person on the vehicle.

Passenger Car Trailers

Brakes: Every trailer of a Gross Vehicle Weight (GVW) of 3,000 lbs. must be equipped with brakes adequate to control the movement of and to stop and hold the vehicle, and so designed as to be applied by the driver of the towing motor vehicle from its cab, or with self-actuating brakes, and a weight-equalizing hitch with a sway control. Every trailer of a GVW of 3,000 lbs. or more must be equipped with a separate, auxiliary means of applying the brakes on the trailer from the cab of the towing vehicle.

Dimensions: Total length: 70 feet (includes bumpers); trailer length: not specified; width: 96 inches (certain roads allow a width of 102 inches (includes bumpers)); height: 14 feet.

Hitch: Weight-equalizing hitches that apply leverage by means of spring bars, coil springs, or torsional bars are approved for use with trailers.
- 5th-wheel types of connections and sway control devices that employ friction, hydraulics, torsional bars, mechanical cams, or electronics are approved to limit side sway.

Lighting: Every trailer having a GVW in excess of 3,000 lbs. must have the following: (1) on the front, 2 clearance lamps, 1 at each side, if the trailer is wider in its widest part than the cab of the vehicle towing it; (2) on each side, 1 side-marker lamp at or near the rear; 2 reflectors, 1 at or near the front and 1 at or near the rear; and (3) on the rear, 2 clearance lamps, 1 at each side; 1 stop light; 1 taillamp; and 2 reflectors, 1 at each side.
- A lighting device or reflector, when mounted on or near the front of a trailer, must not display any other color than white, yellow, or amber.
- No lighting device or reflector, when mounted on or near the rear of any trailer, may display any other color than red, except that the stop light may be red, yellow, or amber.
- Clearance lamps must be mounted on the permanent structure of the vehicle in such manner as to indicate the extreme width of the vehicle or its load.

Mirrors: Any motor vehicle towing another vehicle in such manner as to obstruct the view in a rearview mirror located in the driver's compartment must be equipped with a side mirror located so that the view to the rear will not be obstructed. When the vehicle is not towing another vehicle, the side mirrors must be retracted or removed.

Speed Limits: Rural 55 mph. Interstate 70 mph or as posted.

Towing: When 1 vehicle is towing another, the drawbar or other connection must not exceed 15 feet.
- The drawbar must be of sufficient strength to pull all weight towed and must be fastened to the frame of the towing vehicle in such manner as to prevent side sway. In addition to the principal connection there must be a safety chain which must be fastened as to be capable of holding the towed vehicle should the principal connection fail for any reason.

IA

Miscellaneous Provisions

Accident Reporting: Drivers will no longer be required to fill out a DOT report for an accident resulting in personal injury, death, or damage of $1,000 or more if the accident is investigated by a law enforcement agency.

Bail Bonds: Mandatory recognition of AAA arrest bond certificate up to $1,000 with specifications.

Liability Laws: Has security-type law applicable in event of accident causing property damage in excess of $1,000 or personal injury or death. A person may not drive a motor vehicle on the highways of the state unless the driver has proof of financial liability coverage for the vehicle.

- Liability coverage must be a minimum of $20,000 for bodily injury or death of 1 person in any 1 accident, $40,000 for bodily injury or death of 2 or more persons in any 1 accident, and $15,000 for damage to or destruction of property in 1 accident.
- State has non-resident service of process law.

Weigh Stations: Any peace officer having reason to believe that the weight of a vehicle and load is unlawful is authorized to require the driver to stop and submit to a weighing of the same by means of either portable or stationary scales and may require the vehicle to be driven to the nearest public scales. If the officer determines that the weight is unlawful, the officer may require the driver to stop the vehicle in a suitable place until such portion of the load is removed as may be necessary to reduce the GVW to the permitted limit.

- All vehicles weighing over 6,000 lbs. must stop.

Fees & Taxes

Table 1: Title Fees

Vehicle Type	Fee Amount
All Vehicles Required to Be Titled	$15.00
Replacement	$15.00

Table 2: Registration Fees

Vehicle Type	Registration Fee
Motor Vehicles (except vehicles designed for carrying livestock, freight, or more than 9 passengers; motor homes; ambulances; hearses; motorcycles; motor bicycles; and 1992 model year and older multipurpose vehicles (SUVs and vans))	
Van Equipped for Wheelchair	$60.00
Motor Vehicle Not More Than 5 Model Years Old	1% of the vehicle's value as fixed by the MVD plus $0.40 for each 100 lbs. or fraction thereof the vehicle's weight
Motor Vehicle More Than 5 Model Years Old	part of fee that is based on value of vehicle is 75% of rate fixed when vehicle was new
Motor Vehicle More Than 6 Model Years Old	part of fee that is based on value of vehicle is 50% of rate fixed when vehicle was new
1994 Model Year or Newer Motor Vehicle Once the Vehicle Is 9 Model Years or Older (not applicable until 2003)	$35.00

1993 Model Year or Older Motor Vehicle That Has Been Titled in the Same Person's Name Since the Vehicle Was New or the Title Was Transferred prior to Jan. 1, 2002	part of the fee that is based on value of vehicle is 10% of the rate fixed when vehicle was new	
1969 Model Year or Older Motor Vehicle Transferred to a New Owner or Brought into the State on or After Jan. 1, 2002	$16.00	
1970 through 1989 Model Year Motor Vehicle Transferred to a New Owner or Brought into the State on or After Jan. 1, 2002	$23.00	
1990 through 1993 Model Year Motor Vehicle Transferred to a New Owner or Brought into the State on or After Jan. 1, 2002	$27.00	
Minimum	$10.00	
Other Vehicles		
1992 and Older Model Year SUV or Van	$55.00	
1992 and Older Model Year Van Equipped for Wheelchair	$60.00	
Antique Vehicles for Exclusively Educational, Exhibition, or Entertainment Purposes	$5.00	
Electric Automobiles 5 Years Old or Newer (excluding low speed vehicles)	$25.00	
Electric Automobiles More Than 5 Model Years Old (excluding low speed vehicles)	$15.00	
Motorcycles 5 Model Years Old or Newer	$20.00	
Motorcycles More Than 5 Model Years Old	$10.00	
Motorized Bicycles	$7.00	
Church Buses	$25.00	
Travel Trailers	$0.20 per sq. ft. floor space (75% of this amount after trailer is more than 6 model years old)	
Trailers Excluding Travel Trailers	$10.00	
Motor Homes		
Class A	List Price of $80,000 or More	First 5 Model Years	$400.00
		Each Succeeding Registration	$300.00
	List Price of $40,000 to $79,999	First 5 Model Years	$200.00
		Each Succeeding Registration	$150.00
	List Price of $20,000 to $39,999	First 5 Model Years	$140.00
		Each Succeeding Registration	$105.00
	List Price of Less than $20,000	First 5 Model Years	$120.00
		Each Succeeding Registration	$85.00
Class A Motor Home Which Is a Passenger-Carrying Bus Registered at Least 5 Times as Motor Truck and Converted to Living Quarters		Through 10 Model Years	$90.00
		Each Succeeding Registration	$65.00
Class B		First 5 Model Years	$90.00
		Each Succeeding Registration	$65.00
Class C		First 5 Model Years	$110.00
		Each Succeeding Registration	$80.00
Replacement Registration Certificate	$3.00	

IA

Table 3: License Fees

License Class	Cost
A (Commercial)	$16.00* (2) $40.00* (5)
B (Commercial)	$16.00* (2) $40.00* (5)
C (Commercial)	$16.00* (2) $40.00* (5)
C (Non-commercial-Operator)	$8.00 (2) $20.00 (5)
D (Non-commercial-Chauffeur)	$16.00 (2) $40.00 (5)
M (Motorcycle License-Added to Existing License)	$1.00 per year (2 or 4)
M (Motorcycle License Only-New Issuance)	$10.00 (2 or 4)
Restriction 1 (Motorcycle Instruction Permit-Must be added to an existing license)	$1.00 per year
C-Restriction 1 (Motorcycle Permit Only-New Issuance)	$8.00 (2)
C-Restriction 2 (Instruction Permit)	$6.00 (2)
Restriction 3 (Commercial Instruction Permit-Must be added to an existing license)	$12.00 (6 months)
C-Restriction 4 (Chauffeur's Instruction Permit)	$12.00 (2)
C-Restriction 5 (Motorized Bicycle License-Moped)	$8.00 (2)
C-Restriction 6 (Minor's Restricted License)	$8.00 (2)
C-Restriction 7 (Minor's School License)	$8.00 (2)
Replacement Fee	$3.00

* There are also additional fees for the commercial endorsements.

Table 4: Vehicle Taxes

Tax	Rate
Personal Property Tax	registration fees are in lieu of all taxes
State Sales Tax	5%
Gasoline Tax; (Diesel)	$0.203/gallon; ($0.225/gallon)
Gasohol Tax	$0.19/gallon
Natural Gas Tax for Vehicles	$0.16/gallon

Table 5: Miscellaneous Fees

Fee	Amount
Delinquent Registration Fee	5% of annual registration fee per month; not less than $5.00
Replacement of Registration Plates	$5.00
FCC Licensed Radio Operation Plates	$5.00
Personalized Plates	$25.00
Additional Fee for Re-Registration of Personalized Plates	$5.00
New Registration Plates after Change of County of Registration	$5.00

KANSAS

Contact Information

Division of Motor Vehicles (DMV)
Kansas Department of Revenue
Robert B. Docking Office Building
Topeka, KS 66626

(785) 296-3963
www.ksrevenue.org/dmv.htm

Kansas Highway Patrol
122 SW 7th
Topeka, KS 66603

(785) 296-6800
www.kansashighwaypatrol.org

Kansas Department of Transportation
Eisenhower Building
700 Harrison
Topeka, KS 66603-3754

(785) 296-3566
www.ksdot.org

Vehicle Title

Application: The application shall contain a statement of all liens or encumbrances on the vehicle, and any other information required by the DMV. For new vehicles, a dealer shall execute a manufacturer's statement of origin stating the liens and encumbrances on the vehicle.

- An odometer reading and purchase price is required on a title application except for vehicles over 10 years old or for trucks with a Gross Vehicle Weight Rating (GVWR) over 16,000 lbs.
- All fees for a certificate of title shall be paid to the county treasurer where the applicant resides or has his or her principal place of business.
- A certificate of title will not be granted until the applicant has shown proof that the sales tax on the motor vehicle has been paid.
- Vehicles titled in another state must be inspected by a member of the Highway Patrol prior to receiving a Kansas title.

Transfer of Ownership: The transferor shall endorse an assignment of the title to the transferee with a warranty of title, and shall deliver the assigned title to the buyer within 30 days of delivery.

- The transferee shall then present the assigned title to the DMV when applying for a new title and registration.
- The sale of a vehicle without transfer of the certificate of title is considered fraudulent and void.

Vehicle Registration

Application: Every owner of a motor vehicle, motorized bicycle, trailer, or semitrailer shall apply for registration if the vehicle is based in the state.

- A purchaser of a vehicle currently registered in the state may operate the vehicle with its existing license plates for up to 30 days before applying for a new registration for the vehicle.
- An applicant for registration shall register by mail, in person, or online to the office of the county treasurer where the applicant resides or has a bona fide place of business.

- The application shall contain a brief description of the vehicle and other such information required by the DMV. In addition, the applicant must submit a statement certifying that the applicant has a certificate of title for the vehicle, showing the date and identification number.
- New owners have 30 days to register a vehicle in the state, but must immediately apply for a temporary registration from a dealer or from the county treasurer.
- When an owner of a registered vehicle buys a new vehicle, he can use his registration from the old vehicle for up to 30 days prior to applying for a new registration.
- An application for registration will not be granted until the applicant has shown proof that the sales tax on the motor vehicle and all personal property taxes have been paid, and has proof of insurance.

Non-Residents: Non-residents may operate a vehicle without Kansas registration on a reciprocal basis with the home state. Non-residents must purchase Kansas registration within 90 days of establishing residency in Kansas.

- Military personnel on active duty in Kansas may maintain vehicle registration on a reciprocal basis with the home state. Kansas military personnel on duty out of state may apply for registration at any time without penalty fee.
- Full-time college students (enrolled in at least 9 credit hours per semester) with a valid vehicle registration and a driver's license from their home state are not required to obtain Kansas registration.

Registration Type: Vehicles used as implements of husbandry, all-terrain vehicles, and privately owned fire trucks need not be registered.

- Upon the filing of an application and payment of the required fees, the division of vehicles shall register the vehicle and issue to the owner a registration receipt which contains the registration number.
- Passenger vehicles, pickup trucks with a GVWR less than 12,000 lbs., motorcycles, motorized bicycles, and recreational vehicles are registered for 12 consecutive months from the month of initial registration. The registration expires at 12:00 midnight on the last day of the last month of the 12-month period of registration.
- For all other vehicles, registration expires December 31 of each year.
- In every year where a new license plate is not issued upon registration, the owner will receive a decal to be affixed to the rear license plate indicating the county of registration and the year of expiration.
- Registration expires upon the transfer of ownership, and does not transfer to the new owner.

Safety Inspection: The Kansas Highway Patrol is authorized to conduct a spot inspection of the mechanical condition of any vehicle where signs are displayed requiring such stop, or at any time upon reasonable cause to believe that a vehicle is unsafe or not equipped as required by law.

License Plates

Disbursement: The DMV shall furnish to the owner of every registered vehicle 1 license plate.

- The license plate shall display the registration number assigned to the vehicle, the name of the state, and the year or years for which it is issued.
- In every calendar year ending in a "5" or "0," the DMV shall furnish 1 license plate for each vehicle. In the intervening 4 years, the division shall furnish 1 decal for the

license plate each year showing the expiration date.
- 2 personalized license plates may be issued to the owner of a passenger vehicle or truck up to 20,000 lbs. GVWR upon application for such a plate. Owners of motorcycles may receive 1 personalized plate.
- License plates shall be attached to the rear of the vehicle. Owners of specialized plates shall place 1 in the front of the vehicle and 1 on the rear of the vehicle.
- Veterans with a 100% disability are eligible to receive free, distinctive license plates.
- Holders of amateur radio licenses and owners of antique vehicles are eligible for a specialized license plate, upon payment of a fee.
- Special license plates for handicapped individuals are available upon application, with medical certificate, to County Treasurer's office.

Transfer of Plates: Upon transfer of ownership of any vehicle, the right to use any license plate shall expire immediately and the plate shall be removed by the transferor.
- The transferor of a vehicle may pay a fee to transfer the plate to another vehicle registered to himself.
- The owner of a registration plate has 30 days to transfer it from an old to a new vehicle.

Driver's Licenses

Examination: An applicant for an initial driver's license shall be examined by the DMV prior to the issuance of a license. The applicant must pass a vision test, a test of the applicant's ability to read and understand highway signs and the applicant's knowledge of the traffic laws of the state, and a road test.
- An examination is required when an applicant for a license does not have a valid driver's license, or answers in the affirmative that he has had a prior revocation, suspension, or refusal of a license.
- Eye test (20/40 vision acuity required) and written and driving tests are required for original license.

Graduated Drivers Licensing: State has a system of graduated licensing for teen drivers.
- A person at least 14 years of age may apply for a learner's permit. The applicant must pass all parts of the license examination except the driving test, and must have permission from a parent or guardian. This permit must be held for 6 months.
- Applicants between 16 and 18 years of age shall submit a signed affidavit of either a parent or guardian stating that the applicant has completed at least 50 hours of adult supervised driving, with at least 10 of those hours at night.

Issuance/Application: No person shall operate a vehicle without a valid driver's license.
- Every applicant shall indicate for which category of license he or she is applying.
- Each applicant must provide the following: name, proof of age, sex, address, a brief physical description, whether the applicant has been licensed before, and whether the applicant has ever had a license suspended or revoked.
- Commercial applicants must also provide a social security number, color photograph, and a consent to release driving record information.
- Applicants for driver's licenses to submit their social security or taxpayer identification number. If an applicant does not have either document, the person must submit a sworn statement stating they do not have either one.
- Licensees shall submit to an examination for a license whenever the DMV has good

KS

cause to believe that such person is incompetent or otherwise not qualified to be licensed, or if the person has had a license suspended.
- Upon payment of the required fee, the DMV shall issue to every qualified applicant a driver's license that contains the class or classes of motor vehicles that the licensee is entitled to drive, a distinguishing number that may be a social security number, the name, date of birth, address, brief physical description, color photograph, and signature of the licensee.
- Licenses of persons under age 18, between the ages of 18 through 21, and 21 and over shall be distinguishable from each other.
- Licenses are to be carried and exhibited on demand.
- Social security number on license is not allowed.

Renewal: Licenses issued to persons between the ages of 21 and 65 expire on the 6th anniversary of the date of birth of the licensee that is nearest the date of application.
- Licenses issued to persons less than 21 years of age or more than 65 years of age shall expire on the 4th anniversary of the license that is nearest the date of application.
- Commercial driver's licenses shall expire on the 4th anniversary of the date of birth of the licensee nearest the date of application.
- Every license shall be renewable on or before its expiration upon application and payment of the required fee and successful completion of required examinations.
- Prior to renewal, the applicant shall pass a vision test and written examination of the ability to read and understand highway signs. In lieu of this provision, the applicant can submit a vision test from a licensed physician or optometrist taken within 3 months of the application, and can complete the examination furnished with the notice of expiration of license and submit it with the application.
- For military personnel, the Kansas DMV will renew their driver's licenses regardless of whether their license is currently expired (no time limitation). For military dependents, license is renewed only if it has been expired for less than one year. Licensure terms are the same for military persons as the general public. If they are stationed out of state and expire, they must contact the Kansas DMV, fax a copy of their driver's license and military id, give their current mailing address, and the test and booklet will be mailed to them to complete and return. Dependents use the same process. Their previous photo will be used from the DMV's files to produce the new license.

Types of Licenses:

Commercial Licenses:
- Class A: Motor vehicles including any combination of vehicles with a GVWR over 26,000 lbs., provided the GVWR of the vehicle or vehicles being towed exceeds 10,000 lbs.
- Class B: Motor vehicles including any single vehicle with a GVWR over 26,000 lbs., or any such vehicle towing a vehicle not in excess of 10,000 lbs. GVWR.
- Class C: Motor vehicles including any single vehicle 26,000 lbs. GVWR or less, any such vehicle towing a vehicle not in excess of 10,000 lbs. GVWR, or any vehicle designed to transport 16 or more passengers or any vehicle used in the transportation of hazardous materials that cause the vehicle to be placarded, if the combined weight of the vehicles is 26,000 lbs. GVWR or less.

Non-Commercial Licenses:

- Class A: Motor vehicles including any combination of vehicles with a GVWR over 26,000 lbs., provided the GVWR of the vehicle or vehicles being towed exceeds 10,000 lbs.
- Class B: Motor vehicles including any single vehicle with a GVWR over 26,000 lbs., or any such vehicle towing a vehicle not in excess of 10,000 lbs. GVWR. Class B vehicles do not include vehicles registered as farm trucks in excess of 26,000 lbs. GVWR.
- Class C: Motor vehicles including any single vehicle 26,000 lbs. GVWR or less, any such vehicle towing a vehicle not in excess of 10,000 lbs. GVWR, or any vehicle with a GVWR of 26,000 lbs. or less towing a vehicle in excess of 10,000 lbs. GVWR, or any single vehicle registered as a farm truck with a GVWR exceeding 26,000 lbs.
- Class M: Includes motorcycles.
- In each classification, holders of Class A licenses may drive Class B and C vehicles, and holders of Class B licenses may operate Class C vehicles.
- A restricted Class C or M license may be issued to a person aged 15, but only if he or she has successfully completed an approved driver training course, has held an instructional permit for at least 6 months, has completed at least 25 hours of adult supervised driving, and has written consent of a parent or guardian. The restricted license shall allow a driver to operate a vehicle while going to or from any job, to and from school, at any time when a licensed adult is in the vehicle, or if a motorcycle license, when a licensed adult is in the general proximity of the licensee. At no time shall the holder of a restricted license operate a vehicle with any non-sibling minor passengers.
- Any person at least 14 years of age may apply for an instruction permit. A person with an instruction permit may only operate a vehicle when a licensed parent or guardian is in the adjacent seat.
- Any person between the ages of 14 and 16 and who resides upon or works upon a farm may apply for a farm permit. The farm permit allows the licensee to operate a motor vehicle while going to or from any job, to and from school, at any time when a licensed adult is in the vehicle, or if a motorcycle license, when a licensed adult is in the general proximity of the licensee.

Traffic Rules

Alcohol Laws: Any person who operates a vehicle in Kansas is deemed to have given an implied consent to submit to an alcohol-content test. Open containers are not permitted. Meets TEA-21 requirements.

- Illegal per se BAC level is .08.
- BAC level for people under 21 is .02.
- BAC level for commercial drivers is .04.

Emergency Radio/Cellular: Emergency number is 911 and the cell number *47 or *KTA on turnpike.

- Citizen band radio channel 9 is monitored for emergency calls.

Headsets: Wearing of radio headsets while operating a motor vehicle is permitted.

Occupant Restraints: Every passenger in the front seat of a motor vehicle must be properly restrained by a seat belt.

- Children under the age of 4 must be securely restrained in a child passenger safety restraining system.
- All children between the ages of 4 and 14 must properly wear a seat belt while the vehicle is in operation.
- Violation of the seat belt law is a secondary offense, however violation of the child restraint law is a primary offense.
- It is unlawful for any person under the age of 14 to ride in the back of a pickup truck. Additional gaps in coverage apply; see Occupant Protection Chart.

Railroad Crossing: All drivers must stop between 15 and 50 feet of a railroad crossing in any of the following circumstances: a clearly visible electric or mechanical signal gives warning; a crossing gate is lowered or a human flagman gives warning; a train approaching within 1,500 feet gives an audible signal; or an approaching train is plainly visible and in hazardous proximity to the railroad crossing.

- Buses, motor vehicles carrying hazardous materials, and trucks carrying hazardous materials must stop at all railroad crossings.

School Buses: It is unlawful to pass from either direction a school bus that is stopped with its lights flashing.

- Vehicles on the far side of a divided highway need not stop.
- The maximum speed limit for a school bus is 45 mph on a gravel roadway, 55 mph on a paved roadway.

Vehicle Equipment & Rules

Bumper Height: Modification of original vehicle bumper height is permitted.

Glass/Window Tinting: The windshield may have tinting installed above the AS1 line along the top of the windshield.

- All windows must have a total light transmission of at least 35%. Reflective tinting is prohibited on all windows.

Telematics: No motor vehicle may be equipped with television-type receiving equipment located so that the screen is visible from the driver's seat.

- Vehicle navigation systems, however, are allowed.

Windshield Stickers: Signs, posters, or other non-transparent materials may not be placed on any window that substantially obstructs, obscures, or impairs the driver's clear view of the roadway.

Motorcycles & Mopeds

Equipment: A person operating a motorcycle shall ride only upon the permanent and regular seat, and shall not carry another person unless the motorcycle has either a permanent and regular seat designed for 2 persons or has a second seat and footrests firmly attached to the rear or side of the front driver's seat.

- All persons operating a motorcycle under the age of 18 shall wear a helmet while operating or riding upon a motorcycle or motorized bicycle.

- No person shall operate a motorcycle unless that person is either wearing protective glasses, goggles, or transparent windshields, or whose motorcycle is equipped with a windscreen with a 10 inch minimum height.
- Motorcycles, motor-driven cycles, and motorized bicycles manufactured after January 1, 1978, shall display lighted head- and taillights at all times that such vehicles are operated on roadways.
- All motorcycles and motor-driven cycles shall be equipped with at least 1 headlamp, 1 taillamp and 1 white light capable of illuminating the rear license plate from at least 50 feet.
- All motorcycles and motor-driven cycles shall be equipped with at least 1 red rear reflector, and 1 rear stop lamp.
- All motorcycles shall be equipped with multiple-beam headlights that can reveal persons and vehicles at least 300 feet ahead of the upper beam, and 150 feet ahead of the lower beam.
- All motorcycles and motor-driven cycles shall be equipped with a braking system that will stop the cycle within 40 feet from an initial speed of 20 mph.

Licenses: Operators of motorcycles must obtain a Class M license.
- Applicants for a motorcycle license must fulfill the same requirements as applicants for motor vehicles.

Mopeds: No person shall operate any motor-driven cycle at a speed greater than 35 mph, unless the motor-driven cycle is equipped with a headlamp or lamps adequate to reveal a person or vehicle at a distance of 300 feet.
- Every person operating a moped on a roadway at less than the normal speed of traffic shall remain on the far right side of the roadway, unless overtaking and passing another vehicle, preparing for a left turn, or it is reasonably necessary to avoid hazardous conditions.
- Regular driver's license or motorized bicycle license required; minimum age is 15.

Passenger Car Trailers

Registration: Passenger car trailers shall be registered in accordance with registration of passenger vehicles.
- Trailers with a gross weight of more than 12,000 lbs. may be issued a multi-year registration for a 5-year period upon payment of the appropriate registration fee, with the fee being 5 times the annual fee.
- If the weight of the trailer and load being carried does not exceed 2,000 lbs., no registration is required.

Brakes: Every combination of vehicles shall have a service braking system, which will stop such combination within 40 feet from an initial speed of 20 mph on a level, dry, smooth, hard surface, and shall have a parking brake system adequate to hold such combination on any grade on which it is operated under all conditions of loading.

Dimensions: Total length: 65 feet (includes bumpers); trailer length: not specified; width: 102 inches (allows outside width to exceed 102 inches if excess is attributed to appurtenances); height: 14 feet.

Hitch: Hitch must be capable of towing the trailer safely, with adequate safety chain. If second towed vehicle is attached, first towed vehicle must have an anti-sway mechanism.

Lighting: All trailers shall be equipped with at least 2 taillamps mounted on the rear that emit a red light plainly visible from a distance of at least 1,000 feet.
- There shall be a white lamp that renders the registration plate visible from a distance of 50 feet to the rear.
- Every trailer shall have at least 2 rear red reflectors, 2 stop lamps, and 2 electric turn signal lamps.
- Trailers over 80 inches in width, except for boat and house trailers needing special permits, must have the following:
  - on the front, 2 clearance lamps, 1 at each side;
  - on the rear, 2 clearance lamps, 1 at each side, and on vehicles manufactured after July 1, 1959, 3 identification lamps in a horizontal row between 6 to 12 inches from each other; or
  - on each side, 2 side marker lamps, 1 at or near the front and 1 at or near the rear.

Mirrors: Every motor vehicle shall be equipped with a mirror on the left side and an additional mirror mounted either inside the vehicle in the center or outside the vehicle on the right side.

Speed Limits: No person shall operate a vehicle towing a house trailer at a speed greater than 55 mph.

Other Provisions: No persons shall occupy a house trailer or mobile home while it is being moved on a public roadway.

Miscellaneous Provisions

Bail Bonds: Automobile club (AAA) arrest bond certificates are accepted for up to $1,000, with specified exemptions.
- The guaranteed arrest bond certificate must be signed by the person to whom it is issued and must contain a printed statement that the surety guarantees the appearance of such person and, in the event of failure of such person to appear in court at the time of trial, will pay any fine or forfeiture imposed upon such person not to exceed an amount to be stated on such certificate.

Liability Laws: The minimum insurance coverage required is $25,000 for injury to any 1 person, $50,000 for injury to more than 1 person, and $10,000 for personal property damage.
- Kansas has a non-resident service of process law.
- Kansas has a no-fault insurance law.

Parking Restrictions: No vehicle may park in the following places: on the roadway side of any vehicle stopped or parked at the edge or curb; on a sidewalk; within an intersection; on a crosswalk; between a safety zone and the adjacent curb, or within 30 feet of points on the curb immediately opposite the ends of a safety zone; alongside or opposite any street excavation if that would obstruct traffic; upon any bridge or other elevated structure; within a tunnel; on any railroad tracks; in the median of a divided highway; or where official signs prohibit parking.
- No vehicle may park on the right-of-way of a controlled-access highway, except for disabled vehicles; giving aid in an emergency; in compliance with the directions of a police officer or safety official; due to illness or incapacity of the driver; or in designated parking or rest areas.

Weigh Stations: Any police officer having reason to believe that a vehicle or combination of vehicles is exceeding the legal weight limit may require the driver to stop and submit to a weighing of the vehicle by means of either portable or stationary scales.

- All vehicles registered as trucks are required to stop at motor carrier safety and weight inspection stations when signs direct them to do so.

Fees & Taxes

Table 1: Title & Registration Fees

Vehicle Type	Title Fee	Registration Fee
Motor Vehicle	$10.00	$30.00 for vehicles 4,500 lbs. or less; $40.00 for vehicles over 4,500 lbs.
Trailers	$10.00	$15.00 for trailers weighing up to 8,000 lbs., $25.00 for trailers between 8,000 lbs. and 12,000 lbs., and $35.00 for trailers above 12,000 lbs.
Motorcycles	$10.00	$16.00
Trucks and Truck Tractors 12,000 lbs. or less	$10.00	$40.00
Trucks and Truck Tractors over 12,000 lbs.	$10.00	$102.00 - $1,935.00, depending on weight
Motorized Bicycles		$11.00
Special Plate Registration		$1.00 - $1.50, plus additional registration fees
Duplicates	$16.00	$1.00 for registration receipt, $2.00 for license plates

Table 2: License Fees

License Class	Fee	Driving Test Fees
Any CDL	$25.00*	$3.00
Non-Commercial Class A	$31.00 for those between ages 21-65; $23.00 for those under 21 and 65+*	$3.00
Non-Commercial Class B	$31.00 for those between ages 21-65; $23.00 for those under 21 and 65+*	$3.00
Non-Commercial Class C	$25.00 for those between ages 21-65; $19.00 for those under 21 and 65+*	$3.00
Class M: Motorcycle	$9.00 for those between ages 21-65; $12.50 for those under 21 and 65+*	$3.00
Instruction Permit		$2.00 for non-commercial; $5.00 for commercial
Retaking of One Portion of Test		$1.50
Motorcycle Learner's Permit		$2.00
Duplicate License	$8.00	
Endorsements	$10.00 each	

*Total fee includes license, photo, and exam fees.

Table 3: Vehicle Taxes

Tax	Rate
Motor Vehicle Tax	state motor vehicle personal property taxes are levied on the basis of county ad valorem rates, and are collected by the counties
Compensating Use Tax	4.9% of value of vehicle, minus trade-in, but only on automobiles purchased out-of-state and not subject to state sales tax
State Sales Tax	4.9% on new and used cars
Gasoline Tax; (Diesel)	$0.24/gallon; ($0.26/gallon)

Table 4: Miscellaneous Fees

Tax	Amount	Payable Upon
Security Interest Noted on Title	$2.50	dealer must deliver to DMV within 20 days of sale
Title Application Sent to Kansas Lienholders	$1.50	receipt of application
Assignment of Certificate of Title	$10.00	assignment
Adding Names to Titles or Registrations	$7.00 until July 1, 2002; $6.00 until July 1, 2004; $3.50 thereafter	application
Transferring Registration from Old to New Vehicle	$1.50 plus any additional registration fees	application
License Plate Replacement Fee	$2.00	application

KENTUCKY

Contact Information

Division of Driver's Licensing
501 High Street
Frankfort, KY 40622

(502) 564-6800
www.kytc.state.ky.us/DrLic/home.htm

Kentucky State Police
919 Versailles Road
Frankfort, KY 40601

(502) 695-6300
www.kentuckystatepolice.org

Kentucky Transportation Cabinet (DOT)
501 High Street
Frankfort, KY 40622

(502) 564-4890
www.kytc.state.ky.us

Kentucky Revenue Cabinet
200 Fair Oaks Lane
Frankfort, KY 40620

(502) 564-4581
http://revenue.state.ky.us/

Vehicle Title

Application: Prior to operation of a vehicle on the highways of the state, the owner must obtain motor vehicle insurance, a certificate of registration, and a license plate and apply for a certificate of title.

- The owner of a new vehicle, the transferee of a vehicle, or the owner of a vehicle brought into the state for permanent use in the state must apply for registration within 15 days.
- An application for vehicle title is made to the county clerk in the county in which the owner resides, or, if a new vehicle, in the county in which the dealer has his or her principal place of business.
- Prior to application for a certificate of title, the owner of a vehicle must have the vehicle inspected by a certified inspector in the county in which the application for title is to be submitted to the county clerk. The inspection includes verification of the vehicle identification number, legibility of the application for title, and an odometer reading.
- New motor vehicles sold by a dealer licensed in Kentucky do not require inspection.

Transfer of Ownership: When an owner transfers his interest in a vehicle, the owner must execute an assignment and warranty of title to the transferee.

- Any person other than a dealer who sells a motor vehicle must deliver the certificate of registration and the certificate of title to the county clerk's office and must transfer the vehicle to the new owner within 10 days of the date of sale or transfer. An affidavit attesting to the actual consideration paid may also be required.
- If the transferor learns that the transferee did not promptly submit the necessary documentation to the county clerk within 15 days, as required by law, the transferor must submit an affidavit to the county clerk stating that the owner has transferred his interest in the vehicle.
- A transfer of ownership will not be permitted unless evidence has been presented to the county clerk that all excise taxes imposed on the sale or transfer have been paid.
- A transfer of ownership will not be permitted unless proof of insurance has been presented to the county clerk.

Mobile Homes: Mobile homes must be registered.

- If a mobile home will not be operated upon the highways of the state, the owner must within 15 days apply for a certificate of title, but the owner need not apply for registration until the mobile home is to be operated on the highways of the state.

Vehicle Registration

Application: An application for vehicle registration is made to the county clerk in the county in which the owner resides, or, if a new vehicle, in the county in which the dealer has his or her principal place of business.

- The owner of a new vehicle, the transferee of a vehicle, or the owner of a vehicle brought into the state for permanent use in the state must apply for registration within 15 days.
- The application for registration must be accompanied by a bill of sale and a manufacturer's certificate of title if it is a new vehicle, or the owner's registration receipt if the vehicle was previously registered in Kentucky.
- If the vehicle was last registered in another state, the application must be accompanied by the owner's registration receipt and bill of sale if the previous state of registration does not require an owner to obtain a certificate of title, or the certificate of title if last registered in a state requiring such certificate.
- Renewal of registration may be completed via mail.
- A registration certificate will not be issued if the payment of ad valorem taxes are delinquent.

- An application will not be accepted if it does not contain a vehicle identification number or motor number.
- If a vehicle is destroyed by fire or accident, the owner is entitled to a refund proportionate to the unused amount of the registration fee.
- The owner's copy of the registration receipt must be kept in the vehicle (except motorcycles) at all times.

Non-Residents: A certificate of registration is not needed for a vehicle which is owned by a non-resident and principally operated in another state and currently registered and titled in another state.

- An owner who brings a vehicle in from another state must apply for registration within 15 days and the application must be accompanied by proof of insurance.
- Any full-time college student or member of the armed services who is temporarily maintaining an abode in Kentucky does not need to register his or her vehicle while in school or stationed in Kentucky if he or she maintains residency in his or her home state.

Registration Type: All motor vehicles, including motorcycles, with a Gross Vehicular Weight (GVW) of 6,000 lbs. or less, first registered or needing renewed registration after January 1, 1983, are on a system of year-round registration based upon the birth month of the owner and evidenced by a license plate bearing an adhesive insignia.

- Upon the owner's request and payment of the appropriate pro-rated fee, a vehicle may be registered for 2 years, with the registration and license plate valid through the last day of the owner's second birth month following the month and year in which the owner applied for a certificate of registration.

Emissions Inspection: Vehicle emissions inspection is conducted at the county level and administered on a biennial basis.

- Out-of-state vehicles that can display proof of having passed inspection in another state will be granted an exemption from inspection, but such exemption period will not exceed 1 year.
- A compliance certificate is issued for each vehicle that passes inspection.
- Upon the expiration of a vehicle emissions compliance certificate, the Transportation Cabinet will revoke the registration unless evidence of compliance is received within 30 days.
- Motorcycles are not subject to emissions inspection.

License Plates

Disbursement: One plate is issued for the rear of the vehicle that must be illuminated during hours of darkness.

- The county clerk issues a decal or decals, to be placed on the license plate, corresponding to the month and year of expiration shown on the registration certificate.
- Specialized and personalized plates are available.

Transfer of Plates: When a previously registered motor vehicle changes ownership, the registration plate remains on the vehicle until the expiration of the registration year.

- Upon the sale or transfer of a vehicle bearing a personalized plate, the owner must remove the plate and return it, along with the certificate of registration, to the county clerk. The personalized plate may be re-issued by the county clerk to a vehicle of the same classification and category owned by the same person.

Driver's Licenses

Examination: All examinations are conducted by the state police and are held in the county in which the applicant resides.
- The examination includes a vision test (requires 20/40 visual acuity), a test of the applicant's knowledge of traffic signs, signals, and traffic laws, and a roadside demonstration test.
- Non-residents need not take the examinations provided they hold a valid license from a state that affords a reciprocal exemption to a Kentucky resident.

Graduated Drivers Licensing: State has a system of graduated licensing for teen drivers. At 16, teens are eligible for a learner's permit. During this stage teens may not drive unless supervised by a parent or guardian. Teens must hold the permit for at least 6 months before being eligible for a full license. In Kentucky, the law prohibits learner's permit holders from driving between midnight and 6 a.m. License holders younger than 18 must complete a 4-hour course on safe driving within 1 year of receiving license. Teens are eligible for an unrestricted license at 16 and a half.

Issuance/Application: All licenses are issued by the Transportation Cabinet.
- Only persons with legal INS status are issued Kentucky licenses or I.D.'s.
- Application for original or renewal licenses are made at the office of the circuit clerk in the county wherein the applicant resides.
- The application must contain the person's full name, signature, date of birth, social security number, sex, address, voter application information, and a brief physical description. All licenses bear a color photograph of the applicant.
- An application for a driver's license, motorcycle license, or instruction permit by a person under the age of 18 must be accompanied by the signature of the applicant's parent or legal guardian.
- Non-residents that are at least 16 years old and are licensed in another state may operate a vehicle in Kentucky without obtaining a Kentucky learner's permit or operator's license as long as his or her home state accords similar privileges to licensed residents of Kentucky. If the non-resident's home state does not afford such privileges to licensed residents of Kentucky, the non-resident may operate a motor vehicle, motorcycle, or moped for not more than 30 days in any 1 year without obtaining a Kentucky license.
- Any person under the age of 18 who holds a valid instruction permit but has not graduated high school, is not currently enrolled in high school, or is not being home schooled will not be granted a driver's license.
- Whenever a licensee's address or name is changed from that which appears on a license, the licensee must apply for a corrected license within 10 days of the change.
- License normally includes a color photograph.
- Social security number not displayed on license.
- Non-citizens who are non-residents of Kentucky may drive for 1 year on the license issued by their home country.
- Licenses of non-citizens are linked to the expiration dates of the person's visa.

Renewal: An application for renewal must be made every 4 years within 30 days after the birth date of the applicant.
- An applicant under the age of 21 will be issued a license that is valid until the applicant attains the age of 21 and the applicant must apply for a renewal within 30 days

KY

of his or her 21st birthday.
- Military personnel on active duty out of the state and their dependents may renew their driver's licenses by mail.

Types of Licenses: Licenses are categorized by class and are distinguished as being commercial or non-commercial.
- Class A: Any combination of vehicles with a GVW rating of 26,001 lbs. or more.
- Class B: Any single vehicle with a GVW rating of 26,001 lbs. or more and any vehicle towing a vehicle not in excess of 10,000 lbs.
- Class C: Any single vehicle with a GVW rating of less than 26,001 lbs. or any vehicle towing a vehicle with a GVW rating not in excess of 10,000 lbs.
- Class D: All vehicles not listed in any other class including passenger cars.
- Class E: Mopeds only.
- Class M: Motorcycles and mopeds.

Traffic Rules

Alcohol Laws: State has implied consent law.
- Open containers are not permitted. Meets TEA-21 requirements.
- Illegal per se BAC level is .08.
- BAC level for people under 21 is .02.

Emergency Radio/Cellular: Citizen band radio is not monitored for emergency calls. Cell phone number is 911 or (800) 222-5555.

Headsets: Wearing radio headsets while operating a motor vehicle is permitted.

Occupant Restraints: The driver and all passengers over 40 inches in height must wear a seat belt at all times when the vehicle is being operated on the public roadways.
- Violation of the seat belt law is a secondary offense, however violation of the child restraint law is a primary offense.
- Any driver of a motor vehicle, when transporting a child of 40 inches in height or less must have the child properly secured in a child restraint system.
- Riding in pickup truck beds is permitted.

Railroad Crossing: The operator of a vehicle must stop at a railroad crossing when a signal device warns of the immediate approach of a train, an approaching train is visible and in hazardous proximity, or a human flagman signals the approach of a train.
- The operator of any bus or motor vehicle used for transporting children must stop not less than 10 feet nor more than 30 feet from the nearest track before crossing any railroad, except where crossing is protected by gates or a flagman is employed.

School Buses: If any school or church bus is stopped and has a stop arm and signal lights activated, any vehicle approaching from any direction must stop and may not proceed until the bus has been put into motion. This rule does not apply when approaching a stopped bus from the opposite direction upon a highway of 4 or more lanes.

Vehicle Equipment & Rules

Bumper Height: Modification of original vehicle bumper height is permitted, provided driver's vision is not obscured.

Glass/Window Tinting: Any windows that are forward of or adjacent to the driver's seat may not be composed of, covered by, or treated with any sunscreening material or any product that has the effect of making the windows non-transparent. Sunscreening material is permitted if it has a total solar reflectance of visible light of not more than 25% on the non-film side.

- Any windows that are behind the driver may not be covered by, composed of, or treated with any sunscreening material, but such material may be used if it has a total solar reflectance of visible light of not more than 35% on the non-film side.
- The rear window of any vehicle may not be composed of, covered by, or treated with any sunscreening material unless the vehicle is equipped with side mirrors on both sides.
- Window tinting on the windshield is permitted only along the top strip of the windshield.

Windshield Stickers: Windshield stickers are permitted when required by law.

Motorcycles & Mopeds

Equipment: Every motorcycle or moped must be equipped with at least one headlamp.

Licenses: Any person who already possesses a valid driver's license, or who is at least 18 years old, may apply for an instruction permit to operate a motorcycle.

- An applicant for a motorcycle license must pass a roadside demonstration test.
- Motorcycle rider training courses are provided free of charge to applicants under 18 years of age.
- Successful completion of an approved rider training course, which includes a minimum of 8 hours of hands-on instruction, permits exemption from the licensing skill test for motorcycle license applicants.
- All motorcycles must be equipped with a rearview mirror.
- All persons operating a motorcycle must wear protective eye gear and any person under the age of 21, or any person operating a motorcycle with an instruction permit, or any person who has held a motorcycle license for less than 1 year must wear a safety helmet.

Mopeds: Registration not required.

- Minimum age to ride a moped is 16.
- No safety equipment is required.

Passenger Car Trailers

KY

Brakes: Kentucky law does not specifically require brakes on many passenger car trailers, regardless of weight. However, vehicles singular or in combination must be able to stop within distance specified by statute.

Dimensions: Total length: 63 feet (includes all structural parts); trailer length: not specified; width: 96 inches; height: 13.6 feet (11.5 feet on some roads).

Hitch: Frame mounted on equalizer type hitch is recommended. Safety chain is required.

Lighting: When any vehicle is being towed by another, it must carry at least one light on the left side that is green on the front and red on the back and visible from at least 500 feet.

Mirrors: Every motor vehicle which is so loaded as to obstruct the driver's view to the rear must be equipped with a mirror so located and adjusted as to reflect a view of the highway for a distance of at least 200 feet to the rear.

Speed Limits: Same as passenger cars.

Towing: No vehicle may haul more than two vehicles, connected in such a manner as to keep them evenly spaced, at any one time.

Miscellaneous Provisions

Bail Bonds: Mandatory recognition of AAA club guaranteed arrest bond certificates for amounts up to $500, with specified exemptions.

Liability Laws: Kentucky has no-fault and mandatory liability insurance law.
- Evidence of liability insurance must be kept within the vehicle.
- The minimum liability policy coverage is $25,000 per person with an aggregate limit of $50,000 per accident and $10,000 for all damages to or destruction of property.
- State has non-resident service of process law; does not have guest suit law.

Weigh Stations: Vehicles transporting agricultural products and all commercial vehicles with GVW rating of 10,000 lbs. or more must stop.

Fees & Taxes

Table 1: Title & Registration Fees

Vehicle Type	Title Fee	Registration Fee
All vehicles less than 6,000 lbs. GVW	$6.00	$11.50
Pickup Trucks and Vans	$6.00	$11.50
Vehicles for Hire with 9 Person Capacity	$6.00	$11.50
Motorcycles	$6.00	$9.00
Sidecar Attachments	$6.00	$7.00
Trailers Pulled by Vans or Pickup Trucks	$6.00	$4.50
Trailers Pulled by Vehicles less than 6,000 lbs. GVW	$6.00	$19.50
Motor Homes	$6.00	$20.00
Commercial Vehicles		
6,001 - 10,000 lbs.	$6.00	$24.00
10,001 - 14,000 lbs.	$6.00	$30.00
14,001 - 18,000 lbs.	$6.00	$50.00
18,001 - 22,000 lbs.	$6.00	$132.00
22,001 - 80,000 lbs.	$6.00	$160.00 - $1,260.00
Duplicate Registration Receipt		$3.00
Registration Revocation Fee		$20.00
Replacement/Corrected Title (no fee if correction needed due to error of county clerk)	$4.00	
Transfer of Title Fee	$1.00	
Notarized Affidavit of Consideration	$3.00	

Table 2: License Fees

License Class	Fee
Class D: 4-year Original or Renewal License	$20.00
Class M: 4-year Original or Renewal License	$24.00
Combination Class M and Class D License	$30.00
Under 21 Licenses (valid for up to 5 years if only age 16)	$2.00 per year (up to 5 years if age 16)
Instruction Permit	$12.00
Motorcycle Instruction Permit	$25.00
Motorcycle Endorsement/Motor Vehicle Endorsement	$15.00/$10.00
Duplicate License Fee	$12.00

Table 3: Vehicle Taxes

Tax	Rate
Motor Vehicle Usage Tax	6% of retail price - due upon registration or transfer of ownership
Sales Tax	6% of retail price
Gasoline Tax; (Diesel)	$0.15/gallon; ($0.12/gallon + $0.014 environmental fee)

Table 4: Miscellaneous Fees

Fee	Amount	Payable Upon
Registration Renewal by Mail	$2.00	registration renewal
County Clerk's Registration Fee	$3.00/$4.00 if registration period exceeds 12 months	registration
Personalized License Plates	$25.00	application
Transfer of Vehicle with Personalized Plates/Issuance of New Plates	$14.50	sale/transfer of vehicle
Personalized Plate Reassignment Fee	$2.00	application for reassignment
Duplicate License Plates	$6.00	loss/destruction of old plates
License Plate Reflectorization	$0.50	registration
Vehicle Inspection Fee	$5.00	inspection

LOUISIANA

Contact Information

Office of Motor Vehicles
P.O. Box 64886
Baton Rouge, LA 70896

http://omv.dps.state.la.us/

Louisiana State Police
7919 Independence Boulevard
Baton Rouge, LA 70806

(225) 925-6325
www.lsp.org/index.html

Department of Transportation and Development
P.O. Box 94245
Baton Rouge, LA 70804-9245

(225) 379-1100
www.dotd.state.la.us

Vehicle Title

Application: A person applying for a certificate of title must submit an application provided by the Department with the appropriate fees attached.

- If a Louisiana certificate of title has been previously issued for the vehicle, the application must be accompanied by a properly endorsed and certified certificate of title.
- If a certificate of title has not been previously issued for the vehicle, the application must be accompanied by either a proper bill of sale, a sworn statement of ownership, or any other evidence of ownership the Department may require. If the vehicle is a new vehicle, the application must be accompanied by the manufacturer's certificate.
- The Department will issue a certificate of title to a vehicle even if there is no bill of sale and no current record of ownership upon which to provide a title if the following conditions are met: (1) the vehicle is 25 years or older; (2) the vehicle has not had its registration renewed in any state for 3 years from the date the title was applied for; (3) the applicant has submitted a sworn application that the vehicle has been abandoned for 3 years; and (4) the applicant has provided the Office of Motor Vehicles a statement from the state police auto theft division confirming that based upon a sufficient check the vehicle is not stolen.

Transfer of Ownership: No person can sell a vehicle without delivering a certificate of title to the purchaser.

- An effective transfer of title requires filling out, endorsing, and delivering the certificate of title by the transferor to the transferee and delivering the certificate to the Department with proper transfer and application fees.
- If a certificate of title is held by a lienholder and the lienholder is selling the vehicle, the lienholder can make and deliver to the purchaser at the time of delivery a sales contract and an assignment of certificate of title, on the Department's form. These documents along with the certificate of title must be submitted to the commissioner within 5 days of the sale. The commissioner will then send the appropriate parties an amended certificate of title.
- A vehicle that was previously purchased and titled in another state is allowed a credit against the state and local use taxes imposed in Louisiana.

Mobile Homes: A purchaser of a mobile home must apply for a new certificate of title on or before the 20th day in which the mobile home has been delivered.

Vehicle Registration

Application: Every owner of a motor vehicle, trailer, semitrailer, or other vehicle must apply for registration at the Department in the parish where he or she lives.

- The application will request the following: (1) the address of the owner of the vehicle; and (2) a brief description of the vehicle including the engine number, serial number, and the date of sale of the vehicle.
- All appropriate registration fees and license taxes must be submitted with the application.
- The registration must be kept in the vehicle while it is in operation.
- The registration must always correspond with the vehicle's license plate number.

Non-Residents: Any person that is employed in Louisiana and who drives a vehicle in Louisiana must apply for a certificate of registration within 30 days of the date that the person was employed in Louisiana.

- A non-resident who is in the military and on active duty in Louisiana may operate a vehicle in the state without obtaining Louisiana registration if the following requirements are met: (1) the license plates on the vehicle are from another state; (2) the vehicle registration and license plates are current and issued to the active duty member; or (3) the owner has one of the forms of financial responsibility required by the state.
- A non-resident spouse of an active duty military person can also operate a vehicle in Louisiana without obtaining Louisiana registration if the above requirements are met.

Registration Type: Renewals of registration or the license tax may be made by mail, or online.

Emissions Inspection: Required on an annual basis as part of safety inspection in non-attainment areas only.

Safety Inspection: Every motor vehicle, trailer, semitrailer, and pole trailer registered in Louisiana must have a valid safety inspection certificate issued in the state.

- The commissioner of the Department, any person that the commissioner designates, or the state police can require the driver of an unsafe or improperly equipped vehicle to stop the vehicle and have it submitted to an inspection.
- If the vehicle is found to be unsafe, or in need of repair, the officer will give the driver a notice requiring the driver to have the vehicle repaired so that it is in compliance. This notice will also be sent to the Department.
- The notice will require that a certificate of inspection and approval be obtained within 5 days of the citation. The driver must keep one copy of the official certificate of inspection and approval and send the other official certificate to the Department.

License Plates

Disbursement: The Department issues 1 license plate for private passenger vehicles.

- Every license plate must display the registration number assigned to the owner, the name of the state, and the registration time period.
- Special license plates can be issued for a variety of groups and organizations.
- A special license plate for the disabled is available upon application, with doctor's certificates, to any motor vehicle office.

Transfer of Plates: All regular license plates must be removed and destroyed before the vehicle is transferred to another person. When the license plate has been destroyed, the owner of the vehicle must notify the Department that the license plate has been destroyed and provide the Department with the destroyed license plate number.

- The requirements for determining what special license plates can transfer with a car vary depending on the type of special plate.

Driver's Licenses

Examination: All applicants for a Louisiana license must pass a knowledge-based and a skills-based driving examination. An eye examination is also given (20/40 visual acuity is required).

- The knowledge portion of the examination includes testing a person's understanding of Louisiana motor vehicle laws, highway signs, railroad and highway crossing safety, and knowledge of the classification of motor vehicle the applicant will be driving.

- The skills test will include an on-the-road driving test, and possibly a simulated skills-based driving test.
- The knowledge and skill tests will be administered by the Department or by a 3rd party approved by the Department.

Graduated Drivers Licensing: State has a system of graduated licensing for teen drivers.

- A learner's permit may be issued to a person who is between 15 and 17 years old if that person meets the following conditions: (1) is taking the exam for the 1st time; (2) completes a driver's education course approved by the Department; (3) passes a visual exam; and (4) passes a knowledge test, including rules of the road, signs, signals, and at least 2 questions about railroad and highway crossing safety.
- Permit holders may not drive unsupervised.
- At 16, teens who have held a permit for at least 6 months and have passed a road test or completed an approved driver education course are eligible for an intermediate license.
- Intermediate license holders may not drive unsupervised between the hours of 11:00 p.m. and 5:00 a.m.
- Teens must hold the intermediate license for at least 12 months.
- An intermediate license holder can automatically receive his or her license if he or she meets the following conditions for 12 consecutive months: (1) was not determined to be at fault for causing any accidents; (2) has received no convictions for moving violations; and (3) has received no convictions for violations of the seat belt or curfew laws.
- At 17 years, teens may receive an unrestricted driver's license.
- An intermediate license holder, aged 18 or younger who has violated any of the above provisions can have the time period of the permit extended from 30 days to 180 days.

Issuance/Application: A first-time applicant of at least 17 years of age must also show completion of a full 36-hour driver's education course or an approved 6-hour prelicensing training course.

- New applicants transferring into Louisiana with an out-of-state, foreign, or military license do not have to take a driver's education course or an approved 6-hour prelicensing training course.
- All applicants transferring to Louisiana whose out-of-state license has been expired for 6 months or longer must successfully complete the knowledge test. After 2 year's expiration, the driving test must also be successfully completed.
- Every person 60 years of age or older who is applying for a license must attach to his or her application a detailed medical report from a physician or optometrist discussing the applicant's physical condition and any problems that might impair the applicant's ability to drive. This rule does not apply to people over 60 who apply for a renewal license.
- Every physically or mentally handicapped person applying for a license for the 1st time must include a detailed medical report from a physician indicating the severity of the disability and any problems that might impair the applicant's ability to drive. If the impairment is visual, a report from an optometrist can be attached to application instead of a physician's report.
- License includes a color photo and optional printing of social security number.

- Non-citizens must provide proof of legal presence in the U.S.
- The expiration date of a non-citizen's driver's license is linked to the expiration date of that person's visa.
- Licenses of non-citizens contain a restriction code which declares that the license holder is a legal alien.

Renewal: All motor vehicle driver's licenses expire on the anniversary of the birthday of the applicant which is closest to a period of 4 years subsequent to the issuing of the license, unless this license has been suspended, revoked, or cancelled prior to that time.

- Louisiana driver's license of members of the Armed Forces/Peace Corps and their dependents who serve outside of Louisiana shall remain valid for 60 days after discharge, provided license was valid upon entrance to service and not expired, suspended, or revoked (R.S. 32:412F). The driver's license will be expired/delinquent on the 61st day after discharge. Last license issued and proof of discharge shall be accepted to renew license. This applies to class "E" operator's license only.
- To keep the driver's license record of Military/Peace Corps personnel and dependents active and prevent them from being purged from the computer system, the military flag must be set. This may be accomplished when completing the driver's license transaction on a member of the Armed Forces/Peace Corps or their dependents by setting a "Y" in the military field.
- A resident dependent of any person on active duty with the Armed Forces and stationed within Louisiana, but who is domiciled in another state and has in his immediate possession both a valid license issued to him by his home state and a current military dependent identification card, shall be exempt from obtaining a Louisiana driver's license during the period of residency with the supporting member of the Armed Forces while stationed in Louisiana. Dependents must comply with normal renewal procedure of their home state.

Types of Licenses: There are 3 general types of driver's licenses: (1) the commercial driver's license; (2) the chauffeur's license; and (3) the personal vehicle driver's license.

- The 3 types of commercial drivers are Class A, B, and C licenses.
- Class A Commercial Driver's License – Combination Vehicle permit holder can drive all commercial vehicles or a combination of commercial vehicles with a gross weight of 26,001 lbs. or more. This class of vehicles does not include the operation of motorcycles and motor scooters, unless there is a specific endorsement.
- Class B Commercial Driver's License – Heavy Straight Vehicle permit holder can drive any vehicle within Classes C, D, and E, plus any single vehicle with a gross vehicle weight of more than 26,001 lbs. This class does not include the operation of motorcycles and motor scooters, unless there is a specific endorsement.
- Class C Commercial Driver's License – Light Vehicle permit holder can drive any vehicle within Classes D and E, plus any single vehicle less than 26,001 lbs. This group of vehicles includes vehicles designed to transport 16 or more passengers including the driver, and vehicles used in the transportation of hazardous material as outlined in the Federal Hazardous Materials Transportation Act.
- Class D Chauffeur's License permit holder can drive any vehicle within Class E plus any single motor vehicle used in commerce to transport passengers or property if the motor vehicle has a Gross Vehicle Weight Rating (GVWR) between 10,001 lbs. and 26,000 lbs. This class does not allow a person to transport hazardous material as outlined in the Federal Hazardous Materials Transportation Act.

- Class E Driver's License – Personal Vehicle permit holder can drive any single motor vehicle under 10,001 lbs. GVWR or any such vehicle towing a vehicle not in excess of 10,000 lbs. GVWR. This class does not allow a person to transport hazardous materials.
- Motorcycles, mopeds, and motorized bicycles are not given a separate class, but these vehicles can only be driven if a person fulfills the appropriate requirements to obtain an endorsement to his or her existing license.
- A school instruction permit may be issued to any person who is at least 15 years of age if that person is enrolled in a certified driver education course. This permit is only valid during the driver education course. The permit holder can only drive while he or she is accompanied by the education course instructor.

Traffic Rules

Alcohol Laws: Operation of a motor vehicle gives implied consent to a test of blood, breath, urine, or other bodily substance for determining blood alcohol content, or to determine the presence of any controlled substances. The state's open container law does not meet TEA-21 requirements.

- Illegal per se BAC level is .08.
- Lower BAC level for people under 21 is .02.

Emergency Radio/Cellular: Emergency cell number is 911.

- Citizen band radio channel 9 is not monitored for emergency calls.

Headsets: Wearing headsets while driving is prohibited, except for a motorcycle operator who has a headset in his or her helmet.

Occupant Restraints: Each front seat occupant of a passenger car, van, or a pickup truck over the age of 13 must wear a seat belt. All motor vehicle operators who transport children under the age of 13 must restrain the children in age or size appropriate passenger restraint systems.

- Children under 1 year or less than 20 lbs. must be restrained in a rear-facing child safety seat.
- Children 1 year to 4 years or 20-40 lbs. must be restrained in a forward-facing child safety seat.
- Children 4 and 5 years of age or 40-60 lbs. must be restrained in a booster seat. When the passenger side airbag is active, children younger than 6 or less than 60 lbs. must be in the rear seat, if available.
- Children who are between the ages of 6 and 13 or more than 60 lbs. must be restrained in either a child safety seat or a seat belt.
- Violation of the occupant protection laws is a primary offense.
- No person under 12 years of age can be a passenger in the open bed of a pickup truck unless there is an emergency situation and an adult accompanies the child in the open bed of the pickup truck. Additional gaps in coverage apply; see Occupant Protection Chart.

Railroad Crossing: Any person driving a motor vehicle that approaches a railroad crossing must stop between 15 and 50 feet of the railroad crossing if one of the following occurs: (1) a clearly visible signal device gives warning of the approach of a railroad train; (2) a crossing gate is lowered, or a human flagman stops traffic; (3) a fast moving railroad train approaching within approximately 900 feet of the highway crossing emits a signal; (4) an approaching train is plainly visible and is in hazardous proximity to such crossing; and (5) a stop signal is at the railroad grade crossing.

- Any motor vehicle carrying passengers for hire, school buses, and any vehicle carrying hazardous material must stop between 15 and 50 feet of all railroad crossings and then proceed when it is safe to do so.

School Buses: Vehicles must stop upon meeting, from either direction, a school bus that is stopped for loading or unloading children and displays or has recently displayed a stop signal arm. This rule does not apply if the bus is on the opposite roadway of a divided highway.

Vehicle Equipment & Rules

Bumper Height: Modification of original vehicle bumper height is permitted.

Glass/Window Tinting: A person may not drive a motor vehicle with any tinted windows that obstruct the inward and outward view. The exceptions to this rule are: (1) a sun-screening device used with automotive safety glazing material on the front side window with a light transmission of at least 40%, the side window behind the driver with a light transmission of at least 25% and rearmost windows with a light transmission of at least 12%; (2) a non red or amber transparent material affixed to the top of the windshield not extending more than 5 inches down from the top; (3) an adjustable nontransparent sun visor that is not attached to the glass and mounted forward on the side window; and (4) all vehicles that have windows tinted on or before December 31, 1993, that were in compliance with the law at that time, as long as the owner obtains a certificate stating that the tinting occurred before 1994; a certificate confirming this must be filed with the Department.

Telematics: A person may not operate a motor vehicle that has a television set installed in a manner that allows the person driving the vehicle to see the television set. Retailers may not install a television set at any point forward of the back of the driver's seat.

Windshield Stickers: Prohibited (motor vehicle inspection certificate allowed).

Motorcycles & Mopeds

Equipment: Every motorcycle must have 2 properly equipped white headlights on the front of the motorcycle that emit a white beam.

- Every new motorcycle sold in Louisiana must have 2 red reflectors. All other motorcycles must have at least 1 reflector, which must be mounted properly so that it is visible for at least 100 feet.
- All stop lights and turn signals are required on new motor vehicles.
- All motorcycle riders must wear a properly equipped safety helmet.
- All motorcycle operators must wear protective eye gear, unless the motorcycle is equipped with a windshield of sufficient height to protect the operator's eyes.
- All motorcycles carrying a passenger must have a footrest for that passenger.
- All motorcycle handlebars must be no more than 15 inches above portion of the seat where the operator is sitting.

Licenses: There is no separate class of driver's license for motorcycle riders.

- To operate a motorcycle, a person must obtain an endorsement to his or her regular driver's license. An endorsement can be obtained by passing an operation skills test and a knowledge test. An operation skills test does not have to be taken if the applicant successfully completed the Department-approved Motorcycle Safety, Awareness, and Operation Training Program.

Motor Scooter: There is no separate class of driver's licenses for motor scooter riders.

- To operate a motor scooter, a person must obtain an endorsement to his or her regular driver's license.
- An endorsement can be obtained by passing an operation skills test and a knowledge test. An operation skills test does not have to be taken if the applicant successfully completed the Department-approved Motorcycle Safety, Awareness, and Operation Training Program.
- Only 1 person can ride on a motor scooter.
- The brakes of a motor scooter must be inspected to insure reasonable and reliable performance.

Passenger Car Trailers

Brakes: A trailer or semitrailer that weighs at least 3,000 lbs. must be equipped with brakes adequate to control the movement of and to stop and to hold the towing vehicle and trailer or semitrailer.

- These brakes must be designed so that the driver of the towing motor vehicle can apply the brakes from the towing vehicle itself and adequately stop both the towing vehicle and the trailer or semitrailer.
- Every trailer or semitrailer manufactured after 1962 must be equipped with brakes upon all wheels.
- Every trailer or semitrailer between 3,001 and 5,000 lbs. only requires brakes on one axle.

Dimensions: Total length: 70 feet; trailer length: 40 feet; width: 96 inches (a width of 102 inches allowed on certain roads); height: 13.6 feet.

Hitch: No requirements by law as to type of hitch or mount. Safety chains required on all trailers under 6,000 lbs. Tow bar not required.

Lighting: Trailers and semitrailers 80 inches or more in width must be equipped with 2 front clearance lamps on each side, 2 rear clearance lamps on each side, and 2 side marker lamps and 2 reflectors, 1 of each on the front and on the rear.

- Trailers and semitrailers 30 feet or more in length must have 1 amber side marker lamp and 1 amber reflector, centrally located on each side.
- Every trailer and semitrailer must be equipped with at least 1 red light mounted on the rear that emits a light for at least 1,000 feet.

Mirrors: Every semitrailer or trailer manufactured after December 31, 1972, must be equipped with a mirror mounted on the left side of the vehicle and so located as to reflect to the driver a view of the highway for a distance of at least 200 feet to the rear of the vehicle.

Speed Limits: Boat or utility trailer, same as passenger car; house trailer, 55 mph, day, 50 mph, night for brake-equipped trailers 15-32 feet long and for trailers without brakes less than 15 feet; all others, 45 mph

Towing: The connection between 2 vehicles when 1 is towing the other must be of suffi-

cient strength to pull all weight towed.
- The connection must not exceed 15 feet.
- When the connection between a vehicle and a towed vehicle is a chain, rope, or cable, a red flag or cloth at least 1-foot square must be displayed on the connection between sunrise and sunset, and a red light visible for a distance of at least 500 feet must be visible on the connection between sunset and sunrise.
- Riding in towed trailers is prohibited.
- Maximum of 2 trailers may be towed behind passenger or pleasure vehicles.

Miscellaneous Provisions

Bail Bonds: Mandatory recognition of AAA club arrest bond certificates up to $200, where accepted.

Liability Laws: Motor vehicle operators must carry a motor vehicle liability policy in their car at all times.
- Minimum liability insurance coverage must be at least $10,000 for bodily injury or death of 1 person, $20,000 for the bodily injury to 2 or more persons in any 1 accident, and at least $10,000 for damage to property as a result of any 1 accident.
- State has non-resident service of process law; does not have guest suit law.

Weigh/Inspection Stations: The following vehicles must stop: (1) agricultural vehicles; (2) passenger or specialty vehicles, either single or in combination (towing a trailer) with GVWR of 10,000 lbs. or more; (3) commercial trucks with GVWR of 10,000 lbs. or more.

Fees & Taxes

Table 1: Title & Registration Fees

Vehicle Type	Title Fee	Plate Fee
Motor Vehicle	$18.50	Based upon the selling price of the vehicle. The current rate is 0.1% of the value of the vehicle per year, with a minimum base of $10,000. The license plates are sold in 2-year increments; therefore the minimum price is $20.00
Mobile Home	$18.50	$25.00
Utility Trailer (Up to 500 lbs.)	$18.50	$12.00
Trailers of 10,000 lbs. or less	$18.50	$12.00
Trailers of more than 10,000 lbs.	$18.50	$12.00
Noncommercial Trailers less than 6,000 lbs.	$18.50	$12.00
Motorcycles	$18.50	$12.00
Mopeds	$18.50	$12.00
Duplicates	$18.50	$4.00

LA

Table 2: License Fees

License Class	Fee	Driving Test Fees
A (CDL)	$41.00 (New Orleans $50.00)	$15.00
B (CDL)	$41.00 (New Orleans $50.00)	$15.00
C (CDL)	$41.00 (New Orleans $50.00)	$15.00
D	$27.50 (New Orleans $35.00)* (70 & Older $14.75) (New Orleans 70 & Older $17.50)	
E	$12.50 (70 & Older $4.50)*	
Endorsement to CDL - Hazardous Material	$5.00	
Endorsement to CDL - Tankers	$5.00	
Endorsement to CDL - Passenger Transport	$5.00	
Endorsement to CDL - Double & Triple Trailers	$5.00	
Endorsement to CDL - Combination Haz-Mat	$5.00	
& Trailers	$5.00	
ID card	$10.00*	
Motorcycle Endorsement	$8.00	
Duplicate License Fee	$5.00*	

* $8.00 handling fee added to all transactions.
A parish fee not to exceed $3.00 is assessed in certain parishes.

Table 3: Vehicle Taxes

Tax	Rate
State Sales Tax	The tax is levied from 4% to 9 1/2% depending on the address of the purchaser. The tax must be remitted within 40 days of the date of purchase. After the 40th day, penalty and interest will be assessed for each 30 days or portion thereof. Penalty is assessed at the rate of 5% for 30 days or fraction thereof (maximum 25%) and 1 1/4% interest per month (no maximum) based on the amount of sales tax.
Gasoline Tax; (Diesel)	$0.20 per gallon; ($0.20 per gallon)
Use Fuel Tax	The Use Tax is due on all vehicles imported for use in this state when first registered in Louisiana. This tax is based on the book value of the vehicle. Credit can be given for up to 4% for tax paid in another state providing it is a state with which Louisiana has a reciprocal agreement. The state must have proof of this tax for certain states.

Table 4: Miscellaneous Fees

Fee	Amount	Payable Upon
Title Correction Fee	$18.50	Request
Duplicate Registration	$4.00	Request
License Transfer	$3.00	Request
Handling Fee	$8.00	This handling fee is added to all transactions except CDL classes A, B, and C and duplicate identification cards for applicants aged 60 and older

MAINE

Contact Information

Bureau of Motor Vehicles (BMV)
29 State House Station
101 Hospital Street
Augusta, ME 04333-0029

(207) 624-9000
www.state.me.us/sos/bmv/

Maine State Police
36 Hospital Street
Augusta, ME 04330

(207) 624-7000
www.state.me.us/dps/msp/home.htm

Maine Department of Transportation
16 State House Station
Augusta, ME 04333

(207) 624-3000
www.state.me.us/mdot

Vehicle Title

Application: Application should be made to the Secretary of State.

- Applications must include name, residence and mailing address of the owner, description of the vehicle including make, model, year, vehicle identification number, type of body, current mileage, whether new or used and whether repaired or rebuilt, date of purchase and name and address from whom the vehicle was acquired, names and addresses of lienholders, and a certificate of origin for a new vehicle or previous certificate of title for a used vehicle.

Transfer of Ownership: When vehicle ownership is transferred, an assignment and warranty of title must be given to the new owner. The warranty must include the odometer information.

Vehicle Registration

Application: Applications must be made to the Secretary of State.

- Applications must include legal name, residence and address of registrant, current vehicle mileage, brief description of the vehicle, maker, vehicle identification number, year of manufacture, and type of fuel.
- A new vehicle registration must be signed by the registered owner or owner's legal representative.
- Proof of insurance must be provided to register the vehicle.

Non-Residents: A non-resident does not need to register the vehicle in Maine, provided that the vehicle is properly registered and licensed by the jurisdiction of residence.

Registration Type: Registration expires on the last day of the month, 1 year from the month of issuance.

Safety Inspection: An annual inspection is required on the following equipment: body components; brakes; exhaust system; glazing; horn; lights and directional signals; rearview mirrors; reflectors; running gear; safety seat belts on 1966 and subsequent models; steering mechanism; tires; windshield wipers; catalytic converter on 1983 and subsequent models; and filler neck restriction on 1983 and subsequent models.

- An enhanced inspection that includes the fuel tank cap on 1974 and subsequent models of gasoline-powered vehicles and the on-board diagnostic system on 1996 and subsequent models is required in Cumberland County.
- Upon passage of the inspection, an official sticker is provided that must be placed in the lower left-hand corner of the windshield or in the center of the windshield behind the rearview mirror.

License Plates

Disbursement: License plates are issued by the Secretary of State and are renewed annually.

- License plates must be on the front and rear of each vehicle except for motorcycles and trailers which must have their plate attached to the rear.
- Personalized license plates may be issued and may contain a combination of letters and numbers not to exceed seven characters.
- License plates issued to motorcycles must include the words "Ride Safe."
- Special license plates are available for disabled drivers, upon application, with physician's certificate, to BMV.

Transfer of Plates: License plates expire when the owner of a vehicle transfers the vehicle title.

- The registrant may request that plates and the registration number be assigned to another vehicle in that registrant's name.

Driver's Licenses

Examination: Passage of skills, visual (20/40 visual acuity required) and written examinations are required for licensure.

- A physical examination may be required and may be performed by a licensed physician, physician's assistant, nurse practitioner, or other competent treatment personnel as determined by the medical advisory board.
- A vision test must be passed (1) at the time of the 1st license renewal after age 40, (2) at every 2nd license renewal after initial renewal at age 40 until the person reaches 62 and, (3) at every license renewal after age 62.

Graduated Drivers Licensing: State has a system of graduated licensing for teen drivers. At 15, teens are eligible for a learner's permit.

- Permit holders may not drive unless supervised by a driver who is at least 20 years old and holds a license that has not been suspended or revoked over the past 2 years.
- Permit holders must also accumulate at least 35 hours (5 at night) of parental/guardian supervised driving.
- Teens must hold the permit for at least 6 months before being eligible for a probationary/intermediate license.
- Teens may not transport any passengers under 18, except family members and may not drive unsupervised between midnight and 5:00 a.m., unless supervised by driver at least 20 years old.
- A driver with a permit is prohibited from using a cellular phone while driving.
- Teens are eligible for an unrestricted license at 16 and 6 months.
- Driver education is required for all license applicants under 18.

Issuance/Application: A driver's license is required before driving a motor vehicle in this state.

- A person must apply for a driver's license within 30 days of becoming a resident of Maine.
- A person must be 16 years old to obtain a regular, unrestricted driver's license.
- Social security numbers will be collected and may be used to establish a permanent license number.
- A driver's license is required to have the applicant's name, date of birth, place of resident or mailing address, signature, and permanent assigned license number.
- Full-face color photographs or digital images are required on all licenses except for a temporary license or a person who renews a license on or after the 65th birthday.
- A person under 21 years has a distinctive color-coded license.

Renewal: Prior to expiration of a license, the Secretary of State will send the license holder a renewal application.

- A driver's license for a person under 65 expires at midnight on the license holder's 6th birthday following the date of issuance.
- A driver's license for a person 65 or older expires at midnight on the license holder's 4th birthday following the date of issuance.
- Any valid driver's license issued to a person on active duty with the armed forces, or the person's spouse, is effective without requirement for renewal until 90 days after the date of the person's discharge from the service.

Types of Licenses: A special restricted license may be issued to a person who is 15 years old, has successfully completed a driver education course, and can prove educational or employment need. To prove need, a statement must be provided explaining that no readily available alternative means of transportation exists and use of a vehicle is necessary for transportation to and from school or work. The license allows the holder to drive only between the holder's residence and school or work.

- A Class A license is for the operation of a combination of vehicles with a Gross Vehicle Weight Rating (GVWR) or registered weight of 26,001 lbs. or more, if the GVWR or gross weight of the vehicles being towed is in excess of 10,000 lbs.
- A Class B license is for the operation of a single motor vehicle with a GVWR or registered weight of 26,001 lbs. or more or such a vehicle towing a vehicle with a GVWR or gross weight not in excess of 10,000 lbs.
- A Class C license is for the operation of a single vehicle or combination of vehicles that does not meet the definition of a Class A or Class B license.
- A Class A or Class B license, or a Class C license with endorsements for double or triple trailers, buses, tank trucks, or hazardous materials is a commercial license.
- Operation of a school bus, motorcycle, motor-drive cycle, or moped requires a special endorsement on a license.

Traffic Rules — ME

Alcohol Laws: Open containers are not permitted. Meets TEA-21 requirements. The state requires BAC testing of all drivers involved in accidents resulting in fatalities.

- Maine has an implied consent law.
- Illegal per se BAC level is .08.
- BAC level for people under 21 is .00.
- BAC level for commercial drivers is .04.

Emergency Radio/Cellular: Emergency phone number is *77 or 911.
- Citizen band radio channel 9 is monitored for emergency calls.

Headsets: Wearing of radio headsets while operating a motor vehicle is permitted.

Occupant Restraints: All passengers 18 years or older and the driver are required to wear seat belts.
- Children under 40 pounds must be properly secured in a child safety seat that meets federal standards.
- Children who weigh at least 40 pounds but less than 80 pounds and are under 8 must be properly secured in a booster seat.
- Children between 8 and 18 and more than 4 feet 7 inches in height must be properly secured in a seat belt unless that child is required to be secured in a federally approved child restraint system.
- Children under 12 and under 100 pounds must be in the rear seat of a vehicle, if possible.
- Violation of the seat belt law is a secondary offense, however violation of the child restraint law is a primary offense.
- Passengers under 19 years of age must ride in the passenger compartment of a pickup truck except: (1) workers or trainees engaged in completion of their duties or training or being transported between work or training locations; (2) licensed hunters being transported to or from a hunting location; (3) participants in a parade; or (4) a passenger secured by a seat belt in a manufacturer-installed seat located outside the passenger compartment.

Railroad Crossing: Whenever a person driving a vehicle approaches a railroad crossing and there is a signal indicating an approaching train, the driver must stop not less than 10 feet from the nearest rail of the railroad and must not proceed until he can do so safely.
- A bus transporting passengers, a motor vehicle transporting any quantity of chlorine, a motor vehicle required to be marked or placarded according to federal law, or a cargo tank vehicle whether loaded or empty, must come to a complete stop before crossing any railroad track.
- School buses are required to stop at railroad track crossings not more than 50 feet or less than 15 feet from the nearest rail.

School Buses: Upon meeting or overtaking in either direction a school bus receiving or discharging children, a driver must stop and not proceed until the bus resumes movement or the school bus operator signals to proceed.
- A driver need not stop for a school bus if traveling in a lane separated by curbing or another physical barrier from the lane that the bus is in, or on a limited access highway where pedestrians are not permitted to cross the roadway with the school bus stopped in a loading zone.

Vehicle Equipment & Rules

Bumper Height: Modification of original vehicle frame height permitted, restrictions apply. Lift blocks and spring shackle extensions are prohibited. Door height limits apply.

Glass/Window Tinting: Tinting is permitted only along the top 4 inches of the windshield.

- Side and rear windows may not be covered or treated with tinting that reduces light transmission to less than 50%.
- Reflective material is not permitted on any vehicle windows.
- All windows except the rear window must contain 2-way glass.

Telematics: A motor vehicle may not be operated with a television viewer or screen visible to the driver.

Windshield Stickers: No sign, poster, opaque or semitransparent material or substance may be placed on the windshield that obstructs the driver's clear view of the road or an intersection.

- No more than 1 sticker, except for an inspection sticker, for parking or entry identification may be placed on the windshield of a motor vehicle.
- No portion of an inspection sticker on a motor vehicle windshield may be more than 4 inches from the bottom edge of the windshield.
- If an inspection sticker is located on the lower left hand corner of the windshield, the other sticker must be located to the right of it.

Motorcycles & Mopeds

Equipment: A motorcycle must have 1 front-mounted headlight.

- A motorcycle must have a mirror mounted and adjusted to allow the driver a clear, reflected view of the highway in the rear for a distance of at least 200 feet.
- A driver of a motorcycle may ride only on the permanent and regular attached seat.
- No more than 2 persons may ride on a motorcycle and the passenger must be on a permanent seat provided for said passenger.
- No more than 2 persons may ride in a sidecar, provided that the sidecar is designed with permanent seats for 2 passengers.
- Handlebars of a motorcycle may not be higher than shoulder level of the driver.
- No person under the age of 15 may be a passenger on a motorcycle, or motor-driven cycle without protective headgear.
- A driver of a motorcycle or motor-driven cycle operating with a learner's permit or within 1 year of successfully completing a driving test must wear protective headgear.

Licenses: Operation of a motorcycle, motor-drive cycle, or moped requires a special endorsement on a license.

Noise Limits: A motor vehicle must be equipped with an adequate muffler properly maintained to prevent excessive or unusual noise. Amplification of the noise emitted by the muffler is strictly prohibited.

Mopeds: The following safety equipment is required for a moped: rearview mirror; headlight, tail and brake light, and license plate light. Helmets are required if operating under a learner's permit, or for 1 year after being licensed or for all passengers under age 15.

- Lights must be on at all times while in operation. Mopeds are subject to annual inspection. Not allowed on interstate/turnpike or on a way on which a bicycle is prohibited. May only be operated in single file and as close as practicable to the right.

ME

Passenger Car Trailers

Registration: A trailer exceeding 2,000 lbs. must be registered on the basis of gross weight.

- Any person may apply to the Secretary of State for an 8-year or 12-year semipermanent registration plate for a trailer. The fee is $5 for each trailer of not more than 2,000 lbs. GVWR.

Brakes: A trailer less than 3,000 lbs. gross weight is not required to have brakes.

- A trailer with a gross weight of 3,000 lbs. or greater is required to have adequate brakes acting on all wheels of all axles.

Dimensions: Total length: 65 feet; trailer length: 48 feet; width: 102 inches (mirrors are permitted to extend beyond the total outside width of vehicle); height: 13.6 feet.

Hitch: Safety chains required at least 1/2 inch in diameter.

Lighting: On a vehicle 7 feet wide or wider, all rear lights, reflectors, and signal lights must be within 12 inches of the extreme extension of the vehicle, except for trailers with lights, reflectors, and signals installed by the manufacturer.

- A trailer that is wider than the vehicle towing it must have reflective material or a lamp on each front corner visible to oncoming traffic.

Mirrors: A person may not operate a vehicle so constructed, equipped, loaded, or used that the driver is prevented from having a constantly free and unobstructed view of the way immediately to the rear, unless there is attached a mirror or reflector placed and adjusted to afford the driver a clear, reflected view of the highway to the rear of the vehicle for a distance of at least 200 feet.

Other Provisions: Only 1 trailer or semitrailer may be pulled by a motor vehicle with exception of a truck tractor, semitrailer, and full trailer on the interstate highway system.

- Riding in towed trailer is prohibited.
- Maximum of 1 boat or general/utility trailer may be towed behind passenger or pleasure vehicle; total length of both not to exceed 65 feet.

Miscellaneous Provisions

Liability Laws: Insurance or a bond covering the vehicle is required.

- Minimum insurance requirements are: (1) $350,000 combined single limit for rental vehicles, emergency vehicles and for-hire vehicles transporting freight or merchandise but not passengers; (2) for vehicles for hire used to transport passengers within the state, but not defined as school buses, there is a combined single limit of: (a) $125,000, or split limits of $50,000 per person and $100,000 per occurrence for bodily injury, and $25,000 for property damage for vehicles not under contract with the state, a municipality, or a school district for the transportation of students that are designed to carry no more than 3 passengers behind the driver's seat; (b) $300,000 for vehicles that are designed to carry 4-7 passengers behind the driver's seat, including vehicles under contract with the state, a municipality, or a school district for the transportation of students; (c) $750,000 for vehicles that are designed to carry 8-15 passengers behind the driver's seat; (d) $1,500,000 for vehicles that are designed to carry 16-30 passengers behind the driver's seat; and (e) $2,000,000 for vehicles that are designed to carry 31 or more passengers behind the driver's seat; (3) for vehicles for hire used to transport passengers between points in the state, but not defined as school buses, under contract with the state, municipality, or school district, or for transportation of students, there is a combined single limit of: (a) $1,500,000 for vehicles with 15 or fewer passengers, and (b) $5,000,000 for vehicles with 16 or more passengers; (4) for school buses there is a combined single limit of: (a) $500,000 for buses with up to 30 passengers, and (b) $1,000,000 for buses with 31 or more passengers; (5) for rental trucks with registered gross weight of 26,000 lbs. or less, rented or leased for fewer than 30 days: (a) there is a combined single limit of $125,000; or (b) there is a split limit of $50,000 per person or $100,000 per occurrence for bodily injury and $25,000 for property damage.

- State has non-resident service of process law; does not have guest suit law.

Fees & Taxes

Table 1: Title & Registration Fees

Vehicle Type	Title Fee	Registration Fee
Motor Vehicle	$23.00	$25.00
Mobile Home		$10.50
Motor Home		varies from $21.00 to $469.00 based on gross weight
Trailers of 2,000 lbs. or less		$10.50 to $21.00
Trailers of more than 2,000 lbs.		$18.00 to $36.00
Motorcycles	$23.00	$21.00
Mopeds		$9.00
Duplicates	$23.00	$2.00 cards; $0.50 stickers

Table 2: License Fees

License Class	Fee	Driving Test Fees
6-Year License	$30.00	
Permit	$10.00	
6-Year Commercial License	$41.00	
65 and Older (4 yr.)	$21.00	
65 + Older without Photo	$18.00	
Duplicate License	$5.00	
Endorsements		$10.00, reexamination is $5.00

Table 3: Vehicle Taxes

Tax	Rate
State Sales Tax	7% on the value of rental of living quarters in any trailer camp; 10% on the value of rental for a period of less than 1 year of an automobile
Gasoline Tax; (Diesel)	$0.246/gallon; ($0.257/gallon)
Use Fuel Tax	was previously repealed
Excise Tax for Mobile Homes	25 mills on each dollar of the maker's list price for the first or current year of model; 20 mills for the 2nd year; 16 mills for the 3rd year; 12 mills for the 4th year and succeeding years; The minimum tax shall be $15.00.
Excise Tax for Motor Vehicle or Camper Trailer, Excluding Commercial Vehicles	24 mills on each dollar of the maker's list price for the first or current year of model; 17.5 mills for the 2nd year; 13.5 mills for the 3rd year; 10 mills for the 4th year; 6.5 mills for the 5th year; 4 mills for the 6th and succeeding years. The minimum tax for a motor vehicle other than bicycle with motor attached is $5.00, $2.50 for bicycle with motor attached, $15.00 for a camper trailer and $5.00 for a tent trailer.
Excise Tax for Commercial Vehicles, Model Year 1996 and After	Tax is based on the purchase price in the original year of title rather than on the list price. The initial bill of sale or the state sales tax document provided at point of purchase determines verification of purchase price. The initial bill of sale is that issued by the dealer to the initial purchaser of a new vehicle. Mills remain the same as other motor vehicles.

Table 4: Miscellaneous Fees

Fee	Amount	Payable Upon
Motor Vehicle Inspection	$6.50 for regular inspection $9.50 for enhanced inspection on model years prior to 1996 $12.50 for enhanced inspection on model years 1996 and newer	Completion of Inspection
Special Plates Fee	$15.00	
License Plate Replacement Fee	$5.00 for each plate	
Driver's License Photograph	$3.00	

MARYLAND

Contact Information

Motor Vehicle Administration
6601 Ritchie Highway, NE
Glen Burnie, MD 21062

(800) 950-1682
www.marylandmva.com

Maryland State Police
110 Airport Drive
East Frederick, MD 21701

(301) 644-4151
www.mdsp.maryland.gov/mdsp/default.asp

Maryland Department of Transportation
7201 Corporate Center
P.O. Box 548
Hanover, MD 21076

(410) 865-1142
www.mdot.state.md.us/

Vehicle Title

Application: Certificates of title are required for all vehicles, except trailers weighing less than 2,500 lbs.

- Applications for title must contain the owner's name; address; a description of the vehicle, including make, model, year, vehicle identification number, type of body, and number of cylinders; a statement of the applicant's title to and each security interest in the vehicle, as well as the name and address of each secured party with any security interest in the vehicle; and the applicant's signature.
- Along with the completed application, an applicant must provide the MVA with a certificate of origin, a dealer's reassignment, a dealer's bill of sale, and an odometer disclosure statement.
- An application for title is to be accompanied by any outstanding certificates of title issued for the vehicle.
- Each certificate of title shall include the date of issuance, the name and address of the owner, the names and addresses of all secured parties, in the order of priority, the title number assigned to the vehicle, a description of the vehicle described above, and the classification or weight for which the vehicle is registered.
- Certificates of title will be mailed to the applicant.
- Holders of certificates of title have 30 days to apply for a corrected certificate after a change of name or residence.

Transfer of Ownership: If an owner transfers his interest in a vehicle, he shall, at the time of delivery of the vehicle, execute an assignment and warranty of title to the transferee, with a statement of each security interest, lien, or other encumbrance on the vehicle, in the space provided on the certificate.

- Applicants for certificates of title for a used vehicle purchased from a dealer must have, in addition to a completed application, a properly assigned title, a dealer's reassignment, a dealer's bill of sale, a Maryland safety inspection certificate, and an odometer disclosure statement.
- Applicants for certificates of title for a used vehicle sold by someone other than a dealer must have, in addition to a completed application, a properly assigned certificate of title.

MD

- The transferee shall complete an application for a new certificate of title and mail or deliver it to the MVA.

Vehicle Registration

Application: Each motor vehicle, trailer, semitrailer, and pole trailer driven on a highway shall be registered.

- No vehicle may be registered until the owner of the vehicle has received a certificate of title or an application for a certificate of title.
- A county may be authorized to register vehicles and issue registration plates and cards. Applicants for registration at these facilities must pay an additional fee of $1.00.
- If an application for registration and certificate of title is accompanied by the required fees, the MVA may issue a temporary registration card and plate to permit the vehicle to be driven pending action by the MVA. The card is valid for 15 days.
- The registration card issued by the MVA shall contain the date of issuance, the name and address of the owner, the registration number assigned, and a description of the vehicle.

Non-Residents: A new resident may reside in the state for 60 days before registering the vehicle in Maryland.

- Non-residents who occupy a dwelling in Maryland for at least 30 days, but less than 1 year, must obtain a non-resident's permit from the MVA within 10 days immediately following the 30-day period.
- Military personnel on active duty in Maryland need not register his/her vehicle in Maryland if the vehicle is registered in the state of his/her residence.

Registration Type: A vehicle owner is required to carry the registration card in the vehicle at all times while operating the vehicle.

- A vehicle owner must display the registration card on demand of a police officer.
- Registration expires at midnight on the date indicated on the registration card.
- Holders of vehicle registrations have 30 days to apply for a corrected registration after a change of name or residence.
- The registration of a vehicle expires upon transfer of title, unless the owner gives the transferee written permission to use the existing plates.
- A transferee that has been given permission to use the existing plates may not use them for more than 10 days. Within 10 days, the transferee shall return the plates to the MVA or the former owner.
- The former owner may transfer the plates from one vehicle to another.
- The transferee must apply for and obtain a new registration prior to using the vehicle on a highway.
- Each registration renewal shall be for 2 years for non-commercial vehicles.
- Vehicle registration classifications:
    - Class A: Passenger cars and station wagons.
    - Class B: "For hire" vehicles.
    - Class D: Motorcycles.
    - Class E: Single unit trucks with 2 or more axles (Includes tow trucks).
    - Class F: Truck Tractors.
    - Class G: Trailers and semitrailers.

- Class L: Historic motor vehicles.
- Class M: Multipurpose passenger vehicles.
- Class P: Passenger buses, charter or for hire.

Emissions Inspection: Vehicles must have an exhaust emissions test and emissions equipment and misfueling inspection every 2 years.

- Motorcycles, Class E trucks with a Gross Vehicle Weight (GVW) over 26,000 lbs., historic vehicles, and cars prior to model year 1977 are not required to have an emissions test.
- Vehicles passing the emissions test shall be issued a certificate with the date of inspection, vehicle information, the pass/fail status of all tests; and the expiration date of the certificate.
- Owners must carry the inspection certificate at all times in the vehicle.
- Vehicles that fail the test may be granted a waiver if the owner has incurred an expenditure of $450 towards emissions-related repairs to the vehicle within 120 days after the test, fails a retest, and the owner shows that the repairs made were done so by a certified repair technician.
- Vehicles driven less than 5,000 miles annually and that have special registration plates need not be inspected.

Safety Inspection: An owner of a vehicle shall have the vehicle inspected, maintained, and repaired at least every 25,000 miles or every 12 months, whichever comes first.

- Vehicles that have been in operation for at least 18 years must be inspected at least every 12,500 miles or every 6 months, whichever comes first.
- An inspection is required whenever a used vehicle is sold or ownership is transferred.
- Upon successful completion of an inspection, a certificate shall be issued that contains vehicle information and the certification date.

License Plates

Disbursement: Upon registration of a vehicle the MVA shall issue registration plates. Motorcycles, tractor vehicles, and trailers are to be issued 1 license plate, and every other vehicle shall be issued 2 plates.

- On vehicles for which 2 plates are required, 1 plate shall be attached to the front of the vehicle and the other plate shall be attached to the rear of the vehicle.
- On vehicles receiving just 1 plate, it shall be attached to the rear of the vehicle.
- Validations tabs are to be placed on the registration plates upon renewal of the vehicle registration.
- Owners of passenger vehicles, multipurpose vehicles, and Class E trucks shall be offered stickers that display the owner's county of residence.
- Registration plates may be reflectorized, and shall have a durability of at least 5 years.
- Vehicle dealers may issue 1 temporary registration plate to new owners, with the dates of issuance and expiration clearly written on the tag.
- Temporary plates expire upon the first to occur of the following: receipt of annual registration plates, rescission of the contract to buy the vehicle, or 60 days from issuance.
- Personalized registration plates are available for an additional fee.
- Persons presenting sufficient proof of a disability may obtain special disabled license plates without an additional fee.

Transfer of Plates: Registration plates expire upon transfer of ownership unless the former owner gives written permission to the transferee to use the plates. In such a case, the transferee may use the plates for 10 days prior to returning them to the MVA.

- The former owner of a vehicle may transfer the registration plates from the sold vehicle to his new vehicle.

Driver's Licenses

Examination: Each applicant for an original driver's license shall pass the following exams: a vision test; a test indicating the ability to read and understand highway signs regulating, warning, and directing traffic; a test of the applicant's knowledge of the traffic laws of the state and safe driving practices; and a driving test.

- The vision standards for a driver with restricted license are a visual acuity of 20/40 in at least 1 eye, and a continuous field of vision of at least 110 degrees with at least 35 degrees lateral to the midline of each side.
- The MVA may issue a restricted license for daylight driving only to an applicant with at least 20/70 vision in 1 eye, and a continuous field of vision of at least 110 degrees with at least 35 degrees lateral to the midline of each side. The operator is allowed to operate a vehicle only from one-half hour before sunrise to one-half hour after sunset.
- A driver with a telescopic lens placed at the top of a corrective vision lens is eligible for a Class C license if he or she demonstrates a visual acuity of at least 20/100 in 1 eye and a field of 150 degrees horizontal vision with or without corrective lenses; but if the applicant has vision in only 1 eye, he or she must demonstrate a field of at least 100 degrees horizontal vision. Applicants with a visual acuity of at least 20/70 in 1 eye are also eligible for a Class C license.
- An applicant will be issued a commercial driver's license when he or she has passed the knowledge and skills tests for driving a commercial motor vehicle which complies with the minimum federal standards established by the federal Commercial Motor Vehicle Safety Act of 1986.

Graduated Drivers Licensing: State has a system of graduating licensing for teen drivers.

- At 15 and 9 months, teens are eligible for a learner's permit. During this stage teens may not drive unless supervised by a parent or guardian.
- Teens must hold this permit for at least 6 months and accumulate at least 60 hours (10 nighttime) of parental/guardian certified driving before being eligible for an intermediate license.
- At 16 and 3 months, teens are eligible for an intermediate license. Intermediate license holders may not drive unsupervised during the hours of midnight to 5:00 a.m. For the first 5 months during this stage, teens are prohibited from transporting passengers under the age of 18 (immediate family exempt).
- Teens with a learner's permit or provisional license are prohibited from using a wireless communication device while driving.
- At 17 and 9 months, teens are eligible for an unrestricted license.
- Driver education and certification of practice driving are required of all initial applicants.
- The nighttime driving restriction only applies to intermediate license holders under 18.

Issuance/Application: Each application for a driver's license shall state the full name, address, employer, race, sex, height, weight, general physical condition, and date of birth of the applicant; whether the applicant previously has been refused a license to drive; whether the applicant has previously been licensed to drive, and if so, whether the applicant has ever had a license suspended or revoked; a signature; and proof of age and identity.

- Applications of a minor for a license shall be cosigned by a parent, guardian, or if the minor does not have a parent or guardian or is married, by an adult employer of the applicant or any other responsible adult.
- The MVA shall suspend a license of a minor until he reaches 18 years of age, upon either a request by or the death of the signing adult.
- A new resident may reside in the state for 30 days before applying for a new license, provided that he or she has a valid license from another state, and the individual is at least the same age as Maryland requires for the same class of license.
- A non-commercial Class A, B, C, or M license shall include the name and address of the licensee; date of birth; a description of the licensee, including height, weight, and sex; a color photograph; type or class of vehicles the licensee is authorized to drive; and the signatures of the issuing agent and the licensee.
- The MVA may not include or encode an individual's social security number on the license. License includes color photograph.
- Licenses are to be carried at all times while operating a motor vehicle, and shall be displayed to any uniformed police officer upon demand.

Renewal: A license issued to a driver at least 21 years of age shall expire on the birth date of the licensee in the 5th year following the issuance of the license.

- A license issued to a driver under the age of 21 shall expire 60 days after the driver's 21st birthday.
- The MVA may renew a license within 1 year after the expiration date without requiring a driving test.
- Individuals between 21 and 40 years old may renew their license electronically without a vision test if the applicant has passed a vision test within the previous six years. The MVA shall require every individual applying for renewal of a license to pass a vision test.
- People out of state during the renewal process may renew by mail. A valid without photo license is issued to people who renew by mail. The license must be exchanged for a photo license within 15 days after returning to the state.
- A license held by active military personnel or a dependent outside of the state is valid for 30 days after re-entering the state. The license can also be renewed by mail.

Types of Licenses:

Commercial:

- Class A: authorizes a licensee to drive combinations of tractor and trailer vehicles; and any vehicle that a Class B, C, or D license authorizes its holder to drive.
- Class B: authorizes a licensee to drive vehicles or combinations of vehicles with a registered GVW of more than 25,000 lbs., excluding combinations of tractor and trailer vehicles; and any vehicle that a Class C or D license authorizes its holder to drive.
- Class C: authorizes a licensee to drive buses and any vehicle that a Class D license authorizes its holder to drive.
- Class D: authorizes the licensee to drive any vehicle or combination of vehicles, except combinations of tractor and trailers, vehicles or combinations of vehicles with a registered Gross Combination Weight (GCW) of more than 25,000 lbs., but not including an uncoupled truck trailer; buses over 10,000 lbs. GVW; and motorcycles.

- Class E: authorizes the licensee to drive motorcycles.
- Licensees of Classes A-D may drive any tow truck.

Non-Commercial:
- Class A: authorizes the licensee to drive combinations of tractor and trailer vehicles and any vehicle that a non-commercial Class B license authorizes its holder to drive, except commercial vehicles and motorcycles.
- Class B: authorizes the licensee to drive any single vehicle or combinations of vehicles with a GVW or GCW of 26,001 lbs. and more and any vehicle that a non-commercial Class C driver's license authorizes its holder to drive, except commercial vehicles; motorcycles; and combinations of trucks and trailers.
- Class C: authorizes the licensee to drive any vehicle or combination of vehicles with a GVW less than 26,001 lbs., except commercial vehicles and motorcycles.
- Class M: authorizes the licensee to drive motorcycles.
- Licensees of Classes A-C may tow travel trailers, camping trailers, or boat trailers.

Traffic Rules

Alcohol Laws: Any person operating a vehicle on a highway gives an implied consent for law enforcement to take a test to determine if the person is driving under the influence.
- Open containers not permitted. Meets TEA-21 requirements.
- Illegal per se BAC level is .08.
- BAC level for people under 21 is .02.

Emergency Radio/Cellular: Citizen band radios are not monitored. Emergency cell phone number is 911. Non-emergency number is #77 or #SP.

Headsets: A person may not drive a motor vehicle on any highway while the person is wearing either over or in both ears earplugs, headsets, or earphones.

Occupant Restraints: A person may not operate a motor vehicle unless the person and each occupant 16 years of age or older are restrained by a seat belt in the front seat.
- All children under the age of 6 or weighing 40 pounds or less must be secured in a child safety seat in a motor vehicle registered in the state. If a child is being transported in a motor vehicle registered in another state the child must be secured according to manufacturer instructions for children under 4 or weighing 40 pounds or less.
- Children between 6 and 16 years and more than 40 lbs. must be restrained in a safety belt or child restraint.
- Violation of the occupant protection laws is a primary offense.
- In a truck with a GVW exceeding 10,000 lbs., no person may occupy the area of the vehicle primarily intended to carry cargo.
- A person may not operate a truck on a highway in the state while a passenger under the age of 16 is riding in an unenclosed bed of the vehicle. Additional gaps in coverage apply; see Occupant Protection Chart.

Railroad Crossing: A driver of a vehicle shall stop between 15-50 feet of a railroad crossing whenever a crossing gate is lowered, a flagman signals the approach or passage of a railroad train, a railroad train approaching within 1,500 feet of the crossing gives an audible signal that because of its speed or nearness it is an immediate danger, or a railroad train is plainly visible and is or is approaching dangerously near to the crossing.

- The following vehicles are to stop at all railroad crossings: vehicles carrying passengers for hire; school vehicles carrying any passengers; every bus owned or operated by a church and carrying any passenger; every vehicle carrying flammable liquids or explosives; and every vehicle carrying hazardous materials.

School Buses: If a school vehicle has stopped on a roadway and is operating flashing red lights, the driver of any other vehicle on the roadway shall stop at least 20 feet from the school vehicle, and may not proceed until the school vehicle either resumes motion or the red lights are deactivated.

- Drivers on the opposite side of a divided highway are not required to stop.
- School buses may not be operated at a speed exceeding 50 mph.
- All school buses used for the transportation of children to and from schools shall be equipped with seat back crash pads.
- School vehicles shall be painted national school bus yellow.

Vehicle Equipment & Rules

Bumper Height: A person may not operate a vehicle on any highway if the height of the vehicle's bumpers exceed:

- 20 inches for passenger vehicles;
- 28 inches for multipurpose vehicles and trucks with GVW of 10,000 lbs. or less;
- 30 inches for trucks with a GVW exceeding 10,000 lbs.; or
- 32 inches for trucks used for spraying agricultural crops.
- A bumper may not be modified or extended upward or downward to compensate for vehicle suspension or body alterations or modifications.

Glass/Window Tinting: No window may have tinting applied that does not allow for at least 35% light transmission.

- No tint shall be applied to the windshield of a vehicle below 5 inches from the top of the windshield.

Telematics: A motor vehicle may not be equipped with television-type receiving equipment installed in front of the back of the driver's seat or otherwise visible to the driver.

- Vehicle navigation systems are allowed.

Windshield Stickers: No sign, poster, or other non-transparent material may be placed on the front windshield, other than a certificate or other paper required to be so displayed by law.

Motorcycles & Mopeds

Equipment: The operator of a motorcycle may not carry any other person on the motorcycle unless it has a permanent seat to the side or behind the operator.

- If any motorcycle carries a passenger other than in a sidecar or enclosed cab, the motorcycle shall be equipped with footrests for the passenger.
- A person may not operate a motorcycle with handlebars more than 15 inches in height above the seat.

- An individual may not operate or ride on a motorcycle unless the individual is wearing protective headgear.
- An individual may not operate or ride on a motorcycle unless the individual is wearing protective eye gear, or the motorcycle is equipped with a windscreen.
- All face shields and protective eye gear must allow the wearer an angle of vision of not less than 105 degrees.
- Every motorcycle shall be equipped with 1 or 2 headlamps, which shall be of sufficient intensity so that they can be seen from 100 feet if the motorcycle is traveling less than 25 mph, 200 feet if the motorcycle is traveling between 25-34 mph, and at least 300 feet if the motorcycle is traveling 35 mph or more.
- Every motorcycle shall be equipped with 2 taillamps, visible from a distance of 1,000 feet to the rear.
- Every motorcycle shall be equipped with a white light capable of illuminating the rear registration plate from a distance of 50 feet to the rear.
- Every motorcycle shall be equipped with at least 1 red rear reflector, visible from distances 100-600 feet to the rear.
- Every motorcycle shall be equipped with at least 1 stop lamp mounted on the rear.
- Motorcycles need not be equipped with electric turn signals.
- Every motorcycle shall be equipped with 2 rearview mirrors, 1 each attached on the right and left handlebars.
- A person may not operate a motorcycle that has 1.5 horsepower or less, or a capacity of less than 70 cubic centimeters piston displacement on a roadway where the speed limit is at least 50 mph, or on any expressway or controlled access highway.

Licenses: A Class M license authorizes the licensee to drive motorcycles, but an applicant must be age 16 years 1 month before obtaining a provisional license. The same application procedures for a motor vehicle apply to a motorcycle application.

Noise Limits: Maximum acceptable noise limits for motorcycles:
- Motorcycles manufactured between July 1, 1975 and January 1, 1988: 83 decibels.
- Motorcycles manufactured after January 1, 1988: 80 decibels.

Mopeds: An individual with any valid class of vehicle license may operate a moped.
- A moped operator's permit is available to any individual age 16 or older who does not possess a valid driver's license. The applicant must pass a vision test and a written test and pay the required fees.
- A moped operator's permit is valid for 5 years, and can be renewed upon application and payment of the required fee.

Passenger Car Trailers

Brakes: All trailers must be equipped with parking brakes adequate to hold the vehicle on any grade on which it is operated.
- All trailers with a registered gross weight of at least 10,000 lbs. must be equipped with brakes on all wheels.
- Trailers not exceeding 3,000 lbs. need not have brakes on all wheels, provided that the total weight of the trailers does not exceed 40% of the gross weight of the towing vehicle when connected to the trailer and the combination of vehicles is capable of complying with braking performance requirements.

- Trailers between 3,000–10,000 lbs. need not have brakes on all wheels, provided that the trailer has 2 or more axles, is equipped with brakes acting on all wheels of at least one of the axles, and the combination of vehicles is capable of complying with braking performance requirements.

Dimensions: Total length: 55 feet (includes bumpers); trailer length: 40 feet (includes bumpers); width: 102 inches; height: 13.6 feet.

Hitch: Every full trailer shall be equipped with a towbar and means of attaching the towbar to the towing and towed units.

- The towbar and means of attaching the towbar to the units shall be structurally adequate for the weight drawn; be mounted properly and securely, without excessive slack, but with enough play to allow for universal action of the connection; and have a suitable locking device to prevent accidental separation of the towed and towing vehicles.
- The mounting of the trailer hitch of the towing vehicle shall include sufficient reinforcement or bracing of the frame to provide sufficient strength and rigidity to prevent undue distortion of the frame.
- Every trailer and semitrailer equipped with a towbar and any special mobile equipment being towed shall be coupled directly to the frame of the towing vehicle with 1 or more safety chains or cables, and the chains or cables shall be connected to the towed or towing vehicle and to the towbar to prevent the towbar from dropping to the ground if it fails.

Mirrors: Where the view through the inside mirror is obstructed, 2 outside rearview mirrors are required.

Lighting: Every trailer shall be equipped with at least 2 rear taillamps that emit a red light plainly visible from at least 1,000 feet to the rear.

- Trailers manufactured before June 1, 1971 shall have at least 1 taillamp that emits a red light plainly visible from a distance of at least 300 feet to the rear.
- On a combination of vehicles, only the taillamps on the rearmost vehicle need actually be seen from the required distance.
- Every trailer shall have either a taillamp or separate lamp that illuminates the rear license plate with a white light from a distance of at least 50 feet.
- After July 1, 1971, every trailer shall carry on the rear, either as part of the taillamps or separately, 2 or more red reflectors visible from all distances between 100-600 feet behind the vehicle.
- Before July 1, 1971, every trailer shall carry on the rear, either as part of the taillamps or separately, 1 or more red reflectors visible from all distances between 100-600 feet behind the vehicle.
- Every trailer manufactured after July 1, 1971 shall be equipped with at least 2 stop lamps shaded either red or amber and visible from a distance of 300 feet, while vehicles manufactured before that date must have at least 1 stop lamp.
- Every trailer manufactured after July 1, 1971 shall be equipped with electric turn signals on the front and rear of the vehicle.
- Trailers and semitrailers 80 inches or more in overall width shall have:
    - on the front, 2 clearance lamps, 1 at each side;
    - on the rear, 2 clearance lamps, 1 at each side, and after June 1, 1971, 3 identification lamps grouped in a horizontal row, with lamp centers between 6 and 12

inches apart, and mounted on the permanent structure of the vehicle as close as practicable to the vertical centerline;
- on each side, 2 side marker lamps, 1 at or near the front and 1 at or near the rear; and
- on each side, 2 reflectors, 1 at or near the front and 1 at or near the side.
- Rear reflectors on pole trailers may be mounted on each side of the bolster or load.
- Clearance lamps shall be mounted so as to indicate the extreme width of the motor vehicle, not including mirrors, and as near the top of the vehicle as practicable.
- When rear identification lamps are mounted at the extreme height of the vehicle, rear clearance lamps may be mounted at an optional height.
- When mounting of the front clearance lamps at the highest point of a trailer results in those lamps failing to mark the extreme width of the trailer, they may be mounted at an optional height, but must indicate the extreme width of the trailer.
- Front, side, and rear clearance and identification lamps shall be capable of being seen at all distances between 500 and 50 feet from the front and rear, respectively.

Speed Limits: Same as passenger cars.

Towing: If a trailer is towed by a Class E truck, it must have a GVW of 20,000 lbs. or less.
- If a trailer is towed by a Class A passenger vehicle or a Class M multipurpose vehicle, it must have a GVW of 10,000 lbs. or less.
- Class A and Class M vehicles may only tow the following: boat trailers; camping trailers; travel trailers; house trailers; or utility trailers.
- A person may not occupy any mobile home while it is being towed on a highway.

Miscellaneous Provisions

Bail Bonds: Mandatory recognition of AAA arrest bond certificates up to $500, with specified exceptions.

Liability Laws: Compulsory liability minimum $20,000/40,000/15,000, and uninsured motorist coverage in like amounts. Unless waived by insured, policy shall provide no-fault coverage for medical, hospital, and disability benefits up to $2,500. General damages: no limit.
- Liability insurance coverage is required at all times. Registration plates must be returned to the MVA immediately after cancellation of insurance or transfer of ownership of the vehicle. MVA monitors vehicle insurance status through several enforcement programs. If a vehicle owner is involved in an enforcement program, they must submit verification of their liability insurance to MVA upon request or face suspension of current and future registration privileges. Monetary penalties up to $2,500 are also imposed if vehicle is found to be uninsured.
- State has non-resident service of process law; does not have guest suit law.

Weigh Stations: The Department of State Police shall maintain at least 5 vehicle weighing and measuring stations. At least 1 of the stations shall be on Interstate 95.
- The following vehicles must stop: (1) agricultural vehicles over 10,000 lbs.; (2) all commercial vehicles over 10,000 lbs.; (3) commercial buses carrying over 16 passengers; (4) any hazardous material haulers requiring placards.

Fees & Taxes

Table 1: Title & Registration Fees

Vehicle Type	Title Fee	Registration Fee (Two Year Fee, plus $13.50 annual Emergency Medical Services surcharge)
Class A Passenger Vehicles and Class M Multipurpose Vehicles	$23.00	$128.00 for vehicles 3,700 lbs. or less; $180.00 for vehicles over 3,700 lbs.
Class E Truck not exceeding 7,000 lbs.	$23.00	$154.50
Class E Truck	$23.00	Registration varies by weight, with fees per 1,000 lbs. ranging from $9.00 for trucks between 10,000 - 18,000 lbs. to $22.50 for trucks between 60,001 - 80,000 lbs.
Non-Freight Trailer 3,000 lbs. or less	$23.00	$25.50
Non-Freight Trailer 3,001 - 5,000 lbs.	$23.00	$51.00
Non-Freight Trailer 5,001 - 10,000 lbs.	$23.00	$80.00
Non-Freight Trailer 10,001 - 20,000 lbs.	$23.00	$124.00
Historic Motor Vehicle	$23.00	$51.00
Motorcycles	$23.00	$97.00
Mopeds	$23.00	$59.00
Duplicates	$20.00	$5.00

Table 2: License Fees

License Class	Fee
Learner's Permit	$45.00
Learner's Permit to Provisional License	No fee
Provisional to Regular License	$5.00
Non-Commercial Renewal	$30.00
Commercial Renewal	$50.00*
Exchanging Out-of-State License for Maryland License	$45.00
Changing License Information	$20.00
Duplicate License Fee	$20.00

* Includes a $20.00 CDL information system surcharge.

Table 3: Vehicle Taxes

Tax	Rate
Excise Titling Tax for Vehicles less than 7 years old	5% of the value of the vehicle, but if transferred from a state with a higher tax rate, a flat fee of $100. If transferred from a state with a lower tax rate, the net difference of the tax rate with a minimum tax of $100. If from a state with no tax 5% of the value of the vehicle. All vehicles valued at less than $2,000 will be taxed at the 5% rate.
Excise Titling Tax for Vehicles at least 7 years old	Tax is based on the greater of the purchase price of $640, and taxed at the above rates.
Excise Tax for Trailer	$50.00 if exempt from the titling requirement, otherwise the same tax applies
Gasoline Tax; (Diesel)	$0.235/gallon; ($0.243/gallon)

MD

Table 4: Miscellaneous Fees

Fee	Amount	Payable Upon
Emissions Inspection	$14.00	inspection
Special Plates Fee	Vary from $27.00 to $184.00 plus an $11.00 surcharge for emergency medical services.	issue/annual renewal
Registration Transfer Fee	$10.00 if the registration fee is the same or less than the old vehicle, otherwise $10.00 plus the difference in the registration fees.	transfer
Registration at a County-Run Facility	$1.00	upon application, in addition to regular registration fee
Vehicle Title Security Interest (lien)	$20.00	application
Duplicate Plate	$20.00	application
Plate Fees*	Vary from $27.00 to $184.00	

* Plus an $11.00 surcharge per year for emergency medical services.

MASSACHUSETTS

Contact Information

Registry of Motor Vehicles (RMV)
P.O. Box 199100
Boston, MA 02119-9100

(617) 351-4500
www.massrmv.com

Massachusetts State Police
470 Worcester Road
Framingham, MA 07105

(508) 820-2300
www.state.ma.us/msp

Massachusetts Highway Department
10 Park Plaza
Boston, MA 02116

(617) 973-7800
www.state.ma.us/mhd/

Vehicle Title

Application: Whoever acquires a motor vehicle shall be required to make an application for a certificate of title. Such application shall be made within 10 days from the acquisition of ownership.

- Certificate of title application must be made before registration application.
- Application for the first certificate of title of a vehicle in Massachusetts shall be made by the owner to the RMV on such form as the RMV shall prescribe. The application shall contain: (1) the name, residence, and mailing address of the owner; (2) a description of the motor vehicle including, its make, model, identifying number, type of body, the number of cylinders, the mileage shown on the odometer, and whether the vehicle is new or used; (3) the date of purchase by applicant, the name

and address of the person from whom the vehicle was acquired, and the names and addresses of any lienholders in the order of their priority and the dates of their security agreements; (4) any further information that the RMV may require to identify the vehicle and to enable him or her to determine whether the owner is entitled to a certificate of title; (5) if the application refers to a new vehicle, it shall be accompanied by a certificate of origin; and (6) if the application refers to a vehicle last previously registered in another state or country, the application shall be accompanied by a certificate of title issued by the other state or country.

Transfer of Ownership: If an owner of a vehicle for which a certificate of title has been issued transfers his interest therein, he or she shall, at the time of the delivery of the vehicle, execute an assignment including the actual odometer reading and warranty of title to the transferee in the space provided on the certificate, or such other form as the registrar shall prescribe, and cause the certificate and assignment to be mailed or delivered to the transferee or the registrar.

- The new owner shall, promptly after delivery to him or her of the vehicle, execute the application for a new certificate of title in the space provided on the certificate or on such other form as the registrar shall prescribe and cause the certificate and application to be mailed or delivered to the registrar.

Mobile Home: Mobile homes must be registered.

Vehicle Registration

Application: Application for the registration of a motor vehicle may be made by the owner.

- The application for registration of a motor vehicle shall contain the owner's name, place of residence and address, date of birth, and the number of the applicant's license to operate, if one has been issued.
- The application for registration shall also contain a brief description of the motor vehicle, including the name of the maker, the vehicle identification number, the character of the motor power, and the type of transmission.
- The application for registration shall also include a statement that there are no outstanding excise tax liabilities on said motor vehicle.
- A registration fee shall also accompany an application for registration.
- An application for the registration of a motor vehicle owned by a minor shall, if not made by the minor, be made by his parent or legal guardian for registration in the name of the minor as owner.

Non-Residents: A motor vehicle owned by a non-resident who has complied with the laws relative to motor vehicles, and the registration and operation thereof, of the state or country of registration, may be operated on the public streets without registration in Massachusetts.

- Every non-resident enrolled as a student at a school or college in Massachusetts, who operated a motor vehicle registered in another state or country, shall file in triplicate with the police department in which such school is located, on a form approved by the RMV, a signed statement providing the following information: the registration number and make and model of the motor vehicle and the state or country of registration, the name and address of the owner, the names and addresses of all insurers, the legal residence of such non-resident, and his address while attending such school or college.
- Massachusetts registration is required when a motor vehicle is operated in

Massachusetts for more than 30 days in the aggregate in any 1 year or, in any case where the owner thereof acquires a regular place of abode or business or employment within Massachusetts. Massachusetts registration must be applied for within a period of 30 days.
- Military personnel on active duty in Massachusetts may maintain vehicle registration from home state.

Registration Type: The registration of every motor vehicle shall expire at midnight of the expiration date appearing on said certificate of registration.
- In no event shall a registration be valid for less than a period of 12 months.
- Every person operating a motor vehicle shall have the certificate of registration for the vehicle and for the trailer upon his person or in the vehicle in some easily accessible place.

Emissions Inspection: Vehicles with even numbered model years must also take emissions tests on even years, odd model year vehicles on odd years. Fee is $29 for either annual safety inspection or combined biennial safety/emissions inspection.
- Vehicles failing the emissions test will have 60 days to get repairs and re-inspection. If vehicle still fails after repair, a waiver may be granted if emissions repair expenditures exceed: $400 for vehicles up to 5 model years old; $300 for vehicles 6 to 10 model years old; and $200 for vehicles over 10 model years old.
- Vehicles model year 1983 and older will not be required to have emissions tests.
- New cars will be exempt for their 1st 2 years.
- Visible smoke emitted from the exhaust pipe is considered a safety-related failure, applicable to all vehicles regardless of age.

Safety Inspection: A safety inspection is required annually.

License Plates

Disbursement: License plates are provided upon vehicle registration.
- RMV provides 2 license plates per motor vehicle registration and 1 license plate per trailer registration.
- Handicap plates or placards for the disabled are available upon application with medical certificate to Medical Affairs Section, Registry of Motor Vehicles. Road test may be required if medical professional is unable to certify competency to operate safely.

Transfer of Plates: The owner of a motor vehicle who transfers the ownership or who terminates the registration shall remove from the vehicle any visible evidence furnished to him by the RMV.

Driver's Licenses

Examination: Tests required for obtaining a license include: a written test, a road test, and a vision screening (20/40 visual acuity required), testing both field vision and basic color recognition.

Graduated Drivers Licensing: State has a system of graduated licensing for teen drivers.
- At 16, teens are eligible for a learner's permit. Permit holders may not drive unsupervised.

- At 16 and 6 months, teens who have: (1) held a permit for a period of 6 months; (2) completed an approved driver's education course; (3) completed 12 or more hours of behind-the-wheel experience; and (4) a clean driving record for a minimum of 6 months are eligible for a junior operator's/intermediate license.
- Junior operator's/intermediate license holders are prohibited from driving unsupervised between the hours of midnight and 5:00 a.m.
- For the first 6 months of the junior operator's/intermediate license phase, teens may not transport any passengers (other than family members) under the age of 18 unless supervised by a driver 21 years and older.
- A junior operator's/intermediate license holder who violates the passenger restriction shall be subject to a license suspension of up to 90 days. The 6-month passenger restriction period will stop running when the suspension begins and the remainder of the restriction period will start running again when the suspension is completed.
- Junior operators/intermediate license holders face a license suspension for a 2nd or subsequent offense for speeding or drag racing violations.
- At 18, teens who have held a junior operator's/intermediate license for at least 12 months are eligible for an unrestricted license.

Issuance/Application: Application for license or permit requires the following: social security number, date of birth, full name, sex, height, mailing address, and residential address.

- Applicant must provide a social security number or a valid passport.
- Applicant must also present 3 identifying documents.
- License normally includes photograph.
- License number is usually an assigned number unless social security number is requested.
- Non-citizens who are non-residents of Massachusetts may drive for 1 year on the license issued by their home country.

Renewal: An operator's license is valid for 5 years and expires on the holder's birthday.

- Renewal of license may be done up to 1 year prior to the expiration date.
- Application for renewal includes: social security number, date of birth, license number, full name, mailing address, and residential address of the applicant.
- Active duty military personnel may drive on an expired license for up to 60 days after honorable discharge from military service or return to Massachusetts. Active duty military personnel may be issued renewed non-photo driver's license if stationed outside Massachusetts.

Types of Licenses: Class A: Any combination of vehicles with a Gross Combination Vehicle Weight Rating (GCWR) of 26,001 lbs. or more provided the Gross Vehicle Weight Rating (GVWR) of the vehicle(s) being towed is in excess of 10,000 lbs., except a school bus. With a Class A license and the appropriate endorsements, a driver may operate any vehicle covered within Classes B and C.

- Class B: Any single vehicle with a GVWR of 26,001 lbs. or more, or any such vehicle towing another vehicle not in excess of 10,000 lbs. GVWR, except a school bus. With a Class B license and appropriate endorsements, a driver may operate any vehicle covered within Class C.
- Class C: Any vehicle that is either less than 26,001 lbs. GVWR or any such vehicle

towing a vehicle not in excess of 10,000 lbs. GVWR or a vehicle placarded for hazardous materials or designed to transport 16 or more persons, including the operator, except a school bus.

- Class D: Any single vehicle or combination except a semitrailer unit, truck trailer combination, tractor, or truck having a registered gross weight in excess of 26,000 lbs., a bus, or a school bus.
- Class M: Motorcycle. If operator has a Class D license, he or she may opt for a Class M endorsement on their driver's license.

Traffic Rules

Alcohol Laws: Any person who accepts the privilege of operating a motor vehicle in Massachusetts, is deemed to have given his or her consent to submit to an approved chemical or physical test, if the person is lawfully arrested for any offense allegedly committed while the person was driving or was in actual physical control of a motor vehicle.

- Open containers are not permitted. Meets the requirements of TEA-21.
- Illegal per se BAC level is .08.
- BAC level for people under 21 is .02.

Cellular Telephone Use: No person shall operate a moving school bus while using a mobile telephone except in the case of an emergency.

Emergency Radio/Cellular: Citizen band radio channel 9 is monitored for emergency calls. Emergency cell number is *77 or *SP.

Headsets: No person shall operate a motor vehicle while wearing headphones, unless said headphones are used for communication in connection with controlling the course or movement of said vehicle.

Occupant Restraints: No person shall operate a motor vehicle unless the person is wearing a seat belt and all passengers 12 and older are properly restrained.

- Children under the age of 5 and weighing 40 lbs. or less shall be properly fastened and secured by a child passenger restraint system.
- Children between the ages of 5 and 12 shall wear a safety belt, which is properly adjusted and fastened.
- Violation of the seat belt law is a secondary offense, however violation of the child restraint law is a primary offense.
- Riding in pickup truck beds is prohibited for people 12 and under. Additional gaps in coverage apply; see Occupant Protection Chart.

Railroad Crossing: Every person operating a motor vehicle, upon approaching a railroad crossing shall reduce the speed of the vehicle to a reasonable and proper rate before proceeding over the crossing, and shall proceed over the crossing at a rate of speed and with such care as is reasonable and proper under the circumstances.

- Every person operating a school bus or any motor vehicle carrying explosive substances or flammable liquids as cargo, upon approaching a railroad crossing, shall bring his vehicle to a full stop not less than 15 feet and not more than 50 feet from the nearest track of the railroad and shall not proceed to cross until it is safe to do so.

School Buses: When approaching a vehicle which displays a sign bearing the words "School Bus" and which is equipped with front and rear alternating flashing red signal lamps which are flashing, and which has been stopped to allow pupils on or off of the vehicle, a person operating a motor vehicle shall, except when approaching from the opposite direction on a divided highway, bring his vehicle to a full stop before reaching said school bus and shall not proceed until the warning signals are deactivated.

Vehicle Equipment & Rules

Bumper Height: No person shall alter, modify, or change the height of a motor vehicle with an original manufacturer's GVWR of up to and including 10,000 lbs., by elevating or lowering the chassis or body by more than 2 inches above or below the manufacturer's specified height.

Glass/Window Tinting: The use of non-transparent or sunscreen material or window application is allowed if it has a total visible light reflectance of not more than 35% or a visible light transmittance of not less than 35% on the side windows immediately adjacent to the right and the left of the operator's seat, the side windows immediately to the rear of the operator's seat and the front passenger seat, or on the rear window if the vehicle is equipped with 2 outside mirrors.

- The use of any transparent material is limited to the uppermost 6% along the top of the windshield, provided such strip does not encroach upon the driver's direct forward viewing area.
- A special window treatment or application determined necessary by a licensed physician, for the protection of the owner or operator of a private passenger motor vehicle who is determined to be light or photosensitive, is allowed if the application is made to the RMV. The application must also be supported by a written attestation of a physician licensed to practice in Massachusetts. Upon granting this exemption, the RMV shall issue a sticker to the applicant, which shall be affixed to the side window immediately adjacent to the operator.

Telematics: No person shall drive any motor vehicle equipped with any television viewer, screen, or other means of visually receiving a television broadcast which is located in the motor vehicle at any point forward of the back of the driver's seat or which is visible to the driver while operating such motor vehicle.

Windshield Stickers: No person shall operate any motor vehicle upon any public street with a sign, poster, or sticker on the front windshield, the side windows immediately adjacent to the operator's seat and the front passenger seat, the side windows immediately to the rear of the operator's seat and the front passenger seat, and the rear window in such a manner so as to obstruct, impede, or distort the vision of the operator.

Motorcycles & Mopeds

Equipment: Every motorcycle must be equipped with either a split service brake system or 2 independently actuated service brake systems.

- Every motorcycle must be equipped with 1 white headlamp and 1 red rear lamp.
- Every motorcycle must be equipped with 1 rear stop lamp.
- Every motorcycle must be equipped with a registration plate illuminator.
- Every operator of or rider on a motorcycle must wear protective headgear and eye-goggles if motorcycle is not equipped with a windshield or screen.

- Motorcyclists are exempt from wearing protective headgear when participating in a parade.

Licenses: Class M: A motorcycle or any other motor vehicle having a seat or saddle for the rider and designed to travel with no more than 3 wheels in contact with the ground.

Noise Limits: A motorcycle may not exceed a noise limit of 82 decibels when measured at a speed of 45 mph or less.

- A motorcycle may not exceed a noise limit of 86 decibels when measured at a speed of over 45 mph.

Mopeds: A motorized bicycle shall not be operated on any public highway by any person under 16 years of age.

- A motorized bicycle shall not be operated upon any public highway at a speed of greater than 25 mph.
- A motorized bicycle shall not be operated on any public highway by any person not possessing a valid driver's license or learner's permit.
- Every person operating or riding as a passenger upon a motorized bicycle shall wear protective headgear.

Passenger Car Trailers

Brakes: Every trailer having an unladed weight of more than 10,000 lbs. shall be equipped with air or electric brakes.

Dimensions: Total length: 65 feet; trailer length: 40 feet; width: 102 inches (allows outside width to exceed 102 inches if due to an appurtenance and the state may exclude safety devices); height: 13.6 feet.

Hitch: Every trailer, except a semitrailer, shall, in addition to a regular hitch, be fastened by safety chains to prevent it from breaking away from the towing vehicle.

Lighting: Every trailer shall be equipped with 2 rear lights mounted 1 at each side of the rear of the vehicle so as to show 2 red lights from behind.

- Every trailer shall be equipped with a white light to illuminate and not obscure the rear registration plate.
- Every trailer shall be equipped with 2 stop lights.

Mirrors: Every motor vehicle, including trailers, shall be equipped with at least 1 mirror so placed and adjusted as to afford the operator a clear, reflected view of the highway to the rear and left side of the vehicle.

Speed Limits: Same as passenger cars.

Miscellaneous Provisions

Bail Bonds: Mandatory recognition of AAA arrest bond certificate up to $500, with specified exceptions.

Liability Laws: All drivers are required to have insurance policies of at least $20,000 for an individual's bodily injury; $40,000 for injury to multiple persons; and $5,000 for property damage.

- Compulsory liability insurance law requires at least $20,000/$40,000 limits of public

liability for death or injury, $5,000 for property damage. Policy must cover any person operating vehicle with owner's express or implied consent.
- State has non-resident service of process law.
- State has no-fault, personal injury insurance law. Sale and purchase mandatory. Benefits: medical, funeral, wage loss, and substitute service up to $8,000; wage loss limited to 75% of actual loss. General damages: recover if medical costs exceed $2,000 or in case of death, loss of all or part of body member, permanent and serious disfigurement, loss of sight or hearing, or a fracture.

Weigh Stations: The following vehicles must stop: (1) agricultural vehicles; (2) passenger or specialty vehicles, either single or in combination (towing a trailer) with GVWR of 10,000 lbs. or more; (3) commercial trucks with GVWR of 10,000 lbs. or more.

Fees & Taxes

Table 1: Title & Registration Fees

Vehicle Type	Title Fee	Registration Issuance and Renewal Fees
Motor Vehicle (B)	$50.00 + 5% sales tax	$30.00
Mobile Home (A)		$25.00
Trailers of 3,000 lbs. or less (A)	no title required	$12.00 per 1,000 lbs.; $15.00 minimum
Trailers of more than 3,000 lbs. (A)	$50.00 + 5% sales tax	$12.00 per 1,000 lbs.; $15.00 minimum
Motorcycles (A)	$50.00	$20.00; vanity $70.00
Mopeds up to 2 Years		$20.00
Duplicates	$25.00	$15.00

A = Annual; B = Biennial

Table 2: License Fees

License Class	Fee	Driving Test Fees	Out of State Conversion Fee	Renewal Fee
A (valid for 5 years)	$52.50	$20.00 road test fee	$87.50	$52.50
B (valid for 5 years)	$40.00	$20.00 road test fee	$75.00	$40.00
C (valid for 5 years)	$33.75	$20.00 road test fee	$68.75	$33.75
D (valid for 5 years)	$33.75	$20.00 road test fee	$68.75	$33.75
M (valid for 5 years)	$33.75	$20.00 road test fee	$68.75	$33.75
M Endorsement	$15.00	$20.00 road test fee	$15.00*	$15.00*
D Permit or Junior Driver's License (valid for 2 years)	$15.00			
Commercial Endorsements	$10.00			
Duplicate License	$15.00			

* Plus basic license fee.

Table 3: Vehicle Taxes

Tax	Rate
State Sales Tax	5% of value
Gasoline Tax; (Diesel)	$0.21/gallon; ($0.21/gallon); plus 2.5 cent UST fund tax
Excise Tax	$25.00 per $1,000 valuation based on percentage of vehicle's factory list price. Percentage used to calculate varies from 90%-10% based on year model of car.

MA

Table 4: Miscellaneous Fees

Fee	Amount	Payable Upon
Safety/Emissions Inspection	$29.00	inspection
Reinstatement Fee	$50.00-$1,000.00	upon reinstatement of license or registration
Special Plates Fee	$35.00-$80.00	issue/annual renewal
Plates Transfer Fee	$15.00	transfer
License Plate Replacement Fee	$10.00 per plate	replacement of plates
Excess Weight Permit	$50.00 per 1,000 lbs.	The time of application for registration. Available only at the Marlboro RMV Office

MICHIGAN

Contact Information

Department of State
Driver and Vehicle Records (MDOS)
7064 Crowner Drive
Lansing, MI 48918

(517) 322-1460
www.michigan.gov/sos

Department of State
Motor Vehicle Office
Treasury Building, 1st Floor
430 W. Allegan Street
Lansing, MI 48918-9900

(517) 334-8305
www.michigan.gov/sos

Michigan State Police
714 S. Harrison Road
East Lansing, MI 48823

(517) 332-2521
www.michigan.gov/msp

Michigan Department of Transportation
State Transportation Building
425 W. Ottawa Street
P.O. Box 30050
Lansing, MI 48909

(517) 373-2090
www.michigan.gov/mdot

Vehicle Title

Application: Every motor vehicle, pickup camper, trailer coach, trailer, semitrailer, and pole trailer, when driven or moved upon a highway, is subject to the registration and certificate of title.

- Applications are made to the Secretary of State, upon an appropriate form furnished by the Secretary of State and must include, among other things, the signature of the owner, a description of the vehicle, odometer miles, whether the vehicle has previously been issued a salvage or rebuilt certificate of title from this state or a comparable certificate of title from any other state or jurisdiction, and the names and addresses of the holders of security interests in the vehicle and in an accessory to the vehicle, in the order of their priority.

Transfer of Ownership: The certificate of title will contain a form for assignment of title or interest and warranty of title by the owner with space for the notation of a security interest in the vehicle, which at the time of a transfer must be certified and signed, and space for a written odometer mileage statement that is required upon transfer.

- A person cannot transfer the plates to a vehicle without applying for a proper certificate of registration describing the vehicle to which the plates are being transferred.
- Unless the transfer is made and the fee paid within 15 days, the vehicle is considered to be without registration, the Secretary of State may repossess the license plates, and transfer of the vehicle ownership may be effected and a valid registration acquired thereafter only upon payment of a transfer fee of $15 in addition to the title late fee of $15.
- The transferor must present to the transferee before delivery of the vehicle, a written disclosure of odometer mileage by means of the certificate of title or a written statement signed by the transferor.
- A dealer is required to apply to the Secretary of State for a new title and secure registration plates and certificate of title for the purchaser within 15 days after delivering the vehicle.

Vehicle Registration

Application: Applications are made to the Secretary of State, upon an appropriate form furnished by the Secretary of State.

- The Secretary of State will issue a registration certificate and a certificate of title when registering a vehicle and upon receipt of the required fees.
- The registration certificate is delivered to the owner and must contain on its face the date issued, the name and address of the owner, the registration number assigned to the vehicle, expiration date of plate, and a description of the vehicle as determined by the Secretary of State.
- A temporary registration may be issued to an owner of a vehicle. The registration shall be valid for 30 days or 60 days from date of issue and shall be in a form as determined by the Secretary of State.
- If a person, after making application for or obtaining the registration of a vehicle or a certificate of title, moves from the address named in the application, the person within 10 days after moving must notify the Secretary of State in writing of the old and new addresses.
- The Secretary of State will refuse issuance of a registration or a transfer of registration if the application contains a false or fraudulent statement, the applicant has failed to furnish required information or reasonable additional information requested by the Secretary of State, the applicant is not entitled to the registration of the vehicle under this act, or the applicant has not paid the required fees.

Non-Residents: Non-residents are permitted the operation of a vehicle within this state without registering the vehicle in, or paying any fees to, this state if the vehicle at all times is duly registered in, and displays upon it a valid registration certificate and registration plate or plates issued for the vehicle in the place of residence of the owner.

- A non-resident owner of a vehicle otherwise subject to registration may not operate the vehicle for a period exceeding 90 days without securing registration in this state. This applies to military personnel on active duty.
- Non-resident owners of vehicles used for transportation of persons and property

within the state must be registered and pay corresponding fees.
- MDOS may issue to the non-resident owner a temporary permit authorizing the operation of the foreign vehicle within this state for a period of 72 hours, without registering the vehicle, on the payment of a fee.

Registration Type: Registration must be carried at all times by the driver of the vehicle.
- A vehicle registration issued by the Secretary of State expires on the owner's birthday. If the owner's next birthday is at least 6 months but not more than 12 months in the future, the owner shall receive a registration valid until the owner's next birthday.
- The Secretary of State, upon request, may issue a vehicle registration for more than 1 year.
- The expiration date for a registration issued for a motorcycle is March 31. (Effective 2/1/05 will expire on owner's birthday.)

Safety Inspection: A police officer may stop and inspect any vehicle for suspected equipment and safety violations. Temporary vehicle check lanes may also be established.

License Plates

Disbursement: The Secretary of State shall issue to the owner 1 registration plate.
- The plate is required to be attached to the rear of the vehicle. The plate must be attached at a height of not less than 12 inches from the ground, measured from the bottom of the plate, in a place and position which is clearly visible.
- Special license plate or windshield placard disabled drivers is available upon application with doctor's statement to Secretary of State.

Transfer of Plates: Upon transfer of title, the registration plates issued for the vehicle must be removed, destroyed, or retained and preserved by the owner for transfer to another vehicle upon application and payment of the required fees.
- The registration plate may be transferred to another vehicle upon proper application and payment of a transfer fee.
- A person cannot transfer the plates to a vehicle without applying for a proper certificate of registration describing the vehicle to which the plates are being transferred.

Driver's Licenses

Examination: Vision screening (20/40 visual acuity) and knowledge tests are required to obtain a Level 1 graduated license. If the applicant is age 18 or older, he or she must pass a vision screening and knowledge test to obtain a Temporary Instruction Permit (TIP).
- Teens in the graduated licensing program will take the knowledge test as part of segment 1 of driver education. Knowledge tests will be administered by the Department of State.
- An original license examination without a vehicle group designation or endorsement must include a behind-the-wheel road test.
- Vision screenings are required with each renewal.
- The Secretary of State may waive the requirement of a behind-the-wheel road test, knowledge test, or road sign test of an applicant for an original operator's or chauffeur's license without a vehicle group designation or endorsement who at the time

of the application is the holder of a valid, unrevoked operator's or chauffeur's license issued by another state or country.
- The results of a knowledge test for an original group designation or endorsement shall be valid for 12 months.

Graduated Drivers Licensing: State has a system of graduated licensing for teen drivers.
- At 14 and 9 months, teens who have completed the first segment of driver education, including 6 hours of on-the-road driving with an instructor, and pass a vision test and health standards are eligible for a learner's license/permit.
- At 16, teens who have (1) held the permit for at least 6 months; (2) accumulated 50 hours (10 at night) of parental/guardian certified driving; (3) completed segment 2 of driver education; (4) no convictions/civil infractions, license suspensions, or crashes during the 90-day period immediately prior to applying for an intermediate license; and (5) passed a road test are eligible for an intermediate license.
- Intermediate license holders are prohibited from driving unsupervised between the hours of midnight and 5:00 a.m. unless driving to and from employment.
- At 17, teens who have held an intermediate license for at least 6 months and completed 12 consecutive months of driving without a moving violation, an at-fault crash (even if no citation is issued), a license suspension, or a violation of the graduated license restrictions are eligible for an unrestricted license.
- Throughout graduated licensing program, parents receive a separate notice of traffic offenses from the Department of State.

Issuance/Application: The application must include the applicant's full name, date of birth, residence address, height, sex, eye color, signature, photo, and, to the extent required to comply with federal law, the applicant's social security number.
- A license may not be issued to a person under 18 years of age unless that person successfully passes a driver education course and examination given by a public school, nonpublic school, or an equivalent course approved by the Department of State given by a licensed driver training school.
- A license may not be issued to anyone over 18 years of age who has not held a temporary instruction permit for at least 30 days.
- A student while enrolled in an approved driver education program and who has successfully completed 10 hours of classroom instruction and the equivalent of 2 hours of behind-the-wheel training may be issued a temporary driver education certificate furnished by the Department of State that authorizes a student to drive a motor vehicle when accompanied by a licensed parent or guardian. If the person is over the age of 18, any licensed adult driver may accompany them.
- The Secretary of State may issue an original operator's license and designate level 1, 2, or 3 graduated licensing provisions to a person who is less than 18 years of age and has been licensed in another state or country.
- The licensee shall have his or her operator's or chauffeur's license, in his or her immediate possession at all times when operating a motor vehicle.
- License includes color photograph. Does not include social security number.
- License must include medical information, including blood type, immunization data, hearing ability, medication data, and donor status.
- License may also include a digitized code for voter information.

Renewal: A driver's license expires on the birthday of the driver on the 4th year follow-

ing issuance unless suspended or revoked.
- A first operator's license will expire on the driver's 21st birthday. Under 21 licenses are clearly marked.
- A person holding a license at any time within 45 days before the expiration of his or her license may make application for a new license. However, if the licensee will be out of the state during the 45 days immediately preceding expiration of the license or for other good cause shown cannot apply for a license within the 45-day period, application for a new license may be made not more than 6 months before expiration of the license.
- A person who will be out-of-state for more than 90 days beyond the expiration date of his or her operator's license may apply for a 2-year extension of his or her driving privileges.
- A member of the U.S. armed forces, while on active duty, may use an expired Michigan driver's license in conjunction with his/her military papers for a period not to exceed:
  - 30 days from the person's first leave of absence following the expiration of his/her license (the leave does not have to be to Michigan; this refers to any leave of absence), or
  - 30 days from the date of the person's discharge following the expiration of his/her license.
- Spouses and dependents of active military personnel are not granted the same extension allowed for military personnel. A spouse or dependent's driver's license expires on his/her birthday in the expiration year. The license may be renewed through the mail.

Types of Licenses: A chauffeur's license must be obtained to drive any size motor vehicle used as a common or contract carrier of persons or property, or if the applicant is employed for the principal purpose of driving a motor vehicle with a Gross Vehicle Weight Rating (GVWR) of 10,000 lbs. or more.
- Motorcycle endorsements are separate and distinct for 3-wheeled and 2-wheeled vehicle operating privileges.
- Group A licenses authorize holders to drive a vehicle with a GVWR over 10,000 lbs.
- Group B licenses authorize holders to drive a vehicle with a GVWR of 26,001 lbs. and over.
- Group C licenses authorize holders to drive a vehicle designed to transport 16 or more passengers.
- Group N licenses authorize holders to drive a tank vehicle.
- Group H licenses authorize holders to drive a commercial motor vehicle carrying hazardous materials.
- Group P licenses authorize holders to drive school buses.
- Group F licenses authorize holders to drive a vehicle with a GVWR more than 26,001 lbs. and operated near a farm.
- Group R licenses authorize holders to drive a pick-up truck equipped with a fifth-wheel assembly with an attached semitrailer designed for recreational living purposes or towing an additional trailer.
- Group S licenses authorize holders to drive a school bus with students aboard.

Traffic Rules

Alcohol Laws: Any person who operates a vehicle upon a public highway is considered to have given implied consent to chemical tests of his or her blood, breath, or urine

for determining their blood/alcohol level.
- Open containers are not permitted. Meets TEA-21 requirements.
- Illegal per se BAC level is .08.
- BAC level for people under 21 is .02.
- BAC level for commercial drivers is .04.

Emergency Radio/Cellular: In some areas citizen band radio channel 9 is monitored for emergency calls. Emergency number is 911.

Headsets: Wearing radio headsets while driving is permitted.

Occupant Restraints: Each driver and front seat passenger of a motor vehicle operated on a street or highway in this state must wear a properly adjusted and fastened safety belt.
- Each driver transporting a child less than 4 years of age in a motor vehicle must properly secure that child in a child restraint system.
- Children aged 4 through 15 must wear a seat belt or be in an approved restraint system.
- Violation of the occupant protection laws is a primary offense.
- A person less than 18 years of age may not ride in the open bed of a pick-up truck on a highway, road, or street in a city, village, or township at a speed greater than 15 mph. Additional gaps in coverage apply; see Occupant Protection Chart.

Railroad Crossing: Vehicles must stop between 15 and 50 feet from the nearest rail when a signal indicates the approach of a train or if a train is clearly visible.
- All motor vehicles carrying passengers for hire or hazardous material must stop before crossing.

School Buses: All vehicles must stop not less than 20 feet from a stopped school bus displaying alternately flashing red lights and may not proceed until the school bus has resumed motion or the visual signals are no longer actuated.

Vehicle Equipment & Rules

Bumper Height: A passenger car shall not have a frame height that exceeds 12 inches or a bumper height that exceeds 22 inches. A pickup truck or sport utility vehicle (such as Bronco, Jeep, Explorer, etc.) cannot exceed the following: up to 4,500 GVWR – – 24 inch frame height, 26 inch bumper height; 4,501 to 7,500 GVWR – 24 inch frame height, 28 inch bumper height; 7,501 to 10,000 GVWR – 26 inch frame height, 30 inch bumper height.
- All trucks or sport utility vehicles having an increased suspension must be equipped with a bumper on both the front and rear of the vehicle.

Glass/Tinting: No window application may be used on the front windshield, unless accompanied by a letter from a certified physician stating a medical necessity of the motor vehicle driver.
- A tinted film, however, may be applied no more than 4 inches from the top of the windshield and front side windows.
- Rear and rear side window tinting is allowed.

Telematics: Televisions viewable by drivers are prohibited in motor vehicles.

Windshield Stickers: Prohibited if they interfere with vision.

MI

Motorcycles & Mopeds

Equipment: A motorcycle must be equipped with adequate seats and foot rests or pegs for each designated seating position.

- Handlebars may not be higher than 15 inches from the lowest point of the undepressed saddle to the highest point of the handle grip of the operator.
- A person operating or riding on a motorcycle on a public thoroughfare shall wear a U.S. DOT approved crash helmet.

Licenses: A person, before operating a motorcycle upon a public street or highway in this state, must procure a motorcycle endorsement on the operator's or chauffeur's license.

- Before a person who is less than 18 years of age is issued an original motorcycle endorsement on an operator's or chauffeur's license, the person must pass an examination and a motorcycle safety course.

Noise Limits: At a distance of 50 feet, the noise limit is 86 decibels if the maximum lawful speed on the highway or street is greater than 35 mph and 82 decibels if the maximum lawful speed on the highway or street is not more than 35 mph. There can be no excessive or unusual noise.

Mopeds: Mopeds must be registered but need not be insured.

- A moped registration shall be valid for a 3-year period that begins on May 1 and expires on April 30 of the third registration year.
- A moped or a low-speed vehicle must have permanently affixed to its frame a manufacturer's identification number and registration decal.
- A person, before operating a moped upon a highway, must procure a special restricted license to operate a moped unless the person has a valid operator's or chauffeur's license. A special restricted license to operate a moped may be issued to a person 15 years of age or older if the person satisfies the Secretary of State that he is competent to operate a moped with safety.
- A crash helmet is required for all operators under age 19.
- A moped or low-speed vehicle cannot be operated on a sidewalk constructed for the use of pedestrians.
- A low-speed vehicle must be operated at a speed of not to exceed 25 mph and cannot be operated on a highway, road, or street with a speed limit of more than 35 mph except for the purpose of crossing that highway, road, or street.
- Every moped must be equipped with a head lamp.
- A moped shall not be used to carry more than 1 person at a time.

Passenger Car Trailers

Registration: Registration plates are issued for permanent, non-expiring plates based on the unit's weight as of 10/1/03. New registrations are permanent and do not expire.

Brakes: Independent braking system required when gross weight exceeds 3,000 lbs.

Dimensions: Total length: 65 feet; trailer length: 45 feet; width: 102 inches (allows outside width to exceed 102 inches due to an appurtenance); height: 12.6 feet.

Hitch: The hitch cannot exceed 15 feet in length from 1 vehicle to the other and may not allow either vehicle to deviate more than 3 inches from the other.

- If the connection consists of a chain, rope, or cable, there shall be displayed upon the connection a red flag or other signal or cloth not less than 12 inches both in length and width.

Lighting: All trailers must be equipped with at least 1 rear lamp mounted on the rear that emits a red light plainly visible from a distance of 500 feet to the rear.

- The rear registration plate must be illuminated with white light so as to be visible from a distance of 50 feet to the rear.
- Also required: on the front, 2 clearance lamps, 1 at each side; on each side, 2 side marker lamps, 1 at or near the front and 1 at or near the rear; on each side, 2 reflectors, 1 at or near the front and 1 at or near the rear; and on the rear, 2 clearance lamps, 1 at each side, also 2 reflectors, 1 at each side, and 1 stop light.

Mirrors: Required.

Speed Limits: A person driving a passenger vehicle pulling another vehicle or trailer shall not exceed a speed of 55 mph, unless the vehicle or trailer has 2 wheels or less and weight under 750 lbs. for the vehicle or trailer and load, or the vehicle or trailer is a trailer coach of not more than 26 feet in length with brakes on each wheel and attached to the passenger vehicle with an equalizing or stabilizing coupling unit.

Miscellaneous Provisions

Bail Bonds: State has mandatory recognition of AAA arrest bond certificates up to $1,000 with specified exceptions.

Liability Laws: State has no-fault insurance law. Sale and purchase are mandatory. Motorist must show proof of insurance at request of law enforcement officer. Benefits: medical and hospital, unlimited; funeral up to $2,500; wage loss $4,070 per month for maximum of 36 months; replacement services $20/day payable to victim or survivor. General damages: cannot recover from an insured motorist unless injuries result in death, serious impairment of body function, permanent serious disfigurement. The benefits available to non-residents may depend on whether insurer of non-resident vehicle has filed certificate of no-fault protection. Insurance is compulsory for non-resident vehicle if in state for an aggregate of more than 30 days in any calendar year.

- Minimum insurance requirements are $20,000 for bodily injury to or death of 1 person in any 1 accident; $40,000 for bodily injury to or death of 2 or more persons in any 1 accident; and $10,000 for injury to or destruction of property of others in any 1 accident.
- Proof of financial responsibility must be furnished by filing with the Secretary of State a written certificate of any insurance carrier duly authorized to do business in this state, certifying that there is in effect a motor vehicle liability policy for the benefit of the registration applicant.

Weigh Stations: The following vehicles must stop: (1) vehicles with dual rear wheels transporting agricultural products; (2) trucks over 10,000 lbs. with dual rear wheels and/or towing construction equipment; (3) all tractor/semitrailer combination vehicles.

MI

Fees & Taxes

Table 1: Title & Registration Fees

Vehicle Type	Title Fee*	Registration Fee*
Motor Vehicle	$15.00	If vehicle model is earlier than 1983, depends on weight. If vehicle model is 1983 or later depends on the list price of the vehicle. Range is from $33.00-$148.00 for vehicles priced from $0 - $30,000 for first registration. Registration fee declines by 10% each year until the fifth renewal. $8.00 (transfer fee)
Mobile Home	$45.00	
Trailer Coaches	$15.00	$75.00 (0-2,499 lbs.) $200.00 (2,500-9,999 lbs.) $300.00 (greater than 10,000 lbs.)
Motorcycles	$10.50	$23.00 per year
Mopeds		$15.00 for 3 years

*Some fees provided by the Michigan State Motor Vehicle Office

Table 2: License Fees

License Class	Fee
Operator's License (Graduated License Level 2 and 3)	$25.00 (renewal $18.00)
Chauffeur's License	$35.00 (renewal $35.00)
A	$25.00(original endorsement) + $5.00 per endorsement
B	$25.00(original endorsement) + $5.00 per endorsement
C	$25.00(original endorsement) + $5.00 per endorsement
F	$20.00(original endorsement) + $5.00 per endorsement
N	$20.00(original endorsement) + $5.00 per endorsement
H	$20.00(original endorsement) + $5.00 per endorsement
P	$20.00(original endorsement) + $5.00 per endorsement
R	$10.00 + $5.00 per endorsement
Learner's Permit (Graduated License Level 1)	No charge
Duplicate Fee	$18.00 (chauffeur's) $9.00 (operators)
Motorcycle Endorsement	$13.50/$7.00 additional $5.00 renewal
Moped License	$7.50 additional $6.00 renewal

Table 3: Vehicle Taxes

Tax	Rate
Gasoline Tax; (Diesel)	$0.19/gallon; ($0.15/gallon)
State Sales Tax	6%

Table 4: Miscellaneous Fees

Fee	Amount	Payable
Special Plates Fee	$30.00-$35.00 Personal	
License Plates Transfer Fee	$8.00	Registration
Duplicate Fee		$5.00

MI

MINNESOTA

Contact Information

Driver and Vehicle Services Division
Department of Public Safety
445 Minnesota Street, Suite 195
St. Paul, MN 55101-2156

(651) 296-6911
www.dps.state.mn.us/dvs/

Minnesota State Patrol
444 Cedar Street, Suite 130
St. Paul, MN 55101-2156

(651) 282-6871
www.dps.state.mn.us/patrol/

Minnesota Department of Transportation
Transportation Building
395 John Ireland Boulevard
St. Paul, MN 55155

(651) 296-3000
www.dot.state.mn.us/

Vehicle Title

Application: The Department upon registration of the vehicle issues the certificate of title.

- The application for certificate of title must be made on a form provided by the Department.
- The application must contain the name, date of birth, and address of all owners, a description of the vehicle including the type of make, vehicle model, vehicle year, vehicle identification number, vehicle body type, the date of purchase of the vehicle, the names and addresses of any secured parties, the mileage on the vehicle, any sustained vehicle damage, and any other information that the Department may request.
- If the application refers to a vehicle purchased from a dealer it must contain the name and address of any secured party holding a security interest at the time of sale.
- If the application refers to a new vehicle it must be accompanied by a manufacturer's certificate of origin.
- If the vehicle was previously registered out of state, the application must be accompanied by any certificate of title issued by the other state, any other information the Department reasonably requires to establish ownership, or certification by a person from the Department that the identifying number of the vehicle was inspected and found to conform to the description given in the application.

Transfer of Ownership: An effective transfer of title requires the owner to do the following: (1) execute an assignment and warranty of title to the transferee; (2) state the actual selling price of the vehicle in the space provided on the certificate; (3) complete, detach, and return to the Department the postcard on the certificate entitled notice of sale or transmit this information to the Department through e-mail.

- To receive a new certificate, the transferee must fill out and execute the application for a new certificate of title and mail it to the Department within 10 days of the transfer.

- If a security interest is reserved or created at the time of transfer, a notification of the security interest must be delivered or mailed to the person who becomes the secured party.

Vehicle Registration

Application: Application for an original or renewal registration and listing for taxation is made to the Department on a form provided by the Department.

- The application requests the following information from the vehicle's owner(s): (1) full name; (2) birthday; (3) the address of the primary residence of each owner; (4) the name and address of the person that sold the vehicle; (5) the make and year of the motor vehicle; (6) the manufacturer's identification number; (7) body type; (8) the weight of the vehicle in pounds; (9) for trailer only, its rated load carrying capacity; and (10) any such other information that the Department may require.
- Registration will be refused if the original identification or serial number has been destroyed, removed, altered, covered, or defaced unless the owner can prove in a manner sufficient to the Department that he or she is the owner.
- The motor vehicle of any military person who is on active duty is exempt during the active duty time period, and for 40 days after active duty ends.
- The motor vehicle of any disabled veteran that was furnished to the veteran by the government will be exempt from the vehicle registration tax.

Non-Residents: A non-resident buyer of a motor vehicle in Minnesota can obtain a 31-day temporary vehicle permit. The vehicle owner does not have to pay any registration taxes.

- Non-residents can register vehicles by submitting the vehicle title or registration card from the previous state in which the car was registered along with the registration and license tax form.
- Also, the following documents must be submitted with the application: (1) a valid driver's license; (2) an insurance card with policy number; and (3) the odometer reading on the vehicle.
- Military personnel on active duty in Minnesota may maintain out-of-state vehicle registration if they maintain primary residence in Minnesota.

Safety Inspection: The state does not require vehicle safety inspections, but every municipality has the authority to set up, maintain, and determine the rules for operating vehicle inspection stations.

License Plates

Disbursement: When the applicant pays the registration tax, the Department will issue the license plate bearing the state name and vehicle number assigned.

- Single plates for rear display are issued to trailers, motorcycle/mopeds, dealers in transit, collector classes, and all vehicles 20 years or older.
- Single plates for display on the front of the vehicle are issued to tractors and truck-tractors, tractor-trailer combinations, and farm class vehicles 20 years or older.
- All other classes are required to display registration and will be issued 2 license plates to be displayed on the front and rear of the vehicle.
- Special license plates for the disabled are available upon application with doctor's certificate.

Transfer of Plates: When a motor vehicle is transferred to another person, the transferor must surrender the plates to the Department and assign the paid pro-rated registration tax to the transferee.

- The license plate must be surrendered to the Department within 10 days of the transfer.
- There is a $2 fee for failure to deliver a title transfer within 10 days.
- When the Department has suspended a license plate because the transferee has failed to file the title certificate within 30 days, the transferee must pay a $10 fee before the registration is reinstated.

Driver's Licenses

Examination: Every applicant for a driver's license must include a test of the applicant's eyesight (20/40 visual acuity required), ability to read and understand highway signs, traffic laws, knowledge of the effects of drugs and alcohol while driving, knowledge of a driver's ability to safely and legally operate a motor vehicle, and an actual demonstration of the driver's ability to exercise ordinary and reasonable care while driving the vehicle. The examination can also include anything else that the Department deems necessary.

- The examination will be given either in the county where the applicant resides or at a place (next to the county that is reasonably convenient to the applicant).
- If the applicant has a valid driver's license from a jurisdiction that gives a comparable driving examination, the Department can waive the requirement that the applicant demonstrate the ability to exercise ordinary and reasonable control in the operation of a motor vehicle.
- A driver's license can be renewed when the applicant has passed an eye examination.
- The Department may require any examination to determine the incompetence, physical or mental disability or disease of any licensed driver, or any conditions which would affect the driver from exercising reasonable and ordinary control over the motor vehicle. If, as a result of the examination, the Department believes that the driver is an unsafe person to operate a motor vehicle, the Department may cancel the driver's license.
- No examination shall be required only for the reason that any licensed driver has attained a certain age.

Graduated Drivers Licensing: State has a system of graduated licensing for teen drivers.

- An instruction/learner's permit can be issued to an applicant who is 15 years old or older if that person meets the following requirements: (1) has completed a driver's education course in another state, has previously been issued a valid license from another state, or is enrolled in either a certified public, private, or commercial driver education program; and (2) has completed the classroom phase of instruction in the driver education program and has passed an eye examination, has passed a Department-administered test of the applicant's knowledge, has completed the required application, and has paid the application fees. This instruction permit must be kept for 3 months before the applicant can apply for a license.
- An applicant who is 15, 16, or 17 years old who is issued an instruction/learner's permit must keep the permit for 6 months before applying for a driver's license.

This permit enables a person to operate a motor vehicle, but the applicant must be accompanied by a certified driver education instructor, the permit holder's parent or guardian, or another licensed driver over 21 years of age. The adult licensed driver must be sitting in the passenger seat next to the permit holder. Instruction permit holders must accumulate at least 40 hours (10 at night) of parental/guardian certified driving before being eligible for an unrestricted license.

- Permit holders are prohibited from using a cell phone while driving.
- A person under 18 years of age can only qualify for a driver's license under 1 of the following conditions: (1) the applicant has a valid license from another state; or (2) the applicant has held a provisional license for 12 consecutive months before the license application and has incurred no conviction for a crash-related moving violation, and not more than 1 conviction for a moving violation that is not crash-related; and (3) the application is approved by a parent or guardian.

Issuance/Application: Every application for an instruction permit, for a provisional license, or for a driver's license must be made on a form prescribed by the Department, and every application must be accompanied by the appropriate fee.

- First-time Minnesota applicants must present a primary and a secondary form of identification to verify both identity and residency status.
- Visitors who are in the U.S. as temporary residents will have the words "Status Check" and a visa expiration date on their state-issued cards. Proof of extended authorization to remain in the country will be required when the authorization date indicated on a card expires. Immigrants granted permanent or indefinite residency will not have a status check designation appear on their state-issued cards.
- Social security numbers are not displayed on licenses.
- License includes a color photograph. All applicants must have a full-face photograph taken, with the head and face unobscured, as part of the identification process. This does not require the complete removal of headwear worn for religious or medical reasons. However, individuals are required to pull headwear back far enough so as not to obscure the face and provide the shape of the head.
- Out-of-state driver's licenses are viewed as secondary identification documents.
- An applicant 18 years of age or older who received an instruction permit, and has not been previously licensed to drive in Minnesota or any other jurisdiction, must possess the instruction permit for at least 6 months.
- Any valid driver's license issued to a person on active duty with the armed forces, or the person's spouse, is effective without requirement for renewal until 90 days after the date of the person's discharge from the service.
- Authorizes the Commissioner of Public Safety to waive the road test for licensed military personnel when a license is issued by another jurisdiction that requires a comparable demonstration for license issuance.

Renewal: The license expiration date for drivers under the age of 21 is the 21st birthday of the licensee.

- The license expiration date for drivers over the age of 21 is the birthday of the driver in the 4th year following the date of issuance of the license.

Types of Licenses: There are 4 classes of driver's licenses: D, C, B, and A.

- A Class D license holder can drive the following vehicles: (1) all farm trucks operated by the owner, an immediate family member of the owner, or an employee of the owner; (2) a fire truck, operated by an on-duty firefighter; (3) recreational equipment that is operated for personal use; (4) all single vehicles except vehicles with a Gross Vehicle Weight (GVW) of more than 26,000 lbs., vehicles designed to carry more than 15 passengers including the driver, and vehicles that carry hazardous materials. The holder of a Class D license may also tow vehicles if the combination of vehicles has a GVW of 26,000 lbs. or less.

- A Class C license holder can drive the following vehicles: (1) all Class D vehicles; (2) vehicles with a hazardous material endorsement, transporting materials in Class D vehicles; and (3) with a school bus endorsement, a school bus designed to transport 15 or fewer passengers including the driver.
- A Class B license holder can drive the following vehicles: (1) all Class D and C vehicles; (2) all other single-unit vehicles including, with any passenger endorsement, buses; and (3) can tow vehicles with a GVW of 10,000 lbs. or less.
- A Class A license holder can drive any vehicle or combination of vehicles.

Traffic Rules

Alcohol Laws: Operation of a motor vehicle gives implied consent to a test of blood, breath, urine, or other bodily substance for determining blood-alcohol content.

- Open containers are not permitted. Meets the requirements of TEA-21.
- Illegal per se BAC level is .08.
- If you are under 21, it is illegal for you to operate a motor vehicle when you have consumed any amount of alcohol. BAC level for people under 21 is .00.

Headsets: The operator of a motor vehicle must not use headphones or earphones, which are used in both ears simultaneously for the purposes of receiving or listening to broadcasts or reproductions from radios, tapedecks, or other sound-producing or transmitting devices. This does not prohibit the use of hearing aid devices.

Occupant Restraints: Restraints are mandatory for drivers and front seat passengers and all passengers under the age of 11 riding in any seat. Children under the age of 4 must not be transported in a motor vehicle without being secured by a child passenger restraint system.

- Violation of the seat belt law is a secondary offense, however violation of the child restraint law is a primary offense.
- Riding in the bed of a pickup truck is permitted.

Railroad Crossing: When a stop sign has been erected at a railroad crossing, the driver of a vehicle approaching a railroad crossing must stop between 10 and 50 feet from the nearest track of the crossing and can only proceed upon exercising due care and when the roadway is clear of traffic so that the vehicle can proceed without stopping until the rear of the vehicle is at least ten feet past the farthest railroad track.

- When any person driving a vehicle approaches a railroad grade crossing, the driver must stop at least 10 feet away from the nearest railroad track if a clearly visible electric or mechanical signal device warns of the immediate approach of the railroad train, or an approaching train is visible and is in a hazardous proximity.

School Buses: When a school bus is stopped on any roadway and is displaying an extended stop signal arm and flashing red lights, the driver of a vehicle approaching the bus must stop the vehicle at least 20 feet away from the bus. The driver of the vehicle must not move until the school bus stop signal arm is retracted and the red lights are no longer flashing.

Vehicle Equipment & Rules

Bumper Height: The maximum bumper height (measured from the bottom of the bumper to the ground) for any passenger automobile or station wagon is 20 inches.
- The maximum bumper height of any 4-wheel drive multipurpose vehicle, van, or pickup truck is 25 inches.

Glass/Window Tinting: It is illegal to drive or operate a vehicle when any window on the vehicle is composed of, covered by, or treated with any material which has the following effects: (1) making the windshield more reflective or in any way reducing light transmittance through the windshield; (2) making the windshield have a highly reflective or mirrored appearance; (3) making any side or rear window substantially reduce the driver's clear view through the window by having a light transmission of less than 50% in the visible light range or a luminous reflectance of more than 20%. This does not apply to the following: (1) glazing material which has not been modified since the original installation, or the original replacement windows and windshields that were replaced in conformance with Federal Motor Vehicle Safety Standard 205; (2) windows tinted for medical reasons provided that the driver or passenger of the vehicle is in possession of a prescription or a physician's statement of medical need; and (3) the rear windows of a pickup truck, the rear windows or the side windows on either side behind the driver's seat of a van, the rear and side windows of any vehicle used to transport human remains by a funeral establishment holding a license, and the side and rear windows of a limousine.

Telematics: It is unlawful to drive a motor vehicle equipped with a television, or television-type equipment if the television or television equipment is located where the screen is visible to the driver.
- It is legal to use a screen visible to the driver if the screen is part of a vehicle navigational system or vehicle control system.
- It is legal to have a closed circuit video system used only to help the driver's rear or side visibility.

Windshield Stickers: The only stickers that can be placed on a windshield are transparent stickers or stickers required to be placed on the windshield by law, or authorized by the state director of emergency management, or the commissioner of public safety.

Motorcycles & Mopeds

Equipment: No person can operate a motorcycle if the handlebars extend above the shoulders of the operator while he or she is seated with both feet on the ground.
- An operator of a motorcycle must ride on a permanent and regular seat.
- Any motorcycle with a seat designed or suited for use by a passenger must be equipped with foot rests for the passenger, reachable by both feet.
- A motorcycle operator must not carry more passengers than there are designated seats for those passengers.
- Every motorcycle must be equipped with at least 1 properly adjusted rear view mirror that is adjusted to reflect to the operator a view of the roadway for a distance of at least 200 feet.
- Anyone under the age of 18 operating a motorcycle, all drivers in the first year of licensure, or with instructional permits must wear protective headgear.

MN

- All motorcycle operators must wear protective eye wear.
- Every motorcycle must be equipped with at least 1 hand or foot brake.
- Every motorcycle must be equipped with at least 1 and not more than 2 properly mounted headlamps.

Licenses: A person operating a motorcycle upon a roadway must be granted the rights and is subject to the duties applicable to a motor vehicle as provided by law.

- No person can operate a motorcycle or motor scooter on any street or highway without having a valid standard driver's license with a 2-wheeled endorsement.
- A 2-wheeled endorsement will be issued if the applicant has a valid 2-wheeled vehicle instruction permit and has passed a written examination and road test administered by the Department.
- If the applicant is under 18 years of age, has a valid driver's license, and presents the Department with evidence of successfully completing an approved 2-wheeled vehicle driver safety course, the Department can waive the road test.
- The Department can issue a 2-wheeled vehicle instruction permit to any person over 16 years of age who is in possession of a valid driver's license, is enrolled in an approved 2-wheeled vehicle driver's safety course, has passed a written examination for the permit, and has paid all necessary fees.
- A person who has an operator's permit cannot carry any passengers while operating the motorcycle, cannot drive the motorcycle at night, and cannot drive the motorcycle on any interstate highway.

Noise Limits: It is unlawful to operate a motorcycle in violation of the motor vehicle noise rules adopted by the pollution control agency.

Passenger Car Trailers

Brakes: A trailer or a semitrailer with a gross weight of 3,000 lbs. or more, or a gross weight that exceeds the empty weight of the towing vehicle, must be equipped with brakes that can adequately control the movement of and stop and hold the trailer or semitrailer.

- A trailer or semitrailer with a gross weight of 6,000 lbs. or more, must be equipped with brakes that are constructed so that they can hold the trailer or semitrailer if it becomes detached from the towing vehicle.

Dimensions: Total length: 60 feet; trailer length: 45 feet; width: 102 inches (excludes mirrors and safety devices); height: 13.6 feet.

Hitch: The drawbar or other connection between the 2 vehicles must not be more than 15 feet.

Lighting: Every trailer or semitrailer manufactured after January 1, 1960 must be equipped with at least 2 properly mounted rear headlamps, and at least 2 reflectors. The rear headlamps must emit a red light for a distance of 500 feet. The reflectors must be mounted between 20 and 60 inches from the ground and must be visible from all distances within 300 to 50 feet from the vehicle.

- Trailers or semitrailer manufactured before January 1, 1960 must be equipped with at least 1 properly mounted rear headlamp.

MN

Mirrors: Every motor vehicle, which is connected with another vehicle so that it obstructs the driver's rear view, must be equipped with a rearview mirror that enables the driver to see for a distance of at least 200 feet to the rear of the last vehicle being towed.

Miscellaneous Provisions

Bail Bonds: State has general recognition of AAA club arrest bond certificate up to $500 with specified exceptions.

Liability Laws: State has compulsory/mandatory liability and no-fault insurance proof. State has non-resident service of process law; does not have guest suit law.

- Every driver and every owner of a motor vehicle must carry evidence of financial responsibility in his or her motor vehicle at all times and be ready to present such evidence at the demand of a police officer.
- Minimum liability insurance coverage must be at least $30,000 for bodily injury or death of each person as a result of any 1 accident, $60,000 as a result of injury to 2 or more persons in any 1 accident, and $10,000 if the accident has resulted in injury to or destruction of property, or $70,000 single.

Weigh Stations: All vehicles with a GVW rating in excess of 10,000 lbs. must stop.

Fees & Taxes

Table 1: Title Fees

Fee	Amount	Payable Upon
Initial Title	$4.00	Request
Duplicate Title	$4.00	Request
Corrected Title/Name Change	$2.00	Request
Title Transfer Fee	$2.00	Due with each assignment of a Minnesota title
State Patrol Vehicle Title Transfer Fee	$3.50	Due on initial application for title, transfers, and repossessions where title is being issued.
Motorcycle	$2.00	Request

Table 2: License Fees

License Class	Fee
Class A Regular	$37.50
Class A, Under Age 21	$17.50
Class B, Regular or Under Age 21	$29.50
Class C, Regular or Under 21	$22.50
School Bus Processing Fee–Original and Renewal Applications	$4.00
Class D, Regular or Under Age 21	$18.50
Provisional Driver's License	$9.50
Class D Provisional License Upgrade to Under 21 DL – No Violations on Record ($3.50 credit)	$15.00
Duplicate Driver's License/Identification Card – All Classes	$8.00
Class D Instruction Permit	$9.50
Class A, B, or C Instruction Permit	no fee
Endorsement Examination Fees	$2.50
Motorcycle Instruction Permit/Endorsement Fee	$21.00
Motorcycle Endorsement Renewal (2-wheel only)	$13.00
Standby or Temporary Custodian Designation	$3.50
Revoked License Reinstatement Fees for Alcohol/Drugs	$290.00
Revoked License Fees for Other Offenses	$30.00
Suspended License Fee	$20.00
Motorized Bicycle Operator Permit Knowledge Test and 30-Day Instruction Permit	$6.00
Motorized Bicycle Operator Permit Skill Test and 1 Year Operator's Permit	$6.00
Motorized Bicycle Operator Permit Duplicate of 1 Year Operator's Permit	$3.00
Motorized Bicycle Operator Permit Renewal of 1 Year Permit to Age 21	$9.00
Motorized Bicycle Operator Permit Duplicate of Renewal Permit	$4.50
Motorized Bicycle Operator Permit Renewal, Age 21 or Older	$15.00

Table 3: Vehicle Taxes

Tax	Rate
State Tax for Registered Collector Vehicles	$10.00 regardless of actual purchase price
State Sales Tax	6.5% based on purchase price or fair market value, whichever is higher
Gasoline Tax; (Diesel)	$0.20/gallon; ($0.20/gallon)
In Lieu Tax	$10.00 collected on passenger vehicles 10 years old and older - The purchase price must be under $3,000 and the vehicle cannot be an above market vehicle
Transfer Tax	$4.00 (Exceptions to this tax are motorcycles, 1,500-3,000 lb. utility trailers, vehicles less than 1,000 lbs. GVW, manufactured homes, transfers to dealers, leasing companies, and government agencies)
Registration Annual Ad Valorem Tax	Registration tax system for passenger class vehicles. This means that the tax is determined in part upon the base value of the vehicle as provided by the manufacturer when the vehicle was new, and the age of the vehicle. The first registration renewal of a vehicle will cost no more than $189.00. The second and subsequent renewals will have a cap of $99.00. One can determine the passenger registration tax by going to www.dps.state.mn.us/dv/MotorVehicle/byMakeYearHTML
Bus, Second Class City (2c) Registration Annual Ad Valorem Tax	$2.00
Bus, Private School (SB) Registration Annual Ad Valorem Tax	$26.00
Moped, Registration Annual Ad Valorem Tax	$6.00
Motorcycle Registration Annual Ad Valorem Tax	$10.00
SemiTrailer (ST) Registration Annual Ad Valorem Tax	no registration tax
Classic Car Registration Annual Ad Valorem Tax	$25.00
Collector Car Registration Annual Ad Valorem Tax	$25.00
Street Rod Registration Annual Ad Valorem Tax	$25.00
Pioneer Registration Annual Ad Valorem Tax	$25.00
Classic Motorcycle Registration Annual Ad Valorem Tax	$10.00
Trailer from 0 – 1,500 lbs.	initial registration $7.50
Trailer from 1,500 – 3,000 lbs.	initial registration $9.00

Table 4: Miscellaneous Fees

Fee	Amount	Payable Upon
Grant of Security Interest	$2.00	Request
Release of Security Interest	No Fee	Request
Assignment of Security Interest	$1.00	Request
Repossession	$2.00	Request
A Transaction Filing Fee is due for each Registration Renewal	$4.50	when the transaction is filed
A Transaction Filing Fee is due for any other type of Motor Vehicle Transaction	$7.00	when the transaction is filed
Late Transfer Penalty (Due when transfer is not submitted to Department within 10 days)	$2.00	when the transaction is filed
Grant of Security Interest	$2.00	Request
Passenger Plate Fees	$3.00	Request
Trailer Plate Fees	$2.00	Request
Motorcycle/Moped Plate Fees	$2.00	Request
Truck Double Plate Fees	$3.00	Request
Truck Single Plate Fees	$2.00	Request
Duplicate Registration Stickers	$0.50	Request
Duplicate Registration Card	$1.00	Request
Personalized Plates	$14.00	Request

MISSISSIPPI

Contact Information

Driver Services Bureau
Department of Public Safety
P.O. Box 958
Jackson, MS 39205

(601) 987-1200
www.dps.state.ms.us

Mississippi Highway Safety Patrol
P.O. Box 958
Jackson, MS 39205

(601) 987-1212
www.dps.state.ms.us/

Mississippi Department of Transportation
P.O. Box 1850
Jackson, MS 39215-1850

(601) 359-7001
www.mdot.state.ms.us

Mississippi Tax Commission
P.O. Box 1033
Jackson, MS 39215-1033

(601) 923-7000
www.mstc.state.ms.us/

Vehicle Title

Application: Application for certificate of title for a vehicle, manufactured home, or mobile home should be made to the State Tax Commission.

- All vehicles in the state that are manufactured or assembled after July 1, 1969 or

MS

which are the subject of 1st sale for use after July 1, 1969, and every owner of a manufactured home which is in this state and which is manufactured or assembled after July 1, 1999, or which is the subject of 1st sale for use after July 1, 1999, must make application for a certificate of title.
- Voluntary application for title may be made for any model motor vehicle which is in this state after July 1, 1969, and for any model manufactured home or mobile home which is in this state after July 1, 1999, and any person bringing a motor vehicle, manufactured home, or mobile home into this state from a state which required titling shall make application for title to the State Tax Commission within 30 days after arriving.
- Application for certificate of title for a motor vehicle must include the name, current residence and mailing address of the owner, description of the vehicle including year, make, model, vehicle identification number, type of body, number of cylinders, odometer reading at the time of application and whether new or used, date of purchase by the applicant, name and address of the person from whom the vehicle was acquired, the names and addresses of any lienholders, an odometer disclosure statement made by the transferor, and a certified copy of the manufacturer's statement of origin.
- Application for certificate of title for a manufactured home or mobile home must include the name, current residence and mailing address of the owner, description of the manufactured or mobile home including year, make, model number, serial number and whether new or used, date of purchase by the applicant, name and address of the person from whom the vehicle was acquired, the names and addresses of any lienholders, an odometer disclosure statement made by the transferor, and a certified copy of the manufacturer's statement of origin.

Transfer of Ownership: When an owner transfers the ownership of a vehicle, manufactured home, or mobile home, he must, at the time of delivery, execute an assignment and warranty of title to the transferee in the space provided on the certificate and deliver the certificate and assignment to the transferee.

Vehicle Registration

Application: All vehicles required to pay the road and bridge privilege tax are to be registered with the tax collector in the county or municipality in which they are domiciled or garaged.
- Manufactured or mobile homes must be registered with the tax collector of the county where the home is located, within 7 days of purchase or entry into the county.
- The road and bridge privilege license tax must be paid annually prior to registration or renewal.

Non-Resident: Must obtain Mississippi license after 60 days, unless tourist, out-of-state student, or military personnel.

Registration Type: Passenger car registrations expire on a staggered basis.

Safety Inspection: Vehicles designed and used primarily for the transportation of property or for the transportation of 10 or more persons, may require an inspection upon registration.
- Every motor vehicle, trailer, semitrailer, and pole trailer registered in Mississippi

must be inspected not more than once each year and must obtain an official certificate of inspection and approval.
- Each motor vehicle that has passed inspection must display at all times a certificate of inspection and approval on the lower left-hand corner of the windshield in such a position as to be visible from the outside.
- Every motor vehicle registered in any other state and operated in Mississippi shall be inspected and display a certificate different in color or design from certificates issued for Mississippi registered vehicles. The Commissioner of Public Safety may authorize the acceptance of a certificate of inspection and approval issued under the authority of a qualified agency or department of another state, provided that every municipality, county, and state office in such other state accepts, under a mutually acceptable reciprocal agreement, Mississippi's certificate of inspection and approval.

License Plates

Disbursement: The State Tax Commission is authorized to issue and renew license tags.
- A license tag on a motor vehicle or trailer may be renewed for 5-year periods, except for vehicles registered in excess of 10,000 lbs. Gross Vehicle Weight (GVW).
- During each intervening year of the period tags are issued, the State Tax Commission will issue up to 2 decals, in lieu of tags, that specify the month and year that the tag will expire.
- License decals shall indicate the month and last 2 figures of the year the license tag will expire and shall be color-coded to make it easier to distinguish month from year.
- Personalized license tags may be issued as long as they are the same color as regular license tags and have the name of the county and not more than 7 letters and/or numbers.
- Special license tags, decals, and windshield placards are available upon application to persons with a disability that limits or impairs the ability to walk. Application is to be made to the State Tax Commission.

Transfer of Plates: Upon sale or transfer of a vehicle, the seller shall remove and retain the license plate.

Driver's Licenses

Examination: A driving test will be administered that examines the applicant's ability to read and understand road signs and to give the required signals and the applicant must take a test composed of at least 10 questions relating to the safe operation of a motor vehicle.
- Prior to administration of the driving test, the license examiner will inspect the horn, lights, brakes, inspection certificate, and vehicle registration of the motor vehicle that the applicant expects to operate while being tested. If any of the items are deficient, no license or endorsement shall be issued to the applicant until they have been repaired.
- Any applicant holding a valid driver's license from another state is not required to take a written test.
- An applicant for an original motorcycle endorsement or restricted motorcycle oper-

ator's license is required to pass a written test which consists of questions relating to the safe operation of a motorcycle and a skills test. An applicant may be exempt from the skills test if a certificate of successful completion of an approved course can be provided.
- An applicant is required to pass a vision test (requires 20/40 vision acuity).

Graduated Drivers Licensing: State has a system of graduated licensing for teen drivers. At 15, teens are eligible for a learner's permit.
- Permit holders may not drive unsupervised.
- At 15 and 6 months, teens who have held the permit for at least 6 months are eligible for an intermediate license.
- Intermediate license holders are prohibited from driving unsupervised between the hours of 1:00 a.m. and 6:00 a.m.
- At 16, teens are eligible for an unrestricted license.
- Teens applying for a license for the first time at 17 are exempt from the GDL process.

Issuance/Application: A person must have a driver's license to operate a vehicle in Mississippi.
- To lawfully operate a motorcycle, a person must have a restricted motorcycle license or motorcycle endorsement.
- A person under 18 years of age applying for a driver's license must submit the appropriate form with the application, indicating that the person is attending school or not attending school under acceptable circumstances.
- An application for a driver's license is made to the Department of Public Safety and shall include the name, date of birth, sex, race, color of eyes, color of hair, weight, height, residence address, and information regarding whether or not the applicant's driving privileges have ever been suspended or revoked, whether any previous application has been denied, and whether the applicant has any physical defects that would interfere with the safe operation of a vehicle.
- A social security number must be provided to the Commissioner of Public Safety; however, a licensee may choose to use or not use his or her social security number as his or her driver's license number.
- Each license must contain a full-face color photograph in such form that the license and the photograph cannot be separated.
- A driver's license must contain signatures of the Commissioner, assistant commissioner, or authorized deputy and an ink signature of the applicant.
- No person shall be issued a commercial driver's license unless that person is a resident of Mississippi, is 21 years of age or older, has passed a knowledge and skills test, and has satisfied any additional state or federal requirements.
- A person 17 years of age or older who meets all requirements for a commercial driver's license may be issued an endorsement that authorizes the licensee to operate a commercial vehicle only within the geographic boundaries of Mississippi.
- The licenses of documented aliens that do not possess social security numbers are valid for only 1 year.

Renewal: A driver's license may be renewed electronically according to rules set by the Commissioner of Public Safety.

- All licenses of persons 18 years of age or older shall be issued for a 4-year period and may be renewed any time within 6 months before the expiration, which is midnight on the licensee's birthday.
- All licenses of persons under 18 years of age shall be issued for a 1-year period and may be renewed any time within 2 months before the expiration, which is midnight on the licensee's birthday.
- An expired license may be renewed any time within 12 months after expiration upon application, payment of the required fee, and payment of a delinquent fee in lieu of a driver examination, unless an examination is required.
- Any person in the armed services and their dependents who are out of state due to military service at the time of expiration may renew the license any time within 90 days after being discharged from such military service or upon returning to the state.
- Any person holding a valid license who is going overseas for 2 to 4 years and whose license is going to expire during the overseas stay, may renew the license for 4 years prior to leaving with proper proof of such overseas travel.
- Any person in the armed forces and their dependents who are out of state due to military service at the time of expiration may renew the license any time within 90 days after being discharged from military service or upon returning to the state.

Types of Licenses: A Class A Commercial Driver's License (CDL) allows a licensee to operate a combination of vehicles with a Gross Vehicle Weight Rating (GVWR) of 26,001 lbs. or more, provided the GVWR of the vehicle or vehicles being towed is in excess of 10,000 lbs.
- A Class B CDL allows a licensee to operate any single vehicle with a GVWR of 26,001 lbs. or more, and any such vehicle towing a vehicle not in excess of 10,000 lbs.
- A Class C CDL allows a licensee to operate any single vehicle with a GVWR of less than 26,001 lbs. or any such vehicle towing a vehicle with a GVWR not in excess of 10,000 lbs. comprising (1) vehicles designed to transport 16 or more passengers including the driver; and (2) vehicles used to transport hazardous materials which are required to be placarded.
- A Class D CDL allows a licensee to operate all other vehicles or combination of vehicles which are not included in Class A, B, or C and for which a commercial license is not required.
- Commercial endorsements and restrictions include: (1) "H" authorizing the driver to drive a vehicle transporting hazardous materials; (2) "K" restricting the driver to vehicles not equipped with air brakes; (3) "T" authorizing the driving of double and triple trailers; (4) "P" authorizing the driving of vehicles carrying passengers; (5) "N" authorizing the driving of tank vehicles; (6) "X" representing a combination of hazardous materials and tank vehicle endorsements; and (7) "S" restricting the driver to school buses being operated for the purpose of transporting pupils to and from school or to school-related functions and/or to all other vehicles not requiring a commercial driver's license.
- A restricted motorcycle license can be issued to any applicant who fulfills all the requirements necessary to obtain such a license. The license allows the person to operate a motorcycle and no other motor vehicle.
- A motorcycle endorsement may be issued to any person who holds a valid Mississippi driver's license and meets the requirements for endorsement.

Traffic Rules

Alcohol Laws: Mississippi has an implied consent law.
- Illegal per se BAC level is .08.
- Lower BAC level for people under 21 is .02.
- BAC for commercial drivers is .04.

Emergency Radio/Cellular: Channel 19 is randomly monitored. Cell number is *47.

Headsets: Wearing radio headsets while operating a motor vehicle is prohibited.

Occupant Restraints: The driver and every front-seat passenger over the age of 8 must wear a properly fastened seat belt system.
- Violation of the seat belt law is a primary offense for children under 8 years.
- Violation of the seat belt law is a secondary offense for passengers over 8 years of age.
- Children who are between the ages of 4 and 8 must wear a seat belt.
- Children under the age of 4 years shall be properly restrained in a child passenger restraint device. Violation of the child restraint law is a primary offense.
- Riding in pickup truck beds is permitted.

Railroad Crossing: Whenever a person driving a vehicle approaches a railroad crossing and a clearly visible electric or mechanical signal device gives warning of the immediate approach of a train, the driver of such vehicle shall stop within 50 feet but not less than 10 feet from the nearest track of the railroad and shall not proceed until he can do so safely.
- The driver of a vehicle shall stop and remain standing and not traverse a railroad crossing when a crossing gate is lowered or when a human flagman gives or continues to give a signal of the approach or passage of a train.
- The state highway commission is authorized to designate particularly dangerous highway railroad crossings and to erect stop signs thereat. When such stop signs are erected, the driver of any vehicle shall stop within 50 feet but not less than 10 feet from the nearest track and shall proceed only upon exercise of due care.
- The driver of any motor vehicle for hire carrying passengers or any school bus carrying any school child must stop within 50 feet but not less than 10 feet from the nearest rail of a crossing to listen and look in both directions for any approaching train or signals indicating the approach of a train and shall not proceed until he can do so safely.
- The driver of any motor vehicle for hire carrying passengers or any school bus carrying any school child does not need to stop at a railroad crossing where a police officer or a traffic control signal directs traffic to proceed or at a crossing within a business or residential district.

School Buses: Upon meeting or overtaking a school bus that is stopped to receive or discharge children, the driver of a vehicle must come to a complete stop and shall not proceed until the children have crossed the street and the bus has proceeded in the direction it was going.

Vehicle Equipment & Rules

Bumper Height: Modification of original vehicle bumper height cannot exceed 8 inches total lift with a maximum of 6-inch suspension lift front and rear.

Glass/Window Tinting: No vehicle registered in Mississippi shall have windows that are covered with any glazing material that causes a mirrored effect.

- No person shall drive any motor vehicle registered in Mississippi with any tinted film, glazing material, or darkening material of any kind on the windshield except material designed to replace or provide a sun shield in the uppermost area as authorized to be installed by manufacturers of vehicles under federal law.
- Requires that tinted windows not exceed 20% luminous reflectance and have a light transmittance of 35% or more, and have a label certifying the percentages.
- School buses, buses used for public transportation, any bus or van owned or leased by any nonprofit organization, any limousine owned or leased by a private or public entity, or any other motor vehicle the windows of which have been tinted or darkened before factory delivery as permitted by federal law or regulation, are exempt from all window tinting rules.

Windshield Stickers: Prohibited unless official.

Motorcycles & Mopeds

Equipment: The driver of a motorcycle or motor scooter is required to wear a crash helmet that is designed, inspected, and approved by the American Association of Motor Vehicle Administrators.

Licenses: A restricted motorcycle license can be issued to any applicant who fulfills all the requirements necessary to obtain such a license. The license allows the person to operate a motorcycle and no other motor vehicle.

- A motorcycle endorsement may be issued to any person who holds a valid Mississippi driver's license and meets the requirements for endorsement.

Noise Limits: Every motor vehicle shall at all times be equipped with a muffler in good working order and in constant operation to prevent excessive or unusual noise. No person shall use a muffler cutout, bypass, or similar device upon a motor vehicle on a highway.

Mopeds: License requirements same as motorcycles.

- Required safety equipment includes helmets and rearview mirrors.

Passenger Car Trailers

Registration: Registration is not required for pole trailers or utility trailers of less than 5,000 lbs. Gross Vehicle Weight (GVW).

Brakes: Every trailer carrying over 1 ton, when operated on a highway, shall be equipped with brakes adequate to control the movement of the trailer and to stop and hold the trailer.

- Brakes on a trailer should be designed so that the driver of the towing vehicle from its cab may apply them.
- Brakes on a trailer should be designed and connected so that in case of an accidental breakaway of the towed vehicle, the brakes shall be automatically applied.
- Every new trailer, except a trailer of 2 axles of less than 2,000 lbs. GVW towed by an automobile, hereafter sold in this state and operated on the highways, shall be equipped with service brakes on all wheels of every such vehicle.

Dimensions: Total length: 53 feet; trailer length: 40 feet (includes bumpers); width: 102 inches; height: 13.6 feet.

Hitch: Every trailer which shall be towed on public highways at a speed greater than 20 mph shall be coupled to the towing vehicle by means of a safety chain, chains, cables, or equivalent devices in addition to the regular trailer hitch or coupling.

- No more slack shall be left in any safety chains, cables, or equivalent devices than shall be necessary to permit proper turning. The safety chains, cables, or equivalent devices shall be so connected to the towed and towing vehicles and to the drawbar to prevent the drawbar from dropping to the ground if the drawbar fails and shall be of sufficient strength to control the trailer in the event of failure of the regular trailer hitch or coupling.

Lighting: Means for establishing an electric connection between towing and towed vehicles shall be mechanically and electrically adequate and free of short or open circuits.

- Every motor vehicle, trailer, semitrailer, pole trailer, and any other vehicle which is being pulled in a train of vehicles shall be equipped with at least 1 rear lamp mounted on the rear, which, when lit, shall emit a red light plainly visible from a distance of 500 feet to the rear.

Mirrors: Every motor vehicle that is loaded and obstructs the driver's view to the rear shall be equipped with a mirror located to reflect to the driver a view of the highway for a distance of at least 200 feet to the rear of such vehicle.

Speed Limits: 55 mph unless otherwise posted.

Towing: When 1 vehicle is towing another, the drawbar or other connection shall be of sufficient strength to pull all weight towed. The drawbar or other connection shall not exceed 15 feet from 1 vehicle to the other except the connection between any 2 vehicles transporting poles, pipes, machinery, or other objects of a structural nature which cannot readily be dismembered.

- When 1 vehicle is towing another and the connection consists of a chain, rope, or cable, there shall be displayed upon such connection a white flag or cloth not less than 12 inches square.
- Not more than 3 vehicles in combination shall be towed by saddle-mounts, provided the overall length of the towing and towed vehicles shall not exceed 75 feet in length.
- Not more than 1 motor vehicle shall be towed by a tow bar.

Miscellaneous Provisions

Bail Bonds: Recognition of AAA arrest bail certificate up to $200.

Liability Laws: State has security and future proof type law. Minimum required coverage is $25,000 for bodily injury or death of 1 person in 1 accident; $50,000 for 2 or more persons in 1 accident; and $25,000 for injury or destruction of property in 1 accident.

- A motor vehicle owner may choose to post an indemnity bond in lieu of a liability insurance policy. The bond must guarantee payments in amounts and under the same circumstances as required in a motor vehicle liability policy.
- A motor vehicle owner may choose, in lieu of a liability policy or posting a bond, to deposit cash or securities in the amount of $15,000 to the state treasurer to satisfy proof of financial responsibility.
- State has non-resident service of process law; does not have guest suit law.

Weigh Stations: The State Tax Commission, tax collectors, highway patrol, or another authorized enforcement officer, shall have a right to weigh or have weighed any vehicle to ascertain the accuracy of registration.

Fees & Taxes

Table 1: Title & Registration Fees

Vehicle Type	Title Fee	Registration Fee
Motor Vehicle	$4.00	$13.00
Mobile Home or Manufactured Home	$8.00	$1.00 registration fee
Trailers		
Motorcycles	$2.50	$11.00
Mopeds		
Duplicates for Motor Vehicles	$4.00	$1.00
Duplicates for Mobile or Manufactured Homes	$8.00	

Table 2: License Fees

License Class	Fee	Application or Driving Test Fees
4-Year License	$18.00 plus photograph fee	
1-Year License	$3.00 plus photograph fee	
1-Year License for Non-Citizens	$8.00	
Restricted Motorcycle License	$11.00 plus photograph fee	
Class A Commercial License	$38.00 plus photograph fee	$25.00 application
Class B Commercial License	$38.00 plus photograph fee	$25.00 application
Class C Commercial License	$38.00 plus photograph fee	$25.00 application
Class D Commercial License	$23.00 plus photograph fee	
Duplicate License Fee	$8.00 for 2nd and subsequent duplicates	
Endorsements		
Motorcycle Endorsement	$5.00	
Commercial Endorsement	$5.00 each	
Class "S" CDL Endorsement	$23.00	

Table 3: Vehicle Taxes

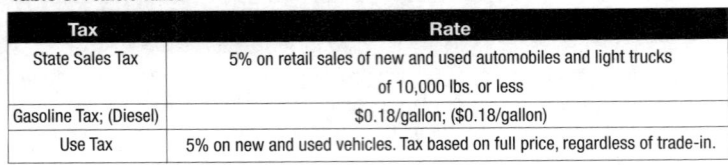

Tax	Rate
State Sales Tax	5% on retail sales of new and used automobiles and light trucks of 10,000 lbs. or less
Gasoline Tax; (Diesel)	$0.18/gallon; ($0.18/gallon)
Use Tax	5% on new and used vehicles. Tax based on full price, regardless of trade-in.

Table 4: Road & Bridge Privilege Taxes

Vehicle Type	Road & Bridge Privilege Tax
Motor Vehicle	$15.00
Trailers	$10.00
Motorcycles	$8.00
Hearses and Ambulances	$25.00
Church and School Buses	$10.00
Taxis	$35.00
Pickup Trucks	$7.20

Table 5: Miscellaneous Fees

Fee	Amount	Payable Upon
Environmental Protection Fee	$0.004 cent per gallon	
Safety Inspection	$5.00 for in-state registered vehicles $10.00 for out-of-state registered vehicles	completion of inspection
Registration or Tag Fee	$5.00 for tag and 2 decals $3.75 for 2 decals	
Personalized License Tag Fee	$30.00 plus the regular cost of tags	application for the tag and at annual renewal thereafter
Duplicate Personalized Tag Fee	$10.00	
License Plate Replacement Fee	$10.00	
Driver's License Photograph	actual cost of photograph rounded to the next highest dollar	
Reinstatement of Driver's License	$25.00 plus license fees	
Reinstatement of Driver's License after Violation of Implied Consent or Uniform Controlled Substances Law	$75.00 plus regular reinstatement and license fees	
Delinquent Driver's License Renewal	$1.00	renewal

MISSOURI

Contact Information

Department of Revenue
Drivers License Bureau (DLB)
301 West High Street, Room 470
P.O. Box 200
Jefferson City, MO 65105-0200

(573) 751-4600
www.dor.state.mo.us

Department of Revenue
Driver and Vehicle Services Bureau (DVSB)
301 West High Street, Room 370
P.O. Box 100
Jefferson City, MO 65105-0100

(573) 751-4509
www.dor.state.mo.us

State Highway Patrol
1510 E. Elm Street
P.O. Box 568
Jefferson City, MO 65102

(573) 751-3313
www.msph.state.mo.us

Missouri Department of Transportation
105 West Capitol Avenue
Jefferson City, MO 65102

(888) 275-6636
www.modot.state.mo.us/

Vehicle Title

Application: No certificate of registration of any motor vehicle or trailer will be issued by the DVSB unless the applicant has applied for and been granted a certificate of ownership of such motor vehicle or trailer.

- An application shall be made within 30 days after the applicant acquires the motor vehicle or trailer upon a blank form furnished by the DVSB and must contain: the applicant's identification number; a full description of the motor vehicle or trailer; the vehicle identification number; and the mileage registered on the odometer at the time of transfer of ownership.
- A statement of the applicant's source of title and of any liens or encumbrances on the motor vehicle or trailer shall accompany the application.

Transfer of Ownership: When a vehicle is sold or transferred, the owner must endorse the certificate of ownership and sign a warranty of title with a statement of all liens or encumbrances on such motor vehicle or trailer, and deliver the same to the buyer at the time of the delivery to him or her of such motor vehicle or trailer.

- The buyer must then present the certificate to the DVSB, at the time of making application for the registration of such motor vehicle or trailer, and a new certificate of ownership shall be issued to the buyer.
- If such motor vehicle or trailer is sold to a resident of another state or country, or if such motor vehicle or trailer is destroyed or dismantled, the owner must immediately notify the DVSB. Certificates when so signed and returned to the DVSB must be retained by the DVSB and all certificates must be appropriately indexed so that at all times it will be possible for the DVSB to expeditiously trace the ownership of the motor vehicle or trailer.

Vehicle Registration

Application: Every owner of a motor vehicle or trailer shall annually file an application for registration.

- The application shall contain the following information: a brief description of the motor vehicle or trailer to be registered, including the name of the manufacturer, the vehicle identification number, the amount of horsepower of the motor vehicle, and whether the motor vehicle is to be registered primarily for business; the name, the applicant's identification number and address of the owner of such motor vehicle or trailer; and the gross weight of the vehicle and the desired load in pounds if the vehicle is a commercial motor vehicle or trailer.
- The DVSB must notify each registered motor vehicle owner by mail, within an appropriate time of the beginning of a new registration period.

Non-Residents: The DVSB shall issue a temporary permit authorizing the operation of a motor vehicle or trailer by a non-resident buyer for not more than 15 days from the date of purchase. Proof of ownership must be presented to the DVSB and the application for such permit shall contain a full description of the motor vehicle, including manufacturer's or other identifying number.

- Military personnel on active duty in Missouri may maintain out-of-state vehicle registration.

Registration Type: Registration for every motor vehicle shall be annual.

Emissions Inspection: Emission inspections, in addition to safety inspections, are required biennially in counties of St. Louis, St. Charles, Jefferson, and St. Louis City (annually in Franklin County). Not required for new vehicles, diesel, propane, or other alternative fuel vehicles, motorcycles, vehicles with gross weights over 8,500 lbs., and model years older than 1970. Vehicles built in even numbered years are subject to test in even number years and vehicles built in odd years are subject to test in odd numbered years, except Franklin County, which requires annual emissions inspection, unless a 2-year emissions inspection was obtained from a St. Louis area emissions inspection station. Fee: $24 ($10.50 in Franklin County).

Safety Inspections: Motor vehicle inspections are required biennially not more than 60 days prior to registration renewal at official inspection stations. Not required for new vehicles not previously titled and registered, or for next succeeding registration required by law. Vehicles built in even numbered years are subject to inspection in even numbered years and vehicles built in odd numbered years are subject to inspection in odd numbered years.

License Plates

Disbursement: The DVSB distributes license plates to each motor vehicle in the state. Each type of vehicle is considered a separate class.

- A set of license plates is issued with the certificate of registration.
- Each set of license plates shall bear the name or abbreviated name of this state, the words "SHOW-ME STATE," the month and year in which the registration shall expire, and an arrangement of numbers or letters, or both, as shall be assigned from year to year by the DVSB.
- Special plates for qualified disabled veterans will have the "DISABLED VETERAN" wording on the license plates in preference to the words "SHOW-ME STATE" and

special plates for members of the national guard will have the "NATIONAL GUARD" wording in preference to the words "SHOW-ME STATE."

Transfer of Plates: When the owner of a motor vehicle moves to another state, he or she must return the license plates to the DVSB within 90 days, or upon the expiration of the period of reciprocity granted by the new state of residence.

- If the owner of a vehicle ceases to operate a vehicle within the state, the plates must be returned to the DVSB within 90 days.
- License plates may be transferred from a motor vehicle which will no longer be operated in the state to a newly purchased motor vehicle.
- Upon the transfer of ownership of a vehicle, the license plates must be removed and the right to use the plates expires. However, the original owner may register another motor vehicle of the same category under the same number, provided the appropriate fee is paid.
- If the transferor of a vehicle cannot register another vehicle under the same number because the vehicle is of a different category, the owner may surrender the plates and receive credit for any unused portion of the original registration fee.

Driver's Licenses

Examination: Any applicant for a license who does not possess a valid license issued pursuant to the laws of the state, another state, or a country which has a reciprocal agreement with the state of Missouri regarding the exchange of licenses must be examined. Any person who has failed to renew his license on or before the date of its expiration or within 6 months after the expiration date must take the complete examination.

- To obtain an Under 21 Full License, an applicant must pass the vision (20/40 visual acuity required) and road sign recognition tests but is not required to take the written and driving tests if the applicant has already passed these tests.

Graduated Drivers Licensing: State has a system of graduated licensing for teen drivers.

- At 15, teens are eligible for a Class F/Instruction/Learner's permit.
- Permit holders may only drive when accompanied by a parent, grandparent, guardian, or Department of Secondary Education or certified driver trainer.
- To be eligible for an intermediate license teens must: (1) be at least 16; (2) hold the permit for at least 6 months; (3) accumulate 20 hours of certified driving; (4) pass the vision, road sign, written, and driving tests if results are over a year old; (5) not have an alcohol-related offense within the last 12 months; and (6) not have a traffic conviction in last 6 months.
- Intermediate license holders may not drive unsupervised between the hours of 1:00 a.m. to 5:00 a.m. (except to and from a school activity, job, or an emergency as defined by the director of revenue).
- Teen drivers and their passengers are also required to wear seat belts.
- To be eligible for a full license, teens must: (1) be at least 18; (2) pass a vision test; (3) not have had the intermediate license suspended, revoked, or denied; and (4) not have any alcohol related offenses or traffic convictions within the last 12 months.
- This system applies to all drivers under 18.
- An applicant cannot receive an Under 21 Full License if his Intermediate License is suspended, revoked, or denied when applying for a full driver's license.

Issuance/Application: An applicant applying for his first Missouri driver license must bring 2 documents for proof of identity. These documents may be 2 primary forms of identification or 1 primary and 1 secondary form of identification. An applicant must also provide proof of a social security number.

- Primary documents acceptable as proof of identity are as follows: (1) U.S. or Canadian photo driver's license; (2) U.S. or Canadian photo identification card; (3) certified microfilm copy or image portfolio of a driver's license or identification card; (4) U.S. or Canadian birth certificate; (5) current approved INS document; (6) Canadian Immigration Record and Visa; (6) military identification; (7) U.S. or Canadian passport (foreign passports must be accompanied by appropriate INS documentation); (8) U.S. or Canadian learner's permit containing a photo; or (9) Canadian Dept. of Indian Affairs identification card.
- Secondary documents acceptable as proof of identity include the following: (1) court order containing full name, date of birth, and court seal; (2) approved INS documents that are expired 1 year or less; (3) U.S. Bureau of Indian Affairs Card/Indian Treaty Card; (4) employer photo identification card; (5) non-English language birth certificate; (6) health insurance card; (7) IRS/state tax form; (8) marriage certificate/license; (9) medical records; (10) military discharge/separation papers; (11) parent/guardian affidavit; (12) gun permit; (13) pilot's license; (14) certified school record/transcript; (15) social security card; (16) student photo identification; (17) vehicle title; (18) photo public assistance card; or (19) prison release documents.
- The following persons are exempt from holding a driver's license: (1) any person operating any farm tractor or implement of husbandry temporarily operated or moved on a highway; (2) a non-resident who is at least 16 years of age and who has in his immediate possession a valid license issued to him in his home state or country; (3) a non-resident who is at least 18 years of age and who has in his immediate possession a valid license issued to him in his home state or country which allows such person to operate a motor vehicle in the transportation of persons or property; and (4) convicted offenders of the department of corrections who have not been convicted of a motor vehicle felony and are operating state-owned vehicles for the benefit of the correctional facilities while accompanied by a correctional officer or other staff person in the vehicle.
- License normally includes a color photograph (unless prohibited by religious beliefs). License also includes a social security number as the license number unless the driver objects.

Renewal: Renewal drivers ages 18-20: 3-year driver license issued that will expire on the applicant's date of birth in the 3rd year after date of issuance. 21-69: during phase-in period, applicants with an odd number year of birth get a 3-year license; applicants with an even number year get a 6-year license. Beginning July 2003, all licenses in this age group will expire on applicant's date of birth in the 6th year after date of issuance. 70 and over: driver license will expire on the applicant's date of birth in the 3rd year after date of issuance.

- Older driver requirements and restrictions: 3-year license issued to persons age 70 and older, driver's license renewal includes a vision test and highway sign recognition.
- All persons renewing their license must pass a vision test and a sign recognition test.
- Military personnel and their dependents out of state when their licenses expire may renew their driver's license by mail.

Types of Licenses: Class A, Class B, and Class C licenses are for large commercial vehicles with a Gross Combination Weight Rating (GCWR) exceeding 26,001 lbs., vehicles designed to transport 16 or more passengers, and vehicles designed to transport hazardous materials. Class E licenses are for drivers whose employment involves transporting property or persons for hire or driving a vehicle owned by another person in the course of their employment.

- **Class F:** Class F licenses are for non-commercial vehicles including recreational vehicles being used solely for personal use. An applicant must be 18 years of age.
- **Under 21 Driver's License:** A person is eligible for an Under 21 Driver's License at 18 years of age.

Traffic Rules

Alcohol Laws: Missouri's implied consent law requires a driver to submit to a chemical test when requested by a law enforcement officer.

- Illegal per se BAC level is .08.
- BAC level for people under 21 is .02.
- BAC level for commercial drivers is .04.

Emergency Radio/Cellular: Citizen band radio channel 9 is monitored for emergency calls. Cell emergency number is *55.

Headsets: Wearing radio headsets while operating a motor vehicle is permitted.

Occupant Restraints: The operator and front seat occupants of all passenger vehicles must wear a properly adjusted and fastened seat belt.

- Violation of the seat belt law is a secondary offense. However, it is primary for people under 16.
- Children under 4 years of age must be protected by a child safety seat when transported in any motor vehicle other than a public carrier for hire.
- A child at least 4 years of age, but less than 16 years of age, must wear a properly adjusted and fastened seat belt when occupying any position of any motor vehicle.
- No person under 18 years of age shall ride in the unenclosed bed of a truck (with a licensed gross weight of less than 12,000 lbs.) when the truck is in operation. Additional gaps in coverage apply; see Occupant Protection Chart.

Railroad Crossing: The driver of a vehicle must approach a railroad crossing in a manner so that he will be able to stop if necessary. The driver must stop the vehicle not less than 15 feet and not more than 50 feet from the nearest rail of the railroad track and must not proceed until he can do so safely if: (1) a clearly visible electric or mechanical signal device warns of the approach of a train; (2) a crossing gate is lowered or a human flagman gives or continues to give a signal or warning of the approach or passage of a train; (3) a train is visible and is in hazardous proximity to the crossing; or (4) any other sign, device, or law requires the vehicle to stop.

- No person may drive any vehicle through, around, or under any crossing gate or barrier at a railroad crossing when a train is approaching while such gate or barrier is closed or is being opened or closed.
- No person may drive a vehicle through a railroad crossing when there is not sufficient space to drive completely through the crossing.
- No person may drive a vehicle through a railroad crossing unless the vehicle has

sufficient undercarriage clearance necessary to prevent the undercarriage of the vehicle from contacting the railroad crossing.

School Buses: The driver of a vehicle upon a highway, upon meeting or overtaking from either direction any school bus which has stopped on the highway for the purpose of receiving or discharging any school children and whose driver has given the signal to stop, shall stop the vehicle before reaching such school bus and shall not proceed until such school bus resumes motion, or until signaled by its driver to proceed.

Vehicle Equipment & Rules

Bumper Height: The maximum height for motor vehicle bumpers is 22 inches for the front and 22 inches for the back.

Glass/Window Tinting: Any person may operate a motor vehicle with front sidewing vents or windows located immediately to the left and right of the driver that have a sun screening device, in conjunction with safety glazing material, that has a light transmission of 35% or more plus or minus 3% and a luminous reflectance of 35% or less plus or minus 3%.

- Except as otherwise provided, any sun screening device applied to front sidewing vents or windows located immediately to the left and right of the driver in excess of the requirements of this section shall be prohibited without a permit pursuant to a physician's prescription as described below.
- A permit to operate a motor vehicle with front sidewing vents or windows located immediately to the left and right of the driver that have a sun screening device, in conjunction with the safety glazing material, which permits less light transmission and luminous reflectance than allowed under the requirements of this subsection, may be issued by the department of public safety to a person having a serious medical condition which requires the use of a sun screening device if the permittee's physician prescribes its use. The permit shall allow the operation of the vehicle by any titleholder or relative (spouse, each grandparent, parent, brother, sister, niece, nephew, aunt, uncle, child, and grandchild).
- This section shall not prohibit labels, stickers, decalcomania, or informational signs on motor vehicles or the application of tinted or solar screening material to recreational vehicles provided that such material does not interfere with the driver's normal view of the road. This section shall not prohibit factory installed tinted glass, the equivalent replacement thereof, or tinting material applied to the upper portion of the motor vehicle's windshield which is normally tinted by the manufacturer of motor vehicle saftey glass.
- A motor vehicle in violation of this section shall not be approved during any motor vehicle safety inspection required pursuant to sections 307.350 to 307.390.
- Any person who violates the provisions of this section is guilty of a Class C misdemeanor.
- Any vehicle licensed with a historical license plate shall be exempt from the requirements of this section.

Windshield Stickers: Labels, stickers, decalcomania, or informational signs on motor vehicles are not prohibited as long as they do not interfere with normal vision of the road.

Motorcycles & Mopeds

Equipment: Every person riding on or operating a motorcycle or motortricycle shall wear protective headgear.

- Every motorcycle shall be equipped with at least 1 and not more than 2 headlamps. Every motorcycle equipped with a sidecar or other attachment shall be equipped with a lamp on the outside limit of such attachment capable of displaying a white light to the front.
- Required equipment: safety helmet; 1 rearview mirror, horn, fuel tank cap, license plate, muffler, registration card, tires approved for highway use, and turn signals (if equipped by manufacturer).

Licenses: It is unlawful to operate a motorcycle or motortricycle unless the operator has a valid license that shows the operator has successfully passed an examination for the operation of the vehicle.

- Any person at least 15 1/2 years of age who, except for age or lack of instruction in operating a motor vehicle, would otherwise be qualified to obtain a motorcycle or motortricycle license or endorsement, may apply, with the written consent of the parent or guardian of such person, for a temporary motorcycle instruction permit to operate a motorcycle or motortricycle.

Mopeds: Registration not required. Minimum age for a driver's license is 16. Valid operator's license required. The following items are required when used on street or highway 1/2 hour after sunset to 1/2 hour before sunrise: (1) headlamp, (2) rear reflectors, (3) pedal reflectors, (4) side-mounted reflectors on front and rear wheels or retro-reflective sidewalls, and (5) equipment required by moped regulation VESC-17.

Passenger Car Trailers

Brakes: Independent braking system not required except on trailers coupled by a 5th-wheel and kingpin.

Dimensions: Total length: 55 feet (65 feet vehicle combinations are allowed on certain roads); trailer length: not specified; width: 96 inches (a width of 102 inches is allowed on certain roads); height: 14 feet (some roads have a 13.6 foot height limit).

Hitch: Safety chains or an equivalent device are required in addition to the primary coupling device, except for 5th-wheel or gooseneck-type vehicles.

Lighting: Each trailer must display on the rear 2 red taillights, 2 red reflectors, and a white license plate light. The reflectors may be incorporated in the taillights.

- Turn signal lights and brake lights are required if visible signals cannot be given by arm and hand; or when the distance from the center of the top of the steering post to the left outside limit of the body, cab, or load exceeds 24 inches; or when the distance from the top of the steering post to the rear limit of the body or load exceeds 14 feet.

Mirrors: All motor vehicles, which are so constructed or loaded that the operator cannot see the road behind such vehicle by looking back or around the side of such vehicle, shall be equipped with a mirror so adjusted as to reveal the road behind and be visible from the operator's seat.

Speed Limits: Same as for passenger cars.

Miscellaneous Provisions

Bail Bonds: Discretionary recognition of AAA arrest bond certificates up to $200, with specified exceptions.

All-Terrain Vehicles: Must be titled and registered with the Department of Revenue. May not be operated on highway except for agricultural or industrial on-premises purposes, or by handicapped persons for short distances occasionally on state secondary roads between sunrise and sunset. Registration decal issued; renewed every 3 years; fee, $10.25.

Liability Laws: No owner of a motor vehicle registered in this state, or required to be registered in this state, may operate, register, or maintain registration of a motor vehicle, or permit another person to operate the vehicle, unless the owner maintains the required liability coverage.

- An insurance identification card shall be carried in the insured motor vehicle at all times. A motor vehicle liability insurance policy, a motor vehicle liability insurance binder, or receipt which contains the policy information is satisfactory evidence of insurance in lieu of an insurance identification card.
- A motor vehicle liability policy must insure the person named in the policy and any other person using the vehicle or vehicles with the express or implied permission of the named insured against liability for damages arising from the ownership or use of the vehicle in the amount of $25,000 because of bodily injury to or death of 1 person in any 1 accident and, subject to the limit for 1 person, $50,000 because of bodily injury to or death of 2 or more persons in any 1 accident, and $10,000 because of injury to or destruction of property of others in any 1 accident.

Weigh Stations: All commercial trucks licensed with a GVWR of over 18,000 lbs. must stop.

Fees & Taxes

Table 1: Title & Registration Fees

Vehicle Type	Title Fee	Registration Fee
Motor Vehicle	$8.50	9 horsepower and less than 12 hp - $18.00
		12 hp and less than 24 hp - $21.00
		24 hp and less than 36 hp - $24.00
		36 hp and less than 48 hp - $33.00
		48 hp and less than 60 hp - $39.00
		60 hp and less than 72 hp - $45.00
		72 hp and more - $51.00
Mobile Home	$8.50	
Non-Commercial Trailer less than 6,000 lbs.		$25.00
Bus		10 passengers or less - $100.50
		11 - 18 passengers - $180.50
Motorcycles	$8.50	$8.50
Mopeds	not required	$8.50
Duplicate Registration		$8.50

Table 2: License Fees

License Class	Fee	Driving Test Fees
A	$22.50 for 3 years $45.00 for 6 years	$25.00 for exam, each subsequent test is the same, $25.00
B	$22.50 for 3 years $45.00 for 6 years	$25.00 for exam, each subsequent test is the same, $25.00
C	$22.50 for 3 years $45.00 for 6 years	$25.00 for exam, each subsequent test is the same, $25.00
Driver's License (Also called Class F)	$10.00 for 3 years $20.00 for 6 years	
Under 21 Driver's License	$7.50 for 3 years	No test needed if results from intermediate license are less than 2 years old
Intermediate License	$7.50 for 2 years	Must pass written test and road test
Instruction Permit	$7.50 for 6 months	Must pass vision and written test
Duplicate Fee	Intermediate License - $5.00 Driver's License - $7.50 Commercial Driver's License - $20.00 Motorcycle - $7.50	
Motorcycle Endorsement	$10.00 for 3 years $20.00 for 6 years	Must have driver's license written, vision, and road sign tests. At age 16, must have an instruction permit for 6 months.

Table 3: Vehicle Taxes

Tax	Rate
Personal Property Tax	Determined and collected by local county or township collector
State Sales Tax	4.225% on new and used vehicles
State Use Tax	4.225% on vehicles purchased outside of the state
Gasoline Tax; (Diesel)	$0.17/gallon; ($0.17/gallon)

Table 4: Miscellaneous Fees

Fee	Amount
Delinquent Registration/Transfer Fee	$5.00 late fee
Registration and Plate Reinstatement Fee	$8.50
Special Plates Fee	$15.00
License Plate Replacement Fee	$8.50
Safety Inspection Fee	$12.00 vehicles; $10.00 motorcycles and trailers
Emission Inspection	$24.00

MONTANA

Contact Information

Motor Vehicle Division (MVD)
Department of Justice (DOJ)
Scott Hart Building, Second Floor
303 N. Roberts
P.O. Box 201430 (406) 444-1773
Helena, MT 59620-1430   www.doj.state.mt.us/department/motorvehicledivision.asp

Title and Registration Bureau
Motor Vehicle Division
1032 Buckskin Drive (406) 846-6000
Deer Lodge, MT 59722   www.doj.state.mt.us/department/motorvehicledivision.asp

Montana Highway Patrol
2550 Prospect Avenue
P.O. Box 201419 (406) 444-3780
Helena, MT 59620-1419   www.doj.state.mt.us/department/highwaypatroldivision.asp

Montana Department of Transportation
P.O. Box 201001
2701 Prospect Avenue (406) 444-6200
Helena, MT 59620-1001   www.mdt.state.mt.us

Vehicle Title

Application: Applications for certificate of ownership are made to the county treasurer. The certificate will contain the date issued, the name and mailing address of the owner or the names and addresses of joint owners, the name and address of any lienholder, and a description of the vehicle including the year built and vehicle identification number.

Transfer of Ownership: The transferor must sign the certificate of ownership in ink, and the signature must be acknowledged before the county treasurer or a notary public.

- Within 20 days after endorsement, the transferee must forward the endorsed certificate of ownership, an odometer mileage statement, and the certificate of registration to the MVD. If the transferee fails to make the application within 20 days, the transferee is subject to a $10 fine.
- Each seller of a motor vehicle must record an odometer reading on the certificate of ownership and a statement or certification that the odometer reading reflects the actual mileage, exceeds the mechanical limit, or differs from the actual mileage and should not be relied upon. Vehicles 10 years old and older are exempted from the odometer statement requirement.
- If the transfer is by operation of law, the transferee must forward a verified or certified statement of the transfer of interest setting forth the reason for the involuntary transfer, the interest transferred, the name of the transferee, the process or procedure for the transfer, and other information requested by the MVD.

Mobile Homes: A manufactured home is subject to the certificate of ownership requirements for a vehicle unless it has been declared an improvement to real property.

- A manufactured home is considered an improvement to real property if the running gear is removed and it is attached to a permanent foundation on land that is owned or being purchased by the owner of the manufactured home or with the permission of the landowner.
- To eliminate the certificate of ownership, the owner may file a statement of intent with the DOJ that includes: (1) the serial number of the manufactured home; (2) the legal description of the real property to which the home has been permanently attached; (3) a description of any liens; and (4) approval from all lienholders of the intent to eliminate the title.
- Upon a transfer of any interest in a mobile home or house trailer, the application for the transfer must be made through the county treasurer's office in the county in which the mobile home or house trailer is located at the time of transfer. The county treasurer may not accept the application unless all taxes, interest, and penalties assessed on the mobile home or house trailer have been paid in full.

Vehicle Registration

Application: Each owner of a motor vehicle operated or driven on the public highways of the state must apply in the office of the county treasurer in the county where the owner permanently resides at the time of making the application for registration or re-registration.

- The application must contain: (1) the name and address of the owner, giving the county, school district, and town or city within whose corporate limits the motor vehicle is taxable, if taxable, or within whose corporate limits the owner's residence is located if the motor vehicle is not taxable; (2) the name and address of any lienholder; (3) a description of the motor vehicle; and (4) the declared weight of all trailers operating intrastate.
- The applicant must pay at the time of making the application to the county treasurer the registration fee and the motor vehicle fees in lieu of tax or registration fees imposed against the vehicle for the current year of registration and the immediately previous year.
- Mobile homes, motor homes, trucks exceeding a 1-ton capacity, trailers, buses, some commercial vehicles, government vehicles, and fleet vehicles are subject to staggered registration.
- Vehicles subject to staggered registration that exceed a 1-ton capacity must be re-registered annually in the month in which they were first registered.
- Owners of vehicles subject to staggered registration with a capacity of 1 ton or less may register the vehicle for a period not to exceed 24 months.
- Owners of vehicles subject to staggered registration that are 11 years old or older may permanently register the vehicle.
- Owners of vehicles subject to staggered registration have a grace period for registration that exists between the 1st and end of the month. Motor vehicles must be registered not later than the last day of the month corresponding to the anniversary registration period.
- The owner of a new or transferred vehicle has a grace period of 20 calendar days from the date of purchase to make application and pay the registration fees, fees in lieu of taxes and other fees, and local option taxes, if applicable, as if the vehicle were being registered for the first time in the registration year.

- If the vehicle was not purchased from a licensed motor vehicle dealer, the purchaser may operate the vehicle on public streets and highways without a certificate of registration for 20 calendar days, provided that at all times during that period, a vehicle purchase sticker obtained from the county treasurer or a law enforcement officer, showing the date of purchase, is clearly displayed in the rear window.
- Failure to apply for a certificate of registration within 20 days subjects the purchaser of a motor vehicle to a penalty of $10.
- Registration fees and new number plate fees do not apply when number plates are transferred to a replacement vehicle.
- Montana residents on active military duty stationed outside Montana are not subject to registration fees and fees in lieu of taxes if they file the appropriate application for the exemption with the MVD.
- All registrations of motor homes expire annually on April 30. Application for registration must be made by June 15. The owner of a motor home is entitled to operate the vehicle between May 1 and June 15 without displaying a registration certificate for the current registration year, if the owner displays the plates, or plate assigned for the previous year.
- The owner of a light vehicle 11 years old or older may permanently register their vehicle upon payment of a $50 fee in lieu of tax, the applicable registration and license fees, a $2 surcharge, and an amount equal to 5 times the applicable fees imposed for: (1) junk vehicle disposal; (2) weed control; (3) former county motor vehicle computer; (4) local option vehicle tax or flat fee; (5) license plates; and (6) senior and disabled persons transportation services. The permanent registration may not be transferred.

Non-Residents: All vehicles registered outside of Montana must carry in plain sight the license plates from state or country of registration.

- A vehicle brought into Montana by a non-resident temporarily employed in the state and used exclusively for transportation of that person is subject to the fee to be paid in lieu of taxes. The county in which the vehicle is located imposes the fee. One-fourth of the annual fee must be paid for each quarter or portion of a quarter of the year that the vehicle is located in Montana. The quarterly fees are due the first day of the quarter.
- Non-residents temporarily employed in the state must obtain a decal from the county treasurer as proof of payment of the required fees. The decal must be displayed in the lower right-hand corner of the windshield. Decals expire each year on December 31 and application for re-registration must be filed no later than February 15.

Registration Type: Registration must be renewed annually, and license fees must be paid annually. Except for vehicles subject to a staggered registration period, all registrations expire on December 31 of the year in which they are issued. The application for registration or re-registration must be filed with the county treasurer not later than February 15 of each year.

Safety Inspection: A person may not drive or permit to be driven on a highway a vehicle or combination of vehicles that is in such unsafe condition as to endanger a person.

- The MVD or its agents may at any time, upon reasonable cause to believe that a vehicle is unsafe or not equipped as required by law or that its equipment is not in proper adjustment or repair, require the driver of such vehicle to stop and submit such vehicle to an inspection.

License Plates

Disbursement: Unless otherwise exempted, a person may not operate a motor vehicle on the public highways of the state unless the vehicle is properly registered and has the proper number plates conspicuously displayed, 1 on the front and 1 on the rear of the vehicle, each securely fastened to prevent it from swinging and unobstructed from plain view.

- A person may not purchase or display on a vehicle a license plate bearing the number assigned to any county other than the county of the person's permanent residence at the time of application of registration.
- All number plates are issued for a maximum period of 4 years. In years when number plates are not issued, the MVD will provide nonremovable stickers bearing appropriate registration numbers that must be affixed to the rear license plate.
- Any purchaser of a motor vehicle may obtain a temporary window sticker from the country treasurer if he or she is unable to complete the process of applying for a Montana title at the time he or she applies for registration of the vehicle because the certificate of ownership is lost, in the possession of third parties, or in the process of reissuance. The sticker is valid for 60 days and must be displayed on the upper left-hand corner of the rear window.
- Personalized license plates are available as are special plates for veterans, collectors, amateur radio operators, disabled veterans, alumni of Montana colleges and universities, and organizations.
- Special permits for disabled are available, as well as disabled plate.

Transfer of Plates: The registration of a motor vehicle expires upon transfer, and it is the duty of the transferor immediately to remove the license plates from the vehicle.

- Number plates issued to a passenger vehicle, truck, trailer, motorcycle, or quadricycle may be transferred only to a replacement passenger vehicle, truck, trailer, motorcycle, or quadricycle.
- The application for transfer of the license plates from the motor vehicle for which the plates were originally issued to a motor vehicle acquired by the same owner must be made within 20 days of acquiring the new vehicle. License plates may be transferred without transferring ownership of the first vehicle, but upon transfer of the plates, the registration of the first vehicle expires, and the certificate of registration for the first vehicle must be surrendered to the county treasurer with the application for transfer.

Driver's Licenses

Examination: Each applicant is subject to a vision test (20/40 visual acuity required), knowledge test, and driving skills test.

- A resident who has a valid driver's license issued by another jurisdiction may surrender that license for a Montana license of the same class, type, and endorsement upon payment of the required fees and successful completion of a vision examination.
- The MVD may impose restrictions on an applicant's license if the MVD determines

that an applicant's ability to exercise ordinary and reasonable control in the safe operation of a motor vehicle on the highway depends on the use of adaptive equipment or operational restrictions.
- A road test may not be given more than once in every 7 days.

Graduated Drivers Licensing: State has a system of graduated licensing for teen drivers (effective 07/01/06).

- At age 14 and 6 months, a teen may apply for a learner's permit and must hold it for at least 6 months and complete 50 hours (10 nighttime) of certified driving.
- At age 15, a teen may apply for an intermediate license and is restricted from transporting more than 1 passenger under age 18 for the first 6 months and more than 3 passengers under age 18 for the second 6 months. Teens are prohibited from operating a vehicle from 11:00 p.m. to 5:00 a.m.
- A full unrestricted license is issued at age 16.

Issuance/Application: Each application must include the full legal name, date of birth, sex, residence address, and social security number of the applicant. The application must include a statement as to when and where the applicant has been previously licensed; whether the applicant has ever had a driver's license suspended or revoked; and whether the applicant has any physical or mental disability that may impair the applicant's ability to maintain ordinary and reasonable control over a vehicle.

- The application of a person who is under 18 years of age must be signed by a parent or by some other responsible person who is willing to assume liability. Any negligence or willful misconduct of a driver under 18 years of age must be imputed to the person who has signed the minor's application. The adult signing the application may later request that the minor's license be cancelled and be relieved from any subsequent liability for the actions of the minor while operating a motor vehicle.
- The MVD will conduct a check of the applicant's driving record through the national driver register.
- A person has 10 days to notify the MVD of change of name or change of address.
- Exempt from license: any person who is a member of the armed forces of the United States, while operating a motor vehicle owned or leased to the United States government and being operated on official business.
- License includes a color photograph and may include a social security number.
- A license issued to a person under the age of 18 is marked as a "provisional license." Any provisional license may be suspended for not more than 12 months if the licensee has been found guilty of careless or negligent driving.

Renewal: When a person applies for renewal of a driver's license, the MVD will conduct a records check through the national driver register and test the applicant's eyesight. The MVD may also require a knowledge and skills test if (1) the applicant has a mental or physical disability that may impair the applicant's ability to operate a vehicle; (2) the expired or expiring license does not include adaptive equipment or operational restrictions appropriate to the applicant's functional abilities; or (3) the applicant wants to remove or modify the restrictions stated on the expired or expiring license.

- A person can apply to renew his or her driver's license within 6 months before or 3 months after the expiration of the person's license.
- A person may renew a driver's license by mail if the person is temporarily out-of-state and submits an approved vision examination and medical evaluation from a licensed physician. The terms of a license renewed by mail is 4 years, and a person may not renew by mail for consecutive terms.

- Except for a license renewed by mail, a license expires on the anniversary of the licensee's birthday 8 years or less after the date of issue or on the licensee's 67th birthday, whichever occurs first.
- A license issued to a person who is 68 - 74 years of age or older expires on the anniversary of the licensee's birthday 6 years or less after the date of issue. All drivers 75 and older receive 4-year licenses.
- A license issued to a person who is under 21 years of age expires on the licensee's 21st birthday.
- Any person who has a valid Montana driver's license at the time of entering active duty with the armed forces may apply for a military renewal. The military renewal is valid so long as the person is assigned to active duty not to exceed 30 days following the date of release from active duty.

Types of Licenses: An endorsement is an addition to a commercial driver's license which indicates that the driver meets all of the qualifications required to operate a vehicle other than a normal passenger car. Type 1 allows a driver to operate a commercial motor vehicle in interstate commerce; Type 2 allows a driver to operate a commercial motor vehicle only within the State of Montana. Vehicles will be categorized by class: Class A is any combination of two or more vehicles, including a trailer(s) in excess of 10,000 lbs., articulated buses with a Gross Vehicle Weight Rating (GVWR) exceeding 26,000 lbs., and all vehicles authorized to be driven under Class B and C, or with a regular driver's license Class D; Class B is any single vehicle in excess of 26,000 lbs. GVWR, or any such vehicle towing a vehicle not in excess of 10,000 lbs. GVWR, or any bus, and any vehicle designed to carry and is capable of carrying more than 16 passengers, including the driver; all school buses and all vehicles under Class C or D; Class C is a single vehicle under 26,000 lbs. GVWR which may tow a trailer under 10,000 lbs. GVWR which hauls hazardous materials in an amount sufficient to require placarding under CFR 291, and any vehicle which hauls 16 or more passengers including the driver; all school buses; Class D is a regular non-commercial license. Endorsements are as follows: N-Tank, H-Hazardous, (T)-Double/triple, P-Passenger, M-Motorcycle, (O)-Endorsement for Other. Restrictions: (A)-Airbrake.

- Military personnel having a valid Montana license upon entry into service may use such license until 30 days following honorable discharge. Must obtain military endorsement.

Traffic Rules

Alcohol Laws: State has implied consent law. Open containers are not permitted.
- Illegal per se BAC level is .08.
- BAC level for people under 21 is .02.
- BAC level for commercial drivers is .04.

Emergency Radio/Cellular: Citizen band radio channel 9 is randomly monitored by the public for emergency calls. Emergency cell number is 911 or (800) 525-5555.

Headsets: Wearing radio headsets while driving is permitted.

Occupant Restraints: No driver may operate a motor vehicle on a highway in the state unless each occupant of a designated seating position is wearing a properly adjusted and fastened seat belt.

- Children under the age of 6 and weighing less than 60 lbs. must be properly restrained in a child restraint device.
- Violation of the seat belt law is a secondary offense, however violation of the child restraint law is a primary offense.
- Riding in pickup truck beds is permitted.

Railroad Crossing: When stop signs are erected at railroad crossings, the driver of a vehicle must stop within 50 feet but not less than 15 feet from the nearest rail of the railroad and may proceed only upon exercising due care.

- At all railroad crossings outside of corporate limits of incorporated cities or towns where a flagman or a mechanical device is not maintained and where the view is obscured or when a moving train is within sight or hearing, the driver must bring the vehicle to a full stop not less than 10 or more than 100 feet from the intersection of the highway and the railroad tracks before crossing the railroad tracks.
- Unless a police officer or traffic-control signal directs traffic to proceed, vehicles carrying 7 or more passengers for hire, school buses, and vehicles carrying explosives or flammable liquids as cargo must stop within 50 feet but not less than 15 feet from the nearest rail of the railroad. The driver must listen and look in both directions along the track for an approaching train and for signals indicating the approach of a train and may not proceed until he or she can do so safely. The driver may not shift gears while crossing the track or tracks.

School Buses: The driver of a vehicle upon meeting or overtaking from either direction any school bus that has stopped on the highway or street to receive or discharge any children: (1) must stop not less than 10 feet before reaching the school bus when the flashing red signal is in operation; and (2) may not proceed until the children have entered the school bus or have alighted and reached the side of the highway or street and until the school bus ceases operation of the flashing red signal.

- The driver of a vehicle on a highway with separate roadways need not stop upon meeting or passing a school bus that is on a different roadway or when the school bus is stopped in a loading zone that is a part of or adjacent to a controlled access highway.

Vehicle Equipment & Rules

Bumper Height: Modification of original bumper height is permitted on pickup trucks and SUVs. Excess of 20 inches requires mudflaps.

Glass/Window Tinting: A windshield may not have sunscreening material that is not clear and transparent below the AS-1 line or sunscreening material that is red, yellow, or amber in color above the AS-1 line.

- The front side windows may not have sunscreening or other transparent material that has a luminous reflectance of more than 35% or has light transmission of less than 24%.
- The rear window or side windows behind the front seat may not have sunscreening or other transparent material that has a luminous reflectance of more than 35% or has light transmission of less than 14%, except for the rear window or side windows behind the front seat on a multipurpose vehicle, van, or bus.
- The highway patrol or local law enforcement may grant a waiver of window tinting standards for medical reasons based on an affidavit signed by a licensed physician.

Windshield Stickers: A person may not drive a motor vehicle with a sign, poster, substance, or other non-transparent material upon the front windshield, sidewings, or side or rear windows of the vehicle that materially obstructs, obscures, or impairs the driver's clear view of the highway or an intersecting highway.

Motorcycles & Motor-Driven Cycles

Equipment: A person operating a motorcycle or quadricycle on public streets or highways may ride only on the permanent and regular seat. The operator may not carry a passenger unless the passenger is seated on a seat designed for two persons or on another seat firmly attached to the side or rear of the operator.

- Motorcycles and quadricycles must be operated with lights on at all times unless the vehicle is registered as a collector's item. If the vehicle is registered as a collector's item, it is only required to be operated with lights at nighttime and during periods of poor visibility.
- Motorcycles, quadricycles, and motor-driven cycles must be equipped with at least 1 properly functioning taillamp mounted on the rear that emits a red light plainly visible from a distance of 500 feet to the rear of the vehicle.
- All operators and passengers under 18 years of age of a motorcycle or quadricycle must wear protective headgear approved by the DOJ.

Licenses: A license is not valid for the operation of a motorcycle or quadricycle unless the holder of the license has successfully completed a road or skills test for a motorcycle or quadricycle and the license has been clearly marked with a motorcycle endorsement.

Motor-Driven Cycles: A person may not operate a motor-driven cycle at speeds of greater than 35 mph at nighttime or during periods of poor visibility unless the motor-driven cycle is equipped with a headlamp or lamps that are adequate to reveal a person or vehicle at a distance of 300 feet ahead.

- The headlamp on a motor-driven cycle must be of sufficient intensity to reveal a person or a vehicle at a distance of not less than 100 feet when operated at any speed less than 25 mph, at a distance of not less than 200 feet when operated at a speed from 25 to 35 mph, and at a distance of not less than 300 feet when operated at a speed of 35 mph or more.

Passenger Car Trailers

Brakes: All trailers and pole trailers with a Gross Vehicle Weight (GVW) of 3,000 lbs. or greater must be equipped with brakes acting on wheels. All trailers and pole trailers with a GVW of less than 3,000 lbs. must be equipped with brakes on all wheels if the total weight of the trailer or trailers does not exceed 40% of the GVW of the towing vehicle.

- Every trailer and pole trailer equipped with air- or vacuum-actuated brakes and every trailer and pole trailer with a GVW in excess of 3,000 lbs. must be equipped with brakes acting on all wheels that are designed to be applied automatically and promptly, and remain applied for at least 15 minutes upon breakaway from the towing vehicle.
- A towing vehicle and all trailers being towed must have one control device that can be used to operate all service brakes.

Dimensions: Total length: 65 feet (includes bumpers); trailer length: not specified; width: 102 inches; height: 14 feet.

- Passenger vehicles less than 2,000 lbs. GVW may tow one trailer; this combination shall not exceed 65 feet. Three-unit combinations shall not exceed 65 feet (includes bumpers). Three-unit combinations permitted if rear unit is equipped with breakaway brakes.

Hitch: A trailer or pole trailer with GVW of 3,000 lbs. or less must be equipped with a steel safety chain or cable with a minimum diameter of one-fourth of an inch must be securely fastened to the towing unit. The safety chain or cable may not be connected to the ball but must be connected to the hitch or other frame member of the towing vehicle to prevent the drawbar from dropping to the ground if the ball, socket, or coupler fails.

Lighting: A trailer with a GVW in excess of 3,000 lbs. must be equipped with: (1) 2 clearance lamps on the front, 1 at each side; (2) 2 side marker lamps and 2 side reflectors, 1 at or near the front and 1 at or near the rear; and (3) 2 clearance lamps and 2 reflectors on the rear, 1 at each side.

- A pole trailer with a GVW in excess of 3,000 lbs. must be equipped with (1) on each side, 1 side marker lamp and 1 clearance lamp that may be in combination, to show to the front, side, and rear; and (2) on the rear of the pole trailer or load, 2 reflectors, 1 at each side.
- A trailer or pole trailer with GVW of 3,000 lbs. or less must be equipped with 2 rear reflectors and 2 stop lights, 1 on each side.

Mirrors: A motor vehicle must be equipped with a mirror that reflects to the driver a view of the highway for a distance of at least 200 feet to the rear of the motor vehicle.

Miscellaneous Provisions

Bail Bonds: Mandatory recognition of AAA arrest bond certificates up to $1,000 with specified exceptions.

Liability Laws: An owner of a motor vehicle that is registered and operated in Montana by the owner or with the owner's permission must continuously provide insurance against loss resulting from liability imposed by law.

- A policy must provide minimum coverage of: (1) $25,000 because of bodily injury to or death of 1 person in any 1 accident and subject to that limit for 1 person; (2) $50,000 because of bodily injury to or death of 2 or more persons in any 1 accident; and (3) $10,000 because of injury to or destruction of property to others in any one accident.
- State has non-resident service of process law; does not have guest suit law.

Weigh Stations: Vehicles transporting agricultural products and trucks with a GVW of 8,000 lbs. or more and new or used RVs being transported to a distributor or dealer must stop.

Fees & Taxes

Table 1: Title Fees

Vehicle Type	Title Fee
Motor Vehicles with a Weight Capacity of 1 Ton or Less (Light Vehicles)	$10.00
Vehicles with a Weight Capacity Exceeding 1 Ton	$10.00
Motorcycle	$10.00

Table 2: Registration Fees

Vehicle Type	Registration Fee
Passenger Vehicles Weighing Less than 2,850 lbs.	$13.75
All Passenger Vehicles Weighing 2,850 lbs. or More	$18.75
All Trucks Designed or Used Primarily for Hauling Property	$23.75
Motor Homes	$22.25
Travel Trailers	$11.75
Trailers with GVW of Less than 2,500 lbs.	$8.25
Trailers with GVW from 2,500 lbs. to 6,000 lbs.	$11.25
Trailers Exceeding 6,000 lbs. GVW	$16.25
Collector's Vehicle More than 30 Years Old over 2,850 lbs.	$10.00
Collector's Vehicle More than 30 Years Old under 2,850 lbs.	$5.00
Off-Highway Motor Vehicles	$9.00
Motorcycles and Quadricycles (Including Motor-Driven Cycles)	$9.75
Permanent Registration Fee for Light Vehicles 11 Years Old or Older	$50.00
Replacement	$5.00

Table 3: License Fees

License Plates	$5.00
Replacement of Number of Plates	$5.00
Replacement of Pioneer Plates	$5.00
Temporary Window Sticker	$2.00
Personalized Plate	$25.00
Amateur Radio Operator Plate	$5.00
Collector Plate	$5.00 - $10.00
Collegiate Plate	$30.00
Transfer of Personalized Plate	$10.00
Non-Resident Decal	$2.00
Non-Commercial Driver's Licenses	$5.00 per year
Motorcycle Endorsement	$0.50 per year or fraction of a year
Duplicate License	$10.00
Identification Card	$8.00

Table 4: Vehicle Fees

Tax	Rate
Fees in Lieu of Poperty Taxes	
Light Vehicle 0-4 Years Old	$195.00
Light Vehicle 5-10 Years Old	$65.00
Light Vehicle 11 Years Old and Older	$6.00
Motor Homes, Travel Trailers, Campers, Trailers, and Pole Trailers Weighing Less Than 26,000 lbs.	
Motor Home Less than 2 Years Old	$250.00
2-Year-Old Motor Home	$230.00
3-Year-Old Motor Home	$195.00
4-Year-Old Motor Home	$150.00
5-Year-Old Motor Home	$125.00
6-Year-Old Motor Home	$100.00
7-Year-Old Motor Home	$75.00
Motor Home 8 Years Old and Older	$65.00
Travel Trailers Less than 3 Years Old	$60.00
Travel Trailers 3 Years Old and Older	$22.50
Campers Less than 3 Years Old	$52.50
Campers 3 Years Old and Older	$22.50
Trailers and Pole Trailers with Declared Weight of Less Than 6,000 lbs.	
Permanent Registration	$25.00
Trailers and Pole Trailers with Declared Weight of More Than 6,001 lbs.	
Permanent Registration	$65.00
Motorcycles and Quadricycles	
Permanent Registration	$40.00

Table 5: Vehicle Taxes

Tax	Rate
Local Option Vehicle Property Tax	up to 0.7% of the value or a local flat fee
Gasoline Tax; (Diesel)	$0.278/gallon; ($0.285/gallon)

NEBRASKA

Contact Information

Nebraska Department of Motor Vehicles (DMV)
Nebraska State Office Building
301 Centennial Mall South
P.O. Box 94789
Lincoln, NE 68509-4789

(402) 471-2281
www.dmv.state.ne.us

Nebraska State Patrol
P.O. Box 94907
Lincoln, NE 68509

(402) 471-4545
www.nsp.state.ne.us

Department of Roads
1500 Nebraska Highway 2
P.O. Box 94759
Lincoln, NE 68509

(402) 471-4567
www.dor.state.ne.us/

Department of Property Assessment and Taxation (DPAT)
1033 "O" Street, Suite 600
Lincoln, NE 68508

(402) 471-5984
http://pat.nol.org

Vehicle Title

Application: An application must be submitted to the DMV.

- The following information is required: Vehicle Identification Number, year, make, model, body style, color, and Gross Vehicle Weight Rating (GVWR). The application also requires the owner's full name, address, mailing address, signature, and any lien information.
- An application for a certificate of title shall include a statement that an identification inspection has been conducted on the vehicle by an inspector designated by the sheriff.
- If the motor vehicle has previously been registered, the application for title must be accompanied by the certificate of title duly assigned.
- If a certificate of title has not been previously issued for the vehicle, the application for title must be accompanied by a manufacturer's or importer's certificate.

Transfer of Ownership: No person shall sell or otherwise dispose of a motor vehicle without delivering to the purchaser or transferee of such vehicle a certificate of title.

- The transferor of any motor vehicle of an age of less than 10 years, which was equipped with an odometer by the manufacturer, shall provide to the transferee a signed statement that the mileage shown on the odometer is accurate to the transferor's best knowledge.

Mobile Home: All applications for a certificate of title for a mobile home shall be accompanied by a mobile home transfer statement prescribed by DPAT.

Vehicle Registration

Application: An application must be submitted to the county office where the vehicle's owner resides.

- An application for vehicle registration includes the owner's name, valid proof of insurance, his or her post office address, a description of the vehicle, and whether and what type of alternative fuel is used to propel the motor vehicle.

Non-Residents: Any non-resident owner whose passenger car is operated in the state for 30 or more continuous days shall register such car in the same manner as a Nebraska resident unless the state of his or her legal residence grants immunity from such requirements to residents of this state operating a passenger car in that state.

Registration Type: The registration period for motor vehicles shall expire on the 1st day of the month 1 year from the month of issuance, and renewal shall become due on such day and shall become delinquent on the 1st day of the following month.

- Any owner who has 2 or more vehicles required to be registered, may register all such vehicles on a calendar-year basis or on an annual basis for the same registration period beginning in a month chosen by the owner.

License Plates

Disbursement: The DMV shall furnish to every person whose motor vehicle is registered, fully reflectorized license plates upon which shall be displayed the registration number consisting of letters and numerals assigned to such motor vehicle in figures not less than 2 and 1-half inches nor more than 3 inches in height, and also the word "Nebraska."

- The DMV shall, without the payment of any extra fee, issue license plates for 1 motor vehicle to any handicapped or disabled person.
- The DMV shall furnish to every person whose motor vehicle is registered, 1 or 2 renewal tabs that shall bear the year for which furnished and be so constructed as to permit them to be permanently affixed to the plates.
- Disabled license plates are available by application through DMV.

Transfer of Plates: The owner of a vehicle bearing personalized message license plates may make an application to the county treasurer to have such plates transferred to a motor vehicle other than the vehicle for which such plates were originally purchased if such vehicle is owned by the owner of the plates.

Driver's Licenses

Examination:

- Vision Test: The DMV vision test measures visual acuity (20/40 required) and field of vision. If corrective lenses are needed to meet the standards, they must be worn at all times while driving, and the license issued will indicate this. If the standards are not met, either an ophthalmologist or optometrist will be required to check the findings. Applicants who cannot meet the minimum vision standards will be denied a license.
- Written Test: There is a separate written test for each class of license. Applicants renewing a valid Nebraska operator's license will have the written test waived if they renew the license prior to expiration or within 1 year after expiration. The

examiner has access to Nebraska driver records and will determine eligibility upon application for renewal.
- Driving Test: The driving test measures the ability to operate a specific class of vehicle under typical driving conditions. Examiners may, at their discretion, give a driving test to any license applicant. The vehicle must be furnished by the applicant for the driving test and it must be representative of the type of license for which he or she is applying.

Graduated Drivers Licensing: State has a system of graduated licensing for teen drivers. At 15, teens are eligible for a learner's permit. During this stage, teens must be accompanied by a licensed driver who is at least 21 years old. Applicant must successfully pass the vision and written tests prior to the LPD being issued. There is no minimum holding period for the learner's permit.

- Sixty days prior to their 16th birthday, teens may apply and take the tests for a provisional license. Teens must hold this license for 1 year.
- During this stage, teens may not drive unsupervised between 12:00 midnight and 6:00 a.m. unless they are driving to or from home to work or a school activity. Individuals may drive anytime if they are accompanied by a parent, guardian, or licensed driver who is at least 21 years old.
- Before individuals can apply for a provisional they must do one of the following: (1) complete a DMV-approved driver safety course and successfully complete written and driving tests given by the driver safety course instructor, or (2) present to the driver's license examiner a 50-hour certification form signed by a parent, guardian, or licensed driver who is at least 21 years old. The 50-hour certification form must be obtained from the DMV.
- Teens are eligible for an unrestricted license at age 17.

Issuance/Application: An application for a driver's license or permit must be made to the DMV and include the applicant's name, residential address, mailing address, physical description, birth information, social security number, and medical history information.

- An application for a driver's license or permit must be accompanied by proof of age and identity. If applicant is under the age of 18, this must be his or her birth certificate. Only original documents will be accepted by the DMV as proof of age and identity.
- A driver's license shall at all times be carried by the licensee when operating a motor vehicle.
- In Nebraska, 14-year olds who live 1.5 miles or more from school and who either live outside or attend school inside a metro area may be issued a learner's permit called an LPE and then a school license. The LPE authorizes supervised driving for the purpose of preparing for the school permit, which allows driving to and from school or any place supervised by a parent or guardian.
- Any valid driver's license issued to a person on active duty, or the person's spouse, is effective without requirement for renewal until 60 days after the date of the person's discharge from the service.
- License does not include social security number.
- License includes color photograph.

Renewal: An operator's license issued to a person 21 years of age or older, on or after January 1, 1999, expires on the licensee's birthday in the 5th year after issuance.

- An operator's license issued to a person under the age of 21 expires on that person's 21st birthday.
- An operator's license issued to a person 21 years of age or older, prior to January 1, 1999, expires on the licensee's birthday in the 1st year after issuance in which his or her age is divisible by 4.
- Upon renewal, a vision test is required. The written and driving tests, however, may be waived by the DMV.
- Operator's licenses issued to persons required to use bioptic or telescoptic lenses shall expire annually on the licensee's birthday.
- The licenses of active duty military and their family members stationed outside of Nebraska are valid while on duty and for 60 days following a discharge or return to Nebraska. A DMV form 07-08 must be attached to the license.

Types of Licenses: Learner's Commercial Permit: The LCP authorizes a person to operate a commercial motor vehicle for learning purposes when accompanied by a person who is at least 21 years of age (applicants must be at least age 18). Applicant must first possess a Class O license or a commercial license from another state.

- Class A Commercial: Any combination of commercial vehicles and towed vehicles with a Gross Vehicle Weight Rating (GVWR) of more than 26,000 lbs. if the GVWR of the vehicles being towed is in excess of 10,000 lbs.
- Class B Commercial: Any single commercial vehicle with a GVWR of 26,001 lbs. or more or any such commercial motor vehicle towing a vehicle with a GVWR not exceeding 10,000 lbs.
- Class C Commercial: Any single commercial motor vehicle with a GVWR of less than 26,001 lbs. or any such motor vehicle towing a vehicle with a GVWR not exceeding 10,000 lbs. This class includes motor vehicles designed to transport 16 or more passengers, including the driver, and motor vehicles used in the transportation of hazardous materials.
- Class M: Motorcycle license.
- School Bus Permit: A school bus permit is required for drivers of all vehicles that transport 1 or more school children provided such transportation is sponsored and approved by a Board of Education.

Traffic Rules

Alcohol Laws: Any person who operates or is in the actual physical control of a motor vehicle upon a highway in Nebraska shall be deemed to have given his or her actual consent to submit to a chemical test or tests of his or her blood or breath for the purpose of determining the amount of alcoholic content in his or her blood or breath.

- Open containers are not permitted. Meets the requirements of TEA-21.
- Illegal per se BAC level is .08.
- Lower BAC level for people under 21 is .02.

Emergency Radio/Cellular: Citizen band radio channel 9 is monitored for emergency calls. Emergency cell phone number is *55.

Headsets: Wearing headsets while operating a motor vehicle is permitted.

Occupant Restraints: Drivers and front seat passengers are required to wear a seat belt.

- Children under age 6 must be properly secured in a child passenger restraint system.
- Children ages 6 up to age 18 are required to ride secured in an occupant protection system in all seating positions.
- Violation of the seat belt law is a secondary offense, however violation of the child restraint law is a primary offense.
- All persons being transported in a motor vehicle operated by a holder of a provisional operator's permit or a school permit are required to ride secured in an occupant protection system.
- Riding in a pickup truck bed or vehicle cargo area is not permitted for passengers under the age of 18. Additional gaps in coverage apply; see Occupant Protection Chart.

Railroad Crossing: Driver shall stop within 50 feet but not less than 15 feet from the railroad track if any of the following conditions are present: (1) a clearly visible electric or mechanical signal device is giving warning of the immediate approach of a train; (2) a crossing gate is lowered or a flag-person is giving warning of an approaching train; or (3) an approaching train is plainly visible or audible and is in hazardous proximity.

- No person shall drive any vehicle through, around, or under any crossing gate or barrier at a railroad crossing while such gate or barrier is closed or being opened or closed.
- The driver of any bus for hire carrying passengers or of any school bus, shall stop such vehicle within 50 feet but not less than 15 feet from the railroad and shall not proceed until he or she can do so safely.

School Buses: Upon meeting or overtaking, from the front or rear, any school bus on which the stop warning signal lights are flashing, the driver of a motor vehicle shall reduce the speed of such vehicle to not more than 25 mph, shall bring such vehicle to a complete stop when the school bus stop signal arm is extended, and shall remain stopped until the stop signal arm is retracted and the school bus resumes motion or until signaled by the bus driver to proceed.

Vehicle Equipment & Rules

Bumper Height: Modification of original vehicle bumper height is permitted.

Glass/Window Tinting: It shall be unlawful for a person to drive a motor vehicle required to be registered in this state upon a highway: (a) if the windows in such motor vehicle are tinted so that the driver's clear view through the windshield or side or rear windows is reduced or the ability to see into the motor vehicle is substantially impaired; (b) if the windshield has any sunscreening material that is not clear and transparent below the AS-1 line [1] or if it has a sunscreening material that is red, yellow, or amber in color above the AS-1 line; (c) if the front side windows have any sunscreening or other transparent material that has a luminous reflectance of more than 35% or has light transmission of less than 35%; or (d) if the rear window or side windows behind the front seat have sunscreening or other transparent material that has a luminous reflectance of more than 35% or has light transmission of less than 20% except for the rear window or side windows behind the front seat on a multipurpose vehicle, van, or bus.

[1] The term "AS-1 line" shall mean a line extending from the letters AS-1, found on most motor vehicle windshields, running parallel to the top of the windshield or shall mean a line 5 inches below and parallel to the top of the windshield, whichever is closer to the top of the windshield.

Telematics: It shall be unlawful to operate upon any highway a motor vehicle which is equipped with or in which is located a television set so placed that the viewing screen is visible to the driver while operating such vehicle.

Towing: The draw-bar or other connection between any 2 vehicles, 1 of which is towing or pulling the other on a highway, shall not exceed 15 feet in length from 1 vehicle to the other.

- The connecting device between any 2 vehicles, 1 towing the other, shall have displayed at approximately the halfway point between the towing vehicle and the towed vehicle a red flag or other signal or cloth not less than 12 inches square.
- Whenever the load on any vehicle extends more than 4 feet beyond the rear of the bed or body, there shall be displayed at the end of such load a red flag not less than 12 inches square.
- Whenever the load on any vehicle extends more than 4 feet beyond the rear of the bed or body, and is being operated between sunset and sunrise, there shall be displayed a red light plainly visible under normal weather conditions at least 200 feet from the rear of the vehicle.

Motorcycles & Mopeds

Equipment: A person shall not operate or be a passenger on a motorcycle unless such person is wearing a protective helmet of the type and design for motorcycle use. The helmet must also be secured properly on the operator or passenger's head with a chin strap.

Licenses: Learner's Permit (LPD or LPE): The applicant must pass a vision screening before obtaining either permit and must also pass a written test for a LPD. The permit authorizes holder to operate a motorcycle if he or she is within visible contact and is under the supervision of a person who is age 21 and a licensed motorcycle operator.

- Class M: Applicant must pass a vision and physical test. Applicant must also successfully complete an examination including the actual operation of a motorcycle. This examination may be waived if the applicant presents proof of successful completion of a motorcycle safety course within the immediately preceding 48 months.

Noise Limits: Every vehicle shall be equipped, maintained, and operated so as to prevent excessive or unusual noise. No person shall drive a motor vehicle on a highway unless such motor vehicle is equipped with a muffler or other effective noise-suppressing system in good working order and in constant operation. It shall be unlawful to use a muffler cutout, bypass, or similar device on any motor vehicle upon a highway. No person shall modify or change the exhaust muffler, the intake muffler, or any other noise-abatement device of a motorcycle in a manner such that the noise emitted by the motorcycle is increased above that emitted by the motorcycle as originally manufactured.

Mopeds: A moped shall be entitled to full use of a traffic lane of any highway with an authorized speed limit of 45 mph or less.

- No person shall operate a moped between lanes of traffic or between adjacent rows of vehicles.
- Mopeds shall not be operated more than 2 abreast in a single lane.
- Any person who operates a moped on a highway shall ride as close to the right-hand side of the road as practicable.

- No person shall operate any moped at a speed in excess of 30 mph.

Passenger Car Trailers

Brakes: All commercial trailers with a carrying capacity of more than 10,000 lbs. shall be equipped on each wheel with brakes that can be operated from the driving position of the towing vehicle.

- All recreational trailers having a gross loaded weight of 3,500 lbs. or more but less than 6,500 lbs. shall be equipped with brakes on at least 2 wheels.
- All trailers with a gross loaded weight of 6,500 lbs. or more shall be equipped with brakes on each wheel. The brakes shall be operable from the driving position of the towing vehicle. Such trailers shall also be equipped with a breakaway, surge, or impulse switch on the trailer so that the trailer brakes are activated if the trailer becomes disengaged from the towing vehicle.

Dimensions: Total length: 65 feet; trailer length: 40 feet (includes bumpers); width: 102 inches (allows outside width to exceed 102 inches if excess is due to an appurtenance); height: 14.6 inches.

Hitch: Safety chains required.

Lighting: Any trailer, in use on a highway, shall be equipped with brake and turn-signal lights in good working order.

Mirrors: No person shall drive a motor vehicle on a highway when the motor vehicle is so constructed or loaded as to prevent the driver from obtaining a view of the highway to the rear unless such vehicle is equipped with a right-side and a left-side outside mirror so located as to reflect to the driver a view of the highway for a distance of at least 200 feet to the rear.

Speed Limits: No person shall operate any motor vehicle when towing a mobile home at a rate of speed in excess of 50 mph.

Miscellaneous Provisions

Bail Bonds: Mandatory recognition of AAA arrest bond certificate up to $200, with specified exceptions.

Liability Laws: State has future proof law. Proof of coverage required at all times. Violators may be charged with a class II misdemeanor.

- Any person operating a motor vehicle must have liability insurance with the following minimum coverage: $25,000 for bodily injury to or death of 1 person in 1 accident; $50,000 for bodily injury to or death of 2 or more persons in any 1 accident; and $25,000 for injury to or destruction of property in any 1 accident.
- State has non-resident service of process law; does not have a guest suit law.

Weigh Stations: All trucks over 1 ton must stop, except a pickup truck pulling a recreational trailer.

Fees & Taxes

Table 1: Title & Registration Fees*

Vehicle Type	Title Fee	Registration Fee
Motor Vehicle	$10.00	$20.00
Mobile Home	$10.00	$18.00 if less than 8,000 lbs. $30.00 if between 8,000 - 12,000 lbs. $42.00 if more than 12,000 lbs.
Trailers of 1,000 lbs. or less	farm/ranch use: title not required non-commercial: title not required commercial: $10.00	$1.00
Trailers between 1,000 - 9,000 lbs.		$1.00 per 1,000 lbs.
Motorcycles	$10.00	$20.00
Duplicates	$14.00	$6.00

* From January 1, 2003, through December 31, 2005, an additional $0.25 for each certificate issued will be charged to pay for the costs of the motor vehicle insurance database.

Table 2: License Fees

License Class	Fee
Learner's Permit	$8.00
School Permit	$8.00
Provisional Operator's Permit	$15.00
Operator's License	$23.75*
Motorcycle License	$23.75*
Commercial License	$50.00
Duplicate License Fee	$11.25
Replacement License Fee	$11.25

* Valid for 5 years

Table 3: Vehicle Taxes

Tax	Rate
State Sales Tax	4.5%
Gasoline Tax	Changes every 3 months

Table 4: Miscellaneous Fees

Fee	Amount	Payable Upon
Motorcycle Plates	$6.00	Registration
Message Plates	$30.00 + registration costs	Registration
Special Plates Fee	$30.00 - $70.00	Registration
License Plate Replacement Fee	$9.10	Replacement
Inspection	$10.00	Testing

NEVADA

Contact Information

Department of Motor Vehicles (DMV)
555 Wright Way
Carson City, NV 89711

(877) 368-7828
www.dmvstat.com

Nevada Highway Patrol
555 Wright Way
Carson City, NV 89711

(775) 684-4808
http://ps.state.nv.us/NHP/

Nevada Department of Transportation
1263 South Stewart Street
Carson City, NV 89712

(775) 888-7000
www.nevadadot.com

Vehicle Title

Application: The certificate of ownership must contain on its front the date issued, the name and address of the registered owner and the owner or lienholder, a description of the vehicle, and a reading of the vehicle's odometer. The rear of the certificate shall contain forms for notice to the DMV of a transfer of title or interest of the owner or lienholder and an application for registration by the transferee.

- If any certificate of ownership is lost, the registrant shall apply immediately for a duplicate.
- When a new vehicle is sold in Nevada for the first time, the seller shall complete and execute a manufacturer's certificate of origin or a manufacturer's statement of origin and a dealer's report of sale. The report of sale must include a description of the vehicle and the names and addresses of both the seller and buyer. If a security interest is taken by the seller or another party, the name and address of the secured party must be entered on the report of sale as well.
- When a used vehicle is sold in Nevada by a dealer to any person, except a licensed dealer, the seller shall complete and execute a dealer's report of sale, that includes a description of the vehicle and the names and addresses of the seller and buyer. If a security interest exists at the time of sale, the name and address of the secured party must also be entered on the report of sale.
- The seller or dealer shall collect the fee for a certificate of title, submit the original of the dealer's report of sale and the manufacturer's certificate or statement of origin, and remit the fee collected to the DMV within 20 days of the execution of the dealer's report of sale for a new vehicle, and 30 days for a used vehicle. For used vehicles, the dealer must also remit the properly endorsed certificate of title or ownership previously issued for the vehicle.
- Upon receipt of the completed application and payment of all fees, the DMV will issue a certificate of ownership. The buyer will receive the certificate if there is no security interest, but if there is, the secured party will receive it.
- If a secured party receives the certificate of ownership, that party shall deliver it to the buyer within 15 days of the completed performance of the security agreement.

Transfer of Ownership: Upon transfer of title, the person or persons whose title or interest is to be transferred and the transferee shall write their signatures with pen and ink upon the certificate of ownership issued for the vehicle, together with the residence address of the transferee in the appropriate spaces provided on the back of the certificate of ownership.

- The transferee shall immediately apply for registration in any county, and shall pay the governmental services tax due.

Vehicle Registration

Application: Applications are to be made in person, and must contain the signature of the owner; his or her residential address; a declaration of the county where he or she intends the vehicle to be based; a brief description of the vehicle, including the make, model, engine, identification or serial number, whether new or used, the last license number, if known and state of issuance; if new, the date of sale to the person first purchasing or operating the vehicle; proof of adequate insurance; and if required, evidence of emission control compliance.

- Applications for new motor vehicles may be made at the dealer where the vehicle is purchased, if that dealer is authorized by the DMV.
- Every vehicle being registered for the first time in Nevada must be taxed for the purposes of the governmental services tax for a 12-month period.
- When registering a vehicle, the applicant must pay all fees for license plates and registration, and pay the applicable taxes. Once this is done, the DMV shall issue the certificate of registration and the license plate or plates.
- Registrations expire on midnight of the day specified on the receipt of registration, and the DMV shall mail applications for renewal to the registrant prior to the date of expiration. The applications shall include the amount of the governmental services tax to be collected and a notice informing the registrant of the need to maintain vehicle insurance.
- Registrants can renew their registration in person at the DMV or at an authorized inspection station or authorized station or by mail or by electronic means.
- If any certificate of registration is lost, the registrant shall apply immediately for a duplicate.

Registration Type: Staggered; expires on a 365-day basis. Any motor vehicle, trailer, or semitrailer operated by a resident must be registered.

- Mobile homes and mopeds need not be registered.
- Motor vehicle registrations are valid for 1 year.

Non-Residents: New residents must register vehicle and have it inspected in Nevada within 60 days of establishing residence in Nevada, or before the out-of-state registration expires, whichever comes first. Residency is established when a person's legal residence is in Nevada, when a person engages in intrastate business so that a vehicle's home state is Nevada, when a person resides in Nevada and is employed in Nevada, or when a person declares himself to be a resident to obtain privileges not given to non-residents.

- Tourists, out-of-state students, border state employees, or seasonal residents need not register their vehicles in Nevada.
- Military personnel on active duty in Nevada may maintain vehicle registration in home state.

Emissions Inspection: Only vehicles in urban and suburban portions of Clark and

Washoe counties are required to be tested.

- New vehicles on their first or second registration, vehicles manufactured before 1967, and alternative fuel vehicles are exempt.
- Tests are required annually with registration renewal.
- If a vehicle fails a required emissions inspection, registration for the vehicle will be cancelled unless the owner has the vehicle repaired so that the vehicle is in compliance within 30 days of the failed test, or if the owner has applied for a waiver. A waiver may be issued to a vehicle owner in Washoe County if the owner has spent at least $200 on repairs, and a vehicle owner in Clark County may be issued a waiver if he spends $450 on repairs.

Safety Inspection: Peace officers and DMV inspectors may require drivers to stop and submit the vehicle to an inspection of the mechanical condition or equipment.

- The DMV director may establish centers for the inspection of motor vehicles for safety at the branch offices of the DMV for the purpose of inspecting vehicles to be registered in Nevada. Inspections will be limited to an examination of tires and brakes on vehicles with a weight of less than 10,000 lbs. and vehicles that are more than 2 years old.
- Inspection is required when registering or titling a vehicle on which a dismantling certificate or bill of sale/salvage has been issued.

License Plates

Disbursement: The DMV shall furnish 2 license plates to every registered motor vehicle other than a motorcycle and 1 should be placed on the front and 1 on the rear.

- The DMV may issue license plate stickers or tabs upon renewal of registration.
- License plates assigned to a passenger car or truck must contain a space for the name of a county or other identification, and a designation which consists of a group of 3 numerals followed by a group of 3 letters.
- One license plate will be assigned to motorcycles; it is to be mounted on the rear of the motorcycle, and shall consist of 5 numerals.
- Each license plate must be of sufficient size to be plainly readable from a distance of 100 feet during daylight, and treated to reflect light and to be at least 100 times brighter than conventional painted number plates.
- Personalized plates are available for an added fee for passenger cars, trucks, motorcycles, or trailers.
- Specially designed plates are available for an added fee for a wide range of themes.
- Special license plates and permits for disabled drivers are available by application to DMV.

Transfer of Plates: The holder of the original registration may transfer license plates to a new vehicle, provided that the vehicle is eligible for that class of license plates and the vehicle registration has been transferred to the new vehicle.

Driver's Licenses

Examination: When a person with a valid license from another state applies for a Nevada license, that application is to be treated as an application for renewal.

- A driver's license examination shall include tests of the applicant's ability to understand official devices used to control traffic and the applicant's knowledge of safe driving practices and traffic laws; a vision test (20/40 visual acuity required) or report from an ophthalmologist, optician, or optometrist; and a road test.

- The DMV may waive an examination for a person holding a valid license from another jurisdiction, unless that person is under the age of 25, has had his or her license suspended, revoked, or canceled in the preceding 4 years, has been convicted of certain crimes in the preceding 7 years, or has restrictions on his or her driver's license.

Graduated Drivers Licensing: State has a system of graduated licensing for teen drivers. At 15 1/2 teens are eligible for a learner's permit. During this stage teens must be supervised by a driver at least 21 years old.

- Teens must hold the permit for at least 6 months, complete an approved driver education course and certify that they've received 50 hours (10 at night) of supervised driving practice before being eligible for an intermediate license.
- Teens are eligible for an intermediate license at 16. Intermediate license holders are prohibited from driving unsupervised from 10:00 p.m. to 5:00 a.m. For the first three months, Intermediate license holders are also prohibited from transporting any teen passengers, family members excepted.
- Teens are eligible for an unrestricted license at 18.

Issuance/Application: Every application for a driver's license must contain the following: the required fee; the full name, date of birth, address, and brief physical description of the applicant; and an indication of whether the applicant has ever been licensed to drive before, and if so, by what state and whether the license has ever been suspended or revoked. In addition, the applicant must furnish proof of age by showing a birth certificate, and also provide proof of his or her social security number.

- Upon passage of the examination and payment of the required fees, the DMV shall issue a license that indicates the type or class of vehicles the licensee may drive, a unique number assigned to the licensee (if issued prior to 1998), a color photograph, and the licensee's social security number, full name, date of birth, mailing address, brief physical description, and the licensee's signature.
- The application of any person under the age of 18 must be signed and verified by a parent or guardian, but if the applicant has neither, by his or her employer or any responsible person willing to assume liability.
- A person shall not drive any motor vehicle upon a highway unless he or she has a valid license.
- The state may refuse to accept a driver's license issued by another state or the District of Columbia if it is determined that the other state or the District of Columbia has less stringent licensing standards.

Renewal: Every driver's license expires on the 4th anniversary of the licensee's birthday nearest the date of issuance or renewal.

- The DMV may require an applicant for a renewal license to pass a vision test.
- Every license is renewable at any time before its expiration upon application and payment of the required fee.
- No later than 30 days before the expiration of a licensee's license, the DMV shall mail an expiration notice.
- The DMV shall allow for renewal of a license by mail, in exchange for an additional fee. The licensee shall provide a vision report from an ophthalmologist, optometrist, or agency of the state taken within 90 days of the application with the application.

- All persons who renew a license after it has expired may be required to complete all portions of the original license examination.

Types of Licenses:

- Class A: any combination of vehicles with a Gross Combination Weight Rating (GCWR) of 26,001 lbs., if the Gross Vehicle Weight Rating (GVWR) of the trailing vehicle is over 10,000 lbs. The holder may also drive a Class B or Class C vehicle, but not a motorcycle unless he or she has an appropriate endorsement.
- Class B: any single vehicle with a GVWR of 26,001 lbs. or more, or any vehicle which is towing another vehicle that does not have a GVWR of more than 10,000 lbs. The holder may also drive a Class C vehicle, but not a motorcycle unless he or she has an appropriate endorsement.
- Class C: any single vehicle, or combination of vehicles, which does not meet the definition of a Class A or Class B vehicle, including passenger vehicles and mopeds. The holder of a Class C license may not drive a motorcycle without the appropriate endorsement, tow a vehicle with a GVWR of less than 10,000 lbs. unless the holder obtains an R endorsement, or drive a combination of vehicles exceeding 70 feet in length.
- Class M: the holder may drive a motorcycle, trimobile, or moped.

License Restrictions:

- M: on Class A-C licenses, licensees need an M restriction before legally operating a motorcycle, trimobile, or moped.
- U: on Class M licenses where the licensee has been tested on a motorcycle that does not exceed 6.5 horsepower or a displacement of 90 cubic centimeters.
- X: on Class M licenses where the licensee has been tested on a motorcycle that has 3 wheels in contact with the ground; also on Class C licenses where the licensee has been tested in a low-speed vehicle. The driver of such a vehicle will not be allowed to drive over 35 mph.
- Z: on Class M licenses where the licensee has been tested on a moped.
- Commercial driver's licenses are required for vehicles that do not meet the requirements of Class A or B licenses, but are designed to transport at least 16 passengers or to transport hazardous material.

Traffic Rules

Alcohol Laws: Any driver operating a vehicle on a highway is deemed to have given consent to a preliminary breath test for alcohol concentration.

- Open containers are prohibited. The federal government recognizes this law as meeting the requirements of TEA-21.
- Illegal per se BAC level is .08.
- BAC level for drivers under 21 is .02.

Emergency Radio/Cellular: Citizen band radio channel 9 is monitored for emergency calls. Emergency cell number is *NHP. (*677), *DUI.

Headsets: Wearing radio headsets while driving a motor vehicle is permitted.

Occupant Restraints: Any person driving and any passenger at least 5 years of age who rides in the front or back seat must wear a seat belt if one is available for that seating position. All children under 5 must be in a child restraint system.

- All persons over the age of 6 or weighing more than 60 lbs. must wear a seat belt. Any child under the age of 6 and who weighs less than 60 lbs. must be secured in a child passenger restraint system.
- Violation of the seat belt law is a secondary offense, however violation of the child restraint law is a primary offense.
- Children under age 18 are prohibited from riding in the back of an unenclosed pickup truck on freeways and roads with 2 or more lanes in 1 direction. Additional gaps in coverage apply; see Occupant Protection Chart.

Railroad Crossing: Whenever a person driving a vehicle approaches a railroad crossing and a clearly visible traffic-control or railroad device gives warning of the immediate approach of a train, the driver shall stop the vehicle 15-50 feet from the nearest track of the railroad.

- A driver is also required to stop whenever a crossing gate is lowered or a flagman gives a signal of the approach or passage of a train, whenever a train approaching within 1,500 feet of the highway crossing emits an audible signal and the train is an immediate hazard, or whenever an approaching train is plainly visible and is in hazardous proximity to such crossing.
- Any motor vehicle carrying passengers for hire, any school bus carrying any school child, any vehicle having a normal operating speed of 10 mph or less, or any vehicle carrying an explosive or flammable liquid must stop 15-50 feet from the nearest track of the railroad at all railroad crossings.

School Buses: The driver of any vehicle may not overtake or pass, from either direction, a school bus that has stopped on the highway and is displaying flashing red lights. This does not apply to vehicles traveling on the opposite side of a divided highway.

- A school bus shall not exceed 55 mph when carrying pupils to and from school or any school activity.

Vehicle Equipment & Rules

Bumper Height: The maximum bumper height for a passenger car is 24 inches.
- The maximum height for other vehicles:
  - Vehicles less than 4,500 lbs.: 28 inches.
  - Vehicles between 4,501 and 7,500 lbs.: 30 inches.
  - Vehicles between 7,501 and 10,000 lbs.: 32 inches.

Glass/Window Tinting: Nonreflective window tinting is allowed on the front side windows if the light transmission is at least 35%, with a tolerance of 7%.
- Rear side windows can have nonreflective tinting, so long as the vehicle has outside mirrors on each side that are so located as to reflect to the driver a view of the highway through each mirror for a distance of at least 200 feet. Vehicles manufactured before 1993 that have tinting prior to 1993 are not subject to this prohibition.
- The windshield may have a transparent material applied, so long as the bottom edge of the material is not less than 29 inches above the top of the driver's seat when the seat is in its rearmost and lowermost position with the vehicle on a level surface, and the material may not be red or amber.

Telematics: No person shall drive any motor vehicle equipped with television-type receiving equipment so located that the screen is visible from the driver's seat.
- Television-type receiving equipment may be visible to the driver if used exclusively

for traffic safety, law enforcement, or navigation of the motor vehicle.

Windshield Stickers: A person shall not drive any motor vehicle with any sign, poster, or other non-transparent material upon the windows of such vehicle, if those objects obstruct the driver's clear view of the highway or any intersecting highway.

- Stickers required to be displayed by the state are allowed to be displayed in the 6-inch square portion of the lower corner of the windshield farthest removed from the driver.

Motorcycles & Mopeds

Equipment: A motorcycle shall not be driven while carrying more than 1 person unless such motorcycle is designed to carry more than 1 person.

- Any passenger on a motorcycle shall ride behind the driver and astride the regular seat that was designed for 2 persons, astride another seat firmly attached to the rear of the driver, or in an attached sidecar. Every motorcycle and moped designed to transport a passenger shall have a footrest for that passenger.
- A person driving a motorcycle or moped shall ride only upon the permanent and regular seat.
- A person shall not operate a motorcycle or moped in such a position that he or she cannot reach the ground with both feet simultaneously when sitting astride the seat in a stopped or upright position.
- Motorcycle and moped handlebars may not extend above the uppermost portion of the driver's shoulders when the driver sits on the seat and the seat is depressed by the weight of the driver.
- The driver of a motorcycle or moped shall drive with at least 1 hand on a handlebar at all times.
- Motorcycles and mopeds are required to have fenders on both wheels.
- Whenever operating a motorcycle, the driver and passenger shall wear a securely fastened helmet and protective glasses, goggles, or face shields.
- If a motorcycle is equipped with a transparent windscreen, the driver need not wear glasses, goggles, or face shields.
- Every motorcycle or moped shall be equipped with at least 1 and not more than 2 headlamps.
- Every motorcycle or moped operated upon a highway at any time from one-half hour after sunset to one-half hour before sunrise, and at any other time when persons and vehicles are not visible from 1,000 feet away, must display lighted lamps and illuminating devices.
- Every motorcycle or moped must be equipped with at least 1 rear taillamp that emits a red light visible from 500 feet to the rear. The lamp must be wired to be lighted whenever the headlamp is lighted.
- Every motorcycle manufactured after January 1, 1973, must be equipped with electric turn signal lamps on both the front and rear of the motorcycle.
- Every motorcycle or moped shall be equipped with at least 1 rear reflector, visible from all distances within 300 feet when directly in front of lower headlamp beams.
- Every motorcycle or moped shall be equipped with brakes.
- Every motorcycle or moped shall be equipped with 2 mirrors, 1 on each handlebar, in positions enabling the driver to view clearly the highway for at least 200 feet to the rear.

Licenses: A person may not apply for a motorcycle license unless he or she is 16 years

of age, has successfully completed any examinations issued by the DMV, and has completed a course of motorcycle safety.
- The other requirements are the same as for a regular license.

Noise Limits: Motorcycles traveling 35 mph or less may not be operated at a noise level above 82 decibels, and motorcycles traveling over 35 mph may not be operated at a noise level above 86 decibels.

Mopeds: Mopeds need not be equipped with turn signals.
- Drivers of mopeds need not wear helmets.

Passenger Car Trailers

Registration: License plates for registered trailers will be manufactured in 2 sizes, with the smaller size being issued to trailers with a GVWR less than 1,000 lbs. The smaller plates will have 1 letter and 4 numbers, and the larger plates will have 1 letter and 5 numbers.

Brakes: Every trailer, semitrailer, or pole trailer at least 1,500 lbs. and manufactured after July 1, 1975 must be equipped with service brakes on all wheels.
- Trailers, semitrailers, house trailers, or pole trailers, manufactured before July 1, 1975 and weighing less than 3,000 lbs. need not have brakes on all wheels.
- Every trailer, semitrailer, house trailer, and pole trailer equipped with air or vacuum-actuated brakes and every trailer, semitrailer, house trailer, and pole trailer exceeding 3,000 lbs. and manufactured after July 1, 1969 must be equipped with brakes acting on all wheels, and of such character as to be applied automatically and remain applied for 15 minutes in the event of a breakaway from the towing vehicle.
- All trailers weighing more than 3,000 lbs. must be equipped with parking brakes adequate to hold the trailer on any grade on which it is operated, and in all conditions.
- Every towing vehicle, when used to tow another vehicle equipped with air-controlled brakes, shall be equipped with 2 means for emergency application of the trailer brakes. One of these means shall apply the brakes automatically in the event of a reduction of the towing vehicle air supply. The other means shall be a manually controlled device for applying and releasing the brakes, readily operable by a person seated in the driver seat.
- Every towing vehicle used to tow other vehicles equipped with vacuum brakes shall have a second control device that can be used to operate the brakes on towed vehicles in emergencies. The second control shall be independent of brake air, hydraulic and other pressure, and independent of other controls, unless the braking system is so arranged that failure of the pressure upon which the second control depends will cause the brakes to be applied automatically.

Dimensions: Total length: 70 feet (excludes safety and energy conservation devices); trailer length: not specified; width: 102 inches (excluding mirrors, lights, and other devices required for safety); height: 14 feet.

Lighting: Pole trailers need only have reflectors, stop lamps, turn signal lamps, and taillamps on the rearmost portion of the load.
- On every trailer or semitrailer at least 80 inches wide, there shall be 2 front clearance lamps, 1 on either side; 2 rear clearance lamps and 3 identification lamps; and

- on each side, 2 side marker lamps and 2 reflectors, with 1 at the front and 1 at the rear.
  - In addition, on every trailer 30 feet or longer, there shall be on each side, 1 amber side marker lamp and 1 amber reflector, centrally located.
  - On every pole trailer there shall be on each side, 1 amber side marker lamp and 1 amber reflector at or near the front of the load.
  - Identification lamps shall be grouped in a horizontal row, with lamp centers spaced between 6 and 12 inches apart, and mounted as close as practicable to the vertical center line.
  - On trailers designed to carry boats, front and rear clearance lamps may be located on each side of the trailer at or near the midpoint of the trailer between the front and rear of the trailer to indicate the extreme width of the trailer.
  - Every reflector required above must be readily visible at nighttime at all distances between 100-600 feet. Every front and rear clearance lamp and every side marker lamp shall be capable of being seen and distinguished at all distances between 50-500 feet.
  - Whenever motor vehicles and other vehicles are operated in combination and lights are required, only the rear vehicle's lamps need be illuminated.

Mirrors: Every truck having a body that obscures a view of the road to the rear shall be equipped with a mirror carried in such a position that the driver of the truck shall be able to see traffic approaching from the rear.
  - All motor vehicles shall have a mirror so located so as to reflect to the driver a view of the highway for a distance of at least 200 feet to the rear of the vehicle.

Speed Limits: As posted.

Hitch: Safety chains are required.

Miscellaneous Provisions

Bail Bonds: Discretionary recognition of AAA arrest bond certificates up to $200, with specified exceptions.

Liability Laws: State has mandatory public liability and property insurance law.
  - Driving without liability insurance is punishable as a misdemeanor. Evidence of insurance must be carried in the motor vehicle.
  - Every owner of a motor vehicle registered in Nevada must have the following insurance coverage for as long as the vehicle is registered: $15,000 for bodily injury to or the death of 1 person in any 1 accident; $30,000 for bodily injury to or the death of 2 or more persons in any 1 accident; and $10,000 for injury to or destruction of property of others in any one accident.
  - State has future proof-type law applicable in event of an accident causing property damage in excess of $750, or personal injury or death.
  - State has non-resident service of process law.

Weigh Stations: The following vehicles must stop: (1) agricultural; (2) passenger or specialty vehicles either in combination (towing a trailer) with GVWR of 10,000 lbs. or more; and, (3) commercial trucks with a GVWR of 10,000 lbs. or more.

Fees & Taxes

Table 1: Title & Registration Fees

Vehicle Type	Title Fee	Registration Fee
Motor Vehicle	$20.00	$33.00 each for first 4 cars, $16.50 for 5-6 cars, $12.00 for 7-8 cars, $8.00 for 9 or more cars.
Travel Trailer	$20.00	$27.00 + $12.00 fee for trailers 1,000 lbs. or less, and $24.00 fee for trailers over 1,000 lbs.
Non-Commercial Trailer less than 6,000 lbs.	$20.00	
Trucks less than 6,000 lbs.	$20.00	$33.00
Trucks 6,000 – 8,499 lbs.	$20.00	$38.00
Trucks 8,500 – 10,000 lbs.	$20.00	$48.00
Trucks 10,001 – 26,000 lbs.	$20.00	$12.00/1,000 lbs.
Trucks 26,001 – 80,000 lbs.	$20.00	$17.00/1,000 lbs., with maximum of $1,360
Motorcycles	$20.00	$6.00 for motorcycle safety course
Duplicates	$20.00	$5.00

Table 2: License Fees

License Class	Fee	Driving Test Fees
License to Person 65 or Older	$14.00	$3.00
License to Person Any Other Age	$20.50	
Renewal License to Any Other Age	$20.50	
Renewal License Issued by Mail to a Person 65 or over	$14.00	
Renewal License Issued by Mail to a Person under 65	$21.00	
Reinstatement of License after Suspension or Cancellation	$40.00 - $65.00, depending on violation	
Change of Photo or Information on License	$10.00	
Additional License Fee	$0.50 flat fee	
Commercial License	$54.00	$30.00
Renewal of Commercial License	$54.00	$30.00
Duplicate License Fee	$14.00	
Duplicate Commercial License	$19.00	
Duplicate Commercial License Fee Endorsements	$5.00 for motorcycle endorsement; commercial endorsements = $14.00	$30.00 for commercial endorsement driving tests

Table 3: Vehicle Taxes

Tax	Rate
Government Services Tax (formerly Vehicle Privilege Tax)	$0.04/$100.00 of the value of the vehicle; and counties may add an additional $0.01/$100.00. Valuation is based on 35% of the manufacturer's suggested retail price for the 1st year of the make and model. Minimum tax = $6.00
State Sales Tax	2% of value
City-County Relief Tax	2.25% of value
Local School Support Tax	2.25% of value
Gasoline Tax; (Diesel)	$0.24/gallon; ($0.27/gallon)

Table 4: Miscellaneous Fees

Tax	Amount	Payable Upon
Certificate of Title for Vehicle Not Present or Registered in Nevada	$20.00	application
Emissions Inspection	$5.00 certificate fee plus:	inspection
-- Clark County	$26.00/$28.50/$28.00 light duty/heavy duty/diesel powered	
-- Washoe County	$22.50/$24.50/$23.00 light duty/heavy duty/diesel powered	inspection
Duplicate License Plates	$10.00	application
Substitute License Plates	$5.00	application
County License Plate Decals	$0.50	application
Other Decal, License Plate Sticker, or Tab	$5.00	application
Registration and Plate Reinstatement Fee due to Insurance Lapse	$50.00	reinstatement of registration and suspended plates due to cancellation or non-renewal of liability insurance policy
Personalized Prestige Plates	$35.00	application
Renewal of Prestige Plates	$20.00	application
Special Plates Fee	$25.00 - $35.00	issue / annual renewal
License Plate Replacement Fee	$5.00	new issued plates

NEW HAMPSHIRE

Contact Information

Division of Motor Vehicles (DMV)
Department of Safety
10 Hazen Drive
Concord, NH 03305

(603) 271-2251
www.state.nh.us/dmv

Division of State Police, Department of Safety
James H. Hayes Safety Building
10 Hazen Drive
Concord, NH 03305

(603) 271-2575
http://webster.state.nh.us/safety/nhsp

New Hampshire Department of Transportation
John O. Morton Building
1 Hazen Drive
Concord, NH 03302-0483

(603) 271-3734
www.state.nh.us/dot

Vehicle Title

Application: An application for a certificate of title shall be made by the owner of a motor vehicle to the DMV, on a form prescribed by the DMV.

- The application shall contain: (a) the name, residence, and mailing address of the owner; (b) a description of the vehicle including, the make, model, vehicle identification number, model year, type of body, the number of cylinders, and whether the vehicle is new or used; (c) the date purchased by the applicant, the name and address of the person from whom the vehicle was acquired and the names and addresses of any lienholders in the order of their priority and the dates of their security agreements; and (d) if a new vehicle, the application shall be accompanied by the manufacturer's or importer's certificate of origin.
- If the application for certificate of title refers to a vehicle last previously registered in another state or country, the application shall be accompanied by any certificate of title issued by the other state or country. The certificate shall either be in English or a notarized translation of the certificate shall be provided.
- Any motor vehicle whose manufacturer's model year is older than 15 years is not required to have a title.

Transfer of Ownership: The DMV, upon receipt of a properly assigned certificate of title, with an application for a new certificate of title and the required fee, shall issue a new certificate of title in the name of the transferee as owner and mail it to the first lienholder named in it or, if none, to the owner.

- If the interest of an owner in a vehicle passes to another other than by voluntary transfer, the transferee shall promptly mail or deliver to the DMV the last certificate of title, if available, proof of the transfer, and the application for a new certificate.

Vehicle Registration

Application: An application for the registration of a vehicle may be made by the owner by mail or in person to the DMV, upon a form prescribed by the DMV.

- The application for the registration of a motor vehicle shall contain: the applicant's

name, mailing address, residential address, birth date, and signature.
- The application of any person under the age of 18 to register a vehicle shall be signed by 1 of his parents or a guardian, or in the event there is no parent or guardian, by another responsible adult. This does not apply to a person under the age of 18 years who is emancipated by marriage or who has presented proof of insurance coverage at the time of the application.
- No certificate of registration shall be issued to any person under 16 years of age.

Non-Residents: When a non-resident has established a bona fide residency in New Hampshire, he or she shall have a maximum of 60 days from the date on which the residency was established to register the vehicle.
- A non-resident who garages a vehicle exclusively in New Hampshire may register such vehicle as a non-resident.

Registration Type: The registration of a motor vehicle shall expire at midnight on the last day of the month in which the first anniversary of the registrant's birth following the date of issue is observed.
- 20-Day Registration: Any resident who intends to purchase a vehicle in another state, from another person, or who is unable to register a vehicle because of limited hours of operation of the town clerk in the town where the person resides, may apply to the DMV for a registration to drive the vehicle on the roads of the state in an unregistered condition. The resident shall appear in person at the DMV to obtain such registration and shall sign under penalty of perjury a statement that the vehicle meets all New Hampshire inspection requirements, and in the case of a person seeking an extension of his registration, that he was unable to register the vehicle because of the limited hours of the town clerk, before the 20-day Registration may be issued. This type of registration is valid for 20 days. Only 1 20-day registration shall be issued during any 1 calendar year for a vehicle.
- In-Transit Registration: The owner of any vehicle intended to be driven upon the roads of the state only for the purpose of transporting the vehicle to another jurisdiction where it is to be registered may apply to the DMV for the issuance of an in-transit registration for such vehicle. The application shall be made on a form furnished by the DMV. If satisfied that the vehicle is to be driven as provided in this section, the DMV shall assign to such vehicle a distinctive number and deliver to the applicant an in-transit registration valid for a period of 20 days from the date of issuance. The registration shall specify the terms and conditions under which the vehicle may be driven upon the roads, and no such vehicle shall be operated in violation of such terms and conditions.

Emissions Inspection: There is no separate emissions test. A visual inspection of several emissions-related vehicle components is part of the existing annual state vehicle inspection. The visual check is performed on vehicles 1975 and newer and is done as part of the normal inspection. No separate sticker is required. In addition to the visual inspection of cars and light-duty trucks, there is a roadside diesel smoke testing program for heavy-duty diesel vehicles.

Safety Inspection: Any vehicle registered by the DMV shall be inspected once a year, during the month of the owner's birth date.
- Trucks and buses exceeding 10,000 lbs. gross vehicle weight and all school buses, public and private shall be inspected semiannually. Newly registered vehicles inspected within 10 days from date of registration.

- An inspection sticker shall be valid for the same duration as the vehicle's registration, which shall not exceed 16 months.

License Plates

Disbursement: The DMV shall design and issue to every person whose vehicle is registered a number plate or plates.

- Every vehicle driven in or on any road, if required to be registered, shall have a number plate displayed with any current validation sticker issued by the DMV.
- All registration plates for passenger vehicles shall display the state motto "Live Free or Die."
- The plate shall be kept clean at all times.
- Special license plates or hanging placards for disabled drivers are available by application to DMV. Letter from physician attesting to disability and possession of New Hampshire driver's license is required.

Transfer of Plates: The new owner of a vehicle may be issued the same registration number as previously given to the vehicle if the owner applies to the DMV for registration and submits the transferor's registration certificate. If the plates are vanity plates, a written statement from the transferor releasing the vanity plates must also be submitted to the DMV.

- The owner of a vehicle may transfer the registration number between vehicles if the owner registers the new vehicle within 30 days of the transfer and is the first person named on the registration certificate bearing that number.

Driver's Licenses

Examination: Vision Screening: The DMV shall issue driver's licenses to applicants whose visual acuity is between 20/40 and 20/70. No license shall be issued to an applicant whose visual acuity is worse than 20/40 in both eyes, or worse than 20/30 if there is vision only in 1 eye, unless special consideration is granted by the DMV.

- Written Examination: The written examination consists of 20 multiple-choice questions. This requirement may be waived by the DMV.
- Road Test: The applicant shall provide the test vehicle for the completion of the road test. This requirement may be waived by the DMV.

Graduated Drivers Licensing: State has a system of graduated licensing for teen drivers.

- At age 15 years 6 months, teens may practice driving if accompanied in the front seat by a parent, legal guardian, or other licensed adult who is 25 years of age or older.
- At age 16 years, teens who have successfully completed driver education are eligible for a Youth Operator's License.
- The Youth Operator's License shall expire 1 month after the first anniversary of its issuance unless the holder is convicted of an offense specified in RSA 259:39. If the holder of a Youth Operator's License is convicted of an offense specified in RSA 259:39 the license shall expire 1 year after the date of the holder's last conviction.
- For the first 6 months following issuance the youth operator is restricted to having only 1 passenger (other than family members) under 25 in the vehicle.
- The youth operator shall not operate a motor vehicle between the hours of 1:00 a.m. and 5:00 a.m.
- No holder of a Youth Operator's License shall operate a motor vehicle when the

number of occupants exceeds the number of passenger restraints in the vehicle.
- Youth operator must accumulate 20 hours of supervised driving.

Issuance/Application: Applicants for a driver's license must provide the following on a form provided by the DMV: (1) legal name; (2) residence address; (3) mailing address; (4) social security number, unless a waiver is requested and granted; (5) date of birth; (6) sex, height, weight, color of eyes, color of hair; (7) class(es) of driver's license(s) desired; (8) where last driver's license, if any, was held; and (9) proof of completion of an approved driver education course as a prerequisite of a non-resident. The following certified statements are also required: the applicant has paid all resident taxes for which he is liable; the applicant, if required, has filed with the DMV an insurance certificate; the applicant has no physical or mental handicap that would be detrimental or incapacitate the applicant from holding a license; the applicant does not hold a license in any other jurisdiction; and the applicant's driving privileges are not subject to or under disqualification, suspension, or revocation by any jurisdiction. The signature of the applicant is also required.

- No person shall drive any motor vehicle unless such person has a valid driver's license.
- Every person driving a motor vehicle shall have their driver's license on their person or in the vehicle in some easily accessible place.
- License normally includes a digital image. License does not include social security number.

Renewal: All licenses shall expire on the 5th anniversary of the license holder's date of birth following the date of issuance.

- The DMV shall notify each holder of a license by mail addressed to the holder's last known address, 45 days prior to the expiration date of a place and time where he or she shall appear for the issuance of a new license.
- An applicant for a renewal driver's license who is under the age of 75 shall complete the vision screening examination. The DMV may require applicants, under the age of 75, for a license renewal to complete a road performance evaluation. Applicants for renewal of their driver's licenses who are 75 years old or older must complete a vision screening, a road performance test, and a physical or mental examination if the DMV has any reason to believe that the applicant may be a hazard to public safety if licensed to drive.
- Any person who is a member of the armed forces of the United States and who, at the time of induction, call to active duty, or enlistment into the armed forces for 2 or more years, was a resident of New Hampshire and was a holder of a valid New Hampshire license to drive a motor vehicle in New Hampshire, is entitled to renewal of such license without cost. The spouse of any resident of New Hampshire on active duty in the armed forces is able to renew his or her driver's license through the mail; however, the fee is not waived.

Types of Licenses: Class D: Non-Commercial Operator's License. May also be "moped only," "motorcycle only," or "motorcycle also."

- Class A Commercial: Authorizes holder to drive a combination of vehicles with a Gross Vehicle Weight Rating (GVWR) of over 26,000 lbs. while towing over 10,000 lbs.
- Class B Commercial: Authorizes holder to drive a single vehicle or a combination of vehicles with a GVWR over 26,000 lbs. while towing under 10,000 lbs.

- Class C Commercial: Authorizes holder to drive a vehicle with a GVWR under 26,000 lbs. while transporting hazardous wastes or 16 or more passengers.

Traffic Rules

Alcohol Laws: Any person who drives a vehicle upon the roads of New Hampshire shall be deemed to have given consent to physical and chemical tests and examinations for the purpose of determining whether such person is under the influence of intoxicating liquor or controlled drugs.

- Open containers are not permitted. Meets TEA-21 requirements.
- Illegal per se BAC level is .08.
- Lower BAC level for people under 21 is .02.

Distracted Driving: Anyone who drives a vehicle negligently or causes a vehicle to be driven negligently, or in a manner that endangers or is likely to endanger any person or property shall be guilty of a violation. Examples—the use of cell phones, reading the paper, eating, drinking, etc.

Emergency Radio/Cellular: Citizen band radio channel 9 is monitored for emergency calls. Cell number is 911.

Occupant Restraints: No person shall drive a motor vehicle on any road with a passenger under the age of 18, unless such person is wearing a seat belt, which is properly adjusted and fastened.

- No person shall drive a motor vehicle on any road while carrying a child less than 6 years of age and under 55 inches, unless such child is properly fastened and secured by a child passenger restraint system.
- No person shall operate a motor vehicle unless all children between the ages of 6 and 18 or under 18 and more than 55 inches in height are properly restrained.
- The state does not have a seat belt law, however violation of the child restraint law is a primary offense.
- Riding in pickup truck beds is permitted.

Railroad Crossing: Whenever any person driving a vehicle approaches a railroad grade crossing under any of the following circumstances, the driver shall stop within 50 feet but not less than 15 feet from the nearest rail of such railroad: a clearly visible electric or mechanical signal device gives warning of the immediate approach of a railroad train; a crossing gate is lowered or a flagman gives or continues to give a signal of the approach or passage of a railroad train; a railroad train approaching within approximately 1,500 feet of the road crossing emits a signal audible from such a distance that such train is an immediate hazard; or an approaching train is plainly visible and is in hazardous proximity to such crossing.

- No person shall drive any vehicle through, around, or under any crossing or barrier at a railroad crossing while such a gate or barrier is closed or is being opened or closed.
- The driver of any vehicle carrying passengers for hire, or any school bus carrying any school child, or of any vehicle carrying explosive substances, before crossing any railroad tracks, shall stop the vehicle within 50 feet but not less than 15 feet from the nearest rail of such railroad and, while stopped, shall listen and look in both directions for any approaching train, and for signals indicating the approach of a train, and shall not proceed until driver can do so safely.

School Buses: The driver of a vehicle upon any road upon meeting or overtaking from either direction any school bus, which has stopped on the highway for the purpose of receiving or discharging school children, shall stop the vehicle before reaching such school bus but at least 25 feet away from such school bus. The driver shall not proceed until such school bus resumes motion, or until flashing red lights cease to operate.

Vehicle Equipment & Rules

Bumper Height: No person shall change the height of a bumper of a private passenger vehicle so that the height of any bumper falls below the minimum distance of 16 inches above the ground or above the maximum distance of 20 inches.

- No person shall change the height of a bumper of any vehicle other than a private passenger vehicle so that the height of any bumper falls below the minimum distance of 16 inches above the ground or above the maximum distance of 30 inches.

Glass/Window Tinting: No person shall drive a vehicle, registered in New Hampshire, which has after-market tinting installed on the windshield or on the windows to the left and right of the driver.

- No person shall drive a vehicle which has after-market tinting applied to the windows to the rear of the driver, unless such vehicle has rearview mirrors located on both the left and right sides of the vehicle. However, the light transmittance of after-market tinted windows shall not be less than 35%.
- Persons who require after-market tinting on the windshield or on the windows to the left and right of the driver for medical reasons may apply to the DMV for a special permit.
- After-market tinting of the 6-inch strip at the top of the windshield of any vehicle is allowed so long as the light transmittance of the strip is not less than 35%.

Telematics: No person shall drive any motor vehicle that is equipped with any television viewer, screen, or other means of visually receiving a television broadcast which is located in the motor vehicle at any point forward of the back of the driver's seat, or which is visible to the driver while driving the motor vehicle.

Windshield Stickers: No person shall drive any vehicle with a sign, poster, sticker, or other non-transparent material upon or adjacent to the front windshield, sidewings, or side or rear windows of such vehicle which shall obstruct the driver's clear view of the road, unless such material is required by law.

Motorcycles & Mopeds

Equipment: No person less than 18 years of age may drive or ride a motorcycle wearing protective headgear that is not equipped with either a neck or chin strap.

- If a motorcycle is not equipped with a windshield or screen which protects the driver's eyes and face when the driver is sitting erect, the driver shall wear either eyeglasses, goggles, or a protective face shield when driving the motorcycle.
- Every motorcycle, driven during the period between one-half hour after sunset to one-half hour before sunrise, and whenever rain, snow, or fog shall interfere with the proper view of the road so that persons and vehicles on the road are not clearly discernible at a distance of 1,000 feet ahead, shall display at least 1 lighted headlamp on the front. The headlamp shall throw sufficient light ahead to make clearly visible all vehicles, persons, or substantial objects within a distance of 150 feet. All headlamps shall be designed to prevent glaring rays. All headlamps shall be located

at a height of not more than 54 inches nor less than 24 inches from the ground.
- It shall be unlawful for any person to drive a motorcycle unless it is equipped with a stop lamp in working order at all times.
- It shall be unlawful for any person to drive a motorcycle registered in New Hampshire, which was manufactured after January 1, 1973, unless such vehicle is equipped with directional signals.
- Every motorcycle shall carry on the rear, whether as part of the tail lamps or separately, 1 red reflector.
- No person shall drive a motorcycle of which the grips are higher than the shoulder level of the driver when in the seat or saddle. It shall be illegal to drive a motorcycle with improvised, defective, or repaired handlebars.
- Every motorcycle shall have footrests for each person driving or riding.
- Every motorcycle shall have a rearview mirror.
- A person operating a motorcycle shall ride only upon the permanent and regular seat attached thereto. Such driver shall not carry any other person nor shall any other person ride on a motorcycle unless such motorcycle is designed to carry more than 1 person.
- A person shall ride upon a motorcycle only while sitting astride the seat, facing forward, with 1 leg on each side of the motorcycle.
- While driving a motorcycle, the driver must keep both hands on the handlebars.

Licenses: Motorcycle Learner's Permit: Upon application, the DMV shall issue a motorcycle learner's permit to a person 18 years of age or older or to a person who is between 16-18 years of age who has successfully completed an approved driver education course. A motorcycle learner's permit shall permit the holder of such permit to drive a motorcycle on any road after sunrise and before sunset. The permit shall be valid for 30 days from the date of issuance or until the holder of the permit obtains a special license to drive motorcycles.

- Class D: Non-Commercial Operator's License. May also be "moped only," "motorcycle only" or "motorcycle also."

Noise Limits: No person shall operate a motorcycle which has a measured noise level of more than 106 decibels when measured 20 inches from the exhaust pipe at a 45 degree angle while the engine is operating at 2,800 revolutions per minute for 1 and 2 cylinder motorcycles and 3,500 revolutions per minute for any motorcycle with 3 or more cylinders.

Mopeds: No person may drive a moped upon any road in New Hampshire without a current valid driver's license issued by any state, a special motorcycle license issued by any state, or a special moped license.

- No person shall drive a moped in the night time at a speed greater than 35 mph unless such moped is equipped with a lighted headlamp or lamps which are adequate to reveal a person or vehicle at a distance of 300 feet ahead.
- Tail lamps and stop lamps are also required for mopeds.
- No person shall operate a moped, except 1 equipped with clipless pedals, unless such moped has pedals equipped with a reflector that is visible from the front and rear of the moped from a distance of 200 feet.
- No person, during darkness, shall operate a moped equipped with clipless pedals unless the operator is wearing either reflectorized leg bands on the lower exterior of either the operator's legs or shoes.

- Every moped shall be equipped with a brake or brakes which will enable its driver to stop the moped within 25 feet from a speed of 10 mph on dry, level, clean pavement.

Passenger Car Trailers

Brakes: Every combination of motor vehicle with a trailer or semitrailer when driven upon the roadways of the state shall at a speed of 20 mph be capable, at all times and under all conditions, of stopping on a dry, smooth, approximately level pavement free from loose material, upon application of the foot or service brake, within a distance of 30 feet.

Dimensions: Total length: not specified; trailer length: 48 feet (includes bumpers); width: 102 inches; height: 13.6 feet.

Hitch: Ball hitch shall be mounted on bumper or secured to frame; safety chain is required.

Lighting: The taillamps and reflectors on trailers may be located at a height of less than 20 inches from the ground, provided they are placed in such a manner as to indicate the extreme width of the vehicle and load, and the visibility of reflectors is not impaired at any time.

- It shall be unlawful for any person to pull any trailer unless it is equipped with a stop lamp in working order at all times.
- It shall be unlawful for any person to pull a trailer registered in New Hampshire, which was manufactured after January 1, 1952, unless such a vehicle is equipped with directional signals.
- Every trailer, when driven at night, shall have on the rear, 1 lamp, displaying a red light visible for a distance of at least 1000 feet, and a white light illuminating the registration plate of such vehicle so that the characters thereon shall be visible for a distance of at least 50 feet. All taillamps shall be located at a height of not more than 72 inches nor less than 20 inches from the ground. On a combination of vehicles, only the taillamp on the rearmost vehicle need actually be seen from the distance specified.
- Every trailer and semitrailer, with a weight of 3,000 lbs. or more, when driven on the roads at night, shall have displayed on the body or load carrying portion of the vehicle, the following: on each side, 1 amber reflector, located at or near the front, and 1 red reflector located at or near the rear. Such reflectors shall be located not less than 24 nor more than 48 inches from the ground. The visibility of any such reflector shall not be impaired at any time.

Mirrors: No person shall drive upon any road any motor vehicle so loaded that the driver is prevented from having a constantly free and unobstructed view of the road immediately in the rear, unless there is attached to the vehicle a mirror or reflector so placed and adjusted as to afford the driver a clear, reflected view of the road in the rear of the vehicle.

Speed Limits: House trailers, 45 mph.

Towing: Every trailer or semitrailer shall have, in addition to the towbar or coupling device, a safety chain or cable to prevent breakaway from the towing vehicle. Each chain or cable shall have an ultimate strength at least equal to the gross weight of the trailer and the load being towed. Chains or cables shall be connected to the towed and

NH

towing vehicle to prevent the towbar from dropping to the ground in the event the towbar fails.

- Except for duly registered wrecking vehicles and transporters or motor vehicles towing with a chain or cable for no more than 1 mile another vehicle which is disabled and unable to proceed under its own power, no motor vehicle shall be used to tow another vehicle on any road unless the 2 vehicles are connected by a tow bar of sufficient strength to control the movements of the vehicle being towed without manual steering of said towed vehicle.
- No vehicle may tow on any road more than 1 vehicle, trailer, or semitrailer, except 1 used exclusively for agricultural purposes or 1 authorized by the DMV to do so.
- No person or persons shall occupy any type of house trailer or automobile utility trailer while it is towed.

NH Miscellaneous Provisions

Bail Bonds: State has recognition of AAA arrest bond certificates of $200.

Liability Laws: State has security-type law applicable in the event of accident causing property damage in excess of $1,000 or personal injury death.

- State also has future proof law requiring motorists to show financial responsibility after conviction of certain serious traffic offenses.
- State has non-resident service of process law; does not have guest suit law.
- All drivers are required to have insurance liability policies of at least $25,000 for bodily injury or death to any 1 person, $50,000 for bodily injury or death to 2 or more persons, and $25,000 for injury to and destruction of property in any 1 accident.

Weigh Stations: The driver of every motor vehicle shall, upon request of any law enforcement officer, stop and submit such to a weighing of said motor vehicle by means of either portable or stationary scales. If such scales are not available at the place where the stopping occurs, upon request of a law enforcement officer, the driver shall drive said motor vehicle to the nearest public scales provided the distance to the public scales does not exceed 10 miles.

Fees & Taxes

Table 1: Title & Registration Fees*

Vehicle Type	Title Fee	Registration Fee
Motor Vehicle up to 3,000 lbs.	$25.00	$25.20
Motor Vehicle between 3,001-5,000 lbs.	$25.00	$37.20
Motor Vehicle between 5,001-8,000 lbs.	$25.00	$49.20
Motor Vehicle over 8,000 lbs.	$25.00	$0.84 per 100 lbs.
Trailers of 1,000 lbs. or less	no title required	$3.00
Trailers of 1,001-1,500 lbs.	no title required	$6.00
Trailers of 1,501-3,000 lbs.	no title required	$12.00
Trailers of 3,001-5,000 lbs.	$25.00	$24.00
Trailers of 5,001-8,000 lbs.	$25.00	$36.00
Trailers of more than 8,000 lbs.	$25.00	$0.60 per 100 lbs.
Motorcycles	$25.00	$13.00
Mopeds	no title required	$3.00
Duplicates	$25.00	$10.00

*A $5.00 fee will be added for each registration processed by electronic means.

Table 2: License Fees

License Class	Fee	Driving Test Fees
A (Commercial)	$60.00	each re-examination in 1 year: $20.00
B (Commercial)	$60.00	each re-examination in 1 year: $20.00
C (Commercial)	$60.00	each re-examination in 1 year: $20.00
D (Non-Commercial)	$50.00 (+ $10.00 per year for non-resident alien)	
Youth Operator's License	$10.00 for the first year	
Motorcycle Learner's Permit	$30.00	
Motorcycle Endorsement	$5.00 for renewal $30.00 for original	
Moped	$8.00	
Duplicate License Fee	$10.00	
Endorsements	$10.00 each	

Table 3: Vehicle Taxes

Tax	Rate
State Sales Tax	State has no sales tax
Gasoline Tax; (Diesel)	$0.18/gallon; ($0.18/gallon)

Table 4: Miscellaneous Fees

Fee	Amount	Payable Upon
Safety Inspection	$25.00	inspection
Transfer Plates	$10.00	transfer
Special Plates Fee	$25.00-$30.00	request for vanity plates
Special Plates Transfer Fee	$10.00	transfer
License Plate Replacement Fee	$7.50	replacement
Duplicate Plates	$4.00 per plate	

NEW JERSEY

Contact Information

Motor Vehicle Commission (MVC)
P.O. Box 009
Trenton, NJ 08666-0009

(888) 486-3339
www.state.nj.us/mvc/

New Jersey State Police
P.O. Box 7068
West Trenton, NJ 08628

(609) 882-2000
www.njsp.org

Department of Transportation
P.O. Box 600
Trenton, NJ 08625-0600

(609) 530-3536
www.state.nj.us/transportation/

Vehicle Title

Application: Application for a certificate of ownership should be made to the director of the MVC within 10 days of purchase of a motor vehicle.

- An application for certificate of ownership should be accompanied by evidence of purchase, either a certificate of origin, certificate of ownership, or bill of sale.
- If a person has a certificate of ownership for a mobile or manufactured home that is located in a mobile home park that is being relocated to land that the owner of the home has an interest in or title to, that person shall file a notice of relocation with the director of the MVC at least 10 days prior to relocation. If the director deems the notice to be complete, the certificate of ownership will be cancelled on the date of relocation.

Transfer of Ownership: Upon the sale of a vehicle, the seller shall execute and deliver an assignment of the certificate of ownership to the purchaser.

NJ Vehicle Registration

Application: Every vehicle driven primarily in New Jersey, whether owned by a resident or non-resident, is required to be registered.

- Applications for vehicle registration must be made to the MVC designated agent in the county of residence.
- Applications for vehicle registration must contain the name, street address of the residence or business of the owner, mailing address, age of the owner, description of the vehicle that includes the manufacturer and vehicle identification or manufacturer's number, name of the vehicle's insurer, and if the vehicle is leased, the name and street address of the lessor.
- Registration may be denied without presentation of a certificate of ownership.

Non-Residents: Non-residents must obtain New Jersey driver's license and registration within 60 days after residence established, unless expiration of out-of-state license comes first, and provided compliance has been made with the license laws of the state of previous residence.

- The owner of a vehicle registered in a foreign country has 20 days to register the vehicle in New Jersey.

Registration Type: Registrations shall expire every four years.

- Renewal of motorcycle registrations will take place on a date set by the director of the MVC, but in no case shall that expiration date be earlier than April 30 nor later than October 31.
- Renewal application forms for passenger automobiles will be sent to the last address of owners on record with the MVC.
- Application for renewal of a passenger automobile or motorcycle registration may be directly made to any agent of the MVC.
- Temporary registration may be issued for a 20-day period to any person purchasing an automobile in New Jersey while en route to another state. Renewal is not permitted.

Emissions & Safety Inspection: Every motor vehicle registered in New Jersey is required to be inspected unless the director determines that passage under a similar program of another state, district, or territory of the United States is sufficient.

- Vehicles are to be inspected on a biennial basis. New cars, trucks, motorcycles purchased after 1/1/03 in New Jersey, 4 years from date of purchase and every 2 years after.
- An approval certificate will be issued once a vehicle successfully passes all required emissions tests and the mechanism, brakes, and equipment are found to be in a proper and safe condition.

License Plates

Disbursement: Issuance of license plates may be denied without presentation of a certificate of ownership.

- Special license plates and windshield placards for disabled drivers are available at no fee by application to the MVC.

Transfer of Plates: License plates may be transferred to another vehicle owned by the same person.

Driver's Licenses

Examination: Every licensed driver is required to pass a vision screening successfully (20/50 visual acuity required) at least once every 10 years as a condition of driver's license renewal.

- When a written examination is given as part of a high school driver education program, a certified driver education instructor, or special education teacher may be allowed to read the examination to any student who has been diagnosed with a deficiency in reading, perception, or other learning disability.

Graduated Drivers Licensing: State has a system of graduated licensing for teen drivers.

- At 16, upon successful completion of driver education, a teen is eligible for a special learner's permit.
- Permit holders may not drive unsupervised. Teens must hold the permit for at least 6 months and pass a road test to be eligible for an intermediate/provisional license.
- Intermediate license holders may not drive unsupervised between midnight and 5 a.m. and may not have more than 1 passenger unless supervised by a driver at least 21 years old (family members are exempted).
- Teens may apply for an examination permit at 17.
- Permit holders may not drive unsupervised.
- Teens must hold the permit for at least 6 months.
- At 17 years and 6 months teens may drive unsupervised but not between midnight and 5:00 a.m.
- At 18, teens are eligible for an unrestricted license.
- Learner's permit and provisional license holders are prohibited from using telecommunications devices including cell phones while driving.
- Permit and provisional license holders and their passengers must always wear safety belts.
- New Jersey's law applies to adults as well. Persons 21 and older must hold permit for at least 3 months. The night and passenger restrictions in the intermediate license are waived for drivers 21 and older.

Issuance/Application: Applications for a driver's license must be made to the MVC designated agent in the county of residence.

- Applications for a driver's license require passage of an eye examination and written and road tests.
- A person must apply within 30 days of establishing residence to transfer a commercial driver's license from another state.
- Expiration date of non-citizen's driver's license and id cards is linked to the expiration date of the person's visa.
- License does not include social security number.
- All applicants for driver licenses must present proof of age, identity, and address using primary and secondary documents outlined under the "6 Point ID Verification System." For more information, contact the MVC.

Renewal: Application for renewal of a passenger automobile or motorcycle driver's license may be directly made to any agent of the MVC.
- A licensed driver has 1 week to notify the MVC of change of residence.
- A driver's license is issued for a 4-year period.
- Active military personnel on duty outside of New Jersey can call the MVC 60 days before the expiration date on the license and request a renewal application be sent to their current address.

Types of Licenses: A Basic Automobile License (Class D) may be issued to a person 18 years of age and older for all types of motor vehicles registered by the MVC, except motorcycles.
- A Commercial Driver's License (Class A, B, C) is for large trucks, buses, and vehicles hauling hazardous materials.
- A Class A Commercial Driver's License (CDL) is necessary for the operation of tractor trailers or any truck or trailer with a Gross Combination Weight Rating (GCWR) of 26,001 lbs. or more, provided the Gross Vehicle Weight Rating (GVWR) of the vehicle being towed is more than 10,000 lbs., and allows the driver to operate all vehicles in the Class B, C, and D categories.
- A Class B CDL is necessary for the operation of any vehicle with a GVWR of 26,001 lbs. or more or a vehicle with a GVWR of 26,001 lbs. or more towing a trailer with a GVWR of less than 10,000 lbs., or a bus with a GVWR of 26,001 lbs. or more designed to transport 16 or more passengers, including the driver, and allows the driver to operate all vehicles in the Class C and D categories.
- A Class C CDL is necessary for any vehicle with a GVWR of less than 26,001 lbs. used and placarded to transport hazardous material, or any bus, including school buses, designed to carry 16 or more passengers, including the driver, and with a GVWR of less than 26,001 lbs. and all school vehicles designed for 15 or less passengers, including the driver, or any bus or other vehicle designed to transport 8 to 15 passengers, including the driver, which is used for hire.
- There are 4 commercial license endorsements available: (1) double and triple trailer which is for operators of vehicles pulling 2 or 3 trailers and requires a Class A license; (2) passenger which is for operators of all buses or similar vehicles used to transport passengers; (3) tank vehicle for operators of vehicles that transport liquids or gas in bulk; and (4) hazardous materials for operators of vehicles transporting hazardous materials.

- A bus driver license shall be issued to a person 18 years of age and older that has passed a satisfactory examination of driving ability and familiarity with the mechanism of the bus and has presented evidence, satisfactory to the director of the MVC of at least 3 years of driving experience, good character, and physical fitness.
- A Motorcycle License (Class E) or Endorsement (M) is for most vehicles with less than 4 wheels, including motor bikes and scooters. The endorsement is for individuals already holding a basic New Jersey automobile license; otherwise, an individual must obtain a separate license.
- A Motorized Bicycle License (Class F) is for unlicensed drivers, 15 years and older, and is not needed if the operator has a Class A, B, C, D, or E license.
- An Agricultural License (Class G) is for farming purposes only and may be granted to persons between 16 and 17 years of age and can be exchanged for a Class D license at age 17.

Traffic Rules

Alcohol Laws: State has an implied consent law.
- Open containers are not permitted. Meets the TEA-21 requirements.
- Illegal per se BAC level is .08.
- BAC level for people under 21 is .01.
- BAC for commercial drivers is .04.

Cellular Telephone Use: No person shall use a hand-held phone while driving. This law is secondarily enforced.
- School bus drivers are prohibited from talking on a cell phone and driving, except in emergencies.

Emergency Radio/Cellular: Citizen band radio channel 9 is monitored for emergency calls.
- Emergency number is #77; aggressive driver hotline is 1-888-723-7623.

Headsets: Wearing of radio headsets while operating a motor vehicle is permitted.

Occupant Restraints: The driver of a passenger automobile and any front seat passenger must utilize the seat belt system.
- All children under the age of 8 years and weighing less than 80 lbs. must be in a child passenger restraint system or booster seat in the rear seat, if possible.
- All children 8 to 18 and at least 80 lbs. must be restrained in a seat belt in all seating positions.
- Violation of the occupant protection laws is a primary offense.
- Riding in the back of an unenclosed pickup truck is illegal, except for employees on duty.

Railroad Crossing: A person driving a vehicle approaching a railroad grade crossing must stop within 50 feet but not less than 15 feet from the nearest rail and shall not proceed until he can do so safely whenever: (1) a clearly visible electric or mechanical signal device gives warning of the immediate approach of a railroad train; (2) a crossing gate is lowered or when a human flagman gives or continues to give a signal of the approach or passage of a railroad train; (3) a railroad train approaching within approximately 1,500 feet of the highway crossing emits a signal audible from such distance and such railroad train, by reason of its speed or nearness to such crossing, is an immediate hazard; or (4) an approaching railroad train is plainly visible and is in hazardous proximity to such crossing.

- No person is permitted to drive any vehicle through, around, or under any crossing gate or barrier at a railroad crossing while such gate or barrier is closed or is being opened or closed.
- Any school bus carrying any child or children must stop within 50 feet but not less than 15 feet from the nearest rail of a railroad crossing to listen and look in both directions for any approaching train or signals indicating the approach of a train.

School Buses: Lap belt type seat belts or other child restraint systems must be available at each seating position on the bus.

- Each passenger on a school bus that is equipped with seat belts shall wear a properly adjusted and fastened seat belt or other child restraint system at all times the bus is in operation.
- On roads that are not divided, the driver of a vehicle approaching or overtaking a school bus that has stopped to receive or discharge any child, must stop not less than 25 feet from the bus and remain stopped until such child has entered the bus or exited and reached the side of the road and until a flashing red light is no longer exhibited by the bus.
- On roads that have a physical separation, the driver of a vehicle overtaking a school bus that has stopped to receive or discharge any child must stop not less than 25 feet from the bus and remain stopped until such child has entered the bus or exited and reached the side of the road, and until a flashing red light is no longer exhibited by the bus. If the driver of a vehicle is on another road approaching a bus that has stopped to receive or discharge a child, the driver must slow his vehicle to not more than 10 mph until the vehicle has passed the bus and any child that may have disembarked from the bus.

Vehicle Equipment & Rules

Bumper Height: Bumpers shall be mounted at a height that meets manufacturer's specifications.

Glass/Window Tinting: The owner or lessee of a vehicle that is driven by or used to transport a person with a medical condition involving ophthalmic or dermatologic photosensitivity may apply to the director of the MVC for permission to have the windshield and windows of that vehicle covered or treated with a product or material that increases its light reflectance or reduces its light transmittance.

- Sunscreening materials that are installed or applied to the windshield of a motor vehicle shall be of a clear film and such material installed or applied to the front side windows of a motor vehicle shall be either a clear or tinted film.
- Any motor vehicle may have the rear window and/or the rear side windows tinted or covered in a manner so as to partially obscure the driver's vision, provided that the vehicle is equipped with an exterior mirror on each side of the vehicle. Any high-mounted rear stoplight shall not be obstructed in any manner.
- Mirror-type material is not permitted on any window of a motor vehicle.

Telematics: It is unlawful to operate a vehicle that has a television set placed so that the screen is visible to the driver while operating the vehicle.

Windshield Stickers: No person shall drive any motor vehicle with any sign, poster, sticker, or other non-transparent material upon the front windshield, wings, deflectors, side shields, corner lights adjoining the windshield, or front side windows other than a certificate or other article required to be so displayed by statute or regulations.

Motorcycles & Mopeds

Equipment: Every motorcycle shall be equipped with at least 1 and not more than 2 headlamps.

- Every motorcycle equipped with a side car shall be equipped with a lamp on the outside edge of the side car, capable of displaying a white light to the front.
- Every motorcycle shall have, in addition to at least 1 headlamp, 1 tail lamp, 1 stop lamp, at least 1 reflector on the rear, adequate license plate illumination, and a white light displaying to the front on any side car or other extension attached to the side.
- Every motorcycle must have at least 1 brake adequate to control the movement of and to stop the motorcycle.
- No person shall operate a motorcycle which has handle bar grips higher than the shoulder height of the operator when seated.
- A person operating a motorcycle shall ride only upon the permanent and regular seat attached to the motorcycle; passengers shall ride on the permanent and regular seat if designed for 2 persons, or on another seat firmly attached to the rear or side of the driver.
- An operator of a motorcycle must not carry any other person unless the motorcycle is designed to carry more than 1 person and has adequate footrests for each passenger.
- A motorcycle operator and passenger must wear goggles or a face shield unless the motorcycle is equipped with a wind screen meeting specifications established by the director and a securely fitted helmet that is equipped with either a neck or chin strap and be reflectorized on both sides.

Licenses: The director of the MVC may waive the road test portion of the examinations required for a motorcycle license or endorsement if the applicant has successfully completed a motorcycle safety education course.

- All applicants for a motorcycle license who have never previously held such license shall be on probation for a period of 2 years following the issuance of their initial license.
- A motorized bicycle license may be issued to any person 15 years of age or older upon proof of identity, date of birth, and passage of a driving examination.

Noise Limits: Every motor vehicle with a combustion motor must at all times be equipped with a muffler in good working order and in constant operation to prevent excessive or unusual noise and annoying smoke and no person shall use a muffler cutout, bypass, or similar device on a motor vehicle.

- Motorcycles shall be equipped with muffler systems designed especially for motorcycles.

Mopeds: Registration and title are required.

- Special motorized bicycle license is issued to 15 and 16 year olds.

- Operator required to have liability insurance covering bodily injury, $15,000; death, $30,000; property damage, $5,000.
- Protective helmet required.

Passenger Car Trailers

Brakes: Every trailer and semitrailer must have brakes that can be automatically applied upon break-away from the towing vehicle, and means shall be provided to stop and hold the vehicle for an adequate period of time.

- In any combination of motor vehicles, means shall be provided for applying the trailer or semitrailer brakes in approximate synchronism with the brakes on the towing vehicles and creating the required braking effort on the wheels of the rearmost vehicle at the fastest rate, or means shall be provided for applying the braking effort first on the rearmost vehicle equipped with brakes.

Dimensions: Total length: 50 feet (includes bumpers); trailer length: 40 feet (includes bumpers); width: 102 inches; height: 13.6 feet.

Hitch: Trailers shall be connected to the towing vehicle by at least 1 chain or cable, in addition to the hitch bar, of sufficient strength to hold the trailer on a hill if the hitching bar becomes disconnected, or be provided with an adequate device to prevent its rolling backward.

Lighting: Every trailer or semitrailer must be equipped on the rear with 2 taillamps, 2 stop lamps, 2 turn signals, and 2 reflectors, 1 of each at each side.

Mirrors: No person shall drive a vehicle that is so constructed, loaded, or covered that the driver does not have a clear view of the traffic following and at its sides, unless the vehicle is equipped with a device that will show the road to the rear and side.

Speed Limits: As posted. No additional restrictions for car with trailer.

Other Provisions: Maximum of 1 boat or general utility trailer may be towed behind passenger or pleasure vehicle. Total length of both not to exceed 62 feet.

Miscellaneous Provisions

Bail Bonds: A bail bond issued by an automobile club or association may not exceed $500.

Liability Laws: All vehicles registered in New Jersey must be covered by an automobile liability insurance policy that insures against loss resulting from liability for bodily injury, death, and property damage where coverage amounts shall be at least: (1) $15,000 for injury or death of 1 person in any 1 accident; (2) $30,000 on account of injury to or death of more than 1 person in any 1 accident; and (3) $5,000 from property damage in any 1 accident.

- A person with an automobile registered in New Jersey may choose a basic automobile insurance policy, as an alternative to the mandatory coverage, that provides the following coverage: (1) personal injury protection coverage that includes the payment of medical expense benefits for reasonable and necessary treatment of bodily injury in an amount not to exceed $15,000 per person per accident, except that, medical expense benefits shall be paid in an amount not to exceed $250,000 for all medically necessary treatment of permanent or significant brain injury, spinal cord injury or disfigurement, or for medically necessary treatment of other permanent or significant injuries rendered at a trauma center or acute care hospital; (2) $5,000 for property damage in any 1 accident, and (3) the option of $10,000 for injury to or death of 1 or more persons in any 1 accident.

- Every standard automobile liability insurance policy issued or renewed shall contain personal injury protection benefits for the payment of benefits without regard to negligence, liability, or fault to the insured and members of his family residing in his house who sustain bodily injury as a result of an accident, or as a pedestrian, caused by an automobile or an object propelled by or from an automobile, to other persons sustaining injury while occupying the automobile with permission of the insured, and to pedestrians sustaining bodily injury caused by the insured's vehicle or by an object propelled by or from that vehicle.
- State has non-resident service of process law; does not have guest suit law.
- State has no-fault insurance law.

Fees & Taxes

NJ

Table 1: Title & Registration Fees

Vehicle Type	Fee
Motor Vehicle Passenger Registration Fee	Fees range from $32.50 to $81.00
Private Utility, House-Type Semitrailers, and Trailers of Gross Load Not in Excess of 2,000 lbs.	$4.00
All Other Utility, House-Type Semitrailers and Trailers	$9.00
Motorcycles	$28.50
Motorized Bicycles	$15.00
Duplicates	$11.00
Title Fee Without a Lien	$20.00
Duplicate Title	$25.00

Table 2: License Fees

License Class	Fee	Driving Test Fees
Basic Driver's License	$24.00 (photo)	
Commercial Driver's License (CDL)	$42.00* (photo)	$35.00
CDL Exam or Learner's Permit for Additional Endorsement or License Class	$2.00 (per endorsement or class)	
Motorcycle License or Endorsement	$24.00 (photo)	
Duplicate License Fee	$11.00	
Endorsements	$2.00 (per endorsement)	
Permit Fee	$10.00	

* Plus $2.00 per endorsement. $16.00 for non photo license

Table 3: Vehicle Taxes

Tax	Rate
State Sales Tax	6%
Gasoline Tax; (Diesel)	$0.145/gallon; ($0.175/gallon)

Table 4: Miscellaneous Fees

Fee	Amount	Payable Upon
Emissions & Safety Inspection	$2.50	payment of registration fees
Emissions & Safety Inspection Approval Sticker	$1.00 for each sticker	upon issuance
Registration and License Reinstatement Fee	$50.00	upon restoration
Special Plates Fee	$15.00 - $50.00 new $0.00 - $10.00 renewal	upon registration or renewal
License Plate Replacement Fee	$6.00 - $11.00	when remade
New Jersey Emergency Medical Service Helicopter Response Program Fund	$1.00	payment of registration fees

NEW MEXICO

Contact Information

New Mexico Motor Vehicle Division (MVD)
Joseph Montoya Building
1100 South St. Francis, P.O. Box 1028
Santa Fe, NM 87504-1028

(888) 683-4636
www.state.nm.us/tax/mvd

New Mexico State Police
P.O. Box 1628
Santa Fe, NM 87501

(505) 827-9000
www.dps.nm.org

New Mexico State Highway and Transportation Department
1120 Cerrillos Road
P.O. Box 1149
Santa Fe, NM 87504-1149

(505) 827-5100
www.nmshtd.state.nm.us

Vehicle Title

Application: Every motor vehicle, trailer, semitrailer, and pole trailer is subject to registration.

- Applications are made to the MVD and shall be made upon the appropriate forms furnished by the MVD.
- The application shall bear the signature of the owner written with pen and ink, the name and address of the owner, a description of the motor vehicle, an odometer reading, and a statement of all liens or encumbrances upon the vehicle.
- The division shall issue a certificate of title that contains the date issued, the name and address of the owner, a description of the vehicle, a statement of the owner's title and of all liens and encumbrances upon the vehicle.
- The certificate of title shall contain a space for the release of any lien, a space for the assignment of title or interest and warranty by the owner, and a space for the notation of liens and encumbrances upon the vehicle at the time of transfer.

Transfer of Ownership: Registration expires upon transfer of title. The previous owner must notify the division on the appropriate form provided by the division.

- The owner must endorse an assignment and warranty of title upon the certificate of title for such vehicle with a statement of all liens or encumbrances thereto and deliver the certificate of title to the purchaser or transferee at the time of delivering the vehicle.
- The person making the transfer shall sign and record on the transfer document the actual mileage of the vehicle as indicated by the vehicle's odometer at the time of transfer.
- When the owner of a registered vehicle assigns title or interest in the vehicle, he or she shall remove and retain the registration plate from the vehicle, and within 30 days of the transfer, he or she shall either apply to have the registration number assigned to another vehicle of the same class or forward the plate back to the MVD.
- The transferee must apply to the division for issuance of a new certificate of title and transfer of registration within 30 days from the date of transfer.
- Any dealer, when transferring a new vehicle to the first purchaser, shall give the transferee the manufacturer's certificate of origin.

Mobile Homes: Mobile homes must be titled and registered upon payment of property tax.

Vehicle Registration

Application: Every motor vehicle, trailer, semitrailer, and pole trailer is subject to registration.

- Applications are made to the MVD and shall be upon the appropriate forms furnished by the MVD.
- The application shall bear the signature of the owner, the name and address of the owner, a description of the motor vehicle, an odometer reading, and a statement of all liens or encumbrances upon the vehicle.
- Any owner of a vehicle subject to registration which has never been registered in this state but which has been registered in another state shall have such vehicle examined and inspected for its identification number or engine number by the division or an officer or designated agent thereof incident to securing registration, re-registration, or a certificate of title from the division. NCIC clearance is also required.
- A copy of the vehicle registration shall be kept in the vehicle at all times and shall be made available upon the request of a law enforcement officer.
- Changes of address notices must be made within 10 business days of move.
- The MVD may refuse registration or issuance of a certificate of title or any transfer of registration upon the ground that the application contains any false or fraudulent statement; the vehicle is mechanically unfit or unsafe to be operated or moved upon the highways; the division has reasonable ground to believe that the vehicle is a stolen or embezzled vehicle; the required fees and/or taxes have not been paid; or because the owner is required to but has failed to provide proof of compliance with a vehicle emission inspection and maintenance program.

Non-Residents: Non-residents may operate a vehicle registered in another state for a period of up to 180 days without registering the vehicle in New Mexico.

- Any person gainfully employed within the boundaries of the state for a period of 30 days or more within a 60-day period shall be presumed to be a resident of the state

unless the owner of the vehicle commutes from another state in which he resides.
- Every nonresident including any foreign corporation carrying on business within the state and owning and regularly operating in that business any vehicle or trailer within the state must register each vehicle and pay the same fees as required residents of this state.

Registration Type: Renewals of registration are for a 1-year period, but may be extended to a 2-year period for vehicles weighing less than 26,000 lbs.
- The MVD will notify each registered vehicle owner by mail at the last known address within an appropriate period prior to the beginning of the registration period to which the owner has been assigned. The notice shall include a renewal-of-registration application form specifying the amount of registration fees due and the specific dates of the registration period covered by the renewal application.
- Every manufactured home must be titled and registered and shall be issued a registration plate.

Emissions Inspection: May be required by a county or municipal ordinance only. At the present time, according to the New Mexico MVD, Albuquerque is the only jurisdiction to require them.

License Plates

Disbursement: One plate must be attached to the rear of the vehicle not less than 12 inches from the ground.
- After the initial registration, license plates are validated by a sticker when the required registration renewal fees have been paid.
- Disabled license plate available by submitting application, accompanied by medical statement from licensed physician attesting to disability to Vehicle Services Bureau. Disabled placards movable from vehicle to vehicle are also available at local field offices with appropriate medical form completed by physician.

Transfer of Plate: The owner must remove the registration plate from the vehicle within 30 days from the date of the transfer and forward the registration plates to the division to be destroyed, or the owner may apply to have the plate and registration number assigned to another vehicle upon payment of all applicable fees. All foreign plates must be delivered to the MVD.

Driver's Licenses

Examination: The MVD is responsible for establishing qualifications and administering examinations.
- Applicants get no more than 3 chances to pass the examination within a period of 6 months from the date of the application.
- All 1st-time applicants must pass a written test and a road test.
- The department is required to test the eyesight of all applicants (20/40 visual acuity is required).

Graduated Drivers Licensing: State has a system of graduated licensing for teen drivers.
- At 15, teens who are enrolled in and are attending or have completed a driver education course are eligible for an instructional/learner's permit.

- Permit holders may only drive when supervised. Permit holders must also accumulate at least 50 hours (10 at night) of parental/guardian supervised driving.
- At 15 and 6 months, teens who have completed a driver education course and held an instruction permit for at least 6 months are eligible for a provisional license.
- Provisional license holders may not operate a motor vehicle upon public highways between the hours of midnight and 5:00 a.m., unless accompanied by a licensed adult, or when traveling to or from work or a school function. Provisional license holders are also prohibited from transporting more than 1 passenger younger than 21 (except family).
- A driver's license may be issued to any person 16 years and 6 months of age who has successfully held a provisional license for at least 12 months.

Issuance/Application: Applications are to be made on forms furnished by and submitted to the MVD.

- Applications must include disclosure of any past DUI/DWI convictions.
- A notice of change of address or name changes should be made to the department within 10 days.
- Applicants must be at least 18 years old to be issued a license except under certain conditions.
- License normally includes a color photograph.
- License application must include social security number or an individual taxpayer identification number (ITIN).
- License applicants younger than 18 must complete driver education.
- Social security number on license is optional.

Renewal: All driver's licenses are issued for a period of 4 years unless the applicant elects to have an 8-year issuance period, and each license shall expire 30 days after the applicant's birthday in the 4th or 8th year after the effective date of the license. Each license is renewable within 90 days prior to its expiration or at an earlier date approved by the department. The department may require an examination upon renewal.

- Military personnel out of the state should request a non-photo renewal via mail 60 days prior to the expiration of their current license. Requests should be mailed to: Driver Services, P.O. Box 1028, Santa Fe, NM 87504.
- Drivers over 75 must renew licenses annually but the license fee is waived.

Types of Licenses: Class A allows the holder to drive any combination of vehicles with a gross combination weight rating of more than 26,000 lbs.

- Class B allows the holder to drive any single vehicle with a Gross Vehicle Weight Rating (GVWR) of more than 26,000 lbs.
- Class C allows the holder to drive any vehicle designed to transport 16 or more passengers or hazardous materials.
- Class D allows the holder to drive any single vehicle weighing less than 26,001 lbs., or vehicles towing 10,000 lbs. or less.

Traffic Rules

Alcohol Laws: Any person who operates a motor vehicle will be deemed to have given consent to chemical tests of his or her breath or blood or both for the purpose of determining the drug or alcohol content of his or her blood.

- Open containers are prohibited. Meets TEA-21 requirements.
- Illegal per se BAC level is .08.
- BAC level for people under 21 is .02.
- BAC level for commercial drivers is .04.

Cellular Telephone Use: Hand-held cellular phones are prohibited in Santa Fe.

Emergency Radio/Cellular: Citizen band radio channel 9 may be monitored for emergency calls. Emergency cell number is 911.

Headsets: Wearing radio headsets while operating a motor vehicle is permitted.

Occupant Restraints: Each occupant of a motor vehicle must wear seat belts at all times while the vehicle is in operation.

- Children under 1 year old must be placed in a rear-facing child safety seat in the rear seat, if it is available. Children 1 through 4 years of age or children who weigh less than 40 lbs. must be properly secured in a child passenger restraint device that meets federal standards. Children ages 5 through 6, or children under 60 lbs., must use a booster seat. Children ages 7 through 12 must be properly restrained in a child restraint until a vehicle safety seat fits properly. Children ages 13 through 18 must be properly restrained in a seat belt.
- Violation of the occupant protection laws is a primary offense.
- Riding in a pickup truck bed is permitted for persons 18 years and older.

Railroad Crossing: Drivers must stop within 50 feet but not less than 15 feet from the nearest rail when signaled to do so or an approaching train is plainly visible and in hazardous proximity to a crossing.

- Vehicles for hire carrying passengers or vehicles carrying hazardous material must stop at all crossings.

School Buses: A driver, upon approaching or overtaking a stopped school bus from any direction that is receiving or discharging any school children, must stop at least 10 feet before reaching the school bus and may not proceed until the special signals are turned off or the bus resumes motion.

Vehicle Equipment & Rules

Bumper Height: Modification of original vehicle bumper height is permitted. Bumper must be at least 13 inches above surface.

Glass/Window Tinting: Tinting cannot extend more than 5 inches from the top of the windshield.

- If the vehicle is equipped with both left and right outside rearview mirrors, nonreflective tinting may be used on side windows and the rear windshield but cannot have a light transmission of less than 20%.

Telematics: Television screens may not be within the normal view of the driver of a motor vehicle unless the television is used solely as an aid to the driver in the operation of the vehicle.

Towing: When one vehicle is towing another and the connection consists of a chain, rope, or cable, there must be displayed upon such connection a white flag or cloth not less than twelve inches square.

- When a combination of vehicles are engaged in transporting poles, pipe, machinery, or other objects of structural nature which cannot readily be dismembered, the load shall be distributed so as to equalize the weights on the axle of each vehicle insofar as possible.

Windshield Stickers: No person is permitted to drive any motor vehicle with any sign, poster, or other non-transparent material upon or in the front windshield, windows to the immediate right and left of the driver, or in the rearmost window if the latter is used for driving visibility.

Motorcycles & Mopeds

Equipment: Persons under the age of 18 are required to wear a helmet while riding on a motorcycle.

- The motorcycle must have a permanent and regular seat for each rider along with footrests and must be equipped with at least 1 headlamp on the front.
- No motorcycle shall be equipped in a manner such that it is incapable of turning a 90° angle within a circle having a radius of not more than 14 feet.

Licenses: First-time applicants for a motorcycle license or an endorsement on their New Mexico driver's license may be required to complete a motorcycle driver education program as prescribed by the rules and regulations of the bureau.

- A restricted motorcycle license may be issued to any person 13 years of age or older who passes an examination prescribed by the department.
- A Class M license allows the holder to operate a 2- or 3-wheeled motorcycle. It carries one of 3 endorsements:
    - W: any 2- or 3-wheeled motorcycle with an engine displacement of more than 100 cc (minimum 15 years of age with the successful completion of an approved driver education course).
    - Y: any 2- or 3-wheeled motorcycle with an engine displacement between 50 and 100 cc (minimum of 13 years of age).
    - Z: any 2- or 3-wheeled motorcycle with an engine displacement below 50 cc (minimum 13 years of age).

Noise Limits: Every motor vehicle must be equipped with a muffler that prevents "excessive or unusual" noise.

Mopeds: Mopeds shall comply with those motor vehicle safety standards deemed necessary and prescribed by the director of motor vehicles.

- While operating a moped, persons must have in their possession a valid driver's license or any class or permit issued to them.
- Operators of bicycles, motorcycles, mopeds, and the like shall comply with the rules for operation of motor vehicles.

Passenger Car Trailers

Registration: Every motor vehicle, trailer, semitrailer, and pole trailer when driven or moved upon a highway is subject to the registration and certificate of title provisions.

- Trailers not used in commerce and weighing less than 6,001 lbs. may be granted permanent registration upon application and payment of fee.

Brakes: Trailers must be equipped with brakes if they have a gross weight of 3,000 lbs. or greater.
- In any combination of motor-drawn vehicles, means shall be provided for applying the rearmost trailer brakes, of any trailer equipped with brakes, in approximate synchronism with the brakes on the towing vehicle.

Dimensions: Total length: 75 feet; trailer length: 40 feet (includes bumpers); width: 102 inches (allows outside width to exceed 102 inches if the excess is due to an appurtenance); height: 14 feet.

Hitch: Hitch must be secured to frame; safety chain required; double safety chain required for gross weight in excess of 3,000 lbs.

Lighting: Trailers must be equipped with at least 1 red light taillamp mounted on the rear that is plainly visible from a distance of 500 feet, and must also be equipped with at least one white light illuminating the license plate so as to make it visible from at least 50 feet from the rear.
- Trailers must have 2 amber clearance lamps mounted on the front of the vehicle, with 1 on either end of the front side.
- Trailers must also be equipped with 2 red reflectors, 1 at each side, and at least 1 red or amber stop/break lamp and must be equipped with at least 1 lamp or mechanical turn-signaling device visible from both the front and the rear.
- Trailers must be equipped with at least 1 lamp or mechanical turn-signaling device visible from both the front and the rear.

Mirrors: Every vehicle must be equipped with a mirror so located as to reflect to the driver a view of the highway from a distance of at least 200 feet to the rear of the vehicle.

Speed Limits: 75 mph or as posted.

Miscellaneous Provisions

Bail Bonds: Mandatory recognition of AAA arrest bond certificates up to $200, by State Magistrate Courts.

Liability Laws: The department will not issue or renew the registration for any motor vehicle not covered by a motor vehicle insurance policy or by evidence of financial responsibility currently valid meeting the requirements of the laws of New Mexico.
- State has compulsory/mandatory liability law applicable in event of accident causing death, personal injury, or property damage exceeding $500, which results in judgment. Driver loses license if unsatisfied judgment. Mandatory financial responsibility law is effective January 1, 1984. Proof of coverage is required at all times. Noncompliance could result in $300 fine.
- Minimum liability: $25,000 bodily injury or death to any 1 person; $50,000 bodily injury or death to any 2 persons; $10,000 for injury or destruction of property.
- Evidence of financial responsibility is required to be carried in a motor vehicle and shall be executed by the owner or operator's insurer, surety, or the New Mexico state treasurer.

Weigh Stations: Trucks with a GVWR of 26,001 lbs. or more must stop.

Fees & Taxes

Table 1: Title & Registration Fees

Vehicle Type	Title Fee*	Registration Fee
Motor Vehicle	$3.50	Range from $21.00 to $42.00 for 1 yr. and $42.00 to $112.00 for 2 years for cars and $112.00 to $172.00 for trucks
Mobile Home	$3.50	Based on Size
Trailers	$3.50	$7.00 plus $1.00 for each 100 lbs. over 500 lbs. (annual) or $33.00 plus $7.00 for each 100 lbs. over 500 lbs. (permanent)
Motorcycles	$3.50	$15.00 (1-year) $30.00 (2-year)
Mopeds	$3.50	
Duplicate Registration		$3.50
Duplicate Plate		$15.00

* Some fees given by the New Mexico MVD.

Table 2: License Fees

License Class	Fee
Driver's	$16.00 (4-year) $32.00 (8-year)
Provisional	$13.00
Learner's Permit	$5.00
Duplicate Fee	$16.00
Motorcycle Endorsement	$16.00

Table 3: Vehicle Taxes

Tax	Rate
Gasoline Tax; (Diesel)	$0.19/gallon; ($0.21/gallon)
Motor Vehicle Excise Tax	4% of the price of the vehicle (Payable upon Application for Title)
State Sales Tax	5%

Table 4: Miscellaneous Fees

Fee	Amount	Payable Upon
Vehicle Transaction	$3.00	Filing for a new title or registration
Tire Recycling Fee	$1.00 (vehicle) $0.50 (motorcycle)	Registration
Driver Safety Fee	$3.00 (4 year) $6.00 (8 year)	License issuance or renewal
"Additional" Registration Fee	$2.00 (per year)	Registration
Registration and Plate Reinstatement Fee	$25.00 (non DUI) or $75.00 (for DUI)	Registration
Special Plates Fee	$15.00-$40.00	Registration

NM

NEW YORK

Contact Information

Department of Motor Vehicles (DMV)
Empire State Plaza
Albany, NY 12228

(518) 474-0841
www.nydmv.state.ny.us

State Police
Public Security Building #22
State Campus
Albany, NY 12226

(518) 457-6811
www.troopers.state.ny.us

New York State Department of Transportation
5-504 Harriman State Office Campus
1220 Washington Avenue
Albany, NY 12232

(518) 457-6195
www.dot.state.ny.us

Vehicle Title

Application: An application for a certificate of title shall be made by the owner of a vehicle to the DMV on a form provided by the DMV.

- The owner must provide his or her name, residential address, mailing address (if different), and social security number on the title application form. The form also requires the owner to give a description of the vehicle including its make, model year, vehicle identification number, body type, and whether the vehicle is new or used. Also required is the date the applicant acquired the vehicle, the name and address of the person from whom the vehicle was acquired, and the names and addresses of any lien holders.
- A title application must also be accompanied by a statement signed by the applicant stating either (a) any facts or information known to him that could reasonably affect the validity of the title or (b) that no such facts or information are known to him. The DMV may also require other information or documents to identify the vehicle and its proper ownership.
- If the application for a title refers to a vehicle previously registered or licensed in another state or country, the application shall contain or be accompanied by, a certificate of title issued by the other state or country.
- Every owner shall apply for the registration of his or her trailer(s). Such registration shall contain a statement showing the manufacturer's number or other identification. No number plate issued for a trailer shall be transferred to or used for any other trailer.

Transfer of Ownership: If an owner transfers his or her interest in a vehicle, the owner shall, at the time of delivery of the vehicle, execute an assignment and warranty of title to the transferee in the space provided therefor on the certificate of title.

- The transferee shall, within 30 days after acquiring the vehicle, execute an application for a new certificate of title at the DMV.

Mobile Home: A certificate of title is not required for a mobile home designated by the manufacturer as being a 1994 or earlier model year.

Vehicle Registration

Application: An application for the registration of a motor vehicle must be made to the DMV upon a form prescribed by the DMV.

- The applicant must provide his or her name, driver's license number, birth date, sex, phone number, mailing address, and residential address as well as the vehicle's identification number, color, weight, make, year, body type, type of fuel, seating capacity, and odometer reading. Also required is a statement on how the vehicle was obtained as well as information concerning any lien holders.
- An applicant for vehicle registration must be at least 16 years of age.
- No motor vehicle shall be registered unless the application for registration is accompanied by proof of financial security, which shall be evidenced by proof of insurance or evidence of a financial security bond, a financial security deposit or qualification as a self-insurer.
- No motor vehicle shall be operated or driven without first being registered.

Non-Residents: A New York registration is not required for a non-resident who is in compliance with the provisions of the law concerning vehicle registration of the foreign country, state, territory, or federal district of his residence. A non-resident owner shall conspicuously display their registration numbers given to him by their place of residence.

- When a non-resident becomes a resident he or she must register his or her vehicles in New York within 30 days.

Registration Type: Vehicle registration expires every 2 years from the date that the vehicle was first registered in New York. Registration renewal may be done by mail, over the phone, online, or at any DMV office. The DMV will send a renewal notice 45-60 days before the expiration date.

- The owner of a vehicle to be operated only for the purpose of transporting the vehicle to a jurisdiction within this state or to any other state, where the vehicle will be registered, may file with the DMV or any county clerk, an application for an in-transit permit. The in-transit registration is valid for 30 days from the date of issuance.

Emissions Inspection: Required annually.

Safety Inspection: Every motor vehicle registered in New York shall be inspected once each year for safety at an official inspection station. This inspection is required to be performed on the brakes, steering mechanism, wheel alignment, lights, odometer, safety belts, and vehicle identification number. An inspection will also be made of the readiness of the inflatable restraint system in any vehicle manufactured on or after September 1, 1997.

License Plates

Disbursement: Upon registration, the DMV will issue 2 numbered plates to the owner of any motor vehicle and 1 numbered plate to the owner of any trailer or motorcycle. The plates shall have a distinct number that corresponds with the registration number on the registration certificate.

- The plates shall be securely fastened on the vehicle, 1 on the front and 1 on the rear, at a height not more than 48 inches and not less than 12 inches from the ground.
- The plates shall be kept in a clean condition so as to be easily readable and shall not be covered by glass or any plastic material.

- The DMV shall assign to such motor vehicle used for transporting persons with disabilities distinctive numbered plates, called disabled person plates.
- The DMV may issue special number plates to applicants in the same manner that regular plates are issued but with the payment of an increased fee.
- Numerous distinctive license plates are available. Please check with the DMV or online at www.nydmv.state.ny.us to view the selection of plates available.
- Disabled license plates available upon application to DMV. Doctor's statement attesting to disability must accompany application.

Transfer of Plates: When a vehicle is sold, the owner must remove the license plates from the vehicle.

- The owner, however, may register another vehicle and use the plates previously issued to him for another vehicle, after registering the new vehicle and paying the applicable transfer of tags fee.
- Special number plates assigned to a vehicle may, in the discretion of the DMV be transferred to any person 1 year after the expiration date of the registration, or to any person within 1 year after the expiration date of the registration with the permission of the prior registrant or his estate.
- Disabled license plates available upon application to the DMV. Doctor's statement attesting to disability must accompany application.

Driver's Licenses

Examination: Knowledge tests are appropriate for the class, license, or license endorsement, are in written format, and are available in either English or Spanish.

- Road tests are required for all classes of licenses, except a learner's permit.
- The vision test may be administered by the DMV or another state's DMV or by a licensed physician, optometrist, ophthalmologist, optician, or registered nurse. Any statement of visual acuity (20/40 required) will only be acceptable if the date of the examination is not more than 6 months prior to the date of submission.

Graduated Drivers Licensing: State has graduated licensing for teen drivers.

- Learner's Permit: The holder must be at least 16 years of age and must pass the vision screening and knowledge tests. The holder may only operate a vehicle between the hours of 5:00 a.m. and 9:00 p.m., when under the immediate supervision of a person who is at least 21 years old and who holds a license valid in New York for the type of vehicle being operated. From 9:00 p.m. until 5:00 a.m. the holder of a permit must be accompanied by a licensed parent, guardian, or driver's education teacher. However, no learner's permit holder may operate a vehicle within the city of New York unless it is between 5:00 a.m. and 9:00 p.m. and the permit holder is accompanied by a driver's education teacher in a vehicle equipped with dual controls. A learner's permit holder may only operate a vehicle in Nassau and Suffolk counties between the hours of 5:00 a.m. and 9:00 p.m. and when accompanied by a licensed parent, guardian, or driver's education teacher. Front seat occupants are limited to the supervising driver and all occupants must wear safety belts. Permit holder may not operate with more than 2 unrelated passengers under 21, and must have held a learner's permit for 6 months while accumulating 20 hours of driving practice with a licensed parent, guardian, driving school instructor, and/or driver education teacher.
- Class DJ: The holder must be at least 16 years of age. The holder may operate only

vehicles which may be operated with a Class D license, except that it shall not be valid to operate a motor vehicle with an unladen weight or a gross vehicle weight rating (GVWR) of not more than 10,000 lbs. or any motor vehicle towing another vehicle with an unladen weight or GVWR of more than 3,000 lbs. The holder may only operate a vehicle alone from 5:00 a.m.-9:00 p.m. or from 9:00 p.m-5:00 a.m. when driving to or from school, or to or from a place of business where the holder is employed, or when accompanied by a parent or guardian. The holders of the DJ license may not drive in the city of New York. Such license shall automatically become a Class D license when the holder turns 18. In Nassau and Suffolk DJ license holders may only drive from 5:00 a.m. to 9:00 p.m. when accompanied unless driving to or from work, school, driver ed or while engaged in farming. All vehicle occupants must be restrained and occupants are limited to 2 unrelated passengers under 21 unless they are family members.

- Limited class DJ or MJ License: Residents of Nassau, Suffolk, the City of New York, Westchester, Putnam, and Rockland Counties are not eligible to receive such license. Elsewhere in the state, such license can be obtained if a road test is successfully completed within the first 6 months of the validity of a learner's permit. Holders of such license cannot operate a vehicle in the above referenced counties without being accompanied by a licensed parent or guardian. License is valid only en route to and from the holder's place of employment, and/or to and from a class or course, a medical exam or treatment for the holder or a member of his or her household, a daycare facility, or when accompanied by a licensed parent or guardian. Limited Class License automatically becomes a class DJ or MJ license after such license singly or in combination with the class DJ or Class MJ learner's permit has been valid for 6 months.

Issuance/Application: The application for a driver's license shall be made to the DMV on a form prescribed by the DMV.

- An applicant for license is required to provide his name, birth date, sex, height, eye color, social security number, phone number, residential address, mailing address, any name change, and if under the age of 18 parental consent unless 17-18 with certificate of driver's education completion.
- Applicants are required to present proof of identity, age, and fitness. Proof of fitness is defined as: (a) the applicant has not lost consciousness within the previous 12 months, (b) applicant has experienced loss of consciousness within the previous 12 months and an applicant submits a statement from a physician confirming that and stating that the condition was due to a change in medication or that the condition will not interfere with such persons safe operation of a vehicle on the highway.
- An applicant for any class of driver's license, except a learner's permit, is required to submit to a photo imaging process as part of the licensing procedure. Such applicant must not wear dark eyeglasses, makeup or any apparel which when photographed would obscure the applicant's face or make identification difficult. An applicant may apply for an exemption from submitting to a photograph if the applicant (a) presents a statement from a licensed physician that states why the applicant can not visit the DMV to have a picture taken or (b) presents satisfactory evidence that the taking of a photograph is a violation of sincerely held religious beliefs forbidding the making of photo images.
- A member of the armed forces who has been issued a license to operate a motor vehicle or motorcycle by the armed forces of the United States of America may

operate a motor vehicle or motorcycle on the highways for a period of 60 days before application for a New York license must be made.
- License normally includes a photograph. License does not normally include a social security number or a social insurance number.

Renewal: A valid driver's license may be renewed if the applicant is qualified for a renewal of the license by making an application on a form provided by the DMV 6 months prior to 2 years after the date of expiration, paying the appropriate fees, passing a vision test, and having his or her photo image taken.

- Driver's licenses are valid for a period of 8 years.
- A valid driver's license is automatically extended when a person is out of state on active military duty. The driver's license of active duty military personnel is also extended for a maximum of 6 months after discharge or return to the state. Active duty military personnel must file form MV-75 (Military Service Notification).

Types of Licenses: Class D: The holder may operate any passenger vehicle, limited use automobile or any truck with a GVWR of not more than 10,000 lbs., or any such vehicle towing another vehicle with a GVWR of more than 10,000 lbs. provided that such combination of vehicles has a GVWR of not more than 16,000 lbs., except it shall not be valid to operate a tractor, a tow truck, a motorcycle other than a Class B or Class C limited use motorcycle, a vehicle used to transport passengers for hire or for which a hazardous materials endorsement is required, or a vehicle defined as a bus. The holder shall be at least 18 years of age, or 17 years of age if he or she has successfully completed a driver's education course.

- Class E: The holder may only operate vehicles allowed under a Class D license, except that in addition the holder may operate any motor vehicle, other than a bus, used to transport passengers for hire. The holder must be at least 18 years of age.
- Class MJ: The holder shall be at least 16 years of age. This license allows holder to operate any motorcycle. The holder may not drive in the city of New York. Such license will automatically become a class M license when the holder turns 18.
- Class M: The holder may operate a motorcycle, or a motorcycle towing a trailer. The holder shall be at least 18 years of age, or 17 years of age if he or she has successfully completed a driver's education course.
- Class C: May be either commercial or non-commercial. The holder may operate any vehicle or combination of vehicles which may be operated with a Class E license and shall be valid to operate any motor vehicle with a GVWR of not more than 10,000 lbs. However, it shall not be valid to operate a tractor or a motorcycle other than a Class B or C limited use motorcycle. The holder must be at least 18 years of age.
- Commercial Class A: The holder may operate any motor vehicle or any combination of vehicles except a motorcycle other than a Class B or C limited use motorcycle. The holder must be at least 21 years of age.
- Commercial Class B: The holder may operate any vehicle or combination of vehicles which may be operated with a Class E license and shall be valid to operate any motor vehicle or any such vehicle, other than a tractor, towing a vehicle having a GVWR of not more than 10,000 lbs. It shall not be valid to operate a motorcycle other than a Class B or C limited use motorcycle. The holder must be at least 18 years of age.

Traffic Rules

Alcohol Laws: Any person who drives on the roads shall be deemed to have given their implied consent for any chemical tests to determine the weight of alcohol in that person's system.

- Open containers are prohibited. Meets TEA-21 requirements.
- Illegal per se BAC level is .08.
- BAC level for people under 21 is .02.
- BAC for commercial drivers is .04.

Cellular Telephone Use: No person shall operate a motor vehicle while using a mobile telephone to engage in a call while the vehicle is in motion, unless that person is using a hands-free device. This does not apply to the use of a mobile telephone for the sole purpose of communicating with any of the following regarding an emergency situation: an emergency response operator, a hospital, a physicians office or health care clinic, an ambulance company, a fire department or a police department. Also does not apply to any of the following persons while in the performance of their official duties: a police officer or peace officer, a member of the fire department, or the operator of an authorized emergency vehicle.

- A violation of this law shall be a traffic infraction and shall be punishable by a fine of not more than $100.

Emergency Radio/Cellular: Citizen band radio channel 9 is monitored for emergency calls. Emergency cell number is 911.

Headsets: It shall be unlawful for any driver to operate a motor vehicle while wearing more than 1 earphone attached to a radio, tape player, or other audio device.

Occupant Restraints: Use of seat belts is mandatory for all front seat occupants.

- All children under the age of 7 must be placed in a child restraint system unless they are 4'9" tall and/or weigh more than 100 lbs.
- Children who are under 4 but weigh more than 40 lbs. can be restrained in a booster seat with a lap and shoulder belt (when available).
- All children who are between the ages of 7 and 16 must wear a seat belt.
- Violation of the occupant restraint laws is a primary offense.
- No operator of a truck shall operate such vehicle in excess of 5 miles while there are more than 5 persons under 18 years old in the body of the truck unless at least 1 person over the age of 18 is also in the body of the truck.

Railroad Crossing: Whenever any person driving a vehicle approaches a railroad grade crossing under any of the following circumstances, the driver of such vehicle shall stop, not less than 15 feet from the nearest rail and shall not proceed until he or she can do so safely. This applies when (1) an audible or clearly visible electronic or mechanical signal device gives warning of the immediate approach of a train; (2) a crossing gate is lowered or a human flagman gives a signal of the approach of a train; (3) a train approaches within 1,500 feet, which by its proximity is a hazard; or (4) a train emits a warning sound, which by its proximity is a hazard.

- No person shall drive any vehicle through, around, or under any crossing gate or barrier while such gate or barrier is closed or being opened or closed.
- The driver of any bus carrying passengers, of any school bus, any vehicle carrying explosive materials or flammable liquids, any crawler-type tractor, steam shovel, derrick roller, or any equipment or structure having a normal operating speed of 10 mph or less, or a vertical body or a load clearance of less than 1/2 inch per foot of the distance between any 2 adjacent axles shall stop such vehicle within 50 feet but not less than 15 feet from the nearest rail of the railroad and while stopped shall listen and look in both directions for any approaching train and shall not proceed until he or she can do so safely.

School Buses: The driver of a vehicle upon meeting or overtaking from either direction any school bus which, while displaying a red visual signal, stopped to receive or discharge any passengers, or which has stopped because a school bus in front of it has stopped to receive or discharge any passengers shall stop their vehicle before reaching the school bus and not proceed until the school bus resumes motion, or until signaled by the bus driver or a police officer to proceed.

Vehicle Equipment & Rules

Bumper Height: No person shall operate a motor vehicle with a model year of 1999 or after, except a motorcycle or special purpose commercial vehicle granted an exception by the DMV, which is so constructed that the body has a clearance at the front end more than 30 inches from the ground when empty, unless the front end is equipped with bumpers or devices so located that (a) some part of the bumper or device must be at least 16 but not more than 30 inches above the ground with the vehicle empty; (b) the maximum distance between the closest points between the bumpers or devices, if more than 1 is used does not exceed 24 inches; (c) the maximum transverse distance from the widest part of the motor vehicle at the front to the bumper or device shall not exceed 18 inches; and (d) the bumpers or devices shall be substantially constructed and firmly attached.

Glass/Window Tinting: No person shall operate any motor vehicle if the front windshield is composed of, covered by, or treated with any material which has a light transmittance of less than 70%, unless such material is limited to the uppermost 6 inches of the windshield.

- No person shall operate any motor vehicle if the sidewings or side windows on either side forward or adjacent to the operator's seat are composed of, covered by, or treated with any material which has a light transmittance of less than 70%.
- No person shall operate any motor vehicle classified as a station wagon, sedan, hardtop, coupe, hatchback, or convertible if any rear side window has a light transmittance of less than 70%.
- No person shall operate any motor vehicle if the rear window is composed of, covered by, or treated with any material which has a light transmittance of less than 70% unless the vehicle is equipped with side mirrors on both sides of the vehicle so adjusted that the driver has a clear and full view of the road and conditions behind their vehicle.

Telematics: No person shall operate a motor vehicle which is equipped with a television receiving set within view of the operator or in which a television receiving set is in operation within the view of the operator. This does not apply to closed-circuit television receiving equipment exclusively for safety and maneuvering purposes.

- A person other than a police or peace officer, who equips a motor vehicle with a radio receiving set capable of receiving signals on the frequencies allocated for police use or who in any way interferes with the transmission of radio messages by the police without first securing a permit to do so, is guilty of a misdemeanor, punishable by a fine not exceeding $1,000, or imprisonment not exceeding 6 months, or both.

Windshield Stickers: Placing stickers on the windshield or rear windows of a motor vehicle, other than those authorized by the DMV, is prohibited.

Motorcycles & Mopeds

Equipment: Every motorcycle shall have adequate brakes in good working order to control the motorcycle at all times. Motorcycles manufactured after January 1, 1971 shall be equipped with brakes acting both on the front and rear wheels.

- Every motorcycle shall have a bell, horn, or other device for signaling.
- Every motorcycle shall have at least 1 red reflector attached to the rear, 1 red or amber stop lamp, and shall, whenever the motorcycle is being operated, display 1 lighted lamp either white or yellow in color, visible for at least 200 feet on the front and 1 red light on the rear visible for at least 50 feet.
- No motorcycle shall be operated with handlebars or grips more than the height of the operator's shoulders.
- No person may operate a motorcycle without a helmet, goggles, or a face shield, and a rearview mirror so adjusted that the driver has a clear view of the road and condition of traffic behind such motorcycle.
- A person operating a motorcycle shall ride only upon the permanent and regular seat attached.
- A person riding upon a motorcycle shall not carry any other person unless the motorcycle is designed to carry more than 1 person.
- A person shall ride a motorcycle only when sitting astride the seat, facing forward with 1 leg on each side of the motorcycle.
- No person shall operate a motorcycle while carrying any article which prevents him from keeping both hands on the handlebars.
- No person riding upon a motorcycle shall attach themselves or the motorcycle to any other vehicle or streetcar on a roadway.

Licenses: Class M or MJ license is required.

- Class MJ: The holder, shall be at least 16 years of age and may operate any motorcycle. The holder may not drive in the city of New York. Such license will automatically become a class M license when the holder turns 18.
- Class M: The holder may operate a motorcycle, or a motorcycle towing a trailer. The holder shall be at least 18 years of age, or 17 years of age if they have successfully completed a driver's education course.
- A 4-hour motorcycle training class required.

Noise Limits: The maximum allowable sound level is 82 decibels for any motorcycle traveling at any speed. This is to be measured at a distance of 50 feet from the center of the lane in which the motorcycle is traveling.

Limited Use Motorcycles (Mopeds): A limited use motorcycle having a maximum performance speed of more than 30 mph but not more than 40 mph shall be a class A limited use motorcycle. A limited use motorcycle having a maximum performance speed of more than 20 mph but not more than 30 mph, shall be a Class B limited use motorcycle. A limited use motorcycle having a maximum performance speed of not more than 20 mph shall be a Class C limited use motorcycle.

- A registration issued to a Class B or Class C limited use motorcycle shall be valid only for operation on roads in the right-hand lane available for traffic, or upon a usable shoulder on the right side of the highway. This does not apply when the motorcycle operator is preparing to make a left turn.
- A limited use motorcycle shall be subject to the equipment requirements that are

applicable to a motorcycle.
- A certificate of title is not required for a limited use motorcycle.
- The following safety equipment is required: approved protective helmet and eye protection, except for moped classified as Class C limited use motorcycles. Brake acting on both wheels, horn, headlamp, taillamp, number plate lamp, tires with at least 2/32-inch tread, 1 rear red reflector, muffler, and rearview mirror.

Passenger Car Trailers

Brakes: Every trailer and semitrailer weighing more than 1,000 lbs. unladen and every trailer and semitrailer manufactured on or after January 1, 1971, having a registered maximum gross weight or an actual gross weight of more than 3,000 lbs. shall be equipped with adequate brakes in good working order.

Dimensions: Total length: 65 feet (includes bumpers); trailer length: 48 feet (includes bumpers); width: 96 inches (102 inches allowed on certain designated roads); height: 13.6 feet.

Hitch: Device of a type approved by Commissioner of Motor Vehicles. Each approved towing system must include safety chains. Ball hitch mounted on bumper permitted.

Lighting: Taillights, brake lights, license plate lights, and turn signals required. On a combination of vehicles the rear signal lamp must be at the rear of the last vehicle in the combination.

Mirrors: Every motor vehicle, when driven or operated upon a public highway, shall be equipped with a mirror or other reflecting device so adjusted that the operator of such vehicle shall have a clear and full view of the road and condition of traffic behind the vehicle.
- Every motor vehicle when driven or operated on a public highway, that has a model year after 1968, shall be equipped with an adjustable side mirror which shall be affixed to the left outside of such vehicle and which shall be adjustable so that the operator of such vehicle may have a clear view of the road and condition of traffic on the left side and to the rear of such vehicle.

Speed Limits: Same as passenger cars.

Towing: No vehicle shall be towed with the use of a dolly, unless the dolly is secured to the towing vehicle by safety chains or cables which will prevent the dolly from separating from the towing vehicle.
- It is unlawful to operate any open truck or trailer transporting loose materials, unless the truck or trailer has a cover, tarpaulin, or other device that covers the opening on the truck or trailer to prevent the falling of any material therefrom. However, if the load is arranged so that no loose material can fall from or blow out of the truck or trailer, the covering is not necessary.

Miscellaneous Provisions

Bail Bonds: State has discretionary recognition of AAA arrest bond certificate.

Liability Laws: State has compulsory liability insurance law. Also has security-type safety-responsibility law and Motor Vehicle Accident Indemnification Corp.
- Proof of financial security is required for every motor vehicle registered.

- The minimum amounts of financial security required are $25,000 because of bodily injury to or $50,000 because of the death of any 1 person in an accident, $50,000 because of bodily damage to or $100,000 because of the death of 2 or more persons in any 1 accident, and $10,000 because of injury to or destruction to property in any 1 accident.
- State has non-resident service of process law; it does not have guest suit law.
- Proof of insurance coverage for New York registered vehicles required. Insurance ID card must be kept with the vehicle to which it applies and it must be produced upon request to any police officer or to any person with whom an accident has occurred. Failure to produce an ID card when required can result in a charge of uninsured operation. Uninsured operation can result in revocation of license and registration privileges.
- State has compulsory no-fault insurance law. Sale and purchase are mandatory. State provides benefits up to a limit of $50,000 per person to drivers, passengers, and pedestrians injured in a motor vehicle accident occurring in this state. Benefits include all reasonable and necessary medical and rehabilitation expenses; wage loss up to 80% of lost earnings, maximum $2,000 per month for 3 years; substitute service $25 per day up to 1 year.

Weigh Stations: State has fixed inspection/weigh stations along with random enforcement through use of portable units.

Fees & Taxes

Table 1: Title & Registration Fees

Vehicle Type	Title Fee	Registration Fee
Non-Commercial Motor Vehicles and Mobile Homes	$5.00	0-2,150 lbs.: $20.50-$27.00
		2,151-2,750 lbs.: $28.50-$35.00
		2,751-3,350 lbs.: $36.00-$42.50
	No title required for mobile homes dated 1994 or earlier	3,351-3,950 lbs.: $44.00-$53.00
		3,951-4,550 lbs.: $55.00-$64.50
		4,551-5,150 lbs.: $66.50-$76.00
		5,151-5,750 lbs.: $78.00-$88.00
		5,751-6,350 lbs.: $90.00-$91.50
		6,351 and up: $101.50-$112.00
	Security interest: $5.00	minimum for a vehicle with 6+ cylinders or for an electric vehicle: $26.00
Commercial Motor Vehicles	$5.00	0-3,000 lbs.: $6.00-$34.50
		3,001-6,000 lbs.: $40.50-$69.00
		6,001-9,000 lbs.: $75.00-$103.50
		9,001-12,000 lbs.: $109.50-$138.00
		12,001-15,000 lbs.: $144.00-$173.00
		15,001-18,000 lbs.: $178.50-$207.50
		For diesel vehicles weighing 9,501 lbs. or more add 2.6% of the listed fee, then round to the nearest $0.25.
Trailer of 1,000 lbs. or less	no title required	$2.88 for each 500 lbs.
Trailers of more than 10,000 lbs.	$5.00	$2.88 for each 500 lbs.
Motorcycles	$5.00	$14.00 annually
Mopeds	not required	$5.00 annually
Duplicates	$10.00	$3.00

Table 2: License Fees

License Class	Fee	Driving Test Fees
D/DJ age 16-21 (includes Learner's Permit)	$42.50-$47.00	
M/MJ age 16-21	$46.00-$52.00	
D/DJ over 21	$38.50-$43.00	
M/MJ over 21	$43.00-$51.00	
E or C (Non-Commercial) over age 18	$64.00-$83.00	
Commercial Class A,B,C	$123.00	$40.00
Endorsements	$5.00	
M endorsement	$8.00	
Duplicate License Fee	$8.00	

Table 3: Vehicle Taxes

Tax	Rate
Vehicle Use Tax	New York City: $30.00-$80.00 for 2 years.
	Bronx, Kings, Queens, and Richmond Counties: $30.00-$80.00 for 2 years.
	Nassau or Westchester County: $30.00-$60.00 for 2 years.
	Albany, Allegany, Broome, Cattaraugus, Chautauqua, Clinton, Cortland, Livingston, Madison, Niagara, Orleans, Oswego, Putnam, Rensselaer, Schenectady, Schoharie, Schuyler, Steuben, Suffolk, Tompkins, Washington, and Yates: $10.00-$20.00 for 2 years.
State Sales Tax	4% counties may impose a supplement tax
Gasoline Tax; (Diesel)	$0.327/gallon; ($0.305/gallon)
Excise Fuel Tax	$0.08

Table 4: Miscellaneous Fees

Fee	Amount	Payable Upon
Emissions Inspection	upstate: $11.00 downstate: $27.00	inspection
In-Transit Registration	$10.00	application
Plates Fee	$5.50	registration
Plates Transfer Fee	$7.75	transfer
License Plate Replacement Fee	$8.50	replacement

NORTH CAROLINA

Contact Information

Division of Motor Vehicles (DMV)
Motor Vehicles Building
1100 New Bern Avenue
Raleigh, NC 27697-0001

(919) 715-7000
www.dmv.dot.state.nc.us

Crime Control and Public Safety Department
State Highway Patrol
512 N. Salisbury Street
Raleigh, NC 27626-0591

(919) 733-7952
www.ncshp.org

North Carolina Department of Transportation
1503 Mail Service Center
Raleigh, NC 27699-1503

(919) 733-2522
www.ncdot.org

Vehicle Title

Application: An application for vehicle title shall be made at the same time as an application for vehicle registration. The application shall contain the following information: the owner's name; mailing and residence addresses; a description of the vehicle, including make, model, type of body, and vehicle identification number; whether the vehicle is new or used, and if new, the dates the manufacturer or dealer sold and delivered the vehicle to the applicant; and a statement of the owner's title and of all liens upon the vehicle, including the names, addresses, and date of all lienholders in order of priority.

- Applications for new vehicles must also be accompanied by a manufacturer's certificate of origin that is properly assigned to the applicant.
- Upon receipt of a valid application for title, the DMV shall issue a certificate of title. The certificate shall contain the name and address of the owner, and a description of the vehicle. If there are more than 2 owners or lienholders, the names, dates of issuance, and all liens or encumbrances shall be included on the title.
- The reverse side of the certificate of title shall contain a form for the assignment of title or interest and warranty by the registered owner or registered dealer.
- A person must notify the DMV of a change of address or name within 60 days of the change.

Transfer of Ownership: In order to assign or transfer a title, the owner must execute, in the presence of a person authorized to administer oaths, an assignment and warranty of title on the reverse of the certificate of title. The form on the back of the title shall include the name and address of the transferee.

- Any person transferring title or interest in a motor vehicle shall deliver the certificate of title to the transferee at the time of delivery of the vehicle. If there is a security interest, the transferor shall deliver the certificate of title to the lienholder and the lienholder shall forward the certificate of title together with the transferee's application for new title and necessary fees to the DMV within 20 days.
- A transferee must apply to the DMV for a new certificate of title within 28 days of the transfer.

Vehicle Registration

Application: All vehicles, unless exempted, must be registered with the DMV before operating the vehicle.

- The following types of vehicles need not be registered: those dealing with manufacturers, dealers, or non-residents; vehicles used only to cross a highway to get from one piece of property to another; implements of husbandry, farm tractors, road construction, or maintenance machinery that are designed for use in work off the highway and are operated on the highway for the purpose of going to and from such non-highway projects; vehicles owned by the U.S. government; farm equipment headed to or from farms or markets; and trailers or semitrailers attached to and pulled by a farm vehicle.
- For the requirements of an application for registration, see the APPLICATION section for Vehicle Title.

Non-Residents: Non-residents are exempted from North Carolina licensing requirements for motor vehicles for the same time and to the same extent as like exemptions are granted by other jurisdictions to residents of North Carolina.

- Military personnel on active duty in North Carolina may maintain home state vehicle registration.

Registration Type: Staggered registration system.
- Upon receipt of a valid application for registration, the DMV shall issue a registration card. The card shall contain the name and address of the owner, space for the owner's signature, the registration number assigned to the vehicle, and a description of the vehicle. The owner shall sign the registration card and keep it in the vehicle at all times.
- The registration must be renewed annually. The owner of a vehicle may renew the registration by filing an application with the DMV and paying the required fee.
- When the DMV renews a vehicle registration, it shall send the owner a new registration card and either a new license plate or a registration renewal sticker for the plate.
- A person must notify the DMV of a change of address or name within 60 days of the change.

Emissions Inspection: Until July 1, 2002, a motor vehicle is subject to an emissions inspection if it meets the following requirements: it is subject to registration with the DMV; it is not either a trailer with a gross weight below 4,000 lbs., a house trailer, or a motorcycle; it is a 1975 model or later; and it is required to be registered in an emissions county, is part of a fleet operated primarily in an emissions county, is offered for rent in an emissions county, is a used vehicle for sale in an emissions county, or is operated on a federal installation in an emissions county and is not a tactical military vehicle; and is not licensed at the farmer rate.
- From July 1, 2002 until July 1, 2003, a motor vehicle is subject to an emissions inspection if it meets the above requirements, and this additional requirement: it is not a new motor vehicle and has been a used motor vehicle for at least 12 months. A motor vehicle that has been leased or rented, or offered for lease or rent, is subject to an emissions inspection when it either has been leased or rented, or offered for lease or rent, for 12 months or more, or it is sold to a consumer-purchaser.
- Effective July 1, 2003, the same requirements apply as above, except that only vehicles that are 1996 models or later are subject to the inspection.
- Until July 1, 2002, an emissions inspection consists of two parts: a visual inspection of the vehicle's emission control devices to determine if the devices are present, properly connected, and the proper type for the vehicle; and an exhaust emissions analysis.
- From July 1, 2002 until July 1, 2003, an emissions test is the same for vehicles with model years between 1975 and 1995. For model years 1996 and later, an analysis is done of data provided by the on-board diagnostic equipment installed by the manufacturer.
- Effective July 1, 2003, the emissions inspections in Cabarrus, Durham, Forsyth, Gaston, Guilford, Mecklenburg, Orange, Union, and Wake counties are the same. For other counties, the emissions inspection consists of the same visual inspection, and an analysis of data provided by the on-board diagnostic equipment installed on the vehicle.
- Upon successful completion of both a safety and emissions inspection, those vehicles required to pass both will receive an inspection sticker that shows the inspec-

tions' expiration date and also contains the date of inspection, odometer reading, and the identification of the mechanic who performed the inspection.
- A vehicle that fails the emissions inspection is eligible for a waiver if the owner has documented repairs made in the amount of $75 for vehicles older than model year 1981, and $200 for vehicles model year 1981 and later.

Safety Inspection: A motor vehicle is subject to a safety inspection if it meets the following requirements: it is subject to registration with the DMV, is not subject to inspection under the Federal Motor Carrier Safety Regulations, and is not either a trailer with a gross weight below 4,000 lbs. or a house trailer.

- A safety inspection ensures that the following equipment is in a safe operating condition: brakes; lights; horn; steering mechanism; windows and windshield wipers (including tinting levels); directional signals; tires; mirrors; and the exhaust system, if the vehicle is not subject to an emissions test.
- Upon successful completion of a safety inspection, the vehicle will receive an inspection sticker that shows the inspection's expiration date and also contains the date of inspection, odometer reading, and the identification of the mechanic who performed the inspection. The inspection sticker shall be a different color than 1 for both inspections.

License Plates

Disbursement: Upon registration, the DMV shall issue 1 registration plate for a motorcycle, trailer, semitrailer, and every other motor vehicle.

- Every license plate shall have the registration number assigned to the vehicle, the name of the state of North Carolina, and year number for which it is issued or for the expiration date.
- Commercial plates must also bear the word "commercial," unless it is a trailer or is licensed for 6,000 lbs. or less.
- Vehicle owners may pay a prorated fee for license plates issued for less than a year. If the plate is issued between April 1 and June 30, the owner will pay 75% of the fee. Between July 1 and September 30, he or she owes 50% of the fee, and from October 1 to December 31, 25% of the fee.
- Handicapped plates are available at DMV branch offices throughout the state.

Transfer of Plates: License plates shall be retained by the owner following the transfer of a vehicle. They may be assigned to another vehicle in the same vehicle class belonging to the owner, upon proper application to the DMV and payment of a transfer fee and any additional fees that may be due because the new vehicle has a greater registration fee.

- If the new vehicle is of a different vehicle class, the owner shall return the plates to the DMV.

Driver's Licenses

Examination: In order to demonstrate an applicant's physical and mental ability to operate a vehicle, an applicant must pass tests issued by the DMV, which may include road tests, vision tests (20/40 visual acuity required), and oral or written tests.

- The DMV may not require a person who is at least 60 years of age to parallel park a motor vehicle as part of a road test.

Graduated Drivers Licensing: State has a system of graduated licensing for teen drivers. At 15, teens who have passed driver education, a written test and have a driving eligibility certificate are eligible for a learner's permit.

- Permit holders may not drive unsupervised.
- For the 1st 6 months, the permit holder may only drive between the hours of 5:00 a.m. and 9:00 p.m. Every person riding in the vehicle operated by a permit holder must either be wearing a properly fastened safety belt or be safely restrained in a child passenger restraint system.
- At 16, teens may obtain a limited provisional license if they have held a learner's permit for at least 12 months, have not been convicted of a moving violation or seat belt infraction during the preceding 6 months, have passed a road test administered by the DMV, and have a driving eligibility certificate or high school diploma. Provisional license holder may drive unsupervised between 5:00 a.m. and 9:00 p.m.
- At all other times, teens must be supervised by a parent, guardian, grandparent, or a person approved by any of them, and must be licensed for at least 5 years.
- Provisional license holders are restricted from transporting more than 1 passenger under 21 unless accompanied by a supervising driver (family exempted). However, provisional license holders transporting family members under 21 may not transport any other passengers under 21 unless supervised. Every person riding in the vehicle operated by a provisional license holder must either be wearing a properly fastened safety belt or be safely restrained in a child passenger restraint system.
- At 16 years and 6 months, teens are eligible for an unrestricted license if they have: (1) held a provisional license for at least 6 months; (2) not been convicted of a moving violation or seat belt infraction during the preceeding 6 months; and (3) have a driver eligibility certificate.

Issuance/Application: A new resident of North Carolina who has a valid driver's license from another jurisdiction must obtain a North Carolina driver's license within 60 days of becoming a resident.

- To obtain a driver's license, an applicant must complete an application, present at least 2 forms of identification, be a North Carolina resident, and demonstrate his physical and mental ability to drive a motor vehicle safely.
- A driver's license application must contain the applicant's full name; mailing address and residence address; a physical description including sex, height, eye color, and hair color; date of birth; social security number; and the applicant's signature.
- The DMV may not issue a license to a person until that person has furnished proof of financial responsibility.
- A driver's license issued by the DMV must be tamperproof and must also contain the following: an identification of North Carolina as the issuer of the license; the license holder's full name; the license holder's residence address; a color photograph of the license holder; a physical description of the holder including sex, height, eye color, and hair color; the license holder's date of birth; an identifying number for the license holder that is not the holder's social security number; the holder's signature; and the dates of issuance and expiration.
- A person whose address or name changes shall notify the DMV within 60 days after the change occurs.
- An application for a commercial license must include the same information as a regular license, as well as a consent to release the applicant's driving record.

- A first driver's license may be issued for period shorter than 4 years if the DMV determines that a license of shorter duration should be issued because the applicant holds a visa of limited duration issued by the United States Department of State.
- The expiration dates on non-citizen's driver's licenses and ID cards are linked to the expiration date of the person's visa.

Renewal: Applicants for renewal prior to the license expiring may not be required to take a written or road test unless the applicant has been convicted of a traffic violation since the person's license was last issued or the applicant suffers from a mental or physical condition that impairs the person's ability to drive a vehicle.

- The first license the DMV issues to a person expires on the person's 4th or subsequent birthday that occurs after the license is issued and on which the individual's age is evenly divisible by 5.
- The first license the DMV issues to a person 17 years old expires on the holder's 20th birthday.
- The first license the DMV issues to a person 62 years old expires on the person's birthday in the 5th year after the license is issued, whether or not the person's age on that birthday is evenly divisible by 5.
- Residents on active duty or their dependents may renew their driver's license by mail no more than two times during a license holder's lifetime. A driver's license with a military designation on it issued to a person on active duty may be renewed up to one year prior to its expiration upon presentation of military or Department of Defense credentials.

Types of Licenses: Non-Commercial:

- Class A: Authorizes the holder to drive any class A motor vehicle exempt from the commercial license requirements, or a class A motor vehicle that has a combined Gross Vehicle Weight Rating (GVWR) of less than 26,001 lbs. and includes as part of the combination a towed unit that has a GVWR of at least 10,001 lbs.
- Class B: Authorizes the holder to drive any class B motor vehicle exempt from the commercial license requirements.
- Class C: Authorizes the holder to drive any class C motor vehicle that is not a commercial motor vehicle, or a class A or B fire-fighting, rescue, or EMS vehicle when operated by a volunteer member of a fire department, rescue squad, or EMS.
- Commercial Drivers' Licenses (CDL):
  - Class A CDL: Authorizes the holder to drive any class A motor vehicle.
  - Class B CDL: Authorizes the holder to drive any class B motor vehicle.
  - Class C CDL: Authorizes the holder to drive any class C motor vehicle.
  - H Endorsement: Authorizes the holder to drive vehicles, regardless of size or class, except tank vehicles when transporting hazardous material that requires the vehicle to be placarded.
  - M Endorsement: Authorizes the holder to drive a motorcycle.
  - N Endorsement: Authorizes the holder to drive tank vehicles not carrying hazardous materials.
  - P Endorsement: Authorizes the holder to drive vehicles carrying passengers.
  - T Endorsement: Authorizes the holder to drive double trailers.
  - X Endorsement: Authorizes the holder to drive tank vehicles carrying hazardous materials.

- Out-of-state restricted license holders who are between the ages of 16 and 18 may be eligible for any of the 3 provisional licenses, depending on the driving experience of the driver.

Traffic Rules

Alcohol Laws: Any person who drives a vehicle in North Carolina gives an implied consent to a chemical analysis if charged with a DUI. Refusal to take a blood alcohol content (BAC) test results in an immediate revocation of the person's driving privilege for at least 30 days and an additional 12-month revocation by the DMV.

- Open containers are not permitted. Meets the requirements of TEA-21.
- Illegal per se BAC level is .08.
- BAC level for people under 21 is .00.
- BAC level for commercial drivers is .04.
- The DMV shall revoke the driver's license of any person under the age of 21 for 1 year if that person has been convicted of underage purchasing of alcohol.

Emergency Radio/Cellular: Citizen band radio channel 9 is not monitored for emergency calls. Emergency cell number is *HP.

Headsets: Wearing of radio headsets while operating a motor vehicle is permitted.

Occupant Restraints: Each front seat occupant who is at least 16 years of age and each driver of a motor vehicle must wear a safety belt while the vehicle is in motion.

- Every passenger 8 until 16 years of age must be secured in either a child passenger restraint system or a seat belt.
- A child under 8 and less than 80 lbs. must be secured in a child passenger restraint system. If the vehicle has a passenger-side air bag and a rear seat, the child must be secured in a rear seat unless the restraint system is designed for use with air bags.
- Violation of the occupant restraint laws is a primary offense.
- No child under the age of 12 may ride in an open bed or cargo area of a vehicle, unless an adult is present and supervising the child or the bed has an approved seat belt. Additional gaps in coverage apply; see Occupant Protection Chart.

Railroad Crossing: The driver of any vehicle shall stop the vehicle within 15-50 feet of a railroad crossing, when there is a clearly visible electrical or mechanical signal device giving warning of the immediate approach of a train, a crossing gate is lowered, a human flagman gives a signal of the approach of a train, a train approaching within 1,500 feet emits a signal audible from that distance and is an immediate hazard, or an approaching train is plainly visible and in hazardous proximity to the crossing.

- The DOT may place a stop sign in front of railroad crossings. In such instances, the driver of a vehicle must stop between 15-50 feet of the railroad crossing.
- The driver of any school bus, activity bus, motor vehicle carrying passengers for compensation, vehicle over 10,000 lbs. that is carrying hazardous materials, and any motor vehicle with a capacity of at least 16 persons shall stop within 15-50 feet of the railroad crossing. Vehicles other than school buses and activity buses do not need to stop at railroad tracks used for industrial switching purposes, where a police officer or flagman directs traffic to proceed, if there is a railroad gate that flashes to indicate an approaching train, or at an industrial or spur line crossing marked with a sign reading "Exempt."

School Buses: The driver of any vehicle approaching a school bus from any direction, when the bus is displaying its stop signal or flashing signal lights, shall stop the vehicle before passing the bus and remain stopped until the signal has been turned off.

- Vehicles traveling on the opposite side of a divided highway do not need to stop.

Vehicle Equipment & Rules

Bumper Height: The manufacturer's specified bumper height of any passenger motor vehicle shall not be elevated or lowered more than 6 inches in the front or back of the vehicle, without prior written approval from the DMV.

Glass/Window Tinting: The windshield of a vehicle may only be tinted along the top 5 inches of the windshield or to the AS1 line, whichever is longer. The tinting must allow a light transmission of at least 35%.

- All other windows must have a light reflectance of 35%, but vehicles measured to have a light reflectance of at least 32% will be presumed to meet the standard.
- All windows must have a light reflectance of 20% or less.
- Exceptions are available to persons with a medical condition causing them to be photosensitive to visible light.

Telematics: No person shall drive any motor vehicle equipped with any television screen or other means of visually receiving a television broadcast which is located at any point forward of the back of the driver's seat, or that is visible to the driver while operating the vehicle.

Windshield Stickers: Prohibited, except those required by law or approved by commissioner.

Motorcycles & Mopeds

Equipment: Every motorcycle and motor-driven cycle shall be equipped with at least one brake operated either by hand or foot.

- No person shall operate a motorcycle, unless it is equipped with a rearview mirror that provides the operator with a clear, undistorted, and unobstructed view of at least 200 feet to the rear of the motorcycle.
- Every motorcycle shall be equipped with either 1 or 2 headlamps, and they shall be lighted at all times when the motorcycle is in operation.
- Every motorcycle or motor-driven cycle manufactured after December 31, 1955, must be equipped with a stop lamp on the rear of the vehicle that displays a red or amber light visible from a distance of at least 100 feet when operated in the sunlight. The stop lamp shall be activated upon application of the foot brake and may be incorporated into a unit with other rear lamps.
- No person shall operate a motorcycle or moped when the number of persons on board exceeds the number it was designed to carry.
- The operator and all passengers of a motorcycle or moped must wear a protective helmet.
- Lights must be on at all times.

Licenses: To drive a motorcycle, a person shall have a full provisional license with a motorcycle learner's permit, a regular driver's license with a motorcycle learner's permit, or either a full provisional license or a regular driver's license with a motorcycle endorsement.

- An applicant must pass a road test, written or oral test concerning motorcycles, and pay the fee to obtain a motorcycle endorsement.
- An applicant must pass a vision test, road sign test, and written test to obtain a motorcycle learner's permit.
- Motorcycle Learner's Permit: A person who is 16 or 17 years old and has a full provisional license, or a person who is at least 18 years old and has a valid license, is eligible for a motorcycle learner's permit.
- A motorcycle learner's permit is valid for 18 months.

Mopeds: To drive a moped, no license is required, but the operator must be at least 16 years of age.

- Mopeds need not be registered.
- Minimum age to drive a moped is 16.
- Safety helmet required. If operated at night, headlight and taillight or reflector and rearview mirror. If moped is registered additional equipment required: horn, brakes, and license plate lamp.

Passenger Car Trailers

Brakes: Every semitrailer, trailer, or separate vehicle attached by a drawbar or coupling to a towing vehicle of at least 4,000 lbs., and every house trailer weighing at least 1,000 lbs., shall be equipped with brakes controlled or operated by the driver of the towing vehicle.

Dimensions: Total length: 60 feet; trailer length: 35 feet; width: 96 inches (excludes mirrors and safety devices); height: 13.6 feet.

Hitch: The towed vehicle, if the primary towing attachment is a hitch, shall also be attached to the towing unit by means of safety chains or cables of sufficient strength to hold the gross weight of the towed vehicle in the event the hitch fails or becomes disconnected.

- Trailers or semitrailers having locking pins or bolts in the towing attachment and semitrailers in combination with vehicles equipped with 5th-wheel assemblies, do not need the safety chains or cables.

Lighting: Trailers whose load does not obscure the directional signals of the towing vehicle from the view of a driver approaching the vehicle from the rear within 200 feet, and trailers with a gross weight of 4,000 lbs. or less, do not need turn signals.

- Trailers with a gross weight of less than 4,000 lbs. need not be equipped with a rear taillamp, provided that the trailer is equipped with 2 red rear reflectors with a diameter of at least 3 inches that are visible from a distance of at least 500 feet when opposed by a vehicle with lighted headlamps.
- In addition to the lighting requirements listed in the vehicle EQUIPMENT section above, all trailers and semitrailers shall be equipped with a red reflector located so as to be visible for at least 500 feet when opposed by a vehicle with lighted headlamps.
- Every trailer or semitrailer with a gross weight of 4,000 lbs. or more must also have the following lighting equipment: on the front, 2 clearance lamps, with 1 on each side; on each side, 2 side marker lamps and 2 reflectors, with 1 of each at or near the front and at or near the rear; and on the rear, 2 clearance lamps and 2 reflectors, with 1 of each at either side, and 1 stoplight.

- Every pole trailer with a gross weight of 4,000 lbs. or more must also have the following lighting equipment: on each side, 1 side marker lamp and 1 clearance lamp (which may be in combination) to show the front, side, and rear; and on the rear, 2 reflectors, with 1 on each side.
- Every trailer, semitrailer, or pole trailer with a gross weight below 4,000 lbs. must also have the following lighting equipment: 2 reflectors, with 1 on each side, on the rear of the vehicle.
- On every trailer or semitrailer 30 feet or more in length and weighing at least 4,000 lbs., 1 combination marker lamp showing amber and mounted on the bottom side rail at or near the center of each side of the trailer is required.
- Mobile home or house trailer lighting equipment shall be designated by the Commissioner of Motor Vehicles.

Mirrors: Vehicles that have an obstructed view of the rear of the vehicle must place a mirror so that it can reflect the view of the highway to the rear of the vehicle.

Speed Limits: 55 mph unless otherwise posted.

Towing: No trailer, semitrailer, or other towed vehicle shall be operated unless such trailer is firmly attached to the rear of the towing unit, and unless so equipped that it will travel in the path of the vehicle towing it without snaking.

Miscellaneous Provisions

Bail Bonds: Mandatory recognition of AAA arrest bond certificates up to $500.

Liability Laws: The minimum liability insurance coverage for a vehicle is $30,000 for bodily injury to or death of 1 person; $60,000 for bodily injury to or death of 1 or more persons; and $25,000 for injury to or destruction of property of others in any 1 accident.

- Vehicle owners are also required to maintain insurance for the protection of persons entitled to recover damages from owners or operators of uninsured drivers and hit-and-run accidents in an amount between $30,000 and $1,000,000 to be selected by the policy holder.
- State has non-resident service of process law; does not have guest suit law.
- Waives civil penalties and restoration fees for any deployed military personnel whose motor vehicle liability insurance lapsed during the period of deployment or within 90 days after the military member returned to the state. The military member must certify to the DMV that the motor vehicle was not driven on the highway by anyone during the period in which the motor vehicle was uninsured and that the owner now has liability insurance on the motor vehicle.

Weigh Stations: A law enforcement officer may stop and weigh a vehicle to determine if the vehicle's weight is in compliance with the vehicle's declared gross weight and weight limits.

- The DOT shall operate between 6 and 13 permanent weighing stations.

Fees & Taxes

Table 1: Title & Registration Fees

Vehicle Type	Title Fee	Registration Fee
Passenger Vehicles for 15 Passengers or Less	$35.00	$20.00 + $1.00 if renewing by mail
Passenger Vehicles for More than 15 Passengers	$35.00	$23.00 + $1.00 if renewing by mail
House Trailers	$35.00	$7.00
Farm Equipment	$35.00	$3.00 + amount based on weight, ranging from $0.23/1,000 lbs. to $0.58/1,000 lbs., and minimum fee = $17.50
Self-Propelled Property-Hauling Vehicles	$35.00	$3.00 + amount based on weight, ranging from $0.46/1,000 lbs. to $1.20/1,000 lbs., and minimum fee = $21.50
Trailers and Semitrailers	$35.00	$10.00, or $75.00 for multiyear registration plate and card valid until transfer of ownership
Motorcycles (1-passenger capacity)	$35.00	$12.00
Motorcycles Equipped to Transport Additional Persons or Property	$35.00	$19.00
Transfer of Registration		$10.00
Duplicates	$10.00	$10.00

Table 2: License Fees

License Class	Fee
A	$4.25/year of license validity
B	$4.25/year of license validity
C	$3.00/year of license validity
Learner's Permit	$10.00
Restoration of License After Suspension or Revocation	$25.00 - $50.00
Commercial A, B, or C License	$10.00/year of license validity
Commercial License Application Fee	$20.00
10-Day Temporary License	$3.00
Duplicate License Fee	$10.00
Endorsements	$1.25/year of license validity

Table 3: Other User Fees Taxes

Tax	Rate
Gasoline Tax; (Diesel)	$0.175/gallon; ($0.175/gallon) + either $0.035/gallon or 7% of avg. wholesale price, whichever is greater
Highway Use Tax	3% of the retail value of a motor vehicle, with a maximum of $1,000

Table 4: Miscellaneous Fees

Fee	Amount	Payable Upon
Safety Only	$8.25 for the inspection, $1.00 for the sticker	testing
Emissions and Safety	$17.00 for the inspection, $2.40 for the sticker	testing
Inspection Fee for Tinted Windows	$10.00	testing at vehicle inspection
Recording Supplemental Lien	$10.00	application
Remove Lien from Title	$10.00	application
One-Day Title Service	$50.00	application
Special Plates Fee	$20.00 - $30.00	application
License Plate Replacement Fee	$10.00	application

NORTH DAKOTA

Contact Information

Motor Vehicle Division
608 East Boulevard Ave.
Bismarck, ND 58505-0700

(701) 328-2500
www.nd.gov/dot

North Dakota Highway Patrol
600 East Boulevard Ave.
Department 504
Bismarck, ND 58505

(701) 328-2455
www.nd.gov/ndhp

Dept. of Transportation (DOT)
608 East Boulevard Ave.
Bismarck, ND 58505 - 0700

(701) 328-2500
www.nd.gov/dot

Vehicle Title

Application: Every owner of a vehicle in North Dakota for which no certificate of title has been issued shall apply to the DOT for a certificate of title to said vehicle.

- All applications for certificate of title must be made to the DOT and contain: (1) a full description of the vehicle, including the name of the manufacturer, either the engine, serial, or identification number and any other distinguishing marks; (2) a statement as to whether the vehicle is new or used; (3) a statement of the applicant's title and any liens upon the vehicle; (4) the name and address of the person to whom the certificate must be delivered; (5) names and addresses of any lienholders; (6) note whether the vehicle is a specialty-constructed, reconstructed, or foreign vehicle; (7) the buyer's street address, city, and county or township and county of residence; and (8) odometer disclosure information.

Transfer of Ownership: The seller of a vehicle must endorse an assignment and warranty of title and include the name of the purchaser and the selling price of the vehicle before delivering the certificate of title to the purchaser.

- The purchaser of a vehicle must present the endorsed and assigned certificate to the DOT within 30 days of receipt and make application for a new certificate of title.

Vehicle Registration

Application: All motor vehicles must be registered annually with the DOT.
- Applications for vehicle registration must be made to the DOT.
- All registration applications must be signed by the owner and contain the owner's county of residence; address; a brief description of the vehicle including name of the maker, engine, serial, or identification number; whether it is new or used; the last license number known and state in which it was issued; and, upon the registration of the vehicle, the date of sale by the manufacturer or dealer to the person first operating the vehicle.
- If the vehicle is being registered from outside the state, the owner must show the certificate of title and registration card or other evidence that satisfactorily proves ownership.
- If the vehicle is new, the certificate of origin from the manufacturer must be attached to the application for registration or certificate of title.

Non-Residents: Passenger motor vehicles registered in another state or territory and displaying current license plates from that state or territory do not have to be registered in North Dakota, provided that the owner or operator is not a resident of North Dakota for any purpose and is not gainfully employed or stationed in North Dakota.

Registration Type: The registration of a motor vehicle whose gross weight does not exceed 10,000 lbs. expires on the last day of the month which is the anniversary of the month it was originally registered and may be renewed annually. This excludes pickups with an open box-type bed not excedding 9 feet (2.74 meters) in length. The registration of a pickup whose gross weight does not exceed 20,000 lbs. expires on the last day of the month which is the anniversary of the month it was originally registered and may be renewed annually.
- Vehicle registration may not transfer upon ownership of the vehicle.
- Temporary registration may be provided to the purchaser of a vehicle valid for 30 days.

Safety Inspection: The DOT may require brake inspections on any motor-driven vehicle and may disapprove any brake that is not designed or constructed to ensure reasonable and reliable performance in actual use.

License Plates

Disbursement: Two number plates are issued by the DOT for each registered motor vehicle, and 1 number plate for each registered motorcycle, trailer, or housetrailer.
- License plates that are marked to indicate the mobility impaired are available without additional charge upon application and payment of the regular license fee.
- Personalized plates with not more than 7 numerals, letters, ampersands, or combination thereof are available upon application. Personalized motorcycle plates may not contain more than 6 characters.
- An annual registration tab or sticker for the current registration year must be displayed on each plate.
- License plates are issued upon payment of registration fees.
- Mobility impaired placard or license plates are issued upon completion of Form SFN 2887 and issued by the Motor Vehicle Division.

Transfer of Plates: License plates must be retained by the owner and may be transferred to a replacement motor vehicle.

Driver's Licenses

Examination: Applicants for a driver's license are required to take a written, road and eye examination (20/40 visual acuity required). The written and road tests may be waived for an applicant who has successfully passed these tests in this or another state.

Graduated Drivers Licensing: State has a system of graduated licensing for teen drivers. At 14, teens are eligible for an instruction/learner's permit.

- Permit holders may only drive when accompanied by a licensed driver who is at least 18 years of age and has had at least 3 years of driving experience and is occupying a seat beside the driver.
- Teens must hold the permit for at least 6 months.
- Minimum age for an unrestricted license is 16.

Issuance/Application: A person must be licensed to operate a motor vehicle in North Dakota.

- Applications for a driver's license must include the full name, date of birth, sex, social security number, residence, and mailing address and brief description of the applicant. Name and date of birth must be verified by a birth certificate or other satisfactory evidence.
- The application of any minor for an instruction permit or driver's license must be signed and verified before a person authorized to administer oaths or the director's agent, and by the parent or guardian or responsible adult willing to assume obligation for the minor.
- A driver's license must contain a distinguishing number assigned to the licensee, a color photograph of the licensee, the full name, date of birth, residence address, a brief description of the licensee, and either a facsimile of the licensee's signature or a space upon which the licensee must sign. The director may not issue a license number that is, contains, can be converted to, or is an encrypted version of the applicant's social security number.
- A licensee has 10 days to notify the director of a name or address change. A corrected license must be obtained in the event of a name change.

Renewal: A driver's license expires at midnight on the 4-year anniversary of the licensee's birthday.

- All applications for renewal of a driver's license must be accompanied by a certificate from either the driver licensing or examining authorities or a physician or optometrist stating the corrected and uncorrected vision of the applicant.
- A North Dakota licensed driver who is a member of the armed forces and stationed out of state may continue to use his or her non-commercial North Dakota driver license until 30 days after separation without renewing, provided the license is accompanied by military identification and has not been suspended, revoked, or cancelled. This extension does not apply to North Dakota military dependents. Upon return to state, leave or separation papers and the North Dakota license must be presented to obtain new license.

Types of Licenses: A Class D license allows a person to operate any single vehicle with a Gross Vehicle Weight Rating (GVWR) of 26,000 lbs. or less or any such vehicle towing a vehicle with a GVWR not in excess of 10,000 lbs., or a truck towing a trailer, semitrailer, or farm trailer not over 16,000 lbs. A house car or a vehicle towing a travel trailer being used solely for personal purposes may be driven with a Class D license.

- A Class M license allows a person to operate a motor vehicle having a seat or saddle for the use of the rider and designed to travel on not more than 3 wheels in contact with the ground, but excluding motorized bicycles, tractors, and vehicles with an enclosed cab. A Class M vehicle may not be operated under a Class A, B, C, or D license.
- A Class M endorsement, giving the holder the same privileges as a Class M license, may be issued to the holder of a Class A, B, C, or D license upon successful completion of an examination.
- A person holding a commercial driver's license (CDL) may drive all vehicles in the class for the license that is issued and all lesser classes of vehicles except motorcycles.
- A Class A, B, or C license may not be issued to anyone under 18 years of age, except that a Class A, B, or C license specially restricted to use for custom harvest purposes may be issued to a person at least 16 years of age who satisfactorily completes the appropriate examinations.
- A Class A CDL allows a person to operate any combination of vehicles with a GVWR of more than 26,000 lbs., provided the GVWR of the vehicles being towed is in excess of 10,000 lbs.
- A Class B CDL allows a person to operate any single vehicle with a GVWR of more than 26,000 lbs., and any such vehicle towing a vehicle not in excess of 10,000 lbs.
- A Class C CDL allows a person to operate any single vehicle with a GVWR of 26,000 lbs. or less or any such vehicle towing a vehicle with a GVWR not in excess of 10,000 lbs., including vehicles designed to transport 16 or more passengers, including the driver, and vehicles used to transport hazardous materials which requires the vehicle to be placarded under federal law.
- Commercial endorsements include: (1) H, authorizing the driver to drive a vehicle transporting hazardous materials; (2) T, authorizing the driving of double and triple trailers; (3) P, authorizing the driving of vehicles carrying passengers; (4) N, authorizing the driving of tank vehicles; (5) X, authorizing the driving of tank vehicles and hazardous material vehicles; and (6) S, authorizing the driving of a school bus.

Traffic Rules

Alcohol Laws: North Dakota has an implied consent law.
- Open containers are not permitted. Meets requirements of TEA-21.
- Illegal per se BAC level is .08.
- Illegal per se BAC level for people under 21 is .02.
- Illegal per se BAC level for commercial drivers is .04.

Emergency Radio/Cellular: Citizen band radio channel 9 is monitored in most areas for emergency calls. Emergency cell number is *2121.

Headsets: Wearing radio head sets while driving is permitted.

Occupant Restraints: All vehicle occupants 18 and older in the front seat must be properly restrained.
- Violation of the seat belt law is a secondary offense, however violation of the child restraint law is a primary offense.
- Children under 7 years of age must be properly secured in a child restraint system unless the child is at least 57 inches and weighs more than 80 lbs.
- Children 7 through 17 years of age must be in an approved child restraint system or buckled in a seat belt.

- Riding in pickup truck beds is permitted.

Railroad Crossing: A person driving a vehicle must stop within 50 feet but not less than 15 feet from the nearest rail of a railroad, and may not proceed until he can do so safely, whenever: (1) a clearly visible electric or mechanical signal gives warning of the immediate approach of a train; (2) a crossing gate is lowered or when a human flagman gives or continues to give a signal of the approach or passage of a train; (3) a train approaching within approximately 1,320 feet emits an audible signal; or (4) an approaching railroad train is plainly visible and is in hazardous proximity to the crossing.

- Driving through, around, or under any crossing gate or barrier at a railroad crossing while such gate or barrier is closed or is being opened or closed is not permitted. Driving past any human flagman is not permitted until the flagman signals that the way is clear.
- A bus carrying passengers or any school bus must stop within 50 feet but not less than 15 feet from the nearest rail or a railroad to look and listen for signals indicating the approach of a train and may not proceed until it is safe.

School Buses: When the flashing red lights or stop sign on the control arm of a school bus are visible, the driver of a vehicle approaching the school bus from any direction must stop before reaching the school bus and may not proceed until the school bus resumes motion, is signaled by the school bus driver, or the flashing red lights and the stop sign are no longer in use.

- The driver of a vehicle on a divided road does not need to stop when approaching or passing a school bus that is on a different road.
- Every school bus must have plainly visible "SCHOOLBUS" signs on the front and rear in letters not less than 8 inches in height, and be equipped with a stop sign on a control arm and red visual signals to be activated by the driver whenever the vehicle is stopped to receive or discharge children.

Vehicle Equipment & Rules

Bumper Height: The maximum bumper height permitted is 27 inches measured from a level ground surface to the highest point on the bottom of the bumper.

Glass/Window Tinting: No person shall operate a vehicle with any windshield tinting that has a light transmittance of less than 70% or window tinting with a light transmittance of less than 50%. Windows behind the operator are exempt if the vehicle has outside mirrors on both sides.

Windshield Stickers: No person may drive a vehicle with any sign, poster, or other nontransparent material on the front windshield, side wings, or side or rear windows which obstructs the driver's clear view of the road.

Motorcycles & Mopeds

Equipment: A person operating a motorcycle shall ride only on the permanent and regular attached seat.

- An operator may not carry more persons than the motorcycle was designed to carry. In the event a passenger may ride, it must be on the permanent and regular seat if designed for 2 persons, or on another seat firmly attached to the motorcycle at the rear or side of the operator.

- A motorcycle must be equipped with footrests for each passenger not in a sidecar or enclosed cab that can support a weight of 250 lbs.
- No person under the age of 18 years may operate or ride on a motorcycle unless a helmet is being worn on the head of the operator and rider. If the operator of a motorcycle is required to wear a helmet, any passenger must also wear a helmet regardless of the age of the passenger.
- Every motorcycle and motor-driven cycle must have at least 1 brake, which may be operated by hand or foot.
- Three-wheeled motorcycles must have a parking brake of a friction type with a mechanical means to retain engagement.
- Motorcycle handlebars must have nonslip handgrips and be no more than 15 inches above the unoccupied seat in a straight-ahead position.
- Every motorcycle must have at least 1 mirror attached to the handlebar that will reflect an image of at least the horizon and the road surface to the rear of the motorcycle with a minimum reflective surface of 10 square inches.
- The seat or saddle for the operator must be securely attached and may not be less than 25 inches above a level road surface when measured to the lowest point on top of the cushion.
- If a gearbox indicator light is on the vehicle it must be located in the driver's field of vision. If a headlamp beam indicator light is on the vehicle it must be located in the driver's field of vision and automatically lit when the high beam of the lamp is on.

Licenses: A person holding an instruction permit for the operation of a motorcycle may operate the motorcycle only during the hours when use of headlights is not required.

- An applicant 16 years of age and older who does not hold a current valid driver's license, may be issued a Class M learner's permit after successful completion of a written examination. The Class M license will be issued after successful completion of a driver's examination or completion of an approved motorcycle safety course.
- Applicants 14 or 15 years of age may be issued a motorcycle learner's permit if enrolled in or have completed an approved motorcycle safety course. The learner's permit must be held for at least 2 months prior to applying for a Class M driver's license, and the permit holder must have completed the safety course and hold a valid motorcycle learner's permit at the time of application. A driver under 16 years of age is restricted to driving a motorcycle with an engine of 250 cubic centimeters, or less, displacement.

Noise Limits: Motorcycles must have an exhaust system with a muffler or other mechanical device to reduce engine noise. Cutouts and bypasses in the exhaust system are prohibited.

Mopeds: Valid driver's license or permit is required. Minimum age is 14. Safety helmet required for persons under 18.

- Headlights and red reflector or red light on rear required for nighttime use.

Motorized Bicycle: A driver's permit for a motorized bicycle may be issued to an applicant who is at least 14 years of age who pays a fee, takes a written examination to test knowledge of traffic laws and general rules of the road, and has adequate eyesight. The permit expires in the same manner as a driver's license. Safety helmet required for persons under 18.

Passenger Car Trailers

Registration: Any trailer, semitrailer, or farm trailer with a gross weight, not including the towing vehicle, not exceeding 1,500 lbs., and not used for hire or commercial use; or when used to transport recreational vehicles or boats and is not for hire or commercial use, is exempt from registration. All other trailers, semitrailers, or farm trailers must be registered annually with the DOT.

Brakes: Every trailer operated at a speed in excess of 25 mph must have safety chains or brakes adequate to control the movement of and to stop and to hold such vehicle and designed so that they can be applied by the driver of the towing vehicle from its cab, and must be designed and connected so that in case of an accidental breakaway the brakes are automatically applied.

Dimensions: Total length: 75 feet (includes bumpers); trailer length: 53 feet (unless registered in the state before July 1, 1987 and includes bumpers); width: 8 1/2 feet (an appurtenance may extend beyond the body of the vehicle no more than 6 inches); height: 14 feet.

Hitch: The drawbar or other coupling device between vehicles, 1 of which is towing the other, must include safety chains connecting the vehicles. The drawbar, coupling device and safety chains must be of a design, strength, and construction so as to prevent the unintentional uncoupling of the vehicles.

Lighting: Taillights, brake lights, license plate lights, turn signals, and reflectors are required.

Mirrors: Every vehicle, operated singly or when towing any other vehicle, must have a mirror located to reflect to the driver a view of the highway for a distance of at least 200 feet to the rear of the vehicle.

Speed Limits: Rural interstate, 75 mph; non-interstate multilane highways, 70 mph; 2-lane highways, 65 mph, if posted. If not posted, 55 mph.

Miscellaneous Provisions

Bail Bonds: There is discretionary recognition of AAA arrest bond certificates up to $200.

Liability Laws: State has security-type law applicable in event of accident causing property damage in excess of $1,000 or personal injury or death; on judgment minimum. Minimum financial responsibility limits: $25,000/$50,000/$25,000. Unsatisfied Judgment Fund Law: applicable to uncollectible judgments exceeding $300.
- State has no-fault insurance law, which is compulsory. Benefits: Economic loss up to $20,000. Motor vehicle liability insurance: $25,000/$50,000/$25,000. Uninsured motorists coverage: $25,000/$50,000.
- State has mandatory liability insurance law. Minimum limits: $25,000/$50,000/$25,000.
- Proof of coverage is required at all times.
- State has non-resident service of process law.
- A person may not drive or operate a motor vehicle that does not have a valid policy of liability insurance.
- Liability insurance must be in the amount of $25,000 for bodily injury to or death of

ND

1 person in any 1 accident, $50,000 for bodily injury to or death of 2 or more persons in any 1 accident, and $25,000 for injury to or destruction of property in any 1 accident.

- In lieu of an insurance policy, a person may also provide a bond or certificate of deposit of money or securities as proof of financial responsibility.

Weigh Stations: All vehicles with a GVWR in excess of 10,000 lbs. must stop. Exception: recreational vehicles used for personal, recreational purposes.

Fees & Taxes

Table 1: Title & Registration Fees

Vehicle Type	Title Fee	Registration Fee
Motor Vehicles	$5.00	Annual Fees range from $49.00 to $274.00 depending on weight of vehicle and first year registered.
Trailers Required to Be Registered		$20.00
Trailers Not Required to Be Registered		$5.00
Motorcycles	$5.00	$28.00
Duplicates	$5.00	not to exceed $5.00

Table 2: Driver License Fees

License Class	Fee	Driving Test Fees
A	$15.00	$5.00 for written test $5.00 for road test
B	$15.00	$5.00 for written test $5.00 for road test
C	$15.00	$5.00 for written test $5.00 for road test
Motorized Bicycle License	$10.00	
Driver's License Renewal or Replacement	$10.00	
Commercial Driver's License Application Fee	$15.00	
Duplicate License Fee	$8.00 if lost, mutilated, or destroyed $3.00 for a name or address change	
Endorsements	$3.00 each	
Non-Driver Photo ID Card	$8.00	

Table 3: Vehicle Taxes

Tax	Tax
State Sales Tax	5% on the gross receipts of retailers from all sales at retail, except mobile homes used for residential or business purposes, including leasing or renting of tangible personal property
	3% on the gross receipts of retailers from all sales at retail of mobile homes used for residential or business purposes
Gasoline Tax; (Diesel)	$0.23/gallon; ($0.23/gallon)
Use/Excise Tax	5% of the purchase price of any motor vehicle purchased or acquired in or outside North Dakota for use on the roads of North Dakota and required to be registered under state law
	3% of the purchase price, on the storage, use or consumption in this state of mobile homes used for residential or business purposes

Table 4: Miscellaneous Fees

Fee	Amount	Payable Upon
Registration Transfer Fee	$5.00	application
Personalized Plates Fee	$25.00	annual registration
Antique Personalized Plates Fee	$100.00	one-time at issuance
License Plate Replacement Fee	not to exceed $5.00	application
Motorcycle Safety Education	$10.00	registration

OHIO

Contact Information

Bureau of Motor Vehicles (BMV)
1970 W. Broad Street
Columbus, OH 43223-1101

614-752-7500
www. ohiobmv.com

Ohio State Patrol
P.O. Box 182074
1970 W. Broad Street
Columbus, OH 43218-2074

614-466-2660
www.state.oh.us/ohiostatepatrol

Office of Governor's Highway Safety
Department of Public Safety
P.O. Box 182081
Columbus, OH 43218-2081

614-466-3250
www.highwaysafetyoffice.ohio.gov/ghsohome.htm

Ohio Department of Transportation
1980 West Broad Street
Columbus, OH 43223

(614) 466-2335
www.dot.state.oh.us

Vehicle Title

Application: Applications are made on a form prescribed by the registrar of motor vehicles and must include among other things the county in which the certificate is issued; an indication that the certificate is an original, memorandum, duplicate, or salvage certificate; the date of issuance of the certificate; the name and address of the owner; the name and address of the previous owner; the previous certificate of title number; the state in which the vehicle previously was titled; the make, body type, year, model, and vehicle identification number of the vehicle; an odometer reading; and disclosure of all liens and encumbrances.

- The application shall be filed with any clerk of the court of common pleas title office if the applicant is a resident of this state or, if not a resident, in the county in which the transaction is consummated. An application for a certificate of title may be filed electronically by a participating e-lien holder.
- The registrar shall prescribe an affidavit in which the transferor shall swear to the true selling price and the true odometer reading of the motor vehicle. If the transferor indicates on the certificate of title that the odometer reading is not the actual mileage, the clerk shall enter the phrase "nonactual: warning - odometer discrepancy" following the mileage designation.
- If the application for a certificate of title refers to a motor vehicle last registered in another state, the application shall be accompanied by a physical inspection certificate issued by the department of public safety verifying the make, body type, model, and manufacturer's vehicle identification number of the motor vehicle for which the certificate of title is desired. The physical inspection certificate shall be in a form as is designated by the registrar of motor vehicles. The physical inspection of the motor vehicle shall be made at a deputy registrar's office, or at an established place of business operated by a licensed motor vehicle dealer.

Transfer of Ownership: The title must be transferred to the new owner upon delivery of the vehicle. It is illegal to buy, sell, or operate any vehicle without a certificate of title.

- In all cases of transfer of a motor vehicle, other than the sale of a motor vehicle to a general buyer by a dealer, the application for certificate of title must be filed within 30 days after the assignment or delivery of the motor vehicle.
- In the case of the sale of a motor vehicle to a general buyer or user by a dealer, the certificate of title shall be obtained in the name of the buyer by the dealer, leasing dealer, or the manufactured home broker, as the case may be, upon application signed by the buyer. The certificate of title shall be issued within 5 business days after the application for title is filed with the clerk. In all other cases such certificates shall be obtained by the buyer.
- If a certificate of title has not previously been issued for the motor vehicle in this state, the application shall be accompanied by a manufacturer's or importer's certificate or by a certificate of title of another state from which the motor vehicle came.

Vehicle Registration

Application: Applications and renewals are made to the office of the registrar of motor vehicles or a deputy registrar on a written or electronic application or a preprinted registration renewal notice for the following year which begins on January 1 of each year and ends on December 31.

- Applications must include a brief description of the motor vehicle to be registered; the name and residence address of the owner; the district of registration; whether the motor vehicle is a new or used motor vehicle; the date of purchase of the motor vehicle; proof of payment of fees; social security number is kept on file on the actual registration form. If the applicant is required to have an emissions inspection, an inspection certificate must accompany the application.

- The application will be refused if the application is not in proper form or registration fees have not been paid. New vehicles only require certificate of title.

Non-Residents: Once a person becomes an Ohio resident, he or she needs to become an official Ohio driver as soon as possible. Ohio law provides no specific grace period for converting an out-of-state driver's license to an Ohio license; however, Ohio courts and police agencies have considered 30 days the maximum time limit. A person is considered an Ohio resident upon obtaining employment; signing a lease; buying a house; registering to vote; or enrolling children in school.

- Military personnel on active duty in Ohio may maintain out-of-state vehicle registration.

Registration Type: Registration must be renewed annually.

- Registration can be renewed within 90 days of expiration. The registrar will mail a renewal notice at least 45 days before the expiration date.

Emissions Inspection: The Director of Environmental Protection implements and supervises a motor vehicle inspection and maintenance program in any county classified as moderate, serious, severe, or extreme nonattainment for carbon monoxide or ozone. Vehicles registered in Butler, Clark, Clermont, Cuyahoga, Greene, Geauga, Hamilton, Lake, Lorain, Medina, Montgomery, Portage, Summit, and Warren counties are required to have enhanced Acceleration Simulation Mode (ASM 25/25) emissions testing.

- Inspections are required to be done biannually. Upon passage of the inspection, the vehicle inspected shall be given an inspection certificate that is needed for registration.
- Motorists may be granted a waiver or conditional pass if the vehicle achieves a 30% improvement from an initial failure and meets the minimum expenditures for repairs of $100 for 1980 and older vehicles or $200 for 1981 and newer vehicles. A repair cap waiver may be granted with emissions repairs totaling at least $300.
- Vehicles over 25 years old and motorcycles are exempt from the emissions inspection.

Safety Inspection: A state highway patrol officer may stop any vehicle and direct it to submit to a safety inspection. Such inspection shall be made with respect to the brakes, lights, turn signals, steering, horns and warning devices, glass, mirrors, exhaust system, windshield wipers, tires, and such other items of equipment as designated by the superintendent of the state highway patrol by rule or regulation.

License Plates

Disbursement: Plates must be displayed on both the front and the rear for all motor vehicles, and on the rear only for motorcycles and trailers. All license plates shall be securely fastened so as not to swing, and shall not be covered by any material that obstructs their visibility. Disability license plates or disability parking placards are available by application with documentation of disability and prescription for disability placard from physician or chiropractor to BMV or local deputy registrars.

Transfer of Plates: Upon the transfer of ownership of a motor vehicle, the registration of the motor vehicle expires and the original owner immediately shall remove the license plates from the motor vehicle, except that if the original owner or surviving spouse of a motor vehicle that has been transferred makes application for the registration of another motor vehicle at any time during the remainder of the registration period for which the transferred motor vehicle was registered, the owner may file an application for transfer of the registration and, where applicable, the license plates. This application must be made within 30 days of the transfer, in which time the transferred plates and registration may be used on the succeeding motor vehicle.

Driver's Licenses

Examination: Written and driving tests are required for all 1st-time applicants.

- The examination shall include a test of the applicant's knowledge of motor vehicle laws, including the laws on stopping for school buses, a test of the applicant's physical fitness to drive, and a test of the applicant's ability to understand highway traffic control devices.
- Vision screening (20/40 visual acuity) is required for all applicants and renewals. The vision screening is conducted at the office of the deputy registrar receiving the application for license renewal.
- The registrar may waive the examination of any person applying for the renewal of a driver's license or motorcycle operator's endorsement issued under this chapter, provided that the applicant presents either an unexpired license or endorsement or a license or endorsement which has expired not more than 6 months prior to the date of application.
- An applicant for a driver's license shall give an actual demonstration of the ability to exercise ordinary and reasonable control in the operation of a motor vehicle by driving the same under the supervision of an examining officer.

Graduated Drivers Licensing: State has a system of graduated licensing for teen drivers.

- Probationary license holders are prohibited from driving unsupervised between the hours of 1:00 a.m. and 5:00 a.m.
- At 17, teens who have completed the probationary license stage and remained traffic and alcohol-violation-free for at least 12 months are eligible for an unrestricted license.
- At 15 and 6 months, teens are eligible for an instruction/learner's permit.
- Permit holders may not drive unsupervised.
- Permit holders must accumulate at least 50 (10 at night) hours of parental/guardian certified driving.
- At 16, teens who have completed the permit phase and a driver training course are eligible for a probationary license.

Issuance/Application: Every application for a driver's license or motorcycle operator's license or endorsement, or duplicate of any such license or endorsement, is made upon the approved form furnished by the registrar of motor vehicles and must be signed by the applicant and filed with the office of the registrar of motor vehicles or of a deputy registrar.

- Notification of change of address is to be made to the registrar within 10 days following the change.
- License includes 2 color photographs, a primary image, and a "ghost" image.
- Social security number printed on license is optional.

- Licenses issued to temporary residents of Ohio are non-renewable/non-transferable and expire on the date indicated on the appropriate document issued by the Immigration and Naturalization Services.

Renewal: Every driver's license expires on the birthday of the applicant in the 4th year after the date it is issued, but for applicants over 16, the license expires on their 21st birthday. The exception being the non-renewable/non-transferable license which should never exceed 4 years.

- The registrar of motor vehicles shall notify each person 40 days prior to expiration of their driver's license and those whose driver's license has expired within 45 days after the date of expiration.
- Every driver's license is renewable within 90 days prior to its expiration upon payment of fees.
- Licenses of active duty military personnel, peace corps volunteers, foreign service employees and their dependents are valid for up to 6 months after their date of discharge or separation.

Types of Licenses: Types of non-commercial licenses are Passenger Class D (Driver's); motorcycle endorsement on a license, and a motorcycle-only license.

- Types of commercial licenses are: Class A—any combination of vehicles with a combined Gross Vehicle Weight Rating (GVWR) of 26,001 lbs. or more, if the GVWR of the vehicle or vehicles being towed is in excess of 10,000 lbs. Class B—any single vehicle with a GVWR of 26,001 lbs. or more or any such vehicle towing a vehicle having a GVWR that is not in excess of 10,000 lbs. Class C—any single vehicle, or combination of vehicles, designed to transport 16 or more passengers, including the driver, or is placarded for hazardous materials and any school bus with a GVWR of less than 26,001 lbs. that is designed to transport fewer than 16 passengers including the driver. Types of endorsements are: H— authorizes the driver to drive a vehicle transporting hazardous materials; K—restricts the driver to only intrastate operation; L—restricts the driver to vehicles not equipped with air brakes; T—authorizes the driver to drive double and triple trailers; P—authorizes the driver to drive vehicles carrying passengers; N—authorizes the driver to drive tank vehicles; S—authorizes the driver to drive school buses; and X—authorizes the driver to drive tank vehicles transporting hazardous materials.

Traffic Rules

Alcohol Laws: Anyone operating a motor vehicle will be assumed to have given implied consent to a chemical test or test of the person's blood, breath, or urine.

- Open containers are not permitted. Meets TEA-21 requirements.
- Illegal per se BAC law is .08.
- BAC level for people under 21 is .02.
- BAC level for commercial drivers is .04.

Cellular Telephone Use: Hand-held cellular telephones are prohibited in Brooklyn.

Emergency Radio/Cellular: Citizen band radio channel 9 is monitored in many areas for emergency calls. Emergency number is *DUI on a cellular phone.

Headsets: It is illegal to operate a motor vehicle while wearing earphones over, or earplugs in, both ears.

Occupant Restraints: Every driver and front seat passenger must wear a seat belt.
- Violation of the seat belt law is a secondary offense, however violation of the child restraint law is a primary offense.
- Every child less than 4 years of age or weighing less than 40 lbs. must be secured in a child restraint system when being transported in a motor vehicle.
- Riding in the back of an unenclosed cargo storage area of a truck or trailer traveling over 25 mph is illegal for persons under age 16. It is illegal for everyone if the tailgate is unlatched.

Railroad Crossing: Vehicles must stop within 50 feet, but not less than 15 feet from the nearest rail if signaled to do so or if an approaching train is plainly visible.
- Special vehicles, buses, or motortrucks transporting employees, buses transporting passengers, school buses, and vehicles transporting hazardous materials are required to stop.

School Buses: Upon meeting or overtaking any bus stopped for the purpose of receiving or discharging school children or people with disabilities, all drivers must stop at least 10 feet from the front or rear of the bus and may not proceed until such bus resumes motion or the driver is signaled to proceed by the school bus driver.
- If driving on a 4-lane roadway, the driver need not stop if on the other roadway.

Vehicle Equipment & Rules

Bumper Height: The minimum bumper height is 4.5 inches in vertical height.
- Maximum bumper heights are 22 inches for passenger vehicles, 26 inches for 4,500 lbs. and under GVWR, 29 inches for 4,501 lbs. to 7,500 lbs. GVWR, and 31 inches for 7,501 lbs. to 10,000 lbs. GVWR.

Glass/Window Tinting: Application of vehicle glass darkening material must meet Director of Public Safety specifications. Reflectorized material prohibited.

Windshield Stickers: Windshield stickers are prohibited, except that there may be in the lower left-hand or right-hand corner of the windshield a sign, poster, or decal not to exceed 4 inches in height by 6 inches in width.

Motorcycles & Mopeds

Equipment: Each rider must ride on a permanently attached regular seat.
- Each rider must wear safety glasses or other protective eye device.
- No person who is under the age of 18 years, or who holds a motorcycle operator's endorsement or license bearing a "novice," shall operate a motorcycle on a highway, or be a passenger on a motorcycle, unless wearing a protective helmet on his or her head, and no other person shall be a passenger on a motorcycle operated by such a person unless similarly wearing a protective helmet.
- One and no more than 2 headlights are required.
- At least 1 taillight/brake light is required.
- A horn that can be heard for at least 200 feet is required.
- At least 1 rearview mirror is required.
- Handlebars may be no more than 15 inches above the seat.
- Motorcycles manufactured after 1968 must be equipped with turn signals.

Licenses: The same age requirements apply to motorcycle licenses as driver's licenses.

- An applicant for a motorcycle operator's endorsement or a restricted license that permits only the operation of a motorcycle shall give an actual demonstration of the ability to exercise ordinary and reasonable control in the operation of a motorcycle by driving the same under the supervision of an examining officer unless the applicant can show proof of successful completion within the preceding 60 days of a course of basic instruction provided by the motorcycle safety and education program approved by the director.

Noise Limits: When operated at a speed of 35 mph or less, the maximum noise limit is 82 decibels based on a distance of not less than 50 feet from the center of the line of travel.

- When operated at a speed of more than 35 mph, the maximum noise limit is 86 decibels.

Mopeds: To become licensed to operate a moped, 14- and 15-year-olds must pass the usual vision and written tests, as well as a road test. This rule also applies to persons not currently holding a valid operator's license, regardless of age.

- Probationary motorized bicycle licenses are required for 14- and 15-year-old operators.
- Operators are required to obtain and display a rear license plate.
- A moped operator must obey the same traffic laws that apply to operators of bicycles and motor vehicles. This includes obeying all traffic signs and signals, traveling the same direction as the rest of the traffic, signaling turns, and yielding the right of way.
- Operators must wear a protective helmet with the chin strap properly fastened if under 18 years of age.
- Mopeds must be equipped with a rearview mirror.
- Mopeds must be operated when practicable within 3 feet of the right edge of the roadway.
- Carrying more than 1 person on a moped is never allowed.

Passenger Car Trailers

Registration: The original owner of any trailer weighing 4,000 lbs. or less and used exclusively for non-commercial purposes shall, upon application for initial registration, obtain and present such evidence of the trailer's weight as the registrar may require.

Brakes: Brakes are required if the trailer has an empty weight of over 2,000 lbs.

Dimensions: Total length: 65 feet; trailer length: 40 feet; width: 102 inches; height: 13.6 feet.

Hitch: When 1 vehicle is towing another vehicle, the drawbar or other connection may not exceed 15 feet from 1 vehicle to the other.

- When the connection consists only of a chain, rope, or cable, there shall be displayed upon such connection a white flag or cloth not less than 12 inches square.
- In addition to a drawbar or other connection, each trailer and each semitrailer which is not connected to a commercial tractor by means of a 5th wheel shall be coupled with stay chains or cables to the vehicle by which it is being drawn.
- Every trailer or semitrailer shall be equipped with a coupling device, which shall be so designed and constructed that the trailer will follow substantially in the path of the vehicle drawing it, without whipping or swerving from side to side.

Lighting: Trailers must carry, either as part of the taillamps or separately, 2 red reflectors.

- Trailers must be equipped with at least 1 red taillamp visible from 500 feet to the rear and a white light to illuminate the license plate and render it visible from at least 50 feet from the rear.
- Trailers must be equipped with at least 2 stoplights, visible from 500 feet to the rear.

Mirrors: A left rearview mirror is required.

Riding: Riding in a travel trailer or non-self-propelled manufactured home is prohibited. Riding in a pickup camper is permitted.

Speed Limits: 55 mph is the maximum speed for any vehicle or vehicle combination that weighs over 8,000 lbs.

Miscellaneous Provisions

Bail Bonds: Discretionary recognition of AAA arrest bond certificates up to $200, with specified exceptions.

Liability Laws: Has compulsory/mandatory liability which prohibits the operation of a motor vehicle unless financial responsibility is maintained. Applicant for a motor vehicle registration or driver's license is required to sign a statement that he or she maintains financial responsibility. Proof of financial responsibility to be provided whenever a police officer issues a traffic ticket, at all vehicle inspection stops, upon every traffic court appearance upon written request by the BMV, and for every motor vehicle crash causing property damage in excess of $400 or personal injury or death.

- Proof of ability to respond in damages for liability, arising out of the ownership, maintenance, or use of a motor vehicle must be obtained in the amounts of $12,500 because of bodily injury to or death of 1 person in any 1 accident, $25,000 because of bodily injury to or death of 2 or more persons in any 1 accident, and $7,500 because of injury to property of others in any 1 accident.
- State has non-resident service of process law.

Fees & Taxes

Table 1: Title & Registration Fees

Vehicle Type	Title Fee	Registration Fee
Motor Vehicle	$5.00 + $1.00 to notarize signatures	Depends on county: $34.50-$54.50
Late Application	Additional $5.00	None
Mobile Home	$5.00 + $1.00 to notarize signatures (no sales tax)	$49.50 in addition to motor vehicle registration fees
House and Travel Trailers		$24.00
Utility and Boat Trailers		Based on weight: 85¢ for each 100 lbs. to 2,000 lbs.; $1.40 each 100 lbs. over 2,000 lbs. up to a maximum of 3,000 lbs.
Motorcycles	$5.00 + $1.00 to notarize signatures	$24.50 base fee $4.00 motorcycle fund fee
Duplicate Registration		$3.50 deputy fee; $1.00 base fee
Replacement Plates		Regular $6.00; Special $8.40

Table 2: License Fees

License Class	Fee
Class D	Depends on exact age. (16) $25.00; (17) $23.75; (18) $22.50; (19) $21.25; (20) $20.00; (21) $23.75
Renewal (Class D)	$24.00
Any Commercial Endorsement	$29.25 first application, $30.25 renewal, $15.00 duplicate
Temporary Permit Packet	$22.00
Duplicate Fee	$19.50
Motorcycle Endorsement only	$11.00
First Motorcycle License	$29.00
Moped	$19.50

Table 3: Vehicle Taxes

Tax	Rate
County License Tax (Non-Commercial Trailers weighing less than 1,000 are exempt)	Counties may levy up to $20 in addition to regular fees
Gasoline Tax; (Diesel)	$0.24/gallon; ($0.24/gallon)
State Sales Tax	6% plus 1%-1.5% depending on county

Table 4: Miscellaneous Fees

Fee	Amount	Payable Upon
Emissions Inspection Fee	Not to exceed $25	inspection at an official site
Physical Inspection Fee	$3.50 + $1.50 (processing fee)	title application for all motor vehicles previously titled in another state
Registration Processing Fee	$3.50	registration
Special Plates Fee	$10.00-$35.00	registration
License Plates Transfer Fee	$1.00	
License Plate and County Identification Fee	$0.25 per plate/$0.25 per sticker	registration

OH

OKLAHOMA

Contact Information

Oklahoma Tax Commission
(Motor Vehicle Registration)
2501 Lincoln Boulevard
Oklahoma City, OK 73194

(405) 522-5632
www.oktax.state.ok.us/mvhome.html

Oklahoma Department of Public Safety (DPS)
Driver's License Service
3600 N. ML King Avenue
P.O. Box 11415
Oklahoma City, OK 73136-0415

(405) 425-2424
www.dps.state.ok.us

Oklahoma Highway Patrol
3600 N. ML King Avenue
Oklahoma City, OK 73136

(405) 425-2424
www.dps.state.ok.us/ohp/

Department of Transportation
200 N.E. 21st Street
Oklahoma City, OK 73105

(405) 522-8000
www.okladot.state.ok.us

Vehicle Title

Application: The owner of every vehicle in the state shall possess a certificate of title as proof of ownership of such vehicle.

- Application for a certificate of title may be made to the Tax Commission or any motor license agent. If the application is made to a motor license agent, the agent shall transmit the application to the Tax Commission either electronically or by mail.
- The application for a certificate of title shall contain the following information: a full description of the vehicle; the manufacturer's serial or other identification number; the motor number and date on which the vehicle was first sold by the manufacturer or dealer to the owner; any distinguishing marks; a statement of the applicant's source of title, and any security interest upon the title.
- If the vehicle is within the last 7 model years, a declaration must be added to the application if the vehicle has been damaged or stolen, if the owner did or did not receive payment for the loss from an insurer, or the vehicle is titled or registered in a state that does not classify the vehicle or brand the title because of damage to or loss of the vehicle similar to the classifications or brands utilized by Oklahoma.
- To obtain an original certificate of title for a vehicle being registered for the first time, the applicant must also provide a manufacturer's certificate of origin, which includes the manufacturer's serial or identification number, the date on which the vehicle was first sold by the manufacturer to the dealer, any distinguishing marks, including the model and year the mark was made, and a statement of any security interests upon the vehicle.
- Out-of-state vehicles being titled in Oklahoma must be inspected prior to issuing a certificate of title. The inspection shall include a comparison of the vehicle identification number on the vehicle with the number recorded on the ownership records, and a recording of the actual odometer reading.

Transfer of Ownership: Any transferor shall give the following written information to the transferee prior to the transfer of ownership of a motor vehicle: the odometer reading at the time of transfer; the date of transfer; the name and current address of the transferor; and the identity of the vehicle, including make, model, year, body type, and vehicle identification number.

- In addition, the transferor shall certify one of the following: that the odometer reading reflects the actual mileage; the odometer reading does not reflect the actual mileage; or the mileage is in excess of the mechanical limits of the odometer.
- The following vehicles are exempted from the odometer disclosure statement: vehicles with a Gross Vehicle Weight Rating (GVWR) of more than 16,000 lbs.; a vehicle that is not self-propelled; a vehicle at least 10 years old; a vehicle sold by the manufacturer to any agency of the United States; or a new motor vehicle prior to its transfer to the first retail purchaser.
- When transferring ownership of a vehicle, the transferor shall endorse on the back of the title a complete assignment with warranty of title, and a statement of all liens or encumbrances on the vehicle, sworn before a notary public, and must deliver the title to the transferee at the time of delivery of the vehicle.
- Within 30 days of the delivery of the vehicle, the transferee shall present the assigned certificate of title and the insurance security verification to the Tax Commission, along with the required fees and any taxes due.

Mobile Homes: Any person purchasing a new or used manufactured home or owning a manufactured home that has not been registered in Oklahoma shall obtain a certificate of title.

- The application for certificate of title shall include the name of the owner; the serial or identification number of the manufactured home; a legal description or address of the location; and the actual retail selling price of the manufactured home excluding taxes.
- Upon receiving a proper application and payment of the required fees and ad valorem taxes, the Tax Commission may issue a manufactured home registration receipt, manufactured home registration decal, and excise tax receipt to the applicant.

Vehicle Registration

Application: Every owner possessing a certificate of title shall make an application for the registration of the vehicle with a motor license agent.

- All applications for registration must contain a full description of the vehicle, including the manufacturer's serial or identification number, and security interest upon the vehicle, an odometer reading (when applicable), and the insurance security verification of the vehicle; the correct name, address, and driver's license number; and the vehicle owner's insurance policy information.
- Upon the filing of a proper application and payment of the required fees, the Tax Commission shall assign a distinctive number to the vehicle and 1 license plate or yearly decal. The decal shall have an identification number and the last 2 numbers of the year of expiration.
- The purchaser of a new or manufactured home shall register the home with the Tax Commission within 30 days of purchase.
- Upon the registration of a manufactured home, the Tax Commission shall obtain the following information: the name of the owner of the home; the serial or identification number of the home; a legal description or address of the location for the

home; the actual retail selling price, excluding taxes; the certificate of title for the home; and the school district in which the home is to be located.

Non-Residents: If the owner of a vehicle becomes employed in Oklahoma, the vehicle is deemed to be subject to tax in the state and, within 30 days from the date of employment, shall be registered in the state.

- Any student certified as a full-time student by an institution of higher learning in Oklahoma who is not a resident of Oklahoma need not register a vehicle in the state.
- Any vehicle, including a manufactured home, that is owned by a visiting non-resident and is properly registered in another state shall become registered in Oklahoma if it remains in Oklahoma for any period in excess of 60 days.
- Military personnel on active duty in Oklahoma may maintain home state vehicle registration. Non-resident military personnel may register any vehicle in Oklahoma for annual fee of $20. Commercial vehicles are excluded.

Registration Type: The certificate of registration shall be carried at all times in the vehicle, and shown on demand of any law enforcement officer.

- The annual registration period for manufactured homes, motorcycles, commercial vehicles, and vehicles registered with permanent nonexpiring license plates begins on January 1 of each year. The full registration fee is required for vehicles registered between January 1 and March 31; 75% of the fee is due for vehicles registered between April 1 and June 30; 50% for vehicles registered between July 1 and September 30; and 25% for vehicles registered between October 1 and November 30. Vehicles registered in the month of December shall be registered for the following year.
- All other vehicles, including passenger vehicles, are registered annually on a staggered system. Twelve registration periods are set up, with each period lasting 1 month.
- A vehicle owner may renew a registration by mail, provided he or she pays an extra fee for the mailing of new plates or decals. The Tax Commission shall provide a postcard form for renewal.

Emissions Inspection: Any person who owns and drives a 1979 or newer model year vehicle up to 8,500 lbs. shall be required to submit the vehicle for a vehicle emission anti-tampering inspection, if he or she lives in or within a county with at least 500,000 people, in a county with fewer than 500,000 people but designated an air quality nonattainment area for auto-related pollutants, or within a metropolitan transport study area.

- Inspections are valid for 1 year.
- Trailers, semitrailers, pole trailers, house trailers, or travel trailers do need to be inspected.
- Manufactured homes, ancient vehicles, and trailers with nonexpiring plates used in interstate commerce need not be inspected.
- Vehicles that fail an emissions inspection have 30 days to make repairs and pass a new inspection.
- An out-of-state vehicle owner has 10 days to have his or her vehicle inspected after registering the vehicle in Oklahoma.

Safety Inspection: Annual safety inspections are no longer required.

- Law enforcement may, upon reasonable cause to believe that a vehicle is unsafe or not properly equipped as required, require that the driver of the vehicle stop and submit the vehicle to an inspection by the officer.

License Plates

Disbursement: The license plate shall be affixed to the rear of the vehicle.
- The yearly decal will validate the license plate for each registration period other than the year the plate is issued.
- The license plate and decal shall be of such size, color, design, and numbering as the Tax Commission directs. Each license plate shall have a space for the placement of the yearly decals. The emblem on the state flag shall be part of all plates issued after December 31, 1998, and all new plates shall have the legend "Oklahoma Native America" to replace "Oklahoma is OK." Letters and numerals shall be green and white.
- For the first year any manufactured home is registered in the state, a metal license plate shall be affixed to the home.
- Temporary license plates placed on newly purchased vehicles are valid for up to 30 days.
- Personalized license plates will be issued with a maximum of 7 letters or numbers, or a combination of 4 letters and 3 numbers. No punctuation marks or symbols are allowed.
- Personalized license plates for motorcycles will be issued with a maximum of 6 letters or numbers, or a combination of 4 letters and 2 numbers.
- Disabled license plates issued upon application to Oklahoma Tax Commission – no additional charge.

Transfer of Plates: The holder of a license plate may transfer that plate to a new vehicle.
- The vehicle owner, after transferring the plate from one vehicle to the next, must also obtain a replacement plate for the 1st vehicle by payment of an additional fee. If the new vehicle was previously registered, the owner shall return the plate from the new vehicle and place the replacement plate on the old vehicle.
- A registration listing the tag as being transferred will be issued, along with a new decal showing the expiration of the registration, following the payment of all required fees.

Driver's Licenses

Examination: Every applicant for an original Class A, B, C, or D license must pass a vision test (20/60 visual acuity required), a written test concerning the applicant's ability to read and understand highway signs and his or her knowledge of the traffic laws of the state, and a road test.
- The DPS may waive any portion of the test for applicants with a valid out-of-state license.
- Holders of Class A, B, or C licenses are eligible for a Class D license without taking another test.
- The written portion of the driving test may be administered by any certified driver education instructor.

Graduated Drivers Licensing: State has a system of graduated licensing for teen drivers. At 15 1/2 teens are eligible for a permit. Permit holders must be supervised at all times by a driver at least 21.
- To be eligible for a permit teens must complete or be enrolled in driver education

or be taking a parent-taught driver education course certified by the Department of Public Safety. Teens who do not take driver's education must wait until age 16 to receive a learner's permit.
- Teens must hold the permit for 6 months and certify that they have received 40 hours (10 at night) of practice driving.
- At 16, teens are eligible for an intermediate license. Intermediate license holders may not drive unsupervised between the hours of 11:00 p.m. and 5:00 a.m. Intermediate license holders are also prohibited from transporting more than 1 passenger unless supervised, family members excepted.
- Teens who complete an approved driver education course must hold the intermediate license for at least 6 months and are eligible for an unrestricted license at 16 1/2. Teens who don't complete an approved driver education course must hold the intermediate license for 1 year before being eligible for an unrestricted license.
- A restricted commercial license will be issued to any person at least 18 years of age who has passed all portions of the commercial driver license examination other than the driving test. The licensee may drive a commercial vehicle only when accompanied by a licensed commercial driver who is at least 21 years of age.

Issuance/Application: All original and renewal licenses are valid for 4 years from the last day of the month in which they are issued.

- Licenses are to be carried in the vehicle at all times, and must be exhibited on demand of a law enforcement officer.
- Every applicant for a driver license shall provide the following information: full name; date of birth; sex; residence address and mailing address, if different from the residence; medical information required by the DPS; whether the applicant is deaf or hard-of-hearing; the license plate number and state of issuance for up to 2 vehicles; a brief physical description of the applicant; whether the applicant has had a license suspended or revoked, and, if so, why; and the applicant's social security number. In addition, the applicant must provide 2 forms of identification. Finger image required as proof of identity.
- Upon payment of the required fee, the DPS may issue to every applicant a Class A, B, C, or D license. The license shall contain a distinguishing number assigned to the licensee, date of issuance, date of expiration, the full name of the licensee, applicant's signature, date of birth, mailing address, sex, a color photograph or computerized image of the licensee and any security features approved by the DPS.
- The DPS may use the applicant's social security number as his or her driver identification number only upon approval by the applicant.
- Any person under the age of 18 will not be issued a license unless he or she is either in school or has successfully passed the 8th grade reading test or is employed for at least 24 hours a week.
- Any person at least age 14 may apply for a restricted Class D license with a motorcycle restriction. After passing all portions of the exam other than the driving test, the licensee may operate a motorcycle with a maximum piston displacement of 250cc between the hours of 4:30 a.m. and 9:00 p.m., when wearing approved headgear, and while accompanied by a licensed adult who is at least 21 years of age and who has a motorcycle endorsement on his or her license. After 30 days, the restricted motorcycle licensee may take the driving test and, if passed, may operate a motorcycle without being accompanied by a licensed adult.
- Licensees have 10 days to apply for a new license after changing addresses or names.

Renewal: A licensee may renew a license by application, furnishing 2 forms of identification, and payment of the required fee.

- Licensees applying for renewal may be required to take an examination if they have proven accident records or apparent physical defects.
- Renewal by mail is available only to Class D licensees.
- In the event a license is lost or destroyed, a replacement may be obtained by paying the required fee and furnishing 2 forms of identification.
- Any person or spouse of a person on active duty with the armed forces of the United States living outside the continental limits of the United States having a valid driver's license issued by the State of Oklahoma for the operation of motor vehicles upon the highways of the state shall have, without additional charge, a valid license for the duration of such service and for a period of 60 days from and after the return of the person or spouse of the person to the continental limits of the United States from such service.

Types of Licenses: Commercial Licenses:

- Class A: must be 18 years of age. The holder of a Class A license may drive any vehicle in Classes A, B, C, or D. A Class A motor vehicle includes any combination of vehicles not listed as a Class D vehicle with a GVWR of at least 26,001 lbs., provided that the GVWR of the vehicle(s) being towed is in excess of 10,000 lbs.
- Class B: must be 18 years of age. The holder of a Class B license may drive any vehicle in Classes B, C, or D. A Class B motor vehicle includes any single vehicle not listed as a Class D vehicle with a GVWR of at least 26,001 lbs., or any such vehicle towing a vehicle with a GVWR of 10,000 lbs. or less. This class also applies to a bus with a GVWR of at least 26,001 lbs. and designed to transport 16 or more persons.
- Class C: must be 18 years of age. The holder of a Class C license may drive any vehicle in Classes C or D. A Class C motor vehicle includes any single or combination of vehicles not listed as a Class D vehicle, other than a Class A or B vehicle, that is either required to be placarded for hazardous materials or designed to transport 16 or more persons.
- No person may drive a hazardous vehicle unless that person is at least 21 years of age.
- Non-Commercial License: A Class D license is given to persons at least 16 years of age who are eligible to drive a Class D non-commercial motor vehicle. Class D vehicles include any vehicle marked and used as a firefighting or law enforcement vehicle; designed and used solely as a recreational vehicle; is a single or combination vehicle with a GVWR of 26,000 lbs. or less; or is a single or combination vehicle with a GVWR of 26,001 lbs. or more, and is used for agricultural purposes.
- In order to operate a motorcycle, licensees must obtain a motorcycle endorsement on their regular license.

Traffic Rules

Alcohol Laws: Any person who operates a motor vehicle in Oklahoma is deemed to have given an implied consent to a test or tests of his or her blood or breath for the purpose of determining the presence and concentration of any intoxicating substances.

- Open containers are not permitted. Meets TEA-21 requirements.
- Illegal per se BAC level is .08.

- Any person under the age of 21 operating a vehicle with any measurable quantity of alcohol is deemed to be operating under the influence.
- BAC level for commercial drivers is .04.

Emergency Radio/Cellular: Citizen band radio channel 9 is not monitored for emergency calls. Emergency cell number is *55.

Headsets: Wearing radio headsets is not permitted.

Occupant Restraints: Every operator and front seat passenger of a passenger car must wear a properly fastened safety belt.
- Children under the age of 6 must be properly restrained in a child passenger restraint system.
- Children at least 6 years of age but younger than 13 must be properly restrained in either a child passenger restraint system or a seat belt.
- A child weighing more than 40 lbs. may be transported in the back seat of the motor vehicle while wearing only a lap belt, if the back seat of the motor vehicle is not equipped with a combination lap and shoulder belt.
- Violation of the occupant protection laws is a primary offense.
- Passengers may ride in the bed area of a pickup truck.

Railroad Crossing: A driver must stop between 15 and 50 feet from a railroad crossing whenever a clearly visible electric or mechanical signal gives warning of the immediate approach of a train; a crossing gate is lowered; a human flagman gives a signal of the approach or passage of a train; a train approaching within 1,500 feet of the crossing emits a signal audible from such distance and the train is an immediate hazard; or when the approaching train is plainly visible and is in hazardous proximity to the crossing.
- The following vehicles are required to stop at all railroad crossings: motor vehicles carrying passengers for hire; commercial and school buses; vehicles carrying explosive substances or flammable liquids; and commercial vehicles carrying hazardous materials.

School Buses: The driver of a vehicle approaching a school bus from either direction must stop his vehicle whenever the bus is stopped to take on or discharge students and has its red loading signals in operation.
- Drivers of vehicles on the other side of a divided highway need not stop for a school bus taking on or discharging students.
- The above rules apply to vehicles approaching church buses as well.

Vehicle Equipment & Rules

Bumper Height: Modification of original vehicle bumper height is permitted. Note: Headlamps cannot be mounted at a height measured from center of the lamp no greater than 54 inches nor less than 22 inches.

Glass/Window Tinting: For model year 1996 and later, side and back windows may have window tinting that allows at least 25% light transmission, and has a luminous reflectance no greater than 25%.
- For model year 1995 and earlier, side windows to the rear of the driver, and back windows may have window tinting that allows at least 10% light transmission, and has a luminous reflectance no greater than 25%.
- Windshields may have transparent material affixed from the top of the windshield

to either the AS-1 line or for a maximum of 5 inches.

Telematics: It is unlawful to install a television set in any location where it is visible from the driver's seat.

Windshield Stickers: No person shall drive any motor vehicle with any sign, poster, or other nontransparent material upon any window that obstructs the driver's clear view of the roadway.

Motorcycles & Mopeds

Equipment: Every person under the age of 18 years must wear a helmet.

- No person shall drive a motorcycle, motor scooter, or motorbicycle unless factory designed for the purpose of carrying additional passengers.
- Lighted lamps and illuminating devices are required at all times.
- Every motorcycle and motor-driven cycle shall be equipped with either 1 or 2 headlamps. Headlamps or lamps shall be capable of revealing a person or vehicle from a distance of at least 100 feet when driving up to 25 mph, a distance of at least 200 feet when driving between 25-35 mph, and 300 feet when driving 35 mph or more.
- 1 stop lamp is required on the rear of the vehicle. At least 1 taillight and 1 rear reflector are also required.
- No driver of any 2-wheeled motor vehicle may carry any other person on the vehicle, unless the vehicle has a wheel diameter of at least 12 inches, and either a double seating device with double footrests or a side car attachment.
- Handlebars on motorcycles and motor scooters shall not exceed 12 inches in height.
- Two rearview mirrors with a reflection surface of at least 3 inches in diameter are required. One mirror shall be mounted on each side of the vehicle, and positioned to allow the operator to clearly view the roadway for a distance of 200 feet to the rear.
- A windshield of such dimensions as to protect the operator from foreign objects is required, unless the operator wears either goggles or a face shield.
- Both wheels must have brakes installed, with separate controls to operate each brake.
- A properly operating speedometer, capable of registering at least the maximum legal speed limit is required.
- A fender is required over each wheel.

Licenses: All motorcycle operators are required to obtain a Class A-D motor vehicle license, with a motorcycle endorsement added. There is no separate license for a motorcycle operator.

- Any new applicant for such a license must complete a written exam, vision exam, and driving examination for a motorcycle to be eligible for a motorcycle endorsement. The driving test may be waived upon proof of completion of a certified Motorcycle Safety Foundation rider course.

Mopeds: No person shall operate a motor-driven cycle or motor scooter at a speed greater than 35 mph.

- Driver's license required; minimum age is 14.
- Operators under 18 must use approved helmet.

OK

Passenger Car Trailers

Brakes: Every trailer, semitrailer, and pole trailer with a GVWR of 3,000 lbs. or more shall be equipped with independent braking system adequate to control the movement of and to stop such a vehicle.

Dimensions: Total length: 65 feet; trailer length: 40 feet; width: 102 inches; height: 13.6 feet.

Hitch: Every trailer, semitrailer (unless drawn by a truck-tractor), or manufactured home shall be equipped with chains or cables to prevent parting from the towing vehicle in the event that the coupling device breaks or becomes disengaged; or chains, cables, or a safety device that provides strength, security of attachment, and directional stability equal to or greater than that provided by safety chains that prevent the parting from the towing vehicle.

Lighting: On every trailer or semitrailer with a GVWR over 3,000 lbs., there must be the following equipment: on the front, 2 clearance lamps, with 1 on each side; on each side, 2 side marker lamps and 2 reflectors, with 1 each at the front and the rear; and on the rear, 2 clearance lamps and 2 reflectors, with 1 each at either side.

- Every trailer, semitrailer, or pole trailer with a GVWR of 3,000 lbs. or less must have 2 reflectors, with 1 on either side of the rear of the vehicle. If the trailer is equipped to obscure the stop lights of the towing vehicle, 1 stop light is required.

Mirrors: Every motor vehicle towing another vehicle must be equipped with a mirror so located as to reflect to the driver a view of the roadway for at least 200 feet to the rear.

Towing: Every trailer, semitrailer, or manufactured home shall be equipped with a coupling device designed and constructed so that the trailer will follow in substantially the same path as the vehicle towing it without whipping or swerving from side to side.

Miscellaneous Provisions

Bail Bonds: Any automobile club may issue guaranteed arrest bond certificates in an amount up to $500.

Liability Laws: State has security-type law applicable in event of accident causing property damage in excess of $500 or personal injury or death.

- The minimum liability coverage limits for a motor vehicle are $25,000 for bodily injury to or death of 1 person in any 1 accident; $50,000 for bodily injury to or death of more than 1 person in any 1 accident; and $25,000 for injury to or destruction of property of others in any 1 accident.
- Applicants for license plates must certify that liability insurance is in effect or deposit a bond of $75,000 or cash of $75,000. Failure to maintain liability insurance bond or security on currently licensed vehicles will cause suspension of license plates and vehicle registration.
- State has non-resident service of process law; does not have guest suit law.

Weigh Stations: Any officer of DPS, the Oklahoma Tax Commission, or any sheriff is authorized to stop any vehicle in order to weigh the vehicle with portable or stationary scales.

Fees & Taxes

Table 1: Title & Registration Fees

Vehicle Type	Title Fee	Registration Fee
Motor Vehicle Up to 8,000 lbs.*	$11.00	$85.00 1st-4th years of registration $75.00 5th-8th years of registration $55.00 9th-12th years of registration $35.00 13th-16th years of registration $15.00 17th + years of registration All vehicles are subject to an additional $5.00 in other fees
Commercial Vehicles	$11.00	Varies by weight, from $95.00-$1,078.00 annually, plus a flat fee of $40.00 for the first registration, and $4.00 flat fee in subsequent years. After 5 years, trucks under 15,000 lbs. will have their fees halved, and halved again after the 7th year of registration. All vehicles are also subject to an additional $5.00 in other fees
Farm Vehicles	$11.00	$30.00
Mobile Home	$11.00	If retail cost is $1,500 or less, the fee is $25.00; if the retail cost is over $1,500, the fee is $25.00 + $0.75/$100.00
Trailers of 10,000 lbs. or less	$11.00	
Trailers of more than 10,000 lbs.	$11.00	$0.00, unless commercial vehicle
Non-Commercial Trailer less than 6,000 lbs.	$11.00	$0.00
Motorcycle	$11.00	
Mopeds	$11.00	
Duplicates	$11.00	

*A fee of $2.00 shall be paid to the Oklahoma Tax Commission for every vehicle registered

OK

Table 2: License Fees

License Class	Application Fee	Issuance Fees	Total Fee
A Commercial	$25.00	$39.00*	$64.00
B Commercial	$15.00	$39.00*	$54.00
C Commercial	$15.00	$29.00*	$44.00
D	$4.00	$19.00*	$23.00
Motorcycle Endorsement	$4.00	replacement fee $9.00	$9.00
Motorcycle License	$4.00	$19.00	$23.00
Motorcycle Learner's Permit	$4.00	$19.00	$23.00
Class D or Motorcycle Endorsement for Drivers age 62 during the year of issuance	$4.00	$11.25	$15.25
Class D or Motorcycle Endorsement for Drivers age 63 during the year of issuance	$4.00	$7.50	$11.50
Class D or Motorcycle Endorsement for Drivers age 64 during the year of issuance	$4.00	$3.75	$7.75
Class D or Motorcycle Endorsement for Drivers age 65+ during the year of issuance	$4.00	Free	$4.00
Duplicate License Fee	$5.00		$5.00

*Effective 7/1/04 license fees will increase $1.00

Table 3: Vehicle Taxes

Tax	Rate
Excise Tax for New Vehicles	3.25% of value of vehicle, minus trade-in
Excise Tax for Used Vehicles	Until June 30, 2002, $20.00 on the first $1,250 in value, and 3.25% of the remaining value of the vehicle. Beginning July 1, 2002, $20.00 on the first $1,500 in value, and 3.25% of the remaining value of the vehicle
Gasoline Tax; (Diesel)	$0.16/gallon; ($0.13/gallon)

Table 4: Miscellaneous Fees

Fee	Amount	Payable Upon
Emissions Inspection Fee	$5.00	Testing
Recording a Security Interest on a Certificate of Title	$13.00	Application
Inspection of Out-of-State	$4.00	Application
Transfer of Ownership Fee	$15.00	Application
Special Plates Fee	Ranges from $5.00 - $25.00 + regular registration fees	Application
Duplicate Plate	$9.00	Application

OREGON

Contact Information

Driver and Motor Vehicle Services (DMV)
1905 Lana Avenue NE
Salem, OR 97314

(503) 945-5000
www.oregondmv.com

Department of State Police
255 Capitol Street NE
400 Public Service Building
Salem, OR 97310

(503) 378-3720
www.osp.state.or.us/

Oregon Department of Transportation (DOT)
355 Capitol Street NE
Salem, OR 97301-3871

1-888-ASK-ODOT
www.odot.state.or.us/home

Vehicle Title

Application: Title is required for most vehicles operated on the roads of the state, unless exempt. Snowmobiles must be titled and registered. ATVs may be optionally titled. Titles are not issued for certain vehicles such as bicycles, emergency fire apparatus providing public fire protection, golf carts, farm tractors and trailers, implements of husbandry, U.S. government owned vehicles, motor assisted scooters.

- An application for title must be in the form specified by the DOT and must include: a full description of the vehicle, including the vehicle identification number (VIN); the name of the owner of the vehicle; the identity of any security interests in order of priority; the identity of the interest of any lessor; a disclosure of whether the vehicle is a replica or is specifically constructed; and any other information the department may require.
- A title does not require renewal and is valid until the vehicle is destroyed, dismantled, or substantially altered. However, any change in ownership interest requires renewal.
- A duplicate or replacement title may be issued if a certificate of title is lost, mutilated, or destroyed.
- The DOT will not grant a title to a vehicle from another jurisdiction or any assembled or reconstructed vehicle until a VIN inspection has been performed and the appropriate fee for such inspection has been paid.
- If the name or address of a person changes from that displayed on the title, the person has 30 days to notify the DOT.

Transfer of Ownership: Upon the transfer of any interest in a vehicle, the transferee must submit an application for title to the DOT within 30 days of the transfer of interest. This provision does not apply if the change involves only a change in the security interest when the security holder is a bank or financial institution, the vehicle is transferred to a vehicle dealer, the vehicle is to be titled in another jurisdiction, or the vehicle has been destroyed.

- Upon the transfer of interest in a vehicle, the transferor must notify the DOT within 10 days of the transfer.

- Upon the transfer of interest in a vehicle, the transferor must also submit an odometer disclosure statement to the transferee, and both parties must sign the statement. This provision does not apply to a vehicle with a Gross Vehicle Weight (GVW) rating of more than 16,000 lbs., a vehicle that is not self-propelled, a vehicle that is at least 10 years old, or a vehicle sold directly by the manufacturer to any agency of the United States.

Vehicle Registration

Application: All vehicles owned by a person in the state are subject to registration except: farm tractors, road rollers, trolleys, and traction engines; bicycles; a vehicle that is not operated on the highways; trailers equipped with pneumatic tires that are not operated with a loaded weight of more than 1,800 lbs.; implements of husbandry; farm tractors; vehicles currently registered and titled in another country, state, or territory, unless the owner is a resident of the state or the vehicle is operated on the highways of the state for profit; vehicles owned and operated by the U.S. government and emergency fire fighting apparatus providing public fire protection.

- An application for registration must contain: the owner's name and residence or business address; a description of the vehicle, including the VIN; an odometer disclosure; and a statement that the applicant is domiciled in the state.
- If the application is for original registration, the applicant must also include a statement that the applicant is in compliance with financial responsibility requirements.
- Registration will not be renewed unless the owner is able to certify compliance with financial responsibility requirements.
- An application for registration will not be granted unless the applicant simultaneously applies for, or has already been issued, title to the vehicle.
- Upon registration, the DOT issues a registration card which contains the name of the owner, the make and model year of the vehicle, the VIN, and the mileage as reported on the odometer at the time of application for registration.
- The owner of a registered vehicle must carry the registration card in the vehicle at all times.

Non-Residents: Non-residents are exempt from both titling and registration requirements. A person becomes a resident when he or she engages in gainful employment or takes any action to indicate the acquiring of residency such as: remaining in the state for 6 months or more; placing children in a public school without paying non-resident tuition fees; maintaining a main office, branch or warehouse in the state; or making a declaration of residency for purposes of acquiring a state license.

- A person who is gainfully employed but takes no further steps to become a resident, such as a student paying non-resident tuition fees, is not considered a resident.
- The owner of a private motor vehicle who lives in an adjoining state is permitted to operate their vehicle in the state without having it registered in the state for so long as the vehicle is registered in an adjoining state.
- Military personnel in active duty in Oregon may maintain out-of-state vehicle registration.

Registration Type: Vehicle registration may be 1 of 5 types:

- Quarterly registration (up to four calendar quarters): heavy motor vehicles, includ-

ing ambulances, buses, self-propelled cranes, hearses, armored cars (8,001 lbs. or more); charitable non-profit (8,001 lbs. or more); manufactured structure toters; trucks registered as farm vehicles.
- Annual registration: tow/recovery; ambulances, armored cars, buses, self-propelled cranes, hearses (8,000 lbs. or less); for rent trailers (also can register for a 5-year period).
- Two year (biennial): campers; low speed; mopeds; motor homes; fixed loads; motorcycles; passenger; snowmobiles; trailers (light, special use, travel).
- Four-year initial registration: Certain new vehicles are required to be issued four-year initial registration if it is a new vehicle (being titled with an MCO) and new plates are being issued at the same time. If a vehicle is subject to four-year registration, the vehicle must have four-year registration; there is no option to obtain only two years, except for vehicles owned by rental/leasing companies.
- Permanent registration: special interest; antique; disabled veteran; heavy trailer; government (until ownership changes); school bus.

Emissions Inspection: Vehicles from the 1975 model year and newer must be submitted for emissions inspection in the Portland Vehicle Inspection Area. In the Medford-Ashland Air Quality Maintenance Area, light duty vehicles that are up to 20 years old and heavy duty vehicles must be submitted for emissions inspection.
- Motor vehicle pollution control systems are required to be tested once during the period for which registration or renewal of registration for a motor vehicle is issued.

Safety Inspection: A state police officer may require a person driving a vehicle or combination of vehicles to stop and submit the vehicle to an inspection of the mechanical condition and equipment of the vehicle.

License Plates

Disbursement: Upon filing of an application for registration and payment of the appropriate fees, the DOT will issue one license plate for a moped, motorcycle, any trailer or camper, or an antique vehicle or vehicle of special interest. Two license plates are issued for all other vehicles.
- In lieu of new plates, the DOT issues stickers upon renewal of registration.
- Special plates are available for special groups and vehicles including veterans' organizations, institutions of higher education, nonprofit groups, amateur radio operators and special vehicles. Personalized plates are also available.
- Disabled person parking placards issued upon application to DMV, with certification by licensed physician attesting to permanent or temporary disability.

Transfer of Plates: In some circumstances, plates may be transferred to another vehicle upon completion of an application for transfer of plates and payment of the appropriate fee.

Driver's Licenses

Examination: Examinations for a license include a test of the applicant's eyesight; a test of the applicant's knowledge of the traffic laws; and a roadside ability test.
- An applicant's visual acuity must be 20/70 or better when looking through both eyes. If an applicant's visual acuity in the applicant's best eye is worse than 20/40, the

applicant will be restricted to daytime driving only.
- All drivers 50 years of age or older must have their eyesight checked by the DMV once every 8 years.
- The demonstration test may also be waived if the person is applying for a commercial driver's license or Class C license, and the applicant holds a valid out-of-state license, or applies for the commercial license or Class C license within 1 year of the expiration of a valid out-of-state license.

Graduated Drivers Licensing: State has a system of graduated drivers licensing for teen drivers. At 15, teens are eligible for an instruction/learner's permit.
- Permit holders may only drive when accompanied by a licensed person who is at least 21 years old and who is occupying the front passenger seat.
- Teens must hold the permit for at least 6 months and accumulate at least 50 hours (100 if teen doesn't take driver education) of certified driving under the supervision of a person who is at least 21 years old who has had a license for at least 3 years driving before being eligible for a provisional/intermediate license.
- At 16, teens are eligible for a provisional/intermediate license.
- The holder of a provisional/intermediate license may not, for the first 6 months after issuance of the license, operate a vehicle that is carrying a passenger under 20 years of age who is not a member of the licensee's immediate family.
- For the second 6 months, the licensee may not operate a motor vehicle that is carrying more than 3 passengers who are under 20 years of age and who are not members of the licensee's immediate family.
- For the first year of the intermediate license, the teens may not drive between midnight and 5:00 a.m. unless driving to and from home and work, to and from home and school, or when accompanied by a licensed driver who is at least 25 years of age.
- At 18, teens are eligible for an unrestricted license.

Issuance/Application: An application for a license must contain: the applicant's name, date of birth, sex, residence address; information relating to any previous license or permit held by the applicant; the class of license sought; and the applicant's social security number. An applicant's social security number is not displayed on the license itself.
- Non-residents are permitted to drive in Oregon without obtaining an Oregon driver's license as long as they possess a current license issued by the person's home jurisdiction.
- Restricted Class C licenses are issued as disability golf cart permits, emergency driver permits, special student driver permits, hardship driver permits, probationary driver permits, Class C instruction permits, and motorcycle instruction driver permits.
- Licenses contain a description of the licensee; the name, date of birth, and residence address of the licensee; the signature of the licensee; an indication of the class of the license; and a photograph of the licensee.
- Whenever a person changes their name or residence address, notice of such change must be sent in writing to the DOT within 30 days of the change.

Renewal: A first license, or renewal of expired license within 1 year is valid for 8 years.
- The DOT is required to provide reasonable notice of pending expiration by mail, unless the person's license has been suspended or revoked, or the person has failed to notify the DOT of a change of address.

- After September 30, 2004, DMV will cease issuing renewal notices that authorize a person to renew by mail in order to complete the transition from 4-year to 8-year licenses.
- An application for renewal of an expired license must be completed within 1 year of expiration, otherwise the licensee does not qualify for renewal and must apply as for an original license.

Types of Licenses: Class A Commercial License: authorizes the operation of any vehicle or combination of vehicles except any vehicle for which an endorsement is required.

- Class B Commercial License: authorizes the operation of any single vehicle and to tow a vehicle that is not in excess of 10,000 lbs. GVW rating.
- Class C Commercial License: authorizes the operation of any vehicle designed to transport 16 or more passengers if the GVW rating of the vehicle is less than 26,001 lbs.; any vehicle owned by a mass transit district, regardless of the number of passengers, if the GVW rating of the vehicle is less than 26,001 lbs.; any vehicle used for the transportation of hazardous material if the GVW rating of the vehicle is less than 26,001 lbs.; and any vehicle that may be operated by the holder of a Class C driver's license.
- Class C Driver's License: authorizes the operation of any vehicle for which a commercial license is not required except those vehicles requiring an endorsement.
- Individual license endorsements permit the operation of various vehicles including a motorcycle, school bus, double and triple trailers, and farm vehicles.

Traffic Rules

Alcohol Laws: Any person who operates a motor vehicle upon public premises or the highways of the state gives implied consent to a chemical test of the person's breath, blood, or urine.

- Open containers are prohibited. Meets the requirements of TEA-21.
- Illegal per se BAC level is .08.
- BAC level for people under 21 is 0.
- BAC level for commercial drivers is .04.

Emergency Radio/Cellular: Citizen band radio channel 9 is monitored for emergency calls. Emergency cell number is 911.

Headsets: Wearing radio headsets while driving is permitted with some local exceptions.

Occupant Restraints: It is unlawful for a driver to operate a motor vehicle unless the driver and all passengers are secured by a safety belt or child safety system.

- A person who is under 4 years of age and weighs 40 lbs. or less must be secured by a child safety system.
- A person who is over the age of 4 but under the age of 6, or weighs between 40 and 60 lbs., must be secured by a child safety system that elevates the person so that a safety belt properly fits the person. Exempts children who are riding in the back seat in a lap belt only vehicle from complying with the booster seat provision.
- A person who is 6 through 16 years of age and weighs 60 lbs. or more must be properly secured with a safety belt.
- Violation of the occupant protection laws is a primary offense.

- Prohibits passengers younger than 18 from traveling in an open truck unless they are strapped in, riding in a parade, working on a farm, or going from one hunting camp to another.

Railroad Crossing: The operator of a vehicle must stop not less than 15 feet or more than 50 feet from the nearest rail of a railroad crossing under any of the following circumstances: an electric signal warning of a coming train is given; a crossing gate is lowered; a flagman indicates the approach of a train; an approaching train is clearly visible; or an approaching train has given an audible signal.

- The operator of a school bus, a school activity vehicle, a worker transport bus, any bus used to transport children to and from church or a church activity, a commercial bus, any vehicle used for transportation of persons for hire for a nonprofit entity, and any vehicle carrying hazardous materials must stop not less than 15 or more than 50 feet from the nearest rail of a railroad crossing and may proceed only if it is safe to do so without changing gears.

School Buses: Color is "National School Bus Yellow." The words "School Bus" are prominently marked on front and rear in letters not less than 8 inches high. When the school bus' red warning lights are flashing, drivers meeting or overtaking a bus from either direction must stop before reaching the bus, and remain stopped until the flashing lights are turned off. However, on a divided highway separated by a median strip, one must stop only if on the same side of the road as the school bus.

Vehicle Equipment & Rules

Bumper Height: Modification of original vehicle bumper height is permitted; lighting equipment must stay within minimum/maximum heights. No portion of the vehicle, except tires, can be lower than the lowest portion of any rim of any wheel in contact with the roadway.

Glass/Window Tinting: Tinting material may be applied to the side and rear windows of a motor vehicle if the material has a light transmittance of 50% or more; a light reflectance of 13% or more; and the total light transmittance through the window is 35% or more.

- Tinting material with a total light transmittance lower than 35% may be applied to the top 6 inches of a windshield, but may not be applied to any other portion of the windshield.
- Tinting material with a total light transmittance lower than 35% may be applied to all windows of a multipurpose passenger vehicle that are behind the driver, but only if the vehicle is equipped with rearview mirrors on each side of the vehicle.
- A signed affidavit by a physician or optometrist may permit the use of tinting material with a total light transmittance lower than 35%.
- Mirror finish tinting, red tinting, yellow tinting, gold tinting, amber tinting, black tinting, or tinting material that is in liquid form and is brushed or sprayed on is prohibited.

Telematics: It is unlawful to operate a motor vehicle on a highway if the vehicle is equipped with any television viewer, screen or other means of visually receiving a television broadcast if such device is located in the vehicle at any point forward of the back of the driver's seat, or is visible to the operator while driving the motor vehicle.

Windshield Stickers: It is unlawful to place any material on a window or windshield if the material, sign, poster, or adhesive film prohibits or impairs the ability to see into or out of the vehicle.

Motorcycles & Mopeds

Equipment: The operator of a motorcycle, and all passengers on a motorcycle, must wear a safety helmet.

- Motorcycles and mopeds must be equipped with at least 1 and no more than 3 headlights, 1 tail light, 1 brake light, a registration plate light, turn signal lights and rear reflectors.
- Motorcycles manufactured before 1973 are not required to be equipped with turn signals.
- A moped may not be equipped with more than 2 headlights.
- At all times that a motorcycle or moped is operated on a highway, it must display a lighted headlight(s). Modulated headlights may be used during daylight hours.
- It is unlawful to carry a passenger on a motorcycle unless the motorcycle is equipped with footrests for the passenger, and the passenger is seated on a permanent and regular seat.

Licenses: A motorcycle endorsement may be issued to the holder of a valid license provided any tests and demonstrations are successfully completed.

- The roadside skills test will be waived if the applicant passes a motorcycle skills test given during a motorcycle rider education course, and the skills test meets or exceeds the motorcycle skills test administered by the DMV.
- A motorcycle endorsement will not be issued to a person under 21 unless that person has successfully completed a motorcycle rider education course established by the DOT.
- A motorcycle instruction permit may be issued only to persons who are at least 16 years old and is valid for 1 year. The holder of a motorcycle instruction permit may only operate a motorcycle during daylight hours, may not carry any passengers, and must wear an approved helmet.

Mopeds: The operator of a moped must wear a safety helmet.

- If a moped is modified such that the moped is capable of reaching speeds in excess of 30 mph, it no longer meets the definition of moped in the law and must surrender moped registration.
- It is unlawful to carry any passenger, other than the operator, on a moped.

Passenger Car Trailers

Registration: Trailers equipped with pneumatic tires that are not operated with a loaded weight of more than 1,800 lbs. are not required to be registered.

- Campers are subject to the same registration and titling requirements as any other vehicle.

Brakes: Independent braking system not required, but combination of vehicles must be able to stop within legal limits. Every motor vehicle and combination of motor vehicles, except motorcycles and mopeds, shall at all times be equipped with a parking brake system.

OR

Dimensions: Total length: 65 feet; trailer length: 45 feet (includes bumpers); width: 102 inches; height: 14 feet.

Hitch: Adequate to control trailer under all conditions of varying speeds and weights; 1 safety chain is required on all trailers with 2 connections to the towing vehicle. The tensile strength of the safety chain must equal the gross weight of the trailer.

Lighting: All trailers are required to be equipped with 2 taillights, registration plate lights, 2 brake lights, turn signal lights, and 2 rear reflectors.

- Any trailer that is 80 inches or more in overall width and less than 30 feet in overall length must be equipped with 2 front and 2 rear clearance lights, and front and rear identification lights.
- Any trailer that is 30 feet or more in overall length must be equipped with 2 front and 2 rear clearance lights, front and rear identification lights, and intermediate side marker lights and side reflectors on each side of the vehicle.

Mirrors: All vehicles must be equipped with mirrors such that the driver has a clear and unobstructed view of the rear at all times and under all conditions of load that will enable the driver to see an approaching vehicle from a distance of not less than 200 feet.

Speed Limits: Any vehicle towing a trailer, any camper, and any vehicle with a registration weight of 8,000 lbs. or more must drive in the right lane of all roadways having 2 or more lanes for traffic proceeding in a single direction.

Towing: It is unlawful for a person to be a passenger in any towed vehicle. This provision does not apply to a 5th-wheel trailer if the 5th-wheel trailer is equipped with safety glazing materials on the windows and doors, an auditory or visual signaling device that may be used to contact the driver, and at least 1 unobstructed exit capable of being opened from both the interior and exterior.

Miscellaneous Provisions

Bail Bonds: State has mandatory recognition of AAA arrest bond certificates up to $1,000, with specified exceptions.

Liability Laws: State has future-proof law for uninsured accidents.

- Antique motor vehicles that have been issued a permanent registration, farm trailers, farm tractors, all-terrain vehicles, special interest vehicles, and implements of husbandry need not comply with the liability provisions.
- The minimum liability policy coverage is $25,000 per person with an aggregate limit of $50,000 per accident and $10,000 for all damages to or destruction of property.
- If a person has been convicted of driving under the influence, the minimum insurance coverage is elevated to $50,000 per person with an aggregate limit of $100,000 per accident.
- State has non-resident service of process law and guest suit law. Mandatory 1 year license suspension for involvement in an uninsured accident.
- State has "add-on," no-fault insurance law. Sale and purchase mandatory. Benefits: Medical $10,000; 70% of wage loss up to $1,250 monthly (maximum 52 weeks); $30 per day loss of services (14-day retroactive waiting period and maximum 52 weeks).
- Owners must certify liability insurance when initially registering, and provide insur-

ance information when renewing.

Weigh Stations: All vehicles or combination of vehicles weighing 26,000 lbs. must stop.

Fees & Taxes

Table 1: Title Fees

Vehicle Type	Title Fee
Heavy Vehicles: Motor vehicles and trucks with a gross vehicle weight rating (GVWR) over 26,000 lbs. and trailers with a loaded weight over 8,000 lbs. (This does not apply to other vehicle types such as motor homes, special use trailers and travel trailers.	
Heavy Vehicle Title Transaction	$90.00
Heavy Vehicle Replacement Transaction Only	$90.00
Heavy Vehicle Replacement Title with Transfer Transaction	$180.00
Salvage Vehicles: Vehicles requiring Salvage Certificate	
Salvage Title Transaction	$17.00
Salvage Replacement Title Transaction Only	$17.00
Salvage Replacement Title with Transfer to Salvage Transaction	$34.00
Replacement Salvage Title with Transfer to Regular Title	$72.00
Replacement Salvage Title with Transfer to Heavy Vehicle Title	$107.00
Regular Replacement Title with Transfer to Salvage Title	$34.00
Heavy Vehicle Replacement Title with Transfer to Salvage Title	$34.00
Regular Vehicles: Vehicles not falling into transactions defined above (Heavy Vehicle or Salvage Vehicle)	
Regular Title Transaction	$55.00
Regular Replacement Title Transaction Only	$55.00
Regular Replacement Title with Transfer Transaction	$110.00

Table 2: License Fees

Type		
Initial License		
Regular Class C driver license, (non-commercial)		$54.50
Commercial Driver License (CDL), class A, B, or C (applicant already has Oregon License)	$25.00	$70.00
Commercial Driver License (CDL), No Oregon License		$124.50
Motorcycle Endorsement		$74.00
Farm Endorsement		$26.00
Moped Restricted Class C driver license		$54.50
Identification Card		$29.00
Disabled Person Parking Identification Card		$29.00
Disabled Person Parking Permit - Individual (including persons holding veteran plates), Program, Family or Decal.	No Fee	No Fee
Regular Class C Instruction Permit (non-commercial)	$18.00	
Motorcycle Instruction Permit	$18.00	
CDL Instruction Permit	$18.00	
Temporary Disabled Person Parking Permit	No Fee	
Renewals		
Regular Class C driver license, (non-commercial)		$34.50
Commercial Driver License (CDL), A, B, or C		$62.50
Regular Class C driver license with Motorcycle Endorsement		$62.50
CDL with Motorcycle Endorsement		$84.00
Regular Class C driver license with Farm Endorsement		$34.50
Moped Restricted Class C driver license		$34.50
Identification Card		$25.00
Disabled Person Parking Identification Card		$25.00
Disabled Person Parking Identification Permit - Individual (including persons holding veteran plates)	No Fee	No Fee
Disabled Person Parking Permit - Program or Family	No Fee	No Fee

Table 3: Vehicle Registration Fees (not including plate fee)

Vehicle Type	2-Year	4-Year
Passenger Vehicles	$54.00	$108.00
Passenger (hybrid-electric or electric powered)	$54.00	$108.00
Motorcycles/Mopeds	$30.00	$60.00
Motorcycles (hybrid or electric powered)	$27.00	n/a
Mopeds (hybrid or electric powered)	$30.00	$60.00
Light Trailers	$54.00	$60.00
Heavy Trailers	$10.00	n/a
Snowmobiles	$10.00	n/a
Low-Speed Vehicles	$54.00	n/a
Custom Plates Surcharge	$50.00	$100.00
Higher Education Group Plate Surcharge	$32.00	$64.00
Non-Profit and Veterans Group Plate Surcharge	$10.00	$20.00
Salmon Surcharge	$30.00	$60.00

Table 4: Vehicle Taxes

Tax	Rate
Gasoline Tax; (Diesel)	$0.26/gallon; ($0.24/gallon)

Table 5: Miscellaneous Fees

Fee	Amount	Payable Upon
Expedited Titling/Registration	$10.00 (maximum)	application for title/registration
VIN Inspection Fee	$7.00	VIN Inspection
License Plates	$3.00 - 1 plate $5.00 - 2 plates	registration
Duplicate/Replacement Plates Between Renewals	$13.00 - 1 plate $15.00 - 2 plates	application for replacement plates
License Plate Transfer Fee	$6.00	application for transfer
Custom Plates	$50.00 plus regular fees	application for plates
Motor Vehicle Accident Fund	$8.00	application for original/renewal license
Motorcycle Safety Subaccount Fee	$28.00	application for original or renewal motorcycle endorsement
Safety Education Fund	$0.25	application for original/renewal license
License Plate Manufacture Fee	$3.00 for a single plate/$5.00 for 2 plates	issuance of plate(s)
Emissions Compliance Certificate	$21.00 (Portland)/ $10.00 (Medford)	at testing

PENNSYLVANIA

Contact Information

Driver and Vehicle Services
Keystone Building
400 North Street
Harrisburg, PA 17120

www.dot4.state.pa.us/

State Police Headquarters
1800 Elmerton Avenue
Harrisburg, PA 17110

(717) 783-5599
www.psp.state.pa.us/

Department of Transportation (DOT)
Keystone Building
400 North Street
Harrisburg, PA 17120

(717) 787-2838
www.dot.state.pa.us/

Vehicle Title

Application: Application for certificate of title must be made on a form provided by the Department.

- Application must contain a full description of the vehicle, the vehicle identification number, odometer reading, date of purchase, the actual or bona fide name and address of the owner, a statement of title of the applicant and any other documents that the Department may require.
- Application for a certificate of title must be made within 20 days of the sale or transfer of a vehicle or its entry into Pennsylvania, whichever is later.
- Any necessary fees and/or taxes must accompany the executed application.

Transfer of Ownership: The transferee must within 10 days of the assignment or reassignment of the certificate of title, apply for a new title.

- Along with the application, the owner must execute a notarized assignment and warranty of title to the transferee in the space provided on the certificate of title.
- The application must be accompanied by the certificate of title and all appropriate fees and any taxes required by the Department.
- If the vehicle was previously titled or registered in another state, the following information must be included with the application: (1) the certificate of title issued by the state or county; (2) a tracing of the vehicle identification number; and (3) any other information or documentation the Department might request.
- If the Department is not satisfied about the ownership of a vehicle the Department may register the vehicle but shall withhold issuance of a certificate of title until the applicant submits the documents which the Department deems necessary to issue the title.

Vehicle Registration

Application: Application for original or renewal vehicle registration must be made on a form provided by the Department.

- The application must contain the full name and address of the owner or owners, the make, model, year and vehicle identification number of the vehicle, and any other documents that the Department may require.
- The vehicle title and a self-certification of financial responsibility must also accompany the application.
- The self-certification form of financial responsibility requires: (1) the name, address, and telephone number of the applicant; (2) the name of the insurance company which is insuring the vehicle; and (3) the policy number, effective date, and expiration date of the vehicle's insurance policy.
- If the vehicle registration application is for a new vehicle, it must be accompanied by the manufacturer's statement of origin for the vehicle.

Non-Residents: A non-resident owner of an out-of-state vehicle can operate a vehicle in Pennsylvania without registering the vehicle in Pennsylvania provided that the vehicle is registered in another state. This out-of-state vehicle cannot be used for transportation services of persons of hire, or regularly operated in carrying on any business in Pennsylvania.

- A person given a citation for not registering his or her vehicle in Pennsylvania must prove that he or she is not a Pennsylvania resident. If he or she can prove that he or she is a non-resident within 5 days of being given the citation, the citation will be dismissed.
- Military personnel on active duty in Pennsylvania may maintain out-of-state vehicle registration.

Registration Type: Vehicle registration expires on the last day of the month as designated on the registration card.

- Application for renewal of registration will be mailed to registrant at least 60 days before the expiration.
- The returned application must be accompanied by a self-certification of financial responsibility and the applicable fees.
- After the Department receives the application, the Department will issue a renewed registration card.
- For a prorated fee, a person that is the owner or lessee of a passenger car, recreational vehicle, motorcycle, truck, or farm vehicle which does not have a Gross Vehicle Weight Rating (GVWR) of more than 9,000 lbs. may register the vehicle with the Department for a period of successive months of less than 1 year.
- Upon receiving the registration card, the registrant must sign his or her name to the card.
- The registration card must be kept with the vehicle at all times.

Emissions Inspection: The Department requires periodic emissions inspections for all motor vehicles except for the following:

- (1) a vehicle that was never permanently registered in any jurisdiction that has less than 5,000 miles on it for which an annual or temporary registration plate was originally issued within the past 12 months; this vehicle will be exempt from an emissions inspection for 1 year from the date of registration.
- (2) A vehicle never registered in any jurisdiction having less than 5,000 miles on it and having a registration plate transferred from another vehicle must pass an emissions inspection before the next registration but not within 9 months of the date of the purchase of the vehicle.
- South Central and Lehigh Valley Region: requires 1996 and newer models to have On-Board Diagnostic (OBD) and gas cap inspections; and requires 1975-1995 models to have gas cap and visual inspections. Northern Region: requires 1975 and newer models to have gas cap and visual inspections. Pittsburgh Region: requires 1996 and newer models to have OBD and gas cap, and requires 1975-1995 models to have gas cap, tailpipe, and visual inspections. Philadelphia Region: requires 1996 and newer models to have OBD and gas cap inspections; and requires 1975-1995 models to have gas cap, tailpipe, and visual inspections. 42 County Non-I/M Region: requires all cars to have a visual inspection.

Safety Inspection: Annual safety inspections are required for all passenger vehicles and light trucks.

- Semiannual inspections are required for school buses, vehicles owned by or under contract to a school and used to transport students to and from school, vans transporting persons for hire or owned by a commercial enterprise for transporting employees, and motor carrier vehicles; there is no set fee. All other vehicles, including passenger cars, light trucks, motorcycles, trailers over 3,000 lbs., emergency vehicles, and private non-commercial vehicles transporting students are inspected annually; there is no set fee. Proof of financial responsibility is required at the time of inspection.

License Plates

Disbursement: The Department will issue 1 license plate when a car is registered in Pennsylvania.

- License plates and motorcycle decals are available to persons with disabilities and severely disabled veterans by application to the Bureau by completing Form MV145 or Form MV145V for veterans. Fee $7.50. Notarization is required.
- Disabled parking placards are available by application to the Bureau of Motor Vehicles. No fee is required. Notarization and Form MV145A or Form MV145V for veterans are needed.

Transfer of Plates: Registration and license plates can be transferred to another vehicle owned or leased by the registrant, or to a vehicle owned or leased by the spouse, parent, or child of the registrant.

- If the transfer is within the same vehicle type, the transferee can keep the previously issued registration and license plate.
- If the transfer is not within the same vehicle type, the transferee must return the license plate to the Department.
- In order to transfer the license plate, the transferee must apply for a temporary vehicle registration card and a transfer of registration.

Driver's Licenses

Examination: Every applicant for a driver's license must be examined for the type or class of vehicle that the applicant desires to drive. The examination includes a physical examination, a screening test of the applicant's eyesight (20/40 visual acuity required), and a test of the applicant's ability to read and understand official traffic-control devices, knowledge of safe driving practices, and knowledge of safe driving practices of Pennsylvania.

- The automobile examination also includes a driving skills test that requires knowledge of controls, ability to parallel park, and on road driving course where the driver's compliance with driving rules of the road are examined. Applicants for a commercial driver's license are required to successfully pass required knowledge tests and a driving skills test that involve pre-trip inspection, basic maneuver skills test, and on road driving. If the Department finds it necessary to further determine an applicant's fitness to operate a motor vehicle safely upon the highways the Department may require one or more of the following types of examinations:
    (1) A vision examination by an optometrist or ophthalmologist
    (2) A physical examination
    (3) A mental examination

Graduated Drivers Licensing: State has a system of graduated licensing for teen drivers. At 16, teens are eligible for a learner's permit.

- A learner's permit holder can drive the class of vehicle the permit allows him or her to drive under the direct supervision of a person who meets the following conditions: (1) is at least 21 years of age, or if a spouse, parent, or guardian of the permit holder is at least 18 years of age; (2) is licensed in Pennsylvania to drive a vehicle of the class then being driven by the holder of the learner's permit; and (3) is actually occupying a seat beside the holder of the learner's permit unless the vehicle is a motorcycle.
- A junior driver's license can be issued to a person 16 or 17 years of age if the person has held a learner's permit for that class of vehicle for 6 months and presents to the Department a certification form signed by the parent, guardian, or spouse of the minor stating that the minor has completed 50 hours of practical accompanied

driving experience. Junior driver's license holders may not drive unsupervised between the hours of 11:00 p.m. and 5:00 a.m.

- A driver's license can be issued to a person 17 1/2 years of age who has successfully completed the following: (1) a driver education course approved by the Department; and (2) for a period of 12 months after receiving a junior driver's license was not the cause of a reportable accident, and has not been convicted of any driving violations.

Issuance/Application: Initial license for new drivers is probationary for ages 16 to 17; 18 for commercial driver's license. The Department will issue the applicant a learner's permit that identifies the class of license applied for by the applicant.

- License application forms are obtainable from DOT Driver License Center and PADOT website.
- Obtaining a license requires passing a knowledge, driving, and eye test, and a physical examination. It also requires a social security card and proof of birth.
- Driving test, knowledge test, and physical exam are waived for new residents with out-of-state driver's license.
- A license includes a color photograph and the height and eye color of the licensee.
- A non-commercial PA driver's license may be issued to a person who is 17 1/2 years old or older, who has a valid driver's license issued by another state that has not expired within 6 months of application. This person must demonstrate visual fitness and the Department must be satisfied that the applicant's experience in driving vehicles which may be driven by holders of the classes of licenses sought by the applicant is sufficient to justify the issuance of the license without further behind the wheel training.
- Social security number not included on license.
- The expiration dates of non-U.S. citizen driver's licenses expire on the same day their immigration visa does.

Renewal: Every driver's license will expire on the day after the licensee's birthday at intervals of 4 years or less, as determined by the Department.

- Licenses of active duty military personnel, their spouses, and children outside of the state are valid for the length of their active duty or 45 days after returning to the state. Service assignments must be carried with expired licenses.

Types of Licenses: A Class A license allows a license holder to operate any combination of vehicles with a GVWR of 26,001 lbs. or more, provided the GVWR of the vehicle or vehicles being towed is more than 10,000 lbs. The holder of a Class A license can drive Class B and Class C vehicles.

- A Class B license allows a license holder to operate any single vehicle with a GVWR of 26,001 lbs. or more or any such vehicle towing a vehicle having a GVWR of 10,000 lbs. or less. The holder of a Class B license can drive Class C vehicles.
- A Class C license allows a license holder to operate any vehicle, or combination of vehicles under 26,000 lbs., except combinations of vehicles involving motorcycles.
- A Class M license allows a license holder to operate a motorcycle.

Traffic Rules

Alcohol Laws: Operation of a motor vehicle gives implied consent to a test of blood, breath, urine, or other bodily substance for determining blood-alcohol content.

- Open containers are not permitted. Meets the requirements of TEA-21.
- Illegal per se BAC level is .08.
- BAC level for people under 21 is .02.

Emergency Radio/Cellular: Citizen band radio channel 9 is monitored for emergency calls by state police patrolling the turnpike system. Emergency phone number is *911.

Headsets: No driver can operate a vehicle while wearing or using one or more headphones or earphones. Exceptions to this rule include the use of hearing aids, and the use of a headset in conjunction with a cellular telephone that only provides sound through one ear and allows surrounding sounds to be heard with the other ear.

Occupant Restraints: Seat belts are required for the driver and all front seat passengers over the age of 18 while the vehicle is in motion. Children 8 through 18 years must be restrained in all seats. Violation of the seat belt law is a secondary offense.

- Children under the age of 4 must be properly restrained in a child passenger restraint system. Violation of this provision is a primary offense.
- Children 4 to 8 years old must be restrained in a booster seat. This provision is secondarily enforced.
- A driver who is less than 18 years of age cannot operate a motor vehicle in which the number of passengers exceeds the number of available seat belts in the vehicle.
- An open bed pickup truck or flatbed truck cannot be driven more than 35 mph if any person is in the bed of the truck.
- A child younger than 18 years of age cannot occupy the bed of a moving pickup truck unless: (1) that child is the child of a farmer who is being transported between parts of a farm owned by the farmer while doing farm work; (2) the child has a valid hunting license and is being transported between hunting sites during hunting season; or (3) that child is a child employed to do farm labor and is being transported on the farm owned or operated by the child's employer.
- People 18 and older may ride in pickup truck beds. Additional gaps in coverage apply; see Occupant Protection Chart.

Railroad Crossing: The driver of a vehicle approaching a railroad crossing must stop within 50 feet but no less than 15 feet under the following circumstances: (1) a clearly visible electric or mechanical signal device gives warning of the immediate approach of a railroad train; (2) a crossing gate is lowered or a flagman gives or continues to give a signal of the approach of a railroad train; (3) a railroad train approaching within approximately 1,500 feet of the highway crossing emits a signal audible from that distance; and (4) the railroad train, by reason of its speed or nearness to the crossing, is a hazard.

School Buses: Color, yellow. "School Bus" signs must be displayed front and rear. Bus must be equipped with red and amber signals on front and rear.

- Traffic must be prepared to stop when amber lights are flashing. A flashing stop sign is displayed near the driver's window when the bus is stopped and lights are activated. Traffic must stop when red signals are flashing, except when the bus is on the opposite side of a highway with a physical separation between the roadways, i.e., a divided highway.

- Every school bus shall be equipped with a crossing control arm on the front of the vehicle. School buses may be equipped with a bright white strobe affixed to the roof.
- Vehicles must stop at least 10 feet upon meeting, from either direction, a school bus that is stopped for loading or unloading children and displays flashing lights and the stop signal arm. This rule does not apply if the bus is on the opposite roadway of a divided highway.

Vehicle Equipment & Rules

Bumper Height: Modification of original vehicle bumper is legal with parameters set by state.

Glass/Window Tinting: No person can drive any motor vehicle with any sunscreening device or other material which does not permit a person to see or view the inside of the vehicle through the windshield, side wing, or side window of the vehicle. Exceptions to this rule include a vehicle which is equipped with tinted windows that were installed by the manufacturer of the vehicle for which a currently valid certificate of exemption has been issued, and a vehicle which is equipped with tinted windows, sunscreening devices, or other materials which comply with all applicable federal regulations for which a currently valid certificate of exemption has been issued.

- The Department can grant a certificate of exemption for a vehicle that is registered in Pennsylvania and is equipped with any prohibited sunscreening devices for a medical condition certified to the Department by a licensed physician or optometrist.

License Plates: It is unlawful for license plates to be obscured in any manner which inhibits the operation of an automatic red light camera.

Telematics: It is unlawful to drive a motor vehicle equipped with a television, or television-type equipment if the television or television equipment is located where the screen is visible to the driver.

- It is legal to use a screen visible to the driver if the screen is part of a vehicle navigational system.

Windshield Stickers: Windshield stickers are permitted to be displayed if they are an inspection sticker, or an officially required sticker.

Motorcycles & Mopeds

Equipment: All motorcycle handlebars must be below the shoulder height of the operator, when the operator is properly seated on the motorcycle.

- Any motorcycle carrying a passenger, other than in a sidecar or enclosed cab, must be equipped with footrests and a handhold for the passenger.
- All motorcyclists under 21 must wear a helmet unless he/she has completed a motorcycle safety course or has had a motorcycle license for two or more years. Passengers who are 21 years of age or older are also exempt.
- All riders and passengers must wear Department-approved protective eye gear.
- An occupant of a 3-wheel motorcycle with an enclosed cab does not have to wear a safety helmet or approved protective eye gear.

Licenses: A motorcycle learner's permit entitles the person to whom it is issued to operate a motorcycle between sunrise and sunset, while under the instruction and immediate supervision of a licensed motorcycle operator. Motorcycle learner's permit holder must not carry any passenger other than an instructor properly licensed to operate the motorcycle.

- If an applicant has successfully completed an approved motorcycle safety course that meets the requirements of the motorcycle operator's license examination administered by the Department, then the examination is waived.

Noise Limits: Every motorcycle must be constructed, equipped, maintained, and operated so that the vehicle does not exceed the sound level for the vehicle.

- Every motor vehicle must be equipped with a muffler or other effective noise suppressing system in good working order. No muffler or exhaust system can be equipped with a cutout, bypass, or similar device.
- A person must not modify the exhaust system of a motorcycle in a manner that will amplify or increase the noise emitted by the motor vehicle above the maximum levels permitted by Department regulations.

Mopeds: Title, registration, and a license plate are required.

- The minimum age to ride a moped is 16.
- The following safety equipment is required: brakes, headlamp, taillamp, side and rear reflex reflectors at night.

Passenger Car Trailers

Brakes: Every vehicle or combination of vehicles, except a motorcycle, operated on a highway shall be equipped with a parking brake system adequate to hold the vehicle or combination of vehicles on any grade and under all conditions for which it is operated.

- Every vehicle and combination of vehicles operated on a highway must be equipped with a service brake system adequate to control the movement of and to stop and hold the vehicle or combination of vehicles on any grade and under all conditions for which it is operated.
- Of every combination of vehicles operated on a highway, the towed vehicle which is equipped with brakes or which has a gross weight in excess of 3,000 lbs. shall be so equipped that, upon breakaway of the towed vehicle, the towed vehicle shall be stopped and held automatically, and the towing vehicle shall be capable of being stopped and held by use of its own service braking system.

Dimensions: Total length: 60 feet (includes bumpers); trailer length: not specified; width: 102 inches (mirrors and sun shades may extend up to 6 inches on each side of vehicle); height: 13.6 feet.

Hitch: Whenever 2 vehicles are connected by a ball-and-socket type hitch, or pintle hook without a locking device, they must also be connected by 2 safety chains of equal length, each safety chain having an ultimate strength at least equal to the gross weight of the towed vehicles. The safety chains must be crossed and connected to the towed and towing vehicle and to the towbar to prevent the towbar from dropping to the ground in the event the towbar fails or becomes disconnected. The safety chains must have no more slack than is necessary to permit proper turning.

Lighting: Trailers and semitrailers do not have to be equipped with headlamps.

- All trailer and semitrailer vehicles operated on a highway must be equipped with a rear lighting system including but not limited to rear lamps, rear reflectors, stop lamps, and a license plate light.

Mirrors: Mirrors may extend on each side a maximum of 6 inches beyond the width of the vehicle or load, whichever is greater.

Speed Limits: As posted. Fixed maximum limits as follows: (1) rural interstate highways – 65 mph; (2) residence districts on most local highways – 25 mph; (3) urban districts – 35 mph; and (4) if not posted with signs – 55 mph.

Towing: When 1 vehicle is towing another, the connection must be of sufficient strength to pull all of the weight towed and the distance between the 2 vehicles must not be more than 15 feet.

- If the distance between the vehicles is more than 5 feet, a red flag or cloth at least 12 inches square must be displayed on the connection between the vehicles. This flag must be centered between the 2 vehicles and light must shine on the flag.
- Every trailer must be attached to the towing vehicle so that the path of the trailer's wheels are no more than 6 inches from the path of the towing vehicle's wheels.

Miscellaneous Provisions

Bail Bonds: Mandatory recognition of AAA club guaranteed arrest bond certificates up to $200, for any motor vehicle law violation except violations involving driving while under the influence of intoxicating liquors, drugs, or narcotics, failure to appear for violations, driving on a suspended/revoked driver's license, hit and run, failure to present evidence of insurance, illegal use or falsification of license or registration, engaging in a felony, attempting to elude/eluding police, or while driving a vehicle used for commercial purposes.

Liability Laws: Pennsylvania has compulsory liability insurance law, sale and purchase are optional.

- Minimum liability insurance coverage must be at least $15,000 for injury or death of 1 person in an accident; $30,000 for the injury or death of more than 1 person in an accident; and $5,000 for damage to the property of another person.
- Proof of financial responsibility must be furnished by filing evidence satisfactory to the Department that all motor vehicles registered in a person's name are covered by motor vehicle liability insurance or by a program of self-insurance as provided by the Department or other reliable financial arrangements, deposits, resources, or commitments acceptable to the Department. Proof of coverage required at all times. Penalty for noncompliance is $300.
- State has non-resident service of process law. Does not have guest suit law.

Parking Restrictions: Except where necessary to avoid other traffic or to protect the safety of another person, it is unlawful to stop, stand, or park a vehicle on the roadway side of any vehicle stopped or parked at the edge of a curb, on a sidewalk, within an intersection, on a crosswalk, upon a bridge, on any railroad tracks, in the area between roadways of a divided highway, any place where official signs prohibit stopping, in front of a public or private driveway, within 15 feet of a fire hydrant, within 20 feet of a crosswalk at an intersection, within 30 feet upon the approach to any flashing signal or traffic sign, where the vehicle would prevent the free movement of a street car, within 50 feet of the nearest railroad crossing, and within 20 feet of the driveway entrance to a fire station.

PA

Weigh Stations: Regardless of size, the following vehicles are subject to inspection and weigh station examinations: (1) agriculture vehicles when using public highways; (2) passenger and specialty vehicles towing large trailers; (3) large recreational vehicles, and (4) trucks.

Fees & Taxes

Table 1: Title & Registration Fees

Vehicle Type	Title Fee	Registration Fee
Motor Vehicle	$22.50	$36.00
Mobile Home (8,000 lbs. or less)	$22.50	$45.00
Mobile Home (8,000 lbs. to 11,000 lbs.)	$22.50	$63.00
Mobile Home (11,001 lbs. or more)	$22.50	$81.00
Trailers of 3,000 lbs. or less	$22.50	$6.00
Trailers of 3,001 lbs. to 10,000 lbs.	$22.50	$12.00
Trailers of 10,001 lbs. or more	$22.50	$27.00
Motorcycles	$22.50	$18.00

Table 2: License Fees

License Class	Fee
Initial Permit and 4-Year License	$31.00
Initial Permit and 2-Year License (age 65+)	$20.50
Initial Motorcycle Permit and 4-Year License	$41.00
Initial Motorcycle Permit and 2-Year License (age 65+)	$30.50
4-Year License Renewal	$26.00
4-Year License Renewal with Motorcycle	$46.00
2-Year License Renewal (age 65+)	$15.50
Duplicate License	$10.00
Duplicate License with Class M (motorcycle class)	$15.00

Table 3: Vehicle Taxes

Tax	Rate
State Sales Tax	7% in City of Philadelphia and Allegheny County, 6% in all other counties
Gasoline Tax; (Diesel)	$0.311/gallon; ($0.351/gallon)

Table 4: Miscellaneous Fees

Fee	Amount	Payable Upon
Duplicate Registration (at any time other than identified above)	$1.50	request
Duplicate Registration (at any time other than identified above)	$4.50	request
Replacement of License Plate or Sticker	$7.50	request
Application for Retired Persons Vehicle Registration	$10.00	request
Replacement / Duplicate Title by Owner or Lienholder	$22.50	request
Replacement / Duplicate Title by a Registered Dealer	$22.50	request
Source Power of Attorney Processing Fee	$15.00	request
Organ Donation Awareness Trust Fund	$1.00	request
License Plate Transfer Fee	$6.00	request

RHODE ISLAND

Contact Information

Division of Motor Vehicles (Division)
Department of Administration
100 Main Street
Pawtucket, RI 02860

(401) 588-3020
www.dmv.state.ri.us

Department of State Police
311 Danielson Pike
N. Scituate, RI 02857

(401) 444-1000
www.risp.state.ri.us

Rhode Island Department of Transportation
Two Capitol Hill
Providence, RI 02903

(401) 222-2481
www.dot.state.ri.us/

Vehicle Title

Application: Every owner of a vehicle registered in Rhode Island must apply for a certificate of title if none has previously been issued.

- An application for the 1st certificate of title of a vehicle must be made to the Division and contain: (1) the name, residence, and mailing address of the owner; (2) a description of the vehicle, including make, model, identifying number, type of body, number of cylinders, and whether new or used; and (3) date of purchase by applicant, name and address of the person who sold the vehicle, and the names and addresses of any lienholders.
- If an application is for a vehicle that was previously registered in another state or country, the application must be accompanied with any certificate of title issued by the other state or country.

Transfer of Ownership: Upon transfer of interest in a vehicle, at the time of the delivery of the vehicle, the owner must execute an assignment and warranty of title to the transferee. The transferee must then promptly execute the application for a new certificate of title.

Mobile Homes: Every deed, instrument, or writing which grants, assigns, transfers, or conveys the interest in any mobile or manufactured home must be filed with the recorder of deeds of the city or town in which the mobile or manufactured home is located, within 10 days after execution of that deed, instrument, or writing.

Vehicle Registration

Application: Every motor vehicle owned by a resident of Rhode Island is required to be registered.

- Every application for vehicle registration must be signed by the owner in ink and contain: (1) the name, city, or town of resident, actual residence address, mailing address as it appears on the owner's driver's license, business address if the owner is a business; (2) a description of the vehicle that includes the make, model, type of body, number of cylinders, and the serial number of the vehicle, and the engine or other number of the vehicle; (3) a statement whether liability insurance is carried on the vehicle and the name of the carrier, policy number, and effective dates of the policy; and (4) the exact mileage reading on the date of application.

Non-Residents: A resident is a person who: (1) owns, rents, or leases real estate with Rhode Island as his or her residence and engages in a trade, business, or profession in Rhode Island, or enrolls his or her children in a Rhode Island school for a period exceeding 90 days; or (2) is registered to vote or is eligible to register to vote in Rhode Island.

- Military personnel on active duty in Rhode Island may maintain out-of-state vehicle registration.

Registration Type: All vehicle registrations, cards, and plates expire at midnight on March 31st each year, unless issued under the staggered registration system.

- Renewal is made to the division at any time prior to expiration of the registration. Upon renewal, a sticker for each plate to be placed at the bottom right-hand corner of the plate will be provided. Owners must be issued a new fully reflective plate no less frequently than every 10 years.
- Before obtaining an original or transferal registration for a vehicle in Rhode Island, the owner must furnish proof of payment of any taxes due.

Emissions Inspection: Emissions inspections are required for all vehicles except: (1) motor vehicles 25 years or older; (2) any class of vehicles that is exempted by regulation because the vehicle presents prohibitive inspection problems or is inappropriate for inspection; (3) vehicles operated exclusively by electric power; (4) new motor vehicles until 24 months after date of purchase or 24,000 miles; and (5) motor vehicles in compliance with an enhanced motor vehicle inspection program operated by another jurisdiction.

- Emissions inspections are required annually.
- Any vehicle that fails the inspection has 30 days to be reinspected and comply with the requirements.
- Vehicles required to be inspected include, but are not limited to, all 1975 and later model year light duty vehicles and light duty trucks up to and including 8,500 lbs. GVWR.

Safety Inspection: The director of the department of administration, members of the state and local police, and other officers and employees of the Division designated by the director of the department of administration may require the seller at retail or driver of a vehicle to stop and submit the vehicle to an inspection or appropriate test.

- At least once, but not more than twice per year, every vehicle, trailer, semitrailer, and pole trailer registered in Rhode Island must be inspected and provided with an official certificate of inspection and approval. The first inspection of any new vehicle must occur within 2 years from date of purchase or before accumulation of 24,000 miles. Inspection shall be made of the mechanism, brakes, and equipment of the vehicle.
- Motor vehicles purchased out of state by a Rhode Island resident must be inspected within 5 business days of registration.
- Trailers or semitrailers with gross weight of 1,000 lbs. or less are exempt from inspection.

License Plates

Disbursement: Plates are provided upon vehicle registration, 1 fully reflective plate for each motorcycle or trailer and 2 fully reflective plates for every other motor vehicle.

- A temporary plate may be issued that allows the operation of a vehicle on the public highways for a period of 5 days from the date of issue.
- On a motor vehicle, plates must be attached 1 in the front and 1 in the rear. On a motorcycle or trailer, plates must be attached at the rear of the vehicle.
- Handicapped parking placards or stickers may be issued upon application and proof of a disability. The placard or sticker shall be renewed every 3 years for individuals with a long-term or permanent disability.

Transfer of Plates: Plates must be removed when selling a vehicle and may be transferred to another vehicle owned by said person within 10 days or must be forwarded to the division.

Driver's Licenses

Examination: All applicants for a license must pass a written test, road test, and eye examination (20/40 visual acuity required). Any person who successfully completes a driver education course who has passed a standardized written driver's license examination does not have to take the written examination.

Graduated Drivers Licensing: State has a system of graduated licensing for teen drivers. At 16, teens who have completed a driver training course and passed a standardized written examination are eligible for an instruction/learner's permit.

- Permit holders must always be in the company of a supervising driver who must sit in the front seat. Permit holders and their passengers must be properly restrained.
- Teen drivers must have 50 hours of supervised driving, including 10 hours during the nighttime.
- At 16 and 6 months, teens who have: (1) held a permit for at least 6 months; (2) passed a road test; and (3) not been convicted of a moving or seat belt violation in the preceding 6 months are eligible for a limited provisional/intermediate license.
- Limited provisional/intermediate license holders are prohibited from driving unsupervised between the hours of 1:00 a.m. and 5:00 a.m.
- Limited provisional/intermediate license holders and their passengers must be properly restrained.
- Teens are prohibited from transporting more than 1 passenger under the age of 21 within the first year of provisional licensure (family members exempt).
- Teens who have held the limited provisional/intermediate license for at least 12 months and have been moving and seat belt violation free during the preceding 6 months are eligible for a full operator's license—minimum age 17 years and 6 months.
- Driver education is required of all license applicants under 18.

Issuance/Application: All persons operating a motor vehicle must have a valid driver's license.

- Any resident is required to obtain a Rhode Island operator's or chauffeur's license within 30 days of establishing residency.
- A person must be at least 16 years of age to apply for an operator's license and 18 years of age to apply for a chauffeur's license.
- All applications for an instruction permit or license must contain: (1) the full name,

date of birth, sex and residence address of the applicant; (2) a brief description of the applicant; (3) whether the applicant has been previously licensed by another state or country; and (4) whether any other previously held license has even been suspended or revoked and for what reason.

- A driver's license must have a distinguishing number assigned to the licensee, the full name, date of birth, residence address, brief description of the licensee, photograph of the licensee, indication of desire to donate tissue or organs, and the licensee's signature.
- License does not normally include a social security number.
- Drug or alcohol offenses may cause postponement of new driver's license eligibility.

Renewal: Every operator's first license is issued as a temporary license valid from the date of issuance until the licensee's birthday in the second year following the issuance of the temporary license. Every operator's license after the temporary license shall expire on the birthday of the licensee 5 years after issuance, with the exception of any person 70 years of age or older whose license shall expire on the birthday 2 years after issuance.

- New license will not be issued during any period of suspension.
- Driver's licenses for active duty military personnel are valid for 30 days after discharge or return to the state of Rhode Island, whichever occurs first.
- Any person serving in the armed forces may apply for a special license that is good until 30 days after discharge.

Types of Licenses: A special license is required to operate a motorcycle or motor scooter.

- A "first license" is issued to a person applying for the first time and is issued for 1 year, after which time a permanent license is issued.
- A chauffeur's license is issued to persons at least 21 years of age for the purpose of driving a school bus to transport children, or any motor vehicle when in use for transportation of persons or property for compensation.
- A commercial driver's license (CDL) issued to persons at least 21 years of age, except for intrastate operations when the applicant must be at least 18 years of age.
- Endorsements on a commercial driver's license include: (1) a tank endorsement; (2) a passenger endorsement; (3) hazmat; (4) doubles; and (5) triples.

RI

Traffic Rules

Alcohol Laws: State has implied consent law.

- Open containers are not permitted. Meets TEA-21 requirements.
- Illegal per se BAC level is .08.
- BAC level for people under 21 is .02.
- BAC level for commercial drivers is .04.

Cellular Phones: School bus drivers are prohibited from using cell phones while driving, except in emergencies.

Emergency Radio/Cellular: Citizen band radio channel 9 is not monitored for emergency calls. Emergency number is 911 or 800-499-3784.

Headsets: Earphones or headsets are not permitted while operating a bicycle or motor vehicle.

Occupant Restraints: Any person operating a motor vehicle and all passengers over the age of 7 must properly wear a seat belt.

- Violation of the safety belt law is a secondary offense; primary for children under 18 (effective July 1, 2005).
- Any child under the age of 7, less than 54 inches in height, and less than 80 lbs. must be properly restrained in a child restraint system and located in the rear seat of the vehicle. If the child is under 7 years old but at least 54 inches in height and at least 80 lbs., the child shall be properly wearing a safety belt and/or shoulder harness and seated in the rear seat of a vehicle.
- Riding in a pickup truck bed is not permitted for people under 16 unless passengers are restrained.

Railroad Crossing: Every vehicle must stop within 50 feet but not less than 15 feet from the nearest rail of a railroad crossing when: (1) a clearly visible electric or mechanical signal device gives warning of the immediate approach of a train; (2) a crossing gate is lowered or a human flagperson gives or continues to give signal of the approach or passage of a train; (3) a train approaching within approximately 1,500 feet of the crossing emits an audible signal; or (4) an approaching train is plainly visible and in hazardous proximity to the crossing. A vehicle may not proceed over the tracks until it is safe to do so.

- No person may drive a vehicle through, around, or under any crossing gate or barrier while it is closed or being opened or closed.
- The driver of any motor vehicle carrying passengers for hire, any school bus carrying any child, any vehicle carrying any cargo or explosive or flammable substances, must stop within 50 feet but not less than 15 feet from the nearest rail of the railroad to listen and look for an approaching train and may not proceed until it is safe to do so.

School Buses: Every school bus must have a stop arm that can be activated when children are being loaded or unloaded.

- The driver of a vehicle upon meeting or overtaking, from any direction, a school bus that has flashing red lights in operation, must stop the vehicle before reaching the bus and may not proceed until the bus resumes motion or the flashing lights are off.
- Stopping for a school bus is not required for drivers of other vehicles when: (1) when the highway is divided by a median strip separating lanes of traffic and the school bus is stopped on the opposite side of the median strip; or (2) when the bus is stopped in a loading zone adjacent to a limited access highway and pedestrians are not permitted to cross the highway.

Vehicle Equipment & Rules

Bumper Height: Modification of original bumper height is illegal unless exempted.

Glass/Window Tinting: Anyone installing a sunscreen device on a motor vehicle must place a label on the front window that contains the installer's name and the percentage of light transmittance.

- The use of non-transparent or sunscreen material or window application on motor vehicles which has a total light transmittance of not less than 70% on the windshield, all side windows, or the rear window is permitted if the vehicle has 2 outside mirrors, 1 on each side, adjusted to provide the driver with a clear view of the highway behind the vehicle.
- The use of transparent material on the uppermost 6 inches of the windshield is permitted.
- Sunscreen material is permitted on windows behind the driver in trailers and mobile homes provided that the vehicle has 2 outside mirrors, 1 on each side.
- Motor vehicles owned or leased by federal, state, and local law enforcement agencies, motor vehicles not required to be registered in Rhode Island, a motor vehicle registered in Rhode Island that is used to transport an individual with a medical need and any vehicle registered and garaged in Rhode Island that has a sole purpose of providing executive security within the state are exempt from window tinting regulations.

Telematics: No television viewer, screen, or other means of visually receiving a television broadcast may be located in the field of view of the driver.

Windshield Stickers: No sign, poster, or other non-transparent material that obstructs the driver's clear view of the road, is permitted on the front windshield, side wings, or side or rear windows of the vehicle. The administrator of the division may permit and specify placement of special stickers on the windshield or any other windows of the vehicle.

Motorcycles & Mopeds

Equipment: Drivers of motorcycles or motor scooters are required to use eye protection when operating the vehicle.
- Any operator under 21 years of age must wear a helmet.
- All new operators, regardless of age, must wear a helmet for 1 year from the date of issuance of the first license.
- Every motorcycle or motor scooter must have a rearview mirror.
- Handlebars are not permitted more than 15 inches in height above the seat.
- No person shall drive a motorcycle at night at a speed greater than 35 mph unless the motorcycle is equipped with a headlamp that is able to reveal a person or vehicle at a distance of 300 feet ahead.
- The operator of a motorcycle shall ride only upon the permanent and regular seat attached.
- A motorcycle shall not carry more persons than it was designed to carry. A passenger must ride on the permanent and regular seat if designed for 2 persons, or on another seat firmly attached to the rear or side of the operator.
- Any passenger on a motorcycle or motor scooter must be in a sidecar or have a separate rear seat, a separate footrest, an appropriate handlebar or grip for his or her use, and a helmet. A passenger under 12 years of age must have a properly secured backrest or equivalent unless seated in a sidecar.
- Every motorcycle must have at least 1 brake that may be operated by hand or foot that is adequate to slow and stop the motorcycle.
- Every motorcycle must have at least 1 and not more than 2 headlamps and at least 1 red reflector on the rear either as part of the taillamps or separately.

- All motorcycles must have stop lamps.
- Motorcycles may have single or multiple beam headlamps, provided that they be of sufficient intensity to reveal a person or vehicle at a distance of not less than 100 feet when the motorcycle is operated at any speed less than 25 mph and at a distance of not less than 200 feet when the motorcycle is operated at a speed of 25 mph or more.

Licenses: No person shall be licensed to operate a motorcycle or motor scooter unless he or she is at least 16 years of age, or unless the person previously has been issued a full operator's license and a motorcycle learner's permit or is already licensed under a prior act of this state.

- All applicants for a motorcycle or motor scooter license must pass written, vision, road sign, and road tests.
- A motorcycle learner's permit may be issued to a person who is at least 16 years old but less than 18 years old and has a limited provisional or full operator's license or is at least 18 years old and has a license. If the holder of the permit has a limited provisional license, the motorcycle may be driven only at times when the holder could drive a motor vehicle without supervision. The permit expires 18 months after issuance.

Noise Limits: Every vehicle must have a muffler in good working order and in constant operation to prevent excessive or unusual noise and annoying smoke. The use of a cutout, bypass, or similar device is prohibited.

Mopeds: Out-of-state residents owning motorized bicycles, whose state of residence does not require registration, shall register the vehicle in the state of Rhode Island.

- The operator of a motorized bicycle is required to have a valid license and must be at least 16 years of age.
- Not permitted on Interstate highways.

Passenger Car Trailers

Registration: Every trailer, tent trailer, and travel trailer owned by a resident of Rhode Island is required to be registered.

Brakes: Every trailer with a gross weight of 4,000 lbs. or more must have brakes that are adequate to slow, stop, and hold the vehicle. Brakes must be designed so they can be applied from the driver of the towing vehicle's normal operating position and that they will be automatically applied in the case of an accidental breakaway. New trailers must have service brakes on all wheels.

- Every trailer must have parking brakes adequate to hold the vehicle on any grade it is operated, under all conditions of loading and on a surface free from snow, ice, or loose material.

Dimensions: Total length: 60 feet; trailer length: not specified; width: 102 inches; height: 13.6 feet.

Hitch: When 1 vehicle is towing another, the drawbar or other connection must be of sufficient strength to pull the weight towed and must not exceed 15 feet in its span from 1 vehicle to the other.

Lighting: Every trailer or vehicle being drawn at the end of a train of vehicles must have at least 1 taillamp mounted on the rear which emits a red light plainly visible from a distance of 500 feet to the rear.

Mirrors: Every vehicle that is so loaded that it obstructs the driver's view to the rear, must have a mirror located for the driver so that it reflects a view of the highway for a list 200 feet to the rear.

Speed Limits: Same as for passenger cars.

Towing: A tow truck or any vehicle towing another, except when designed to be in combination, when on any public highway divided into multiple lanes for travel in the same direction, may travel only in the right lane of a 2-lane highway, or the 2 right lanes of a 3- or more lane highway.

Miscellaneous Provisions

Liability Laws: State has security-type law applicable in event of accident causing property damage in excess of $500 or personal injury or death.

- Motor vehicle insurance is required in the amounts of $25,000 because of bodily injury to or death of 1 person in any 1 accident; $50,000 because of bodily injury to or death of 2 or more persons in any 1 accident; and $25,000 because of injury to or destruction of property in any 1 accident or $75,000 combined single limit.
- State has non-resident service of process law; it does not have guest suit law.

Rhode Island Traffic Tribunal (RITT): Most traffic violations and offenses, except driving under the influence of liquor or drugs, driving to endanger, reckless driving, driving with a suspended license, leaving the scene of an accident, and municipal parking violations are decriminalized under Rhode Island state law. Speeding and all other minor traffic violations are handled by RITT. Most fines may be paid by mail, but some require a personal appearance before a judge or magistrate of the RITT.

Weigh Stations: Agricultural vehicles and trucks with a gross vehicle weight rating over 10,000 lbs. must stop.

Fees & Taxes

Table 1: Title & Registration Fees

Vehicle Type	Title Fee	Registration Fee
Motor Vehicle	$25.00	$30.00
Trailers of 3,000 lbs. or less		$5.00
Trailers of more than 3,000 lbs.		$1.50 per 1,000 lbs.
Motorcycles	$25.00	$13.00
Duplicates	$25.00	$1.00

Table 2: License Fees

License Class	Fee	Fee
Limited Instruction Permit or Limited Provisional License	$10.00	
Operator's License	$12.00	$5.00 for the first license examination
Renewal of Operator's License	$30.00 or $8.00 for those persons over 70 years of age	
Commercial Operator's License	$30.00	$10.00 for every written and/or oral examination, $25.00 for every skill test
Renewal of Commercial Operator's License	$50.00	
Duplicate License Fee	$10.00	
Endorsements/Classifications/Restrictions	$10.00	

Table 3: Vehicle Taxes

Tax	Rate
State Sales Tax	7%
Gasoline Tax; (Diesel)	$0.31/gallon; ($0.31/gallon)
Excise Tax	To be phased out in increments until 2006
Mobile Home Conveyance Tax	For transactions in excess of $100.00, the tax is $1.40 per $500.00 or fractional part of which is paid for the purchase of the home

Table 4: Miscellaneous Fees

Fee	Amount	Payable Upon
Emissions Inspection	$47.00	At the time of inspection
Certificate of Inspection	$4.00	At the time of inspection
Transfer of Registration	$15.00 if the vehicle is of the same class or $15.00 plus the difference in registration fees if the vehicles are of a different class	Upon application
Plate Issuance Fee	$6.00 plus registration fees	Upon application
License Plate Registration Fee with No Number Change	$5.00	Upon application
License Plate Replacement Fee with Number Change	$5.00	Upon application
Temporary License Plate	$10.00	Upon issuance
Certified Copy of Application for Driver's License or Registration or Driver's License or Registration	$10.00	
Motorcycle Driver Education Course	$20.00	
Personalized Plates	$30.00 or $50.00	

SOUTH CAROLINA

Contact Information

Department of Motor Vehicles (Department)
955 Park Street
Columbia, SC 29201

(803) 737-4000
www.scdmv.org/

South Carolina Highway Patrol
5400 Broad River Road
Columbia, SC 29212

(803) 896-7920
www.schp.org/

Department of Transportation (DOT)
955 Park Street
P.O. Box 191
Columbia, SC 29202-0191

(803) 737-2314
www.dot.state.sc.us/

Vehicle Title

Application: Every owner of a vehicle in South Carolina for which the Department has issued no certificate of title must apply for a certificate of title.

- An application for a certificate of title for a vehicle must be made by the owner to the Department on the form it prescribes and must contain or be accompanied by: (1) the name and residence and mailing address of the owner; (2) a description of the vehicle, including, so far as the following data exists, its make, model, year, vehicle identification number, type of body, odometer reading at the time of application, and whether the vehicle is new or used; (3) the date of acquisition by applicant, the name and address of the person from whom the vehicle was acquired, and the names and addresses of any lienholders in the order of their priority and the dates of their security agreements; (4) an odometer disclosure statement made by the transferor of the vehicle and acknowledged by the transferee; and (5) any further information or documentation the Department reasonably requires.
- If the application is not for the 1st certificate of title, the last certificate of title previously issued for the vehicle must accompany it.
- If the application refers to a vehicle purchased from a dealer, it must contain the name and address of any lienholder holding a security interest created or reserved at the time of the sale signed by the dealer as well as the owner, and the dealer must promptly mail or deliver the application to the Department. If the application refers to a new vehicle purchased from a dealer, the application must also be accompanied by the manufacturer's certificate of origin.

Transfer of Ownership: Whenever an owner transfers his ownership in a motor vehicle, he or she must immediately notify the Department in writing of the transfer by providing the Department with the name and address of the new owner and the date of transfer.

- Whenever any person purchases a vehicle which was registered in South Carolina, the person receiving the vehicle must make an application with the Department for the transfer of the vehicle within 30 days of the date of transfer.

Vehicle Registration

Application: Every motor vehicle, trailer, and semitrailer operated on South Carolina highways must be registered.

- Application for registration must be made on the form prescribed by the Department. Every application must contain the following: (1) the name, residence, and mailing address of the owner or business address of the owner if a firm, association, or corporation and the county, municipality, if applicable, and school district in which the applicant resides; (2) a description of the vehicle including the make, model, type of body, number of cylinders, serial number, and engine or other number of the vehicle, whether the vehicle is new or used, the date of sale by the manufacturer or dealer to the person intending to operate such a vehicle, in the event a vehicle is designed, constructed, converted, or rebuilt for the transportation of property, a statement of the load capacity for which it is to be registered; and (3) any additional information as may reasonably be required by the Department to enable it to determine whether the vehicle is lawfully entitled to registration and licensing.
- In addition to the information required above, if the application is for a motor vehicle which has been transferred from a previous registrant to the applicant, the applicant must complete the odometer disclosure statement on the application.
- In addition to the other registration requirements, the Department must collect a federal employer identification number or social security number when a vehicle is registered with a Gross Vehicle Weight (GVW) of more than 26,000 lbs. or as a bus common carrier.
- A signed statement must accompany the application stating that all county and municipal taxes legally due by the applicant on the vehicle being registered have been paid.

Non-Residents: A non-resident owner of a vehicle that is registered in another state has to register his or her vehicle in South Carolina when that non-resident becomes a resident or if that person has operated the vehicle in South Carolina over 150 days.

- Military personnel on active duty in South Carolina may maintain out-of-state vehicle registration.

Registration Type: A vehicle must be registered every 2 years.

- A person cannot renew his or her motor vehicle registration if he or she has not paid his or her property taxes.

License Plates

Disbursement: The Department upon registering and licensing a vehicle must issue to the owner one license plate. This license plate must be attached to the outside rear of the vehicle, except that on truck tractors and road tractors the license plate must be attached to the outside front of the vehicle.

- A disabled license plate or placard is available from DPS by completion of DMVB-16. $1 fee for each placard. Two placards may be issued to each applicant.

Transfer of Plates: Whenever the owner of a registered and licensed vehicle transfers his or her ownership, he or she must immediately notify the Department in writing, giving the name and address of the new owner and the date of transfer. The license plate issued for the vehicle must remain with the prior owner. Within 30 days of the transfer, the prior owner must either apply to transfer the plates to another vehicle or return the plates to the Department. In either event, the registration card must be concurrently returned to the Department.

- The Department, upon application and payment of a fee, must transfer the license plate previously assigned to an owner or lessee for one vehicle to another vehicle of the same general type owned or leased by the same person.

Driver's Licenses

Examination: The Department must examine every applicant for a driver's license, unless the Department waives this requirement. The examination must include a test of the applicant's eyesight (20/40 visual acuity required), his or her ability to read and understand highway signs and all South Carolina traffic laws. This test must also include an actual demonstration of the applicant's ability to exercise ordinary and reasonable control in the operation of the type motor vehicle for which a license is sought. The Department may require a further physical and mental examination if it considers this necessary to determine the applicant's fitness to operate a motor vehicle. The Department must make provisions for giving an examination in the county where the applicant resides.

Graduated Drivers Licensing: State has a system of graduated licensing for teen drivers. At 15, teens are eligible for a beginner's permit. The beginner's/learner's permit allows the teen to drive under the following conditions: (1) during daylight hours (between 6:00 a.m. and 6:00 p.m.) and (2) when accompanied by a licensed driver 21 years of age or older who has had at least 1 year of driving experience and occupies the front passenger seat of the vehicle while the permit holder drives, except when the permit holder is operating a motorcycle.

- At 15 and 6 months, teens who have passed a certified driver's education course, successfully passed the road test, acquired 40 hours (10 hours at night) of supervised driving, or other requirements the Department may prescribe, and satisfied the school's attendance requirement are eligible for a provisional/intermediate license.
- Intermediate license holders may not drive unsupervised (only with a licensed adult 21 years of age or older) between the hours of 6:00 p.m. and 6:00 a.m. EST and 8:00 p.m. and 6:00 a.m. EDT. Intermediate license holders are also prohibited from driving unsupervised with more than 2 passengers.
- At 16 and 6 months, teens are eligible for an unrestricted license.
- A person who has never held a driver's license must first obtain a beginner's permit and then must hold the permit for 90 days before becoming eligible to obtain a full license.
- A provisional driver's license holder may drive a motor scooter or light motor-driven cycle of 5-brake horsepower or less, during daylight hours.

Issuance/Application: Every application for a driver's license or permit must: (1) be made upon the form furnished by the Department; (2) be accompanied by the proper fee and any identification required by the Department; (3) contain the full name, date of birth, sex, race, and residence address of the applicant and briefly describe the applicant; (4) state whether the applicant has been licensed as an operator or chauffeur and, if so, when and by what state or country; and (5) state whether a license or permit has been suspended or revoked or whether an application has been refused and, if so, the date of and reason for the suspension, revocation, or reason for refusal.

- School attendance is a condition for the issuance of a provisional license. The Department may not issue a provisional license to a person unless the person has a high school diploma or certificate, or a General Education Development Certificate, or is enrolled in a public or private school which has been approved by the State Board of Education or a member school of the South Carolina Independent School's Association, a parochial, denominational, church-related school, or other programs which are accepted by the State Board of Education. Also to obtain a provisional license a person must do the following: (1) conform to the attendance laws, regulations, and policies of the school, school district, and the State Board of Education, as applicable; and (2) the person must not be suspended or expelled from school.
- The Department may issue a special restricted driver's license to a person who is between 16 years of age and 17 years of age, who has held a beginner's permit for 90 days and who has successfully passed the road test or other requirements the Department may require. The special restricted driver's license allows the license holder to operate the vehicle between 6:00 a.m. and 6:00 p.m. The holder of a special restricted driver's license may not drive between midnight and 6:00 a.m., unless accompanied by the holder's licensed parent or guardian. The restrictions on a special restricted license may be modified or waived by the Department if the restricted licensee proves to the Department's satisfaction that the restriction interfere with the license holder's employment, opportunity for employment, or ability to attend school.
- License includes a color photograph. Social security number is not displayed on license.
- The following persons do not have to obtain a beginner's/learner's permit to operate a motor vehicle: (1) students regularly enrolled in a South Carolina high school which conducts a driver's training course while the student is participating in the course and when accompanied by a qualified instructor of the course; and (2) a person 15 years or older enrolled in a driver training course conducted by a licensed driver training school. This person must be accompanied by an instructor of the school and can only drive the school's automobile.
- The expiration dates on non-citizens' driver's licenses and I.D. cards are linked to the expiration date of the person's visa.
- Licenses issued to non-citizens shall not be issued for less than 1 year or more than 5 years.

Renewal: Every license expires on the licensee's birth date on the 5th year after the year in which the license was issued. Every license is renewable on or before its expiration date by filling out an application and the payment of the required fee.

- The Department requires all applicants to take a vision test. The vision examination can be waived if the license holder submits a certificate from a person authorized by law to examine eyes.
- The Department may renew a driver's license of a resident by mail upon payment of the required fee, if the renewal is a digitized license.
- Any person licensed to drive a motor vehicle in this State who is involved in 4 accidents in any 24-month period, may in the discretion of the Department, be required to take any portion of the driver's license examination. Any person who has had 4 accidents and fails to submit to such test within 30 days after having been notified

by the Department, will have his or her driver's license suspended until he takes and passes the examination.
- Any valid driver's license issued to a person on active duty out of the state, or the person's spouse, is effective without requirement for renewal until 60 days after the date of the person's discharge from the service.

Types of Licenses: Class D vehicles are passenger vehicles and all non-commercial vehicles that do not exceed 26,000 lbs. Gross Vehicle Weight (GVW).
- Class E vehicles are non-commercial single unit vehicles that do not exceed 26,000 lbs. GVW.
- Class F vehicles are non-commercial combination vehicles that exceed 26,000 lbs. GVW.
- Class M vehicles are motorcycles.
- Class G vehicles are mopeds.

Traffic Rules

Alcohol Laws: State has implied consent law.
- Open containers are prohibited. Meets the requirements of TEA-21.
- Illegal per se BAC level is .08.
- BAC level for people under 21 is .02.
- BAC level for commercial drivers is .04.

Emergency Radio/Cellular: Citizen band radio channel 9 is monitored for emergency calls in some areas.

Headsets: Wearing radio headsets while driving is permitted.

Occupant Restraints: The driver and every occupant of a motor vehicle must wear a fastened safety belt, which complies with federal law.
- Violation of the seat belt law is a primary offense.
- Children less than 1 year or less than 20 lbs. must be properly restrained in a rear-facing child seat.
- Children from 1 until 6 years and weighing 20 to 40 lbs. must be properly restrained in a forward-facing child seat.
- Children 1 to 6 years old and weighing 40 to 80 lbs. must be properly restrained in a booster seat.
- Children 1 through 6 years and weighing 80+ lbs. must be restrained in a seat belt or any child under 6 years who can sit with his knees bent over the vehicle seat edge when sitting up straight with his back firmly against the seat may wear a seat belt.
- All children under the age of 6 must ride in the rear seat of the vehicle. This does not apply if all rear seats are taken by children under 6.
- Riding in pickup truck beds is permitted. However, children 15 and under are prohibited from riding in pickup truck beds with certain exceptions. Additional gaps in coverage apply; see Occupant Protection Chart.

Railroad Crossing: Whenever any person driving a vehicle approaches a railroad grade crossing, the driver of the vehicle must stop within 50 feet, but not less than 15 feet, from the nearest rail of the railroad and must not proceed until he or she can do so safely. The previous mentioned requirements apply when: (1) a clearly visible electric or mechanical signal device gives warning of the immediate approach of a railroad train; (2) a crossing gate is lowered or when a flagman gives or continues to give a signal of the approach or passage of a railroad train; (3) a railroad train approaching within approximately 1,500 feet of the highway crossing emits a signal audible from such distance and the train, by reason of its speed or nearness to the crossing, is an immediate hazard; or (4) an approaching railroad train is plainly visible and is in hazardous proximity to the crossing.

- A person must not drive any vehicle through, around, or under any crossing gate or barrier at a railroad crossing while the gate or barrier is closed or is being opened or closed.
- The DOT and local authorities with the approval of DOT, may designate particularly dangerous highway grade crossings of railroads and erect stop signs at those crossings. When such signs are erected, the driver of any vehicle must stop between 15 and 50 feet from the nearest rail of the railroad and must proceed with care.
- Notwithstanding the indication of a traffic signal to proceed, a driver must not enter an intersection, a marked crosswalk, or drive onto a railroad grade crossing unless there is sufficient space on the other side of the intersection, crosswalk, or railroad grade crossing to accommodate the vehicle the driver is operating without obstructing the passage of the other vehicles, pedestrians, or railroad trains.
- When stopping as required at a railroad crossing, the driver must keep as far to the right of the highway as possible and must not form 2 lanes of traffic unless the roadway is marked for 2 or more lanes of traffic on the driver's side of the center line of the highway.

School Buses: The driver of a vehicle meeting or overtaking from either direction any school bus stopped on the highway must stop before reaching the bus if the bus's flashing red lights are in operation, and the driver must not proceed until the bus resumes motion or the flashing red lights are no longer on.

- The driver of a vehicle does not have to stop upon meeting a stopped school bus when the bus is in a passenger loading zone completely off the main travel lanes and when pedestrians are not allowed to cross the roadway, and on highways where the roadways are separated by an earth or raised concrete median.
- The driver of a vehicle must stop upon meeting or passing a stopped school bus on any 2-lane highway, on any 4-lane or multi-lane highway where the opposing highway is separated only by painted lines on the roadway or a narrow gravel median, or when overtaking a school bus which has its red or amber signal lights on.

Vehicle Equipment & Rules

Bumper Height: It is illegal to elevate or lower passenger vehicle more than 6 inches from the original height.

Glass/Window Tinting: A sunscreening device must be nonreflective and may not be red, yellow, or amber in color.

- A sunscreening device may be used only along the top of the windshield and may not extend downward beyond the AS1 line. If the AS1 line is not visible, no sunscreening device may be applied to the windshield.
- A single sunscreening device may be installed on the sidewings or side windows, or both, located at the immediate right and left of the driver and the side windows

behind the driver. The sunscreening device must be nonreflective and the combined light transmission of the sunscreening device with the factory or manufacturer-installed sunscreening material must not be less than 27%.

- A single sunscreening device applied to the rearmost window must be nonreflective and the combined light transmission of the sunscreening device with the factory or manufacturer-installed sunscreening material must not be less than 27%. If a sunscreening device is used on the rearmost window, 1 right and 1 left outside rearview mirror is required.
- Each vehicle equipped with an after-factory sunscreening device, whether installed by a consumer or professional, at all times must bear a certificate of compliance containing the following information: the percentage of light transmission allowed by the sunscreening device; the identity of the installer by name, address, and telephone number; and the date of installation.
- The light transmittance requirement of this section applies to windows behind the driver on pickup trucks but does not apply to windows behind the driver on other trucks, buses, trailers, mobile homes, multipurpose passenger vehicles, and recreational vehicles.

Telematics: A person must not drive a motor vehicle equipped with any television screen which is visible to the driver while he or she is operating the motor vehicle.

Windshield Stickers: A person must not drive a motor vehicle with any sign, poster, or other non-transparent material on the front windshield which obstructs the driver's clear view of the highway.

Motorcycles & Mopeds

Equipment: Any motorcycle carrying a passenger, other than in a sidecar or enclosed cab, must be equipped with footrests for that passenger.

- A person must not operate any motorcycle with handlebars more than 15 inches in height above that portion of the seat occupied by the operator.
- A person must not operate a motorcycle unless it is equipped with a rearview mirror which will afford the operator ample rear vision at all times.
- It is illegal for any person under the age of 21 to operate or ride on a motorcycle or a moped unless he or she wears a protective helmet approved by the Department. Such a helmet must be equipped with either a neck or chin strap and be reflectorized on both sides.
- It is illegal for any person under the age of 21 to operate a moped or a motorcycle unless he or she wears goggles or a face shield of a type approved by the Department.
- The provisions with respect to goggles and face shields do not apply to the operator of moped or a motorcycle equipped with a wind screen.
- Any person who operates a motorcycle or moped must have the headlights on at all times.
- Every motorcycle and every moped must have at least one rear reflector.
- Every motorcycle and every moped must be equipped with at least one and not more than 2 headlamps.
- The headlamp or headlamps upon every motorcycle and moped may be of the single-beam or multiple-beam type and must be of sufficient intensity to reveal a person or a vehicle at a distance of at least 100 feet when the motorcycle or moped is

operated at any speed less than 25 mph and at a distance of at least 200 feet when the motorcycle or moped is operated at a speed of 25 mph.

Licenses: A motorcycle vehicle examination will be provided where the knowledge and skills examination for a commercial driver's license is offered.

Mopeds: A person may not ride on a moped other than on or astride a permanent and regular seat attached to the moped.

- A moped may not be used to carry more persons at 1 time than the number for which it is designed and equipped.
- It is unlawful for a person to operate a moped without: operable pedals if the moped is equipped with pedals; at least 1 rearview mirror; operable running lights; and brake lights which are operable when either brake is deployed.
- The operator of a moped must have the operating lights turned on at all times while the moped is in operation on the public highways and streets of South Carolina.
- It is unlawful for a person to modify or change the equipment of a moped so that the vehicle exceeds 2 brake horsepower and produces speeds in excess of 30 mph on level ground.
- It is illegal for a person to operate a moped without displaying the metal identification plate, which must be attached to the vehicle.
- To ride a moped, a person must either have a valid driver's license or a moped license.
- A person must be at least 14 years old to obtain a moped license.

Passenger Car Trailers

Brakes: Every combination of vehicles must be equipped with service brakes that are capable and adequate to control the movement of and to stop and hold the vehicle with any load and on any grade on which it is operated.

- Every vehicle manufactured or assembled after June 7, 1949 must be equipped with brakes on all wheels except trailers and semitrailers of a gross weight less than 3,001 lbs. as long as the total weight on and including the wheels of the trailers does not exceed 40% of the gross weight of the towing vehicle when connected to the trailer.
- Every motor vehicle manufactured after July 1, 1964 and used to tow a trailer or semitrailer must be equipped with a means for providing that the towing vehicle is capable of being stopped by the use of its service brakes.
- Every motor vehicle, trailer, or semitrailer must be equipped with brakes that have a braking system arranged so that one control device can be used to operate all service brakes.

Dimensions: Total length: not specified; trailer length: 48 feet; width: 102 inches (allows total width to exceed 102 inches if the excess is due to an appurtenance); height: 13.6 feet.

Hitch: Drawbar or other connection must be of sufficient strength to pull all weight towed. Drawbar or other connection must not exceed 15 feet from one vehicle to the other except when transporting objects which cannot readily be dismembered. When 1 vehicle is towing another vehicle and the connection consists of a chain, rope, or cable, there must be displayed upon such connection a white flag or cloth not less than 12 inches square.

Lighting: Tail, license plate, and brake lights are required. Turn signals and reflectors are also required.

Mirrors: Every motor vehicle that is constructed or loaded so that the driver's rear view is obstructed, the driver's position must be equipped with a rearview mirror that reflects the driver's view of the highway for at least 200 feet.

Speed Limits: Manufactured, modular, or mobile homes must not be transported at a speed in excess of 10 miles below the maximum posted speed limit when the maximum posted speed limit is in excess of 45 mph, and never in excess of 55 mph.

- A person driving a vehicle towing a house trailer must not drive faster than 45 mph.

Miscellaneous Provisions

Bail Bonds: Mandatory recognition of AAA arrest bond certificates up to $500.

Liability Laws: Non-compulsory insurance state law for all motor vehicles subject to registration in South Carolina. Motor vehicle owners must certify when they register the vehicle and each year upon re-registration that they have and will maintain the required coverage or be registered as an uninsured motorist by paying a $550 fee. Driver must meet certain criteria. This fee is not liability insurance, it is for the privilege to drive and operate an uninsured vehicle in South Carolina.

- All motor vehicles must have liability insurance as follows: (1) $15,000 for bodily injury to 1 person in any 1 accident; (2) $30,000 for bodily injury to 2 or more persons in any 1 accident; and (3) $10,000 for injury to or destruction of the property of others.
- Instead of paying the above insurance requirements, a vehicle owner can pay a $550 uninsured motorist fee. Payment of this fee gives the motor vehicle operator the privilege to drive and operate an uninsured motor vehicle on South Carolina roads. To qualify, the applicant and every driver in the applicant's household must have held a driver's license for 3 or more years. A person cannot qualify as an uninsured motorist if he or she has been convicted of certain violations within the past 3 years.
- Owners must maintain proof of financial responsibility in the motor vehicle at all times and it must be displayed upon demand by a police officer or any other person duly authorized by law.
- State has non-resident service of process law and has no guest suit law.

Weigh Stations: If the Department has reason to believe that the weight of a vehicle and load is unlawful, it may require the driver to stop and submit to a weighing of the vehicle and load either by means of portable or stationary scales and may require that the vehicle be driven to the nearest public scales.

- Whenever an officer upon weighing a vehicle and load determines that the weight is unlawful, he may require the driver to stop the vehicle in a suitable place and remain standing until the portion of the load necessary to reduce the axle weight, or gross weight of the vehicle, or both is removed.
- All material unloaded must be cared for by the owner or operator of the vehicle at his own risk. The scaled weights of the gross weight of vehicles and combinations of vehicles cannot be closer than 10% to the true gross weight.

Fees & Taxes

Table 1: Title & Registration Fees

Vehicle Type	Title Fee	Registration Fee
For persons 65 years of age or older or person who is handicapped, the fee for every private passenger vehicle	$10.00	$20.00
For persons under the age of 65, the fee for every private passenger vehicle, excluding trucks	$10.00	$24.00
For persons 65 years of age or older, the biennial registration fee for a property-carrying vehicle with a gross weight of 6,000 lbs., or less	$10.00	$30.00
For persons who are 65 years of age, the biennial registration fee for a private passenger motor vehicle excluding trucks	$10.00	$22.00
For every common carrier passenger vehicle under 2,001 lbs.	$10.00	$18.00
Common Carrier Passenger Vehicles 2,001 - 2,500 lbs.	$10.00	$24.00
Common Carrier Passenger Vehicles 2,501 - 3,000 lbs.	$10.00	$30.00
Common Carrier Passenger Vehicles 3,001 - 3,500 lbs.	$10.00	$36.00
Common Carrier Passenger Vehicles 3,501 - 4,000 lbs.	$10.00	$42.00
Common Carrier Passenger Vehicles 4,001 - 4,500 lbs.	$10.00	$48.00
Common Carrier Passenger Vehicles 4,501 - 5,000 lbs.	$10.00	$54.00
Common Carrier Passenger Vehicles over 5,000 lbs.	$10.00	$54.00 plus $6.00 for each 500 lbs. of weight or fraction over 5,000 lbs.
Every House Trailer	$10.00	$12.00
Every Camper or Travel Trailer	$10.00	$10.00
Every Motorcycle, 3-Wheel Vehicle or Moped	$10.00	$10.00
Semitrailers, Regular Trailers, and Utility Trailers	$10.00	$75.00

Table 2: License Fees

License Class	Fee	Driving Test Fees
Class D: Passenger Vehicle and all Non-Commercial Vehicles that do not exceed 26,000 lbs. GVW	$12.50	Knowledge test $2.00 Beginner's permit $2.50
Class E: Non-Commercial Single Unit Vehicles that do not exceed 26,000 lbs. GVW	$12.50	Knowledge test $2.00 Beginner's permit $2.50
Class F: Non-Commercial Combination Vehicles that exceed 26,000 lbs. GVW	$12.50	Knowledge test $2.00 Beginner's permit $2.50
Class M: Motorcycles	$12.50	Knowledge test $2.00 Beginner's permit $2.50
Class G: Mopeds	$12.50	Knowledge test $2.00 Beginner's permit $2.50

Table 3: Vehicle Taxes

Tax	Rate
State Sales Tax	5%; $300.00 maximum
Gasoline Tax; (Diesel)	$0.16/gallon; ($0.16/gallon)
State Use Tax	5%

SC

Table 4: Miscellaneous Fees*

Fee	Amount
Transfer of Title	$10.00
Issuance of a Duplicate Certificate of Title	$10.00
Regular License Plates	$24.00
Regular License Plates for a Person that is 64 years old	$22.00
Regular License Plates for a Person that is 65 years or older	$20.00
Penalties for Late Registration 45 to 60 days	$10.00
Penalties for Late Registration 61 to 75 days	$25.00
Penalties for Late Registration 76 to 135 days	$50.00
Penalties for Late Registration over 135 days	$75.00
Penalties for Late Registration Renewal first 14 days	$10.00
Penalties for Late Registration Renewal 15 to 30 days	$25.00
Penalties for Late Registration Renewal 31 to 90 days	$50.00
Penalties for Late Registration Renewal over 90 days	$75.00
Copy of Driver's Record	$6.00
Commercial Driver's License Application	$15.00
Replacement License	$3.00
Duplicate Registration	$1.00
Specialty Plates	$30.00 plus registration fee (for personalized). Other plate fees vary by specialty.

*Fees payable upon request.

SOUTH DAKOTA

Contact Information

South Dakota Department of Revenue and Regulation
Division of Motor Vehicles
445 E. Capitol Ave.
Pierre, SD 57501-3185
(605) 773-3541
www.state.sd.us/drr/revenue.html

South Dakota Department of Public Safety
Office of Driver Licensing
118 W. Capitol Ave.
Pierre, SD 57501
(605) 773-6883
www.state.sd.us/dps/dl

South Dakota Highway Patrol
118 W. Capitol Ave.
Pierre, SD 57501
(605) 773-3105
http://hp.state.sd.us/

South Dakota Department of Transportation
700 E. Broadway Ave.
Becker-Hansen Building
Pierre, SD 57501
(605) 773-3265
www.sddot.com

Vehicle Title

Application: An application for a certificate of title must be made to the applicant's county treasurer on a form prescribed by the Department. This application must contain all of the following: (1) a full description of the vehicle; (2) the vehicle identification number; (3) a statement of the vehicle's title including all liens and encumbrances on the vehicle; (4) the county in which the vehicle is to be kept; (5) the addresses of the holders of all liens; and (6) any other information as the Department may require. If a certificate of title has previously been issued for the motor vehicle, trailer or semitrailer in this state or any state, the application must be accompanied by that certificate of title.

- A person is not required to obtain a certificate of title for a moped.
- Each trailer or semitrailer pulled by a non-commercial motor vehicle upon which fees were paid under the non-commercial declared gross weight fee schedule must have a license plate displayed in a conspicuous manner. The license plate is valid for the useful life of the trailer or semitrailer. However, if the title to the trailer or semitrailer is transferred, the new owner must make an application for a new identification plate within 30 days of the date of transfer.

Transfer of Ownership: A motor vehicle cannot be sold without delivering the purchaser or transferee a certificate of title indicating the date that the vehicle was purchased.

- The certificate of title can be transferred by completing the certificate.
- Once the certificate has been completed and approved by the Department, the Department must issue the owner a new certificate of title. This new certificate of title will list all of the unreleased liens, if any on the vehicle. All lienholders will be mailed notification of their security interest.
- A damage disclosure statement must be submitted when transferring a titled car from another state.

Mobile Home: Any new mobile home must, upon its purchase, be initially registered and titled. If the mobile home or manufactured home is sold by a dealer, the dealer must deliver to the county treasurer the manufacturer's statement of origin, the manufacturer's certificate of origin or the title for the mobile home, together with the required fees and completed forms necessary to accomplish the initial registration within 30 days of the sale. The purchaser shall register and title the mobile home within 30 days.

Vehicle Registration

Application: Every owner of a motor vehicle, motorcycle, truck tractor, road tractor, trailer or semitrailer, or recreational vehicle or trailer, which is operated or driven on the public highways must present to the county treasurer an application for the registration of that vehicle.

Non-Residents: A non-resident does not have to register his or her vehicle as long as the non-resident is in compliance with the registration procedures in his or her home jurisdiction. The owner must conspicuously display his or her license plate.

- A person who stays in South Dakota for more than 90 days is determined to be a resident and must register his or her vehicle in South Dakota.
- Military personnel on active duty in South Dakota may maintain home state vehicle registration.

Registration Type: Annual registration of non-commercial vehicles is staggered throughout the year, excluding the months of April, October, and December.

License Plates

Disbursement: Once a vehicle has been properly registered, the county treasurer will issue the vehicle's owner 2 license plates to be placed on the front and rear of the vehicle. The county treasurer will mail the license plates to an applicant upon request if that applicant pays the appropriate fees.

- Disabled license plates available upon application to the department.

Driver's Licenses

Examination: The Department must examine every applicant for an operator's license, unless the Department determines that the examination is not necessary.

- The examination must include a test of the applicant's eyesight (20/40 vision acuity is required), ability to read and understand highway signs regulating, warning, and directing traffic, and knowledge of South Dakota's traffic laws. An actual demonstration of the applicant's ability to exercise ordinary and reasonable control in the operation of a motor vehicle is also required, but may be waived for an applicant who is at least 16 years old and who has successfully passed an actual ability test in his or her state.
- Operators' examinations must be given either in the county where the applicant resides or a place next to the county that is reasonably convenient. The test will be given within 30 days of the date in which the application was received. The Department may require any other physical or mental examination that it deems to be appropriate.

Graduated Drivers Licensing: State has a system of graduated drivers licensing for teen drivers. At 14, teens are eligible for an instruction/learner's permit. From 6:00 a.m. to 10:00 p.m. the permit holder must be accompanied by a person holding a valid operator's license who is at least 18 years of age, that has at least 1 year of driving experience, and who is occupying the front seat beside the applicant. From 10:00 p.m. to 6:00 a.m. a parent/legal guardian must accompany the permit holder.

- Anyone applying for a driver's license for the 1st time who is under 18 years of age must meet the instruction permit requirements.
- At 14 years and 6 months (14 years and 3 months with approved driver education) teens who have: (1) held the permit for at least 6 months (3 months if successfully completed an approved driver education course); (2) passed all applicable tests; and (3) not been convicted of a traffic violation during the past 6 months are eligible for a restricted minor's permit/intermediate license.
- A restricted minor's permit/intermediate license holder is prohibited from driving unsupervised between the hours of 10:00 p.m. and 6:00 a.m.
- At 16, teens who have not been convicted of a traffic violation during the 6 months prior to application are eligible for an unrestricted license, once they have completed the instruction permit requirements.

Issuance/Application: Every application must state the full name, date of birth, sex, social security number, residence, mailing address, a brief description of the applicant, and any other information the Department may request. The proper fee must accompany the application.

- The applicant must state whether he or she has been previously licensed in another jurisdiction, and if so when and by what state or country. If the application was refused, the Department will want to know the date that the application was refused and the reasons for refusal.
- The applicant's father, mother, or guardian must sign the application of any person under the age of 18. If there is no parent or guardian, then the application must be signed by another responsible adult.
- Any student enrolled in a driver education class which has been approved by the South Dakota Department of Education may drive a motor vehicle without a license if the student is accompanied by an approved driver education instructor who is occupying the seat next to the student driver.
- License includes photograph. License number is social security number or 8-digit assigned number.
- Special licensing arrangement for resident military personnel. Military personnel with valid South Dakota license on entry into service may use license until 30 days after honorable discharge while absent from the state, unless license is suspended or revoked. Licensee must have discharge or separation papers in immediate possession.
- State agencies may not accept "matricula consular" cards from Mexico as a form of identification.

Renewal: Each operator's license, motorcycle operator's license, restricted minor's permit, or motorcycle restricted minor's permit expires on the licensee's birthday in the 5th year following the date the license was issued, or on the same date as the expiration date on the valid documents authorizing the applicant's presence in the United States, whichever occurs first.

- Any license issued to a person under 21 expires 30 days after the person's 21st birthday.
- Each operator's license, motorcycle operator's license, restricted minor's permit, or motorcycle restricted minor's permit is renewable 180 days before its expiration.
- The Department will waive the knowledge and driving tests for renewal, if the licensee applies and makes payment of the required fee within 30 days following the license expiration date.
- If the licensee applies and makes payment of the required fees 31 or more days after the expiration date of the license, the licensee must take the knowledge test.
- For renewal of an operator's license, motorcycle operator's license, restricted minor's permit, and motorcycle restricted minor's permit, the Department requires an eye examination.
- The licenses of active duty military personnel remain valid for the length of their service outside the state and 30 days following the date on which the holder of such license is honorably separated from such service or returns to this state, unless revoked for cause as provided by law. The license is valid only when in the immediate possession of the licensee while driving; and if the licensee has been discharged, his separation papers must also be in his immediate possession. This extension does not apply to military dependents.

Types of Licenses:

- Class 1 - Car/Light Truck/Moped/Non-CDL Vehicles
- Class 2 - Class 1 and Motorcycles
- Class 3 - Motorcycles only

- The holder of a valid commercial driver's license may drive any vehicle in the class for which that license is issued, and any lesser class of vehicle, except a motorcycle. No person may drive a vehicle requiring an endorsement unless the proper corresponding endorsement appears on that person's commercial driver's license. A commercial driver's license may be issued with the following classifications:
  - Class A Combination Vehicle. Any combination of commercial motor vehicles and towed vehicles with a gross vehicle weight rating of 26,001 lbs. or more if the gross vehicle weight rating of the vehicles being towed is in excess of 10,000 lbs. This class includes:
    - (a) Any vehicle designed to transport 16 or more passengers, including the driver; and
    - (b) Any vehicle used in the transportation of hazardous materials that require the vehicle to be placarded under 49 C.F.R. Part 172, Subpart F, as amended through January 1, 1993.
  - Class B Heavy Straight Vehicle. Any single commercial motor vehicle with a gross vehicle weight rating of 26,001 lbs. or more or any such commercial motor vehicle towing a vehicle with a gross weight rating not exceeding 10,000 lbs. This class includes:
    - (a) Any vehicle designed to transport 16 or more passengers, including the driver; and
    - (b) Any vehicle used in the transportation of hazardous materials which require the vehicle to be placarded under 49 C.F.R. Part 172, Subpart F, as amended through January 1, 1993.
  - Class C Small Vehicle. Any single vehicle, or combination of vehicles, that meet's neither the definition of class A nor that of class B as contained in this section. This class includes any vehicle designed to transport 16 or more passengers, including the driver, or is used in the transportation of hazardous materials which require the vehicle to be placarded under 49 C.F.R. Part 172, Subpart F, as amended through January 1, 1993.

Traffic Rules

Alcohol Laws: State has implied consent law.
- Open containers are not permitted. Law meets TEA-21 requirements.
- Illegal per se BAC level is .08.
- BAC level for people under 21 is .02.
- BAC level for commercial drivers is .04.
- Any driver under the age of 21 that is convicted of underage purchase, possession, or consumption of alcohol will have his or her driving privileges suspended for 6 months.

Emergency Radio/Cellular: Citizen band radio channel 9 is monitored for emergency calls. Emergency cell number is 911.

Travel Restrictions/Weather Information: Dial 511.

Headsets: Wearing radio headsets while driving is permitted.

Occupant Restraints: Every driver and front seat passenger must wear a properly adjusted and fastened seat belt.

- Children under the age of 5 and weighing less than 40 lbs. must be properly restrained in a child restraint system.
- A motor vehicle operator must assure that passengers between the ages of 5 and 18 who weigh 40+ lbs. are wearing a properly adjusted and fastened seat belt.
- Violation of the seat belt law is a secondary offense, however violation of the child restraint law is a primary offense.
- Riding in pickup truck beds is permitted.

Railroad Crossing: If any person driving a motor vehicle approaches a railroad grade crossing and a clearly visible or audible signal gives warning of the immediate approach of a railway train, he or she must bring the vehicle to a complete stop 15 to 50 feet from the nearest rail of the railroad. The driver must not proceed until it is safe to do so.

School Buses: The driver of a vehicle on a two-lane highway or private road meeting, from either direction, any school bus that is flashing amber lights must reduce the speed of the vehicle to no more than 20 mph and proceed past the bus with caution.

- The driver of a vehicle on meeting, from either direction, any school bus flashing red lights must stop the vehicle at no closer than 15 feet before reaching the school bus. The driver may not proceed until the flashing red lights are no longer activated.
- The driver of a motor vehicle on a highway with separate roadways does not have to stop when meeting or passing a school bus which is on a different roadway.

Vehicle Equipment & Rules

Bumper Height: Modification of original bumper height is permitted.

Glass/Window Tinting: The windows on a vehicle cannot be cracked, broken, shattered, or distorted to the extent that it significantly impairs the driver's vision.

- A vehicle must not have any adhesive film or glaze on the front windshield, sidewing vents, side windows on either side forward of or next to the operator's seat which reduces the light transmission of the window below 35%.

Telematics: A person may not drive a motor vehicle equipped with a television screen that is located in a position where the driver of the vehicle can see it.

Windshield Stickers: These are prohibited unless official.

Motorcycles & Mopeds

Equipment: Every motorcycle must be equipped with at least 1 but no more than 2 headlamps.

- The handlebars of a motorcycle must be no higher than the shoulder height of the person operating the motorcycle.
- All persons under the age of 18 must wear motorcycle safety helmets that are approved by the Department of Transportation.
- A person riding in an enclosed cab attached to a motorcycle does not have to wear a safety helmet.

- A motorcycle operator must wear an eye protective device unless the motorcycle is equipped with a windscreen of sufficient height and design that protects the motorcycle operator. When headlights are required to be on, a motorcycle operator cannot wear protective eye devices that are tinted or shaded to reduce the light transmission of the device below 35%.
- Motorcycles must have at least 1 taillamp, which when lighted emits a red light visible for a distance of 500 feet. A motorcycle may display a blue light of up to one-inch diameter as part of the motorcycle's rear brake light.

Licenses: A person may not operate a motorcycle, except a moped, without a motor vehicle driver's license or permit upon which a state testing officer has certified that such person is qualified to operate the motorcycle. However, the operator of a moped must have a valid motor vehicle operator's license or permit.

- The Department may waive the motorcycle testing requirements upon completion of an approved motorcycle safety course.
- Any minor who has successfully completed the Department approved motorcycle safety education courses, and a driver education course of another state that the Secretary of Public Safety has determined is acceptable, can qualify for a restricted minor's permit in 30 days.
- A motorcycle restricted minor's permit may be issued, upon application and payment of the proper fee, to a minor who is at least 14 years of age but less than 18 years of age. The applicant must have successfully passed all applicable tests and completed the requirements of an instruction permit and must have not been convicted of any traffic violation during the previous 6 months.
- A motorcycle restricted minor's permit entitles the holder to operate a motorcycle during the hours of 6:00 a.m. to 8:00 p.m. standard time if the motorcycle is being operated with the permission of the holder's parents or guardian.

Noise Limits: Every motorcycle must at all times be equipped with a muffler in good working order and in constant operation to prevent excessive or unusual noise.

Mopeds: Valid driver's license required; minimum operator age is 14 for instruction permit and 14 years and 6 months (3 months with approved Driver Ed course) for restricted permit.

- Helmet required under age 18.
- A moped must be equipped with a single beam headlamp. The headlamp must be of sufficient intensity to a person clearly discernable at a distance of at least 100 feet.
- Mopeds must have at least 1 taillamp, which when lighted emits a red light that is visible for a distance of 250 feet.

Passenger Car Trailers

Brakes: Every trailer and semitrailer, must be equipped with a braking system that is arranged so that 1 control device can be used to operate all of the service brakes.

- Trailers, semitrailers or pole trailers of a maximum gross weight of less than 3,000 lbs. and trailer and semitrailers not exceeding 7,000 lbs. manufactured before July 1, 1974 do not have to be equipped with brake action on all wheels provided that: (1) the total weight on and including the wheels of the trailer or trailers does not exceed 40% of the gross weight of the towing vehicle when connected to the trailer or trailers; and (2) the combination of vehicles consisting of the towing vehicle and its total towed load is capable of complying with all performance requirements.

Dimensions: Total length, trailer length, and width: not specified; height: 14 feet.

Hitch: Either ball hitch mounted on bumper or secured to frame is permitted; safety chain is required.

Lighting: Trailers and semitrailers manufactured before July 1, 1973 can have 1 red taillamp mounted on the left-hand side which emits a light from a distance of 500 feet.

Mirrors: Every motor vehicle when towing another vehicle must be equipped with a mirror located so that the driver has a rear view for a distance of at least 200 feet to the rear of the vehicle.

Speed Limits: 65 mph on secondary highways except where posted. 75 mph on interstate except where posted.

Towing: In addition to the regular trailer hitch or coupling device, every trailer that is towed on the public highways at a speed of more than 20 mph must be coupled to the towing vehicle with a safety chain, chains, cables, or an equivalent device. This requirement does not apply to a semitrailer having a connecting device composed of a 5th wheel and kingpin assembly that meets the requirements of the Interstate Commerce Commission.

Miscellaneous Provisions

Bail Bonds: State has discretionary recognition of AAA club arrest bond certificates up to $200.

Liability Laws: Every person who drives or owns a motor vehicle required to be registered in South Dakota shall maintain financial responsibility and must provide proof if requested by law enforcement. Proof of financial responsibility, in form of SR-22 filing, must be filed with the state following conviction for certain vehicle offenses.

- All motor vehicle operators must have motor vehicle insurance in the following amounts: $25,000 for bodily injury to or the death of 1 person in any 1 accident; $50,000 for bodily injury to or the death of 2 or more persons in any 1 accident; and $25,000 for injury to or destruction of property of other in 1 accident.
- State has non-resident service of process law.
- State has mandatory uninsured and under-insured motorist coverage.
- State has "add-on" supplemental insurance law. Sale mandatory. Purchase optional. Benefits: medical, $2,000; wage loss, $60/week (14-day waiting period, 52-week maximum); death, $10,000. General damages, no limit.

Weigh Stations: The following trucks must stop: (1) agricultural vehicles with a GVW rating over 8,000 lbs.; (2) trucks over 8,000 lbs.; (3) driveaway operations in excess of 8,000 lbs. GVW rating.

Fees & Taxes

Table 1: Title & Registration Fees

Vehicle Type	Title Fee	Registration Fee
1 - 2,000 lbs./0 - 4 yrs. old	$5.00	$2.500 per month
1 - 2,000 lbs./5 yrs. plus	$5.00	$1.7500 per month
2,001 - 4,000 lbs./0 - 4 yrs. old	$5.00	$3.5000 per month
2,001 - 4,000 lbs./5 yrs. plus	$5.00	$2.4500 per month
4,001 - 6,000 lbs./0 - 4 yrs. old	$5.00	$4.5833 per month
4,001 - 6,000 lbs./5 yrs. plus	$5.00	$3.2083 per month
6,001 - 10,000 lbs./0 - 4 yrs. old	$5.00	$5.4167 per month
6,001 - 10,000 lbs./5 yrs. plus	$5.00	$3.7917 per month
Motorcycle less than 350 cc, 0 - 4 yrs. old	$5.00	$0.7919 per month
Motorcycle less than 350 cc, 5 yrs. plus	$5.00	$0.5542 per month
Motorcycle 350 cc plus, 0 - 4 yrs. old	$5.00	$1.000 per month
Motorcycle 350 cc plus, 5 yrs. plus	$5.00	$0.700 per month
Mobile Home Initial Registration Fee	4% of the purchase price of a mobile home	
Duplicate Title	$10.00	

Table 2: License Fees

License Class	Fee
Instruction Permit	$8.00
Restricted Minor's Permit	$8.00
Operator's License	$8.00
Motorcycle Instruction Permit	$8.00
Motorcycle Restricted Minor's Permit	$8.00
Motorcycle License Fee	$8.00 for car/truck test plus $8.00 for Motorcycle test
Duplicate License Fee	$6.00

Table 3: Vehicle Taxes

Tax	Rate
Motor Vehicle Excise Tax	3.0%
Gasoline Tax; (Diesel)	$0.22/gallon; ($0.22/gallon)
Solid Waste Fee	$0.25 per wheel not to exceed $1.00
County Wheel Tax	$4.00 per wheel

Table 4: Miscellaneous Fees

Fee	Amount	Payable Upon
Registration Transfer Fee	$5.00	Application
Identification Card	$8.00	Application
Duplicate	$10.00	Application
Speciality Plates	$10.00 for historical	

SD

TENNESSEE

Contact Information

Tennessee Department of Safety (DOS)
Motor Vehicle Services
1150 Foster Avenue
Nashville, TN 37249

(615) 741-3954
www.tennessee.gov/safety/

Tennessee Highway Patrol
1150 Foster Avenue
Nashville, TN 37249-1000

(615) 251-5175
www.state.tn.us/safety/thp.html

Department of Transportation
Commissioner's Office
James K. Polk Building, Suite 700
Nashville, TN 37243-0349

(615) 741-2848
www.tdot.state.tn.us/

Vehicle Title

Application: An application for certificate of title is made to the county clerk of the county where the vehicle is to be registered.

- The application must contain: the applicant's full name; the applicant's residential address; a description of the vehicle, including the odometer reading, the make, model, type of body, vehicle serial number, whether the vehicle is new or used, and a statement of the vehicle's gross vehicle weight (GVW) rating.
- If the application refers to a new vehicle, the applicant must include a statement by the dealer or a bill of sale showing any lien retained by the dealer and a manufacturer's certificate of origin.
- If a certificate of title is lost, mutilated, or becomes illegible, the owner must make immediate application for a replacement title.

Transfer of Ownership: In order for a transfer to be effective, the owner must endorse an assignment and warranty of title upon the certificate of title with a statement of all liens and encumbrances on the vehicle and must deliver the certificate of title to the purchaser or transferee at the time of delivery of the vehicle.

- The transferee must apply for and obtain a registration and a certificate of title before the vehicle may be operated on the highways.

Mobile Homes: A mobile home, when occupied, requires a certificate of title.

- A mobile home or house trailer with a length exceeding 35 feet may not be moved upon the highways of the state unless the owner obtains a permit for such transportation.
- A separate permit is required for each individual mobile home or house trailer.
- A mobile home or house trailer that is assessed as real property or as an improvement upon land is not subject to registration requirements.

Vehicle Registration

Application: An application for registration must be made to the county clerk in the county of the residence of the owner, or where the vehicle is to be based or operated.

- The owner must have proper title to a vehicle prior to registration.
- The application for renewal is made to the county clerk of the county of the owner's residence.
- The application for renewal may be made via mail and must be postmarked not later than 20 days before the expiration date.
- Upon receipt of a registration certificate, the owner must sign the certificate and it must be carried at all times in the vehicle to which it refers or by the person driving. The use of a duplicate or facsimile, in order to ensure the preservation of the original, is acceptable.
- Whenever the address of a vehicle owner changes from that named on a registration or title certificate, the owner must, within 10 days, notify the DOS of the change.

Non-Residents: Non-resident owners of a vehicle registered in any state or territory of the United States, Canada, or Mexico may operate the vehicle in Tennessee for a period of 30 consecutive days without having to register the vehicle in Tennessee.

- A non-resident owner of a mobile home or house trailer may operate the same in Tennessee for a period of 60 consecutive days.
- Military personnel on active duty in Tennessee may maintain home state vehicle registration.

Registration Type: Registration is based on a staggered system and the registration period is valid for 12 months and expires on the last day of the last month of the registration period.

- If ownership of a vehicle is transferred prior to the expiration of the registration period, the registration expires and the new owner must apply to have the vehicle registered. The previous owner may apply to the DOS, through the county clerk, for the registration of another vehicle under the old registration number.

Emissions Inspection: Residents of Davidson, Rutherford, Sumner, Williamson, and Wilson counties in Middle Tennessee and residents of Memphis in West Tennessee must have their vehicles pass an emissions inspection prior to registration renewal. All Shelby County residents who have an address inside the city limits of Memphis must also have their vehicles inspected prior to title and registration.

- Inspection is not required for vehicles of model year 1974 and older in Middle Tennessee. However, an inspection is required for vehicles of all model years in Memphis.
- A new vehicle which has never before been titled is not required to undergo emissions testing before application for the new title. You need only present the Manufacturers' Certificate of Origin (MCO) when you title and register the new vehicle at your county clerk's office. Each year thereafter, however, the vehicle must undergo emissions testing before registration can be renewed.

License Plates

Disbursement: The county clerk issues 1 plate per motor vehicle upon successful application for registration.

- The license plate issued for passenger cars, including trucks with a manufacturer's ton rating not exceeding 1/2 ton and having a pickup body style, motorcycles, trailers, and also those issued for motor homes, must be attached to the rear of the vehicle. License plates issued for all other vehicles must be attached to the front of the vehicle.

- Disabled license plates are available by application through the county clerk's office with physician's statement attesting to disability. Placards are available through county clerk or Department of Safety.

Transfer of Plates: Whenever the owner of a vehicle transfers the vehicle, the registration expires and the plates must be removed from the vehicle.

- The transferor of a vehicle may apply for reassignment of the plates to another vehicle owned by the transferor.
- If the transferor of a vehicle applies for registration reassignment to a new vehicle of a different weight or classification which requires payment of a higher fee, the applicant must surrender both the certificate of registration and the plate or plates to the county clerk.

Driver's Licenses

Examination: Every applicant for any type of license or learner's permit must pass a written examination that tests the applicant's ability to read and understand highway signs as well as the applicant's knowledge of traffic laws and must demonstrate actual ability to exercise ordinary care in the operation of a motor vehicle. All applicants must also submit to an eye exam (20/40 visual acuity required).

- The knowledge and skills tests may be waived for a non-resident who is licensed in another state and has established residency in Tennessee.
- An applicant who presents evidence that the applicant has completed a driver education and training course offered for Class D vehicles at a public school or commercial driver training school is deemed to have satisfactorily completed the licensing examinations required by the department.

Graduated Drivers Licensing: State has a system of graduated licensing for teen drivers.

- At 15, teens are eligible for a learner's permit. A teen with a learner's permit is prohibited from using a cell phone while driving.
- A permit holder may only drive when supervised and may not drive between 10:00 p.m. to 6:00 a.m.
- At 16, teens who have: (1) held a permit for 6 months; (2) accumulated 50 hours (10 at night) of parental/guardian supervised driving; (3) not accumulated 6 or more points on the permit, are eligible for an intermediate license.
- Allows teens that move to Tennessee to be eligible for an intermediate license if they have held a valid learner's permit for at least 6 months in another state. A teen with an intermediate license is prohibited from using a cell phone while driving.
- A person that has been issued an intermediate driver's license may not operate a motor vehicle between the hours of 11:00 p.m. and 6:00 a.m. unless accompanied by a parent or legal guardian or by a licensed driver who is at least 21 and has been designated by the person's parent or guardian.
- A person issued an intermediate driver's license may not operate a motor vehicle with more than 1 passenger unless: 1 or more passengers is 21 or older and possesses a valid unrestricted license; or the additional passengers are siblings of the driver.
- At 17, teens who have held an intermediate license for at least a year, have maintained a safe driving record with no less than 6 points, and have not contributed to an accident are eligible for an unrestricted license.

- Safety belt use is mandatory for all GDL license holders and passengers 4 to 17.

Issuance/Application: Every application for any type of license or instruction permit must be accompanied by a birth certificate or other proof of the applicant's date of birth, and the applicant's name, sex, county of residence, address, height, weight, hair and eye color, and social security number.

- A license bears an assigned number, as well as the licensee's date of birth, address, full name, signature, and a brief description and a color photograph of the licensee. A licensee's social security number will not be used as the license number unless specifically requested by the applicant.
- Whenever a licensee moves, the licensee must notify the DOS within 10 days of a change of address.
- Licenses must be in a person's immediate possession when in operation of a motor vehicle and must be displayed upon demand of a police officer.
- Prohibits the issuance of driver licenses to anyone who is not legally in the United States.

Renewal: Every driver's license is valid for 5 years and expires on the licensee's birthday, excluding Class P licenses which expire 1 year from the date of issuance.

- If a licensee is under the age of 18, the license expires on the licensee's 21st birthday.
- Licenses are renewable on or before their expiration date upon application and payment of the appropriate fee.
- An application for renewal that is filed more than 30 days carries a late renewal fee and if a license is expired for more than 5 years, the license holder must apply as for an original license.
- Licenses may be renewed up to 12 months before the expiration date.
- A driver's license issued to someone who is on active military duty and stationed outside of Tennessee does not expire "so long as such person's service continues and such person is stationed outside this state." Military personnel (not military dependents) may have a "Code 30" added to their license which will give it a non-expiring status.

Types of Licenses: Class A: Valid for the operation of any combination of motor vehicles with a Gross Combination Weight (GCW) rating in excess of 26,000 lbs., provided the vehicles being pulled have a Gross Vehicle Weight (GVW) rating in excess of 10,000 lbs.; and for the operation of Class B, C, and D vehicles.

- Class B: Valid for the operation of any vehicle with a GVW rating in excess of 26,000 lbs., or any such vehicle towing a vehicle not in excess of 10,000 lbs. GVW; also valid for the operation of Class C and D vehicles.
- Class C: Valid for the operation of any single vehicle with a GVW rating of 26,000 lbs. or less or any combination of vehicles with a GCW rating of 26,000 lbs. or less and includes vehicles requiring a placard for carrying hazardous materials and vehicles designed to transport more than 15 passengers; and for the operation of Class D vehicles.
- Class D: Valid for the operation of vehicles with a GVW rating of less than 26,000 lbs. or any combination of vehicles with a GCW rating less than 26,001 lbs. except vehicles in Class A, B, or C.
- Class H: Issued to a minor between 14 and 16 years of age and restricts the holder to operation of a passenger car during the hours of daylight and only for travel to and from authorized destinations.

- Class M: Valid for all motorcycles.
- Class P: Issued as an instruction permit in conjunction with another class and is valid only for operation of that class of vehicle; the holder of a class P permit must be accompanied at all times by a parent or guardian or certified instructor, who is at least 21 years of age and has been licensed in the state for at least 1 year.

Traffic Rules

Alcohol Laws: Any person who drives any motor vehicle in the state is deemed to have given implied consent to a test of the person's blood.

- Open containers are permitted.
- Illegal per se BAC level is .08.
- BAC level for people under 21 is .02.
- BAC level for commercial drivers is .04.

Cellular Telephone Use: School bus drivers are prohibited from talking on a cell phone and driving, except in emergencies.

Emergency Radio/Cellular: Citizen band radio channel 9 is monitored for emergency calls. Emergency cell number is *THP (847).

Headsets: Wearing radio headsets while driving is permitted.

Occupant Restraints: All drivers and front seat passengers must be secured by a seat belt.

- Violation of the occupant protection laws is a primary offense.
- Children less than 1 year or less than 20 lbs. must be properly restrained in a rear-facing child seat.
- Children 1 through 3 years weighing greater than 20 lbs. must be properly restrained in a forward-facing child seat.
- Children who are between 4 and 9 years old and are less than 4'9" tall must be properly restrained in a booster seat.
- Children who are 9 until 16 years old or under 13 years and over 4'9" must be properly restrained in a seat belt.
- The law requires all children under 9 to be seated in the rear seat of the vehicle, if available and recommends that children 9-13 be seated in the rear seat of the vehicle, if available.
- Riding in pickup truck beds is permitted for people older than age 12. Additional gaps in coverage apply; see Occupant Protection Chart.

Railroad Crossing: At railroad crossings that have been deemed particularly dangerous and marked with stop signs, all vehicles must stop within 50 feet but not less than 15 feet from the nearest rail of the railroad, and may proceed only upon exercising due care.

- The driver of any vehicle carrying passengers for hire, or of any school bus, or of any vehicle carrying hazardous materials, must stop such vehicle within 50 feet but not less than 15 feet from the nearest rail of the railroad, and must not proceed until it is safe to do so.

School Buses: The driver of any vehicle must, upon meeting or overtaking from either direction, any school bus which has stopped on the highway for purpose of receiving

or discharging any school children, must stop and may not proceed until the bus resumes motion or is signaled by the bus driver to proceed, or the school bus has deactivated its stop signals.
- When a school bus is stopped on a separate roadway, a driver meeting or approaching the school bus from a different roadway need not stop.
- Failure to obey these provisions may result in a fine of at least $250 but not more than $1,000.

Vehicle Equipment & Rules

Bumper Height: Modification of original vehicle bumper height is legal with restrictions.

Glass/Window Tinting: It is unlawful to operate a vehicle with window tinting that has a visible light transmittance of less than 35% or reduces the visible light transmittance in the windshield below 70%.

License Plates: No tinted materials may be placed over a license plate even if the information on the license plate is not concealed.

Telematics: No television screen or other device of a similar nature shall be installed or used when in any position in a motor vehicle where it may be visible to the driver.

Windshield Stickers: Stickers are permitted, but cannot interfere with visibility.

Motorcycles & Mopeds

Equipment: Any motor-driven cycle, which produces not more than 5 horsepower, may not be driven at a speed of more than 35 mph unless the cycle is equipped with a headlamp which is adequate to reveal a person or vehicle at a distance of 300 feet ahead.
- Every motorcycle must be equipped with at least 1 and not more than 2 headlamps.
- It is unlawful to operate a motorcycle unless the person is seated upon the permanent and regular seat with one leg on each side and with the headlamp illuminated.
- It is unlawful to carry a passenger on a motorcycle unless a proper seat for the passenger is installed on the motorcycle.
- All motorcycle operators and passengers on a motorcycle must wear a safety helmet, unless the person is in an enclosed cab.
- Every motorcycle must be equipped with a windshield, or the operator and any passenger must wear safety goggles, face shields, or glasses containing impact resistant lenses.
- All motorcycles must be equipped with a rearview mirror and securely attached footrests.

Licenses: A person who is at least 16 years of age and a legal resident of Tennessee may apply for a motorcycle license.
- Minors who are 15 years of age and legal residents of Tennessee may apply for a motorcycle learner's permit. Permit holders may only operate during daylight hours, are limited to a 20 mile radius of the permit holder's home, may not operate a motorcycle on the Interstate system, may not operate a motorcycle with an engine size greater than 650cc, and may not carry any passengers.

- Applicants who have successfully completed a motorcycle rider training course may be exempted from taking the licensing skills test and/or the knowledge test.

Mopeds: Registration is required.
- License plate required if used on roadway.
- If operator is between 14 and 16, must have motorized bicycle license; if over 16, valid operator's license required.
- The following safety equipment is required: safety helmet, headlamp, taillamp, stop lamp, brakes, mirror, horn, muffler, and windshield or eye protection devices required. Headlights are required to be on during operation at all times.

Passenger Car Trailers

Registration: Homemade and materially reconstructed trailers may not be registered or titled unless the DOS certifies that such trailer complies with applicable safety standards.

Brakes: Every trailer or semitrailer of a gross weight of 3,000 lbs. or more must be equipped with brakes that may be applied by the driver of the towing vehicle from the cab and must be of a design such that in case of an accidental breakaway of the towed vehicle, the brakes will be automatically applied.

Dimensions: Total length and trailer length: not specified; width: 102 inches (allows outside width to exceed 102 inches if excess is due to appurtenance); height: 13.6 feet.

Hitch: Any vehicle being towed by another vehicle must be connected to the towing vehicle with a chain that is reasonably capable of maintaining the attachment of the 2 vehicles in case of failure of any other attachment device.

Lighting: Every vehicle being towed by another vehicle must carry at the rear a lamp of type which exhibits a yellow or red light plainly visible under normal atmospheric conditions from a distance of 500 feet to the rear.

Mirrors: Required if vision from inside mirror is obstructed.

Speed Limits: Rural interstate, 70 mph or as otherwise posted.

Miscellaneous Provisions

Bail Bonds: Mandatory recognition of AAA arrest bond certificates up to $1,000, with specified exceptions.

Liability Laws: The Commissioner of Safety must revoke the license and registration of all operators of motor vehicles involved in an accident unless proof of financial responsibility in the amount of no less than $500 is presented to the Commissioner. Acceptable forms of proof include the filing of written proof of insurance coverage, a cash deposit, or the filing of a bond.
- A driver need not provide proof of financial responsibility to the Commissioner after an accident if the person had in effect at the time of the accident an automobile liability policy or bond with respect to the vehicle involved in the accident.
- Minimum permissible insurance coverage consists of either: single-limit coverage of $40,000 for any 1 accident; split-limit coverage of $25,000 for injury or death of

any 1 person and $50,000 for injury or death of any 2 persons and not less than $10,000 for damage to property in any 1 accident; a deposit of cash with the Commissioner in the amount of $40,000; or the filing of a bond in the amount of $40,000 with the Commissioner.
- State has non-resident service of process law; does not have guest suit law.

Weigh Stations: Exist statewide, checking federal and state restrictions related to size and weight, safety, and drivers regulations.

Fees & Taxes

Table 1: Title & Registration Fees

Vehicle Type	Title Fee	Registration Fee
Passenger Vehicle	$8.00	$25.00*
Antique Vehicle		$25.00
Motor Homes		$18.75
Motorcycle	$8.00	$11.75
Low Speed Vehicle		$9.50
Mobile Homes & House Trailers 8' wide or less		$21.75
Mobile Homes & House Trailers more than 8' wide		$33.75
Vehicles with not more than 7 seats		$33.75
Vehicles with 8-15 seats		$78.75
Vehicles with 16-25 seats		$138.75
Vehicles with 26-35 seats		$213.75
Vehicles with over 35 seats		$288.75
Private Carriers not more than 9,000 lbs. GVW		$38.00
Private Carriers 9,000 - 80,000 lbs. GVW		$64.00 - $1,332.50
Public Carriers not more than 9,000 lbs. GVW		$47.50
Public Carriers 9,000 - 80,000 lbs. GVW		$102.50 - $1,332.50
Registration Renewal by Mail		$2.00 (for plates) + $1.00 for decals

* Includes $1.00 mailing fee.

Table 2: License Fees

License Class	Fee
Class A	$46.00 for original or renewal
Class B or C	$41.00 for original or renewal
Class D for birthday divisible by 5 otherwise call for amount	$19.50 for original or renewal
Motorcycle	$20.50
Learner's Permit	$5.50
Intermediate License	$5.00 + $2.00
Endorsements	$2.50 plus original license fee
Commercial Upgrades (from class C to B, or B to A)	$15.00
Replacement/Duplicate Fees	$8.00 for initial duplicate, $12.00 subsequent
Late Renewal Fee	$5.00 (up to 6 months) $10.00 (after 6 months & up to 5 years)

Table 3: Vehicle Taxes

Tax	Rate
Sales Tax	6% + 1.75% - 2.25% (depending on county)
Gasoline Tax; (Diesel)	$0.20/gallon; ($0.18/gallon + $0.04/gallon - environmental assurance fee)

Table 4: Miscellaneous Fees

Fee	Amount	Payable Upon
Unexpired Registration Portion Reassignment Fee	$1.00	application for reassignment of registration
Computerized Titling and Registration Fee	$1.00	registration
License Plate Fees	$1.00 + $.75 + $1.00	application for registration/renewal of registration
Licence Plate Replacement Fee	$10.00	application for new plates
Special/Personalized Plate Fee	$25.00	application and renewal
Mobile Home Movement Permit	$3.00 if less than 50 feet $5.00 if 50 feet or more	application for permit
Emissions Test	$10.00	

TEXAS

Contact Information

Texas Department of Public Safety (DPS)
Driver License Issuance Bureau
P.O. Box 4087
Austin, TX 78773-0371
(512) 424-2000
www.txdps.state.tx.us/

Highway Patrol Service
5805 N. Lamar Boulevard
Austin, TX 78773
(512) 424-2000
www.txdps.state.tx.us/hp/index.htm

Texas Department of Transportation
125 E. 11th Street
Austin, TX 78701-2483
(512) 463-8588
www.dot.state.tx.us/txdot.htm

Comptroller of Public Accounts
P.O. Box 13528, Capitol Station
Austin, TX 7811-3528
(800) 531-5441
www.window.state.tx.us

Vehicle Title

Application: The owner of a motor vehicle must apply for a certificate of title to the county assessor-collector in the county in which the owner lives, the motor vehicle is purchased, or the loan to purchase the motor vehicle is obtained.

- An applicant for an initial certificate of title must provide the vehicle's description, odometer reading, previous owner's name and city and state of residence, name and complete address of the applicant, name and mailing address of any lienholder,

TX

if applicable, signature of the seller of the motor vehicle, signature of the applicant, and the applicant's social security number.
- An applicant for a certificate of title on the first sale of a motor vehicle must provide the county assessor-collector with a manufacturer's certificate showing the applicant as the last transferee.
- A person may obtain a certificate of title without registering a vehicle or providing proof of insurance, but the applicant must surrender the license plates and any validation stickers issued for that vehicle.
- Before a motor vehicle that was last registered or titled in another state or country may be titled in Texas, the applicant must furnish the county assessor-collector with a verification of safety and emissions inspections.
- The owner must record the vehicle's current odometer reading on an application for a certificate of title.

Transfer of Ownership: The owner of a vehicle must transfer the certificate of title to the new owner at the time of the sale. At the time of transfer there may be no liens on the vehicle except those shown on the certificate of title.

- The seller of a motor vehicle must provide the buyer with the vehicle's odometer reading on a DOT form for that purpose. However, an odometer disclosure statement is not required for the sale of a motor vehicle that is new, is 10 or more years old, is not self-propelled, or has a manufacturer's rated carrying capacity of more than 2 tons.
- A person, whether acting for that person or another, may not sell, trade, or otherwise transfer a used vehicle required to be registered under the law of Texas unless at the time of delivery the vehicle is registered in the state.
- The buyer or transferee of a vehicle must file the license receipt and certificate of title with the county assessor-collector within 20 working days of taking delivery of the vehicle and the documents.

Mobile Homes: Manufactured housing is not defined as a vehicle under Texas law.

Vehicle Registration

Application: The owner of a motor vehicle or trailer must apply for the registration of the vehicle for each registration year in which the vehicle is used or to be used on a public highway. The application must be made to the DOT through the county assessor-collector of the county in which the owner resides.

- Military personnel, who are residents of Texas, were stationed in another nation, and own a vehicle that was either registered by a branch of the armed forces of the United States or in the nation where the person was stationed, have 90 days to register the vehicle upon their return to Texas.
- An application for a vehicle registration must contain the full name and address of the owner of the vehicle, a brief description of the vehicle, and be signed by the owner.
- An application for registration of a new motor vehicle must include the vehicle's trade name; year model; style and type of body; weight, if the vehicle is a passenger car; net carrying capacity and gross weight, if the vehicle is a commercial motor vehicle; vehicle identification number; and date of sale by the manufacturer or dealer to the applicant.
- An applicant for registration of a commercial motor vehicle or trailer must submit

an affidavit showing the weight of the vehicle, the maximum load to be carried on the vehicle, and the gross weight for the vehicle which is to be registered.
- The DOT will not register or renew the registration of a motor vehicle for which a certificate of title is required unless the owner obtains a certificate of title or presents satisfactory evidence that a certificate of title was previously issued to the owner by the Texas DOT or another jurisdiction.
- The owner of a motor vehicle must present proof of insurance or other evidence of financial responsibility before a vehicle will be registered.
- The owner of a motor vehicle may pay registration fees for a designated period of 12, 24, or 36 months.
- An application for registration must be made during the 2 months preceding the date on which the registration expires.
- A county assessor-collector or the DOT may refuse to register a motor vehicle if the assessor-collector or the DOT receive information that the owner of the vehicle owes the county money for a fine, fee, or tax that is past due.

Non-Residents: A non-resident owner of a privately owned vehicle that is not registered in the state may not make more than 5 occasional trips in any calendar month in the state using the vehicle. Each occasional trip into the state may not exceed 5 days.

- A non-resident owner of a privately owned passenger car that is not registered in the state or country in which the person resides and that is not operated for compensation may operate the car in this state for the period in which the car's license plates are valid.
- A resident of an adjoining state or country may operate a privately owned and registered vehicle to go to and from the person's place of regular employment and to make trips to purchase merchandise if the vehicle is not operated for compensation.
- Military personnel on active duty in Texas may maintain home state vehicle registration as long as the plates are current.

Emissions Inspection: Designated vehicles registered in designated counties must pass an emissions inspection prior to registration. The emissions inspection is required annually, in conjunction with a safety inspection.

- Until May 1, 2002 the designated counties are limited to Dallas, Tarrant, Harris, and El Paso counties. Effective May 1, 2002 through April 30, 2003, the designated counties will include Denton and Collin counties. Effective May 1, 2003 and thereafter, the designated counties will also include Ellis, Johnson, Kaufman, Parker, and Rockwall counties.
- Designated vehicles are vehicles capable of being powered by gasoline, from 2 years old to and including 24 years old, and registered in or required to be registered in and primarily operated in a designated county.
- A vehicle is eligible for a waiver if it failed both its initial emissions inspection and re-test, and the owner incurred emission-related repair expenses of at least $450.

Safety Inspection: An annual safety inspection is required as a prerequisite to registering a vehicle.

- The initial safety inspection period for new passenger cars and light trucks is 2 years.
- A trailer or travel trailer with a gross weight of 4,500 pounds or less is exempt from the safety inspection requirement.

- The DOT may refuse to register a motor vehicle and may revoke a registration if the DOT determines that the vehicle is unsafe, improperly equipped, or otherwise unfit to be operated on a public highway.
- A motor vehicle, trailer, pole trailer, or mobile home registered in the state must be inspected at an inspection station or by an inspector.
- Proof of insurance or financial responsibility is required before a inspection certificate will be issued.
- A vehicle that is inspected and is subsequently involved in an accident affecting the safe operation of an item of inspection must be reinspected following repair. The reinspection must be at an inspection station and must be treated and charged as an initial inspection.
- Vehicles required to be registered in Texas will be required to be inspected at an official vehicle inspection station and obtain a vehicle identification certificate before the registration process can be completed. Valid out-of-state safety inspection certificates will not be honored on vehicles that are required to be registered.

License Plates

Disbursement: License plates are issued for a 5-year period. Validation stickers are issued each year after the 1st year when a license plate or set of plates was issued.

- The validation stickers must be attached to the inside of the vehicle's windshield within 6 inches of the place where the motor vehicle inspection sticker is required to be placed. If the vehicle does not have a windshield, the DOT will issue a sticker for attachment to the rear license plate.
- Numerous specialty license plates are available.
- Permanently disabled drivers have the option of applying for specially designated plates or placards designed to hang from the rearview mirror. An applicant may receive 2 disabled person plates or 1 placard and/or 1 set of plates. An additional set of plates may be obtained for specially equipped vehicles for persons who have lost the use of 1 or both legs.

Driver's Licenses

Examination: Unless otherwise exempt, an applicant for a driver's license must pass a vision test (20/40 vision acuity required), a sign recognition test, a knowledge test, and a driving skills test.

- A licensed driver education school may administer the vision, sign recognition, and knowledge tests.
- Knowledge and skills tests are waived for persons holding a valid out-of-state license when applying for a Texas license of the same or lower type.

Graduated Drivers Licensing: State has a system of graduated driver licensing for teen drivers.

- At 15, a teen who is enrolled in driver education and has passed vision, sign recognition, and knowledge tests is eligible for a learner's permit.
- A permit holder may only operate a vehicle when supervised by a person occupying the seat next to the operator who holds a license that qualifies the operator to operate that type of vehicle, is 21 years old, and has at least 1 year of driving experience.

- At 16, teens who have held a learner's permit for at least 6 months are eligible for an intermediate license.
- Intermediate license holders may not drive unsupervised between the hours of midnight and 5:00 a.m., may not transport more than 1 passenger (except family) and are prohibited from using a cell phone.
- At 16 years and 6 months, teens who have successfully completed the intermediate license phase are eligible for an unrestricted license.

Issuance/Application: An application for an original license must state the applicant's full name and place and date of birth. This information must be verified by presentation of proof of identity. The application must include the applicant's thumbprint or index fingerprint and a brief description of the applicant. The applicant must state the applicant's sex; the applicant's residence address; whether the applicant has been licensed to drive a motor vehicle before; if previously licensed, when and by what state or country; whether that license has been suspended or revoked or a license application denied; the date and reason for the suspension, revocation, or denial; whether the applicant is a citizen of the United States; and the county of residence of the applicant.

- A person who is at least 15 years old but less than 18 years old must be enrolled in school to obtain a learner's permit.
- A person must be at least 18 years old to apply for a commercial driver's license.
- If the person has not passed an approved driver training course, they must be 18 years old to apply for a Class A or Class B license.
- If the applicant owns a motor vehicle, he or she must provide proof of insurance or financial responsibility.
- The following persons are exempt from holding a Texas driver's license while operating a vehicle in the state: a person in the military forces operating an official vehicle in the scope of that service; a person operating a non-commercial road machine or piece of farm equipment on a highway; a non-resident on active duty in the U.S. armed forces who holds a license issued by the person's state or Canadian province of residence; and a person who is the spouse or dependent child of a non-resident on active military duty who holds a license issued by the person's state or province.
- A person who enters Texas as a new resident may operate a motor vehicle in the state for no more than 30 days after the date on which the person enters the state if the person is at least 16 years of age and has in his possession a driver's license issued to him by his state or country of previous residence.
- A non-resident who is at least 18 years old and who has in his possession a license issued to him by his state or country of residence that is recognized by the DPS that is similar to a Class A or Class B driver's license issued by the state of Texas is not required to hold a Class A or Class B driver's license if that state or country of residence recognizes a Class A or Class B license issued by the state of Texas and exempts the holder from securing a license issued by the state or foreign country.
- A non-resident who is at least 16 years old and who holds a driver's license issued by the person's state or Canadian province of residence may operate a type of motor vehicle that is permitted to be operated with a Class C or Class M driver's license in Texas if the license held by the non-resident permits operation of that type of vehicle in the person's state or province of residence.
- All original applicants for driver's licenses must present proof of identity satisfactory to the DPS including a valid or expired Texas driver's license or identification

with photo; a U.S. passport; a U.S. citizenship certificate with identifiable photo; an INS document with verified data and identifiable photo; a valid photo driver's license or identification issued by another U.S. state, Puerto Rico, the District of Columbia, or a Canadian province; or a U.S. military ID card with an identifiable photo.
- A person must notify the DPS of a change of address or change of name within 30 days.
- License normally includes a photograph.
- License does not include a social security or social insurance number.

Renewal: A driver's license expires on the 1st birthday of the license holder occurring after the 6th anniversary of the date of the application. A provisional license expires the earlier of the 18th birthday of the license holder or the 1st birthday of the license holder occurring after the date of the application. An instruction permit expires on the 1st birthday of the license holder occurring after the date of the application.

Types of Licenses: A Class A driver's license authorizes the holder to operate a vehicle or combination of vehicles with a Gross Vehicle Weight Rating (GVWR) of 26,001 lbs. or more.
- A Class B driver's license authorizes the holder to operate a vehicle with a GVWR of more than 26,000 lbs. or a bus with a seating capacity of 24 passengers or more. The vehicle may tow a trailer with a GVWR of not more than 10,000 lbs. or a farm trailer of not more than 20,000 lbs.
- A Class C driver's license authorizes the holder to operate a vehicle or combination of vehicles with a GVWR not in excess of 26,000 lbs., a bus with a seating capacity of 23 passengers or less, and tow a farm trailer with a GVWR of not more than 20,000 lbs.
- A Class M driver's license authorizes the holder to operate a motorcycle or moped.
- A provisional license is issued to anyone under 18 years old.

Traffic Rules

Alcohol Laws: State has implied consent law.
- Open containers are not permitted. Meets TEA-21 requirements.
- Illegal per se BAC level is .08
- Anyone under 21 with a detectable amount of alcohol in their system will have their license suspended.
- BAC Level for commercial drivers is .04.

Emergency Radio/Cellular: Citizen band radio is not monitored for emergency calls. Emergency number is 800-525-5555 and 911.

Headsets: Wearing radio headsets while driving is permitted.

Occupant Restraints: Drivers and passengers 17 and older in the front seat must be properly restrained.
- A child under age 5 and less than 36 inches must be restrained in a child safety seat.
- A child who is at least 5 but younger than 17 years old or younger than 5 and at least 36 inches in height must be secured by a safety belt provided that the child is occupying a seat equipped with a safety belt.

- Violation of the occupant protection laws is a primary offense.
- A child younger than 18 years of age is not permitted to ride in an open-bed pickup truck, on an open flatbed, or on a flatbed trailer unless the vehicle is being operated in a parade or an emergency; the vehicle is transporting farm workers from 1 field to another on a farm-to-market road, ranch-to-market road, or country road outside a municipality; the vehicle is being operated on a beach; the vehicle is the only vehicle owned or operated by the members of a household; or the vehicle is being used in a permitted hayride.

Railroad Crossing: A driver approaching a railroad crossing must stop not closer than 15 feet or farther than 50 feet from the nearest rail if: (1) a clearly visible railroad signal warns of the approach of a railroad train; (2) a crossing gate is lowered, or a flagger warns of the approach of a railroad train; (3) a railroad engine approaching within approximately 1,500 feet of the highway crossing emits a signal audible from that distance and the engine is an immediate hazard because of its speed or proximity to the crossing; (4) an approaching railroad train is plainly visible and is in hazardous proximity to the crossing; or (5) the driver is required to stop by a traffic-control device or signal. A driver must remain stopped until permitted to proceed and it is safe to proceed.

- The driver of a vehicle who approaches a railroad crossing equipped with railroad crossbuck signs without automatic, electric, or mechanical signal devices, crossing gates, or a flagger warning of the approach or passage of a train must yield the right-of-way to a train in hazardous proximity to the crossing, and proceed at a speed that is reasonable for the existing conditions. If required for safety, the driver must stop at a clearly marked stop line before the grade crossing or, if no stop line exists, not closer than 15 feet or farther than 50 feet from the nearest rail.
- A driver may not drive around, under, or through a crossing gate or a barrier at a railroad crossing while the gate or barrier is closed, being closed, or being opened.

School Buses: A driver, when approaching from either direction a school bus stopped on the highway to receive or discharge a student, must stop before reaching the school bus when the bus is operating a stop signal. The driver may not proceed until the school bus resumes motion, the driver is signaled by the bus driver to proceed, or the visual signal is no longer activated.

- A driver on a highway with separate roadways is not required to stop for a school bus that is on a different roadway. A driver on a controlled-access highway is not required to stop for a school bus that is in a loading zone that is a part of or adjacent to the highway and where pedestrians are not permitted to cross the roadway.

Vehicle Equipment & Rules

Bumper Height: A person may not operate on a public roadway a passenger or commercial vehicle that has been modified from its original design or weighted so that the clearance between any part of the vehicle other than the wheels and the surface of the level roadway is less than the clearance between the roadway and the lowest part of the rim of any wheel in contact with the roadway.

Glass/Window Tinting: A windshield sunscreening device that has a light transmission of less than 25% or more, a luminous reflectance of less than 25%, that is blue, red, or amber, or extends downward beyond the AS-1 line or more than 5 inches from the top of the windshield is prohibited.

- A sunscreening device in the front side wing vent or window, a side window to the rear of the vehicle operator, or a rear window is prohibited if it has a light transmission of less than 35% or a luminous reflectance of more than 35%.

Telematics: A motor vehicle may be equipped with video receiving equipment, including a television or similar equipment, only if the equipment is located so that the video display is not visible from the operator's seat. Equipment used exclusively for receiving digital information for commercial purposes is permitted, as is a monitoring device that produces an electronic display used exclusively in conjunction with a mobile navigation system installed in the vehicle.

Windshield Stickers: A person may not place on or attach to the windshield or side or rear window an object or material that obstructs or reduces the driver's clear view.

Motorcycles & Mopeds

Equipment: The DOT may refuse to register a motorcycle and may suspend or revoke the registration if the DOT determines that the motorcycle's braking system does not comply with safety requirements.

- An operator of a motorcycle must ride on the permanent and regular seat attached to the motorcycle.
- A passenger may ride only on the permanent and regular seat, if designed for 2 persons, or on another seat firmly attached to the motorcycle behind or to the side of the operator.
- A motorcycle, including a motor-driven cycle, must be equipped with not more than 2 headlamps, at least 1 taillamp, a separate rear license plate lamp, at least 1 stop lamp, and at least 1 rear red reflector.
- A motorcycle, other than a motor-driven cycle, must be equipped with multiple-beam headlamps.
- A motorcycle may not be operated at any time unless at least 1 headlamp is illuminated.
- The operator and any passenger on a motorcycle or moped are required to wear an approved helmet. However, a person is exempt from wearing a helmet if the person is at least 21 years old, and has successfully completed a motorcycle operator and training safety course or is covered by at least $10,000 in medical benefits for injuries incurred as a result of an accident while operating or riding on a motorcycle.

Licenses: A Class M driver's license authorizes the holder to operate a motorcycle or moped.

- An applicant required to take a motorcycle road test must provide a passenger vehicle and licensed driver to convey the license examiner during the road test.

Noise Limits: A motor vehicle must be equipped with a muffler in good working condition that continually operates to prevent excessive or unusual noise. A person may not use a muffler cutout, bypass, or similar device on a motor vehicle.

TX

Motor-Driven Cycles: Texas law defines a "motor-driven cycle" as a motorcycle equipped with a motor that has an engine piston displacement of 250 cubic centimeters or less.

- A motor-driven cycle may not drive at a speed of more than 35 mph during nighttime or periods of poor visibility unless the cycle is equipped with a headlamp or lamps that reveal a person or vehicle 300 feet ahead.
- A motor-driven cycle must be equipped with either multiple-beam headlamps or single beam headlamps sufficient to reveal a person or vehicle at a distance of 100 feet when the cycle is operated at a speed of less than 25 mph, at a distance of at least 200 feet when the cycle is operated at a speed of 25 mph or more, and at a distance of at least 300 feet when the cycle is operated at a speed of 35 mph or more.

Mopeds: Texas law defines a moped as a motor-driven cycle that cannot attain a speed in 1 mile of more than 30 mph and the engine of which: (1) cannot produce more than 2-brake horsepower; and (2) if an internal combustion engine, has a piston displacement of 50 cc or less and connects to a power drive system that does not require the operator to shift gears.

- For the purpose of registration, mopeds are treated as motorcycles.
- A person may not operate a moped unless the person holds a driver's license. An applicant for a moped license must be 15 years of age or older.

Passenger Car Trailers

Brakes: A trailer or pole trailer is required to have brakes if its gross weight exceeds 4,500 lbs. A trailer with a gross weight between 4,500 lbs. and 15,000 lbs. is not required to have brakes if it is towed at a speed of not more than 30 mph.

Dimensions: Total length: 65 feet (includes bumpers); trailer length: not specified; width: 102 inches (excludes mirrors and safety devices); height: 13.6 feet.

Hitch: The drawbar or other connection between a vehicle towing another vehicle and the towed vehicle must be strong enough to pull all weight towed and may not exceed 15 feet between the vehicles except for the connection between 2 vehicles transporting poles, pipe, machinery, or other objects of a structural nature that cannot be readily dismembered.

- A driver towing another vehicle and using a chain, rope, or cable to connect the vehicles must display on the connection a white flag or cloth not less than 12 inches square.
- A driver of a passenger car or light truck may not tow a trailer, semitrailer, house trailer, or another motor vehicle unless safety chains of a type approved by the DPS are attached in an approved manner from the trailer, semitrailer, house trailer, or towed motor vehicle to the towing vehicle.

Lighting: A trailer, pole trailer, or vehicle that is towed at the end of a combination of vehicles must be equipped with at least 2 tail lamps, at least 2 stop lamps, electric turn signal lamps, and at least 2 red reflectors.

- A trailer that is at least 80 inches wide must be equipped with 2 front clearance lamps, 1 on each side; 2 rear clearance lamps, 1 on each side; 4 side marker lamps, 1 on each side at or near the front and 1 on each side at or near the rear; 4 reflectors, 1 on each side at or near the front and 1 on each side at or near the rear; and hazard lamps.
- A trailer that is at least 30 feet long must be equipped with 2 side marker lamps, 1 centrally mounted on each side; 2 reflectors, 1 centrally mounted on each side; and hazard lamps.

- A pole trailer must be equipped with 2 side marker lamps, 1 at each side at or near the front of the load; 1 reflector at or near the front of the load; and 1 combination marker lamp that emits an amber light to the front and a red light to the rear and side and is mounted on the rearmost support for the load to indicate the maximum width of the trailer.

Mirrors: A motor vehicle, including a motor vehicle used to tow another vehicle, must be equipped with a mirror located to reflect to the driver a view of the highway for a distance of at least 200 feet from the rear of the vehicle.

Speed Limits: Same as for passenger cars.

Towing: A person may not ride in a house trailer while it is being towed.

Miscellaneous Provisions

Bail Bonds: State has mandatory recognition of AAA arrest bond certificates up to $200 with specified exceptions.

Border Inspections: On demand of a peace officer within 250 feet of the Mexican border at a checkpoint, the driver of a vehicle must produce a driver's license and proof of insurance.

Liability Laws: The minimum amounts of motor vehicle liability insurance coverage required are $20,000 for bodily injury to or death of 1 person in 1 accident, $40,000 for bodily injury to or death of 2 or more persons in 1 accident, and $15,000 for damage to or destruction of property of another in 1 accident.

- Has future-proof-type law applicable in event of accident causing property damage of $1,000 or more to any vehicle or personal injury or death. Must show financial responsibility if in accident with more than $1,000 property damage and there is a reasonable probability of judgement against the driver. Uninsured motorist coverage at least equal to minimum financial responsibility limits issued on all insurance policies unless insured rejects coverage. Liability insurance mandatory. Current proof of liability insurance required upon request of law enforcement officer and to receive or renew motor vehicle registration or vehicle safety inspection. Proof of liability insurance required only of original drivers license applicants.

Weigh Stations: All commercial vehicles must stop when directed by sign or police officer.

Fees & Taxes

Table 1: Title Fees

Vehicle Type	Fee
Certificate of Title - All Vehicles	$13.00
Duplicate Certificate of Title	$2.00

Table 2: Registration and Plate Fees

Vehicle Type	Fee
Passenger Motor Vehicles of 6,000 lbs. or less & more than 6 Model Years Old	$40.50
Passenger Motor Vehicles of 6,000 lbs. or less & 4 to 6 Model Years Old	$50.50
Passenger Motor Vehicles of 6,000 lbs. or less & 3 Model Years Old or less	$58.50
Passenger Motor Vehicles of more than 6,000 lbs.	$25.00 + $0.60 for each 100 lbs.
Commercial Motor Vehicle of 1-6,000 lbs., Equipped with Pneumatic Tires	$0.44 per 100 lbs.
Commercial Motor Vehicle of 1-6,000 lbs., Equipped with Solid Tires	$0.55 per 100 lbs.
Commercial Motor Vehicle of 6,001-8,000 lbs., Equipped with Pneumatic Tires	$0.495 per 100 lbs.
Commercial Motor Vehicle of 6,001-8,000 lbs., Equipped with Solid Tires	$0.66 per 100 lbs.
Commercial Motor Vehicle of 8,001-10,000 lbs., Equipped with Pneumatic Tires	$0.605 per 100 lbs.
Commercial Motor Vehicle of 8,001-10,000 lbs., Equipped with Solid Tires	$0.77 per 100 lbs.
Trailer of 1-6,000 lbs., Equipped with Pneumatic Tires	$0.33 per 100 lbs.
Trailer of 1-6,000 lbs., Equipped with Solid Tires	$0.44 per 100 lbs.
Trailer of 6,001-8,000 lbs., Equipped with Pneumatic Tires	$0.44 per 100 lbs.
Trailer of 6,001-8,000 lbs., Equipped with Solid Tires	$0.55 per 100 lbs.
Trailer of 8,001-10,000 lbs., Equipped with Pneumatic Tires	$0.55 per 100 lbs.
Trailer of 8,001-10,000 lbs., Equipped with Solid Tires	$0.66 per 100 lbs.
Motorcycles and Mopeds	$30.00
Personalized License Plates	$40.00
Duplicate Registration Receipt	$2.00

Table 3: Driver's Licenses

Service	Fee
Issuance or Renewal of Class A, B, or C License	$24.00
Additional Authorization to Operate a Motorcycle	$15.00
Renewal of Class M License or License Includes Authorization to Operate a Motorcycle	$32.00
Issuance or Renewal of Provisional License or Instruction Permit	$5.00
Examination to Change from Lower to Higher Class of License	$10.00
Issuance of Commercial Driver's License or Commercial Learner's Permit	$60.00
Renewal of Commercial Driver's License or Commercial Learner's Permit that Includes Authorization to Operate a Motorcycle	$45.00
Change of Name or Address	$10.00
Duplicate License	$10.00
Duplicate Commercial License or Learner's Permit	$10.00

Table 4: Vehicle Taxes

Tax	Rate
Personal Property Tax	no state tax; may be applied locally
State Sales Tax	6.25%
Tax on Motor Vehicles Purchased Outside of State	6.25%
Tax on Motor Vehicle Brought into State by New Resident	$90.00
Tax on Even Exchange of Motor Vehicles	$5.00
Tax Imposed on Recipient of Gift of Motor Vehicle	$10.00
Gasoline Tax; (Diesel)	$0.20/gallon; ($0.20/gallon)

TX

Table 5: Miscellaneous Fees

Fee	Amount
Safety Inspection of a Motor Vehicle other than a Moped	$12.50
Safety Inspection of a Moped	$5.75
Safety Inspection of a Commercial Motor Vehicle	$50.00
Safety Inspection Verification Form for Vehicles Brought into the State	$1.00
Emissions Inspection	not to exceed $27.00
Service Charge for Registration by Mail or Electronic Means	$1.00
Additional Fees Added to All Registration and License Plate Fees	$1.30
Additional Fee for Certain Non-Passenger Vehicles with a Diesel Motor	Registration fee increased
Optional County Registration Fees	by 11%
Transfer Fee	not to exceed $11.50
Replacement of Standard License Plates	$3.50

UTAH

Contact Information

Motor Vehicle Division (DMV)
Utah State Tax Commission
210 North 1950 West
Salt Lake City, UT 84134

(801) 297-7780
http://dmv.utah.gov

Driver License Division (DLD)
P.O. Box 30560
Salt Lake City, UT 84130-0560

(801) 965-4437
http://driverlicense.utah.gov/

Utah Highway Patrol - Headquarters
P.O. Box 141775
Salt Lake City, UT 84114-1775

(801) 965-4518
http://highwaypatrol.utah.gov

Department of Transportation (DOT)
P.O. Box 148240
Salt Lake City, UT 84114

(801) 965-4559
www.dot.state.ut.us

Vehicle Title

Application: The application for a certificate of title shall be made to the DMV on a form prescribed by the DMV.

- The application for certificate of title shall contain: the signature of each person to be recorded on the certificate as an owner; the name, residence and mailing address of the owner, or business address of the owner if the owner is an association or business; a description of the vehicle, including the make, model, body type, the model year as specified by the manufacturer; any other information required by the DMV to enable it to determine if the owner is entitled to a certificate of title; a statement of any lien or encumbrance on the vehicle; the names and addresses of all persons having any ownership interest in the vehicle; and if the application for certificate of title is for a new vehicle, it shall be accompanied by a statement by

the dealer or a bill of sale showing any lien retained by the dealer.
- An applicant for a certificate of title must provide evidence of: title or ownership evidenced by a properly assigned certificate of title or a manufacturer's certificate of title if the vehicle has not been titled before. If the vehicle is from another state or foreign country that does not issue or require certificates of title, the owner shall submit a bill of sale or a sworn statement of ownership; payment of sales tax evidenced by a receipt from the DMV showing that the sales tax has been paid however, if a licensed dealer has made a report of a sale, no receipt is required; payment of all applicable fees; an identification number inspection; and an odometer statement signed by the transferee or automobile dealer.

Transfer of Ownership: The transferee, before operating or permitting the operation of a transferred vehicle on a highway, shall present to the DMV the certificate of registration and the certificate of title, properly endorsed, and shall apply for a new certificate of title and obtain a new registration for the transferred vehicle.

- At the time of any sale or transfer of a motor vehicle, the transferor shall furnish to the transferee a written odometer disclosure statement in a form prescribed by the DMV, usually on the face of the certificate of title issued to the transferor. This statement shall be signed and certified as to its truthfulness by the transferor, stating: the date of the transfer; the transferor's name and address; the transferee's name and address; the identity of the motor vehicle, including its make, model, year, body type, and identification number; the odometer reading at the time of the transfer; and that to the best of the transferor's knowledge, the odometer reading reflects the amount of miles the vehicle has actually been driven or a warning if the transferor knows of a discrepancy. Each transferor and transferee shall acknowledge receipt of the odometer disclosure statement by signing it.
- The odometer mileage does not need to be disclosed if: the vehicle is a single motor vehicle having a manufacturer specified gross laden weight rating (GLWR) of more than 16,000 lbs., or a motor vehicle registered in Utah with a GLWR of 18,000 lbs. or more; a motor vehicle that is 10 years old or older; a new motor vehicle prior to its first transfer for purposes other than resale.

Mobile Homes: The owner of a manufactured home or mobile home shall apply to the DMV for a certificate of title if mobile home is not attached to any property, or an Affidavit of Mobile Home Affixture if the mobile home is attached to any property.

- An owner of a manufactured home or a mobile home previously issued a certificate of title who attached that home to property shall apply for an Affidavit of Mobile Home Affixture within 30 days of attaching to property.
- The owner of a manufactured home or mobile home previously issued an Affidavit of Mobile Home Affixture who separates that home from the property shall apply for a certificate of title within 30 days of the separation, prior to any transfer of ownership of that home.

Vehicle Registration

Application: A person may not operate, and an owner may not give another person permission to operate a motor vehicle unless it has been registered.

- An application for the registration of a motor vehicle shall be made by the owner of the vehicle to the DMV on a form furnished by the DMV.
- The application for registration shall include: the signature of an owner of the vehicle to be registered; the name, residence and mailing address of the owner, or

business address of the owner if the owner is a firm, association, or corporation; a description of the vehicle including the make, model, body type, the model year as specified by the manufacturer, the number of cylinders, and the identification number of the vehicle; and any other information required by the DMV to determine whether the owner is entitled to register the vehicle.
- The DMV shall require that the applicant or person making the application for registration has a valid driver's license.
- Prior to registration a vehicle must have: an identification number inspection done by a licensed dealer or a qualified identification number inspector; passed the safety inspection, if required in the current year; passed the emissions inspection, if required in the current year; paid property taxes, the fee, or received a property tax clearance; paid the automobile driver education tax; paid the uninsured motorist fee, if applicable; and a valid certificate of title for the vehicle being registered.
- A registration card shall be signed by the owner in ink in the space provided and carried at all times in the vehicle to which it was issued.
- The application for registration shall not contain any false or fraudulent statements. Such statements shall result in refusal of registration to the applicant.

Non-Residents: Registration is not required for any vehicle registered in another state and owned by a non-resident.
- Registration of any vehicle is required within 60 days of the owner establishing residency.
- In order to be eligible for a license, the applicant must be a resident of the state and remain in the state for six months or more during a calendar year.
- Military personnel on active duty in Utah may maintain home state vehicle registration.

Registration Type: Registration renewal is on a staggered system. Every vehicle is registered for a 12-month time period beginning with the 1st day of the calendar month of registration and expiring on the last day of the same month in the following year. If the last day of the registration period falls on a day in which the county offices are not open for business, the registration of the vehicle is extended to midnight of the next business day. The application for registration renewal shall be accompanied by an emissions inspection and safety certificate.

Emissions Inspection: Most diesel- and gas-powered cars and trucks manufactured in 1968 or later must have an annual emissions test, which can be completed at most service stations. New vehicles, motorcycles, and vehicles with a model year of 1967 and older are exempt from this requirement.
- Emission certificates are required in Davis, Salt Lake, Utah, and Weber counties and are valid for 60 days. This certificate must be submitted to the appropriate DMV office as a condition of registration.
- The frequency of the emissions inspection shall be determined based on the age of the vehicle as determined by model year and shall be required to the extent allowed under the current federally approved state implementation plan. In accordance with the federal Clean Air Act, 42 U.S.C. Sec. 7401 et seq., the legislative body of a county shall only require the emissions inspection every 2 years for each vehicle that is less than 6 years old on January 1, 2003.
- If an emissions inspection is only required every 2 years for a vehicle, the inspection shall be required for the vehicle in odd-numbered years for vehicles with odd-

numbered model years or in even-numbered years for vehicles with even-numbered model years.

Safety Inspection: The frequency of the safety inspection shall be determined based on the age of the vehicle determined by model year and shall be required each year for a vehicle that is 8 or more years old on January 1, 2003; or every 2 years for each vehicle that is less than 8 years old on January 1, 2003 in odd-numbered years for a vehicle with an odd-numbered model year; and in even-numbered years for a vehicle with an even-numbered model year.

License Plates

Disbursement: The DMV upon registering a vehicle shall issue to the owner 1 license plate for a motorcycle, trailer, or semitrailer and 2 identical license plates for every other vehicle. Each license plate shall have displayed on it: the registration number assigned to the vehicle for which it is issued; the name of the state; a designation of the county in which the vehicle is registered; and a registration decal showing the date of expiration.

- Each original license plate that is not a special issuance plate shall be a statehood centennial license plate or a Ski Utah license plate. A person who is the registered owner of a vehicle may, upon payment of a fee, apply to the DMV for personalized license plates.
- The owner of a motor vehicle that is a model year 1973 or older may apply to the DMV for permission to display an original issue license plate of a format and type issued by the state in the same year as the model year of the vehicle.
- Every license plate shall at all times be securely fastened in a horizontal position at a height not less than 12 inches from the ground and maintained free from foreign materials and clearly legible from a distance of at least 100 feet during daylight.
- Disabled plates and placards are available by application to Customer Service Division. Affidavit by owner and disability certification by physician are required to accompany application.

Transfer of Plates: If the owner of a registered vehicle transfers his title or interest to the vehicle, the vehicle registration expires. The owner shall remove the license plates from the transferred vehicle. Within 20 days from the date of transfer the owner shall forward the plates to the DMV to be destroyed or may have the plates and the registration number assigned to another vehicle.

Driver's Licenses

Examination: The DLD shall examine every applicant for a license by testing the applicant's eyesight by the DMV or by allowing the applicant to furnish to the DLD a statement from a physician or optometrist licensed in Utah. The Division requires the applicant be able to read and understand highway signs regulating, warning, and directing traffic. The state requires 20/40 vision and peripheral fields (side vision) of 120 degrees in each eye to pass the vision test. It also requires the applicant to be able to read and understand simple English used in highway traffic and directional signs and to have knowledge of the state traffic laws. The Division is also allowed to assess other physical and mental abilities it finds necessary to determine the applicant's fitness to drive a motor vehicle safely on the highways. The applicant must be able to exercise ordinary and reasonable control while driving a motor vehicle.

Graduated Drivers Licensing: State has a system of graduated licensing for teen drivers. At 15 and 6 months, teens are eligible for a practice/learner's permit. The permit is valid for 6 months (but a mandatory holding period does not exist) for a student enrolled in an approved driver education course. The student must pass the written test before the permit may be issued.

- The permit allows the student to operate a private motor vehicle when accompanied by the student's parent, legal guardian, or adult spouse who must be a licensed driver and who is occupying a seat next to the practice driver.
- Driver's education students must complete at least six hours of behind-the-wheel driving using a dual-control motor vehicle with a certified driving instructor seated next to the student.
- Teens must also accumulate at least 40 (10 at night) hours of parental supervised driving before being eligible for a Class D/Intermediate license. At 16, teens are eligible for a Class D/Intermediate license. For the first 6 months, Class D/Intermediate license holders may not transport any passenger who is not an immediate family member unless accompanied by a licensed driver at least 21 years of age or with the written consent of the driver's parent or guardian to drive to and from the driver's school, a school-sponsored activity, or a religion-sponsored activity.
- The holder of a Class D/Intermediate license who is under the age of 17 may not operate a motor vehicle upon any highway between the hours of 12:00 a.m. and 5:00 a.m. unless accompanied by a licensed driver at least 21 years of age or with the written consent of the driver's parent or guardian to drive to and from the driver's school, a school-sponsored activity, or a religion-sponsored activity; or to and from the driver's place of employment and their place of residence.
- At 17, teens are eligible for an unrestricted license.

Issuance/Application: An application for any original license, provisional license, or endorsement shall be made at the DLD on a form furnished by the DLD.

- Regardless of age, permit applicants must be enrolled in driver education and license applicants must complete driver education.
- The application for a license shall contain: the applicant's full legal name, birth date, sex, social security number, and a brief description of the applicant; a statement of whether the applicant has previously been licensed to drive a motor vehicle and, if so, by what state or country; the applicant's signature; and the mailing and residential address of the applicant.
- The application form must be accompanied by proof of the applicant's name and birth date by at least 1 of the following means: current driver's license; birth certificate; Selective Service registration; or other proof, including church records, family Bible notations, school records, or other evidence approved by the DLD.
- When the DLD issues a new driver's license, the applicant is assigned a distinguishing number. A photograph of the licensee is required.
- The licensee shall have his license in his immediate possession at all times when driving a motor vehicle.

Renewal: A renewal or extension of a license expires on the birth date of the licensee in the 5th year following the year the license was issued or the date of expiration of the applicant's foreign visa or permit. The license may be renewed at any time within 6 months before the license expires. The vision test is required once every 10 years, and the DLD may require the applicant for renewal to take a written examination.

- Drivers eligible for renewal by mail will be contacted by the DLD approximately 90 days prior to the expiration of their driver's license.

- Military personnel who had a valid Utah license at the time of entry into the service may continue to use that license up to 90 days after discharge (this provision applies only to those military members stationed outside of Utah).

Types of Licenses:

- Class A license (Commercial) is issued to drive any combination of vehicles with a GVWR of 26,001 pounds or more, if the GVWR of the 1 or more vehicles being towed is in excess of 10,000 pounds.
- Class B license (Commercial) is issued to drive any single motor vehicle with a GVWR of 26,001 pounds or more, including that motor vehicle when towing a vehicle with a GVWR of 10,000 pounds or less.
- Class C license (Commercial) is issued to drive any single motor vehicle with a GVWR of less than 26,001 pounds or that motor vehicle when towing a vehicle with a GVWR of 10,000 pounds or less when the vehicle is designed or used:
    - to transport more than 15 passengers, including the driver;
    - as a school bus, and weighing less than 26,001 pounds GVWR; or
    - to transport hazardous materials.
- Class D license (Non-Commercial) is issued to drive motor vehicles not defined as commercial motor vehicles or motorcycles.
- Class M license (Non-Commercial) is issued to drive a motorcycle.
- Endorsements: H-hazardous materials; K-restricted to intrastate operation of commercial vehicles; L-restricted to vehicles not equipped with air brakes; M-motorcycle; N-tank vehicle; P-passenger vehicle; S-school bus; T-double or triple trailers; X-hazardous materials and tank combination; and Z-taxi.

Traffic Rules

Alcohol Laws: A person operating a motor vehicle in Utah is considered to have given their implied consent to a chemical test or tests of their breath, blood, or urine for the purpose of determining whether he was operating or in actual physical control of a motor vehicle while under the influence of alcohol or any other drug.

- Open containers are not permitted. Meets TEA-21 requirements.
- Illegal per se BAC level is .08.
- Second DUI offense and greater legal limit is .05, if transporting childen.
- BAC level for people under 21 is .00.

Cellular Telephone Use: In Sandy, Utah, an ordinance was adopted by the City Council that levies up to a $300 fine if a motorist engages in a distracting activity that contributes to a crash.

Emergency Radio/Cellular: Citizen band radio is monitored for emergency calls. Emergency cell number is 911. Non-emergency cell number is *11.

Headsets: Wearing radio headsets when driving is permitted.

Occupant Restraints: The driver of a motor vehicle and passengers 16 years and older shall wear a properly adjusted and fastened seat belt in all seats.

- Violation of the seat belt law is a secondary offense, but it is primary for people under 19.
- The driver of a motor vehicle shall provide for the protection of each person younger than 5 years old by using a child restraint system in the manner prescribed by the manufacturer of such device.

- The driver of a motor vehicle shall provide for the protection of each person ages 5 to 16 by using or requiring them to use an appropriate child restraint device or seat belt.
- The passenger restraint requirements do not apply if all seating positions are occupied by other passengers.
- No person shall ride, and no person driving a motor vehicle shall knowingly permit any person to ride, upon any portion of any vehicle not designed or intended for the use of passengers. This does not apply to any vehicle driven elsewhere than upon a highway or to an employee engaged in the necessary discharge of his duty.

Railroad Crossing: Whenever any person driving a vehicle approaches a railroad grade crossing, the driver of the vehicle shall stop within 50 feet but not less than 15 feet from the nearest rail of the railroad track and may not proceed if: a clearly visible electric or mechanical signal device gives warning of the immediate approach of a train; a crossing gate is lowered, or a human flagman gives a signal of the approach of a train; a railroad train approaching within approximately 1,500 feet of the highway crossing emits a signal audible from such a distance and the train by reason of its speed or nearness to the crossing is an immediate hazard; an approaching train is plainly visible and is in hazardous proximity to the crossing; or there is any other condition which makes it unsafe to continue through the crossing.

- A person may not drive any vehicle through, around, or under any crossing gate or barrier at a railroad crossing while the gates or barrier is closed or is being opened or closed.

School Buses: The operator of any vehicle upon a highway, upon meeting or overtaking any school bus which is displaying alternating flashing amber warning light signals, shall slow his vehicle, but may proceed past the school bus using due care and caution at a speed not greater than 20 mph.

- The operator of any vehicle upon a highway, upon meeting or overtaking any school bus that is displaying alternating flashing red lights visible from the front or rear shall stop immediately before reaching the bus and may not proceed until the flashing red light signals cease operation.
- The operator of a vehicle need not stop upon meeting or passing a school bus displaying alternating flashing red light signals if the school bus is traveling in the opposite direction when: traveling on a divided highway; the bus is stopped at an intersection or other place controlled by a traffic-control signal, or by a peace officer; or upon a highway of 5 or more lanes.

Vehicle Equipment & Rules

Bumper Height: Lift kits are permitted. 4 inch tires, 4 inch lift on 100-inch+ wheel base: under 100-inch wheelbase, height is determined by formula.

Glass/Window Tinting: Front windows must allow 70% light transmittance; windshield banners are allowed on the top of the windshield as long as they do not exceed 4 inches from the top of the windshield or go below the AS-1 line. Windows to the left and right of the driver must still allow 43% light transmittance. Windows behind the driver may be as dark as the owner wishes. Mirrored and reflective tint is still prohibited. A right side mirror is required on all vehicles with window tint. The third brake light may not be covered by window tint.

Telematics: A motor vehicle may not be operated on a highway if the motor vehicle is equipped with a video display located so that the display is visible to the operator of the vehicle.

- This does not apply to television-type receiving equipment used for safety or law enforcement purposes approved by the DMV, or motor vehicle navigation.

Windshield Stickers: A person may not operate a motor vehicle with any sign, poster, or other non-transparent material on the windshield except a certificate or other paper required to be displayed by law or the vehicle's identification number displayed or etched.

- Nontransparent materials may be used when: along the top edge of the windshield area not to exceed 3 inches to the right or left of the center of the windshield if the materials do not extend downward more than 4 inches from the top edge of the windshield; in the lower left-hand corner of the windshield provided they do not extend more than 3 inches to the right of the left edge or more than 4 inches above the bottom edge of the windshield; in the lower left-hand corner of the rear window provided they do not extend more than 3 inches to the right of the left edge or more than 4 inches above the bottom edge of the window.

Motorcycles & Mopeds

Equipment: A person under the age of 18 may not operate or ride, unless within an enclosed cab, a motorcycle upon a highway unless that person is wearing protective headgear.

- Every motorcycle shall be equipped with the following items: 1 headlamp; 1 taillamp; either a taillamp or a separate lamp shall be so constructed and placed as to illuminate with a white light the rear registration plate; 1 red reflector on the rear, either as part of the taillamp or separate; 1 stop lamp; a braking system; a horn or warning device; and a mirror.
- A person operating a motorcycle shall ride only upon the permanent seat attached to the motorcycle and such operator shall not carry any other person unless the motorcycle is designed to carry more than 1 person.
- A person shall ride a motorcycle while sitting astride the seat, facing forward.
- No person shall operate a motorcycle while carrying anything preventing him or her from keeping both hands on the handlebars.
- No operator shall carry any person, nor shall any person ride, in a position that will interfere with the operation or control of the motorcycle or the view of the operator.
- Every motorcycle shall be equipped with footrests for each passenger and no person shall operate any motorcycle with handlebars above shoulder height.

Licenses: A person who has been issued a motorcycle learner's permit may drive a motorcycle only during daylight hours and only without passengers.

- Motorcycle endorsement on all classes of license or motorcycle only, Class M, license required; valid for 5 years; expires on licensee's birthday in the 5th year.

Mopeds: A peace officer may at any time upon reasonable cause to believe that a moped is unsafe or not equipped as required by law, or that its equipment is not in proper adjustment or repair, require the person riding the moped to stop and submit the moped to an inspection and a test as appropriate.

UT

- A moped may not be used to carry more persons at 1 time than the number for which it is designed or equipped, except that an adult rider may carry a child securely attached to his person in a back pack or sling.
- A person operating a moped upon a roadway at less than the normal speed of traffic shall ride as near as practicable to the right-hand edge of the roadway.
- A person under the age of 18 may not operate or ride a moped upon a highway unless that person is wearing protective headgear.

Passenger Car Trailers

Registration: A trailer of 750 lbs. or less unladen weight and not designed, used, and maintained for hire or for the transportation of property or persons is not required to be registered.

Brakes: Every motor vehicle and every combination of vehicle shall have a service braking system which will stop the vehicle or combination within 40 feet from an initial speed of 20 mph on level, dry, smooth, hard surface.
- Every motor vehicle and combination of vehicles shall have a parking brake system adequate to hold the vehicle or combination of any grade on which it is operated under all conditions of loading on a surface free from snow, ice, or loose material.

Dimensions: Total length: 65 feet (includes bumpers); trailer length: 40 feet (includes bumpers); width: 102 inches (can exceed 102 inches if excess is due to an appurtenance); height: 14 feet.

Hitch: Every towed vehicle shall be coupled by means of a safety chain, cable, or equivalent device, in addition to the regular trailer hitch or coupling. The safety chain or cable shall be securely connected with the chassis of the towing vehicle, the towed vehicle, and the drawbar. The safety chain or cable shall be of sufficient material and strength to prevent the 2nd vehicle from becoming separated and shall have no more slack than is necessary for proper turning. The safety chain or cable shall be attached to the trailer drawbar so as to prevent it from dropping to the ground, and to assure the towed vehicle follows in the course of the towing vehicle in the case the vehicles become separated. The requirement for chains or a cable does not apply to a semi-trailer having a connecting device composed of a 5th-wheel and kingpin assembly, nor to a pole trailer.

Lighting: Tail, brake, and license plate lights are required. Turn signals and 2 or more red reflectors are also required. A trailer over 80 inches must have clearance lights.

Mirrors: Every motor vehicle shall be equipped with a mirror mounted on the left side of the vehicle and so located as to reflect to the driver a view of the highway to the rear of the vehicle.
- Every vehicle shall be equipped with a mirror mounted either inside the vehicle approximately in the center or outside the vehicle on the right side and so located as to reflect to the driver a view of the highway to the rear of the vehicle.

Speed Limits: Same as passenger cars unless posted.

Towing: Every towed vehicle shall be coupled by means of a safety chain, cable, or equivalent device, in addition to the regular trailer hitch or coupling. The safety chain or cable shall be securely connected with the chassis of the towing vehicle, the towed vehicle, and the drawbar. The safety chain or cable shall be of sufficient material and strength to prevent the 2 vehicles from becoming separated and shall have no more slack than is necessary for proper turning. The safety chain or cable shall be attached to the trailer drawbar so as to prevent it from dropping to the ground, and to assure the towed vehicle follows in the course of the towing vehicle in case the vehicles become separated. The requirement for chains or a cable does not apply to a semi-trailer having a connecting device composed of a 5th-wheel and kingpin assembly, nor to a pole trailer.

- Whenever the load upon any vehicle extends to the rear 4 feet or more beyond the bed or body of the vehicle there shall be displayed at the extreme rear end of the load, between 1/2 hour after sunset and 1/2 hour before sunrise, 2 red lamps and 2 red reflectors located so as to indicate maximum width and maximum overhang. At all other times, there shall be displayed red flags, not less than 12 inches square, marking the extremities of the load.
- Vehicles drawing trailers are prohibited from operating in the left-most general purpose lane on highways with more than 3 lanes traveling the same direction.

Miscellaneous Provisions

Bail Bonds: Mandatory recognition of AAA club guaranteed arrest bond certificate up to $200 with specified exceptions.

Liability Laws: State has security-type law applicable in event of accident causing property damage in excess of $1,000 or personal injury or death; no judgment minimum.

- Every driver of a motor vehicle must have a minimum insurance coverage of $25,000 for injury or death to any 1 person in an accident, $50,000 for injury or death to 2 or more people in any accident, and $15,000 for the damage to any property in 1 accident. Proof of financial responsibility required after driver's license suspension or revocation or when department is notified that an uninsured owner or operator has been involved in an accident. Failure to show proof may result in suspension or revocation of driver's license.
- State has non-resident service of process law.
- State has uninsured insurance law. Sale and purchase are mandatory. Benefits: medical and hospital, $3,000; wage loss, 85% of gross income up to $250/week for 52 weeks; substitute service, $20/day, maximum 365 days; funeral, $1,500; survivors, $3,000, 3-day waiting period for wage and service loss where total disability is less than 2 weeks.
- State has no fault insurance law.

Weigh Stations: Any peace officer having reason to believe that the height, width, length, or weight of a vehicle and its load is unlawful may require the operator to stop the vehicle and submit to a measurement or weighing of the vehicle and load. A peace officer may require the vehicle to be driven to the nearest scales or port-of-entry within 3 miles.

Fees & Taxes

Table 1: Title & Registration Fees

Vehicle Type	Title Fee	Registration Fee
Motor Vehicle	$6.00	$21.00 under 12,000 lbs. $49.50 between 12,000 - 14,000 lbs. $18.50 for each 2,000 lbs. over 14,000 lbs.
Mobile Home	$6.00	$21.00 under 12,000 lbs. $49.50 between 12,000 - 14,000 lbs. $18.50 for each 2,000 lbs. over 14,000 lbs.
Trailers of 750 lbs. or less	$6.00	Not required for non-commercial $8.50 for commercial
Trailers over 750 lbs.	$6.00	$11.00
Motorcycles	$6.00	$22.50
Vintage Vehicle	$6.00	$20.00
Duplicates	$6.00	$4.00

Table 2: License Fees

License Class	Fee	Driving Test Fees
Commercial A & B	test fees	$35.00 knowledge; $55.00 skills
C or D under age 21	$25.00	
C or D over age 21	$20.00	
Motorcycle under age 21	$27.50	
Motorcycle over age 21	$22.50	
Motorcycle Endorsement	$7.50	
Duplicate License Fee	$13.00	
Endorsements	$5.00	

Table 3: Vehicle Taxes

Tax	Rate
State Sales tax	5.75-6.75% based on the net sale price of the vehicle
Personal Property Tax	based on the age of the vehicle; $10.00-$150.00
Gasoline Tax; (Diesel Tax)	$0.245/gallon; ($0.245/gallon)

Table 4: Miscellaneous Fees

Fee	Amount	Payable Upon
Safety Inspection	$15.00 or less for motor vehicles, $7.00 or less for motorcycles, and $20.00 or less for 4 wheel drives	Inspection
Emissions Inspection	Up to $7.50	Inspection
Delinquent Registration/Transfer Fee	$20.00	Registration
Personalized Plate Fee	$50.00	Registration
Special Plate Fee	$0.00-$50.00	Registration
License Plate Fee	$5.00	Registration
Replacement Plate Fee	$5.00	Replacement

VERMONT

Contact Information

Department of Motor Vehicles (DMV)
120 State Street
Montpelier, VT 05603-0001

(802) 828-2000
www.aot.state.vt.us/dmv/dmvhp.htm

Vermont State Police Headquarters
Department of Public Safety
103 S. Main Street
Waterbury, VT 05671-2101

(802) 244-7345
www.dps.state.vt.us/vtsp/index_main.html

Department of Transportation
1 National Life Drive
Drawer 33
Montpelier, VT 05633-0001

(802) 828-2657
www.aot.state.vt.us

Vehicle Title

Application: Application for vehicle title is required for all vehicles that are less than 15 years old.

- Applications shall contain the name, residence, and address of the owner; a description of the vehicle including, its make, model, identification number, odometer reading, or hubometer; the date of purchase by the applicant; the name and address of the person from whom the vehicle was acquired; and the names and addresses of any lienholders in the order of their priority and the dates of their security agreements.
- For new vehicles, the application shall be accompanied by a manufacturer's or importer's certificate of origin.
- The certificate of title shall be mailed or personally delivered, upon proper identification of the individual, to the first lienholder named in it or, if none, to the owner.

Transfer of Ownership: At the time of transfer of a vehicle, the transferor must execute an assignment and warranty of title to the transferee and a reading of the odometer at the time of delivery and must mail or deliver the certificate to the transferee or to the commissioner of the DMV.

Vehicle Registration

Application: Application is made to the commissioner of the DMV, and the application must show that the vehicle is equipped and in good mechanical order. Along with the application, the applicant should also send the required registration fees and evidence of ownership.

- The DMV will issue a certificate of registration on which will appear the name of the registrant, his address, a brief description of the vehicle registered, and the date of registration. The DMV also will assign to each motor vehicle registered a distinctive license plate.
- A person shall not operate a motor vehicle nor pull a trailer or semitrailer unless the registration certificate is carried in some easily accessible place in such motor

vehicle. In case of the loss, mutilation, or destruction of such certificate, the owner of the vehicle shall notify the DMV and remit a fee whereupon a duplicate certificate shall be furnished to the owner.

- A person who registers a motor vehicle of which he is not the bona fide owner shall be fined $500, or imprisoned for not more than 2 years, or both.
- Residents must register motor vehicles owned or leased for a period of more than 30 days and operated by them. A "resident" is any legal resident of the state and any person who accepts employment or engages in a trade, profession, or occupation in the state for a period of at least 6 months (except for a person who lives in another state and returns to that state on at least a weekly basis). Also any foreign partnership, firm, association, or corporation having a place of business in the state is considered to be a resident with regard to all vehicles owned or leased and which are garaged or maintained in the state. A new resident must register a vehicle within 60 days of moving to the state.

Non-Residents: If a non-resident owner or operator has complied with the laws of the foreign country or state of his residence relative to the registration of motor vehicles and the granting of operators' licenses, the non-resident shall be considered as registered and a non-resident operator shall be considered as licensed in this state.

- Military personnel on active duty in Vermont may maintain out-of-state vehicle registration.

Registration Type: Registration must be renewed each year. Each registration is in effect for a period of 12 months.

Emissions Inspection: Vermont adopted the California Low Emission Vehicle (LEV) Program, which requires dealerships to sell the cleanest cars available to Vermont residents.

- All new vehicles with a model year 2000 and later, and sold in Vermont with a weight rating of less than 6,000 lbs., have to be California-certified.

Safety Inspection: Except for school buses and motor buses which shall be inspected twice during the calendar year at 6-month intervals, all motor vehicles registered in this state shall be inspected once each year.

- Any motor vehicle, trailer, or semitrailer not currently inspected in this state shall be inspected within 15 days from the date of its registration in Vermont. The inspections shall be made at garages or qualified service stations, designated by the commissioner as inspection stations, for the purpose of determining whether those motor vehicles are properly equipped and maintained in good mechanical condition.
- A person shall not operate a motor vehicle unless it has been inspected and has a valid certification of inspection affixed to it. The month of next inspection for all motor vehicles shall be shown on the current inspection certificate affixed to the vehicle.

License Plates

Disbursement: The DMV shall issue to each motor vehicle a distinctive number that shall be displayed on plates.

- All number plates shall be the property of the state.

- A motor vehicle operated on any highway in this state shall have displayed in a conspicuous and un-obscured place either 1 or 2 plates. If 1 plate is issued, the plate shall be attached securely to the rear of the vehicle. If 2 plates are furnished, 1 shall be secured to the rear and 1 shall be secured to the front of the vehicle.
- Specialized plates are available.
- Disabled cards and license plates are available by application to DMV.

Transfer of Plates: Upon the transfer of ownership of a vehicle, the registration number plates may be attached to another vehicle that is being leased or purchased by the registrant for a period greater than 30 days.

- Upon the termination of a lease of a vehicle, the registration number plates may be attached to another vehicle that is owned, being leased, or being purchased by the lessee. Full registration fees are due.

Driver's Licenses

Examination: Before an operator's license is issued for the 1st time in this state, or if an applicant's previous Vermont license has expired over 3 years ago, then the applicant must pass a satisfactory examination consisting of oral, road, written, and vision tests (20/40 visual acuity required).

- If an applicant holds a valid out-of-state license, he or she is only required to take a vision test. If the out-of-state license has been expired for more than 1 year, the applicant also must take the written and road tests.

Graduated Drivers Licensing: State has a system of graduated licensing for teen drivers. At 15, teens are eligible for a learner's permit.

- Permit holders may not drive unless supervised by: (1) a licensed unimpaired parent or guardian; (2) a licensed or certified and unimpaired driver education instructor; or (3) a licensed and unimpaired individual who is at least 25 years of age.
- Permit holders must also accumulate at least 40 hours (10 at night) of parental/guardian supervised driving.
- At 16, teens who have held the permit for at least 1 year and have been crash and conviction free for at least 6 months are eligible for a junior/intermediate license.
- For the 1st 3 months of the junior/intermediate license, teens may not transport any passengers unless supervised (see requirements in permit stage above). During the 2nd 3 months, teens may not transport any passengers except siblings unless supervised.
- At 18, teens are eligible for a full license if they have been crash and conviction free for at least 6 months.
- Driver education is required for all license applicants under 18.

Issuance/Application: An individual must be 18 years of age to obtain an operator's license and must not have had any recalls, suspensions, or revocations during the previous 6-month period.

- A license that is issued to an individual under the age of 18 shall be distinguishable by color from a license that is issued to an individual over the age of 21.
- Each applicant for an original learner's permit or operator's license is required to show documentary proof of identity and date and place of birth. Proof of identity must be 1 primary document and 1 secondary document or 2 primary documents.

- Primary documents include: photo driver's license or state, province, or territory issued photo ID that is not expired more than 1 year; U.S. or Canadian birth certificate; approved INS documents; court order containing full name, date of birth, and court seal; military ID; Vermont issued learner's permit; and Canadian Dept. of Indian Affairs ID card.
- Secondary documents include: photo driver's license or ID card expired more than 1 year; court order; employer or student ID; social security card; marriage certificate or license; parent or guardian affidavit; vehicle title; and certain other approved documents.
- First time license holders must have a photograph on their license. Current license holders are grandfathered. Does not include social security number.
- A licensee must notify the DMV within 30 days of any change of mailing address, legal name, or legal residence.
- If a person holds a license from another state or Canada, they must surrender that license when applying for a Vermont license.

Types of Licenses: Class I: A non-commercial operator's license, which permits the operation of any vehicle except a motorcycle, a school bus, or commercial Class A, B, or C vehicle.

- Class A: Allows operation of a vehicle over 26,001 lbs. and towing over 10,000 lbs.
- Class B: Allows operation of a vehicle over 26,001 lbs. and towing under 10,000 lbs.
- Class C: Allows operation of a vehicle under 26,000 lbs. and transporting hazardous materials or carrying more than 16 or more passengers.

Renewal: An operator's license must be renewed after 4 years. At least 15 days before a license expires, the DMV shall mail an application for license renewal.

- A person may not operate a motor vehicle if their license has expired.

Traffic Rules

Alcohol Laws: Every person who operates, attempts to operate, or is in actual physical control of any vehicle on a highway in this state is deemed to have given consent to an evidentiary test of the person's breath for the purpose of determining the person's alcohol concentration or the presence of other drugs in the blood. The test shall be administered under the direction of a law enforcement officer. Open containers are permitted.

- Illegal per se BAC level is .08 or 0.02 if the person is operating a school bus.
- Lower BAC level for people under 21 is .02.
- Open containers are not permitted. Law meets TEA-21 requirements.

Emergency Cellular/Radio: Emergency number is 911 or *DWI for unsafe driving.

Headsets: Wearing of radio headsets while driving is permitted.

Lane Restrictions: Whenever a roadway had been divided into 2 or more clearly marked lanes the following rules shall apply: a vehicle shall be driven entirely within 1 lane; upon a roadway which is divided into 3 lanes and provides for 2-way movement of traffic, a vehicle may be driven in the center lane only when overtaking and passing another vehicle traveling in the same direction or in preparation for making a left turn; official traffic-control devices may be erected directing specified traffic to use a designated lane; and, official traffic-control devices may be installed prohibiting the changing of lanes on sections of roadway.

- A vehicle may not be driven over, across, or within any dividing space, barrier, or section dividing the roadway sections of a divided highway except at established openings in the physical barrier or dividing section or space, or at a crossover or intersection.

Occupant Restraints: A driver and passengers 16 years or older should wear a seat belt in all seats.
- Children under 1 year and less than 20 lbs. must be restrained in a rear-facing infant seat.
- Children 1 until 8 years and more than 20 lbs. must be properly restrained in a federally approved child passenger restraint system.
- Children 8 until 16 years must be restrained in a child safety seat or seat belt.
- Violation of the seat belt provision is a secondary offense, however violation of the child restraint law is a primary offense.
- Riding in the back of an unenclosed pickup truck is permitted.

Railroad Crossing: When an electronic or mechanical signal device gives warning of an approaching train, a crossing gate is lowered, a train approaching emits a signal that is audible, or a stop sign has been erected, then a driver approaching a railroad crossing shall stop within 50 feet of such crossing and may not proceed until he can do so safely.
- The driver of any motor vehicle carrying passengers, any bus, any vehicle carrying explosive substances or flammable liquids shall stop within 50 feet, but no less than 15 feet, from the nearest rail of the railroad crossing.

School Buses: Vehicles from both directions must stop when approaching a school bus when its red lights are flashing.
- The driver of a vehicle need not stop on a highway with separate roadways upon meeting or overtaking a school bus which is on a different roadway, or on a controlled access highway where the school bus is stopped in a loading zone which is a part of or adjacent to the highway at a point where pedestrians are not permitted to cross the roadway.

Vehicle Equipment & Rules

Bumper Height: Modification of the original vehicle bumper height is illegal.

Glass/ Window Tinting: Application of after-market vehicle glass-darkening material is illegal in driver's compartment only.

Telematics: No person may operate upon a highway in this state a motor vehicle having installed or carried in the front or driving compartment or in a manner visible to the operator, a television receiver, screen, or other means of visually receiving a television broadcast.

Windshield Stickers: A person shall not paste, stick, or paint advertising matter or other things on or over any transparent part of a motor vehicle windshield, vent windows, or side windows located immediately to the left and right of the driver, except in a space not over 4 inches high and 12 inches long in the lower right-hand corner of the windshield, or in such space as the DMV may specify for location of any government sticker, and further shall not hang any object other than a rearview mirror in back of the windshield of a motor vehicle.

Motorcycles & Mopeds

Equipment: No person may operate or ride upon a motorcycle upon a highway unless he or she wears upon his head protective headgear reflectorized in part and of a type approved by the commissioner. The headgear shall be equipped with either a neck or chin strap.

- Any motorcycle or moped carrying a passenger, other than in a sidecar or enclosed cab, must be equipped with footrests for such passenger.
- No person may operate any motorcycle or moped with handlebars more than 15 inches in height above that portion of the seat occupied by the operator.
- All motorcycles and mopeds must be equipped with at least one headlight, taillight, brake light, and license plate lamp.

Licenses: Any applicant for a permit or an operator's license valid for operating a motorcycle, except a renewal applicant or an applicant who surrenders a valid motorcycle license issued by another state, shall successfully complete the rider training course.

Noise Limits: Any exhaust system on a motorcycle will be deemed defective if any changes, modifications, alterations, deletions, or adjustments have been made which would cause the exhaust system to generate a higher sound level than would be generated by the exhaust system customarily installed by the manufacturer as original equipment.

Mopeds: A moped may be operated only by a licensed driver at least 16 years of age.

Passenger Car Trailers

Brakes: Trailers, semitrailers, trailer coaches, or pole trailers of a gross weight not exceeding 3,000 lbs. need not have brakes provided the total weight on, and including, the wheels of the trailer, semitrailer, or pole trailer shall not exceed 40 percent of the gross weight of the towing vehicle when connected to the trailer, semitrailer, or pole trailer.

- Every trailer, semitrailer, or trailer coach of a gross weight of more than 3,000 lbs. but less than 6,000 lbs. when operated upon a highway shall be equipped with brakes on the wheels of at least 1 axle, adequate to control the movement of and to stop and to hold the vehicle and so designed as to be applied by the driver of the towing motor vehicle from its cab. The brakes shall be so designed and connected that, in case of an accidental break-away of the towed vehicle, the brakes shall be automatically applied and remain applied for not less than 15 minutes.
- Every trailer, semitrailer, or trailer coach of a gross weight of 6,000 lbs. or more, when operated upon the highways of this state, shall be equipped with brakes on all wheels adequate to control the movement of and to stop and to hold the vehicle and so designed as to be applied by the driver of the towing motor vehicle from its cab. The brakes shall be so designed and connected that in case of an accidental breakaway of the towed vehicle, the brakes shall be automatically applied and remain applied for not less than 15 minutes.
- Every vehicle, trailer, semitrailer, pole trailer, or any other vehicle being drawn at the end of a combination of vehicles shall be equipped with at least 2 taillamps on the rear, unless the vehicle is only equipped with 1.

Dimensions: Total length: 65 feet; trailer length: 45 feet; width: 102 inches (allows outside width to exceed 102 inches if excess is attributed to appurtenance); height: 13.6 feet.

Hitch: In addition to a hitch, trailer coaches must be secured to the towing vehicle, while in operation on any highway, by a safety chain. The hitch on any motor vehicle towing a trailer coach and the corresponding coupling on the coach and safety chain must be adequate to ensure the public safety.

Lighting: Taillights, required; brake lights, at least 1 required, if equipped with 2 both must work; license plate light, required; turn signals, required if trailer coach manufactured after January 1, 1955; reflectors required.

Mirrors: Required.

Speed Limits: Same as for passenger cars.

Towing: There must be carried on each trailer coach at least 1 fire extinguisher of a type approved by the state fire marshal, in good usable condition and easily accessible.
- No person may occupy a trailer coach while it is being moved on a public highway.
- Maximum of 1 boat or general utility trailer may be towed behind passenger or pleasure vehicle.

Miscellaneous Provisions

Bail Bonds: The bond shall be held by the commissioner to satisfy an execution issued against such person in a case arising out of damage caused by the operation of a motor vehicle owned by such person.

Liability Laws: No owner or operator of a licensed motor vehicle shall operate or permit the operation of the vehicle upon the highways of the state without having in effect an automobile liability policy or bond in the amount of at least $25,000 for 1 person killed or injured in an accident; $50,000 for 2 or more persons killed or injured in any 1 accident; and $10,000 for damages to property in any 1 accident.
- State has Non-resident Service of Process Law.

Fees & Taxes

Table 1: Title Fees

Type	Fee
Certificate of Title for All Vehicles Subject to Registration	$15.00
Each Security Interest or Loan Noted on Title	$7.00
Certificate of Title after Release of Security Interest	$15.00
Duplicate Certificate of Title	$15.00
Corrected Certificate of Title	$15.00

Table 2: Registration & Title Fees

Vehicle Type	Registration Fee
Automobile/Motor Home/Truck under 6,100 lbs. - Gasoline Fueled	$50.00 or $92.00 biennially*
Automobile/Motor Home/Truck under 6,100 lbs. - Diesel Fueled	$27.00 or $50.00 biennially
Automobile/Motor Home/Truck under 6,100 lbs. - Other Fuel	$74.50 or $138.50 biennially
Trailer - (Trailer & Load of 1,499 lbs. or less)	$15.00
Trailer - (Trailer & Load of 1,500 lbs. or more)	$30.00
Motorcycles - Gasoline & Diesel	$31.00*
Motorcycles - Other Fuel	$53.50*
Moped - Gasoline & Diesel	$21.00*
Moped - Other Fuel	$36.00
Electric Powered - All Vehicle Types	$42.00
Antique & Exhibition	$16.00*
Duplicate Registration Certificate	$7.00
Conservation Plate	$20.00
Safety Organization Plate	$10.00 one-time
Vanity Plate	$15.00
Duplicate Plate	$10.00 for each plate
Sample Plate	$15.00
Title Fee	$15.00

* Includes $1 clean air fees per year.

Table 3: Driver License Fees

License and/or Service	Fee
Learner Permit - First Test and Permit	$30.00
Learner Permit - Second Test and Permit	$25.00
Junior Operator - First Test and License	$39.00
Junior Operator - Subsequent Test and License	$34.00
4 Year Operator License - (If Applicant Has Valid Learner Permit or Operator License)	$30.00
2 Year Operator License - (If Applicant Has Valid Learner Permit or Operator License)	$18.00
Second Operator License Test - (If Applicant Has Valid Learner Permit)	$15.00
Administrative Fee to Convert License from Another State	$15.00
Commercial Driver License Test	$30.00
Subsequent Commercial Driver License Test	$25.00
Commercial Endorsement Test	$10.00
Commercial Class Upgrade Test	$25.00
4 Year Commercial Driver License	$60.00
2 Year Commercial Driver License	$40.00
Commercial Instruction Permit (Includes Photo Fee)	$12.00
Commercial Skill Test Scheduling Fee (Applied to New License)	$20.00
Duplicate Driver License 1CDL	$10.00
Corrected Driver License	$10.00
Photo Fee	$5.00
Motorcycle Endorsement (per year)	$2.00

Table 4: Vehicle Taxes

Tax	Rate
Purchase & Use Tax	6% on new and used motor vehicles
Gasoline Tax; (Diesel)	$0.20/gallon; ($0.26/gallon)

VIRGINIA

Contact Information

Virginia Department of Motor Vehicles (DMV)
P.O. Box 27412
Richmond, VA 23269

(800) 435-5137
www.dmv.state.va.us

Department of State Police
Administrative Headquarters
7700 Midlothian Turnpike
Richmond, VA 23235

(804) 674-2000
www.vsp.state.va.us/index.htm

VDOT Information Center
1221 East Broad St.
Richmond, VA 23219

(804) 786-2801
http://virginiadot.org/

Vehicle Title

Application: The owner of a vehicle, or his or her duly authorized attorney-in-fact, must apply for a certificate of title in the name of the owner on appropriate forms prescribed and furnished by the Commissioner of the DMV.

- Certificate of title must contain all liens, security interests, or encumbrances on the vehicle.
- The certificate of title shall contain the date issued; the registration number assigned to the motor vehicle, trailer, or semitrailer; the name and address of the owner; a description of the registered motor vehicle, trailer, or semitrailer; and other statements of fact as may be determined by the DMV.
- Whenever any person who has applied for or obtained the registration or title to a vehicle moves from the address shown in his or her application, registration card, or certificate of title, he or she shall notify the DMV of his or her change of address within 30 days.
- Every certificate of title issued under this chapter shall be valid for the life of the motor vehicle, trailer, or semitrailer so long as the owner to whom it is issued shall retain legal title or right of possession of or to the vehicle.

Transfer of Ownership: When transferring or assigning a title or interest, transferor must fully and correctly endorse the assignment on the certificate of title to its purchaser, with a statement of all security interests on it, and shall deliver the certificate to the purchaser or transferee at the time of delivery.

- The transferee shall write his or her name and address in ink on the certificate of title and must within 30 days forward the certificate to the DMV with an application for the registration of the motor vehicle, trailer, or semitrailer and for a certificate of title.
- Every owner or transferor of any motor vehicle, including a dealer, shall, at the time of transfer of ownership of any motor vehicle by him or her, record on the certificate of title, if one is currently issued on the vehicle in the Commonwealth, and on any application for certificate of title the reading on the odometer or similar device plus any known additional distance traveled not shown by the odometer or similar device of the motor vehicle at the time of transfer.

- The registration card contains forms for providing notice to the DMV of a transfer of the ownership of the motor vehicle, trailer, or semitrailer.
- It is illegal to sell, trade, or offer to sell or trade any vehicle without an accompanying certificate of title issued to its owner.

Mobile/Manufactured Homes: The owner of a mobile/manufactured home must register the vehicle with the DMV and obtain from the DMV a registration card and certificate of title.

Vehicle Registration

Application: The registration application must include a description of the vehicle and a statement of all liens of the vehicle.

- No motor vehicle subject to an emissions test may be registered until it has passed such test or been issued a waiver.
- Whenever any person who has applied for or obtained the registration or title to a vehicle moves from the address shown in his or her application, registration card, or certificate of title, he or she shall notify the DMV of the change of address within 30 days.
- The DMV may reject an application for the registration of a motor vehicle, trailer, or semitrailer or certificate of title when the applicant has neglected or refused to furnish the DMV with the information required on the appropriate official form or other information required by the DMV; the required fees have not been paid; the vehicle lacks required equipment or contains prohibited equipment; or there is reason to believe that the application or accompanying documents have been altered or contain false statements.

Non-Residents: Non-residents may operate a motor vehicle in the state without registering or paying any fees to the Commonwealth for a period not to exceed 6 months if the vehicle is registered in another state.

- Other than for purposes of pleasure (any purpose other than to conduct business), a non-resident regularly operating within the Commonwealth must register his or her vehicle(s) with the Commonwealth.
- Any owner who operates or permits to be operated one or more of these vehicles either simultaneously or alternately as often as 4 times in any 1 month shall be considered to be regularly operating them in the Commonwealth.
- Military personnel on active duty in Virginia may retain vehicle registration in their home state.

Registration Type: Registration expires on the last day of the 12th or 24th month next succeeding the date of registration.

- Every registration shall be renewed annually or biannually on application by the owner and by payment of the fees required by law.
- The operator of any motor vehicle, trailer, or semitrailer being operated on the highways in the Commonwealth, shall have in his or her possession the registration card issued by the DMV or the registration card issued by the state or country in which the motor vehicle, trailer, or semitrailer is registered; and his or her driver's license, learner's permit, or temporary driver's permit.
- The registration card shall contain the date issued; the registration number assigned to the motor vehicle, trailer, or semitrailer; the name and address of the

owner; a description of the registered motor vehicle, trailer, or semitrailer; and other statements of fact as may be determined by the DMV.

Emissions Inspection: Motor vehicles having a gross weight of 10,000 lbs. or less that are registered in the Northern Virginia region must have emissions inspections.

- Inspections must be done on a biennial basis at official emissions inspection stations. This rule does not apply to motorcycles, "clean fuel" vehicles, hybrid cars (that get at least 50 miles per gallon in city driving), or antique vehicles.
- A vehicle will qualify for a waiver if it has failed an initial inspection and subsequently fails a reinspection if the owner provides written proof that at least $175 was spent on improvements to a pre-1980 model vehicle or $200 for 1980 and newer vehicles; and that any emissions control system which has been removed, damaged, or rendered inoperable has been replaced and restored to operating condition.

Safety Inspection: Motor vehicles, trailers, and semitrailers, except for antique vehicles, are required to be inspected for safety and must be reinspected within 12 months of the month of the first inspection and at least once every 12 months thereafter. New motor vehicles that have been inspected in accordance with the manufacturer or distributor are exempt from the safety inspection.

- Safety inspection stickers must be displayed on the windshield of vehicles.

License Plates

Disbursement: Plates must be attached to both the front and the rear of the motor vehicle.

- For a motorcycle or trailer, the plate must be attached to the rear of the vehicle.
- Handicapped license plates are available by application to DMV or Customer Service Center.

Transfer of Plates: An owner who sells or transfers a registered motor vehicle may have the license plates and the registration number transferred to another vehicle titled in the owner's name.

- An application for transfer of plates must be made to the DMV accompanied by a fee or, if the other vehicle requires a greater registration fee than that for which the license plates were assigned, on the payment of a fee plus the amount of the difference in registration fees between the 2 vehicles.

Driver's Licenses

Examination: Every applicant must submit to an examination to determine his or her mental and physical qualifications and ability to drive.

- A written examination and road test are required for first-time applicants.
- Any person under the age of 18 who applies for a driver's license and fails the motor vehicle knowledge test shall not be eligible for retesting for at least 15 days.
- Vision screening with a 20/40 or better vision in one or both eyes is required.

Graduated Drivers Licensing: State has a system of graduated licensing for teen drivers. At 15 years and 6 months, teens are eligible for a learner's permit.

- Permit holders may not drive unsupervised, between the hours of midnight and 4:00 a.m or with more than 1 passenger under 18.
- Teens must hold the permit for at least 9 months (minimum age — 16 years and 3

months) and accumulate at least 40 (10 at night) hours of parental/guardian supervised driving before being eligible for an intermediate license.
- Provisional license holders may not drive unsupervised between the hours of midnight and 4:00 a.m.
- Provisional license holders under 18 are prohibited from transporting more than 1 passenger under 18 for the first year they hold their license. After the first year, provisional license holders who are 17 are prohibited from transporting more than 3 passengers under 18 until they reach age 18. Family members are exempted from all passenger restrictions.
- At 18, teens are eligible for an unrestricted license.

Issuance/Application: Application information must include whether or not the applicant has previously been licensed as a driver and, if so, when and by what state, and whether or not his or her license has ever been suspended or revoked and, if so, the date of and reason for such suspension or revocation. Applicant must also provide signature and disclosure of whether or not the applicant has ever been convicted of a felony.

- Initial applicants older than 19 years of age must have held a learner's permit issued by the DMV for at least 30 days or have completed driver's education before issuance of a driver's license.
- A resident must notify the DMV within 30 days of a change of address. Persons moving to Virginia have 60 days to obtain a Virginia license.
- License includes a photograph or a statement "valid without photo pending licensee's return to Virginia."
- Licenses issued 07/01/03 and after are prohibited from displaying a social security number.
- When applying for a DMV document, applicants may not use immigration visas and written statements (whether notarized or not) where another person "vouches" for the applicant's Virginia residency.

Renewal: Every driver's license expires on the last day of the birth month of the applicant in years in which the applicant attains an age equally divisible by 5. Licenses issued 07/01/03 and after expire on date of birth.

- Any driver's license may be renewed by application, which must include the applicant's certification of Virginia residency, after the applicant has taken and successfully completed all required examinations.
- Applicants 80 years of age or older must undergo vision examinations either in person or provide a report of the examination to renew a driver's license.
- License may be renewed online, by phone, or by mail every other time.
- Out-of-state military personnel can apply for a license extension in the mail. Licenses must be renewed within 60 days of returning to the Commonwealth.

Types of Licenses: Types of non-commercial licenses are driver's licenses, driver's licenses with a Class M motorcycle, and a motorcycle-only license.

Types of commercial licenses are:
- Class A: Any combination of vehicles with a Gross Combination Weight Rating (GCWR) of 26,001 lbs. or more if the vehicle(s) being towed has a GVWR of more than 10,000 lbs. If an operator holds a Class A license and has the correct endorsements, he or she may also operate vehicles listed in Classes B and C.
- Class B: Any single vehicle with a GVWR of 26,001 lbs. or more. Any single vehicle

with a GVWR of 26,001 lbs. or more towing another vehicle with a GVWR of 10,000 lbs. or less.
- Class C: Any vehicle that is not included in Classes A or B that carries hazardous materials or is designed to carry 16 or more passengers, including the driver.
- Types of endorsements are: H — permits driving a vehicle that transports hazardous materials; N — permits driving a tank vehicle; P — permits driving a passenger-carrying vehicle; S — permits driving a school bus; or T — permits driving a double or triple trailer.

Traffic Rules

Alcohol Laws: A person who drives a motor vehicle in this state is deemed to have given implied consent to a blood or breath test to determine the person's blood alcohol level.
- A police officer may assume that a driver has been drinking alcohol and driving if he observes that an open container is located in the passenger area of a motor vehicle, the alcoholic beverage in the open container has been at least partially removed, and the appearance, conduct, odor of alcohol, speech, or other physical characteristic of the driver may be reasonably associated with the consumption of an alcoholic beverage. A violation of drinking alcohol and driving is punishable as a Class 4 misdemeanor. The law does not meet TEA-21 requirements.
- Illegal per se BAC level is .08.
- BAC for people under 21 is .02.
- BAC for commercial drivers is .04.

Emergency Radio/Cellular: Citizen band radio channel 9 is monitored for emergency calls. Some areas have 911 cellular capabilities. Other cell emergency number is #77.

Headsets: It is unlawful to operate a motor vehicle, bicycle, electric power-assisted bicycle, or moped while using earphones.

Occupant Restraints: All persons age 16 and older and occupying the front seat of a motor vehicle are required to wear seat belts.
- Violation of the seat belt law is a secondary offense, however violation of the child restraint law is a primary offense.
- Every child under the age of 6 must be secured in a child restraint or booster seat.
- Every child between 6 and 16 years of age must be secured in a child restraint, booster seat, or safety belt.
- Transportation of persons younger than 16 years old in pickup truck beds is prohibited.

Railroad Crossing: All vehicles must stop within 50 feet but not less than 15 feet from the nearest rail on a railroad crossing if either signaled to do so or if an approaching train is plainly visible.
- Except in cities or towns, the driver of any motor vehicle carrying passengers for hire, or of any vehicle carrying explosive substances or flammable liquids must stop within 50 feet but not less than 15 feet from the nearest rail of a railroad.

School Buses: A person shall be guilty of reckless driving who fails to stop when, approaching from any direction, any school bus which is stopped on any highway or school driveway for the purpose of taking on or discharging children, the elderly, or mentally or physically handicapped persons. Drivers must also remain stopped until all such persons are clear of the highway or school driveway and the bus is put in motion.

VA — Vehicle Equipment & Rules

Bumper Height: Modification of original bumper height is permitted but must meet state standards.

Glass/Window Tinting: Glass tinting is allowed only if the vehicle is equipped with 2 side mirrors, and the following conditions apply: rear side windows or rear windows tint cannot reduce the total light transmittance of such window to less than 35%; and front side windows tint cannot reduce total light transmittance of such window to less than 50%.

- No tints may have a reflectance of light exceeding 20% or produce a holographic or prism effect.
- No film or darkening material may be applied to the windshield except to replace the sunshield in the uppermost area of the windshield.
- Any greater reduction of light transmittance of any window requires written authorization from the Commissioner of the DMV.

Telematics: No television receiver may be visible to the driver.

- Provides an exemption by allowing rear-view closed circuit video monitors (to assist a driver in backing up).

Windshield Stickers: Stickers are not allowed on any windshield, except for inspection and county tax decals.

Motorcycles & Mopeds

Equipment: Each passenger is required to have a permanently affixed seat and footrest.

- Every person operating a motorcycle must wear a face shield, safety glasses, or goggles, or have his motorcycle equipped with safety glass or a windshield at all times while operating the vehicle.
- Operators and any passengers thereon must wear protective helmets.
- Handlebars may not be higher than 15 inches above the level of the motorcycle's seat.

Licenses: Applicants must pass a special examination including a written examination and a road test before being issued a license.

Noise Limits: The exhaust system must be no louder than the original factory equipment.

Mopeds: Moped drivers must ride as close as is practical to the right curb or edge of the roadway or, if posted, may be required to use an adjacent bike trail.

- No moped may be driven on any highway or public vehicular area faster than 30 mph or by any person under the age of 16.
- All drivers must carry identification that includes their name, address, and date of birth.
- Local ordinances may require riders of mopeds to wear helmets and other protective equipment.
- All rear red reflectors must be visible from 600 feet.

Passenger Car Trailers

Registration: Trailers must be registered the same as vehicles.

Brakes: Trailers must be equipped with brakes if the gross weight exceeds 3,000 lbs.
- Trailers must be equipped with at least 1 red brake light on the rear of the vehicle.

Dimensions: Total length: 65 feet (includes coupling in the combination measurement); trailer length: 45 feet; width: 102 inches (allows outside width to exceed 102 inches if excess is attributed to appurtenance); height: 13.6 feet.

Lighting: Trailers must carry at the rear a red light plainly visible in clear weather from a distance of 500 ft.
- Alternatively, a separate white light shall be so mounted as to illuminate the rear license plate from a distance of 50 feet to the rear of such vehicle.
- Reflectors must be affixed to the rear end of the trailer.

Mirrors: Mirrors are required to give view of not less than 200 feet to rear of the vehicle; 1 outside and 1 inside. If inside view is obstructed to rear, then 1 on each side of the vehicle on the outside is required.

Speed Limits: 65 mph or as posted.

Towing: No person may occupy a house trailer or camping trailer while it is being towed on a public highway.

Miscellaneous Provisions

Bail Bonds: Mandatory recognition of AAA club guaranteed arrest bond certificates up to $1,000, with specified exceptions.

Liability Laws: Has security-type law applicable in event of accident causing property damage of $1,000 or more or personal injury or death.
- Vehicle owners are required to pay a $500 UMV fee if registering an uninsured motor vehicle; all policies must include "uninsured motorist" coverage.
- Every motor vehicle's owner's policy must insure the insured or other person against loss from any liability imposed by law for damages, including damages for care and loss of services, because of bodily injury to or death of any person, and injury to or destruction of property caused by accident and arising out of the ownership, use, or operation of such motor vehicle or motor vehicles within the commonwealth, any other state in the United States, or Canada.
- The insurance amounts, with respect to each motor vehicle, are $25,000 because of bodily injury to or death of 1 person in any 1 accident and, subject to the limit for 1 person; to a limit of $50,000 because of bodily injury to or death of 2 or more persons in any 1 accident; and to a limit of $20,000 because of injury to or destruction of property of others in any 1 accident.
- State has non-resident service of process law and guest suit law.

Weigh Stations: Trucks must stop if their registered gross weight exceeds 7,500 lbs.

Fees & Taxes

Table 1: Title & Registration Fees

Vehicle Type	Title Fee	Registration Fee
Motor Vehicle, Private Passenger Car, or Motor Home Weighing 4,000 lbs. or less	$10.00	$30.50
Motor Vehicle, Private Passenger Car, or Motor Home Weighing more than 4,000 lbs.	$10.00	$35.50
Duplicate Title	$5.00	
Trailers of 1,500 lbs. or less	$10.00	$10.00 (1 year); $20.00 (2-year) $52.00 (permanent)
Trailers of 1,501-4,000 lbs.	$10.00	$20.50 (1 year); $41.00 (2-year) $52.00 (permanent)
Trailers of greater than 4,001 lbs.	$10.00	$25.50 (1 year); $51.00 (2-year) $52.00 (permanent)
Trailer Safety Inspection		$1.50 (1 year); $3.00 (2-year) $4.00 (permanent)
Motorcycles	$10.00	$28.50
Additional Registration Fee for All Vehicles		$2.00
Duplicate Registration Fee		$2.00

Table 2: License Fees

License Class	Fee
Driver's	$4.00/year; for additional year up to an age divisible by 5
Commercial	$7.00/year
Learner's Permit	$3.00 plus yearly cost
CDL Endorsements/Classifications	additional $1.00/year
Duplicate Fee	$10.00
Motorcycle Endorsement	additional $2.00/year
Reexamination	$2.00
School Bus Permit	maximum additional $3.00/year
Photo Identification Card	$10.00

Table 3: Vehicle Taxes

Tax	Rate
Gasoline Tax; (Diesel)	$0.175/gallon; ($0.16/gallon) additional 2% in Northern VA Metro Area
State Motor Vehicle Sales and Use Tax	3%

Table 4: Miscellaneous Fees

Fee	Amount	Payable Upon
Emissions Inspection Fee	$2.00	registration
Emission Inspection Station Charge	Capped at $28.00	inspection
Safety Inspection Fee	$15.00	registration
Safety Inspection Station Charge	$15.00 per vehicle weighing less than 26,000 lbs.; $5.00 per motorcycle; $1 per reinspection	inspection
Uninsured Motorist Fee	$500.00	registration
Special Plates Fee	$10.00 one-time fee	

WASHINGTON

Contact Information

Department of Licensing (DOL)
1125 Washington Street, SE
P.O. Box 9020 (360) 902-3600
Olympia, WA 98507-9020 www.dol.wa.gov

Driver Examining
P.O. Box 9030 (360) 902-3900
Olympia, WA 98507-9030

Vehicle Licensing
P.O. Box 9909 (360) 902-3770
Olympia, WA 98507-8500

Washington State Patrol
General Administration Building
P.O. Box 42600 (360) 753-6540
Olympia, WA 98504-2600 www.wa.gov/wsp/index.htm

Washington State Department of Transportation (DOT)
Transportation Building
310 Maple Park Avenue, SE
P.O. Box 47300 (360) 705-7000
Olympia, WA 98504-7300 www.wsdot.wa.gov

Department of Ecology (DOE)
Air Quality Program - Vehicle Emission
P.O. Box 47600 (800) 272-3780
Olympia, WA 98504-7600 www.ecy.wa.gov

Vehicle Certificate of Ownership

Application: The application for a certificate of ownership must contain: (1) a description of the vehicle including the VIN, odometer reading at the time of delivery, and any distinguishing marks of identification; (2) the name and address of the registered owner and any lienholders; (3) and any other information the DOL may require.

- If a vehicle is titled in another state, the application must be accompanied by the most current title issued by that state. The DOL will accept a copy of the current title when it is being held by the lienholder and is not available.
- If a certificate of ownership is lost, stolen, mutilated, or destroyed or becomes illegible, the first priority secured party or, if none, the owner or legal representative of the owner named in the certificate must promptly apply for a duplicate.
- It is unlawful for any person under the age of 18 to be the registered or legal owner of any motor vehicle unless the person is emancipated or became the registered or legal owner of a motor vehicle while a non-resident of the state.
- It is unlawful for any person to convey, sell, or transfer the ownership of any motor vehicle to any person under the age of 18.

Transfer of Ownership: If an owner transfers his or her interest in a vehicle, other than by the creation, deletion, or change of a security interest, the owner must, at the time of the delivery of the vehicle, execute an assignment to the transferee and provide an odometer disclosure statement, and deliver the certificate and assignment to the buyer or transferee. The seller must notify the DOL of the date of the sale or transfer, the name and address of the buyer, the buyer's driver's license number if available, and a description of the vehicle including the VIN or the license plate number or both. The seller must file the notice within 5 business days of the transfer.

- The new owner must apply for a new certificate of ownership within 15 days after delivery of the vehicle.
- An odometer disclosure statement must accompany every application for a certificate of ownership unless the vehicle has a declared Gross Vehicle Weight (GVW) of more than 16,000 lbs., the vehicle is not self-propelled, the vehicle is 10 years old or older, the vehicle is sold directly by a manufacturer to a federal agency, or the vehicle is a new vehicle before its first retail sale.

Mobile Homes: The Housing Division of the CTED is responsible for all titling functions pertaining to mobile homes.

- The certificate of ownership for a manufactured home may be eliminated or not issued when the manufactured home is registered as real property. When the certificate of ownership is eliminated or not issued, the application for license must be recorded in the county property records of the county where the real property to which the home is affixed is located. All license fees and taxes applicable to the mobile home as a vehicle must be collected prior to recording the ownership with the county auditor.
- When the ownership of a mobile home is transferred and the new owner applies for a new certificate of ownership, the DOL or county auditor must notify the county assessor of the county where the mobile home is located of the change in ownership including the name and address of the new owner and the name of the former owner. A certificate of ownership for a mobile home will not be transferred or issued until the DOL has verified that any property taxes due on the mobile home have been paid.
- In order to transfer ownership of a mobile home, all registered owners of record must sign the title certificate releasing their ownership.
- Any person moving a mobile home on public highways must obtain a special permit from the DOT and local authorities. A special permit will not be valid until the county treasurer of the county in which the mobile home is located has endorsed or attached his certificate to the permit certifying that all property taxes on the mobile home have been satisfied.

Vehicle Registration

Application: Registration applications must be made to the DOL or an agent of the DOL including county auditors.

- Vehicle license plates and registration will not be issued unless the applicant simultaneously applies for a certificate of ownership or proves that a certificate of ownership has already been issued.
- A resident of the state must register a vehicle that is to be operated on the highways of the state. New Washington residents have 30 days from the date they become residents to register their vehicles. A resident is a person who shows

intent to live or be located in the state on more than a temporary or transient basis. Evidence of residency includes but is not limited to registering to vote in the state, receiving public assistance benefits from the state, or declaring residency for the purpose of obtaining a state license or in-state tuition.

- Temporary permits are available when an application is pending and also may be issued by an authorized vehicle dealer. The temporary permit must remain affixed to the vehicle until the receipt of permanent license plates.
- Temporary dealer licenses are effective for 45 days.
- Vehicle licenses and license plates may be renewed for the subsequent registration year up to 18 months before the current expiration date and must be used and displayed from the date of issue or from the day of the expiration of the preceding year, whichever date is later.
- All parking fines must be paid before a registration can be renewed.
- The certificate of license registration must be signed by the owner and carried in the vehicle at all times.

Non-Residents: The registration and license plate requirements of the state do not apply to any vehicles owned by non-residents of the state if the owner has complied with the vehicle registration requirements in his or her state of residency and that state grants similar privileges to Washington residents. Foreign businesses owning, maintaining, or operating places of business in the state must register motor vehicles used in connection with the business in the state.

- Non-resident military personnel on active duty in Washington may maintain home state registration or they may obtain a Washington license.

Emissions Inspection: Vehicles 5 through 25 years old registered in the areas of Seattle, Bellevue, Spokane, Tacoma, Vancouver, or Everett must pass an emission inspection test every 2 years. Vehicles with even-numbered model years must be inspected in even-numbered years, and vehicles with odd-numbered model years must be inspected in odd-numbered years.

- A vehicle will be granted a certificate of acceptance if: (1) it failed its first inspection; (2) it failed a reinspection; (3) it has been used for more than 50,000 miles; (4) all primary emission control components installed by the vehicle manufacturer, or its appropriate replacement are installed and operative; and (5) the owner has provided receipts for repairs performed by an authorized emission specialist between the first and last inspections. Repairs for a pre-1981 vehicle must be at least $100, and repairs for a 1981 or newer vehicle must total at least $150.

Safety Inspection: Commercial motor vehicles are subject to periodic inspections.

- No person may operate a motor vehicle or permit someone to operate a motor vehicle that is in such unsafe condition as to endanger any person, or which does not contain the parts and equipment, in proper condition and adjustment, as required by law.

License Plates

Disbursement: All motor vehicles, except trailers and motorcycles, are issued 2 license plates. Trailers and motorcycles are issued 1 plate.

- If a vehicle is issued 2 plates, 1 plate must be displayed on the front of the vehicle, and 1 plate must be displayed on the rear. If 1 plate is issued, that plate must be displayed on the rear of the vehicle. Each vehicle license plate must be placed or hung in a horizontal position at a distance of not less than 1 foot or more than 4 feet from the ground and must be kept clean so as to be plainly seen and read at all times. Any holders, frames, or any materials that in any manner change, alter, or make the vehicle license plate illegible are prohibited.

- Current registration tabs are affixed to the rear license plate as indicated on the license plate to identify the registration expiration month or year for a specific vehicle.
- Numerous specialty license plates are available.
- Disabled license plates or placards are available by application to the Department of Licensing or authorized agents located throughout the state. Proof of disability must be provided by the department and signed by both the disabled person and his or her physician.

Transfer of Plates: The right to license plates attached to a vehicle pass to the purchaser or transferee of a motor vehicle unless the vehicle is licensed to a public entity or the plates are specialty or personalized plates.

- When any person who has been issued personalized license plates sells, trades, or otherwise releases ownership of the vehicle upon which the personalized license plates have been displayed, he or she must immediately report the transfer of the plates to a new vehicle or camper eligible for the plates, or he or she must surrender such plates to the DOL and release his or her rights to the letters or numbers displayed on the plates.
- A person may not purchase a vehicle bearing foreign license plates without removing and destroying the plates unless the out-of-state vehicle is sold to a Washington resident by a resident of a jurisdiction where the license plates follow the owner. The buyer may also return the plates to the jurisdiction of issuance.

Driver's Licenses

Examination: The driver's licensing examination includes a vision test (20/40 visual acuity is required in at least one eye), a written knowledge test, and a driving skills test.

- No person may be issued a commercial driver's license unless that person has passed a knowledge and skills test for driving a commercial motor vehicle that complies with minimum federal standards.
- All applicants for a driver's license or renewal must take a vision test administered by the DOL.
- An applicant for a basic driver's license is not required to take the knowledge and driving skills tests if the applicant is surrendering a valid driver's license issued by the applicant's previous home state, has not failed a Washington driving test, or has not failed a Washington knowledge test.

Graduated Drivers Licensing: State has a system of graduated licensing for teen drivers. A person is eligible for a permit at 15 years of age if the person is enrolled in an accredited traffic safety education program. At 15 1/2 teens who do not enroll in driver's education are eligible for a learner's/instruction permit.

- A person holding a permit may drive a motor vehicle, other than a motorcycle, on the public highways if an approved instructor or a licensed driver with at least 5 years of experience occupies the seat beside the driver.
- At 16, teens who have held a permit for at least 6 months are eligible for an intermediate license. Teens must also pass a driving skills examination and an accredit-

ed traffic safety education program to receive an intermediate license.
- Parents, guardians, or employers must also certify that intermediate license applicants have at least 50 hours of driving experience (10 at night).
- Intermediate license applicants must not have been adjudicated for an offense involving the use of drugs or alcohol during the period the applicant held a permit.
- For the first 6 months, the intermediate license holder may not operate a motor vehicle that is carrying any passengers under the age of 20 who are not members of the licensee's immediate family.
- For the next 6 months, the licensee may not operate a motor vehicle that is carrying more than 3 passengers who are under the age of 20 and are not members of the licensee's immediate family.
- Intermediate license holders are also prohibited from driving unsupervised between the hours of 1:00 a.m. and 5:00 a.m. except when accompanied by a parent, guardian, or a licensed driver who is at least 25 years of age.
- An intermediate licensee may drive at any hour with any number of passengers in the vehicle if, for the 12-month period following the issuance of the intermediate license, the licensee has not been involved in an automobile accident and has not been convicted of a traffic offense.
- After 1 year of driving without collisions or traffic citations, teens are allowed to drive without limitation as to the time of day or the age and number of passengers.
- At age 18 the intermediate license automatically becomes a regular license.

Issuance/Application: When transferring from another state an applicant must have at least a current or recently expired (60 days or less), license, identification card or instruction permit from their previous state and 2 additional documents for identification. Most Federally issued documents with photo and signature are accepted without additional documentation. If further documentation is required Washington Drivers License Offices have a brochure to assist in the identification process.

- License includes a color photograph.
- DOL has plans to implement a voluntary biometrics matching system to verify the identity of an applicant for the issuance, renewal or duplicate license or identification card.
- License does not include a social security number or social insurance number but a social security number is required on application.
- New residents must obtain a valid Washington driver's license within 30 days from the date they become residents. To qualify for a Washington driver's license, a person must surrender to the DOL all valid driver's licenses that any other jurisdiction has issued to him or her.
- The parent or guardian of a minor applicant must show proof of identity and proof of relationship to the applicant. When last names are different, additional documents that show the link between the minor and the parent will be required.
- All applicants for a driver's license or instruction permit must provide their name of record and date of birth as established by 1 of the required identification documents; their sex; their Washington residence address; their description; and their driving licensing history.
- A student who maintains his or her legal home of record at a location outside Washington state, or the spouse or dependent of the student, who is at least 16 years of age, is exempt from holding a Washington driver's license. The student must be enrolled as a full-time non-resident student at an accredited institution of higher learning in Washington.

WA

Renewal: A person's 1st Washington driver's license expires on the person's 5th birthday after it was issued.

- A license may be renewed at any Licensing Services Office (LSO). The applicant must appear in person and pass a vision test. If the license has a corrective lens restriction, and the applicant would like to have it removed, he or she may request that his or her vision be tested without corrective lenses.
- A license may be renewed as much as 90 days ahead of its expiration date.
- A Washington driver's license issued to a service member, or the spouse or dependent child living with the service member, remains in effect while the person is serving in the armed forces on active duty.
- The license is valid until 90 days after the honorable discharge from service duty, unless it is suspended, cancelled, or revoked for cause as provided by law. If separation from the service is other than honorable, the military expiration is immediately void and you must apply for a renewal license. A license with a military expiration issued to a reservist who has been called to active duty, or the spouse or dependent child of the reservist, only remains in effect while the person remains on active duty.

Types of Licenses: A basic non-commercial driver's license is issued to a driver who has sufficient experience operating a non-commercial passenger vehicle.

- A Class A commercial driver's license is for a combination of vehicles with a Gross Combined Weight Rating (GCWR) of more than 26,000 lbs. if the Gross Vehicle Weight Rating (GVWR) of the vehicle being towed is in excess of 10,000 lbs.
- A Class B commercial driver's license is for a combination of vehicles with a GCWR of more than 26,000 lbs. if the GVWR of the vehicle being towed is not in excess of 10,000 lbs.
- A Class C commercial driver's license is for a single vehicle with a GVWR of less than 26,001 lbs. or any such vehicle towing a vehicle with a GVWR not in excess of 10,000 lbs.

Traffic Rules

Alcohol Laws: Any person who operates a motor vehicle within the state is deemed to have given consent to a test or tests of his or her breath or blood for the purpose of determining the alcohol concentration or presence of any drug in his or her breath or blood if arrested for any offense, where at the time of the arrest, the arresting officer had reasonable grounds to believe the person had been driving or was in actual physical control of a motor vehicle while under the influence of intoxicating liquor or any drug.

- Open containers are not permitted. Meets the requirements of TEA-21.
- Illegal per se BAC level is .08.
- BAC level for people under 21 is .02.

Emergency Radio/Cellular Use: Citizen band radio channel 9 is monitored for emergency calls. Emergency cell number is 911.

Headsets: No person may operate any motor vehicle on a public highway while wearing any headset or earphones connected to any electronic device capable of receiving a radio broadcast or playing a sound recording and which headset or earphones muffle or exclude other sounds.

Occupant Restraints: Every person 16 years of age or older operating or riding in a motor vehicle must wear a seat belt.

- Violation of the occupant protection laws is a primary offense.
- Children less than 1 year of age or less than 20 lbs. must be properly restrained in a rear-facing infant seat.
- Children 1 to 4 years of age or 20-40 lbs. must be properly restrained in a forward-facing child restraint system.
- Children under 8 years must be properly restrained in a booster seat, unless the child is at least 57 inches.
- Children under 6 or less than 60 lbs. must be in the rear seat if the vehicle has a passenger airbag.
- Children 8 until 16 years or 57 inches or taller must be properly restrained with a seat belt or booster seat. Children under 13 years must be restrained in the back seat if possible.
- Riding in pickup truck beds is permitted.

Railroad Crossing: A driver must stop within 50 feet but not less than 15 feet from the nearest rail of a railroad under any of the following circumstances: when a clearly visible electric or mechanical signal device gives warning of the immediate approach of a train; when a crossing gate is lowered or a human flagman gives or continues to give a signal of the approach or passage of a train; or when an approaching train is plainly visible and is in hazardous proximity to such crossing. The driver must not proceed until the crossing can be made safely.

- No person may drive any vehicle through, around, or under any crossing gate or barrier at a railroad crossing while the gate or barrier is closed or is being opened or closed.
- When a stop sign is erected at a railroad crossing, the driver of a vehicle must stop within 50 feet but not less than 15 feet from the nearest rail of the railroad and must proceed only upon exercising due care.

School Buses: Upon overtaking or meeting from either direction any school bus which has stopped on the roadway for the purpose of receiving or discharging any school children, the driver of any other vehicle must stop before reaching the school bus if the bus has its flashing red lights activated or a stop sign extended. The driver must not proceed until the school bus resumes motion or visual signals are no longer activated.

- The driver of a vehicle on a divided highway or on a highway with 3 or more marked traffic lanes need not stop upon meeting a school bus that is proceeding in the opposite direction.

Vehicle Equipment & Rules

Bumper Height: A passenger vehicle may not be modified from the original design so that any portion of the vehicle other than the wheels has less clearance from the surface of a level roadway than the clearance between the roadway and the lowermost portion of any rim of any wheel the tire on which is in contact with the roadway.

Glass/Window Tinting: The maximum level of film sunscreening material to be applied to any window, except the windshield, must have a total reflectance of 35% or less, and a light transmission of 35% or more. Installation of more than a single sheet of film sunscreening material to any window is prohibited.

- A greater degree of light reduction is permitted on all windows and the top 6 inches of windshields operated by or carrying as a passenger a person who possesses a written verification from a licensed physician that the operator or passenger must be protected from exposure to sunlight for physical or medical reasons.
- A greater degree of light reduction is permitted on the top 6-inch area of a vehicle's windshield. Clear film sunscreening material that reduces or eliminates ultraviolet light may be applied to the windshield.
- The following types of film sunscreening material are not permitted: mirror finish products; red, gold, yellow, or black material; or film sunscreening material that is in liquid preapplication form and brushed or sprayed on.

Telematics: No person may drive any motor vehicle equipped with any television viewer, screen, or other means of visually receiving a television broadcast that is located in the motor vehicle at any point forward of the back of the driver's seat, or which is visible to the driver while operating the motor vehicle.

Towing: No vehicle towing a trailer may be driven in the left-hand lane of a limited access roadway having 3 or more lanes for traffic moving in 1 direction except when preparing for a left turn.

Windshield Stickers: These are prohibited unless official and cannot obstruct vision.

Motorcycles & Mopeds

Equipment: Every motorcycle and motor-driven cycle must have its headlamps and taillamps lighted whenever the vehicle is in motion on a highway.

- Every motorcycle and every motor-driven cycle must be equipped with at least 1 headlamp. Every motorcycle other than a motor-driven cycle must be equipped with multiple-beam road-lighting equipment.
- Every motorcycle and motor-driven cycle must be equipped with a license plate lamp, a rear red reflector, and a stop lamp.
- Any motorcycle 25 years old or less must be equipped with mirrors on the left and right side of the motorcycle that provide the driver a complete view of the highway for a distance of not less than 200 feet to the rear of the motorcycle.
- Any person riding or operating a motorcycle, motor-driven cycle, or moped must wear an approved helmet.
- No person may transport a person under the age of 5 on a motorcycle or motor-driven cycle.
- No person may operate any motor-driven cycle during nighttime or periods of poor visibility at a speed of greater than 35 mph unless the motor-driven cycle is equipped with a headlamp or lamps which are adequate to reveal a person or vehicle at a distance of 300 feet ahead.
- A person operating a motorcycle must ride only upon the permanent and regular seat, and the operator must not carry any other person nor may any other person ride on a motorcycle unless the motorcycle is designed to carry more than 1 person. The motorcycle must contain foot pegs for each person the motorcycle is designed to carry.
- No person may operate on a public highway a motorcycle with handlebars or grips that are more than 30 inches higher than the seat of the saddle for the operator.

Licenses: No person may drive a motorcycle or motor-driven cycle unless such person has a valid driver's license specially endorsed by the DOL to authorized the holder to drive such vehicles.

- A person holding a valid driver's license who wishes to learn to ride a motorcycle may apply for a motorcycle instruction permit. The DOL will issue an instruction permit after the applicant has passed all parts of the motorcycle examination other than the driving test.
- A person holding a motorcycle instruction permit may drive a motorcycle on the public highways if the person has immediate possession of the permit and a driver's license. A permit holder may not carry passengers and may not operate a motorcycle during hours of darkness. A motorcycle instruction permit is valid for 90 days.
- The DOL may waive all or part of the motorcycle endorsement examination for persons who satisfactorily complete the voluntary motorcycle operator training and education program.

Noise Limits: No person may modify the exhaust system of a motorcycle in a manner that will amplify or increase the noise emitted by the engine of the vehicle above that emitted by the muffler originally installed on the vehicle.

Mopeds: No person may operate a moped on the highways of the state unless the moped has been assigned a moped registration number and properly displays that number.

- A person 16 years of age or older, holding a valid driver's license of any class issued by the state of the person's residence, may operate a moped without taking any special examination for the operation of a moped. No driver's license is required for operation of an electric-assisted bicycle if the operator is at least 16 years of age. Persons under 16 years of age may not operate an electric-assisted bicycle.
- A moped may not be operated on a bicycle path or trail, bikeway, equestrian trail, or hiking or recreational trail.
- No person may operate a moped or an electric-assisted bicycle on a limited access highway or on a sidewalk.
- Removal of any muffling device or pollution control device from a moped is unlawful.

Passenger Car Trailers

Brakes: Every trailer and pole trailer, and every vehicle combination must be equipped with service brakes adequate to control the movement of and to stop and hold the vehicle under all conditions of loading, and on any grade incident to its operation. Every trailer and pole trailer must be equipped with brakes acting on wheels except for those not exceeding a Gross Weight (GW) of 3,000 lbs. if the total weight on and including the wheels of the trailer or trailers does not exceed 40% of the GW of the towing vehicle when connected to the trailer.

Dimensions: Total length: 60 feet; trailer length: not specified; width: 8 1/2 feet; height: 14 feet.

- Permits rearview mirror to extend 5 inches and safety appurtenances and appliances such as clearance lights, door latches, door hinges, and turn signal brackets to extend 4 inches and an awning to extend 6 inches.

Hitch: A vehicle towing a trailer must use safety chains.

- The drawbar or other connection between vehicles in combination must be of sufficient strength to hold the weight of the towed vehicle on any grade where operated. No trailer may whip, weave, or oscillate or fail to follow substantially in the course of the towing vehicle.

Lighting: Tail, brake, and license plate lights are required. Turn signals and reflectors are also required.

Mirrors: Every motor vehicle must be equipped with mirrors mounted on the left and right side of the vehicle and so located to reflect to the driver a view of the highway for a distance of at least 200 feet to the rear of such vehicle.

Speed Limits: Same as posted for trucks.

Towing: No person may occupy any trailer while it is being moved on a public highway, except a person occupying a proper position for steering a trailer to be steered from a rear-end position.

Miscellaneous Provisions

Bail Bonds: Statutory recognition of AAA arrest bond certificates for traffic infractions. Does not cover driving while intoxicated.

Liability Laws: State has mandatory liability insurance law and has security and future-proof type law applicable in event of accident causing property damage in excess of $700 to 1 person's property or personal injury requiring attention of doctor or causing death.

- No person may operate a motor vehicle subject to registration in the state unless the person is insured under a motor vehicle liability policy with a liability limit of not less than $25,000 because of bodily injury to or death of 1 person in any 1 accident and, subject to that limit for 1 person, a limit of not less than $50,000 because of bodily injury to or death of 2 or more persons in any 1 accident, and a limit of not less than $10,000 because of damage to property of others in any 1 accident.
- Motorists must carry on their person proof of auto insurance or financial responsibility. Law carries a $475 fine for noncompliance and applies to out-of-state motorists with similar proof-of-insurance cards.
- State has non-resident service of process law.

Weigh Stations: Agricultural vehicles and trucks with a GVWR over 10,000 lbs. must stop.

Fees & Taxes

Table 1: Certificate of Ownership and Registration Fees

Service	Fee
Certificate of Ownership	$5.00
Additional Fee for Vehicles Previously Titled in Another State or Country	$15.00
Temporary Permit	$5.00
Annual Registration and License Tab Fees for Passenger Motor Vehicles and Personal Trailers	$30.00
Non-Commercial Passenger Car Trailers of 2,000 lbs. Gross Weight or Less Previously Registered in the State	$4.50 initial $3.25 renewal
Moped Registration	$30.00
Trucks, Buses, and For-Hire Vehicles Between 4,000 and 10,000 lbs. GW	$37.00 - $62.00
Trucks, Buses, and For-Hire Vehicles over 10,000 lbs. GW	contact DOL
Commercial Trailers	$36.00
Additional Annual Fee for Each Truck, Motor Truck, Truck Tractor, Road Tractor, Tractor, Bus, Auto Stage, and For-Hire Vehicle with Seating Capacity of More than 6	$1.00
Additional Annual Fee for Each Auto Stage and For-Hire Vehicle with Seating Capacity of 6 or Less	$15.00
Additional Annual Fee for Each Trailer, Semitrailer, and Pole Trailer	$1.00
Duplicate Certificate of Ownership	$5.00
Duplicate Certificate of License Registration	$1.25
Duplicate Windshield Emblem	$1.00 per pair of tabs
Motorcycle Title Fee	$5.25 + $6.50 emergency medical services fee
Motorcycle Registration Fee	$30.00
Title Transfer Fee	$5.00
Trailer Registration Fee	$30.00

WA

Table 2: Driver's License Fees

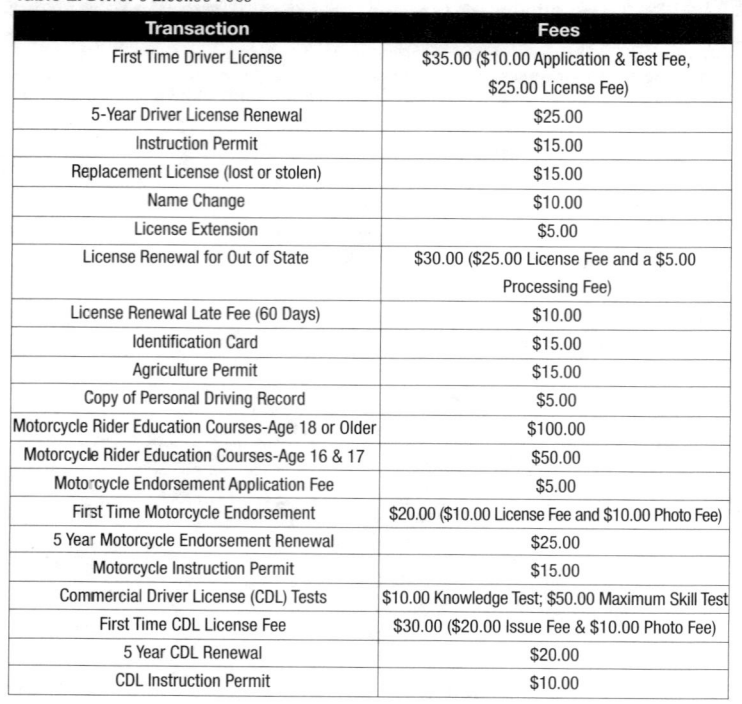

Transaction	Fees
First Time Driver License	$35.00 ($10.00 Application & Test Fee, $25.00 License Fee)
5-Year Driver License Renewal	$25.00
Instruction Permit	$15.00
Replacement License (lost or stolen)	$15.00
Name Change	$10.00
License Extension	$5.00
License Renewal for Out of State	$30.00 ($25.00 License Fee and a $5.00 Processing Fee)
License Renewal Late Fee (60 Days)	$10.00
Identification Card	$15.00
Agriculture Permit	$15.00
Copy of Personal Driving Record	$5.00
Motorcycle Rider Education Courses-Age 18 or Older	$100.00
Motorcycle Rider Education Courses-Age 16 & 17	$50.00
Motorcycle Endorsement Application Fee	$5.00
First Time Motorcycle Endorsement	$20.00 ($10.00 License Fee and $10.00 Photo Fee)
5 Year Motorcycle Endorsement Renewal	$25.00
Motorcycle Instruction Permit	$15.00
Commercial Driver License (CDL) Tests	$10.00 Knowledge Test; $50.00 Maximum Skill Test
First Time CDL License Fee	$30.00 ($20.00 Issue Fee & $10.00 Photo Fee)
5 Year CDL Renewal	$20.00
CDL Instruction Permit	$10.00

Table 3: Vehicle Taxes

Tax	Rate
State Sales Tax	6.5%
Local Sales and Use Tax	not to exceed 1.425%
Gasoline Tax; (Diesel)	$0.375/gallon; ($0.375/gallon)
Personal Property Tax	on mobile homes only

Table 4: Miscellaneous Fees

Service	Fee
Emission Inspection	$15.00
Inspection Prior to Issuance of Certificate of Ownership	$50.00
Medical Services Fee Upon Retail Sale or Lease of Any New or Used Vehicle	$6.50
Late Application for Certificate of Ownership	$25.00 plus $2.00 for each additional day late not to exceed $100.00
Additional Fee for Personalized Plates	$30.00
Renewal of Personalized Plates	$10.00
Specialty Plate Transfer	$5.00
Duplicate License Plates	$3.00 per plate
Duplicate Motorcycle License Plate	$2.00
License Plate Transfer Fee	$10.00

WEST VIRGINIA

Contact Information

Division of Motor Vehicles (DMV)
Building 3, Capitol Complex
1800 Kanawha Boulevard East
Charleston, WV 25317

(304) 558-3900/1-800-642-9066 (in-state)
www.wvdot.com/6_motorists/dmv/6G_dmv.htm

West Virginia State Police
725 Jefferson Road
Charleston, WV 25309-1698

(304) 746-2100
www.wvstatepolice.com

West Virginia Department of Transportation
Building 5
1900 Kanawha Boulevard East
Charleston, WV 25305

(800) 642-9066
www.wvdot.com

Vehicle Title

Application: The application for a certificate of title must be made on a form furnished by the DMV and must contain the following: (1) a full description of the vehicle, which includes a manufacturer's serial identification number, or any other number as determined by the Commissioner, and any distinguishing marks; (2) a statement of the applicant's title and of any liens or encumbrances upon the vehicle; (3) the names and addresses of the holders of the liens; (4) the signature of the applicant; and (5) any other information as required by the DMV.

- A certificate of title or a vehicle registration may not be issued to the owner of a new vehicle purchased outside the state unless the application is accompanied by a certificate of title or a manufacturer's certificate of origin, or, if the state of purchase does not require a certificate of title, the application must be accompanied by a manufacturer's certificate of origin with documentation to prove that the seller is a bona fide dealer of the state where the vehicle was purchased.
- The DMV may issue a temporary permit to operate a vehicle for which the application for registration and certificate of title is pending.
- The certificate of title issued by the Commissioner shall contain, on its face: (1) the date of issuance; (2) the name and address of the owner; (3) a description of the vehicle; (4) a statement of the owner's title and of all the liens and encumbrances of the vehicle; and (5) a seal of the DMV. On the reverse side of a certificate of title, the following information shall be included: (1) the signature of the owner; and (2) forms for the assignment of the title or interest to a vehicle.

Transfer of Ownership: Certificates of title remain valid until the transfer of any interest in the vehicle.

- When the owner of a registered vehicle assigns or transfers the vehicle title, or interest, the registration of the vehicle expires.
- When the owner of a registered vehicle assigns or transfers the vehicle title or interest, the owner must endorse an assignment and warranty of title upon the certificate of title for the vehicle with a statement regarding all liens and encumbrances. Within 60 days of the sale, the owner must deliver the certificate of title to the purchaser or transferee.

- When the transferee of a vehicle is a dealer, the dealer is not required to obtain a new registration of the vehicle until the dealer transfers the title or interest to another. Upon transfer, the dealer must execute and acknowledge an assignment and warranty of title upon the certificate of title, and deliver the title not later than 60 days from the date of sale.
- When the title or interest of a vehicle passes to another other than by a voluntary transfer, the registration expires and the vehicle may not be operated upon the highway unless and until the person entitled to the operation of the vehicle applies for and obtains a registration. The exception to this requirement is that the person in possession of the vehicle or the legal representative may operate the vehicle on the highway for a distance not to exceed 75 miles, or to transport the vehicle to a garage or warehouse for purposes of demonstrating or selling the vehicle.

Mobile Homes: Mobile homes or manufactured homes are exempt from the annual registration, license plates, and fee requirements.

Vehicle Registration

Application: Every owner of a vehicle subject to registration requirements must make an application to the DMV on the forms provided. The application must contain: (1) the signature of the owner or authorized agent; (2) the name, bona fide residence, and mailing address of the owner; (3) the county where the owner resides; (4) a description of the vehicle including the make, model, type of body, the manufacturer's serial or identification number, or any other number, as determined by the DMV; and (5) a statement verifying that the vehicle is insured for the period of the registration.

- A certificate of registration or registration plates may not be issued unless the applicant has received, or at the same time makes an application and is granted, a certificate of title for the vehicle.
- A transferee of a vehicle title or interest may operate the vehicle under the registration of the previous owner for a period of 10 days from transfer. The transferee must at the same time present the endorsed certificate of title to the DMV.
- Unless otherwise specified, every motor vehicle, trailer, semitrailer, pole trailer, and recreational vehicle when driven or moved on the highway is subject to the registration and title requirements.
- House trailers may be registered and licensed.
- Factory-built homes are subject to title requirements.
- Upon registration, the DMV shall issue a registration card to the owner containing the following information: (1) the name and address of the owner; (2) the date of issuance; (3) the registration number assigned to the vehicle; and (4) a description of the vehicle.

Non-Residents: A non-resident owner of a vehicle registered in a foreign state or country may operate the vehicle for a period of 30 days if the vehicle meets the registration requirements of the respective state or country, and the vehicle is not operated for commercial purposes.

- A person attending a college, university, or other educational institution in the state, if the person has a domicile in another state with a valid operator's license and vehicle registration from the state of domicile, and members of the armed forces stationed in the state provided that their vehicles are properly registered in that state or country, are not required to register their vehicle.

- Every non-resident carrying on business within the state and owning and regularly operating in the business a motor vehicle, trailer, semitrailer, or mobile equipment is required to register each vehicle.

Registration Type: Every vehicle registration card and plate expires at midnight on the last day of the month when the registration period ends.
- The expiration dates of registrations is staggered throughout the year.

Emissions Inspection: No motor vehicle may be issued a DMV registration certificate, or the existing registration certificate shall be revoked, unless the motor vehicle has been found to be in compliance with the state emission standards.

Safety Inspection: Every motor vehicle, trailer, semitrailer, and pole trailer registered in the state must be inspected annually and must obtain an official certificate of inspection.

License Plates

Disbursement: The DMV shall issue to the owner 1 registration plate for a motorcycle, trailer, semitrailer, or other motor vehicle upon registration.
- Registration plates must be of a reflective material and display the registration number for the vehicle, the state (which may be abbreviated), and the year when the plate expires.
- The registration plate must be legible from a distance of 150 feet during daylight.
- The registration number for plates shall begin with the number 2.
- Registration plates must be attached to the rear of the vehicle, except for truck tractors and road tractors designed and constructed to pull trailer and semitrailers when plates on the rear would not be visible. In that case, plates must be on the front.
- The registration plate must be securely fastened in a horizontal position and must be at a height of not less than 12 inches from the ground.
- Disabled license plates and placards are available by application to DMV, accompanied by statement of disability from physician or prescribed form.

Transfer of Plates: If the owner of a vehicle has made an application within 60 days from the date of purchase of a vehicle to have the registration plates transferred to another vehicle owned by him or her, then he or she may operate the vehicle for a period of 60 days while application is pending.
- Upon the transfer of a vehicle, the original owner must retain the plates and notify the DMV of the transfer and deliver the certificate of registration. The DMV shall issue a new registration certificate that indicates the use for the plates. The owner may then use the plates on another vehicle as indicated by the registration certificate.
- The owner of a set of registration plates may surrender them to the DMV along with the registration card and receive, upon the payment of fees, a set of plates and a registration card for a vehicle of a different class.

Driver's Licenses

Examination: Upon presenting a valid birth certificate or a certified copy of a birth certificate, the DMV shall examine applicants for a license to operate a motor vehicle.

- The examination shall include a test of the applicant's eyesight (20/40 visual acuity or better); ability to read and understand highway signs regulating, warning, and directing traffic; knowledge of traffic laws; and knowledge of the effects of alcohol on persons operating vehicles.
- The examination shall include an actual demonstration of the ability to exercise ordinary and reasonable control in the operation of a vehicle, and any physical or mental examination as the DMV considers necessary to determine the applicant's fitness to operate a motor vehicle safely.

Graduated Drivers Licensing: State has a system of graduated licensing for teen drivers.

- At 15, teens are eligible for an instruction learner's permit.
- An applicant for permit must pass a vision and written test administered by the DMV.
- A permit allows a person to operate a motor vehicle when accompanied by a licensed driver who is occupying a seat beside the driver. The other driver must be at least 21 years of age, or be a driver education or driving school instructor acting in an official capacity.
- Permit holders under 18 may not drive between 11:00 p.m. and 5:00 a.m. and may not carry more than 2 passengers in addition to the supervisory driver.
- At 16, teens are eligible for an intermediate license.
- To receive an intermediate license, applicants must: (1) pass a road test; (2) have held a permit for 6 months; (3) must not have received infractions for 6 months preceding the date of application for an intermediate license; and (4) must have a 30-hour certifcation form completed and certified by a parent or legal guardian, or a driver education card.
- If a driver with an intermediate license receives 2 or more moving violations, the license will be suspended until the person's 18th birthday.
- Intermediate license holders may drive a vehicle without a supervising adult between 5:00 a.m. and 11:00 p.m. or with a licensed individual over 21 years of age in the front seat at any time.
- Intermediate license holders are prohibited from transporting more than 3 passengers under the age of 19 not including family members.
- At 17, teens are eligible for an unrestricted license. Teens must have an intermediate license and have been infraction-free for 1 year.

Issuance/Application: The application for a license or permit must contain the applicant's: (1) full name, date of birth, sex, and residence address; (2) description; and (3) license history and status.

- Each license issued shall contain the following: (1) a coded number assigned to the licensee; and (2) the full name, date of birth, residence address, description, signature, and color photograph of the licensee.
- The license must indicate the type, general class, or class of vehicles the licensee is authorized to operate.
- Driver's licenses shall be issued in different colors for drivers under the age of 18, those drivers between the ages of 18 and 21, and those adult drivers over 21. Does not include social security number.
- The DMV must not issue a license to a person who holds a valid license to operate a motor vehicle issued by another jurisdiction or state unless the applicant surren-

ders the license, or has submitted an affidavit verifying that the person has surrendered the license to the DMV.
- Within 30 days of taking up residence in the state, a driver must apply to the DMV for a driver's license unless exempt from the requirement.
- A person must present his or her social security card to the DMV when applying for a license or instruction permit.

Renewal: A driver's license is valid for a period of 5 years.
- A renewal license must contain a new photograph of the licensee.
- The DMV shall notify each person who holds a valid driver's license 30 days before the license expires and shall include in the notice a renewal application form.
- A Level 1 Instruction Permit is not renewable.
- An instruction permit is valid for 60 days and may be renewed once for a period of 60 days.
- The driver's license of any person in the armed forces is extended for a period of 6 months from the date the person is out-of-state under honorable circumstances from active duty in the armed forces.

Types of Licenses: A license may authorize the use of the following vehicles as indicated by the respective letters: "A"–Combination Commercial Vehicles over 26,000 lbs.; "B"–Single Commercial Motor Vehicles over 26,000 lbs.; "C"–All other Commercial Vehicles and Buses; "D"–Non-Commercial Vehicles for Hire; "E"––Passenger Vehicles; "F"–Motorcycles Only; and "X"–No Vehicles/Non-Driver.

Traffic Rules

Alcohol Laws: A person who drives a motor vehicle in this state is deemed to have given consent to a preliminary breath analysis and secondary chemical test of blood, breathe, or urine to determine the person's blood alcohol content.
- Open containers are not permitted. Does not meet the requirements of TEA-21.
- Illegal per se BAC level is .08.
- BAC level for people under 21 is .02.
- BAC level for commercial drivers is .04.

Emergency Radio/ Cellular: Citizen band radio channel 9 is not monitored for emergency calls. Emergency cell number is *SP.

Headsets: Wearing radio headsets while driving is permitted.

Occupant Restraints: The operator of a motor vehicle and all front seat passengers over the age of 18 years must wear a seat belt. Passengers 9 until 18 years must be in a seat belt in all seats.
- Violation of the seat belt law is a secondary offense, however violation of the child restraint law is a primary offense.
- An operator of a motor vehicle driven on a highway must ensure that a passenger under age 8 is restrained in a child passenger safety device unless the child is 4' 9" or taller.
- Passengers 8 through 17 must be in a safety belt in all seats.

Railroad Crossing: The driver of a vehicle must stop within 50 feet but not less than 15 feet from the nearest rail of a railroad when: (1) a clearly visible electric or mechanical signal device gives warning of the immediate approach of a railroad train; (2) a crossing gate is lowered or when a human flagman gives or continues to give a signal of the approach of the passage of a railroad train; (3) a railroad train approaching within 1,500 feet of the highway crossing emits a signal audible from such a distance; or (4) an approaching railroad train is plainly visible and is in hazardous proximity to such a crossing.

- It is not permissible to drive a vehicle through, around, or under a crossing gate or barrier at a railroad crossing while a gate or barrier is closed, or is being opened or closed.
- The driver of a motor vehicle carrying passengers for hire, or of any bus, or of any vehicle carrying explosive substances, flammable liquids, or hazardous materials as cargo, or any vehicle owned by an employer which, in carrying out business, is carrying more than 6 employees of the employer must, before crossing at any track or tracks of the railroad, stop the vehicle within 50 feet but not less than 15 feet of the nearest rail. While stopped, the driver shall listen and look in both directions for an approaching train, or signals of an approaching train, and must not proceed until it is safe to do so. The driver must cross the tracks in a gear that does not require changing of the gears, and must not change gears while crossing.

School Buses: The driver of a vehicle meeting or overtaking from either direction any school bus that has stopped for the purpose of receiving or discharging school children, must stop the vehicle before reaching the school bus when the school bus is displaying flashing warning signal lights, and must not proceed until the school bus resumes motion, is signaled by the school bus driver to proceed, or the visual signals are not longer actuated. The driver of a vehicle upon a controlled access highway need not stop upon meeting or passing a school bus that is on a different roadway or adjacent to such highway and where pedestrians are not permitted to cross the roadway.

- Every school bus for the transportation of school children must bear on the front and rear a plainly visible sign that contains the words "school bus" in letters not less than 8 inches in height.
- Every school bus must display lighted headlamps when on the highway.

Vehicle Equipment & Rules

Bumper Height: The front and rear bumper height of motor vehicles with a Gross Vehicle Weight Rating (GVWR) of 10,000 lbs. or less must be not less than 6 inches and not more than 31 inches.

Glass/Window Tinting: A sunscreening device, when used in conjunction with the automotive safety glazing materials on the side wings or windows located to the immediate right and left of the driver shall be of a non-reflective type with a reflectivity of not more than 20% and with a light transmission of not less than 35%.

- The side windows behind the driver and the rear windows may have a sunscreening device that has a light transmission of not less than 35% and a reflectivity of not more than 20%.

Telematics: It is not permissible to operate a motor vehicle equipped with a television receiver unless the receiver is placed so that the screen or picture tube is visible only in the rear and does not fall within the view of the operator of the vehicle.

Windshield Stickers: It is not permissible to drive a motor vehicle with any sign, poster, or other non-transparent material on the front windshield, side wings, or side or rear windows that obstructs the driver's clear view of the highway.

Motorcycles & Mopeds

Equipment: Every motorcycle, motor-driven cycle, and moped must display lighted headlamps at all times when on the highway.

- Every motorcycle, motor-driven cycle, and moped must be equipped with: (1) at least 1 but not more than 1 headlamps; (2) at least 1 brake operated by hand or foot; and (3) a rearview mirror affixed to the handlebars or fairings, and adjusted so that the operator has a clear view of 200 feet.
- The operator or passengers on a motorcycle or motor-driven cycle must wear a protective helmet with a neck or chin-strap; and safety, shatter-resistant eye-glasses, eye goggles, or face shields.
- If any motorcycle, motor-driven cycle, or moped is equipped with a windshield or windscreen, the windshield or windscreen must be constructed of safety, shatter-resistant material.
- It is not permissible to operate a motorcycle, motor-driven cycle, or moped with handlebars or grips that are more than 15 inches higher than the uppermost part of the operator's seat.
- An operator of a motorcycle, motor-driven cycle, or moped may carry as many passengers as the vehicle or sidecar is designed for.

Licenses: A separate motorcycle examination is required to obtain a license that authorizes the operation of a motorcycle, that tests the applicant's knowledge of the operation of a motorcycle, any traffic laws relating to the operation of a motorcycle, and includes an actual demonstration of the ability to drive a motorcycle.

- Upon successful completion of an examination and paying the required fees, the DMV shall include a motorcycle endorsement on the license of the applicant or shall issue a special motorcycle-only license if the applicant does not possess a license.
- Minimum age to operate a moped is 16.

Mopeds: Valid license required. Minimum age is 16.

- Required safety equipment includes: headlamp, taillamp, stop lamp, mirrors, horn, muffler, and brakes.

Passenger Car Trailers

Brakes: Every trailer or semitrailer with a gross weight of 3,000 lbs. or more when operated on a highway must be equipped with brakes adequate to control the vehicle, and designed to be applied by the driver of the towing vehicle. The brakes must be connected in such a way that in the case of an accidental breakaway of the towed vehicle, the brakes apply automatically.

- In any combination of motor-driven vehicles, the means shall be provided for applying the rearmost trailer brakes, of any trailer equipped with brakes, in approximate synchronism with the brakes of the towing vehicle and developing the required braking effort on the rearmost wheels at the fastest rate; means must be provided for applying the braking effort on the rearmost trailer equipped with brakes; or both of the means provided if used in the alternate.

- A motor vehicle or combination of motor-drawn vehicles must be capable of stopping at the following rates as if on a dry, smooth, level free road: (1) vehicles or combinations of vehicles with brakes on all wheels must be able to decelerate at a speed of 14 feet per second; and (2) vehicles or combinations of vehicles not having brakes on all wheels must be able to decelerate at a speed of 10.7 feet per second.

Dimensions: Total length: 75 feet (includes bumpers); trailer length: 40 feet; width: 96 inches (the width may extend to 102 inches on certain roads and excludes mirrors and safety devices); height: 13.6 feet.

Hitch: A drawbar or connection must be of sufficient strength to pull the weight towed and must not exceed 15 feet from one vehicle to another except when transporting poles, pipe, machinery, or other objects of a structural nature that cannot be dismembered.

- When a vehicle is towing another, and the connection consists of a chain, rope, or cable, a white flag or cloth not less than 12 inches square must be displayed.

Lighting: Tail and brake lights are required. License plate lights and reflectors are also required. Turn signals are required where trailer obscures towing vehicle.

Mirrors: When a motor vehicle is constructed or loaded in such a way as to obstruct the driver's view to the rear, mirrors must be equipped on the vehicle to give a view on the rear of at least 200 feet.

Speed Limits: 55 mph, 70 mph where posted.

Miscellaneous Provisions

Bail Bonds: Mandatory recognition of AAA arrest bond certificates up to $500, with specified exceptions.

Liability Laws: Has security-type law applicable in event of accident causing property damage in excess of $500 or personal injury or death.

- The minimum liability coverage is: (1) $20,000 for bodily injury or death to 1 person in 1 accident; (2) $40,000 for bodily injury or death to 2 or more persons in 1 accident; and (3) $10,000 because of injury or destruction of property of others in any 1 accident.
- Compulsory liability insurance is required.
- Proof of coverage is required at all times. Noncompliance could result in fine, jail, and license suspension.
- State has non-resident service of process law and guest suit law.

Weigh Stations: A police officer or motor carrier safety enforcement officer may require that the driver of a vehicle or combination of vehicles stop and submit to a weighing with a portable or stationary weighing device, or to drive to the nearest weighing station if within a distance of 2 miles from where vehicle is stopped.

Fees & Taxes

Table 1: Title & Registration Fees

Type	Amount
Title Fee	$10.00
Registration Fee for Class A Vehicles (and Pickup Trucks Weighing 8,000 lbs. or Less)	$30.00
Registration Fee for Class B Vehicles	$28.00 (For weight of 8,001 lbs. to 16,000 lbs., plus $5.00 for each 1,000 lbs. or fraction thereof that exceeds 8,000 lbs.); $78.50 (For weight of 16,000 lbs. but less than 55,000 lbs., plus $10.00 for each 1,000 lbs. or fraction thereof that exceeds 16,000 lbs.); $737.50 (For weight of 55,000 lbs. or more, plus $15.75 for each 1,000 lbs. or fraction thereof that exceeds 55,000 lbs.)
Registration Fee for Class C Vehicles	$51.00 (Permanent)
Registration Fee for Class G Vehicles	$16.00
Registration Fee for Class H Vehicles	$5.00 (Except for vehicles engaged in interstate transportation of persons)
Registration Fee for Class J Vehicles	$86.50 (Except for ambulances and hearses, which are exempt)
Registration Fee for Class M Vehicles	$18.50
Registration Fee for Class R Vehicles	$39.00 (3 Years)
Registration Fee for Class T Vehicles	$27.00 (3 Years)
Registration Fee for Farm Truck	$31.50 (8,000 - 16,000 lbs.) $61.50 (16,001 - 22,000 lbs.) $91.50 (22,001 - 28,000 lbs.) $116.50 (28,001 - 34,000 lbs.) $161.50 (34,001 - 44,000 lbs.) $206.50 (44,001 - 54,000 lbs.) $251.00 (54,001 - 80,000 lbs.)
Registration Fee for Vehicles (and Pickup Trucks Weighing 8,000 lbs. or Less)	$30

Table 2: Under 21 Driver's License and Identification Cards

Age	Class E & F	Class A, B, C (with 2 years' driving experience)	Class D (with 1 year driving experience)	Class X (Identification Cards Only)
16	$5.00			$12.50
17	$10.50			$10.00
18	$8.50	$26.25	$19.25	$7.50
19	$5.50	$17.50	$13.00	$5.00
20	$3.00	$8.75	$6.75	$2.50

Table 3: License Renewal Fee Table

2nd digit age	License or Identification renewed for:	Class E* Regular Operator's	Class D* Chauffeurs	Class D A,B,C** CDL	Class F Motorcycle Only	Class X Identification Card Only
1 or 6	4 years	$10.50	$25.50	$35.00	$10.50	$10.00
2 or 7	3 years	$8.00	$19.25	$26.25	$8.00	$7.50
3 or 8	7 years	$18.00	$44.25	$61.25	$18.00	$17.50
4 or 9	6 years	$15.50	$38.00	$52.50	$15.50	$15.00
5 or 0	5 years	$13.00	$31.75	$43.75	$13.00	$12.50

*Includes $0.50 voter registration fee
** Fees vary depending on endorsements

Table 4: Vehicle Taxes

Tax	Amount
Consumer Sales and Service Tax	6%
Gasoline Tax; (Diesel)	$0.257/gallon; ($0.257/gallon)
State Privilege Tax	5%

Table 5: Miscellaneous Fees

Type	Amount
Combined Voter Registration and Driver's Licensing Fund	$0.50
Duplicate Decal or Registration Card	$5.00
Duplicate License Plate	$5.50
Highway Litter Control Fund	$1.00
Motorcycle Safety Fee	$6.50
Duplicate License	$5.00
Special Plates Fee	Personalized plates: $15.00 in addition to regular plate fee, $1.00 litter fee and $0.50 insurance and regular registration fee; scenic graphic plates have a 1-time $10.00 fee; wildlife plates 1st-time fee $55.00, each additional year: $45.00.

WISCONSIN

Contact Information

Division of Motor Vehicles
4802 Sheboygan Avenue
P.O. Box 7915
Madison, WI 53707

(608) 264-7184
www.dot.wisconsin.gov/drivers

State Patrol
Hill Farms State Transportation Building
4802 Sheboygan Avenue, Room 551
P.O. Box 7912
Madison, WI 53707-7912

(608) 266-3212
www.dot.wisconsin.gov/statepatrol/index.htm

Department of Transportation (DOT)
4802 Sheboygan Avenue
P.O. Box 7910
Madison, WI 53707-7910

(608) 266-1466
www.dot.wisconsin.gov/

Vehicle Title

Application: A certificate of title must be applied for regardless of whether a vehicle is operated on the highways of Wisconsin, if it is a newly acquired vehicle, or if the owner of a vehicle applies for registration of the vehicle but does not hold a valid title in the owner's name.

- Application is made to the DOT and must include: the name and address of the owner; a description of the vehicle, including make and identification number; the date of purchase of the vehicle; the name and address of the person by which the vehicle was acquired, or the signature of the dealer who sold the vehicle if it is a new vehicle being registered for the first time; and the applicant's social security number.

Transfer of Ownership: The DOT will refuse to issue a certificate of title if the applicant has failed to furnish the mileage disclosure form from the most recent titled owner and of all subsequent non-titled owners.

- The owner of a vehicle that is being transferred must execute an assignment and warranty of title to the transferee at the time of delivery of the vehicle and must mail or deliver the certificate to the transferee.
- The transferee must promptly execute an application for a new certificate of title once the vehicle has been delivered to him or her.
- No transferor may transfer ownership of a motor vehicle without disclosing the vehicle's mileage in writing to the transferee by specifying the odometer reading.
- Mopeds, vehicles that are 10 years old or older, and vehicles with a gross vehicle weight (GVW) rating of more than 16,000 lbs. are exempted from the odometer disclosure requirements.

Mobile Homes: Mobile homes or manufactured homes built on a permanent chassis and designed to be used as a dwelling are exempt from registration.

Vehicle Registration

Application: Application for original and renewal registration is made to DOT, and application forms are available at the county clerk's office.

- Application for original registration must contain the name and birth date of the owner; the name of the town, city, or village in which the owner resides; the owner's business or residential address; and a description of the vehicle, including make, model, color, and identification number.
- An application for registration will not be accepted unless a valid certificate of title has been issued to the applicant.
- At least 30 days prior to expiration of the registration, the DOT must mail a notice of renewal and an application form for renewal to the last known address of the registrant.
- If the applicant for registration is under 18 years old, the application must be accompanied by signed statement from the applicant's parents or person having legal custody which states the applicant has their consent to register the vehicle.
- Whenever a person moves from the address named in the application for registration, or when the person's name changes, the person has 10 days to notify the DOT in writing of the old and new addresses or names.

Non-Residents: Any vehicle registered in another state is exempt from the laws of Wisconsin pertaining to registration if the vehicle carries a license plate indicating it has been registered in another state, the vehicle is owned by a non-resident, and the state in which the vehicle is registered accords similar privileges to Wisconsin residents.

- If a non-resident moves to Wisconsin or sells or leases his vehicle to a Wisconsin resident, the vehicle becomes immediately subject to Wisconsin's registration laws.
- Military personnel on active duty in Wisconsin may maintain out-of-state vehicle registration.

Registration Type: Wisconsin follows a staggered registration system.

- Following the initial registration of a new vehicle by a retail purchaser, a minimum of one model year must elapse before the vehicle is subject to emission inspection once again.
- Registration is usually annual or biennial, but may also be done on a quarterly or consecutive monthly basis for certain vehicles.
- Motorcycles, mopeds, and farm trucks weighing 12,000 lbs. or less are registered only on a biennial basis.

Emissions Inspection: In Kenosha, Milwaukee, Ozaukee, Racine, Sheboygan, Washington, and Waukesha counties, all nonexempt vehicles subject to inspection must have the inspection completed at an inspection station not more than 90 days prior to renewal of annual registration. The emissions inspection is initially required during the 2nd year after the vehicle's model year and every 2 years thereafter.

- If a vehicle is more than 5 model years old at the time of an ownership change, the vehicle must be submitted for inspection within 45 days of an ownership change registration issuance, unless the vehicle passed inspection within 180 days prior to the ownership change registration.

Safety Inspection: All vehicles are subject to inspection by any traffic officer or motor vehicle inspector to ensure the vehicle meets emission requirements and to ensure its equipment is in proper adjustment or repair.

- Required on salvaged vehicles. One time, $80 fee. Compulsory spot check frequently conducted by state and local officers for defective or missing equipment. Inspection is required, but no fee is charged for homemade and reconstructed vehicles.

License Plates

Disbursement: The DOT issues, upon registration, 2 plates for an automobile, motor truck, motor bus, school bus, self-propelled recreational vehicle or dual purpose motor home and one plate for other vehicles.

- When 2 plates are issued, 1 must be attached to the front and the other to the rear of the vehicle. When 1 plate is issued it must be attached to the rear unless issued for a motor truck, truck tractor, or road tractor, in which case it must be attached to the front.
- A decal, indicating the period of registration, is issued by the DOT and must be affixed to the rear plate.
- Special plates are issued for persons with disabilities, veterans, amateur radio station licensees, and various special groups.
- Personalized plates may also be issued upon application.

Transfer of Plates: If a vehicle being transferred is a motorcycle, a motor home, a motor truck, or a dual purpose motor home or dual purpose farm truck with a GVW of not more than 8,000 lbs., the owner must remove the license plates and keep them for use on another vehicle. If the vehicle being transferred is any other type of vehicle, the plates remain with the vehicle.

Driver's Licenses

Examination: Examination includes a knowledge test, including ability to read and understand highway signs, a driving skills demonstration test, and a vision test (20/40 visual acuity required).

Graduated Drivers Licensing: State has a system of graduated licensing for teen drivers. Instruction/learner's permits are issued to persons at least 15 years and 6 months of age who have passed the appropriate knowledge test. During this stage, teens may drive only when supervised by a parent or guardian or a person meeting the requirements of those permitted to travel with the holder of an instruction permit.

- Teens must hold this permit for at least 6 months and accumulate at least 30 hours (10 at night) of parental/guardian supervised driving.
- Permittees may not operate a motor vehicle during the hours of darkness unless accompanied by a licensed person who is 25 years of age or more, has at least 2 years of licensed driving experience and is occupying the front passenger seat, or is a qualified instructor.
- At 16, upon successful completion of the permit stage, teens are eligible for an intermediate license. Intermediate license holders may not drive unsupervised between the hours of midnight and 5:00 a.m. and may not transport more than 1 passenger (family members exempted). The intermediate license stage lasts for 9 months.
- Enrollment in driver education is required for Wisconsin permit applicant younger than 18. Driver education is required for license applicants younger than 18.
- At 19 years teens are eligible for a full unrestricted license.

Issuance/Application: An application for a license must include the full name and address of the applicant, the applicant's date of birth, eye color, hair color, sex, height, weight, race, and social security number.

- If an applicant is under the age of 18, the application must also include documentary proof that the applicant is enrolled in a school program or high school equivalency program, or has graduated from high school or is enrolled in a home-school program. The applicant must also have accumulated at least 30 hours of behind-the-wheel driving experience, including 10 hours of driving during darkness, and the application must be signed by the applicant's parent, step-parent, or adult sponsor.
- A special restricted license may be issued to a person who is at least 14 and physically disabled, or at least 16 years old, and has passed all required examinations. Special restricted licenses are issued only for motor bicycles or mopeds, or specially designed vehicles having a maximum speed of 35 mph. A special restricted license expires 2 years after the date of issuance.
- Non-residents who are at least 16 years of age and hold a valid driver's license from their home jurisdiction need not apply for a Wisconsin driver's license.
- Persons operating a motor home, a vehicle towing a 5th-wheel mobile home, or a single-unit recreational vehicle need not obtain a commercial driver's license if the vehicle is operated and controlled by the person and is transporting only members of the person's family, guests, or their personal property.
- Licenses must be carried at all times while operating a motor vehicle.
- Licenses must include color photograph. Social security number is not required.
- A restricted license may be issued to a person under 18 but at least 14 years of age if the DOT is satisfied that it is necessary to allow the applicant to operate a vehicle, the applicant has appeared in person with his or her parent or guardian with a birth certificate showing the applicant to be at least 14 years of age, and the applicant has passed all necessary examinations. A restricted license is valid until the applicant obtains a regular driver's license or reaches the age of 18 and does not permit operation of any authorized vehicle during the hours of darkness.

Renewal: All original licenses, reinstated licenses, and probationary licenses expire 2 years from the date of the applicant's next birthday. All other licenses and license endorsements expire 8 years after the date of issuance.

- A renewal photograph must also be taken every 8 years.
- The DOT is responsible for mailing an notice of expiration at least 30 days in advance to the licensee's last known address.
- Upon change of address or name, a licensee must apply for a duplicate license within 10 days of the change.
- Any license issued to a person on active military duty does not expire. Active duty military licenses expire 30 days after return to Wisconsin or 90 days after discharge from active duty, whichever is earlier. This extension does not apply to military dependents.

Types of Licenses: Driver's licenses are separated into the following classes:

- Class A: Commercial license permits the operation of any combination of vehicles with a Gross Vehicle Weight (GVW) rating of over 26,000 lbs. if the GVW rating of the vehicle or vehicles being towed is in excess of 10,000 lbs.
- Class B: Commercial license permits the operation of any single vehicle with a GVW rating of over 26,000 lbs. and any such vehicle towing a vehicle or vehicles with an aggregate GVW rating of 10,000 lbs.

- Class C: Commercial license permits the operation of any single vehicle with a GVW rating of 26,000 lbs. or less, including any such vehicle towing a vehicle with a GVW rating of less than 10,000 lbs. if the vehicle is designed to transport more than 16 passengers or the vehicle is transporting hazardous materials.
- Class D: Permits operation of any motor vehicle not included in Class A, B, C, or M.
- Class M: Permits operation of a motorcycle.

Traffic Rules

Alcohol Laws: Wisconsin has implied consent law. Blood, breath, and urine test authorized.
- Open containers are not permitted. Meets TEA-21 requirements.
- Illegal per se BAC level is .08.
- BAC level for people under 21 is .00.
- BAC level for commercial drivers is .04.

Emergency Radio/Cellular: Citizen band radio channel 9 is monitored for emergency calls. Cell phone number is 911.

Headsets: Wearing radio headsets while operating a motor vehicle is permitted. Must be able to hear emergency vehicle sirens.

Occupant Restraints: All drivers and passengers 4 years and older in the front seat are required to be restrained by a safety belt. All passengers 4 years and older in a non-front seat position are required to be restrained by a safety belt in any position equipped with a shoulder belt.
- No person may transport a child under the age of 4 unless the child is properly restrained in a child safety restraint system.
- No person may transport a child who is at least 4 but less than 8 years old unless the child is properly restrained in a child safety restraint system or by a safety belt.
- Violation of the seat belt law is a secondary offense, however violation of the child restraint law is a primary offense.
- No person may transport a child who is at least 4 but less than 16 years unless that child is properly restrained, except in the case of non-front seat positions equipped with a shoulder belt.
- With certain exceptions, it is unlawful to operate a motor truck having a GVW of 10,000 lbs. or less when any child under the age of 16 is in an open cargo area.
- Riding in pickup truck beds is prohibited, except for employees on duty, parades, hunting, and farm operations.

Railroad Crossing: The operator of a vehicle must stop at a railroad crossing when a traffic officer or railroad employee signals stop or when a warning device signals stop.
- A motor bus transporting passengers, school buses, and any vehicle transporting hazardous materials must stop within 50 feet, but not less than 15 feet from the nearest rail of a railroad crossing. Such stop need not be made when a police officer or flagman directs traffic to proceed, or a traffic control signal directs traffic to proceed.

School Buses: Vehicles approaching a school bus from the front or rear that has stopped and is displaying flashing red warning lights, must stop not less than 20 feet from the bus and must remain stopped until the bus resumes motion. This provision does not apply to operators of vehicles proceeding in the opposite direction on a divided highway.

Vehicle Equipment & Rules

Bumper Height: Modification of original vehicle bumper height is permitted 4 inches above or below manufacturer's specs.

Glass/Window Tinting: All glass used for the vent, side, or rear windows must be safety glass. Vent and front side windows may be tinted to a degree that permits 50% of visible light to pass through. Rear windows may be tinted to a degree that permits 35% of visible light to pass through.

Telematics: No person shall drive any vehicle equipped with any device for visually receiving a television broadcast when such device is located at any point forward of the back of the operator's seat, or when such device is visible to the operator of the vehicle.

Towing: No vehicle with a load or fixture which extends more than 4 feet beyond the rear of the bed or body of the vehicle may be operated during the hours of darkness unless a red light or lantern, visible from a distance of 500 feet, is displayed on the extreme rear of the load or fixture. When such vehicle is operated at a time other than during the hours of darkness, a red flag not less than 12 inches square must be displayed on the extreme rear of the load or fixture.

- A motor vehicle may be towed without being equipped with brakes if the GVW of the towed vehicle is not more than 40% of the GVW of the towing vehicle and the towing vehicle has brakes adequate enough to stop the combination of vehicles.
- It is unlawful for a single vehicle to tow more than one vehicle unless the vehicles are being towed by the drive-away method in saddlemount combination and their overall length does not exceed 65 feet.

Windshield Stickers: No sticker, other than a certificate or other sticker issued by order of a government agency, may be placed on the front windshield of any motor vehicle. Permitted stickers may not cover more than 15 square inches of glass surface and must be placed in the lower left-hand corner of the windshield.

Motorcycles & Mopeds

Equipment: Motorcycles must be equipped with footrests or pegs such that any passenger can rest his or her feet when the motorcycle is in motion.

- Every motorcycle must be equipped with at least 1 and not more than 2 headlamps.
- The headlamps on a motorcycle must be in use whenever the motorcycle is in operation.
- A headlamp modulator is permissible, but may not be used during the hours of darkness.
- All motorcycles must be equipped with at least 2 direction signal lamps to the front and 2 direction signal lamps to the rear which must be visible from a distance of 300 feet.
- No person who holds an instruction permit or who is under the age of 18 may operate a motorcycle unless the person is wearing protective headgear, and no person may carry a passenger under 18 years of age unless the passenger is wearing protective headgear.
- No person may operate a motorcycle without wearing a protective face shield attached to headgear, glasses, or goggles.
- It is unlawful to operate a motorcycle if the handgrips are more than 30 inches above the lowest point of the top of the driver's seat.

Licenses: Persons under the age of 18 will not be issued a Class M license unless the person has successfully completed an approved basic rider course.

- Failure of the driving skills test on 2 previous occasions necessitates successful completion of an approved rider course before a license will be issued.
- Motorcycle permits are available and are valid for 6 months. A permit holder may only transport passengers who hold a license endorsed for operation of a motorcycle and have at least 2 years of driving experience and may operate a motorcycle during the hours of darkness only when accompanied by such a passenger who is at least 25 years old.
- The driving skills test may be waived by persons who hold a motorcycle permit and have completed an approved basic driver course.

Noise Limits: No person may operate a motorcycle without a functioning muffler.

Mopeds: Operation of a moped requires possession of a valid operator's license of any class, or a restricted license, or a special restricted license, for persons under 18 years of age but at least 14 years of age.

- It is illegal for any passenger, other than the operator, to ride on a moped.
- A moped instruction permit is available, but holders of such permits may operate a moped only during daylight hours and may not carry any passengers.
- Mopeds are required to observe the lighting requirements imposed on motor vehicles and must have at least 1 and not more than 2 headlamps.

Passenger Car Trailers

Registration: Trailers and camping trailers weighing 3,000 lbs. or less and trailers that are not operated in conjunction with a motor vehicle are exempt from registration.

Brakes: Any trailer, semitrailer, or other towed vehicle with a GVW of 3,000 lbs. or more and manufactured after January 1, 1942, must be equipped with brakes adequate enough to stop the vehicle.

Dimensions: Total length: 60 feet; trailer length: not specified; width: 102 inches (excludes mirrors and safety devices); height: 13.6 feet.

Hitch: The drawbar or other connection between 2 vehicles may not exceed 12 feet in length.

- In addition to the hitch, every towed vehicle must be coupled to the towing vehicle by means of safety chains, leveling bars, or cables. This provision does not apply to a vehicle equipped with a 5th-wheel and kingpin assembly.

Lighting: A mobile home, trailer, or semitrailer must be equipped with at least 1 red taillamp, mounted on the rear that is plainly visible from a distance of 500 feet. If a vehicle was originally equipped with 2 red taillamps, it is unlawful for such vehicle to be operated or towed unless both taillamps are in proper working order.

- All mobile homes, trailers, and semitrailers sold after January 1, 1968 must be equipped with at least 2 direction signal lamps to the front and 2 direction signal lamps to the rear which must be visible from a distance of 300 feet.
- Any trailer having a width at any part of 80 inches must be equipped with 2 amber clearance lamps mounted on the front of the vehicle, 2 red clearance lamps mounted on the rear of the vehicle, and 2 red reflectors mounted on the rear.
- It is unlawful to tow or operate any trailer during the hours of darkness if not equipped with 1 red reflector on each side of the rear of the trailer.

Mirrors: Any vehicle must be equipped with a mirror or mirrors sufficient to reflect to the operator a view of the roadway for a distance of 200 feet to the rear of the vehicle.

Speed Limits: Same as for passenger cars.

Towing: It is unlawful for any person to operate a motor vehicle towing any mobile home or boat on a trailer when any person is in such mobile home or boat.
- It is unlawful for any person to operate a motor vehicle towing a 5th-wheel mobile home when any person under the age of 12 is in the 5th-wheel mobile home, unless that person is accompanied by at least 1 person who is at least 16 years old. It is unlawful to operate a motor vehicle towing a 5th-wheel mobile home while passengers are in the 5th-wheel mobile home unless there is a 2-way communication device capable of providing voice communications between the operator of the motor vehicle and the occupants of the 5th-wheel mobile home.

Miscellaneous Provisions

Bail Bonds: State has mandatory recognition of AAA and other arrest bond certificates up to $200 or $1000 trucking violations with specified exceptions.

Liability Laws: State has security-type law applicable in event of accident causing property damage in excess of $1,000 or personal injury or death.
- Minimum financial responsibility limits: $25,000/$50,000/$10,000. Noncompliance could result in revocation of operating/registration privileges.
- State has non-resident service of process law; it does not have guest suit law.

Weigh Stations: Trucks over 8,000 pounds gross vehicle weight must stop.

Fees & Taxes

Table 1: Title & Registration Fees

Vehicle Type	Title Fee	Registration Fee
Automobiles	$35.00	$55.00
Camping Trailers/Recreational Vehicles over 3,000 lbs. GVW	$35.00	$15.00
Trailers between 3,000 & 12,000 lbs. GVW	$35.00	1/2 the fee prescribed for a motor truck of the same weight
Motorcycles / Mopeds	$35.00	$23.00 - biennial fee
Motor Homes	$35.00	$48.50 - $119.50 depending on GVW
Motor Trucks / Truck Tractors		$48.50 - $1,969.50 depending on GVW plus $18.00 surcharge
Permanent Semitrailer Registration	$35.00	$50.00
County/Municipality Registration Fees		Varies depending upon county/municipality
Late Registration Fee		$10.00
Reinstatement of Revoked Registration		$25.00 - $50.00
Duplicate Registration Certificate		$2.00
Title Transactions Only	$5.00	
Registration Transactions Only		$5.00 ($3.00 if registration renewal)
Title and Registration Transactions	$5.00	
Replacement/Corrected Title	$8.00	
Transfer of Title Fee	$25.00	
Reinstatement of Revoked Title	$25.00	
Duplicate Registration		$2.00

Table 2: License Fees

License Class	Fee
Class D	$18.00 original/$24.00 renewal
Class D Instruction Permit	$25.00
Class M	$12.00 original/$8.00 renewal
Class M Instruction Permit	$22.00
Class A, B, C	$64.00
Endorsements	
Class A, B, or C Endorsement to a Class D license	$64.00
Reinstatement of a Revoked/Suspended License	$50.00
Duplicate License Fee	$4.00
Late Renewal Fee	$5.00
Driving Skills Test Fee	$20.00 commercial/$15.00 any other vehicle

Table 3: Vehicle Taxes

Tax	Rate
Use Tax	5% imposed on sales price of tangible personal property / an additional 0.5% and/or 0.1% may also be levied depending upon the county
Gasoline Tax; (Diesel)	$0.285/gallon; (0.285/gallon) (annually indexed in April to the rate of inflation, $0.03 for petroleum inspection fee)

Table 4: Miscellaneous Fees

Fee	Amount	Payable Upon
Personalized Plates	$15.00 initial and $15.00 each year of renewal (biennial renewal available)	application
Replacement Plates	$2.00 regular plates $5.00 personalized plates $6.00 special plates	proof of loss or destruction
Quarterly Registration Supplement	$5.00	registration
Consecutive Monthly Registration Supplement	$15.00	registration

WYOMING

Contact Information

WYDOT Motor Vehicle Services
5300 Bishop Boulevard
Cheyenne, WY 82009-3340

(307) 777-4714
http://wydotweb.state.wy.us/web/vehicle_services/

WYDOT Driver Services
5300 Bishop Boulevard
Cheyenne, WY 82009-3340

(307) 777-4800
http://wydotweb.state.wy.us/web/driver_services/index.html

Highway Patrol Division

(307) 777-4305
http://whp.state.wy.us/

Wyoming Department of Transportation (WYDOT)
5300 Bishop Boulevard
Cheyenne, WY 82009-3340

http://wydotweb.state.wy.us

Vehicle Title

Application: Applications for certificate of title must contain the name and address of the owner, the vehicle description, certification of applicant's ownership and any liens, and the vehicle's value. Applications for new vehicles must also include the manufacturer's certificate of origin and certification by the dealer that the vehicle was new when sold to the applicant.

- Applications for used vehicles must contain an assignment and warranty of title and an odometer statement.
- In the case of a vehicle registered or titled in another state, the application must include a current statement made by a Wyoming law enforcement officer or licensed Wyoming dealer that the vehicle's VIN is correct. If the vehicle is not in Wyoming at the time of application, an authorized law enforcement officer in that jurisdiction may make the statement.
- The applicant must also present a receipt for payment of sales or use tax.

Transfer of Ownership: The seller or transferor must endorse an assignment of warranty of title on the certificate of title with a statement of all liens and encumbrances. The endorsement must be notarized, and the seller must deliver the certificate of title to the buyer or transferee at the time the vehicle is delivered.

- The transferee must present the certificate of title to a county clerk and apply for a new certificate of title within 45 days.
- The transferee is not required to deliver the certificate of title with the application if he delivers a signed, notarized bill of sale from the transferor with a description of the vehicle, including VIN, the name of the transferor, and a promise from the transferor to deliver a properly executed title free of all liens unless otherwise specified in the bill of sale.
- If the transfer is by operation of law, the transferee must include a verified or certified statement of the transfer of interest with the application.

Mobile Homes: Every owner of a mobile home is required to obtain certificate of title within 30 days of being brought into the state or upon being transferred.

- If a mobile home is installed on a permanent foundation and is taxable as real property, the certificate of title or manufacturer's certificate of origin, if any, must be surrendered to and canceled by the county clerk. However the certificate of title will not be canceled unless all liens on the home have been released.
- An applicant for a duplicate certificate of title for a mobile home must file an affidavit describing the loss along with the application. A duplicate certificate will not be issued until 11 days after the application is filed. The applicant must also deposit an indemnity bond with the state of Wyoming in an amount of not less than double the value of the mobile home.

Vehicle Registration

Application: The application must contain the name and address of the owner, a description of the vehicle including the VIN, the value of the vehicle, the unladen weight if required to compute fees and taxes, the purpose for which the vehicle is used, the color of the vehicle, and any other information WYDOT may require.

- No motor vehicle may be registered without proof that the vehicle is covered by a motor vehicle liability policy in full force and effect.
- The owner must apply for registration upon transfer of ownership within 45 days if transferred and temporary license permits were issued by a licensed dealer, auctioneer, or within 45 days if transferred by an out-of-state dealer.
- For all non-dealer transfers, registration must be applied for within 30 days. Vehicles may be operated by the transferee during this 30-day period when accompanied by a properly executed title for the vehicle transferring interest in the vehicle to the transferee or when accompanied by a notarized bill of sale.
- An owner must apply for registration upon becoming a resident.
- A non-resident owner of a motor vehicle, or any owner upon transfer of ownership or lease, may, as an alternative to registration, obtain not more than 1 temporary registration in a 12-month period authorizing operation of the vehicle on the highways of the state for a period not to exceed 90 days.

Non-Residents: Vehicles owned by a non-resident, validly registered in another state or country, and displaying registration numbers or plates in accordance with the laws of that state or country are not required to be registered in Wyoming if the vehicle is not operated for gain or profit in Wyoming, used for transportation to or from employment in Wyoming, not owned or operated by a person employed in the state, operated primarily by a student enrolled at a licensed post-secondary educational institution, or used for transportation of non-resident seasonally employed agricultural workers.

- An operator of a vehicle operated in the state must apply immediately for registration if the operator of the vehicle is employed in the state; not a daily commuter from another jurisdiction which exempts vehicles of daily commuters from Wyoming from registration; and not a full-time student at a licensed school in the state offering post-secondary education.
- Military personnel on active duty in Wyoming may maintain out-of-state vehicle registration.
- Non-residents vacationing in Wyoming may drive on home state plates for 120 days.

Registration Type: Every owner of a non-commercial vehicle must apply for registration of and license plates for the vehicle annually not later than the last day of the annual registration month if the vehicle is currently registered by that owner in the state.

- "Annual registration month" means: (1) for a vehicle currently registered in this state, the month in which the registration expires; (2) for a newly acquired vehicle, the month of acquisition; and (3) for any other vehicle, the month in which the vehicle was initially required to be registered in the state.

Safety Inspection: No person may drive or move on the highway any vehicle unless the equipment on the vehicle is in good working order and adjustment and unless the vehicle is in such safe mechanical condition as not to endanger the driver or other occupant or any person on the highway.

License Plates

Disbursement: Upon receipt of an approved application and payment of fees the county treasurer will issue to the applicant 1 license plate or validation sticker for motorcycles, and trailers, including house trailers, and 2 license plates or proper validation stickers for any other vehicle.

- License plates must be conspicuously displayed and securely fastened to be plainly visible, secured to prevent swinging, attached in a horizontal position no less than 12 inches from the ground, and maintained free from foreign materials and in a condition to be clearly legible. Motorcycles and trailers must display 1 license plate on the rear of the vehicle, and all other vehicles must display 1 license plate on the front of the vehicle and 1 one license plate on the rear of the vehicle.
- Applications for a specific license plate number must be made to the county treasurer by the last day of the annual registration month.
- License plates and stickers may be delivered by mail if the applicant so desires, but the mailing cost may be required to be paid by the applicant.
- Any person who registers 2 or more vehicles may select 1 currently existing registration month for all of those vehicles.
- License plates are also available for amateur radio operators, antique motor vehicles, disabled veterans, former prisoners of war, Pearl Harbor survivors, National Guard members, and Purple Heart recipients.
- WYDOT will issue a special tamper-resistant removable windshield placard to an applicant submitting a letter from his or her physician stating that the applicant has a disability that is expected to last a minimum of 12 months that limits or impairs the ability to walk. The placard is also available to any person responsible for the transportation of eligible persons. An eligible person may also apply for special license plates.

Transfer of Plates: Unless otherwise provided, upon transfer of ownership of a vehicle the registration of the vehicle expires and the original owner must immediately remove the license plates from the vehicle. Within 30 days (45 days for transfer executed by autioneer) after acquiring another vehicle, the original owner may apply to transfer the license registration number to the new vehicle. The owner must pay the fees based on the amount that would be due on the new vehicle less any credit for the unused portion of the original registration fees.

- If a vehicle held in joint ownership between 2 or more joint owners is transferred to 1 or more of the owners, or by a person to the person's spouse, child, brother, sister, or parent, the same license plates may be kept on the vehicle. The transferee must file an application and pay the proper fee to the county treasurer.
- Upon application and payment of the proper fee, license plates may also be transferred from leased vehicle to a replacement leased vehicle and from a vehicle when sold by the owner to a replacement leased vehicle.

Driver's Licenses

Examination: WYDOT examines every applicant for a driver's license and instruction permit. The examination includes a test of the applicant's eyesight, knowledge, and driving skills.

- WYDOT may waive the knowledge and driving skills test for any person applying for a renewal license.
- Visual acuity of 20/40 or better with or without corrective lenses is required.

Graduated Drivers Licensing: State has a system of graduated licensing for teen drivers.

- At age 15, a teen may apply for a permit and must hold it for at least 10 days and complete 50 hours (10 nighttime) of certified driving.
- At age 16, a teen may apply for an intermediate license and is restricted from transporting more than 1 person under the age of 18 (family is excluded) and from operating a vehicle from 11:00 p.m. to 5:00 a.m.
- A full unrestricted license is issued at age 16 and a half (with driver's education) or age 17 (without driver's education).

Issuance/Application: No person, unless otherwise exempt, may drive, steer, or exercise any degree of physical control of any motor vehicle or a vehicle being towed by a motor vehicle on a highway in the state unless the person has been issued a driver's license for the class and type and applicable endorsements valid for the motor vehicle being driven.

- No person may have more than 1 valid driver's license at any time. A person must surrender to WYDOT all valid driver's licenses in his or her possession before receiving a Wyoming driver's license.
- The following persons are exempt from licensing requirements: (1) a non-resident who has a valid license issued by the licensing authority in his or her possession; (2) a non-resident on active duty in the armed forces of the United States who has a valid license issued by his or her state of residence and the non-resident's spouse or dependent child who has a valid license issued by the person's state of residence; (3) any person on active duty in the armed forces of the United States who has in his or her immediate possession a valid license issued in a foreign country by the armed forces but only for a period of 45 days; and (4) a non-resident full-time student at a licensed institution offering post-secondary education.
- A resident possessing a driver's license issued by a member state of the Driver's License Compact (of which Wyoming is a member) is exempt from the licensing requirement for 1 year.
- Every application for an instruction permit or license must include the full legal name and current mailing address of the applicant; a physical description of the applicant including sex, height and weight; date of birth; a color photograph; the applicant's social security number or other numbers or letters deemed appropriate; the applicant's signature; whether the applicant has previously been licensed as a driver specifying the state or country; and information regarding suspension, revocation, or cancellation of a driver's license.
- If the applicant has not been previously issued a license in Wyoming or another jurisdiction, the applicant must supply a certified copy of the applicant's birth certificate.
- The application of any person under the age of 18 for an instruction permit or driver's license must be signed by a parent or guardian having custody of the appli-

cant. If there is no parent or guardian the application may be signed by the circuit court judge of the applicant's county of residence upon petition to the court and upon a finding that the applicant is sufficiently mature to handle the responsibilities of driving a motor vehicle.
- A licensee has 10 days to notify WYDOT of a change of name or address.
- Social security number on license is optional.

Renewal: Every driver's license will expire on the licensee's birthday in the 4th year following the issuance of the license. Every driver's license is renewable within 120 days before its expiration. An applicant may renew his or her license more than 120 days before its expiration if the applicant states in writing that he or she will not be in the state during the 120 days before the license expires.
- Every person applying for renewal of a driver's license must take and successfully complete an eyesight test.
- The state is prohibited from issuing a license to a person whose physician or optometrist has concluded he or she is not capable of safely operating a motor vehicle.
- The driver's license of any person who had not attained his or her 21st birthday may be renewed within 30 days prior to the date of his or her 21st birthday.
- Resident military personnel and their dependents temporarily out of state may obtain an extension on their license, extending it for 4 years from the date of expiration. The fee is $15. Nonresident military personnel may use home state driver's license.

Types of Licenses: Classes A and B: For vehicles with a gross vehicle weight rating (GVWR) of more than 26,000 lbs. Class S: For drivers operating a school bus.
- Class C: For vehicles with a GVWR of less than 26,000 lbs. excluding motorcycles, designed to transport less than 16 passengers including the driver, and not placarded for the transportation of hazardous materials.
- Class I: Instruction permit.
- Restricted License: WYDOT may issue a restricted Class C or M license to a person who is between the ages of 14 and 16 if the applicant can show "extreme inconvenience" which includes the following: (1) the person must drive to school and the person's residence is more than 5 miles from school; (2) the person has a regular job more than 5 miles from the person's residence; (3) the person must have the license to work in his or her parent's business; or (4) any other circumstance that the highway patrol finds is an extreme inconvenience. The licensee may drive a vehicle only between the hours of 5:00 a.m. and 8:00 p.m.

Traffic Rules

Alcohol Laws: State has implied consent law.
- Open containers are permitted.
- Illegal per se BAC level is .08.
- BAC for people under 21 is .02.

Emergency Radio/Cellular: Citizen band radio channels 9 and 19 are monitored for emergency calls. Emergency cell numbers are #HELP (#4357) and 911.

Headsets: Wearing radio headsets while driving a motor vehicle is permitted.

Occupant Restraints: Each driver and passenger of a motor vehicle operated in the

state must wear a properly adjusted and fastened safety belt.
- Violation of the seat belt law is a secondary offense, however violation of the child restraint law is a primary offense.
- Children under 9 years of age must be secured in a child safety restraint system. The child must be restrained in the rear seat unless the vehicle has only 1 row of seats or if other seats are occupied, then the child may be secured in a child safety restraint system in the front seat. Any child under 9 years who fits properly in a seat belt does not need to use a child restraint.
- Riding in pickup truck beds is permitted.

Railroad Crossing: The driver of a vehicle must stop within 50 feet but not less than 15 feet from the nearest rail of the railroad and must not proceed until he or she can do so safely when: (1) a clearly visible electric or mechanical signal device gives warning of the immediate approach of a train; (2) a crossing gate is lowered or a flagman gives a signal of the approach or passage of a train; and (3) a train is approaching within approximately 1,500 feet of the highway and by reason of its speed or nearness is an immediate hazard.

- No person may drive a vehicle through, around, or under any crossing gate or barrier at a railroad crossing while the gate or barrier is closed or is being opened or closed.

School Buses: The driver of a vehicle upon meeting or overtaking from either direction any stopped school bus must stop before reaching the school bus when the school bus's flashing red lights are in operation. The driver must not proceed until the stopped bus resumes motion or the flashing red lights are no longer in operation.

Vehicle Equipment & Rules

Bumper Height: Modification of original vehicle bumper height is permitted.

Glass/Window Tinting: No person may operate an enclosed motor vehicle that is required to be registered in the state on any public highway, road, or street that has a sunscreening device on the windshield, the front sidewings, and side windows adjacent to the right and left of the driver and windows adjacent to the rear of the driver that do not meet the following requirements: (1) a sunscreening device in the windshield must be non-reflective and may not be red, yellow, or amber in color, and must not extend downward beyond the AS-1 line or more than 5 inches from the top of the windshield, whichever is closer to the top of the windshield; and (2) a sunscreening device used on the sidewings, side windows, and rear windows must be a non-reflective type and have total light transmission of not less than 28%.

- No sunscreening device or tinting film may be applied or affixed to any window of a motor vehicle that has a luminous reflectance of light exceeding 20%.
- If any sunscreen device or tinting film has been added to any windows behind the operator, 1 left and 1 right outside rearview mirror are required.
- Any person with a medical condition requiring tinted windows may obtain a certificate from WYDOT upon WYDOT's receipt of a signed statement from a licensed physician or optometrist.

Telematics: No motor vehicle operated on Wyoming highways may be equipped with television-type receiving equipment located so that the screen is visible from the driver's seat. However, television-type receiving equipment used exclusively for safety or law enforcement purposes and electronic displays used in conjunction with vehicle navigation systems are permitted.

Motorcycles & Mopeds

Equipment: A person operating a motorcycle must ride only upon the permanent and regular seat and must not carry any other person unless the motorcycle is designed to carry more than 1 person.

- Any motorcycle carrying a passenger, other than in a sidecar or enclosed cab, must be equipped with footrests for the passenger.
- Handlebars must not be positioned so that the grips are above the shoulder height of the operator.
- Drivers 18 years or under operating a motorcycle on public streets, highways, or thoroughfares must wear protective headgear.
- Any person operating a motorcycle must have the headlamps activated at all times including daylight hours.
- A motorcycle, motor-driven cycle, or moped must be equipped with at least 1 headlamp, at least 1 taillamp, a white light that illuminates the license plate, at least 1 rear red reflector, and at least 1 stop lamp.

Licenses: Class M licenses are issued for motorcycles. The designation may be added to a license valid for any other class or may be issued as the only class on a license if the applicant is not licensed for any other classification.

Noise Limits: Every vehicle must be equipped, maintained, and operated so as to prevent excessive or unusual noise. Every motor vehicle must at all times be equipped with a muffler or other effective noise suppressing system in good working order and in constant operation. No person may use a muffler cutout, bypass, or similar device.

Mopeds: Any person licensed to drive any class of vehicle may also drive a moped on public streets or highways.

- Mopeds are not required to be registered.

Passenger Car Trailers

Brakes: Every combination of vehicles must have a service braking system that will stop the combination of vehicles within 40 feet from an initial speed of 20 mph on a level, dry, smooth, hard surface.

- Every combination of vehicles must have a parking brake system adequate to hold the combination of vehicles on any grade on which it is operated under all conditions of loading on a surface free from snow, ice, or loose material.

Dimensions: Total length: 65 feet; trailer length: 45 feet; width: 102 inches (excludes safety devices approved by the state); height: 14 feet.

Hitch: Ball hitch mounted on bumper is permitted.

Mirrors: Two mirrors are required, 1 on the left-hand side and 1 on the center of the windshield or the right-hand side. If the mirror on the windshield is obstructed, a right-hand mirror is required. It must be positioned to reflect to the driver a view of the highway to the rear of the trailer.

Speed Limits: Same as for passenger cars.

Towing: No person may occupy a house trailer while it is being towed on a public highway.

Miscellaneous Provisions

Bail Bonds: Discretionary recognition of AAA club arrest bond certificate up to $200.

Liability Laws: State has security-type law applicable in the event of an accident causing property damage in excess of $1,000 or personal injury or death—no judgment minimum. Compulsory automobile insurance. Proof of coverage is required at all times.

- A vehicle owner's policy of liability insurance must insure the person named and, except for persons specifically excluded, any other person, as insured, using any covered motor vehicle with the express or implied permission of the named insured against loss from the liability for damages as follows: $25,000 because of bodily injury to or death of 1 person in any 1 accident and subject to the limit for 1 person; $50,000 because of bodily injury to or death of 2 or more persons in any 1 accident; and $20,000 because of injury to or destruction of property of others in any 1 accident.
- State has non-resident service of process law and guest suit law.

Fees & Taxes

Table 1: Title Fees

Vehicle Type	Title Fee
Original and Duplicate Certificate of Title	$9.00
Duplicate Mobile Home Certificate	$3.00
Motorcycle	$6.00

Table 2: Registration Fees

Vehicle Type	Registration Fee
Passenger Cars	$15.00
House Trailers	$15.00
Motorcycles	$12.00
Other Non-Commercial Vehicles Based on Unladen Weight	
1,000 lbs. or less	$2.00
1,001 to 3,500 lbs.	$15.00
3,501 to 4,500 lbs.	$20.00
4,501 to 5,500 lbs.	$30.00
5,501 to 6,500 lbs.	$40.00
6,501 or more.	$60.00
County Registration	as follows, or $5.00, whichever is greater
Vehicles Less than 1 Year Old	3% of 60% of the factory price
Vehicles 1 to 2 Years Old	3% of 50% of the factory price
Vehicles 2 to 3 Years Old	3% of 40% of the factory price
Vehicles 3 to 4 Years Old	3% of 30% of the factory price
Vehicles 4 to 5 Years Old	3% of 20% of the factory price
Vehicles 6 Years and Older	3% of 15% of the factory price
Duplicate	$4.00

Table 3: License Fees

Duplicate License Plates	$8.00
Duplicate Validation Stickers	$6.00
Personalized License Plates	$30.00
Following Transfer of Ownership between 2 or More Joint Owners, or by an Owner to his Spouse, Child, Brother, Sister, or Parent	$4.00
Antique Motor Vehicles	$10.00
Driver's License	$20.00
Instruction Permit	$20.00
Restricted License	$10.00
Duplicate Driver's License or Renewal	$15.00
Driver's License Extension or Renewal	$15.00
Initial or Renewal of Class M Driver's License Designation	$3.00
Duplicate License	$15.00

Table 4: Vehicle Taxes and Fees

Tax	Rate
Personal Property Tax	none
State Sales Tax	4%
Local Option Sales Tax	2%
State Use Tax	4%
Local Option Use Tax	2%
Gasoline Tax; (Diesel)	$0.14/gallon; ($0.14/gallon)

AMERICAN SAMOA

Contact Information

Office of Motor Carrier Safety Assistance Program, Support Services Bureau
Department of Public Safety (DPS)
Government of American Samoa (684) 633-1111 x27
Pago Pago, American Samoa USA 96799

Commissioner of Public Safety (Commissioner)
Department of Public Safety
Government of American Samoa (684) 633-1111
Pago Pago, American Samoa USA 96799

Department of Administrative Services
Director of Administrative Services (Director)
American Samoa Government (684) 633-4156
Pago Pago, American Samoa 96799 USA

Vehicle Title

Transfer of Ownership: Upon transfer of ownership, seller must endorse and deliver certificate to buyer for surrender to the Office of Motor Vehicles, Office of Traffic Safety (OMV) for recording within 30 working days to avoid penalties.

Vehicle Registration

Application: A person may not operate a motor vehicle on the highway without a valid registration and a vehicle license tag.

- If an owner's registration is suspended, the registration may not be transferred to another until the Director is satisfied that the transfer was conducted in good faith.
- A person whose vehicle license or registration is suspended, or whose vehicle insurance or bond policy has been canceled or terminated, must return the license and registration to the Director.

Non-Resident: Military personnel on active duty in American Samoa must comply with inspection and insurance law of the territory and may maintain registration with home state or register vehicle with government and pay the same license fee.

Registration Type: Staggered depending on first digit of license plate number.

Safety Inspection: A safety inspection is required for the initial registration and annually for all motor vehicles.

License Plates

Disbursement: An application for a motor vehicle license must include: (1) the license fee; (2) a valid inspection certificate; (3) a certificate of insurance coverage; and (4) a motor vehicle registration form.

- Upon submittal of an application for a motor vehicle license, 2 decals shall be given to the applicant that specify the period for which the registration is effective; decals must be placed on the license tags.
- License plates must be displayed on the front and back of vehicles, and must be illuminated by a rear lamp or a separate lamp that projects a white light on the rear tag and that makes it visible from 50 feet.
- Motor vehicle licenses expire annually at the time designated by the Commissioner.
- The Commissioner may allow a 30-day grace period to obtain the vehicle inspection certificate after the expiration of a license.
- Exemptions from the licensing requirement include motor vehicles: (1) owned and operated by the government of American Samoa or the U.S.; (2) with a valid license in any state for a period not exceeding the expiration of the plate or 1 year, whichever comes first; (3) owned by or in the custody of licensed dealers or importers while being transported from the point of entry to the premises of the dealer or importer; and (4) traveling to or from the vehicle inspection station for purposes of obtaining a motor vehicle license.
- A person who is an active member of the U.S. military may operate a motor vehicle with a foreign registration and license plates in a jurisdiction permitting; a person may apply and receive a registration certificate, and license plates from the Commissioner.

Driver's Licenses

Examination: An applicant for an operator's license must pass: (1) the traffic rules and signs examination;(2) the vision test with an acuity of 20/40 corrected; and (3) a road test.

Graduated Drivers Licensing: Territory does not have a system of licensing for teen drivers.

Issuance/Application: A driver's license is required to operate a motor vehicle. Exceptions to this requirement are as follows: (1) individuals over the age of 18 who are non-resident members of the U.S. armed forces on active duty and their families who possess licenses issued by their home state may operate a vehicle; and (2) non-residents who possess a driver's license issued by another jurisdiction may operate a vehicle for a period of 30 days from their arrival in American Samoa.

- A person with a valid driver's license or learner's permit must have it in their immediate possession when operating a motor vehicle on the public highway.
- The age requirement for a private operator's license is 16 years of age if an individual has completed a course in driver's education.
- An applicant for an operator's license must: (1) provide legal proof of age and identification; (2) pass an examination on traffic rules and signs; (3) pass a vision test with a minimum acuity of 20/40 corrected; (4) pass a road test; (5) pay required fees; and (6) if under the age of 18, provide verification of parental or guardian consent and financial responsibility.
- A person who holds a valid license from another jurisdiction, which includes any place other than American Samoa, may be issued an operator's license if the license or appropriate documentation from the other jurisdiction is presented at the OMV.
- For a learner's permit, a person must be 18 years old, or 16 years old if they are enrolled in a driver's education course.
- An applicant for a learner's permit must: (1) provide legal proof of age and identification; (2) pass an examination of traffic rules and signs; (3) pass a vision test with a minimum acuity of 20/40 corrected; (4) pay required fees; and (5) submit a written consent form signed by a parent or guardian verifying financial responsibility.
- An individual with a learner's permit must be in possession of the permit and be accompanied by a competent, licensed driver in the front seat of the vehicle while learning to operate a vehicle.
- If a person is not qualified for a private driver's license, a provisional license may be obtained provided that the person: (1) is 18 years of age or older; (2) passes the driving skills and knowledge examination; and (3) pays the required fees.
- A driver's license must contain the following information: (1) the type or general class of vehicles the licensee is authorized to operate; (2) the distinguishing number assigned to the licensee; (3) the name, birth date, residential address, description, and photograph of licensee; and (4) the licensee's signature.

Renewal: A private driver's license is valid for 3 years from issuance and may be renewed on or before the expiration period; the renewal requirements include the payment of the required fees and the completion of the examinations as required by the Commissioner.

- A provisional driver's license is valid for 2 years; upon expiration, licensee is eligible for a private driver's license.

Types of Licenses: The only 2 types of licenses issued are a provisional driver's license and private driver's license.

Traffic Rules

Alcohol Laws: A person who operates a motor vehicle on the highways is presumed to have given consent to breath, blood, urine, or saliva tests to determine alcohol content in blood. Open containers are not permitted.

- Illegal per se level is .08.
- A person who drives a motor vehicle on the highways under the influence of an intoxicating liquor, any narcotic drug, or any other drug that renders a person incapable of operating a vehicle safely shall be guilty of a misdemeanor.

Barefoot Driving: Barefoot driving is permitted.

Headsets: Wearing of radio headsets while operating a motor vehicle is permitted.

Left Foot Braking: Left foot braking is permitted.

Occupant Restraints: Safety restraints are required for a vehicle operator, and front seat passengers between the ages of 4 and 15, if traveling.

- This violation is considered a primary offense.
- A person operating a motor vehicle must ensure that: (1) a child 2 years of age and under is properly restrained by a child restraint system approved by the U.S. Department of Transportation (DOT); or (2) a child 3 years of age but under 4 is either in a child restraint system approved by the DOT or restrained by a seat belt.
- The penalty for the failure to ensure that a child under the age of 4 is properly restrained is $25 for the first offense, $50 for the second offense, and $75 for the third or further offense; the penalty for the failure to use safety restraints for individuals 4 years of age and older is $25.
- Any child less than 12 years of age must not travel in the bed or back of a truck or pickup truck, unless accompanied by a person 18 years of age or older.

School Buses: Upon meeting or overtaking a school bus that has stopped to receive or discharge children, the driver of a vehicle must stop before reaching the bus when the visual signals are displayed and must not proceed until the lights are turned off, or until the bus proceeds.

- School buses must be equipped with signal lamps that are placed as high and as widely spaced laterally as possible, and that are visible at a distance of 500 feet in normal sunlight.
- School buses must bear on the front and rear a sign that displays "school bus" in letters of not less than 8 inches in height.

Vehicle Equipment & Rules

Bumper Height: Modification of original vehicle bumper height is permitted.

Glass/Window Tinting: Application of after-market vehicle glass darkening material is permitted.

Windshield Stickers: A person may not display any sign, poster, or other non-transparent material upon the front windshield, sidewings, or side or rear windows of a motor vehicle that materially obstructs, obscures, or impairs the driver's clear view.

Motorcycles & Mopeds

Equipment: Motorcycles must be equipped with a lamp on the front to emit a light visible at 500 feet.

- A motorcycle or bicycle with a motor attached must be equipped with one brake that may be operated by hand or foot.

- The operator and passengers of a motorcycle or motor scooter must wear: (1) a safety helmet secured with a chin strap; (2) safety glasses, goggles, or a face shield when the motor cycle or motor scooter is not equipped with windscreens or windshields; and (3) other devices as required by the Commissioner.
- The maximum engine size for a motorcycle is 1,200 cubic centimeters.

Licenses: Valid operator's license required.

Passenger Car Trailers

Brakes: Any combination of motor vehicles, trailers, semitrailers, or other vehicles must be equipped with at least 1 or more brakes upon 1 or more of the vehicles.

Lighting: A vehicle pulled by another must be equipped with 1 or more rear lamps exhibiting a red light at a distance of 500 feet.

Towing: A maximum of 1 boat or general utility trailer may be towed behind passenger or pleasure vehicle.

Miscellaneous Provisions

Accident Reporting: A written report must be made to the DPS within 24 hours of an accident if damage to property is $100 or more, or if injury or death to a person results.

Liability Laws: The minimum required coverage for motor vehicles is: (1) $10,000 for bodily injury or death to 1 person in 1 accident; (2) $20,000 for 2 or more persons in 1 accident; and (3) $10,000 for the destruction of property in 1 accident.

- The minimum required coverage for a vehicle used in the transportation of passengers for hire, including taxicabs, is: (1) $10,000 for the bodily injury or death of 2 or more persons in 1 accident; and (2) $10,000 for destruction of property in any 1 accident.

Parking Restrictions: The stopping of a motor vehicle at a place where it is likely to obstruct traffic or to create a dangerous condition to traffic is permitted.

Weigh Stations: A police officer may require the driver of a vehicle to stop and submit to a vehicle inspection and test if the officer has reason to believe that the vehicle is unsafe, not equipped as required by law, or that the equipment is not in proper adjustment or repair.

Fees & Taxes

Table 1: Motor Vehicle License Fees

Vehicle Type	Fee
Motor Vehicle	$25.00 plus $5.00 per ton of weight
Bicycle	$2.00

Table 2: License Fees

Type of License	Fee
Motor Vehicle Driver's License (valid for 3 years)	$7.00
Learner's Permit (valid for 6 months)	$1.00
Visitor's Motor Vehicle Driver's License	$5.00
Provisional License (Valid for 2 Years)	$5.00

Table 3: Other User Fees

Tax	Rate
Gasoline Tax (Diesel)	Excise Tax is $0.95/gallon ($1.69/gallon)

GUAM

Contact Information

Guam Department of Public Works (PW)
Office of Highway Safety
542 North Marine Drive   (671) 647-5059 or 3229
Tamuning, GU 96910

Guam Police Department (PD and DPS)[1]
Building 233, Central Avenue   (671) 475-8463
Tiyan, GU 96913

Guam Department of Revenue and Taxation (DRT)
Government of Guam
Building 13-1 Mariner Avenue   (671) 475-5000
Barrigada, GU 96913

Vehicle Title

Application: Upon vehicle registration, the DRT shall issue a certificate of ownership to the legal owner, and a registration card to the owner, or both to the owner when there is no legal owner.[2]

- A registration application is required for the issuance of a certificate of ownership.
- A certificate of ownership contains: (1) the name and the address of the owner and legal owner, if applicable; (2) the registration number assigned to the vehicle; and (3) a description of the vehicle.
- The certificate of ownership remains valid until it is suspended, revoked, or canceled by the DRT for cause or upon a transfer of interest.
- A legal owner may transfer a title or interest in a vehicle to another person other than the owner without the consent and without affecting the interest of the owner; upon receipt of certificate of ownership endorsed by the legal owner and transferee of legal ownership, and the registration card, the DRT shall issue a new certifi-

---

[1] P.L. 17-78:1 repealed § 5102 that provided for the Department of Public Safety and reenacted § 5102 that established the Guam Police Department. The references made to the "Director of Public Safety" were changed to the "Chief of Police," and the "Department of Public Safety" were changed to the "Guam Police Department."

[2] An owner is a person with all incidents of ownership including the legal title, whether or not the person lends, rents, or pledges the vehicle. A legal owner is a person holding legal title to a vehicle under a conditional sale contract, the mortgagee of a vehicle, or the renter or lessor of a vehicle to the government under a lease, lease-sale, or rental purchase agreement that grants the possession of the vehicle for a period of 12 months or more.

cate of ownership to the new legal owner and a new registration card to the owner.
- When a transfer of title or interest occurs other than by voluntary transfer, the new owner or legal owner may obtain a transfer of registration upon (1) submittal of application; (2) presentation of last certificate of ownership; (3) registration card issued; and (4) any other information or documents as required by law or by the DRT.

Transfer of Ownership: If a legal owner or owners of a vehicle registered in Guam transfer any interest in a vehicle, the certificate of ownership must contain: (1) the signature of the person transferring the interest; (2) the date of transfer; and (3) the name and the address of the person receiving the interest.

Vehicle Registration

Application: A person may not drive or move an unregistered vehicle on the public highway.
- A motor vehicle driven on the public highways must comply with registration requirements.
- Exemptions to the registration requirement include when: (1) moving or operating a vehicle not registered upon arrival in Guam from the port of entry to the dealer or distributor's place of business, to the owner's residence, or to the place of vehicle registration; (2) moving or operating a vehicle not registered from a dealer or distributor's place of business to a place that alters or supplies essential parts of the vehicle; (3) transporting a vehicle on the highway when no part of the vehicle is in contact with the highway; (4) moving a disabled vehicle for repair purposes; (5) moving or operating a vehicle for purposes of dismantling or wrecking it with the intention of permanently removing the vehicle from the highway; and (6) moving or towing a vehicle that is not registered and is used off the highway or roadway for recreation.
- When the owner of a registered vehicle transfers or assigns title or interest, the registration of vehicle expires.
- The owner of a vehicle may operate it on highways for a period of 10 days after transfer without a registration.
- A dealer who holds a vehicle for resale is not required to register the vehicle.
- If a transfer occurs by operation of law, the registration expires and the vehicle may not be operated on the highways unless the new owner registers the vehicle.
- The DRT may issue a temporary permit to operate a vehicle while a registration application is pending.
- A registration application made to the DRT must contain: (1) the name and the residence or business address of the owner, and the legal owner, if applicable; (2) a description of vehicle; (3) the motor number of the vehicle; (4) the date the vehicle was first sold by the manufacturer or dealer to a consumer; and (5) any other information as reasonably required by the DRT.
- Upon the receipt of an application, the DRT shall refer the vehicle to the DPS for inspection.
- A vehicle inspection by DPS is required prior to the issuance of a vehicle registration.
- A vehicle must be within Guam at the time of the application for original registra-

tion; the exception to this requirement is a new vehicle not within Guam if the application includes: (1) an affidavit signed by both the seller and purchaser with their respective names and addresses; (2) a description of the vehicle; and (3) a statement verifying that the vehicle is purchased for use in Guam and not for resale, that all taxes payable in Guam have been paid, and that the sale and tax payments have been arranged for or secured by the appropriate Guam authorities.

- For vehicles previously registered outside of Guam, the application must contain: (1) a verification of prior registration; (2) the name and the address of the government officer, agency, or authority that registered the vehicle; and (3) other information as reasonably required by the DRT. The applicant must surrender unexpired license plates, seals, certificates, and other evidence of foreign registration. The DRT shall grant full faith and credit to a current valid title certificate from a state or territory where the vehicle was last registered.
- Military personnel on active duty in Guam may maintain home state vehicle registration, but must register with government of Guam.

Registration Type: A vehicle's registration and registration card must be renewed annually.

Emissions Inspection: Investigated by Guam Environmental Protection Agency.

Safety Inspection: Motor vehicles, trailers, semitrailers, and pole or pipe dollies must be inspected by an official inspection station authorized or established by the DRT: (1) upon the original application for registration; (2) annually; and (3) following a collision or accident if extensive repairs are needed.

- A vehicle inspection is conducted to determine whether the vehicle meets both equipment and safety standards.

License Plates

Disbursement: Upon vehicle registration, the DRT shall issue 2 license plates to the owner; one plate is to be displayed on the front of the vehicle and the other on the rear.

- The license plate must display: (1) the registration number; (2) the word "Guam"; and (3) the year of registration.
- At original registration and at annual re-registration, the DRT shall issue suitable plates or devices that indicate the vehicle's registration status.
- The license plate must be illuminated so as to be visible at a distance of 50 feet.
- The DRT may issue special license plates or windshield placards for persons with disabilities.
- License plates must be at a minimum distance of 12 inches from the ground.

Transfer of Plates: Upon the expiration of title or interest in a motor vehicle, the owner must either remove the plates and send them to the DRT, or assign them to another vehicle.

Driver's Licenses

Application: The application for a license or permit must be made to the DRT, and must contain the applicant's: (1) full name, age, sex, and both mailing and residence addresses; (2) height, weight, and eye color; (3) license type; (4) license status history; (5) physical qualifications; (6) confirmation of traffic and signal knowledge; (7) acknowledgement of information by parent or guardian if applicant is under 18 years of age; (8) signature; and (9) certificate verifying completion of driver education course if applicant is under 18 years of age or applying for license for the first time.

- An applicant for a new operator license or instruction permit must: (1) possess a certificate verifying the completion of a driver education course; and (2) meet the age requirements. For a new license or the renewal of an existing license, the applicant must be 18 years of age or older, and for an instruction permit, the applicant must be 16 years of age and have the consent of a parent or guardian.
- A student enrolled in a driver education program offered by a secondary level school and over the age of 15 1/2 years may apply for a student permit. The application must be: (1) signed by the applicant; and (2) accompanied by a consent statement signed by the parent or guardian.
- An applicant for a chauffeur's license must: (1) be 18 years of age or older; and (2) if applying for new license, have a certificate verifying the completion of a driver education course.

Examination: An applicant must: (1) pass a traffic test; (2) demonstrate the ability to operate a vehicle; and (3) pass a hearing and vision examination.

- An applicant may bring an interpreter to translate the commands of a tester during the driving test; the expense of an interpreter must be incurred by the applicant.

Graduated Drivers Licensing: Guam does not have a system of graduated licensing for teen drivers.

Issuance: A license or permit must include the following information: (1) the type of license issued; (2) the identifying number; (3) the name, date of birth, residence address, height, weight, eye color; (4) photograph of licensee; (5) signature of individual; and (6) information concerning restrictive requirements. The chauffeur's license must also include either general or restrictive license status, and for restrictive status licenses, the type of vehicle or vehicle combinations permitted.

- A licensee or permittee must carry their license or permit in their immediate possession when driving a motor vehicle on the public highway.
- A student permit allows a person to operate a motor vehicle during a driver training instruction course, and at the discretion of the instructor. The permit is valid for the period of the course, but for no longer than 1 year after issuance. Student permits must be returned upon the cancellation or completion of the course.
- An instruction permit may be issued to a student 16 years of age or older who has completed a driver education course and has the written consent of a parent or guardian. An alternate provision enables an individual who is 15 and has completed a written driver education course to obtain a permit valid until the individual's 16th birthday, if granted consent by the parent or guardian.
- A person employed by or operating a U.S. vehicle is exempt from the requirement to obtain an operator or chauffeur license.
- A person with a valid operator's or chauffeur's license from a U.S. state, territory, or commonwealth; Japan; the Republic of China (Taiwan); the Republic of Korea; the Republic of the Philippines; or Australia is permitted to operate a vehicle for 30 days from the date of arrival. At the expiration of the 30-day period, an individual must: (1) apply for license; and (2) pass a written test.

- A temporary operator or chauffeur license is valid for a period of 30 days after issuance.
- An instruction permit is valid for a period of 90 days after issuance. An individual with an instruction permit must be accompanied by a licensed operator or chauffeur.

Renewal: An operator or chauffeur license is valid for 3 years after the first anniversary of an applicant's birth date after issuance.

- An operator or chauffeur license may be renewed 90 days prior to the license expiration.

Types of Licenses: The types of licenses issued include an operator license; a chauffeur license; an instruction permit; a student permit; and a temporary license.

Traffic Rules

Alcohol Laws: A person who operates a motor vehicle on the public highways is deemed to have given consent to a blood or breath test for the purpose of determining the presence of alcohol or of a controlled substance. Open containers are not permitted.

- Illegal per se level is .08.
- Lower BAC level for people under 21 is .04.
- It is unlawful for a person under the influence of an alcoholic beverage, a controlled substance, or both to be in physical control of a motor vehicle.

Occupant Restraints: The driver of a car, van, or pickup must secure a child under 2 years of age in a child passenger restraint system that meets federal motor vehicle standards during transit. If a child has outgrown a standard size restraint system, the driver must secure the child with federally approved safety belts or safety harnesses.

- The driver of a car, van, or pickup truck must secure a child 2 years of age or older, but under 12 years of age, with a restraint system that meets federal motor vehicle safety standards, or with federally approved safety belts or safety harnesses.
- Any driver or front seat passenger in a car, van, or pickup truck must wear a properly adjusted and fastened seat belt.

School Buses: Every school bus operating on a public highway must be equipped with signal lamps mounted as high and as laterally spaced as practicable. The lamps must be capable of displaying: (1) 2 alternating red lights to the front; and (2) 2 alternating red lights to the rear. The red lights must be visible at a distance of 500 feet from the front or rear of the vehicle.

- A school bus must display on the front and rear a sign stating "School Bus Stop" in letters not less than 8 inches in height.

Vehicle Equipment & Rules

Bumper Height: Modification of original vehicle bumper height is permitted.

Glass/Window Tinting: A person may not drive a motor vehicle on a public highway with an object or a material, such as tinted glass, that obstructs the visibility through the windshield, or side or rear windows of a vehicle.

Windshield Stickers: Objects such as signs, posters, cards, stickers, or other non-transparent material that exceed 7 inches square must not be placed on the front windshield, sidewings, windwings, side or rear windows. Objects less than 7 inches square may be placed on the windshield on the lower corner farthest from the driver, and on side windows to the rear of the driver provided the driver's view is not obstructed.

Motorcycles & Mopeds

Registration: The owner of a bicycle equipped with a motor must register the bicycle with the DRT and must display the license plate.

- A bicycle with motor must be registered annually.

Equipment: Motorcycles must be equipped with: (1) at least 1 but not more than 2 headlamps; and (2) not more than 1 spot lamp that directs the light at a distance of not greater than 100 feet.

- Every motorcycle operating on a public highway must be equipped with 1 brake that may be operated by hand or foot.
- The operator of a motorcycle is not permitted to carry more than 1 passenger.
- The operator may not carry a passenger on a motorcycle if the motorcycle is not equipped with a seat, footrests, and hand grips for passenger.
- The operator and passenger of a motorcycle must wear a safety helmet when riding on a motorcycle.

Licenses: A person must obtain an operator's license prior to operating a motorcycle on the highway. The exception to this requirement is that a person with a valid motorcycle operator's license issued by a U.S. state or territory, or by a foreign country, may operate a motorcycle for a period of 30 days from date of arrival in Guam.

- A person less than 15 years of age may not operate a bicycle with motor.

Mopeds: Registration is required.

- The minimum age to ride a moped is 15.
- A driver's license is not required.
- Driver must be on extreme right side of the street. Speed not to exceed 35 mph.

Passenger Car Trailers

Registration: With certain exceptions, any semitrailer, pole or pipe dolly, and any dolly used to support the weight of a semitrailer driven on the public highways must comply with registration requirements.

Brakes: A vehicle or combinations of vehicles must be equipped with: (1) brakes capable of stopping the vehicle when traveling at a speed of 20 mph within a distance of 30 feet or at a rate corresponding to this performance on a dry, hard level surface where the grade does not exceed 1 percent; (2) an emergency brake adequate to stop the vehicle at a distance of 55 feet or adequate to hold stationary a vehicle on the grade; and (3) for 2-wheel brake vehicles, a service brake adequate to stop a vehicle at a distance of 40 feet and an emergency brake adequate to stop a vehicle at 55 feet.

Dimensions: Dimension restrictions include vehicle load and loading devices: the width limit is 102 inches; the height limit is 13 feet, 6 inches; and the length limit is 40 feet, with front and rear bumpers.

- A combination of 2 vehicles must not have an overall length in excess of 60 feet; a truck-tractor semitrailer may haul 1 trailer and this combination must not exceed 65 feet.

Hitch: When a vehicle is towing another, the drawbar or connection must not exceed 15 feet from one vehicle to another.

- A chain, rope, or a cable, when used to tow another vehicle, may not be less than 10 feet in length, and a white flag or cloth not less than 12 inches square must be displayed on the connection.

Lighting: Trailers, semitrailers attached to motor vehicles, and vehicles drawn in a combination must carry a rear lamp that emits a light visible at a distance of 500 feet.

- A rear lamp, or a separate lamp, must be placed to illuminate the plate at a distance of 50 feet from the rear under normal atmospheric conditions.

Mirrors: When towing a vehicle impairs the visibility of the driver to the rear, the motor vehicle towing must be equipped with a mirror to reflect a distance of 200 feet to the rear.

Speed Limits: When a vehicle is towing another, the speed limit is 25 mph or the posted speed limit, whichever is less.

Towing: Maximum of 1 boat or general utility trailer may be towed behind passenger or pleasure vehicles.

- Personally operated devices (4-wheel dollies and lift arms) for towing a vehicle behind any vehicle other than a tow truck are permitted.
- Drawbar may not exceed 15 feet.
- Chain, rope, or cable must be between 10 and 15 feet.

Miscellaneous Provisions

Accident Reporting: Accidents involving property damage exceeding $100 must be reported to PD within 24 hours. For accidents involving injuries or death, operators must stop immediately at the scene of the accident.

Liability Laws: The minimum amount of liability insurance required for a motor vehicle is $20,000 for property damage in any 1 accident; $25,000 for each person injured in 1 accident; and $50,000 in aggregate for all persons injured in any 1 accident.

Weigh Stations: Police officer may require driver of a vehicle to stop and submit the vehicle to weighing by portable scales if officer has reason to believe that weight of vehicle, either unladen or with load, is unlawful; if question of weight arises, officer may require vehicle to be driven to the nearest official scales.

Fees & Taxes

Table 1: Annual License & Registration Fees

Vehicle Type	Annual License & Registration Fee
Under 1,000 lbs.	$40.00
1,000 - 1,499 lbs.	$40.00
1,500 - 1,999 lbs.	$40.00
2,000 - 2,499 lbs.	$40.00
2,500 - 2,999 lbs.	$40.00
3,000 - 3,499 lbs.	$40.00
3,500 - 3,999 lbs.	$40.00
4,000 - 4,499 lbs.	$40.00
4,500 - 4,999 lbs.	$40.00
5,000 - 5,499 lbs.	$40.00
5,500 - 5,999 lbs.	$40.00
6,000 - 6,499 lbs.	$40.00
6,500 - 6,999 lbs.	$40.00
7,000 - 7,499 lbs.	$40.00
7,500 - 7,999 lbs.	$40.00
8,000 lbs. and over	$38.00 plus $2.50 for every 500 lbs. or fraction in excess of 7,999[3]
Bicycle Equipped with Motor	$10.00 (initial fee)/$15.00 (annual fee)

Table 2: License Fees

License Class	Fee
A - Operator (new/renewal)	Free
B - Chauffeur (new/renewal)	$5.00
C - Tractor (new/renewal)	$5.00
D - Bus (new/renewal)	$5.00
E - Taxi (new/renewal)	$5.00
F - Motorcycle (new/renewal)	$5.00
G - Minibus (new/renewal)	$5.00
H - Other (new/renewal)	$5.00
Taxi Identification Card (renewal/replacement)	$25.00
Replacement Fee for Licenses: A, B, C, D, E, F & G	$1.00

Table 3: Vehicle Taxes

Tax	Amount
Gasoline Tax (Diesel)	$0.11/gallon ($0.10/gallon)
Vehicle Transfer Tax	$2.00 plus 2% of actual market value of vehicle as determined by the DRT in excess of $100.00

[3] In computing these fees, the model year of the vehicle is taken into account. For 1949 and earlier model vehicles, 50% of the fee is required, for 1950 through 1953 vehicles, 75% of the fee is required; and for 1954 and subsequent year vehicles, 100% of the fee is required.

Table 4: Miscellaneous Fees

Fee	Amount
Abandoned Vehicle and Street Fund (imposed annually on any vehicle subject to registration)	$5.00
Duplicate Certificate of Ownership	$1.00
Duplicate Registration Card	$1.00
Duplicate Equipment Identification Receipt	$1.00
Duplicate License Plate	$1.00
Duplicate Operator and Chauffeur License	$1.00

PUERTO RICO

Contact Information

Driver Services (DS)
Apartado 41243
Minillas Station (787) 294-2424
Santurce, PR 00940

Traffic Division Puerto Rico Police (PD)
Puerto Rico Police
Apartado 70166 (787) 793-1234
San Juan, PR 00936

Transportation & Public Works (TPW)
P.O. Box 41269
Minillas Station (787) 725-7112
Santurce, PR 00940

Vehicle Title

Application: If application is made for new motor vehicle,[1] ownership is established by (1) notarized bill of sale; (2) manufacturer's statement of origin; or (3) other documents, as provided by regulation.

- If application is made for used vehicle, ownership is established by (1) title document, for title system states; (2) registration document, for states not using title system; (3) public auction document; (4) release certificate; (5) bill of sale from insurance company; or (6) other documents, as provided by regulation.
- Vehicle may not be operated on public highway without certificate of title, except for transferring vehicle from one private party to another.
- Prior to issuance of certificate of title, verification of excise tax payment must be presented.

Transfer of Ownership: Transfer requires signature or mark of both vehicle owner and acquirer.

---

[1] A motor vehicle is a self-propelled vehicle and does not include vehicles operated on private property.

- Execution of transfer noted on back of motor vehicle or tow truck license, and on title certificate.
- Transfer must include (1) statement verifying owner's will to transfer and acquirer's acceptance of property; and (2) address of acquirer.
- When motor vehicle distributor or dealer takes used units for purposes of down payment, transfer occurs through the signing of a sworn statement by distributor or dealer, provided owner has stated will to transfer or has transferred by placing signature on back of license and certificate of title. Sworn statement requires (1) date of transfer; (2) name and address of previous owner; (3) means of identification; and (4) detailed description of vehicle.
- Once transfer is executed, it must be filed within 10 days.

Vehicle Registration

Application: For registry of motor vehicle, content information must include (1) vehicle description; (2) name and address of owner; (3) information relating to alienating act or lien; (4) identification information assigned; (5) authorized use verification; and (6) annual license fee payment.

- Provisional registry allows vehicle owner to register car without document of ownership and to operate vehicle on public thoroughfares for a period of 30 days.

Non-Residents: For vehicle owners authorized to operate in U.S. or abroad, but not in Puerto Rico, motor vehicle or trailer license may be issued for private non-commercial use for a period of 120 days within a 12-month period.

Registration Type: Owner of motor vehicle or trailer may not operate vehicle on public highway unless vehicle is registered, except when transferring vehicle from one private party to another.

- For vehicles or trailers registered for the first time, payment of fees is based on staggered system.
- Annual renewal and payment of fees are due on the month vehicle was first registered in the motor vehicle registry system.

Emissions Inspection/Safety Inspection: Vehicles operating on public highways are subject to mechanical inspections at a frequency of not more than once every 6 months, and not less than once in a 1-year time period.

- Part of periodic inspection includes evaluation and diagnosis of emissions control system.
- Inspection is prerequisite for renewal.

License Plates

Disbursement: License plates are issued by TPW only after vehicle is recorded in motor vehicle registry.

- New plates are required when use of vehicle changes and different identification number is required or when individual acquiring vehicle does not possess plates.
- Plates must be displayed with illuminated light at night.

Transfer of Plates: Plates issued to individual for vehicle may be used in the future when another vehicle is acquired.

Driver's Licenses

Examination: Practical examination is required prior to granting of license to show ability to operate vehicle safely.
- Individual applying for learner's permit must take and pass traffic and public safety examination.

Graduated Drivers Licensing: Territory does not have a system of graduated licensing for teen drivers.

Issuance/Application: Driver's license is valid for a period of 6 years.
- For license, operator must be 18 years of age; for learner's permit, operator must be 16 years of age and will be able to get driver's license after passing a road test.
- For license, operator must (1) be mentally and physically able; (2) know how to read and write; and (3) hold learner's permit that, on the day of examination, is not more than 2 years, but not less than 1 month, before the date of issuance.
- A person who is unable to read or write may be issued license if individual (1) passes oral course and examination on highway and traffic safety rules; (2) holds learner's license; and (3) passes practical examination.
- Driver's license must contain: (1) name and descriptive data of operator; (2) identification of license; (3) issuance and expiration date of license; and (4) operator's photograph.
- For driver's license, a new medical certificate is required if more than 2 years have passed since submittal of previous certificate; if applicant exempted from learner's permit requirement, certificate is required.
- For learner's permit, applicant must submit medical certificate verifying his or her physical and mental fitness for license.
- Non-resident who is authorized to drive a motor vehicle in a U.S. state or foreign country with similar laws may operate vehicle for 120 days from date of arrival; but after 120 days, he or she must meet license requirements. Persons exempt from license requirement include members of the U.S. armed forces, the U.S. reserve, and the National Guard of Puerto Rico.
- Learner's license permits an operator over 16 years of age but under 18 to operate automobile under patria potestas[2] for private use. Person with patria potestas over minor is liable for damage or losses resulting from operation of vehicle by minor. Permit valid for 2 years.

Renewal: After expiration of license but before 2 years and 1 month from expiration date, license may be renewed without examination provided fees are paid. After that period a written test is required.

Types of Licenses: Driver's license grants individual authority to operate private motor vehicles, with the exception of heavy motor vehicles, without pay.
- Chauffeur's license authorizes individual to operate motor vehicles, except for heavy motor vehicles, with or without pay.
- Heavy motor vehicle driver's license authorizes individual to operate any motor vehicle, subject to certain statutory provisions.
- Motorcycle driver's license authorizes the operation of motorcycles, motor-driven bicycles, or motor scooters.

[2] The term patria potestas refers to the custody or guardianship over a non-emancipated child.

- Learner's license authorizes individual to drive motor vehicle if accompanied by authorized individual.

Traffic Rules

Alcohol Laws: Person authorized to drive a motor vehicle is deemed to have consented to initial breath tests and to chemical analysis of blood, breath, and any other substance of body except for urine. Open containers are not permitted.
- Illegal per se BAC is .08.
- Person under the influence of intoxicating drinks may not operate motor vehicle; person under the effects of narcotic drugs, marijuana, or depressing or stimulating substances may not operate vehicle when substance makes driver unable to operate vehicle safely.

Barefoot Driving: Barefoot driving is permitted.

Emergency Cellular: The emergency phone number is 911.

Lane Restrictions: Vehicles may not travel or park on exclusive lanes, which are those lanes reserved for the Metropolitan Bus Authority.
- Vehicles may not pass or attempt to pass another vehicle on the acceleration or deceleration lanes, which are respectively those lanes provided to accelerate when coming on, or to decelerate when going out of turnpike.

Left Foot Braking: Left foot braking is permitted.

Occupant Restraints: Any person who drives or rides as a passenger in a motor vehicle, which should be equipped with safety belts, shall be bound to fasten said belt around his or her body while the vehicle is being driven along the public thoroughfares.
- Children under the age of 4 years traveling on public highways must be in protective car seat (exempts handicapped or incapacitated children) or must be using seat belt properly; person operating vehicle is responsible for compliance with provision and subject to penalty for failure to comply.
- For all 1965 and subsequent year motor vehicles, 2 safety belts that adjust over the lap in front seat of vehicle must be installed.
- For all 1968 and subsequent year motor vehicles, safety belts that adjust over the lap must be equipped in all seats that belt is designed for, and with 2 safety belts that adjust over the lap and shoulders in the front seat.
- For all 1971 and subsequent year commercial vehicles, buses, tractors, trailers, or heavy motor vehicles, safety belts that adjust over the lap and shoulders must be installed in front seat.

Railroad Crossing: Driver of vehicle may not stop, stand, or park vehicle at a distance of 15 meters or less of the nearest rail of railroad crossing.

School Buses: In rural zone, driver must stop vehicle when facing or overtaking school bus receiving or discharging children and must not proceed until bus moves or signal is no longer displayed.
- School buses must have at front and rear, a visible signal that states "SCHOOL BUS" in letters not less than 8 inches in height and signal lights installed high and laterally spaced; lights must be able to emanate at a distance of 500 feet on normal sunny days.

- Driver operating on public highway with separate roadway zones need not stop (1) for school bus on different roadway zone, or (2) when bus is stopped on loading or unloading zone that is part of public highway and pedestrian crossing is not allowed.

Vehicle Equipment & Rules

Glass/Window Tinting: Use of unidirectional vision glass prohibited on motor vehicles.
- Application of tints or other material that reduces visibility to less than 35% is prohibited.

Telematics: No television may be located in a motor vehicle in a position so that the driver can watch a televised program.

Windshield Stickers: Objects such as advertisements, cards, pasquinades, decalcomania, signs, or other non-transparent material must not exceed a square of 7 inches by 7 inches, and must be placed on the lower corner farthest from the driver's seat, or on the lateral windows behind the driver so as not to obstruct visibility.

Motorcycles & Mopeds

Equipment: Operators or passengers of motorcycles, motor-driven bicycles, or motor scooters[3] must use helmet while vehicle is moving.
- Driver must use eyeglasses or spectacles, or must install windshield.
- Minimum of 1 but not more than 2 white lamps must be equipped on front.
- One red reflector must be displayed on rear.

Licenses: Motorcycle driver's license authorizes operation of motorcycles, motor-driven bicycles, or motor scooters.

Riding Between Lanes: Motorcycles, motor-driven bicycles, or motor scooters have right to full use of lane and must not drive so as to deprive full use from other vehicles.
- Not permitted to operate motorcycle, motor-driven bicycle, or scooter between traffic lanes, or between adjacent lines or rows of vehicles.

Moped: Registration and valid driver's license are required.
- Minimum age to ride a moped is 16.
- Goggles and a safety helmet are required.

Special Speed Provision: It is not permitted to operate motor scooter a half hour before sunset to a half hour after sunrise at a speed of higher than 35 mph unless scooter is equipped with front light that emits light visible at distance of 300 feet.

Passenger Car Trailers

Registration: For registry of trailers, content information must include (1) identification assigned to trailer; and (2) information relating to owner, liens, and use characteristics.[4]

---

[3] Motor-driven bicycle or scooter includes a scooter or motor scooter, if the engine capacity does not exceed 5 horsepower, and a bicycle with an engine attached.

[4] A trailer, for these purposes, is a vehicle not propelled by motor power and drawn by another vehicle.

Brakes: Trailer brakes must be constructed so as to operate independently of vehicle towing.

Dimensions: Height from ground must not exceed 13 feet, 6 inches; length, including load, must not exceed 40 feet; and width must not exceed 8 feet, 6 inches.

- Overall length of 2 vehicles coupled together may not exceed 75 feet, including load.
- Weight: Overall GVW may not exceed 110,000 lbs.

Hitch/Signals: Vehicle drawbar or connection for towing or pulling another vehicle must not exceed 15 feet in length.

- If towing connection is chain, rope, or cable, it must display red cloth or similar signal that is not less than 12 inches square.

Lighting: Trailer with total width of 80 inches or more must display 2 lights on front and 2 lights on rear, in addition to those required of motor vehicle.

- For platform-type trailers, additional lights must be displayed on permanent structure of vehicle and must indicate width.
- All trailers must display 2 red reflectors in rear, placed as far apart as possible, to indicate width.

Speed Limits: Same as for passenger cars according to the zone, but maximum speed for heavy motor vehicles is 10 mph less than permitted in any zone.

Miscellaneous Provisions

Liability Laws: Upon obtaining or renewing motor vehicle license, must pay premium amount for compulsory liability insurance.

- Initial premium for compulsory liability insurance is $99.00 for private passenger vehicle and $148.00 for commercial vehicle.
- Traditional liability insurance, assuming coverage is equal to or greater than that required by compulsory liability insurance, may be used to meet requirement of compulsory liability insurance.
- Automobile Accident Compensation Administration compensates individuals who suffer bodily injury, sickness, or death as a result of maintenance or operation of motor vehicle; benefits received may be reduced by insurance coverage amounts. Premium for AACA is $35.00.

Parking Restrictions: Stopping, standing, or parking is not permitted on public highway unless (1) it is necessary to avoid traffic conflict; or (2) it is required by law, directive of police officer, or signal.

- In rural zone, it is not permitted to stop, stand, or park vehicle on highway, either attended or unattended, when it is reasonable to place vehicle off the roadway.
- Standing or parking is not permitted on public highway for the purpose of vehicle or merchandise sale, advertisement, demonstration, or rent; or for washing, cleaning, greasing, or repairing vehicle unless in the event of an emergency.

Fees & Taxes

Table 1: Title & Registration Fees

Vehicle Type	Title Fee	Registration Fee
Motor Vehicle	$10.00	$40.00
Trailers of 2 tons or less	$10.00	$25.00
Trailers of more than 2 tons	$10.00	$65.00
Motorcycles	$10.00	$21.00 private / $33 commercial
Mopeds	$10.00	required

Table 2: License Fees

License Class	Fee
Code 1 (Learner's Permit)	$10.00
Code 2 (Motorcycles)	$10.00
Code 3 (Operators)	$10.00
Code 4 (Chauffeur)	$10.00
Code 5 (Heavy Motor Vehicle)	$10.00
Code A (Hazmat)	$10.00

Table 3: Vehicle Taxes

Tax	Rate
Excise Tax	$750 if price of auto <$5,769
	$750+ 13% of excess of price over $5,769 if price of auto is $5,769-$10,000
	$1,300+ 25% of excess of price over $10,000 if price of auto is $10,000-$20,000
	$3,800+ 40% of excess of price over $20,000 if price of auto is $20,000-$42,000
	30% of suggested sale price of auto if price of auto is over $42,000
Gasoline Tax	$0.16 per gallon
Inspection Fee	$11.00 - Inspection either private or by the government

Table 4: Miscellaneous Fees

Fee	Amount	Payable Upon
Plates Transfer Fee	$10.00	transfer

VIRGIN ISLANDS

Contact Information

Office of Highway Safety
Lagoon Street Complex (340) 776-5820
Frederiksted, St. Croix, VI 00840

U.S. Virgin Islands Police Department (PD)
Office of the Police Commissioner (340) 774-2310
8172 Sub Base St. Thomas, VI 00802

Traffic Division
Patrick Sweeney Headquarters
RR-02 Kingshil (340) 778-22111
St. Croix, VI 00850

Bureau of Internal Revenue (BIR)
9601 Estate Thomas (340) 774-5865
Charlotte Amalie, St. Thomas, VI 00802

Vehicle Title

Application: The owner of a vehicle with no certificate of title must make a title application to the PD; exceptions to this requirement include: (1) a vehicle owned by the U.S. government; (2) a vehicle owned by a manufacturer or dealer, and held for resale; (3) a vehicle used by a manufacturer for testing; (4) a vehicle owned by a non-resident, which is not required to be registered; (5) a vehicle moved solely by human or animal power; (6) an implement of husbandry; (7) special mobile equipment; (8) a self-propelled wheelchair or tricycle used by a handicapped person; and (9) a pole trailer.

- The title application must contain: (1) the owner's name, residence, and mailing address; (2) a description of the vehicle; (3) the date of purchase; (4) the name of the person the vehicle is acquired from; (5) the name and the address of any first priority lienholder with the date of the security agreement; (6) the prior title with assignments made to the applicant purchaser, and (7) a statement verifying the mileage and the truck weight, if the vehicle weighs 16,000 lbs. or more.
- If the vehicle is purchased from a dealer, the application must contain: (1) the name and the address of the lienholder; (2) the date of the security agreement; and (3) the signature of the dealer and the owner.
- If the vehicle is previously registered in another state, territory, or country, the title application must contain: (1) the certificate of title issued by the other state, territory, or country; (2) a certificate verifying the vehicle's inspection, description, and proof of identity; and (3) other information and documents as required by the PD to establish the ownership and existence of security interests.
- If the vehicle was last previously registered in another country by a member of the U.S. armed forces on active duty, a form verifying the information issued by the U.S. Department of Defense is sufficient to establish ownership.

- The certificate of title contains: (1) the issuance date; (2) the name, residence, and mailing address of the owner; (3) the name and address of any lienholders; (4) the vehicle title number; (5) the vehicle description; (6) the mileage; (7) a statement verifying that title cancellation must be executed by the PD; and (8) any other information as required by the PD.

Transfer of Ownership: If a dealer buys a car to resell, and obtains a certificate of title within 10 days of delivery, the dealer must execute the assignment and warranty of title at the time of vehicle delivery to the new owner, except if the transfer occurs through a security interest.

- If an owner's interest is terminated or a vehicle is sold through a security interest, the title application must contain: (1) the last certificate of title issued; and (2) an affidavit certifying that the vehicle was repossessed and that the interest was lawfully terminated or sold pursuant to a security agreement.

Vehicle Registration

Application: Motor vehicles may not be operated on public highways unless a registration license has been issued.

- The registration application must be made to the Police Commissioner ("Commissioner").
- Applications must contain either: (1) a copy of the prior registration license, for all vehicles previously registered, or (2) a copy of the certificate issued by the Bureau of Internal Revenue, for vehicles not registered in the Virgin Islands.
- For motor vehicles that entered the Virgin Islands prior to July 1, 1971 and were not registered prior to that date, registration may occur: (1) without the vehicle's license or certificate of title; or (2) with the approval of the Commissioner.
- A certificate of title is required prior to registration.
- A registration license includes the following information: (1) a distinctive or personalized license number assigned by the Commissioner; (2) a brief description of the vehicle; (3) the name, age, and address of the owner; and (4) any other information as deemed necessary by the Commissioner.
- The registration license must be in the possession of vehicle operator or within the vehicle when the vehicle is being operated on public highways.
- If ownership is transferred, the Commissioner must be notified within 24 hours. The cancellation is effective 48 hours after the notice is made to the Commissioner; after the 48-hour time period has passed, the motor vehicle may not be operated unless a registration license and the license plates have been issued. These provisions do not apply to dealers selling vehicles that have not previously been registered.
- Proof of liability insurance and a safety inspection is required prior to the registration of a motor vehicle.

Emissions Inspection: The Commissioner is authorized to regulate the inspection and testing of motor vehicles for purposes of ensuring compliance with emissions standards.

- Motor vehicles must be in compliance with the standards provided in the Clean Air Act.

Safety Inspection: The Commissioner oversees vehicle safety inspections, which are required prior to the issuance of title certificates and registration licenses.

- Motor vehicles must be in compliance with the federal motor vehicle safety requirements.
- Annual inspection required: $5 fee.

License Plates

Disbursement: Motor vehicles, bicycles, and trailers must be equipped with license plates when traveling on public highways.

- License plates are valid for a year and expire on the last business day of the month of the succeeding registration year.
- When deemed appropriate by the Commissioner, a license plate may be issued for an additional number of years and will expire on the last business day of the month displayed by the last digit of the number of the license plate. License plates that are deemed valid for an additional number of years must display a registration sticker or a tag on either the plate or windshield.
- License plates or revalidation stickers are issued in conjunction with vehicle inspections.
- Motor vehicles, motorcycles, mopeds, bicycles, and trailers must display the license plate in a position visible from the rear.
- License plates for vehicles must be illuminated by a taillamp or a separate lamp that makes the plate clearly legible from a distance of 50 feet.

Transfer of Plates: Generally, license plates may not be transferred from one vehicle to another unless the owner complies with the procedural requirements of registration. Dealer's license plates and temporary license plates, and transit and commercial trailer license plates need not comply with the registration requirements imposed for transfers.

Driver's Licenses

Examination: Prior to obtaining an operator's license, an applicant must take an examination testing the applicant's knowledge of vehicle laws and regulations, and an examination testing their competency to operate a vehicle.

- The Commissioner may require proof that the applicant is physically and mentally fit to operate a motor vehicle.
- Applicants must pass a vision and physical examination.
- Upon request, an applicant who speaks Spanish may take the examination in Spanish or may use an interpreter selected by the Commissioner.

Graduated Drivers Licensing: The Virgin Islands do not have a system of graduated licensing for teen drivers.

Issuance/Application: An applicant is required to be at least 18 years of age to be issued an operator's license.

- An applicant's social security number may be requested on the driver's license application.
- Operator's license contains: (1) a distinguishing number; (2) the expiration date; (3) the name, age, and residence of licensee; (4) a brief description and a photograph of the licensee; and (5) a signature.
- Operator's license expires on the operator's birth date on the 3rd calendar year after issuance.

- Licensees must have license in their possession when operating a motor vehicle.
- Upon the request of an applicant, the notice of an anatomical gift may be imprinted on a license.
- Learner's permit authorizes an individual to operate a motor vehicle in areas specified by the Commissioner, if accompanied by a licensed operator.
- For issuance of a learner's permit, an applicant must: (1) be 16 years of age or older; (2) have successfully completed a driver education program; and (3) have the written consent of a parent or guardian verifying the assumption of financial responsibility for any damages resulting from applicant's operation of the vehicle.
- A person who holds a valid operator's license from a state or territory of the U.S. is permitted to operate a motor vehicle for a period of 90 days from date of arrival in the Virgin Islands. After 90 days, the operator must meet license requirements.
- A person who holds a valid operator's license from a foreign country may obtain a temporary permit authorizing the individual to operate a vehicle for a period of 30 days.

Types of Licenses: The types of licenses issued include an operator's private license; an operator's public license; an operator's badge for Automobiles-for-Hire; a learner's permit; a temporary permit for an individual with a license from a U.S. state or territory; and a temporary permit for an individual with a license from a foreign country.

Traffic Rules

Alcohol Laws: A person who drives, operates, or physically controls a motor vehicle is deemed to have consented to blood, breath, or urine tests to determine alcohol or drug content of blood.
- Open containers are permitted.
- It is unlawful to drive, operate, or physically control a motor vehicle with a blood alcohol level of .08 or higher.

Barefoot Driving: Barefoot driving is permitted.

Emergency Radio/Cellular: The emergency cell number is 911.
- Citizen band radio channel 9 is monitored for emergency calls.

Headsets: Wearing radio headsets while operating a motor vehicle is permitted.

Lane Restrictions: When traveling on a two-way highway or a street with 4 or more lanes of moving traffic, the operator of a vehicle must not drive to the right of the center line of the highway or street unless authorized by an official traffic-control device. This provision does not prohibit crossing the center lane to make a right turn into or from an alley, private road, or driveway.
- Right lanes on divided highways are not restricted to passing maneuvers.

Left Foot Braking: Left foot braking is permitted.

Occupant Restraints: Operators and passengers seated in the front must be restrained by a safety belt.
- Children under 5 years of age must use detachable or removable seats that comply with federal motor vehicle safety standards; children between the ages of 3 and 5 may meet this requirement by riding with a seat belt in the rear of the vehicle.

- Riding in the bed of pickup trucks is permitted.
- The fine for noncompliance with restraint requirements may not be less than $25 but not greater than $100.

School Buses: The operator of a motor vehicle must stop the vehicle at a distance of not less than 10 feet from the front of the bus[1] when approaching, or from the rear when overtaking or following the bus when the flashing signals of a bus are displayed.

- A vehicle stopped for a bus must not proceed until the flashing lights are no longer displayed.
- At an intersection, a vehicle may not proceed in the direction of a bus receiving or discharging passengers.
- A vehicle traveling on a highway need not stop upon meeting or passing a bus on a different roadway.
- A school bus, when transporting school children, must display a sign on the front and rear that states "school bus" in 8 inch letters.

Vehicle Equipment & Rules

Bumper Height: On passenger vehicles, the horizontal bumper bar must be between 16-20 inches above the ground level.

- On multipurpose passenger vehicles and light trucks, the horizontal bumper must be between 16-20 inches above the ground level.

Glass/Window Tinting: Approved safety glazing[2] must be used on every windshield, window, or wing of a passenger car or light truck.

- Tinting is not permitted.

Windshield Stickers: Signs, posters, or other non-transparent materials that obstruct, obscure, or impair a driver's clear view of the highway, road, or any intersecting highway or road are not permitted.

- Signs, posters, or other non-transparent materials on the windshield or front side windows of a motor vehicle are not permitted unless officially approved and properly located.
- Non-transparent material that extends more than 3 1/2 inches from the lowest exposed portion of the rear window, rear side windows, or rear wings is not permitted.

Motorcycles & Mopeds

Equipment: Motorcycles[3] must be equipped with: (1) adequate brakes to control the motorcycle at all times; (2) a bell, horn, or other device for signaling; (3) handlebars that are no more than 15 inches higher than the seat or saddle; (4) a muffler to pre-

---

[1] The term bus includes any school bus or bus clearly marked "Senior Citizens" or "Disabled Persons."

[2] As used, approved safety glazing means any sunscreen material that has a total solar reflectance of visible light of not more than 25% as measured on the non-film side and a light transmittance of at least 35% in the visible light range, when tested on 1/8 inch of clear glass.

[3] The term motorcycle means every motor vehicle, inclusive of motor scooters and mopeds, with a seat or saddle for the rider and not having more than 3 wheels.

vent excessive or unusual noises, and excessive fumes or smoke; (5) a fuel tank cap; (6) turn signal lamps; and (6) tires equipped for highway use.

- From half an hour after sunset to half an hour before sunrise, the operator must display a lighted lamp in the front and the rear. When a passenger or truck is attached to the side or the front of the motorcycle, 2 lamps must be displayed with 1 on the front and 1 on the rear; and every motorcycle must be equipped with a red light visible from the rear.
- The operator must wear a protective helmet with a neck or chinstrap, and must be secured to the seat when operating or riding a motorcycle.

Licenses: Licenses may be issued to persons 15 years of age or older to operate motor scooters, motorcycles, mopeds, or motor bicycles that weigh less than 300 lbs. and are powered by a motor of not more than 250 cc.

- The license plate must be displayed.
- Motorcycles must be inspected in August of each calendar year.

Noise Limits: The unnecessary racing of motorcycle engines and the making of unreasonable or unnecessary noise are prohibited.

Mopeds: Driver's license is required. License expires every 5 years on operator's birthday. Minimum age for a license is 15. Helmets are required for operators and passengers.

Passenger Car Trailers

Registration: A trailer may not be operated on the public highway unless: (1) a registration license has been issued and (2) the trailer is equipped with license plates.

- The registration application must be made to the Commissioner.
- A registration license must contain the following information: (1) a distinctive or personalized license number assigned by the Commissioner; (2) a brief description of the vehicle; (3) the name, age, and address of the owner; and (4) other information as deemed necessary by the Commissioner.
- The license plate must be displayed in a position clearly visible from the rear.

Brakes: No special requirements.

Dimensions:

- Total length: 20 feet.
- Trailer length: 8 feet.
- Width: 7 feet.
- Height: 14 feet.

Hitch: Safety chain and towbar required on roadway.

Lighting: Trucks pulling a trailer shall have front lights, and a rear light on the rear of the trailer, which shall clearly show its license number.

- Trucks pulling 2 trailers shall have front and rear lights, and in addition a lighted lantern on the last trailer.
- Trucks and trailers must have 2 reflectors not less than 3 inches in diameter attached to the rear of the vehicle; and a green one in the front and a red one in the back placed as high as the structure will permit.

Mirrors: Right and left rearview mirrors are required.

Speed Limits: Same as for passenger cars.

Miscellaneous Provisions

Accident Reporting: When operating a motor vehicle or bicycle that is involved in an accident causing bodily injury or property damage, the operator must report the accident to the nearest police station.

Bail Bonds: There is no mandatory recognition of AAA arrest bond certificates.

Liability Laws: Territory has compulsory insurance law.
- The minimum required coverage for private passenger vehicles, trucks with a carrying capacity of 3/4 ton or less, and other passenger-carrying vehicles is: (1) $10,000 for the bodily injury of 1 person in 1 accident; (2) $20,000 for the bodily injury of 2 or more persons in 1 accident; and (3) $10,000 for property damage in 1 accident.
- The minimum required coverage for a motorcycle and other 2 or 3-wheeled motorized vehicles is: (1) $10,000 for the bodily injury of 1 person in 1 accident; (2) $20,000 for the bodily injury of 2 or more persons in 1 accident; and (3) $10,000 for property damage in 1 accident.
- The owner of a motor vehicle is required to display a sticker identifying that the vehicle is covered by insurance.
- Has guest suit law. Does not have unsatisfied judgment fund.

Parking Restrictions: If not otherwise controlled by specific law or regulations, parking on highways and roads must be in accordance with parking signs.

Speed Checking Devices and Radar Detectors: Radar is used by law enforcement. Warning signs are not required. Radar detectors are permitted.

Fees & Taxes[4]

Table 1: Title & Registration Fees

Vehicle Type	Title Fee	Registration Fee
Private Use Automobiles (Annual)		
- not exceeding 2,500 lbs.	$27.00	N/A
- from 2,500 to 3,500 lbs.	$27.00	$39.50
- for each additional 100 lbs. or part thereof to exceed 3,500 lbs.	$27.00	$12.00
- for personalized license number (in addition to fees for automobile weight)	$27.00	$27.00
Trucks, Mobil Cranes, Tractors, Pickup Trucks, and Trailers (except for horse or boat trailers) by unladen weight (Annual):		
- Under 3,000 lbs.	$27.00	N/A
- From 3,000 lbs. to 4,000 lbs.	$27.00	$72.00
- For each additional 1,000 lbs. or part thereof	$27.00	$32.00
Horse and Boat Trailers (Annual)	$27.00	$37.00
Bicycles		$5.50
Motorcycles	$27.00	$14.00
Duplicate Certificate of Title		$12.00
Duplicate Registration		$9.00

Table 2: License Fees

License Class	Fee	Driving Test Fees
Operator's Private (3 years)	$17.00	
Operator's Public (3 years)	$27.00	
Learner's Permit	$5.00	
Temporary Permit	$5.00	
Duplicate Operator's License	$7.00	
Road Test		$12.00
Written Exam		$12.00
Medical Forms		$4.00

Table 3: Vehicle Taxes

Tax	Rate
Highway User Tax	$0.11 per pound; the minimum amount for any vehicle is $25.00
Motor Fuel Tax	$0.14 on each gallon of gasoline and diesel fuel

Table 4: Miscellaneous Fees

Tax	Amount
Transfer of Vehicle	$12.00
Expired License Plates (Passenger)	$17.00
Expired License Plate (Cycle)	$3.50
Trailer Plate	$17.00

[4] Applicable taxes to motor vehicles include the highway user tax and the motor fuel tax. Personal property and sales taxes are not applicable in the Virgin Islands.

ALBERTA

Contact Information

Registrar of Motor Vehicle Services and Assistant Deputy Minister
Alberta Government Services
3rd Floor, Brownlee Building
10365 97 Street   (780) 427-0937
Edmonton, AB T5J 3W7

There are over 220 private registry agent locations throughout Alberta that provide motor vehicle related services as well as other registry services. For a listing of registry agents, please visit www3.gov.ab.ca/gs/services/mv.

Vehicle Registration/ Permit

Application: A person may not operate a motor vehicle or trailer on the highway unless a certificate of registration has been issued.

- A temporary registration in the form of an in-transit permit issued by another jurisdiction in Canada permits the operation of a motor vehicle in Alberta if: (1) the operator carries the in-transit permit while operating the vehicle; (2) the operator of the vehicle acts in accordance with the terms and conditions of the in-transit permit; and (3) the owner of the vehicle possesses a valid financial responsibility card (insurance/pink card).
- Prior to obtaining a certificate of registration or permit for a motor vehicle or trailer, the Registrar or license issuer may require that the applicant produce: (1) proof of ownership; (2) a financial responsibility card (insurance/pink card); (3) an inspection certificate, as required; and (4) personal identification.
- Persons under the age of 18 may only be issued a certificate of registration upon satisfying the application requirements: (1) the application is signed by a parent or guardian; or (2) the applicant proves self-supporting ability or proof of marriage.
- The driver, owner, or person with the care and control of a motor vehicle must produce the vehicle registration certificate or permit on demand of any police officer.

Non-Residents: If the owner of a vehicle registered in a jurisdiction outside of Alberta has complied with registration and licensing requirements of the respective jurisdiction, then the vehicle may be operated in Alberta for 90 days in 12 consecutive months or for the period of current vehicle license and registration, whichever is shorter, so long as the owner: (1) displays the license plates assigned to the vehicle; and (2) has a valid financial responsibility card (insurance/pink card).

- If the owner of a vehicle with a maximum gross weight of 3,650 kg or less is a resident of an outside province and has complied with the laws of respective province, then the vehicle is deemed registered for purposes of Alberta law if: (1) the license plates for the current year are displayed on the vehicle; and (2) the vehicle is brought into Alberta temporarily for the sole purpose of towing or for pleasure.
- A resident of the province of Saskatchewan may operate a vehicle in Alberta so long as the vehicle does not travel an area greater than 17 km from the Alberta/Saskatchewan border if the vehicle is registered, licensed in Saskatchewan, and displays the appropriate license plates and has a financial responsibility card (insurance/pink card).

- A person that ordinarily resides in another province, or in a state or country outside Canada, but who moves to and resides in Alberta for a period greater than 3 months to attend a school, university, or college as a full-time student and includes a student who is working as part of an Alberta-based co-op program of study, may operate a vehicle in Alberta if: (1) the vehicle meets the registration requirements of the respective province, state, or country; (2) the operator carries a certificate of registration; (3) license plates are displayed; (4) the vehicle is covered by public liability and property damage insurance as evidenced by a financial responsibility card (insurance/pink card); and (5) the vehicle is registered in the student's name.
- Military personnel on duty in Alberta must register their personal vehicles.

Registration Type: A certificate of registration must be renewed annually and may be reissued before its expiration date.

- Vehicle registration expires on the last day of the expiry month for persons or organizations according to the following. The date is established by associating the first and/or second character of the applicant's last name or the company name. The prefix 'The' in a company name shall be ignored when establishing the expiry date, and the first character after the word 'The' will be used. All numerical named applicants shall be assigned the expiry month of January. January=A, I, J, Ke, U, X, #*; February=M, Q; March=B, Y; April=D, G; May=C, N; June=Cl, H, Sc; July=Av, Be, L, Sz, V, Z; August=E, Gr, R; September=F, Po, T; October=S; November=K, P; December=Me, O, W.
- Registration period shall normally be no longer than eighteen months. Vehicles registered in a passenger class category shall be the only exception, with a 30 month maximum registration period. Commercial plates with an annual fee of more than $500 may qualify for a quarterly registration program.

Transfer of Ownership: When the ownership of a registered vehicle is transferred to another person by an act of the owner or by operation of law, the registration of the vehicle expires and the registered owner must remove the plates from the vehicle and retain.

- When the ownership of a vehicle passes by reason of death, the registration of the vehicle does not expire for that registration year and the following persons may operate the vehicle under the deceased person's registration: (1) spouse of the deceased; (2) a person having proper temporary custody of the vehicle until the grant of probate; and (3) the personal representative of the estate of the deceased.

License Plates

Disbursement: Upon the issuance of a certificate of registration, the Registrar shall issue vehicle license plates in the number and design specified by the Registrar.
- The Registrar may authorize the use of a license plate for more than 1 year if validated by an appropriate tab.
- License plates may be issued prior to the expiration date specified.
- A license plate with a validation tab is valid for so long as the respective certificate of registration is valid.

Transfer of Plates: During the registration year for which license plates are issued, the person may apply to the Registrar to use the plates on another vehicle registered in the same person's name, provided that the application is made within 14 days after acquiring ownership of the vehicle. Persons may display plates on the newly acquired vehicle during the 14-day period.

- When the ownership of a registered vehicle passes by act of the owner or by operation of law, the new owner must return the license plates to the Registrar if the previous registered owner does not remove the license plates.
- When a vehicle is registered to a lessor and lessee, and the lessee ceases to have an interest in the vehicle, the lessor must retain the license plates and may apply within 14 days after having leased the new vehicle to include the name of the new lessee.
- When a dealer takes possession of a motor vehicle to sell it on behalf of the owner, the owner must remove the license plates and retain them, or cancel.

Personalized License Plates: A personalized license plate (also known as vanity plates) can have up to seven characters, either letters or numbers. Personalized plates can be issued for almost every registration class except Dealer, Antique, or Disabled. Alberta Government Services reserves the right to reject requests for personalized plates for any reason, which includes ethnic slurs, religious slurs, or foul language.

Driver's Licenses

An operator's license shall only be issued to an Alberta resident who meets the eligibility requirements as defined in legislation. An interim license valid for 30 days will be issued, followed by a new, highly secure card in the mail. The interim license does not contain an image and may not be used for identification purposes. For additional information on Alberta's new driver license program, please visit www.albertadriverslicence.ca

Examination: An applicant must: (1) complete and pass a knowledge examination for the appropriate class of license required; (2) complete and pass a road examination for the appropriate class of license required.

Graduated Drivers Licensing: Province has a system of graduated licensing for new drivers. The program consists of two stages: learner and probationary. A minimum of three years is necessary to complete both stages; four years is required if the individual applies for a learner's license at 14 years of age.

- Learner's licenses (class 7) are issued to persons 14 years of age or older who pass a vision test and a written knowledge test on the rules of the road. Parental consent is required for persons under 18 years of age.
- Licensees must hold a learner's license (class 7) for at least one year and must be accompanied by a fully licensed (non-GDL probationary) driver who is 18 years of age or older, and who is seated next to the driver.
- Individuals are not permitted to drive from the hours of midnight to 5:00 a.m., have no more passengers than available seat belts, and have a zero alcohol level at all times while operating a motor vehicle. Fewer demerit points are allowed than for fully licensed drivers.
- To obtain a probationary license, the driver must be 16 years of age or older and pass the standard Alberta road test. Licensees must spend a minimum of two years as a probationary driver, have no more passengers than available seat belts, and

have a zero alcohol level at all times while operating a motor vehicle. Fewer demerit points are allowed than for fully licensed drivers. Drivers cannot upgrade to a commercial license while under probation and cannot serve as an accompanying driver to a learner licensee.

- To become a fully licensed driver (class 5), the individual must be suspension free for the last year of the 2-year probationary stage and pass an advanced road test. The minimum age for a full unrestricted license is 18.

Issuance/Application: A person may not operate a motor vehicle unless the person holds a valid operator's license.

- A person holding a valid license or permit issued to that person in a jurisdiction outside of Alberta is exempt from the requirement to obtain a license if the person does not remain in Alberta for more than 90 days in 12 consecutive months.
- A non-resident who: (1) holds an international driver's license issued outside of Canada; and (2) does not remain in Alberta for more than 12 consecutive months is exempt from the requirement to obtain a license.
- For the issuance of an operator's license, the Registrar or license issuer: (1) shall require that the applicant provide personal identification; and (2) shall capture a digital photo and signature image.
- A person applying for a license must pay the appropriate fee.
- A person that applies for or holds a Class 1, 2, or 4 operator's license must submit a medical report with the initial and subsequent renewal applications.
- An operator's license must contain the following information on the licensee: (1) surname and first name; (2) date of birth; (3) signature; (4) photograph; (5) height, weight, eye color, hair color, and sex; (6) operator's license number; (7) class of license; (8) expiration date of license; and (9) mailing address.
- An operator's license may be issued to a person under the age of 18 upon satisfying the application requirements: (1) the application is signed by a parent or guardian; or (2) the applicant proves self-supporting ability or proof of marriage.
- Any person who holds an operator's license or makes an application for an operator's license must disclose to the Registrar any medical condition or disability that may interfere with the safe operation of a motor vehicle.
- Any person 75 years of age or older must provide a medical report upon application and renewal. The Registrar may issue a license under conditions or periods as deemed necessary based on the results of the medical report.
- The members of Her Majesty's forces, or the forces of a country other than Canada who are in Canada under the Status of Forces Agreement (NATO) may operate a privately owned vehicle with a driver's license issued by their home state or country until the expiration of the license.

Renewal: Renewal notices for operator's licenses are generally mailed to drivers six to eight weeks before the expiry date. Renewal application must be done in person at any registry agent office. Only residents of Alberta are eligible to renew. Anyone 75 years or older is required to submit a medical report and have their vision screened. Medical reports are also required for holders of class 1, 2, and 4 licenses and for all licenses with a condition code "C".

Types of Licenses: Class 1 license permits an operator to drive: (1) any motor vehicle, or combination of vehicles, other than a motorcycle; and (2) class 6 type vehicles, for learning only. The minimum learning or licensing age is 18.

- Class 2 license permits an operator to drive: (1) any motor vehicle, or combination of vehicles, that the holder of a Class 3, 4, and 5 operator's license may operate; (2) any bus; and (3) classes 1 and 6 type vehicles, for learner only. The minimum learning or licensing age is 18. Requirements: vision screening; written and road test; medical report; airbrake certificate for vehicle with airbrakes. Vehicle for road test: a bus with a seating capacity exceeding 24, including the operator.
- Class 3 license permits an operator to drive: (1) any motor vehicle, or combination of vehicles that the holder of a class 5 operator's license may operate; (2) a single motor vehicle with three or more axles; (3) a motor vehicle with three or more axles towing a trailer with one or more axles, if the trailer is not equipped with airbrakes; (4) classes 2 and 4 type vehicles without passengers; and (5) all motor vehicles included under class 1, 2, and 6, for learning only. No holder of a class 3 operator's license shall operate a motor vehicle: (1) that has a seating capacity of more than 15, while that vehicle is transporting any person in addition to the operator; and (2) to transport passengers for hire. The minimum learning or licensing age is 18. Requirements: vision screening; written and road test; airbrake certificate if the vehicle is equipped with airbrakes. Vehicle for road test: any single motor vehicle having three or more axles.
- Class 4 license permits an operator to drive: (1) a taxi, ambulance, or bus (including school or kindergarten buses) where seating capacity is not over 24, excluding the operator; (2) all motor vehicles included under class 5; and (3) all motor vehicles included under classes 1, 2, 3, and 6, for learning only. The minimum learning or licensing age is 18. Requirements: vision screening; written test; medical report; road test required if operator does not hold a class 1, 2, or 3 license. Vehicle for road test: any two axle motor vehicle, excluding a motorcycle.
- Class 5 license permits an operator to drive: (1) a two axle single motor vehicle, excluding a motorcycle; (2) a two axle motor vehicle towing a trailer with one or more axles, if the trailer is not equipped with airbrakes; (3) a recreational vehicle or any combination of a recreational vehicle and a trailer, if the trailer has not more than two axles and is not equipped with airbrakes; (4) a moped; and (5) classes 1, 2, 3, 4, and 6 type vehicles, for learning only. No holder of a class 5 operator's license shall operate a motor vehicle: (1) that has a seating capacity of more than 15, while that vehicle is transporting any person in addition to the operator; and (2) to transport for hire. The minimum learning age is 14. The minimum licensing age is 16. Requirements: road test. Vehicle for road test: any two axle motor vehicle, excluding a motorcycle.
- Class 6 license permits an operator to drive: (1) a motorcycle or a moped; and (2) all motor vehicles under class 5, for learning only. The minimum learning or licensing age is 16. Requirements: written test and vision screening, and a road test for applicants with a class 7 or if no license presented. Written test, vision screening, and skill test for applicants with a class 5 or better. Vehicle for road test: motorcycle without sidecar.
- Class 7 license permits an operator to drive: (1) a moped; (2) a motor vehicle referred to in the class 5 category, as a learner only; and (3) a motorcycle, as a learner only, if the operator is at least 16 years of age. The minimum learning or licensing age is 14. Requirements: written test and vision screening.
- Province has a limited occupational hardship license law.

Traffic Rules

Alcohol Laws: Province has implied consent law. The legal drinking age is 18.
- It is a criminal offense to operate a motor vehicle when a person's ability is impaired by alcohol or drugs; or person has an alcohol blood concentration that exceeds 80 mg of alcohol in 100 ml of blood.
- A person with a learner's license may not drive a motor vehicle if there is alcohol in the person's blood.
- It is illegal to transport an open alcoholic beverage container in a vehicle.

Barefoot Driving: Barefoot driving is permitted.

Emergency Radio/Cellular: Citizen band radio channel 9 is monitored for emergency calls.
- Use of cellular telephone while driving is permitted. Emergency number is 911.

Headsets: Wearing radio headsets is permitted.

Left Foot Braking: Left foot braking is permitted.

Occupant Restraints: It is not permissible to operate a vehicle with a child passenger unless: (1) the motor vehicle is equipped with a child seating assembly; (2) the child seating assembly is properly installed; and (3) the child is occupying and properly secured in the child seating assembly.
- In a motor vehicle equipped with a seat belt assembly, the driver and the passengers over 16 years of age must wear the complete seat belt assembly.
- It is not permissible to operate a motor vehicle on the highway with a passenger at least 6 years of age but under 16 years, or a child weighing more than 18 kgs., to occupy a seating position with a seat belt assembly unless the passenger is wearing the complete seat belt assembly.
- A child from birth up to 9 kgs. can be in either a rear-facing infant seat or a rear-facing convertible seat, used and installed according to the manufacturer's instructions.
- A child weighing 9 to 18 kgs. must be in a forward-facing child safety seat and be properly secured by using the vehicle seat belt and the child safety seat tether strap.
- When a child is over 18 kgs., an approved booster seat for the vehicle or the vehicle seat belt may be used.
- It is not permissible to remove, render partly or wholly inoperative, or modify a seat belt assembly in a motor vehicle to reduce its effectiveness.
- A person may ride in the box of a truck: (1) when the nature of the person's occupation requires the person to ride in the box; or (2) when the person is engaged or employed in agricultural, horticultural, or livestock raising operations and riding in the box of the truck is related to one of these operations.

Railroad Crossing: At a railroad crossing when: (1) a clearly visible electrical or mechanical signal device gives warning of a railway train; (2) a crossing gate is lowered or a flagman is giving a signal to indicate the approach or passage of a railway train; (3) a railway train within 500 meters of the crossing is approaching and either sounds an audible signal or is visible; or (4) a railway train is visible and approaching the crossing and by reason of its speed or nearness is an immediate hazard; the driver approaching the crossing must stop the vehicle no closer than 5 meters from the nearest rail of the railway and must not proceed until the train has passed the crossing or has come to a stop.

- It is not permitted to drive through, around, or under a crossing gate or barrier at a railway crossing when the gate or barrier is closed or being opened or closed.
- If a stop sign is erected at a railway crossing, a driver approaching the crossing must stop the vehicle at no closer than 5 meters and no further than 15 meters from the nearest rail of the railway and must not proceed until he can do so safely.
- At a railway crossing not controlled by a traffic control signal, the driver of a vehicle that: (1) is a school bus; (2) is carrying explosive substances as cargo; or (3) is used for inflammable liquids or gas, must stop the vehicle at no closer than 5 meters and no farther than 15 meters from the nearest railway. The driver must remain stopped, listen and look in both directions along the railway for an approaching train and for signals indicating the approach of a train, and must not proceed unless the vehicle can cross safely. In the case of a school bus, the driver before proceeding must open the front door and if practicable to do so with one hand, must open the window immediately to the left.
- When a driver is stopped at a railroad crossing, the driver must cross the tracks in a gear that will not need to be changed while crossing the tracks and must not shift gears while crossing.

A B **School Buses:** When a school bus is displaying alternating flashing amber lights, the operator of a vehicle approaching the bus must: (1) when approaching the bus from the rear, if the school bus is on a highway divided by a median into two separate roadways, or (2) when approaching the school bus from the front or rear, if the school bus is on a highway not divided by a median in two separate roadways, reduce the speed so if the vehicle passes the school bus it does so in a cautious manner.

- When a school bus is displaying alternating flashing red lights, the operator of a vehicle approaching the bus must: (1) when approaching the bus from the rear, if the school bus is on a highway divided by a median into 2 separate roadways, or (2) when approaching the school bus from the front or rear, if the bus is on a highway that is not divided by a median into 2 separate roadways, stop the vehicle before it reaches the bus. The operator must not pass the bus until the operator of the bus indicates by signal that the vehicle may proceed or the alternating flashing red lights stop flashing.

Vehicle Equipment & Rules

Bumper Height: A bumper may not be installed or altered on a passenger car unless the bumper is mounted in substantially the same manner as by the manufacturer.

- The passenger car bumper may not be altered so that the main structural component of the bumper is not more than 50 cm or less than 40 cm above the ground. This provision does not apply to passenger cars manufactured before April 1, 1976. However, no person may alter a bumper so that it is more than 10 cm higher or lower than it was when the car was manufactured.

Glass/Window Tinting: It is not permitted to place or install on a motor vehicle a transparent, translucent, or opaque material on or in place of a windshield glazing or side window glazing that is beside or forward of the driver on the right- and left-hand side of the motor vehicle.

- It is not permitted to place or install in a motor vehicle a transparent, translucent,

or opaque material on or in place of a rear window glazing unless the motor vehicle is equipped with rearview mirrors on the right and left of the motor vehicle.
- Glazing installed by the manufacturer of the motor vehicle, clear untinted frost shields, and window stickers that do not impair the operator's field of vision are permitted.
- It is not permissible to place or install any material on or in place of any window glazing that casts a glare on other vehicles on the highway.

Telematics: It is permissible to drive on a highway any motor vehicle that is equipped with a television/video entertainment set, provided the driver cannot see the screen while the vehicle is moving.

Motorcycles & Mopeds

Equipment: Every headlamp of a moped must have a single beam light that when illuminated reveals persons and vehicles at a distance of 60 meters.
- Every motorcycle, moped, or power bicycle must be equipped with at least 1 but not more than 2 headlamps; 1 taillamp mounted at the rear of the vehicle; and at least 1 stop lamp mounted on the rear of the vehicle.
- Stop lamps on every motorcycle, moped, or power bicycle must be permanently mounted on the rigid part of the vehicle, and the distance between the ground and the center of the lamp must not be less than 38 cm or more than 185 cm. Lamps must be located on the vertical center line unless more than 1 stop lamp is used. If more than 1 stop lamp is used, they must be symmetrically disposed about the vertical center line. These provisions do not apply to vehicles manufactured before January 1, 1971.
- Every motorcycle, moped, and power bicycle must not travel on the highway unless each wheel is equipped with an adequate service brake.
- Service brakes on a moped or power bicycle must be capable of bringing the vehicle to a standstill within 12 meters on a level surface consisting of dry paving of asphalt or concrete free of loose materials at a speed of 30 km/h.
- Operators and passengers on a motorcycle, moped, or bicycle must wear a safety helmet.
- Every motorcycle, moped, or power bicycle must be equipped with a horn or bell to warn persons on or approaching the highway in the immediate vicinity.

Licenses: Driver's license required; minimum age 16; Class 6; valid for 5 years; expires on operator's birth date.
- License plates required; the duration and expiration are the same as regular motor vehicle registration.

Mopeds: Any class license – must be at least 14. Required equipment includes: headlight while in operation, brake lights, turn signals, taillight, rearview mirror, safety helmet, and side and rear reflex reflectors.

Passenger Car Trailers

Registration: A person may not operate a trailer on the highway unless there is an existing certificate of registration.

Brakes: Private trailers weighing more than 910 kg (2,000 lbs.) and more than half of the actual weight of the towing vehicle, need to be equipped with a braking device that can stop and control the trailer.

- No breakaway device required.

Dimensions: Total length: 20 meters; trailer length: none; width: 2.6 meters, mobile living accommodations 3.05 meters; height: 4.0 meters.

Hitch: Two separate means of attachment (i.e., tow bar and safety chains) are required so that the failure of 1 will not affect the other.

Mirrors: Side view mirror (2) required on towing vehicle where rearview obstructed by trailer.

Speed Limits: 100 km/h or as posted.

Towing: Riding in a holiday trailer, fifth-wheel trailer, or truck box, with or without a canopy, is not permitted. Riding in a camper is permitted.

Miscellaneous Provisions

Border Inspections: American visitors crossing the border, either way, may be asked to verify their citizenship with a passport or birth certificate. Naturalized U.S. citizens should carry a naturalization certificate, and permanent U.S. residents who are not citizens should carry their Alien Registration Receipt Card.

- Children under 18 years of age should have their birth certificate, and if the parents are separated or divorced, the parent crossing the border should have proof of custody or a letter from the other parent. Persons under 18 years of age who are not accompanied by a parent should bring a letter from their parent or guardian giving them permission to cross the border.
- A visitor is permitted to bring a reasonable amount of personal effects, a reasonable supply of food, and a full tank of gas. Reasonable means enough for personal use during the length of stay in Canada. Any unreasonable amounts are subject to duty.
- A visitor must have a rabies vaccination certificate signed by a licensed veterinarian to bring dogs or cats into Canada.

Liability Laws: Contracts evidenced by the motor vehicle liability policy insure, to a limit of not less than C$200,000 exclusive of interests and costs, against liability resulting from bodily injury to or the death of 1 or more persons, and loss of or damage to property.

- Insurance is compulsory for residents. Proof is required at all times.
- Province does not have non-resident service of process law. Province has guest suit law.

Weigh Stations: Peace officer may require the operator of a motor vehicle to submit the vehicle together with its equipment and trailer, if any, to examination and tests to determine that the equipment and trailer are fit and safe for operation.

Fees & Taxes

Table 1: Registration Fees (Canadian Dollars)*

Vehicle Type	Fee Amount
Antique Motor Vehicle	$37.49
Dealer Plates (12 Months)	$157.49
Duplicate Registration Certificate	$20.49
Motorcycles, Scooters, and Mopeds (12 Months)	$43.49
Private Passenger Vehicles (12 Months)	$68.49
Trailer Used in Conjunction with Licensed Motor Vehicle	$107.49
Vehicle Owned and Operated by Charitable Organization (12 Months)	$33.49

Table 2: License Fees (Canadian Dollars)*

License Type	Fee Amount
First Application of Operator's License	$62.49 for 5 years
Renewal Application of Operator's License	$62.49 for 5 years
Duplicate Operator's License	$20.49
Refund for Unexpired Portion of License	Pro-rated

Table 3: Vehicle Taxes (Canadian Dollars)

Tax	Amount
Federal Goods and Services Tax	7%
Provincial Gasoline Tax; (Diesel)	$0.09/liter; ($0.09/liter)

Table 4: Miscellaneous Fees (Canadian Dollars)*

Fee	Amount
Exchange of License Plates for Replacement or to Obtain a New Class of License	$20.49
In-Transit Permit	$22.49
Transfer of License Plates and Registration	$20.49

*Fees shown include Agent Service Fee, Motor Vehicle Accident Claim Fund Fee, and GST.

BRITISH COLUMBIA

Contact Information

Insurance Corporation of British Columbia (ICBC)
151 West Esplanade
North Vancouver, BC V7M 3H9

(604) 661-2800; 1-800-663-3051
www.icbc.com

Vehicle Registration

Application: An application for registration and licensing must be made to an ICBC Appointed Agent (an Autoplan Agent). In British Columbia, registration refers to maintaining a registry of vehicle ownership and licensing refers to annual licensing/operating authority and annual fee payment.

Non-Residents: An out-of-province motor vehicle may be operated for touring purposes in British Columbia for up to 6 months. All out-of-province vehicles used for other than touring purposes must be registered, licensed and insured in BC within 30 days. Students attending a BC university, college or educational institution, and armed forces personnel may be exempted from registration, licensing and insurance in BC upon providing proof of financial responsibility from their out of province insurer. This exemption is not automatic. Contact ICBC at 1-800-661-1866 or 604-443-7357 for additional details.

- Commercial use vehicles, other than those operating under an interjurisdictional licensing agreement, must be registered, licensed and insured immediately.
- Motor vehicles imported into British Columbia and that are registered, licensed, or titled outside of British Columbia may, as a condition of issuing the registration, require the vehicle to first pass a mechanical safety inspection. ICBC may require the applicant to surrender the existing certificate of registration and the current license plate(s) issued for the motor vehicle outside of British Columbia before ICBC will register the car in British Columbia.

Registration Type: Passenger vehicles must be registered, licensed and insured within 30 days of arrival if in BC for non-touring purposes.

- If the vehicle is to be imported into BC from another country, contact the Registrar of Imported Vehicles (WWW.RIV.CA or 1-888-848-8240) to determine the importation procedures and requirements.
- BC License and insurance expires at midnight on the date indicated on the insurance certificate and on the license plate decal. No grace period.

Emissions Inspection: Light-duty vehicles, 5,000 kg and under, licensed for use in and around Vancouver (the Lower Mainland and the Fraser Valley) must be tested at an AirCare Inspection Centre. 1991 and older vehicles require an annual AirCare inspection. Most 1992 and newer vehicles require an AirCare inspection every two years. Further information can be obtained at http://www.aircare.ca/ or by contacting the AirCare Program information line at (604) 433-5633.

- The emissions program (AirCare) does not apply to vehicles licensed for use outside of the Lower Mainland region.

Safety Inspection: Used passenger vehicles imported from out-of-province must pass a safety inspection before ICBC will register the motor vehicle. Some vehicles may be exempt. Contact the Commercial Vehicle Safety and Enforcement Division, Compliance and Consumer Services Branch, Ministry of Public Safety & Solicitor General, at (250) 952-0577 for details.

- BC registered vehicles that are rebuilt from salvage or amalgamated must undergo an inspection before a license is issued. Most homebuilt (Ubilt) vehicles must also pass an inspection before being registered.
- Commercial vehicles with a licensed GVW in excess of 8,200 kg, all taxis and commercial or business-insured buses, heavy commercial trailers, and all vehicles that require a Passenger Transportation License must be periodically inspected under the Commercial Vehicle Inspection Program.
- The safety inspection will determine whether the vehicle complies with the standards for motor vehicles and whether the frame of the motor vehicle has been compromised.

License Plates

Disbursement: Front and rear license plates must be displayed on all BC licensed passenger vehicles except motorcycles and trailers, which require a rear plate only. BC utilizes an expiration decal that includes the month, year and date of expiration of the vehicle license and insurance. A decal is applied to the rear plate for passenger cars and trailers (front for commercial trucks and buses over 5,500 kg GVW) indicating expiry of license and insurance. Vehicle licenses are issued for periods ranging from 3 months to 12 months.

Transfer of Plates: License plates remain with the original registrant when a vehicle is sold. The new owner must register the vehicle within 10 days by submitting a transfer form (APV9T) signed by the previous owner along with the previous registration, and pay provincial sales tax and applicable transfer fee. License plates no longer in use may be disposed of, returned to ICBC for recycling and a refund of the unexpired portion of the licensing fee, or attached to a replacement vehicle if the transfer is registered with ICBC within 10 days of the plates being attached to the replacement vehicle.

Driver's Licenses

Examination: Every applicant for a driver's license may be required to pass a vision and medical screening, knowledge test, and road test to obtain the class of license applied for.

- The basic knowledge test contains 50 multiple-choice questions that test the applicant's understanding of material in the ICBC driving guide including rules of the road and traffic signs.
- The test is available in English, French, Arabic, Cantonese, Croatian, Farsi, Mandarin, Punjabi, Russian, Spanish, and Vietnamese.

Graduated Drivers Licensing: British Columbia's Graduated Licensing Program applies to new drivers of any age. At 16, teens are eligible for a Learner's License.

- The Learner's License includes the following conditions/restrictions: must be accompanied by a qualified supervisor (at least 25 years of age who holds a valid full-privilege driver's license); the supervisor must sit beside the learner; a Learner Driver (L) sign must be displayed in the back windshield or on the rear of the vehicle; the learner must not drive after consuming any amount of alcohol (Zero Blood Alcohol Content); only 2 passengers may be in the vehicle – the supervisor and 1 additional passenger; the learner may only drive between 5 am and midnight.
- After holding the Learner's License for at least 12 months (9 with approved driver education), the learner is eligible to take a road test to graduate to the Novice stage.
- The Novice stage includes the following conditions/restrictions: a Novice Driver (N) sign supplied by ICBC must be displayed in the back windshield or on the rear of the vehicle; the novice must observe Zero Blood Alcohol Content; must not carry more than 1 passenger other than immediate family members unless accompanied by a qualified supervisor at least 25 years of age who holds a valid full-privilege driver's license.
- After holding the Novice License for at least 24 consecutive months without a prohibition, the driver is eligible to take a Class 5 or 6 road test to graduate to a full-privilege license. The minimum age for an unrestricted license is 19.

Issuance/Application: A new resident may use their out-of-province driver license for the first 90 days they reside in British Columbia.

- An applicant for a driver's license must: be at least 16 years old, obtain parental/guardian consent if under 19; provide primary identification (e.g., birth certificate or certain immigration documents) and secondary identification (e.g., Passport, school ID, credit card).
- Knowledge and road testing may be waived for applicants surrendering a valid Canadian, American, Austrian, German, Japanese, South Korean or Swiss driver's license.
- An applicant for a full-privilege BC driver's license must provide proof that they have held a driver's license for at least 24 months. Otherwise, the applicant will be placed in British Columbia's Graduated Licensing Program.
- License includes photograph, but not social security number.

Renewal: License renewal is generally every 5 years from the birthday of the applicant nearest the date the license was issued. A new photo is taken and an interim license issued to use until new photo license is received by mail.

Types of Licenses: The types of licenses are classes 1 through 8.

- A Class 1 license holder can drive a semitrailer truck and all motor vehicles or combinations except motorcycles.
- A Class 2 license holder can drive all buses and vehicles in Classes 4 and 5.
- A Class 3 license holder can drive trucks with more than 2 axles, including dump trucks, large tow trucks, and Class 5 vehicles.
- A Class 4 license holder can drive taxis, limousines, ambulances, special buses used to transport people with disabilities, and also Class 5 vehicles.
- A Class 5 or 7 license holder can drive 2-axle vehicles except for Class 4 vehicles and motorcycles. These include cars, vans, 2-axle trucks and utility vehicles, motor homes (including those with more than 2 axles), limited speed motorcycles (e.g., mopeds or mini-scooters), all-terrain vehicles, construction vehicles, trailers 4,600 kg or less, and buses or vans seating not more than 10 people.
- A Class 6 or 8 license holder can drive motorcycles, all-terrain cycles, and all-terrain vehicles.

Traffic Rules

Alcohol Laws: Open containers are prohibited. The legal drinking age is 19.

- The maximum legal blood alcohol content is 80 mg of alcohol in 100 millilitres of blood, or .08 percent.
- A Class 7 or 8 Learner's or Novice Driver's License holder cannot have any alcohol in his or her system while operating a motor vehicle (Zero Blood Alcohol Content).

Barefoot Driving: Barefoot driving is not prohibited.

Emergency Radio/Cellular: Citizen band radio channel 9 is not monitored for emergencies.

Headsets: Wearing radio headsets while driving is not prohibited.

Left Foot Braking: Left foot braking is not prohibited.

Occupant Restraints: Where a vehicle is fitted with seat belts, the complete seat belt must be worn properly unless the person has an official exemption form signed by a medical practitioner.

- A person must not drive a motor vehicle other than a taxi with a passenger aged 6 to 15 and over 18 kg. who is not wearing a seat belt (taxis are exempt). A child under 18 kg. must use an approved child seat.
- A parent driver, of a child under 18 kg., must ensure their child is in an approved child seat. Taxis, buses, rental vehicles and vehicles not licensed in British Columbia are exempt.
- It is recommended that children under 12 be in the back seat, that a child under 1 year be in a rear-facing position in the back seat; that 1-4 year olds be in a forward-facing child seat with a tether strap and older children (up to 8 years) in a booster seat with the proper seat belt fitting.

Railroad Crossing: Must yield to train. Must stop if a signal or flag person so indicates and not proceed until it is safe to do so, or the flag person signals you to go. Stop between 5 and 15 meters from the closest rail. If there is a crossing gate down, must wait for it to go up before proceeding.

School Buses: Must stop for school bus with flashing lights whether approaching from the front or rear. Must not proceed until the school bus moves on or the driver turns off the lights or pulls in the stop sign.

Vehicle Equipment and Rules — BC

Bumper Height: A motor vehicle, except a motorcycle, must be equipped with a front and rear bumper (where originally installed by the manufacturer) and where a replacement bumper has been installed, the replacement must give substantially the same protection as the original bumper. In addition, if the suspension height (bumper height) of a vehicle is altered more than 10 cm [4"], the vehicle must be inspected.

Glass/Window Tinting: The rear window may be tinted, as may side windows behind the driver. Only the top 75mm [3"] of the front windshield may be tinted. If the rear window is deeply tinted to limit visibility to the rear, both left and right side mirrors must be fitted and functioning. Tinted manufactured glass on the front windshield must meet the minimum light transmittancy requirements under the Canadian Motor Vehicle Safety Standards.

Telematics: It is unlawful to drive a motor vehicle equipped with a television if the television can be viewed by the driver, unless the screen displays information solely designed to assist the driver's ability to safely drive the vehicle.

- A person cannot drive a vehicle with a television unless the television is safely and securely mounted so that it does not obstruct the driver's ability to operate the vehicle.

Windshield Stickers: Must not drive on a highway if a windshield sticker obstructs driver's view.

Motorcycles & Mopeds

Equipment: All riders and passengers must wear a motorcycle safety helmet.

Motorcycle handlebars must be below the shoulder height of the operator when the operator is properly seated on the motorcycle.

- All motorcycles and mopeds must be equipped with at least 1 headlamp and 1 stop lamp. Those manufactured after December 31, 1974 must be equipped with a headlamp or headlamps, which automatically turn on when the motorcycle's engine is started. The headlamp(s) must remain on as long as the engine is running.
- Any motorcycle carrying a passenger must be equipped with footrests.

Licenses: A Class 6 Learner's License is valid for 12 months (Class 8 Graduated Licensing Program Learner's License is valid for 24 months) and permits the holder to ride under the following conditions: must ride within sight of a qualified supervisor 19 or older who holds a valid Class 6 license (25 or older for Class 8 Learner's License); must not carry a passenger; must not exceed 60 km/h; permitted to ride only during daylight hours, that is, between sunrise and sunset. A Class 8 motorcycle learner's license also requires the holder to observe Zero Blood Alcohol Content and display a Learner Driver (L) sign to the rear of the motorcycle.

- After passing the Motorcycle Skills Test, the supervision and speed restrictions are removed.

After passing the motorcycle road test, a Class 6 or 8 driver's license is issued.

- If the test is taken using a motorcycle with an engine displacement of 200cc or less, the license issued does not permit carrying a passenger on the motorcycle; if the test is taken on a motor scooter, the license is restricted to motor scooters only; if the test is taken on a motorcycle with sidecar or a trike, the license is restricted to 3-wheeled motorcycles only.
- A Class 8 driver's license also requires the holder to observe Zero Blood Alcohol Content and display a New Driver (N) sign to the rear of the motorcycle.

Noise Limits: A motorcycle must have a properly functioning muffler.

Mopeds: Mopeds and other limited speed motorcycles (e.g., most 50cc motor scooters) must be registered, licensed and insured. May be operated with any class of driver's license. Minimum licensing age is 16. Motorcycle safety helmet must be worn.

- Motor Assisted Cycles (bicycles with small electric assist motors) are not required to be registered, licensed or insured, and a driver's license is not required. Minimum age of operator is 16. Bicycle safety helmet must be worn. Further details on MAC definitions and requirements can be obtained by contacting ICBC.

Passenger Car Trailers

Registration: All trailers operated in BC must display a valid license plate. Out-of-province licenses of trailers are treated the same as motor vehicle licenses as outlined above.

Brakes: Independent trailer braking system required where licensed weight of a trailer (excluding tow dollies) exceeds 1,400 kg or over 50% of licensed weight of towing vehicle; not required with motorhome towing with a towbar a motor vehicle weighing less than 2,000 kg that is also less than 40% of motorhome GVWR.

- Tow dolly braking systems are required where the aggregate net weight of the tow dolly and the GVW of the towed vehicle exceeds 1,400 kg except where the GVWR on the towing vehicle is greater than the combined net weight of the tow dolly, the GVW of the motor vehicle being towed and the GVW of the towing vehicle.

Vehicle Length: A person must have a permit to operate a trailer whose length is 12.5 meters or more. A person must have a permit to operate a semitrailer having an overall length greater than 14.65 meters.

Lighting: Trailer must be equipped with taillights, brake lights, turn signals, license plate light and reflectors. Clearance lights and reflectors required if overall width 2.05 meters or more or gross weight over 1,400 kg.

Mirrors: Two mirrors required; if trailer obstructs view through inside mirror, then two outside mirrors required.

Speed Limits: 80 km/h on provincial highways, and 50 km/h in populated areas, or as posted.

Towing: A person must not drive or operate a motor vehicle and trailer unless the following occurs: the drawbar or other connection between the motor vehicle and trailer holds them together; the device which couples the trailer to the motor vehicle is firmly attached to a structurally adequate integral part of the frame of each vehicle; and the vehicles are equipped and connected with an auxiliary coupling device consisting of a chain or metal cable equal in strength to the principal coupling device. This provision does not apply where the coupling device is a 5th-wheel and kingpin assembly used to couple a semitrailer to a truck.

- Except when the combination of vehicles consists of a motor vehicle and a pole trailer, the length of the drawbar or other connection between the motor vehicle and the trailer must be 5 meters or less to operate without a permit.
- Tow dollies displaying valid license plates are exempt from BC licensing requirements for a period of up to six months.

Hitch: Must be secured to frame; safety chain required.

Miscellaneous Provisions

Border Inspections: American visitors crossing the border, either way, may be asked to verify their citizenship with a passport or birth certificate. Naturalized U.S. citizens should carry a naturalization certificate, and permanent U.S. residents who are not citizens should carry their Alien Registration Receipt Card.

- Children under 18 years of age should have their birth certificate, and if the parents are separated or divorced, the parent crossing the border should have proof of custody or a letter from the other parent. Persons under 18 years of age who are not accompanied by a parent should bring a letter from their parent or guardian giving them permission to cross the border.
- A visitor is permitted to bring a reasonable amount of personal effects, a reasonable supply of food, and a full tank of gas. Reasonable means enough for personal use during the length of stay in Canada. Any unreasonable amounts are subject to duty.
- A visitor must have a rabies vaccination certificate signed by a licensed veterinarian to bring dogs or cats into Canada.

Liability Laws: Vehicle insurance is compulsory for vehicles operating in BC.

- The minimum third party legal liability insurance limit is C$200,000 exclusive of interest and costs indemnifying for legal liability arising from bodily injury or death to 1 or more persons, or loss of or damage to property in 1 accident.
- Claims by residents or by tourists for damage to vehicles or injuries to occupants caused by 'uninsured' or 'hit-and-run' vehicles when operated on a highway in BC are payable by ICBC subject to a maximum of C$200,000. However, the payment to a tourist is limited to the lesser of either C$200,000 or the maximum amount that would be available, under similar circumstances, to a BC resident touring in the tourist's home jurisdiction. All claims for property damage by a hit-and-run vehicle in BC are subject to a C$750 deductible.
- Tourists visiting BC are required to produce proof of financial responsibility if their vehicle is involved in an accident in BC. In that case the tourist should be able to produce a "financial responsibility card." The tourist should obtain the card before entering Canada. The financial responsibility card is obtained from the insurer providing the current insurance on the vehicle used by the tourist. That insurer must have undertaken to pay claims arising in Canada in accordance with the compulsory insurance laws in the jurisdiction where the accident occurs.
- Tourists and non-residents can maintain their out-of-province insurance if the respective vehicle is licensed outside of BC and it complies with the BC licensing exemptions noted above.

Weigh Stations: Commercial vehicles, agricultural vehicles, and buses over 5,500 kg must stop at weigh scales as directed. Upon entry, into the province, commercial vehicles must attend the first weigh station and obtain a non-resident commercial permit (temporary license) if they are not licensed for travel in BC under an interjurisdictional licensing agreement.

Fees and Taxes

Table 1: Registration Fees and Annual License Fees (Canadian Dollars)

Vehicle Type	Annual License Fee	Initial Registration Fee
Private Passenger Vehicles including Station Wagons but not including Motorcycles or Mobile Homes	$46.00 to $142.00 based on vehicle weight	$18.00
Motorcycle	$33.00	$18.00
Motor Home	$63.00 to $125.00 based on vehicle weight	$18.00
Trailer	$23.00 to $99.00 based on vehicle weight	$18.00

Table 2: Driver License Fees (Canadian Dollars)

License Class	Fee
Photo Learner's License	$10.00
Duplicate (replacement) Driver's License Learner's Permit	$10.00
2-year Original Driver's License or Renewal	$31.00
5-Year Original License or Renewal	$75.00
5-Year Original License or Renewal, Seniors (Drivers aged 65 years or older)	$17.00
Knowledge Test	$15.00
Road Test: Passenger Vehicles/Motorcycles - Class 7, 8	$35.00
Road Test: Passenger Vehicles/Motorcycles - Class 5, 6	$50.00
Road Tests: Commercial Vehicles; Class 1	$60.00
Road Tests: Class 2 or 3	$50.00
Road Test: Class 4	$40.00
All Exams for Drivers aged 65 years or older	No Charge

Table 3: Vehicle Taxes (Canadian Dollars)

Tax	Rate
Provincial Sales Tax	7.5% on passenger vehicles up to $47,000; 8% $47,001 - $48,000; 9% $48,001 - $49,000; 10% over $49,000
Gasoline Tax	20.5¢ per litre inside Greater Vancouver Transportation Service Region
	17¢ inside Victoria Regional Transit Service Area
	14¢ remainder of British Columbia
	Tax included in pump price

Table 4: Miscellaneous Fees (Canadian Dollars)

Fee	Amount
License Plate Fee	$18.00
Transfer of Registration	$28.00
Transfer of Salvage Vehicle Registration	$28.00
Duplicate Replacement permits	$18.00
Surcharge for short term (less than 12 months) vehicle license	$10.00
Initial application for Personalized Number Plate	$100.00
Annual renewal for Personalized Number Plate	$40.00
Temporary Operation Permit	$4.00 per day ($12.00 minimum)
Search of current ownership, name only	$5.00
Search of current ownership, name and address	$7.00
Search of ownership as of a specific date, name and address only	$15.00
For each copy of a record or document	$10.00
AirCare emissions test 1991 and older model year vehicles	$24.00
AirCare emissions test most 1992 and newer model year vehicles	$48.00
AirCare emissions test 1992 and newer model year vehicles that cannot be tested on a dynamometer receive an annual idle-only test	$24.00
AirCare emission re-inspection	$24.00

MANITOBA

Contact Information

Driver Licensing & Vehicle Registration (Registrar)
1075 Portage Avenue
Winnipeg, MB R3G 0S1

(204) 945-6850
www.mpi.mb.ca/

Minister, Manitoba Transportation and Government Services
209 Legislative Building
450 Broadway Avenue
Winnipeg, MB R3C 0V8

(204) 945-3768
www.gov.mb.ca/tgs

Vehicle Registration

Application: With exceptions, it is not permissible to operate a motor vehicle or a trailer on the highway without a valid registration card issued in Manitoba.

- An application for registration certificate must be made to the registrar.
- The registrar may require proof of vehicle ownership; personal identification; or birth date verification prior to issuing a registration certificate.
- A vehicle shall not be registered unless the insurance premium required by law has been paid and a vehicle inspection certificate has been filed with the registrar.
- The registrar may issue a combined registration card and insurance certificate.
- A person under 16 years of age may not register a vehicle.
- A person under the age of 18 may not register a vehicle unless the application is signed: (1) by both parents; (2) by a parent if the other parent is deceased; (3) by the legal guardian; or (4) by the applicant's employer, if the applicant's parents are deceased and there is no legal guardian.
- A vehicle may only be registered in the name of the vehicle owner who: (1) alone or jointly with others has exclusive use of the vehicle, or exclusive use of the vehicle under a lease or other agreement for a period of more than 30 days; and (2) is a resident of Manitoba; has an office or principal place of business outside of Manitoba but is engaged in business in the province where the vehicle is primarily used; or is the operator of a public service vehicle or commercial truck.

Non-Residents: If the owner of a vehicle complies with the laws of a jurisdiction outside of Manitoba as to the registration and licensing of the vehicle, and the number plates are displayed on the vehicle, the owner may use or permit the use of the vehicle in Manitoba for 3 months or the period of registration for the vehicle in the outside jurisdiction, whichever is shorter. The owner or driver of the vehicle must carry certificate of registration and the license required under the laws of the jurisdiction when operating the vehicle, as well as a financial responsibility (liability insurance) card.

- A non-resident who enters and resides in Manitoba for more than 3 months to attend a university, college, technical training school, or high school as a full-time student may operate or permit another person to a operate a vehicle if: (1) the owner is in compliance with the registration and licensing laws of the respective jurisdiction where the vehicle is registered; (2) the number plate or plates authorized for the jurisdiction are displayed; (3) the certificate of registration, the license, and the financial responsibility card are carried by the owner or driver when operating the vehicle; and (4) a valid student identification sticker is displayed on, or carried in, the vehicle.

- The owner or driver of a vehicle with a valid in-transit permit or other temporary registration issued by another jurisdiction in Canada may operate the vehicle in Manitoba if the owner or driver: (1) carries the in-transit permit or registration, and proof of financial responsibility in the vehicle; and (2) operates the vehicle in accordance with the in-transit permit or registration requirements.

Safety Inspection: Compulsory. Truck tractors 21,953 kg. and over semiannually; buses exceeding 10 passengers and school buses, semiannually; semitrailers, trailers, trucks, and truck tractors between 4,500-21,953 kg, annually. Random CVSA inspections.

- All motor vehicles changing ownership require a valid inspection certificate prior to registration by the new owner. Does not apply to sales or gifts between immediate family.
- New residents to Manitoba must have their vehicle inspected at a certified government station prior to registration. If vehicle recently inspected in former home jurisdiction, and inspection substantially similar to that in Manitoba, valid inspection certificate will be accepted.
- Any motor vehicle that has been declared a total loss by an insurer and has been designated as salvageable must pass a body integrity inspection before it can be registered. If the insurer has designated the vehicle irreparable, registration is prohibited.

License Plates

Disbursement: When issuing a registration card for a vehicle, the registrar shall issue a vehicle plate or plates, and a registration card with the appropriate validation sticker or registration class sticker.

- Validation stickers are to be affixed to the license plate as evidence of a valid registration.
- A plate remains the property of the Crown.
- It is not permissible to operate a vehicle on the highway unless the number plate or plates are clearly visible and legible.

Transfer of Plates: When the interest of a vehicle passes from the registered owner to another person by an act of the owner or by operation of law, the registration of the vehicle expires immediately and the registered owner shall return the number plate or plates to the registrar. The registrar may retain them or allow the person who was the registered owner to retain them.

- The registered owner of a vehicle may within 7 days of the passing of the interest in a vehicle or the expiration of the registration of the vehicle, whichever is shorter, apply to the registrar to use the number plate or plates issued for the vehicle on another vehicle that the person has newly acquired and intends to register.
- When the interest of a vehicle passes by reason of death, the registration does not expire until the period specified in the vehicle registration. If an application is made before the vehicle expires, the spouse of the registered owner, if the ownership passes to the spouse or the personal representative of the owner, may obtain a transfer of registration and the appropriate number plate or plates.

Driver's Licenses

Examination: The registrar may not issue a license of any class unless the person passes an examination as required by the registrar.

- Except for a learner's permit, the registrar may exempt an applicant for a driver's license from taking any examination if: (1) the applicant holds a valid driver's license issued by a competent authority in a reciprocal jurisdiction; (2) the applicant is a member or a family member of NATO personnel, and holds a valid driver's license in the country where the member permanently resides; (3) the applicant holds a valid driver's license of any class issued under the authority of the Commander of the Canadian Forces Europe; or (4) in the 3-month period preceding the application, the applicant held a valid driver's license issued by a competent authority of a province or territory of Canada.
- The registrar may issue a license of any class without requiring the applicant to take an examination if the person has not allowed the license to lapse for a period of more than 4 consecutive years.
- The examination must include: (1) a test of the person's eyesight, ability to read and understand highway traffic signs, and knowledge of highway traffic laws; and (2) a test of the person's ability to exercise ordinary and reasonable care when operating a motor vehicle.

Graduated Drivers Licensing: Province has a graduated licensing program for novice drivers. At 15 1/2, teens enrolled in a high school driver education course with at least 8 completed hours of classroom instruction are eligible for a learner's permit.

- A learner's permit authorizes a person to drive a motor vehicle, except for a motorcycle, when accompanied and supervised by a person who: (1) holds a valid license for the type of vehicle being operated; (2) has held the license for a period of at least 24 months; (3) occupies the seat nearest the driver; and (4) is conscious and in a condition to assume responsibility of vehicle operation.
- Novice drivers must hold the learner's license for at least 9 months before being eligible for an intermediate license.
- Intermediate license holders may not drive between midnight and 5:00 a.m. with more than one passenger unless there is a qualified supervising driver in the front seat.
- Drivers must complete 15 months in the intermediate stage before graduating to the full license stage.
- Drivers in the full stage must continue to maintain zero blood alcohol content for the first 12 months.
- The minimum age for an unrestricted license is 17 years and 6 months.

Issuance/Application: A valid driver's license is required prior to operating a motor vehicle on the highway.

- The driver must keep a valid driver's license in his or her possession while operating a vehicle.
- An applicant for a license or permit of any kind must: (1) apply in the form required by the registrar; (2) pay the prescribed fee and surcharges; and (3) be photographed for the issuance of a license that includes a photo identification card.
- A driver's license or permit includes a photo identification card, and a license certificate. When the driver is exempted by regulation from the requirement to be photographed, the registrar shall issue a photo identification card without a photograph.
- The registrar may require that the applicant present proof of birth date.

- The registrar may require an applicant or holder of a license to be examined and to provide a report from a medical practitioner, an optometrist, or another expert regarding his or her ability to operate a motor vehicle safely; or a report from an agency as to whether the individual has a disease or disability in the form of an alcohol or drug-related problem that may interfere with the safe operation of the vehicle.
- An applicant for any class of license must make a declaration regarding his or her competency to drive a motor vehicle and any existing disease or disability.
- A person who becomes a resident of the province may operate a vehicle for a period of 3 months after the residency is established if the person holds a valid license from a competent authority outside of Manitoba.

Non-Residents: A non-resident who: (1) has complied with the law of the place of residency; (2) is 16 years of age or older; (3) does not reside or carry on business in the province for more than 3 consecutive months in a year or who is a member of NATO forces personnel; and holds a valid license of any class or permit issued by a competent authority of the jurisdiction where the person resides may operate a vehicle in the province without holding a license issued pursuant to Manitoba law.

- A person temporarily residing in Manitoba for the purpose of attending a university, college, or technical school on a full-time basis may operate a motor vehicle if the person has complied with the licensing laws of the jurisdiction where the person permanently resides, if the license was issued in Canada or the U.S., or if the person is from another country and the person meets conditions imposed by the registrar.

Renewal: Manitoba has a 2-part driver's license consisting of a paper license certificate (part 1) and a photo identification card (part 2). The license certificate expires on the last day of birth month; renewed annually. The photo ID card is renewed every 4 years. Both the license certificate and photocard must be carried together to be valid.

Types of Licenses: A Class 1 license authorizes the holder to operate semitrailer trucks and all motor vehicles or a combination of vehicles in Classes 2, 3, 4, and 5.
- A Class 2 license authorizes the holder to operate a bus, including a school bus, with a seating capacity of over 24 passengers while carrying passengers; includes all vehicles in classes 3, 4, and 5.
- A Class 3 license authorizes a person to operate a truck with more than 2 axles, including any combination of vehicles, or a truck with not more than 2 axles towing a trailer with a registered Gross Vehicle Weight (GVW) of more than 4,540 kg except for semitrailer trucks; includes all vehicles in classes 4 and 5.
- A Class 4 license authorizes the holder to operate taxis, ambulances, and other emergency vehicles; buses with a seating capacity between 10 and 24 passengers (while carrying passengers); school buses with a seating capacity between 10 and 36 passengers (while carrying passengers); includes class 5 vehicles.
- A Class 5 license authorizes a holder to operate passenger cars; a bus while not carrying passengers; a truck with not more than 2 axles; any combination of vehicles consisting of a truck with not more than 2 axles and a towed vehicle with a registered GVW of not more than 4,540 kg; Class 5 and 3 trucks registered as farm trucks; and mopeds.
- A Class 6 license authorizes the holder to operate a motorcycle and a moped. The operation of vehicles in Classes 1 to 5 are prohibited, unless the motorcycle Class 6 license is held in combination with Classes 1, 2, 3, 4, or 5 licenses.

- A Class 5A or 5L license authorizes the holder to drive as a learner within Class 1 to 5, if authorization in that class is shown on the license, and if supervised by a driver who has held the license for that class for 24 months.

Traffic Rules

Alcohol Laws: Open containers are not permitted. The legal drinking age is 18.

- It is a criminal offense to operate a motor vehicle when a person's ability is impaired by alcohol or drug or a person has an alcohol blood concentration that exceeds 80 mg of alcohol in 100 ml of blood.

Barefoot Driving: Barefoot driving is permitted.

Emergency Radio/Cellular: Citizen band radio channel 9 is not monitored for emergency calls. Cell number is 911.

Headsets: It is not permissible to operate a motor vehicle or drive a bicycle while wearing headphones on both ears.

Left Foot Braking: Left foot braking is permitted.

Occupant Restraints: The driver and passengers of a motor vehicle must wear passenger restraints when the vehicle is driven on the highway. When a passenger restraint consists of a separate pelvic and torso restraint, the driver and passengers may wear the pelvic restraint only.

- It is not permissible to operate a motor vehicle when a passenger at least 5 but not yet 18 years of age, or a passenger under the age of 5 that weighs over 23 kg., is not wearing a passenger restraint. When the passenger restraint consists of a separate pelvic and torso restraint, the driver and passengers may wear the pelvic restraint only.
- It is not permissible to operate a motor vehicle with a passenger under 5 years of age or under 23 kg. who is not fastened in a child restraint device.
- Failure to comply with the passenger restraint requirements may result in a fine of not more than $2,000.
- It is not permissible to ride on a vehicle or on any portion not designed or intended for the use of passengers.

Railroad Crossing: A driver approaching a railway crossing where a stop or warning sign has been erected must stop the vehicle: (1) not less than 5 meters from the nearest rail of the railway if the crossing is a restricted area; and (2) not less than 15 meters from the nearest rail if the crossing is not in a restricted speed area, and may not proceed until the driver can do so safely.

- When a traffic control device gives warning of an approaching train, the driver must stop the vehicle and not proceed while the signal continues to give a warning.
- When a crossing gate is lowered or a flagman gives warning of an approaching train, the driver must not proceed until the crossing gate is raised or the flagman gives a signal.
- The driver of a vehicle carrying passengers for compensation, a school bus carrying children, or a vehicle carrying flammable liquids or gas, whether or not full, who is approaching a railway crossing must: (1) stop and look in both directions; (2) listen for signals indicating the approach of a train; and (3) in the case of a bus, open the door of the vehicle. The driver must not proceed unless the driver can do so safely.

- It is not permissible to cross the railway tracks in a gear that needs to be changed while crossing the track.
- It is not permissible to drive through, around, or under a crossing gate or barrier at a railway crossing while the gate or barrier is closed, or being opened or closed.

School Buses: When a school bus is stopped on a highway and the lamp or other warning devices are displayed, the driver of a vehicle approaching the school bus from any direction must bring the vehicle to a stop no less than 5 meters from the school bus; the driver must not proceed unless the bus resumes motion, or the warning signals cease to operate.

- The driver of a vehicle upon a divided highway need not stop upon meeting or overtaking a school bus that is on a different roadway.

Vehicle Equipment & Rules

Bumpers: All passenger cars must be equipped with a front and rear bumper designed to minimize damage to the vehicle.

Glass/Window Tinting: It is not permissible to spray or coat the windshield of a motor vehicle with any substance that reduces the amount of light that is capable of being transmitted through the windshield.

- It is not permissible to apply a plastic film or a substance to the windshield, or side or rear windows that reduces the transmission of light below the minimum level prescribed, or that causes a reflection of light above the maximum level prescribed.
- It is not permissible to equip a motor vehicle with glass of the type that transmits light in only one direction.

Splashguards: Every motor vehicle or trailer, except for a farm trailer, must be equipped with splashguards or fenders adequate to reduce effectively the wheel spray or splash of water from the roadway to the rear when traveling on the highway. The exception to this requirement is when the body of the motor vehicle or the trailer adequately affords such protection.

Telematics: It is not permissible to drive on a highway with a television set unless it is: (1) mounted or positioned behind the seat occupied by the driver; and (2) the screen is not visible directly or indirectly from the driver's seat.

Windshield Stickers: Motor vehicles may be equipped with frost shields.

Motorcycles & Mopeds

Equipment: Every motorcycle and moped must display one but no more than 2 headlamps.

- Every moped must carry one reflector on the back having a diameter of not less than 75 mm, and that illuminates a red reflection visible from 150 meters.
- Motorcycles must carry front and rear lamps that signal that the vehicle is to turn right or left. Front lamp must cast a white or amber light; and rear lamp must cast a red or amber light. The requirement to have signal lamps does not apply to a motorcycle of 1974 or earlier model, or to a moped.
- Motorcycles of the model year 1975 or later and mopeds must light headlamps at all times when operating on the highway.

- Every moped must be equipped with 1 headlamp that reveals persons and vehicles at a distance of 30 meters.
- Every moped must be equipped with brakes on the front and rear wheels. Each set of brakes must have a separate means of application.
- A motorcycle and moped must have brakes capable of stopping movement when traveling at a speed of 30 km/h within a distance of 9 meters as if on a dry, smooth, level road, free from loose material.
- Every motorcycle or moped must have pneumatic rubber tires in safe operating condition; free from bulges, cracks, or cuts that might render the tire hazardous; and the tire must have at least .8 mm of tread when measured on a tire tread wear indicator device at 3 points of the circumference of the tire.
- Motorcycles must be equipped with handlebars with a width of not more than 920 mm and not less than 530 mm. The height of handlebars and the controls must not be more than 390 mm above the portion of the seat occupied by the operator.
- The operator and passenger of a motorcycle, moped, or motor-assisted bicycle must wear a helmet when driving on the highway. Safety helmet is not required when the motorcycle is equipped with a cab that encloses the operator and passengers.

Licenses: A person must hold a valid motorcycle license (class 6 learner, intermediate, or full stage license) prior to operating a motorcycle on the highways.

- A person in the graduated licensing program must pass a written test and complete a motorcycle safety course prior to being issued a motorcycle learner's license.
- Must wait 9 months before taking the road test.
- Persons holding a learner's license must have a zero blood alcohol concentration.
- Class 5 learner or class 6 learner license permits the operation of a moped.

Mopeds: When traveling on a highway, the operator of a moped must: (1) ride as close as practicable to the right-hand edge or curb of the roadway, except for when passing or overtaking another vehicle; (2) ride in a single line with another moped, bicycle, or motorcycle; and (3) keep at least 1 hand on the handlebars at all times.

- It is not permissible to carry or transport any object or thing on the front or rear of the moped that interferes with the proper operation of the moped, or that constitutes a hazard to traffic.
- It is permissible to carry an infant on a moped on a seat designed to carry infants on mopeds.
- It is not permissible to operate a moped on a provincial trunk highway where the maximum speed limit is greater than 80 km/h; however, a moped may cross an intersection if such crossing is the most direct route.

Passenger Car Trailers

Brakes: Every semitrailer or trailer that is attached to a semitrailer truck, and every trailer with a gross weight in excess of 910 kg that is attached to a motor vehicle must be equipped with brakes that are capable of stopping movement when traveling at a speed of 30 km/h at a distance of: (1) 7.6 meters for a passenger car type vehicle; (2) 9 meters for a single-unit vehicle or combination of vehicles if the weight is less than 4,540 kg; (3) 12.2 meters for a single-unit 2-axle vehicle if the weight is 4,540 kg or greater; and (4) 15.3 meters for all other vehicles and combinations thereof if the weight is 4,540 kg or greater.

Dimensions: The trailer length limit is 12.5 meters; the width limit is 2.6 meters; and the height limit is 4.15 meters.

Hitch: A drawbar connection must not exceed 5 meters.

Lighting: A motor vehicle with a trailer attached that has width in excess of 2.05 meters on any part must carry at least 4 clearance lamps or reflectors located as near the top as practicable: 1 must be placed on each side of the front that casts a green or amber light forward, 1 placed on each side of the back of the vehicle that casts a red light to the rear; and placed on that part of the vehicle that projects farthest to the left and to the right. Lamps must be visible from a distance of 150 meters to the rear of the vehicle.

- For every trailer attached to a motor vehicle, or if more than 1 is attached, the rearmost vehicle must carry at the back: (1) at least 1 stop lamp that casts a red light; and (2) a stop signal lamp; and (3) a left and right rear amber or a red turn signal light.

Mirrors: Interior and left exterior mirrors are required when towing loads wider than the towing vehicle. Buses, trucks, and truck tractors require a left and right exterior mirror.

Speed Limits: 90 km/h in rural areas and 50 km/h in urban areas, unless otherwise posted.

Towing: It is not permissible to operate a motor vehicle that is towing a trailer on the highway unless: (1) the motor vehicle and trailer are connected by a drawbar; (2) the drawbar connection must not exceed 5 meters; (3) the attachment for connecting the drawbar, except for when towing a vehicle with a gross weight in excess of 900 kg, is securely affixed to the frame of the towing vehicle; (4) the coupling connection of the drawbar to the motor vehicle is secure; and (5) the drawbar and connection are adequate to prevent the vehicle from swaying, whipping, or weaving on the highway.

- In addition to a drawbar and a coupling connection, the towing vehicle must also have an additional safety chain or cable to: (1) prevent complete disconnection of the vehicle and trailer in the case of accidental disconnection of the primary coupling connection; and (2) prevent the drawbar from dropping to the ground in the event that the primary coupling device becomes disconnected and the additional safety chain or cable must not be fastened or connected to the ball, socket, eye, hook, or any other fasteners common to the primary coupling connection.
- It is not permissible to occupy a house trailer while the trailer is traveling upon a highway.

Miscellaneous Provisions

Border Inspections: American visitors crossing the border, either way, may be asked to verify their citizenship with a passport or birth certificate. Naturalized U.S. citizens should carry a naturalization certificate, and permanent U.S. residents who are not citizens should carry their Alien Registration Receipt Card.

- Children under 18 years of age should have their birth certificate, and if the parents are separated or divorced, the parent crossing the border should have proof of custody or a letter from the other parent. Persons under 18 years of age who are not accompanied by a parent should bring a letter from their parent or guardian giving them permission to cross the border.

- A visitor is permitted to bring a reasonable amount of personal effects, a reasonable supply of food, and a full tank of gas. Reasonable means enough for personal use during the length of stay in Canada. Any unreasonable amounts are subject to duty.
- A visitor must have a rabies vaccination certificate signed by a licensed veterinarian to bring dogs or cats into Canada.

Liability Laws: The minimum amount is not less than C$200,000, exclusive of interest and costs, in respect to liability arising from bodily injury or death to 1 or more persons, or loss of or damage to property in 1 accident.

- Has security-type law applicable in event of property damage in excess of C$1,000 or personal injury or death. Minimum financial responsibility limits: C$200,000 inclusive.
- Insurance: Vehicle insurance is compulsory through Manitoba Public Insurance, and must be purchased when vehicle is registered and upon annual renewal of registration. An insurance premium is also charged with the driver's license fee, and increases on a sliding scale with the accumulation of 6 or more demerit points.
- Compulsory government insurance for all residents.
- Manitoba does not have non-resident service of process law; has guest suit law.

Weigh Stations: A peace officer may require the operator of any vehicle to submit to a vehicle weighing by driving to a weigh station or by using a portable scale.

Fees & Taxes

Table 1: Registration Fees (Canadian Dollars)

Vehicle Type	Fee Amount
Private Passenger Vehicle	$99.00
Motorcycle	$69.00
Moped	$69.00
Motor Home	$99.00
Utility Trailer/Boat Trailer	Variable
Duplicate Registration	$15.00

Table 2: License Fees (Canadian Dollars)

Vehicle Type	Fee Amount
Driver's License (Includes all Classes and Learners)	$60.00 (basic fee)/fee varies on merit-based system
Written Examination	$10.00
Class 1 Road Test	$50.00
Class 2 and 3 Road Test	$45.00
Class 4 Road Test	$35.00
Class 5 and 6 Road Test	$30.00
Replacement Fee for License	$10.00

Table 3: Taxes (Canadian Dollars)

Tax	Amount
Federal Goods and Services Tax	7%
Manitoba Provincial Sales Tax	7%
Gasoline Tax; (Diesel)	$0.115/liter; ($0.109/liter)

Table 4: Plate Fees (Canadian Dollars)

Type	Fees
Personalized	$100.00 + $7.00 for GST (Goods and Services Tax)
Personalized License Plate Replacement	$25.00 + $1.75 for GST
New Plate	$7.00 pair; $4.00 single
Semi-trailer	$6.00 (2 years)

NEW BRUNSWICK

Contact Information

Department of Public Safety
Minister of Public Safety (Minister)
Registrar of Motor Vehicles (Registrar)
P.O. Box 6000   (506) 453-3992
Fredericton, NB E3B5H1

New Brunswick Department of Transportation
P.O. Box 6000   (506) 453-3939
Fredericton, NB E3B5H1

Service New Brunswick
City Centre
432 Queen Street
P.O. Box 1998   (506) 460-6136
Fredericton, NB E3B5G4

Vehicle Title

Transfer of Ownership: When the owner of a registered vehicle transfers or assigns interest and the possession of a vehicle to another, the owner must sign the application for transfer and endorse the name and address of the transferee or assignee, and the date of transfer upon the reverse side of the registration certificate. This certificate must be forwarded to the Registrar.

- Before operating of a vehicle, the transferee or assignee must apply for a transfer of registration.
- When the title or interest in a motor vehicle transfers from the owner to another, except for by voluntary transfer or death, the vehicle may only be operated as necessary to the residence or place of business of the person entitled to the vehicle, or to the garage, if it does not exceed a distance of 120 km, unless the person is entitled to the possession applies and obtains a new registration.
- Every dealer or manufacturer upon transferring a vehicle by sale, lease, or otherwise to a person, except to another manufacturer or dealer, must give written notice to the Registrar of the transfer date, the name and address of the transferor and transferee, and a description of the vehicle.

Vehicle Registration

Application: The application must be made to the Registrar on the appropriate form, must bear the applicant's signature, and must be written in ink.

- The application must contain: (1) the name, bona fide residence and mailing addresses of the owner; (2) a description of the vehicle including the make, model, type of body, serial, or identification number; and (3) any other information reasonably required by the Registrar.
- Upon vehicle registration, the Registrar shall issue a registration certificate to the owner of the vehicle.
- The registration certificate shall contain: (1) the name and address of the owner; (2) the registration number assigned to the vehicle; (3) a description of the vehicle; and (4) on the reverse side of the certificate, an endorsement form for vehicle transfer.
- A registration certificate for a vehicle leased for over 30 days must contain, in place of the name of the owner, the name of the owner together with the name and address of the lessee under the lease.
- It is not permissible to operate a motor vehicle unless a registration certificate has been issued for the vehicle, and the original or photostatic copy of the registration certificate is carried in the vehicle or on the driver at all times.
- A motor vehicle liability insurance card must be carried in the vehicle or on the driver when the vehicle is operated on the highway.
- The Registrar may issue a permit to an applicant to operate the vehicle in New Brunswick on a temporary basis.

Non-Residents: A private passenger vehicle that is owned by a non-resident and registered in the owner's home province or state may be operated on the highways without being registered in New Brunswick.

- The registration of a vehicle is required for: (1) a non-resident who uses a vehicle to solicit business, remains for more than 30 days during any 1 year, and uses the vehicle to make deliveries; (2) a non-resident who resides or remains for more than 6 months in any year; (3) a non-resident who allows a vehicle to be operated for more than 30 days, except for a chauffeur, by a person who is a resident or ordinarily a resident in New Brunswick; or (4) a non-resident gainfully employed in the Province.

Registration Type: The registration for vehicles expires on midnight of the same day one year after the day of initial vehicle registration, except for commercial vehicles with a weight in excess of 4,500 kg and vehicles engaged exclusively for the hauling of unprocessed farm products.

- The registration, registration certificate, and registration plate are valid for a 1-year period.

Safety Inspection: An annual vehicle safety inspection is required prior to registration.

License Plates

Disbursement: Upon registering a vehicle, the registrar shall issue to the owner 1 registration plate for a motorcycle, trailer, or semitrailer, or 2 registration plates for every other motor vehicle.

- A registration plate must display the registration number assigned; the name or abbreviation of the province; the number of the issuance year; and any other information required by the Minister. The letters and numbers on the registration plate must be visible from a distance of 30 meters in the daylight.
- The registration plates issued remain at all times the property of the Crown.
- When 2 registration plates are issued for a motor vehicle, except for a motorcycle, 1 must be displayed on the front and 1 on the rear. When only 1 registration plate is issued for a motorcycle or other vehicle required to be registered, the plate must be displayed on the rear except for a truck tractor, which must display the plate on the front.
- The Registrar may issue, in lieu of registration plate or plates for 1 year, a device or sticker that may be attached to the registration plate, windshield, or other parts of the vehicle.
- The Registrar may issue to disabled persons identification plates, permits, or placards to be displayed on or in vehicles used for the transportation of disabled persons.

Driver's Licenses

Examination: The examinations for an original license include tests of the applicant's eyesight; the ability to read and understand highway signs regulating, warning, and directing traffic, and the knowledge of the traffic laws of the province; and, an actual demonstration of the ability to exercise ordinary and reasonable control of the vehicle.

Graduated Drivers Licensing: Province has a system of graduated licensing for teen drivers.

- A stage 1 learner's license may be obtained if a person is at least 16 years of age, has successfully passed a visual test and a road traffic knowledge examination, and pays all required fees.
- A stage 1 learner's license authorizes a driver to operate a vehicle if accompanied and supervised by a licensed driver who holds a valid license for the type of vehicle operated, other than a learner's license, while occupying the seat beside the driver or if there is no seat beside the driver, a seat inside the motor vehicle.
- A driver is qualified to hold a stage 2 driver's license when the driver has: (1) held a stage 1 learner's license without interruption for the preceding 4 or more calendar months, has successfully passed a licensed driver training course during the previous 2 years, and has passed the required road test; or (2) held a stage 1 learner's license without interruption for the preceding 12 or more calendar months and has passed the required road test.
- Teens are eligible for an unrestricted license at 16 years and 4 months.

Issuance/Application: It is not permissible to operate a motor vehicle on the highways without a valid driver's license.

- Persons are exempt from the license requirement when operating or driving: (1) a motor vehicle in the service of the Army, Navy, or Air Force of Canada; (2) a vehicle designed for and used in the construction, maintenance, or repair of the highways, except for a truck, while the vehicle is being used at the actual site of construction; (3) an instrument of husbandry, other than a farm tractor, incidentally operated or moved on the highway; and (4) a motor vehicle at the time of, and in the course of a driving test.

- A non-resident at least 16 years of age and with a valid driver's license from the non-resident's home province or country may operate a motor vehicle except for: (1) a resident of another province or country who resides and carries on business in New Brunswick for more than 6 consecutive months in a year; or (2) a non-resident driver who was formerly a resident of New Brunswick and whose license was revoked and driving privileges suspended.
- Every application for a license must contain: (1) the full name, date of birth, sex, and residence address of the applicant; and (2) a brief description of the applicant. If the applicant is applying for the first time, the application must include the applicant's birth certificate, baptismal certificate, or other proof of age. Photo is optional.
- A person not previously licensed to operate a motor vehicle in New Brunswick is required to obtain a license before driving in New Brunswick. Upon applying for a new license, the applicant must surrender the license issued by the other jurisdiction.

Renewal: License expires on the licensee's birthday in the year of expiration.

Traffic Rules

Alcohol Laws: Province has implied consent law.
- Presumptive level is .08.
- It is not permissible for a driver with a learner's permit while operating a vehicle to have consumed alcohol in the quantity that exceeds the concentration of more than 0 milligrams of alcohol in 1 hundred milliliters of blood.
- The legal drinking age is 19.

Barefoot Driving: Barefoot driving is permitted.

Emergency Radio/Cellular: Citizen band radio channel 9 is not monitored for emergency calls.

Headsets: Wearing radio headsets while driving a motor vehicle is permitted.

Left Foot Braking: Left foot braking is permitted.

Occupant Restraints: Every driver and passenger of a motor vehicle driven on the highway in which a seat belt assembly is provided must wear the complete seat belt assembly.
- A person driving a motor vehicle on a highway with a passenger 5 - 16 years and more than 18 kg must ensure that the passenger: (1) is wearing the complete seat belt assembly in a properly adjusted and securely fastened manner, or (2) is occupying and properly secured in a child seating and restraint system.
- A person driving a motor vehicle on a highway must ensure that passengers under 5 years of age or with a weight of 18 kg (40 lbs.) or less occupy and are properly secured in an appropriate child seating and restraint system. Children who weigh less than 9 kg (20 lbs.) are required to be secured in either an infant carrier or convertible seat adjusted to the rear-facing position while riding in vehicles where there is an available seating position fitted with a seat belt.
- It is not permissible to operate a motor vehicle on a highway with a person in any portion of the motor vehicle not designed or used for carrying passengers, or to ride in a motor vehicle in the portion not designed for carrying passengers unless the motor vehicle is: (1) used in a parade approved by an appropriate government authority; (2) transporting persons who are working while being transported on the

motor vehicle; or (3) transporting persons to or from a work site.

Railroad Crossing: The driver of a vehicle approaching a railroad crossing must stop the vehicle at least 15 meters, but not less than 5 meters, from the nearest rail of the railroad, when: (1) an electric or mechanical signal device is exhibiting a warning signal; (2) a crossing gate is lowered or when a human flagman gives or continues to give a signal of the approach of a train; (3) a train is approaching within 500 meters of the crossing that emits an audible signal; and (4) an approaching train is plainly visible and is in hazardous proximity to the crossing. The driver must not cross until the signal is no longer given or the train traffic ceases to exist.

- The driver of a motor vehicle carrying passengers for hire, of any bus, or any vehicle carrying explosive substances, or flammable liquid as cargo must stop within 15 meters, but not less than 5 meters from the nearest rail of the roadway. At a stop, the driver must listen and look in both directions for any visible or audible signals of an approaching train, and must not proceed until the driver can do so safely. The driver of these vehicles must not cross in gears that must be shifted when traversing and the driver must not shift gears while crossing.
- It is not permitted to drive any vehicle through, around, or under any crossing gate or barrier while the gate or barrier is being opened or closed or is closed.

School Buses: The driver of a motor vehicle meeting or overtaking a stopped school bus on a highway when the bus is displaying flashing red lights must stop vehicle at not less than 5 meters from the bus and not pass until lights cease to flash. This provision does not apply to the driver of a motor vehicle meeting a bus on a highway divided by a median.

Vehicle Equipment & Rules

Bumper Height: Modification of original bumper height is permitted.

Glass/Window Tinting: It is not permissible to operate a motor vehicle with windshields or windows that have been treated, coated, or covered with a color spray, other colored material, or any opaque or reflective material that prevents more than 30% of any light from passing through the window in either direction when measured by a photometer.

Windshield Stickers: Except as otherwise specified, it is not permissible to operate a motor vehicle on the highway with a non-transparent material on the front windshield, side wings, or side or rear windows, or having on the exterior or interior an ornament that obstructs or is liable to obstruct the driver's clear view of the highway.

Motorcycles & Mopeds

Registration: The owner of a motor-driven cycle must register the cycle. Upon registration, the owner shall be issued 1 registration plate.

- The age requirement for the registration of a motorcycle is 16 years of age or older.

Equipment: Every motorcycle and motor-driven cycle must be equipped with at least 1 but not more than 3 headlamps displaying white lights. The height of the headlamps must be not more than 140 cm and not less than 60 cm from the ground.

- The driver and any passenger of a motorcycle and motor-driven cycle must wear a safety helmet.

- Every motorcycle and motor-driven cycle must be equipped with a least 1 brake that may be operated by either hand or foot.
- A person may not operate a motor-driven cycle on the highway unless the cycle weighs less than 55 kg, and is equipped with: (1) wheels having rims that measure 25 cm or more in diameter; (2) a seat or saddle being 70 cm above the level surface where the vehicle stands; (3) a motor not capable of propelling the motor-driven cycle at a speed in excess of 55 km/h; (4) at least 1 and not more than 3 headlamps displaying a white light; (5) at least 1 tail lamp that when lit emits a light visible to 150 meters; and (6) an automatic transmission.
- The headlamp or headlamps of a motorcycle or motor-driven cycle may be either a single-beam or multiple-beam type, but must be of a sufficient intensity to reveal a person or a vehicle at a distance of not less than: (1) 30 meters when operated at any speed less than 40 km/h; (2) 60 meters when operated between the speeds of 40 and 60 km/h; and (3) 100 meters when operated at a speed of more than 60 km/h.
- No person may operate a motor-driven cycle at night at a speed greater than 60 km/h unless the motor-driven cycle is equipped with a headlamp or lamps that reveal a person or a vehicle at a distance of 100 meters.
- A person operating a motorcycle may only ride on the permanent and regular seat attached, and the driver may not carry any other person unless the motorcycle is designed to carry more than 1 person, or a sidecar is attached.

Licenses: It is not permissible to drive a motorcycle on the highway unless the person possesses an endorsed license that is either "valid for motorcycle" or "valid for motorcycle use only," as the case may be.

Mopeds: Class 9 license required. Minimum age is 14. Helmets are required. Other required equipment: headlamp, taillamp, stop lamp brakes (either hand or foot), mirror, horn, and muffler.

NB

Passenger Car Trailers

Brakes: Every trailer or semitrailer with a gross mass of 1 1/2 tons or more must be equipped with brakes that may be applied by the driver of the towing motor vehicle, in the case of a trailer or semitrailer equipped with air brakes, and the brakes must be designed and connected so that in the case of an accidental breakaway, the brakes will automatically apply.

- In a combination of motor-driven vehicles in which a trailer is equipped with brakes, the brakes must be designed so that the brakes of the rearmost trailer are applied in approximate synchronism with the brakes of the towing vehicle, and so that the brakes on the trailer exude the required braking effort on the rearmost wheels at the fastest rate; the braking effort applies first on the rearmost trailer equipped with brakes; or, must include both of the above systems so installed as to be used alternately.
- Every combination of motor-drawn vehicles must be equipped with service foot brakes adequate and effective under all conditions of traveling: (1) to stop within 10 meters when all wheels are equipped with brakes, and 12 meters otherwise when traveling at a speed of 30 km/h; and (2) to decelerate the vehicle or combination thereof at a rate of 426 cm per second when all wheels are equipped with brakes; and, (3) otherwise at a sustained rate of 326 cm per second, as if on a dry, smooth, level roadway.

Dimensions: The maximum trailer dimensions are: (1) a width of 2.6 meters; (2) a height of 4.15 meters; and (3) a total length of 23 meters and trailer length of 16.2 meters. The exception to the length requirement is a box length of 23 meters for an A-Train Double, a B-Train Double, and a C-Train Double Trailer.

Hitch: The drawbar or connection used to tow must not exceed 5 meters from 1 vehicle to another except for vehicles transporting poles, pipes, machinery, or other objects that because of their structure cannot be dismembered.

- When a vehicle is towing another and the connection consists of a chain, rope, or cable, a white flag or cloth not less than 30 cm must be displayed on the connection.

Lighting: Every semitrailer, or trailer 2 meters or more in overall width must be equipped with: (1) 2 amber clearance lamps on the front mounted at each side; (2) 2 red clearance lamps on the rear mounted 1 at each side; and (3) on each side, an amber reflector at or near the front and a red reflector at or near the rear.

- Every semitrailer, or trailer may be equipped with the following: (1) on the front, 3 amber identification lamps; and (2) on the back, 3 red identification lamps. The identification lamps must be mounted in a row either vertically or horizontally.
- Clearance lamps must be mounted on the permanent structure of the vehicle to indicate its extreme width.

Mirrors: Must give unobstructed view 60 meters to rear.

Speed Limits: 80 km/h unless otherwise posted.

Towing: Every motor vehicle, trailer, semitrailer, pole trailer, and any other vehicle drawn at the end of a train of vehicles must be equipped with at least 2 tail lamps, mounted 1 on either side of the rear of the vehicle, that when lit emits a red light plainly visible from a distance of 150 meters

- Every vehicle towed must be equipped with a tail lamp or a separate lamp constructed and placed to illuminate a white light to the rear registration plate and render it visible from a distance of 15 meters.

Miscellaneous Provisions

Bail Bonds: No restriction of AAA arrest bond certificates.

Border Inspections: American visitors crossing the border, in or out, may be asked to verify their citizenship with a passport or birth certificate. Naturalized U.S. citizens should carry a naturalization certificate, and permanent U.S. residents who are not citizens should carry their Alien Registration Receipt Card.

- Children under 18 years of age should have their birth certificate, and if the parents are separated or divorced, the parent crossing the border should have proof of custody or a letter from the other parent. Persons under 18 years of age who are not accompanied by a parent should bring a letter from their parent or guardian giving them permission to cross the border.
- A visitor is permitted to bring a reasonable amount of personal effects, a reasonable supply of food, and a full tank of gas. Reasonable means enough for personal use during the length of stay in Canada. Any unreasonable amounts are subject to duty.
- A visitor must have a rabies vaccination certificate signed by a licensed veterinarian to bring dogs or cats into Canada.

Liability Laws: Province has future-proof law applicable to accidents resulting in death, bodily injury, or property damage of C$1,000 or more. Minimum financial responsibility limits: C$200,000 (exclusive of interests and costs) for private passenger vehicles. Proof is required at all times. Fine for noncompliance is C$287.50.

- Province does not have non-resident service of process law; it has no guest suit law.

Weigh Stations: When directed by a traffic control device or sign on the highway, or when ordered by a peace officer, the operator of the specified vehicle must drive the vehicle to the location of the massing station or scales and submit the vehicle to a weighing.

Fees & Taxes

Table 1: Vehicle Registration (Canadian Dollars)

Registration Type	Amount
Fee for Private Passenger Vehicle Based on Weight	$45.00 (0-1,000 kg)
	$57.00 (1,100-1,200 kg)
	$68.00 (1,201-1,400 kg)
	$81.00 (1,401-1,600 kg)
	$92.00 (1,601-1,800 kg)
	$106 (1,801-2,000 kg)
	$121 (2,001-2,200 kg)
	$142 (2,201 kg and up)
Fee for the Replacement of a Registration Certificate, Registration Plate, and Sticker for a Registration Plate	$12.00 (Non-Personalized Registration Plate/$29.00 (For Personalized Plate)
Motorcycles	$23.00
Motor-Driven Cycle	$16.00
Registration Plate	$12.00
Semitrailer attached to Truck Tractor in Semipermanent Way or Trailer Used in Combination with Semitrailer and Truck Tractor	$16.00
Snowmobiles	$64.00

Table 2: Driver's License (Canadian Dollars)

Type	Amount
Replacement for Driver's License of Any Class	$8.00
Fee for Reproducing a Photograph for a License	$8.00
License Examination Fee	$25.00
License Re-Examination Fee	$14.00
Fee for a Class 1, 2, 3, 4, 5, 6, 7, 8, 9 Driver's License	$7.00
Renewal	$52.00

Table 3: Vehicle Taxes (Canadian Dollars)

Tax	Fee
Harmonized Sales Tax	15% of the Fair Market Value of the Vehicle
Gasoline Tax; (Diesel)	$0.145/liter; ($0.169/liter)

Table 4: Miscellaneous Fees (Canadian Dollars)

Fee	Amount
Unsatisfied Judgment Fund Fee	$8.00
Inspection Fee for a Utility Trailer	$7.00
Inspection Fee for a Commercial Vehicle or Farm Truck with an Unladen Curb Mass of 2,250 kg to and including 3,499 kg, Semitrailer, Trailer, or Pole Trailer with an Assigned or Configured Gross Mass of 1,500 kg or More, or Bus with an Unladen Curb Mass of 3,499 kg or Less.	$25.00
Inspection Fee for a Private Passenger Vehicle, Family Motor, or Motor Vehicle Converted to Family Motor Coach or Similar Vehicle, Taxicab, Antique Vehicle, Commercial Vehicle, or Farm Truck with Unladen Curb Mass of 2,249 kg or Less, or a Recreational Trailer	$15.00

NEWFOUNDLAND & LABRADOR

Contact Information

Government Services and Lands
Registrar of Motor Vehicles (Registrar)
5 Mews Place
P.O. Box 8700
St. John's, NL A1B 4J6

(709) 729-3688
www.gov.nf.ca/gsl/gs/mr/driver_licensing.stm
www.gov.nf.ca/gsl/gs/mr/vehicle_registration.stm

Vehicle Title

Transfer of Ownership: The seller is required to notify the registrar within 10 days of the sale of the motor vehicle.

- To transfer ownership, a seller must have the following documents: the seller's vehicle registration permit, a bill of sale and/or a sworn affidavit, a completed signed insurance declaration, and a motor vehicle safety inspection report.
- A notice of vehicle sale must be filed with the registrar within 10 days of the date of sale of a vehicle and may be sent to any Motor Registration Office in the province.

Vehicle Registration

Application: Before a motor vehicle can be operated in Newfoundland and Labrador, it must be registered on a form prescribed by the registrar. The application will request the following: (1) the name, place of residence, and mailing address of the owner of the vehicle; (2) a description of the vehicle including but not limited to the make, model, type of body, the manufacturer's serial number, and the date of sale; (3) the weight of the vehicle; (4) where the owner is applying for the first time for the registration of the vehicle described in the application, the amount of the purchase price, and whether any taxes have been paid; and (5) any other information the registrar may require.

- The appropriate fees must accompany the application.

Non-Residents: Non-residents can operate a passenger vehicle for a maximum period of 3 months in 1 year without registering a vehicle in Newfoundland and Labrador.

- A person who enters the province to become a resident must register his or her vehicle within 30 days.

Registration Type: Vehicle renewal applications are mailed approximately 45 days prior to the expiration of the vehicle registration.

- The vehicle registration expires the last day of the month shown on the registration document.
- The application for renewal includes the registration fee and any additional fees owed to the government such as outstanding fines or reinstatement fees.
- Vehicles can be registered online.

Safety Inspection: Before a vehicle can be registered, an official inspection station must inspect it and issue a vehicle inspection certificate.

- The registrar may accept an inspection for a vehicle if the vehicle was inspected and received a vehicle inspection certificate and inspection sticker in another Canadian jurisdiction with which an agreement has been made to recognize and accept inspections.
- The registrar may accept an inspection for a vehicle that has passed an inspection in another jurisdiction where the registrar considers the inspection to be equivalent to Newfoundland's and Labrador's inspection.
- The registrar may permit the registration of a vehicle for which there is no vehicle inspection certificate when the vehicle is subject to periodic inspection under a preventive maintenance program approved by the registrar.
- The registrar can allow vehicle registration without an inspection if there has been a transfer of ownership in the following cases: (1) a genuine gift between family members; (2) under a valid separation agreement or court order; or (3) another situation that, in the registrar's opinion, renders an inspection unnecessary. Before granting an exemption the registrar may require an affidavit setting out various particulars of the proposed transfer. Otherwise, a vehicle must always be inspected before it is transferred.
- The registrar, a police officer, or a traffic officer may demand a vehicle inspection certificate for a vehicle and the registrar may suspend the registration of a vehicle which fails the inspection or where the vehicle owner fails to submit an inspection certificate within the specified period stated on the demand.

License Plates

Disbursement: A driver or owner of a vehicle must ensure that the license plates are securely fastened to the vehicle at least 30 centimeters from the ground in a position that, in the case of a motorcycle, is clearly visible from the rear; a trailer, the plate is clearly visible from the rear; and all other motor vehicles, the front plate is clearly visible from the front, and the rear plate is clearly visible from the rear.

Transfer of Plates: When a vehicle is sold or transferred, the license plates are transferred with the car to the new owner.

- A valid license plate is in force as long as the registrar determines that it should be in force.

Driver's Licenses

Examination: Depending on the individual's particular circumstances, an applicant for a Newfoundland and Labrador driver's license may have to take a written test, a driving test, a vision screening examination, and a medical examination.

Graduated Drivers Licensing: Province has some form of graduated licensing for teen drivers. At 16, teens are eligible for a Class 5, Level 1 Permit.

- During this stage: (1) teens may only drive when supervised by a licensed driver with at least 4 years of experience; (2) teens may not transport any passengers, except accompanying driver or licensed instructor; (3) teens may not drive between midnight and 5:00 a.m.; and, (4) teens must drive with a sign on the rear of the vehicle with 5 cm (2 inches) black on white lettering.
- Teens must hold the Class 5 Level I license for a minimum of 12 months unless an approved driver education program is completed; the time requirement is then reduced to 8 months. Teens must also pass a road test before progressing to the next stage.
- After successful completion of the Class 5, Level I license teens (17 or 16 and 8 months) are eligible for a Class 5, Level II license permit.
- During this stage, the number of passengers must be restricted to the number of seat belts in the car. Teens may only drive between midnight and 5:00 a.m. if a licensed driver with at least 4 years of driving experience accompanies them or if the permit holder works and can provide the police with proof of his or her working schedule.
- Novice driver must have a zero blood alcohol concentration.
- Teens must hold the Class 5, Level II permit for 12 months without suspension before being eligible for an unrestricted license (minimum age 17 and 8 months).

Issuance/Application: The applicant must present (at the time he or she is applying for the learner's permit) proof of age in the form of a birth certificate, baptismal certificate, or passport. All documents must be originals. Photocopies are not accepted unless certified.

- All licenses include a photograph, but not a social security number.
- The applicant is then required to pass a written and vision test. The written test consists of questions about the rules of the road, safe driving practices, and road sign recognition. A mark of 85% is a passing grade for the written test.
- If the applicant is under 19 years of age, he or she will be required to get parental or guardian consent before a learner's permit will be issued.
- If the applicant is a 16-year-old driver presenting a valid driver license from another jurisdiction which has a graduated driver's licensing program, the applicant will be placed in Class 5, Level I. If the applicant takes an approved drivers education course, he or she will be given a 4-month credit and upon reaching 16 years 8 months, he or she will receive a Class 5, Level II driver's license. If the applicant has not taken a driver education course he or she will remain at Level I until his or her 17th birthday, at which time the applicant will graduate to a Class 5, Level II license. A road test is not required since the applicant already passed a road test in another jurisdiction, which Newfoundland and Labrador recognizes.
- If a 17-year-old or older applicant for a Newfoundland and Labrador license is from another Canadian province or the United States, the applicant can exchange his or her existing license for a Newfoundland and Labrador license without taking a written, vision, or road test provided that he or she has an existing license that is valid or that has not expired in the last 5 years.
- All other licensed drivers taking up residence in the province will have their experience rated against the Newfoundland and Labrador system and will be placed in the appropriate phase. Age, driving experience, and class of license currently held will determine placement.

Renewal: A driver must renew a driver's license every 5 years on or before his or her birthday.
- If a driver's license has expired or lapsed in less than 5 years, it can be renewed without taking a written, vision, or road test by filling out a questionnaire and paying all applicable fees.
- Medical tests for age 75: First medical required for class 5 or 6 license.
- Medical tests for age 80: Second medical required.
- Medical tests for age 82+: Every 2 years thereafter.

Types of Licenses: A Class 8 license permits the holder to operate traction engine vehicles only.
- A Class 6 license permits the holder to operate a motorcycle.
- A Class 5 license permits the holder to operate all motor vehicles with no more than 2 axles and a combination of vehicles where the towed vehicles do not exceed 4,500 kg; buses, taxis, and ambulances while not carrying passengers; self-propelled motor homes with 2 or more axles; farm tractors; fork lifts and emergency vehicles excluding ambulances; trucks designed for off-highway use; and vehicles commonly known as backhoes.
- A Class 4 license permits the holder to operate taxis, ambulances, all Class 5 motor vehicles, and buses up to 24 passengers.
- A Class 3 license permits the holder to operate trucks with 3 or more axles including a combination of vehicles and other classes as shown by endorsements.
- A Class 2 license permits the holder to operate all buses over 24 passengers and other classes as shown by endorsements.
- A Class 1 license permits the holder to operate all semitrailer trucks and other classes as shown by endorsements on the license.

Traffic Rules

NL

Alcohol Laws: Open containers are prohibited.
- Presumptive BAC level is .08.
- The legal drinking age is 19.

Barefoot Driving: Barefoot driving is permitted.

Emergency Radio/Cellular: Citizen band radio 9 is not monitored for emergency calls.

Headsets: Wearing of radio headsets while operating a motor vehicle is permitted.

Left Foot Braking: Left foot braking is permitted.

Occupant Restraints: All drivers and front seat passengers must wear properly fastened seat belts unless a person is driving a vehicle in reverse, a person holds a certified report by a qualified physician stating that for medical reasons the person cannot wear a seat belt, or the person is engaged in work that requires the person to re-enter the vehicle frequently, provided that he or she is driving below 50 km/h.
- A child who is under the age of 5 and weighs 18 kg or less must be properly restrained in a child seating and restraint system. This does not apply if the driver holds a certified report by a qualified physician stating that the child cannot be placed in the restraint system because of medical reasons.
- A child who is between the ages of 5 and 16 and weighs more than 18 kg must wear

a properly secured and fastened seat belt. This does not apply if the driver holds a certified report by a physician stating that the child cannot be placed in the restraint system because of medical reasons.
- Riding in pickup truck beds is permitted.

Railroad Crossing: When a driver of a vehicle is approaching a railway crossing at a time when a clearly visible electrical or mechanical signal device gives warning of the approach of a railway train, a crossing gate is lowered or a person holding a flag is giving a signal of the approach or passage of a railway train, or a railway train in dangerous proximity to a crossing is approaching the crossing and emits an audible signal or is visible, the driver must stop the vehicle at least 5 meters from the nearest rail of the railway and must proceed only when it is safe to do so.

- A driver must not drive a vehicle through, around, or under a crossing gate or barrier at a railway crossing while the gate or barrier is closed or is being opened or closed.
- If a stop sign has been erected at a railway crossing, the driver of a vehicle must stop the vehicle at least 5 meters from the nearest rail and proceed only when it is safe to do so.
- The driver of a vehicle approaching the track of a railway must proceed with caution to avoid a collision between the vehicle and an approaching train.

School Buses: The driver of a vehicle meeting or overtaking, from either direction, a school bus that has stopped or is about to stop to discharge or pick up school children must stop the vehicle before reaching the bus, and must not proceed until the school bus resumes motion or the driver of the bus signals that it is okay for the vehicle to proceed.

Vehicle Equipment & Rules

Bumper Height: Vehicle bumpers on passenger cars manufactured after April 1, 1976 must be between 35 cm and 55 cm from the ground when the vehicle is unloaded.
- Bumpers manufactured before April 1, 1976 must not be more than 10 cm higher or lower than when the vehicle was originally manufactured.

Glass/Window Tinting: A person must not install non-transparent, translucent, or opaque material on or in place of the windshield glazing, or on any other window so that the motor vehicle no longer conforms with the requirements of the Motor Vehicle Safety Act.
- This does not apply to replacement of glazing installed by the manufacturer.
- Clear untinted frost shields are permitted as long as they do not impair the safe operation of the motor vehicle.

Telematics: A person must not drive on a highway a motor vehicle that is equipped with a television set which is located where the driver can see it while he or she is operating the motor vehicle. This does not apply to a closed circuit television system consisting of a camera and a monitor or to a visual display unit used to help the driver safely operate the vehicle.

Windshield Stickers: Windshield stickers are permitted as long as they do not impair the operator's field of vision, or prevent the safe operation of the motor vehicle.

Motorcycles & Mopeds

Equipment: A motorcycle must be equipped with at least 1 but not more than 2 headlamps. These headlamps must be lighted at all times when the vehicle is in motion on the highway.

- A motorcycle on a highway must be equipped with headlamps arranged so that when the motorcycle is traveling less than 40 km/h a white light will be emitted to reveal a person or a vehicle at a distance of 30 meters; when a motorcycle is travelling more than 40 km/h a white light will be emitted to reveal a person or a vehicle at a distance of 60 meters.
- The headlamps of a motorcycle must be arranged and directed so that the high-intensity portion of the beams of light are emitted by the headlamps at a distance of 7.5 meters from the lamps higher than the height of the lamp.
- Every motorcycle and moped must be equipped with at least one taillamp mounted at the rear of the vehicle which will emit a red light visible from a distance of 150 meters to the rear.
- A motorcycle assembled before December 31, 1958 must be equipped with 1 stop lamp. A motorcycle assembled after December 31, 1958 must be equipped with 2 stop lamps.
- Motorcycles must be equipped with adequate brakes, and each wheel must be equipped with an adequate service brake.
- A person riding on a motorcycle must wear a helmet that complies with all safety regulations and the helmet must be properly worn by the motorcycle rider.

Licenses: A Class 6, Level I is a learner's permit for a motorcycle rider. A holder of this license must keep it for 12 months unless an approved motorcycle education course is completed; the time requirement is then reduced to 8 months. A Class 6, Level I learner's permit allows the holder to operate a motorcycle under the following conditions: (1) accompanied by a licensed driver with 4 years of motorcycle driving experience; (2) the novice driver must have a blood alcohol level of 0% and an accompanying driver cannot have a blood alcohol level exceeding .05%; (3) no passengers can ride on the motorcycle; (4) cannot upgrade to a commercial class of license; (5) not permitted to drive 30 minutes before sunset and 30 minutes after sunrise; (6) not permitted on highways where the posted speed limit exceeds 80 km/h; and (7) must pass a road test to exit this level. A Class 6, Level II novice driver permits the holder to operate a motorcycle under the following conditions: (1) must spend 12 months at Level II; (2) no driving between midnight and 5 a.m.; and (3) novice driver must have blood alcohol concentration of 0%.

Mopeds: Registration and driver's license required if driven on the highway.
- Minimum age for highway driving is 16; no minimum age for off-highway use.
- Helmet and goggles are required.

Passenger Car Trailers

Registration: Trailers must be registered in Newfoundland and Labrador.

Brakes: The service brakes on a combination of vehicles must be capable of bringing the motor vehicle and a fully loaded combination of vehicles to a standstill at 30 km/h under the following conditions: (1) in a straight line; (2) within 10 meters from the point at which the brakes were applied; and (3) on a dry and level paved surface made of either asphalt or concrete that is free from loose materials.

- The emergency or parking brake on a fully loaded combination of vehicles must be capable of bringing the combination of vehicles to a standstill within 16 meters from the point at which the brakes were applied either on a dry and level paved surface made of concrete or asphalt and free from loose materials, or at a speed of 30 km/h. Additionally the emergency brakes must be capable of holding the combination of vehicles at a standstill while they are fully loaded and facing up or down at a 20% grade.

Dimensions: Total length: 23 meters; trailer length: combination not to exceed 23 meters; width: 2.6 meters; height: 4.1 meters.

Hitch: Hitch and safety chain or metal cable equal in strength to the principal coupling device required.

Lighting: Tail, brake, and license plate lights required. Turn signals and reflectors also required.

Mirrors: The towing vehicle in every combination of motor vehicles must be equipped with 2 mirrors, 1 placed on each side of the motor vehicle to provide the driver with a clear view of the roadway to the rear of the combination of vehicles.

Speed Limits: 90 km/h and posted 100 km/h.

Towing: A motor vehicle towing a trailer must be securely held together by a drawbar or other connection.

- The device, which attaches the trailer to the motor vehicle, must be firmly attached to a structurally adequate and integral part of the frame of each vehicle. If the towed vehicle is a gross vehicle mass less than 900 kg the device which attaches the trailer to the motor vehicle must be firmly attached to a structurally adequate part of the towing vehicle and to an integral part of the frame of the towed vehicle.
- A motor vehicle towing a trailer must also be equipped and connected with an auxiliary coupling device that consists of a chain or metal cable equal in strength to the principal coupling device. This rule does not apply if the coupling device is a 5th-wheel and kingpin assembly used to couple a semitrailer to a truck tractor and that assembly is securely attached to the towing vehicle. Also, the vehicle must not be operated with fewer bolts than were provided by the manufacturer or with any cracks or breaks in the securing attachments.
- If a towing motor vehicle is equipped with a 5th-wheel assembly, the jaw closure mechanism and locking components must function properly and the frame assembly must be fitted with slide rails properly mounted to ensure that the trailer kingpin is securely engaged.

Miscellaneous Provisions

Border Inspections: American visitors crossing the border, either way, may be asked to verify their citizenship with a passport or birth certificate. Naturalized U.S. citizens should carry a naturalization certificate, and permanent U.S. residents who are not citizens should carry their Alien Registration Receipt Card.

- Children under 18 years of age should have their birth certificate, and if the parents are separated or divorced, the parent crossing the border should have proof of custody or a letter from the other parent. Persons under 18 years of age who are not

accompanied by a parent should bring a letter from their parent or guardian giving them permission to cross the border.
- A visitor is permitted to bring a reasonable amount of personal effects, a reasonable supply of food, and a full tank of gas. Reasonable means enough for personal use during the length of stay in Canada. Any unreasonable amounts are subject to duty.
- A visitor must have a rabies vaccination certificate signed by a licensed veterinarian to bring dogs or cats into Canada.

Liability Laws: Every motorist must have insurance in the amount of C$200,000 for a single accident.

- Has security-type law applicable in event of accident resulting in death, personal injury, or property damage exceeding C$1,000. Minimum financial responsibility limits: C$200,000.
- Unsatisfied judgment fund law: "Judgment Recovery Nfld" operates a fund for payment of uncollectible judgments exceeding C$200 (property damage only).

Weigh Stations: An inspector can stop a vehicle by placing a sign on the roadway ordering all vehicles or all vehicles of a certain class to stop for weighing, by signaling the driver to stop the vehicle, or by ordering the driver to drive the vehicle to the nearest weigh station. This weigh station must be within 16 kilometers of where the vehicle was stopped. The driver must perform all other acts that the inspector requires or considers necessary for weighing the vehicle and its load.

- Where the maximum gross mass or the axle mass of the vehicle exceeds that permitted by the regulations or by a sign applicable to that portion of the highway on which the vehicle was stopped, the inspector may order the driver of the vehicle to remove as much of the load as is necessary to bring the maximum gross mass or the axle mass of the vehicle within the mass permitted on that portion of the highway.

Fees & Taxes

Table 1: Title & Registration Fees (Canadian Dollars)*

Vehicle Type	Registration Fee
Passenger Class and Small Pickup Trucks less than 3,000 kg	$140.00
All Utility/Camper Trailers	$38.00 per year
Motorcycle	$50.00
Duplicate Vehicle Registration	$15.00

*The registration for all other vehicles is based on the weight of the vehicle.

Table 2: License Fees (Canadian Dollars)*

License Class	Fee
Class 1 License	$105.00 every 5 years
	(additional $1.75 for every mo. over 5 yrs.)
Class 2 License	$100.00 every 5 years
	(additional $1.70 for every mo. over 5 yrs.)
Class 3 License	$90.00 every 5 years
	(additional $1.50 for every mo. over 5 yrs.)
Class 4 License	$85.00 every 5 years
	(additional $1.45 for every mo. over 5 yrs.)
Class 5 License	$89.00 every 5 years
Class 5 Level I License	$30.00/2 yrs.
Class 5 Level II License	$80.00/5 yrs.
	(additional $1.35 for every mo. over 5 yrs.)
Class 6 Level I License	$30.00/2 yrs.
Class 6 Level II License	$80.00/5 yrs.
	(additional $1.35 for every mo. over 5 yrs.)
Motorcycle Endorsement to License	$5.00 every 5 years
Class 6 or Class 8 License	$80.00 every 5 years
Beginner's Permit Fee	$15.00
Driver's License Fee for Original License	$50.00
Duplicate Driver's License	$15.00
Road Test	$50.00

Table 3: Vehicle Taxes (Canadian Dollars)*

Tax	Rate
Gasoline Tax; (Diesel)	$0.165/liter; ($0.165/liter)
Goods and Service Tax	7% of the value of the vehicle

Table 4: Miscellaneous Fees (Canadian Dollars)*

Fee	Amount
Transfer of Registration	$15.00
Duplicate Registration Certificate	$15.00
Duplicate Plates	$20.00

* The information was obtained by calling the motor registrar's office because the information could not be found in the statutes, regulations, or motor registrar's website.

NORTHWEST TERRITORIES

Contact Information

Road Licensing & Safety Division (RLSD)
Box 1320 (867) 873-7406
Yellowknife, NT X1A 2R3

Royal Canadian Mounted Police
"G" Division
Bag 5000 (867) 669-5210
Yellowknife, NT X1A 2R3

Highway Patrol
Hay River, NT (867) 874-5007

Vehicle Registration

Application: The owner of a non-commercial motor vehicle may apply to the RLSD to have a certificate of registration, license plate, or validation sticker issued for the motor vehicle.

- An applicant must provide a postal address for the owner in the Territories and supply satisfactory proof of insurance for the vehicle.
- The RLSD will not issue a certificate of registration for a motor vehicle if there are more than 90 days before the date of expiration unless there are extenuating circumstances.
- An owner of a motor vehicle that is registered under the laws of another jurisdiction must obtain a certificate of registration for the vehicle by the day that vehicle has been in the Territories for 91 consecutive days regardless of whether the vehicle is operated on a highway.
- A non-dealer certificate of registration expires on the earliest of the following days: (1) the day specified by the RLSD in the certificate; (2) the day that the vehicle is transferred to a new owner; or (3) 60 days after the death of the person named in the certificate, or, where the owner is a corporation, 90 days after the dissolution of the corporation.
- The certificate of registration and proof of insurance must be carried in the vehicle.

Non-Residents: A person is not required to register a vehicle in the Territories when: (1) the owner of the motor vehicle has complied with the laws of a jurisdiction other than the Territories respecting registration, license plates, and validation stickers; and (2) the vehicle has been in the Territories for a period not exceeding 90 consecutive days, or the owner of the vehicle is temporarily in the Territories for the purpose of attending an educational institution as a student in an exchange program or other approved educational program.

Registration Type: A person may apply for a certificate of registration for a private vehicle, motorcycle, or trailer for a minimum period of 7 months and a maximum period of 18 months.

- Commercial vehicles may be registered in 1 month increments to a maximum term of 12 months.

- The certificate of registration for a private vehicle expires on the last day of the month of expiration assigned to the owner based on the 1st letter of the surname of an individual or the 1st letter of the name of the organization that owns the vehicle.
- The RLSD issues annual validation stickers for the renewal of expired certificates of registration.

Transfer of Ownership: When a person purchases or acquires a motor vehicle already registered in the Territories, the person has 30 days to obtain a new certificate of registration.

- When the certificate of registration of a motor vehicle expires because of transfer of ownership, the seller or transferor must immediately remove the license plate attached to the vehicle and sign the notice of transfer on the certificate of registration and give this notice to the new owner. The new owner must submit the notice of transfer to the RLSD within 10 days.

Safety Inspection: No person may operate, on a highway, a vehicle that is in such a condition that the operation of the vehicle is likely to endanger the safety of the driver, a passenger in the vehicle, or the public.

- An officer may direct a person operating a vehicle on a highway to stop and park the vehicle to inspect the vehicle and any vehicle safety item to determine if the vehicle and item comply with the law.
- No person may operate a vehicle unless it complies with the applicable Canadian Motor Vehicle Safety Standard.

License Plates

Disbursement: The license plate must be attached to the rear bumper of a motor vehicle, to the rear fender of a motorcycle, or to the back of a trailer at a position not lower than the rear axle.

- When a motor vehicle liability policy expires or is cancelled and the person named in the certificate of registration covered by the policy does not immediately obtain a new motor vehicle liability policy or equivalent coverage, the person named in the certificate of registration for the vehicle must deliver or mail to the RLSD the license plates issued for that vehicle.
- Personalized license plates are available.

Transfer of Plates: If a person sells or otherwise transfers a motor vehicle, the person named in the certificate of registration for the motor vehicle may transfer the license plate with a validation sticker to another vehicle that he or she owns.

- When a person transfers a license plate to another vehicle owned by that person, the person must obtain a new certificate of registration for the vehicle within 14 days of the transfer and advise the RLSD of numbers or letters on the license plate attached to the vehicle.

Driver's Licenses

Examination: A person who has not been issued a driver's license and wishes to obtain 1 or wishes to increase the privileges associated with his or her existing license must pass a written and a practical driving examination for that class of driver's license.

Graduated Drivers Licensing: Province has a system of graduated licensing for teen drivers. A learner's permit can be obtained at age 15 and must be held for 30 days. An unrestricted license can be obtained at 17.

Issuance/Application: A person must be at least 18 years of age to hold a Class 1, 2, 3, or 4 driver's license.

- A person is not required to have a driver's license issued by the Territories if the person has a valid driver's license issued under the laws of a jurisdiction in Canada or the United States that authorizes the person to operate the class of motor vehicle he or she is operating, and the person (1) has been a resident of the Territories for less than 30 days, (2) is not a resident of the Territories and has been in the Territories for less than 90 consecutive days, or (3) is not a resident and is in the Territories for the purpose of attending an educational institution or participating in an exchange program or other recognized educational program.
- A person who is not a resident of Canada or the United States, who does not remain in the Territories for more than 12 consecutive months, and who holds a valid international driving permit, is not required to obtain a driver's license.
- A person holding a driver's license issued by another jurisdiction may apply for a driver's license issued by the Territories upon surrender of his or her existing license.
- When operating a motor vehicle on a highway, a person must carry his driver's license with him.
- A person holding a driver's license must notify the RLSD within 15 days of a change of name or address.

Renewal: A person who (1) has a valid driver's license, (2) a valid driver's license that has expired for a period of less than 1 year, or (3) a driver's license that has been cancelled for certain reasons for less than 1 year may apply to the RLSD for a new driver's license of the same class as the person previously held or for a class with fewer privileges.

- The RLSD will not issue a driver's license to a person named on a valid driver's license if there are more than 90 days before the date of expiration unless the RLSD is satisfied that there are circumstances that justify issuing a license earlier than 90 days before the expiration date.
- Driver's licenses are issued for a 5-year term.

Types of Licenses: Class 1 permits the operation of semitrailers and tractor trailers; any vehicle in Class 2, 3, 4, or 5; and any vehicle in Class 6 while the driver is learning to operate it.

- Class 2 permits the operation of a bus of any seating capacity; a vehicle or any combination of vehicles in Class 3, 4, or 5; any combination of vehicles without air brakes where the towed vehicles exceed a Gross Vehicle Weight Rating (GVWR) of 4,500 kg; and any vehicle in Class 1 or 6 while the driver is learning to operate it.
- Class 3 permits the operation of a single vehicle with 3 or more axles; any combination of vehicles where the towed vehicles in the combination do not exceed a GVWR of 4,500 kg; any combination of vehicles without air brakes where the towed vehicles exceed a GVWR of 4,500 kg; a vehicle or any combination of vehicles in Class 4 or 5; and any vehicle in Class 1, 2, or 6 while the driver is learning to operate it.

- Class 4 permits the operation of a bus having a seating capacity not exceeding 24 passengers; a taxi; an ambulance; any vehicle in Class 5; and any vehicle in Class 1, 2, 3, or 6 while the driver is learning to operate it.
- Class 5 is the standard license for passenger vehicles. Class 5 permits the operation of a 2-axle vehicle other than a motorcycle, bus, taxi, or an ambulance; any combination of a 2-axle towing vehicle and towed vehicle where the towing and towed vehicles do not exceed a GVWR of 4,500 kg; a recreational vehicle; a moped; certain construction vehicles with no more than 2 axles; and any vehicle mentioned in Class 1, 2, 3, 4, or 6 while the driver is learning to operate it.
- Class 6 permits the operation of a motorcycle and any vehicle in Class 5 while the driver is learning to operate it. A person must be at least 16 years old to have these types of licenses.
- Class 7 permits the operation of any vehicle in Class 5 or 6 while the driver is learning to operate it. A person must be at least 15 years old to have this type of license.

Traffic Rules

Alcohol Laws: Open containers are not permitted. The legal drinking age is 19.
- Illegal per se BAC level is .08.

Emergency Radio/Cellular: Citizen band radio channel 9 is monitored for emergency calls.

Headsets: Wearing of radio headsets while operating a motor vehicle is permitted.

Occupant Restraints: Seat belts are required for all drivers and passengers.
- Children under 18 kg. are required to be in a child restraint system.
- No person may ride and no driver may permit a person to ride in the box of a truck unless the box is totally enclosed, or the truck is being operated within a municipality or settlement at less than 30 km/h.

Railroad Crossing: When a driver approaches a railway crossing and a warning device or flag operator indicates that a train is approaching, or a train that is approaching is visible or is emitting an audible signal and it is not possible to cross the railway crossing in safety, the driver must stop his vehicle not less than 5 meters from the nearest rail of the railway. The driver must not proceed across the railway crossing until it is safe to do so.
- No driver may drive through, around, or under a crossing gate or barrier at a railway crossing when the gate or barrier is closed or is being opened or closed.
- Where a stop sign has been erected at a railway crossing, a driver must stop his or her vehicle not less than 5 meters from the nearest rail of the railway and must not proceed until it is safe to do so.
- A driver approaching a railway crossing must listen and look in both directions of the crossing for an approaching train.

School Buses: A driver, on meeting a school bus that is headed in the same or opposite direction as the driver and has its flashing lights in use, must stop his or her vehicle before it reaches the bus and not proceed until the flashing lights are no longer in use.

Vehicle Equipment & Rules

Bumper Height: Bumpers on passenger cars must be positioned on the vehicle so that the center part of the bumper is not more than 550 mm or less than 380 mm above the road surface. On vehicles other than passenger cars, the lowest part of the bumper must be not more than 750 mm above the road surface.

Glass/Window Tinting: Windshields must be free from a coating of sunscreen or reflective material other than that applied by the vehicle manufacturer.

Telematics: No person may operate a vehicle on a highway that is equipped with a cathode ray tube display screen or similar viewing screen if the screen is located in front of the driver's seat or is visible to the driver while the driver is operating the vehicle.

Towing: No person operating a vehicle of 4,500 kg GVWR or less may tow more than 1 vehicle.

Windshield Stickers: No person may operate, on a highway, any motor vehicle with a sticker, sign, poster, or other non-transparent material placed over, or affixed to the windshield or a side or a rear window that unduly obstructs the driver's view of the highway or an intersecting highway.

Motorcycles & Mopeds

Equipment: No passenger may ride on a motorcycle unless the motorcycle is designed and equipped with a seat to carry more than 1 person, and the person rides on that seat, or the passenger rides in a side car that is attached to the motorcycle.

- No person may drive or ride on a motorcycle unless the person is wearing a helmet.
- No person may operate a motorcycle unless it is equipped with at least 1 headlight capable of clearly illuminating objects at a distance of 100 meters between sunset and sunrise.
- No person may operate a motorcycle unless it is equipped with 1 red taillight at the rear of the vehicle.
- No person may operate a motorcycle designed to carry passengers unless it is equipped with the footpegs for the passenger.
- A motorcycle must be equipped with a drive chain, drive belt or driveshaft guard to prevent injury to the operator and passenger from moving parts.

Licenses: A Class 6 license permits the operation of a motorcycle.

- A person learning to operate a motorcycle may be unaccompanied if the instructor has a minimum of 2 years of experience operating a motorcycle, follows the person in or on another vehicle, and keeps the person in view.
- A person learning to operate a motorcycle may not operate a motorcycle after sunset or in a speed zone of 70 km/h or greater.
- A motorcycle must be equipped with 1 stop light at the rear of the vehicle.

Noise Limits: No person may operate a vehicle unless the muffler on the exhaust system is designed to prevent unnecessary engine noise.

Passenger Car Trailers

Brakes: No person may operate a trailer manufactured before 1985 unless the service brakes apply to the wheels on the opposite ends of 1 axle, or a trailer manufactured after 1984 unless the brakes apply to the wheels on opposite ends of each axle.

Hitch: A towing vehicle must be equipped with a coupling device in the form of a 5th-wheel hitch, pintle hook, drawbar hitch, ball hitch, or other approved coupling device that is designed to support the trailer the person intends to tow.

- Any coupling device, other than a 5th-wheel hitch, must be equipped with an alternate coupling device that is designed to support the same weight as the main coupling device.
- No person may operate a vehicle equipped with a coupling device unless it is securely mounted to the frame of the vehicle, has no missing or ineffective fasteners, and is free of cracks or breaks in the assembly.

Lighting: No person may operate a trailer less than 760 mm wide unless it is equipped with 1 red taillight and 1 red stop light at the rear of the vehicle.

Mirrors: No person may operate a vehicle unless it has at least 2 mirrors attached to the vehicle each of which gives the operator a clear view at least 60 meters behind the vehicle.

Speed Limits: 90 km/h or as posted.

Towing: The certificate of registration for a trailer must be kept in the trailer or in the vehicle towing the trailer.

- No person may occupy and no driver whose motor vehicle is pulling a trailer may permit a person to occupy a trailer while it is being moved on a highway.

Other Provisions: Maximum of 1 boat or general utility trailer may be towed behind passenger or pleasure vehicles. Total length of both not to exceed 25 meters (70 feet).

Miscellaneous Provisions

Liability Laws: No person may operate or park a motor vehicle on a highway unless there is a motor vehicle liability policy in force that meets the minimum coverage requirements.

- Every person who owns and operates a motor vehicle on a highway must maintain an insurance policy that provides liability coverage, in respect of any 1 accident, to the limit of not less than C$200,000 exclusive of interest and costs, against liability resulting from bodily injury to or the death of 1 or more persons and loss of or damage to property.
- Claims arising out of bodily injury or death must have priority to the extent of C$190,000 over claims arising out of loss of damage to property, and claims arising out of loss of or damage to property must have priority to the extent of C$10,000 over claims arising out of bodily injury or death.

Fees & Taxes

Table 1: Private Vehicle Certificate of Registration & License Plate Fees (Canadian Dollars)[1]

Vehicle Type	Registration & Plate Fee (combined)
Private Motor Vehicle (Other than a Motorcycle or Motor Home)	$5.00 per month for 7-18 months
Motorcycle - 12 Months or Less	$20.00
Motorcycle - Over 12 Months	$30.00
Trailer - 12 Months or Less	$20.00
Trailer - Over 12 Months	$30.00
Motor Home - Class A	$90.00
Motor Home - Class B	$70.00
Motor Home - Class C	$60.00

Table 2: Commercial Vehicle Registration Permit & License Plate Fees (Canadian Dollars)

Vehicle Type	Registration Permit Fee	License Plate Fee
Commercial Vehicle - Up to 2,500 Kg GVWR	$70.00	$70.00
Commercial Vehicle - 2,500 Kg up to 5,000 Kg GVWR	$70.00 plus $10.00 for every 500 Kg over 2,500 Kg GVWR	$70.00 plus $10.00 for every 500 Kg over 2,500 Kg GVWR
Commercial Vehicle - Over 5,000 Kg GVWR	$70.00 plus $29.00 for every 1,000 Kg over 5,000 Kg GVWR	$70.00 plus $29.00 for every 1,000 Kg over 5,000 Kg GVWR

Table 3: License Fees (Canadian Dollars)

License	Fee
All Classes of Driver's License (5-year Term)	$75.00
Driver's License for Person 60 Years of Age or Older	$37.50
Class 1 Driver's License Examination	$35.00
Class 2, 3, or 4 License Examination	$30.00
Class 5, 6, or 7 License Examination	$25.00
License Examination - All Classes for Persons 60 Years of Age or Older	$5.00
Driver's License Manual	$5.00
Professional Driver's License Manual	$5.00
Air Brake Manual	$12.00

Table 4: Vehicle Taxes (Canadian Dollars)

Tax	Rate
Personal Property Tax	none
Provincial Sales Tax	none
Federal Goods and Services Tax	7%
Gasoline Tax (Diesel)	$0.107/liter ($0.910/liter)

Table 5: Miscellaneous Fees (Canadian Dollars)

Service	Fee
Personalized License Plate (in Addition to Other Fees)	$150.00
In Transit Permit	$10.00
Replacement of Lost or Damaged Registration Permit or Certificate	$10.00
Replacement of Lost or Damaged License Plate	$10.00
Replacement of Lost or Damaged Personalized License Plate	$25.00
Replacement of Lost or Damaged Validation Sticker	$5.00
Reservation of License Plate	$75.00
Certificate of Registration without License plate	$10.00
Transfer of Certificate of Registration to Spouse	$10.00
Transfer of Certificate of Registration from One Vehicle to Another	$10.00
Change of Name on Driver's License	$10.00
Change of Name for Person 60 Years of Age or Older	$1.00
Change of Class of Driver's License	$10.00
Change of Driver's License Class for Person 60 years of Age or Older	$1.00
Replacement of Lost, Damaged, or Stolen License	$10.00

NOVA SCOTIA

Contact Information

Registrar of Motor Vehicles (RMV)
Department of Service Nova Scotia and Municipal Relations
P.O. Box 2734   (902) 424-5851
Halifax, NS B3J 3P7   www.gov.ns.ca

Royal Canadian Mounted Police
"H" Division
P.O. Box 2286   (902) 426-3940
Halifax, NS B3J 3EI

Vehicle Registration

NS

Application: Unless an exemption is granted by law, every motor vehicle in Nova Scotia must be registered with the Department.

- The application for a certificate of registration must be on a form prescribed by the Department. This form must contain the following information: the name and make of the vehicle; the vehicle's serial number; any distinguishing marks on the vehicle; whether it is new or used; and any other information the Department requires.
- When a vehicle is registered, the Department will issue the owner a permit which will include the vehicle registration number, the name and address of the owner, a description of the registered vehicle, and anything else the Department determines is necessary.

Non-Residents: A passenger motor vehicle owned by a non-resident who does not carry on business in Nova Scotia is exempt from registration for 90 days from the date that the vehicle was first operated in Nova Scotia. Only one 90-day exemption period is allowed in any registration year.

- A passenger motor vehicle registered in the province of New Brunswick or Prince Edward Island is exempt from registration as long as the registered owner does not live in Nova Scotia.
- A single trip permit can be bought for a single 30-day entrance into Nova Scotia.
- A non-resident who becomes a resident and who is the owner of a motor vehicle, trailer, or semitrailer must register his or her vehicle within 30 days of becoming a resident.
- Military personnel on active duty in the province receive a 90-day extension of time for obtaining a vehicle registration.

Registration Type: Registration is for a 24-month time period from the date that the vehicle was registered.
- Registration renewal is based on a staggered system.

Safety Inspection: All motor vehicles must have a vehicle inspection from an approved vehicle inspection station.
- When a vehicle passes an inspection, it will be issued an approval sticker, which must then be placed on the vehicle's windshield.
- This approval sticker will be valid for 12 months from the date that it was issued. In subsequent years the vehicle must be inspected by the date shown on the approval sticker.
- When a vehicle fails an inspection, the necessary repairs must be made to the vehicle and the vehicle must be returned to an official testing station within 10 days from the date on which it was rejected.
- A vehicle purchased outside of the province that is required to be registered in the province must be immediately inspected at an official testing station in the province.

License Plates

Disbursement: When a vehicle is registered, the Department must assign the vehicle 2 number license plates, with the same numbers. Two plates will be issued to a camper, farm truck, commercial fisherman, truck, service truck, self-powered miscellaneous equipment, a vehicle to bear firefighter plates, personalized plates, and antique plates. All other motor vehicles will be issued 1 number license plate.
- Handicapped identification plates are issued upon application to the RMV.

Transfer of Plates: When a vehicle is sold or transferred, the seller must remove the vehicle license plates. The plates may be put on a new vehicle; however, if not placed on a new vehicle, they must be returned to the Department.

Driver's Licenses

Examination: The registrar may not issue a license of any class unless the person passes an examination as required by the Department.
- The examination must include a test of the person's eyesight; a test of ability to read and understand highway traffic signs; knowledge of highway traffic laws; and a test of the person's ability to exercise ordinary and reasonable care when operating a motor vehicle.
- The Department may at its discretion issue a driver's license without an examination to any applicant who is of sufficient age to receive the license applied for and

who at the time of the application has a valid unrevoked license similar to the kind issued by another province or state that requires the licensing and examination of drivers.

Graduated Drivers Licensing: Nova Scotia has a system of graduated licensing for newly licensed drivers.

- A person must be 16 to obtain a learner's permit. This permit must be held for 6 months unless a driver education course is taken; then it must only be held for 3 months.
- Conditions of the learner's permit are: (1) no passengers, except an experienced driver who holds at least a Class 5 license; and (2) zero blood alcohol level for the learning driver. Suspensions will delay graduation to the newly licensed driver stage by the minimum time requirement.
- Once a road test has been successfully completed, the learner enters the newly licensed stage for a minimum of 2 years.
- Conditions of the newly licensed stage are: (1) zero blood alcohol level for the newly licensed driver; (2) only 1 front seat passenger, and rear seat passengers limited to the number of available seat belts; (3) no upgrade beyond a Class 5 driver's license; and (4) no driving between midnight and 5:00 a.m., unless accompanied by an experienced driver.
- A newly licensed driver may apply for an exemption from the nighttime driving curfew for employment purposes. The driver must take the most direct route to and from work, and is not permitted to have any passengers in the vehicle.
- To graduate from the newly licensed stage, the driver must successfully complete a 6-hour defensive driving course, or complete the full driver training course which consists of 25 hours of theory and 8 hours of driving time. A copy of the applicant's graduation certificate must be provided, in person or by mail, to any Registrar of Motor Vehicles office for recording purposes. An unrestricted license can be obtained at 18 years and 3 months.
- The Department will not issue a license to a person under the age of 18 unless his application is signed by a parent or custodial guardian of the applicant; the employer of the applicant if his or her mother and father are dead and he or she has no guardian; or the spouse of an applicant if the spouse is 18 years or older.

Issuance/Application: A non-resident who is 16 years of age or older and has in his or her immediate possession a valid driver's license issued by his or her home province or country, is permitted, without taking an exam, to drive a motor vehicle of a type or a class authorized by such a license for a period of 90 days from the date the non-resident first entered the province.

- License includes a photograph, but not a social security or social insurance number.

Renewal: A driver's license must be renewed every 5 years.

Types of Licenses: Class 1 permits the operation of semitrailer and tractor-trailer combinations and all type of vehicles in Classes 2, 3, 4, 5, and 8. Class 1 permit holders may not drive vehicles with air brakes, school buses or school purpose buses, or motorcycles or mopeds without appropriate endorsement.

- Class 2 permits the operation of buses having a seating capacity of more than 24 passengers, and all types of vehicles in Classes 3, 4, 5, and 8. Class 2 permit holders may not drive vehicles with air brakes, school buses or school purpose buses, or motorcycles or mopeds without appropriate endorsement, or Class 1 vehicles (except as a learner).

- Class 3 permits the operation of any single vehicle in excess of 14,000 kg and any combination of vehicles other than semitrailer or tractor-trailer combinations in excess of 14,000 kg Gross Vehicle Weight (GVW) where the towed vehicle in that combination does not exceed a GVW of 4,500 kg, and vehicles in Classes 4, 5, and 8. Class 3 permit holders may not drive vehicles with air brakes, school buses or school purpose buses, motorcycles or mopeds without appropriate endorsement, Class 1 or 2 vehicles (except as a learner), or public passenger vehicles (unless 19 years of age or older).
- Class 4 permits the operation of buses under 24 passengers, taxis, ambulances, and all types of vehicles in Classes 5 and 8. Class 4 permit holders may not drive vehicles with air brakes, school buses or school purpose buses, motorcycles or mopeds without appropriate endorsement, Class 1, 2, or 3 vehicles (except as a learner), or public passenger vehicles (unless 19 years of age or older).
- Class 5 permits the operation of any single vehicle not in excess of 14,000 kg GVW, any combination of vehicles other than semitrailer or tractor-trailer combinations not exceeding 14,000 kg and the towed vehicle in that combination not exceeding a GVW of 4,500 kg, and Class 8 vehicles. Class 5 does not permit the operation of vehicles with air brakes, motorcycles or motor-driven cycles without an appropriate endorsement, or Class 1, 2, 3, or 4 vehicles (except as a learner).
- Class 6 permits the operation of motorcycle and motor-driven cycles and Class 8 vehicles. Class 6 does not permit the operation of Class 1, 2, 3, 4, or 5 vehicles (except as a learner), and may be restricted to the operation of motor-driven cycles (mopeds) and motorcycles 100 cc and under.
- Class 7 is a learner's license which is valid only while holder is accompanied by a licensed driver in the class of vehicle being operated except Class 6 or 8. Class 7 does not permit the operation of Class 1, 2, 3, 4, or 5 vehicles (except as a learner).
- Class 8 permits the operation of farm tractors. It does not permit the operation of any other class of vehicle except as a learner at age 16.
- The following endorsements may be added to a driver's license to allow the driver to operate additional vehicles or combinations of vehicles when the respective minimum requirements have been met: valid for any motorcycle or motor-driven cycle; valid for a school bus; valid for any motorcycle and any school bus; valid only for a motorcycle with engine size of 100 cc or less or motor-driven cycle; valid for school bus and motorcycle with engine size of 100 cc or less or motor-driven cycle; valid for a vehicle equipped with air brakes.

Traffic Rules

Alcohol Laws: Illegal per se BAC is .08.

- A newly licensed driver may operate a vehicle only if he or she has a zero blood alcohol level.
- The legal drinking age is 19.

Barefoot Driving: Barefoot driving is permitted.

Emergency Radio: Citizen band radio channel 9 is not monitored for emergency calls.

Headsets: Wearing radio headsets while operating a motor vehicle is permitted.

Left Foot Braking: Left foot braking is permitted.

Occupant Restraints: All passengers under the age of 16 must wear a seat belt or an age-appropriate child restraint seat.
- All passengers over the age of 16 must wear a seat belt.
- Children at least 27 kg are required to be in a child restraint or seat belt. Child restraints are required for children under 27 kg.
- A vehicle registered in a jurisdiction which does not require the use of a child restraint system for a toddler must secure the toddler in a lap belt, if a lap belt is available to that child.
- Except for employees engaged in the necessary discharge of a duty passengers are not permitted to be transported in space intended for merchandise unless the trucks have secure seating accommodation and all such persons are seated while being so transported.

Railroad Crossing: Whenever a person driving a vehicle approaches a railway crossing that gives a clearly visible signal warning of an oncoming train, the driver must stop before crossing the railroad tracks.
- A driver must not enter a highway or railway crossing unless there is enough space on the other side to accommodate the vehicle without obstructing the oncoming railroad trains.

School Buses: The driver of a vehicle must stop the vehicle before passing a school bus that is exhibiting flashing red lights and is stopped on or near a highway. This vehicle must remain stopped until the school bus proceeds.
- When a school bus is equipped with and exhibits flashing amber lights, the driver of a motor vehicle that intends to pass the school bus must proceed with caution.

Vehicle Equipment & Rules

Bumper Height: All passenger cars and station wagons must be equipped with a front and rear horizontal bumper of the same type and design as originally equipped.
- The top of the bumper measured from the ground must be at least 14 inches high. The bottom of the bumper measured from the ground must be no more than 22 inches high.

Glass/Window Tinting: Windshield tinting is allowed as long as the windshield was tinted during the manufacture of the glass, and not applied afterward.
- A windshield may be equipped with clear untinted frost shields.
- A windshield must not be tinted in a way that prevents the safe operation of the vehicle.

Windshield Stickers: The inspection sticker must be placed on the lower left-hand interior of the windshield.

Motorcycles & Mopeds

Equipment: Every motorcycle must be equipped with securely fastened handlebars, which are not more than 12 inches in height measured vertically from where the handlebars are attached to the frame.
- The frame or forks must not be altered in any way that will prevent the safe opera-

tion of the motorcycle.
- Every motorcycle must be equipped with footrests for the driver and footrests for any passengers. These footrests must be properly positioned.
- The motorcycle must have a chain or a drive-shaft guard, or the motorcycle must be constructed to protect the operator and any passengers from the chain or drive-shaftguard.
- The brakes must be in good working condition.
- All operators and passengers on motorcycles must wear safety helmets conforming to a safety standard.
- Every motorcycle must be equipped with at least 1 and not more than 2 properly mounted white headlamps.

Licenses: Anyone who resides in Nova Scotia and wants to operate a motorcycle must obtain a separate motorcycle driver's license, or an endorsement to his or her regular license.

- A person that wants to obtain a separate motorcycle driver's license must go through Nova Scotia's graduated license program: a learner motorcycle driver's license, a newly licensed motorcycle driver's license, and an unrestricted motorcycle driver's license. To obtain a learner's license, the applicant must pass a vision test and a knowledge test (this test has a special section on motorcycles). To obtain a newly licensed license, the applicant must have a learner motorcycle license, and pass an advanced skills test. This test may be taken after 6 months, or after 3 months if the driver has passed an approved motorcycle driver training course. To obtain an unrestricted motorcycle driver's license, the applicant must have a newly licensed motorcycle driver's license, complete a waiting period of at least 2 years, and pass an approved motorcycle driver improvement program.
- To obtain a regular motorcycle endorsement, the applicant must: (1) apply for and receive a learner's motorcycle license; (2) wait for a period of 3 months (which may be reduced to 1 month if the applicant passes an approved motorcycle training course); and (3) pass an advanced skills test. If the applicant passes an approved motorcycle training course, he or she will not have to take the road test.

Noise Limits: A person cannot start, drive, turn, or stop any motor vehicle in a manner which causes any loud and unnecessary noise from the engine, exhaust, or braking system or from the contact of tires with the roadway.

NS

Passenger Car Trailers

Brakes: All trailers and semitrailers with a gross weight of load and vehicle of more than 4,000 lbs. must have properly functioning brakes controlled by the operator of the motor vehicle.

Dimensions: Trailer length: 14.65 meters; total length: 23 meters (75 feet); width: 2.6 meters (8 feet, 6 inches); height: 4.15 meters (14 feet).

Hitch: Ball hitch mounted on bumper, on 1/2 ton, and 1-ton units is permitted. The drawbar shall not exceed 4.6 meters in length from one vehicle to the other vehicle. Safety chains are required.

Lighting: Every semitrailer or trailer must be equipped with rear lamps that shine a red light for a distance of 150 meters to the rear of the vehicle. A white light for a distance of 15 meters must illuminate the license plate.

Mirrors: If the rearview mirror in a vehicle is obstructed or interfered with by a trailer or semitrailer attached to the motor vehicle, a rearview mirror must be attached to each side of the motor vehicle and placed so that the driver has a clear rear view for 60 meters on each side.

Speed Limits: 80 km/h or as posted.

Towing: The attachment of a towing structure to a vehicle or trailer must be reinforced or braced to prevent distortion of the frame or point of attachment of the vehicle or trailer and have a strength equal to or greater than that of the trailer hitch.

- A passenger cannot ride in a travel trailer or a mobile home while it is being towed on the highway.

Other Provisions: Towing vehicle may not follow other vehicles closer than 60 meters. Riding in a towed trailer is prohibited.

- Maximum of two boats or general utility trailers may be towed behind passenger or pleasure vehicles. Total length of all combined not to exceed 23 meters (75 feet).

Miscellaneous Provisions

Border Inspections: American visitors crossing the border, either way, may be asked to verify their citizenship with a passport or birth certificate. Naturalized U.S. citizens should carry a naturalization certificate, and permanent U.S. residents who are not citizens should carry their Alien Registration Receipt Card.

- Children under 18 years of age should have their birth certificate, and if the parents are separated or divorced, the parent crossing the border should have proof of custody or a letter from the other parent. Persons under 18 years of age who are not accompanied by a parent should bring a letter from their parent or guardian giving them permission to cross the border.
- A visitor is permitted to bring a reasonable amount of personal effects, a reasonable supply of food, and a full tank of gas. Reasonable means enough for personal use during the length of stay in Canada. Any unreasonable amounts are subject to duty.
- A visitor must have a rabies vaccination certificate signed by a licensed veterinarian to bring dogs or cats into Canada.

Liability Laws: Every operator of a motor vehicle must have insurance coverage in the amount of C$200,000 dollars in respect to 1 accident.

- Province has non-resident service of process law; does not have guest suit law.

Weigh/Inspection Stations: All vehicles over 3,000 kg (6,613 pounds) registered weight must stop.

Fees & Taxes

Table 1: Registration Fees (Canadian Dollars)

Vehicle Type	Registration Fee
Passenger Vehicles	Ranges from $115.00 to $268.00 (2 years) depending on weight
Motorized Home/Other Vehicles Converted to a Camper	Ranges from $71.00 to $134.00/yr. depending on weight
Trailers	Ranges from $37.00 to $134.00/yr. depending on weight
Semitrailer	$37.00 (2 years)
Motorcycle	$37.00/yr.
Moped	$16.00/yr.

Table 2: License Fees (Canadian Dollars)

License Class	Fee	Driving Test Fees
Class 1	Initial fee for license is $84.60 license must be renewed every 5 years for $84.60	
Class 2	Initial fee for license is $79.60 license must be renewed every 5 years for $79.60	
Class 3	Initial fee for license is $74.60 license must be renewed every 5 years for $74.60	
Class 4	Initial fee for license is $69.60 license must be renewed every 5 years for $69.60	
Class 5	Initial fee for license is $63.60 license must be renewed every 5 years for $63.60	
Class 6	Initial fee for license is $63.60 license must be renewed every 5 years for $63.60	road test $40.25
Class 7	Initial fee for license is $20.25 license must be renewed every 5 years for $20.25	knowledge test $11.50 road test $40.25
Class 8	Initial fee for license is $57.60 license must be renewed every 5 years for $57.60	
To Upgrade License from Any Higher Class 1, 2, 3, 4, 5, 6, or 8	$9.60	
To Upgrade License from Class 7	$52.95	

Table 3: Other User Fees Taxes (Canadian Dollars)

Tax	Rate
Motor Vehicle Harmonized Sales Tax	15% of the value of the vehicle
Gasoline Tax; (Diesel)	$0.135/liter; ($0.154/liter)

Table 4: Miscellaneous Fees (Canadian Dollars)

Tax	Amount	Payable Upon
Duplicate Driver's License	$20.25	request
Nova Scotia Driver's Handbook	$7.97	request
Endorsement Fee for A,B,C,D, and E	$9.60	request
Name Change on Driver's License	$20.25	request

NS

ONTARIO

Contact Information

Ministry of Transportation of Ontario (MTO)
1201 Wilson Avenue
Building A, Main Floor, Room 178
Toronto, ON M3M 3E6

General Information	(416) 235-4686 or (800) 268-4686
	www.mto.gov.on.ca
Licensing Administration Office	(416) 235-2999 or (800) 387-3445

Ontario Provincial Police
Lincoln M. Alexander Building
777 Memorial Avenue   (888) 310-1122
Orillia, ON L3V 7V3

Ministry of the Environment	(416) 503-6679 or (888) 758-2999
Drive Clean (Emissions Inspections)	www.driveclean.com

Vehicle Title and Registration

Application: Ontario does not issue titles to vehicles.

- No person may drive a motor vehicle on a highway unless there is a currently validated permit for the vehicle and number plates are displayed on the vehicle.
- Vehicle owners must apply for vehicle permits and inform the MTO of name changes at a Driver and Vehicle License Issuing Office (DVLIO). Vehicle owners may change their address and obtain validation stickers and license plates at a Service Ontario kiosk.
- The owner or lessee of a vehicle has 6 days to notify the MTO of a change of name or address.
- Upon becoming a resident of Ontario, a person has 30 days to obtain an Ontario permit and plates for the person's vehicle provided that person has complied with the registration provisions of the person's former jurisdiction.
- All applicants must provide the original copy of the vehicle registration permit and a bill of sale if the permit is not in the owner's name, a Safety Standards Certificate (SSC), a Drive Clean Vehicle Emissions Pass Report if required, proof of Ontario insurance, and a sales tax receipt or exemption declaration.
- Validation of a permit will be refused if there are any outstanding fees or taxes, parking fines, or photo-radar red light camera fines related to the vehicle.
- A permit for a passenger car, a motorized mobile home, an historic vehicle, a motorcycle, or a motor-assisted bicycle may be validated for a period of not less than 3 months and not more than 26 months.

Transfer of Ownership: When the owner or lessee of a vehicle transfers ownership or ceases to lease the vehicle, the owner or lessee must remove the number plates from the vehicle and complete and sign the transfer application on the permit. The permit must be delivered to the new owner or the lessor with the vehicle.

- Every new owner of a motor vehicle or trailer must apply for a new permit within 6 days.
- Every person who sells or transfers a used motor vehicle must obtain a used vehicle information package from the MTO and deliver that package to the buyer or transferee at the same time as delivery of the vehicle. The purchaser or transferee must deliver the used vehicle information package to the MTO before applying for a new permit.

Non-Residents: A non-resident is not required to register his or her motor vehicle in Ontario if the person is a resident of another Canadian province, does not reside or carry on business in Ontario for more than 6 consecutive months each year, the vehicle is properly registered in the province in which the person resides, and the province provides similar exemptions for vehicles owned by residents of Ontario.

- A non-resident from a foreign country is not required to register the person's vehicle in Ontario if the person does not reside or carry on business in Ontario for more than 3 months in any 1 year, the vehicle is properly registered in the jurisdiction in which the owner resides, and the person's state or country of residence provides similar exemptions to residents of Ontario.

Emissions Inspection: Owners of vehicles weighing 4,500 kg or less in the Drive Clean program area must pass an emissions test every 2 years prior to renewing the sticker on the license plate. This applies to vehicles that are more than 3 model years old and less than 20 model years old. An owner will be notified up to 90 days before the deadline for renewing vehicle license plates.

- Motorcycles and motor-assisted bicycles are excluded from the emissions inspection requirement.
- Drive Clean applies to the Greater Toronto Area (City of Toronto and the Regions of Halton, Peel, Durham, and York), the City of Hamilton, and other urban centers and their commuting zones from Peterborough to Windsor. On July 1, 2002, the program expanded to include Ottawa, Kingston, Cornwall, and Chatham-Kent.
- Passing an emissions test is required to transfer ownership.
- Testing at registration alternates between odd-year models and even-year models. Odd-year models must be tested in 2002; even-year models must be tested in 2003.
- A vehicle is not required to comply with emissions standards if after the test, the vehicle is taken to an Ontario Drive Clean repair facility and work costing at least a set amount has been performed to bring the vehicle more nearly in compliance with the maximum emissions standards. The minimum cost of repairs must be $200 in urban and commuter areas until Jan. 1, 2003. The minimum cost of repairs must be $200 in the expanded program area until Jan. 1, 2004. The minimum cost of repairs will be $450 in urban and commuter areas beginning Jan. 1, 2003 and in the expanded program area beginning Jan. 1, 2004.

Safety Inspection: The owner of a vehicle must obtain a SSC issued within the preceding 36 days before the vehicle can be registered unless the vehicle is new and has never been registered.

- Every police officer may require the driver or owner of any motor vehicle or motor-assisted bicycle to submit the vehicle together with its equipment and any attached trailer to the examinations and tests that the officer may consider expedient.

License Plates

Disbursement: No number other than that on the number plate furnished by the MTO may be exposed on any part of a motor vehicle or trailer in such a position or manner as to confuse the identity of the number plate.

- The license plates for a motor vehicle, other than a motorcycle or motor-assisted bicycle, must be attached to and exposed in a conspicuous position on the front and rear of the motor vehicle.
- The license plates for a motorcycle, motor-assisted bicycle, or trailer must be attached to and exposed in a conspicuous position at the rear of the vehicle.
- A current validation sticker must be affixed to the upper right-hand corner of 1 of the rear plates.
- Renewal applications are mailed to the owner approximately 60 days prior to the expiration date of the validation sticker. The expiration date is usually the owner's birthday.
- The number plates must not be obstructed by any device that prevents the entire plate from being accurately photographed by a photo-radar or red light camera system or from being identified by an electronic toll system.
- Personalized plates and over 40 different graphic plates are available.
- Disabled person parking permit is issued by the Ministry of Transportation. Application must be completed and signed by medical practioner.

Transfer of Plates: Vehicle plates stay with the owner, not with the vehicle. If an owner does not intend to use the plates issued to him or her on a replacement vehicle, the owner must return the plates to a Driver and Vehicle License Issuing Office.

Driver's Licenses

Examination: An applicant for an Ontario driver's license must take vision, knowledge, and driving skills examinations unless otherwise exempted.

- A resident of Ontario is not required to take the written and driving skills examinations for a Class G or M driver's license if he or she holds a valid driver's license issued by another Canadian province or territory of an equivalent class, has at least 24 months' driving experience, and surrenders that license.
- A person with a valid driver's license from the United States, Japan, South Korea, Austria, Germany, Switzerland, or Canada Forces Europe may get full Class G license privileges if they have at least 24 months' driving experience. The applicant is not required to take a knowledge or driving test but must pass a vision test.
- A resident of Ontario who applies for a Class G driver's license is not required to take the written and driving skills examinations if he or she holds a valid driver's license of equivalent class issued by a jurisdiction with a reciprocal exchange agreement with Ontario or Japan and he or she surrenders that license.
- A driver from any other country with 2 or more years of driving experience within the last 3 years must pass a vision and knowledge test to be issued a G1 license. The person may then immediately book a G2 road test, and if they pass, they will receive full driving privileges. If the person does not pass the G2 road test, they may immediately book a G1 road test.
- A driver from any other country with less than 2 years of driving experience is subject to the same graduated licensing procedure as new drivers but may receive credit for their experience.

- Diplomats and their immediate family members are not required to take the written and driving skills examinations when applying for a Class G license.

Graduated Drivers Licensing: Province has some form of graduated licensing for teen drivers. At 16, teens are eligible for G1 license. Two-step licensing program takes 20 months to complete.

- G1 license holders must: (1) maintain a 0% blood alcohol concentration; (2) be accompanied by a fully licensed driver, who has at least 4 years' driving experience and a BAC of less than .05%; (3) ensure the accompanying driver is the only other person in the front seat; (4) ensure the number of passengers in the vehicle are limited to the number of working seat belts; (5) refrain from driving on "400-series" highways or high speed expressways; and (6) refrain from driving between midnight and 5:00 a.m. A new driver must hold a G1 license for a minimum of 12 months before attempting a G1 road test. This time can be reduced to 8 months if the licensee successfully completes an approved driver education course.
- A G2 licensee may drive on any highway but must maintain a zero BAC while driving and ensure that the number of passengers in the vehicle are limited to the number of working seat belts.
- A G2 driver must hold a G2 license for a minimum of 12 months before taking the G2 road test. The minimum age for an unrestricted license is 16 years and 8 months.

Issuance/Application: A new resident has 60 days to obtain an Ontario driver's license if the person holds a valid driver's license issued by the jurisdiction where they resided immediately prior to moving to Ontario.

- A non-resident who is at least 16 years of age and holds a valid driver's license from the person's province, state, or country of residence or a valid International Driver's Permit is not required to obtain an Ontario driver's license.
- No person under the age of 16 may operate a motor vehicle on a highway in the province, and no person may employ a person under the age of 16 to operate a motor vehicle on a highway in the province.
- An applicant for a Class G1 or M1 license must pass a knowledge and vision test before being issued a license. The applicant must pass 2 road tests before being issued a full Class G or M license.
- An applicant for any Ontario driver's license is required to produce 2 pieces of identification, at least 1 with the person's signature. Personal identification is also required. The following documents are acceptable proof of personal identification: citizenship card; passport; immigration card with photo; birth certificate; and baptismal certificate.
- License usually includes name, address, signature, date of birth, gender, height, license issue, expiry dates, and codes showing class of vehicle allowed to driver and under what conditions. License also includes digital photo, driver's signature, and magnetic information strip.

Renewal: An applicant for a Class D, G, or M license is not required to take the knowledge, driving skills, and vision examinations if he or she held an Ontario driver's license that expired within 1 year of making the application.

- An applicant for a Class D, G, or M license is not required to take the knowledge and driving skills examinations if he or she held an Ontario driver's license that expired between 1 and 3 years of making the application.
- A driver 80 years of age and over must pass a vision and knowledge test, and the

driver must participate in a 90-minute group education session. The counselor at the group education session will determine whether the driver must take a road test. Upon successful completion of the course, the driver's license will be renewed for 2 years.

Types of Licenses: Class A: Towed vehicles exceeding 4,600 kg, excluding a bus carrying passengers; also authorized for Class D and G.

- Class B: School buses with a seating capacity for more than 24 passengers; also authorized for Class C, D, E, F, and G.
- Class C: Buses, excluding school buses, with a seating capacity for more than 24 passengers; also authorized for Class D, F, and G.
- Class D: Motor vehicles and combinations exceeding 11,000 kg gross weight or Registered Gross Weight (RGW); also authorized for Class G, provided the towed vehicle is not over 4,600 kg.
- Class E: School buses with seating capacity of not more than 24 passengers; also authorized for Class F and G.
- Class F: Buses, excluding school buses, with a seating capacity of not more than 24 passengers and ambulances; also authorized for Class G.
- Class G: Any motor vehicle or combination, including a motor-assisted bicycle, not exceeding 11,000 kg RGW and towed vehicles where the towed vehicle does not exceed a Total Gross Weight (TGW) of 4,600 kg; does not include motorcycles, buses carrying passengers, or ambulances in the course of providing ambulance services.

Traffic Rules

Alcohol Laws: Containers of liquor are prohibited in a motor vehicle, whether it is in motion or not, except under the authority of a license or permit unless the container is unopened and the seal unbroken or the liquor is packed in baggage that is fastened closed or is not otherwise readily available to any person in the vehicle.

- A person may not operate a motor vehicle or have the care or control of a motor vehicle, whether it is in motion or not, while the person's ability to operate the vehicle is impaired by alcohol or a drug or if the person's BAC exceeds .08%.
- The legal drinking age is 19.

Occupant Restraints: Every person who drives on a highway a motor vehicle in which a seat belt assembly is provided for the driver must wear the complete seat belt assembly in a properly adjusted and securely fastened manner.

- Every person who is a passenger on a highway in a motor vehicle in which a seat belt assembly is provided for the seating position occupied by the passenger must wear the complete seat belt assembly in a properly adjusted and securely fastened manner.
- Use of seat belts is not required for a person who: (1) is driving a motor vehicle in reverse; (2) holds a certificate signed by a legally qualified medical practitioner certifying that the person is unable to wear a seat belt because of a medical condition or physical limitations; or (3) is actually engaged in work that requires him or her to alight from and re-enter the vehicle at frequent intervals and is not driving at a speed exceeding 40 km/h.
- Children 8 until 16 and 36 kg or more or taller than 145 cm are required to be in a seat belt; child restraint required for children under 8 and under 36 kg or under 145 cm.

Railroad Crossing: When the driver of a vehicle is approaching a railway crossing at a time when a clearly visible electrical or mechanical signal device or a flagman is giving warning of the approach of a railway train, he or she must stop the vehicle not less than 5 meters from the nearest rail of the railway and must not proceed until he or she can do so safely.

- No person may drive a vehicle through, around, or under a crossing gate or barrier at a railway crossing while the gate or barrier is closed or is being opened or closed.

School Buses: Every driver, when meeting on a highway, other than a highway with a median strip, a stopped school bus that has its overhead red signal lights flashing, must stop before reaching the bus and must not proceed until the bus moves or the overhead red signal lights have stopped flashing.

- Every driver, when approaching from the rear a stopped school bus that has its overhead red signal lights flashing, must stop at least 20 meters before reaching the bus and must not proceed until the bus moves or the overhead red signal-lights have stopped flashing.

Speed Limits: The speed limit is 80 km/h on controlled-access highways and highways outside of a city, town, village, police village, or developed area.

- The speed limit is 50 km/h on highways within a city, town, village, police village or developed area.
- The speed limit is 40 km/h in designated school zones.
- No motor vehicle may be driven on a highway at such a slow rate of speed as to impede or block the normal and reasonable movement of traffic thereon except when the slow rate of speed is necessary for safe operation under the circumstances.
- No person may operate a slow moving vehicle unless a slow moving vehicle sign is attached to the rear of the vehicle or to the rearmost trailer, if 1 or more trailers is being towed. A slow moving vehicle is a vehicle (other than bicycles, motor-assisted bicycles, and disabled motor vehicles in tow) that is not capable of attaining a speed greater than 40 km/h on level ground when operated on a highway.

Vehicle Equipment & Rules

Bumper Height: Modification of original vehicle bumper height is permitted. May be restricted by local ordinance.

Glass/Window Tinting: Windshields and windows may not be coated with any color spray or other color coating that obstructs the driver's view of the highway or any intersecting highway.

- Windshields and windows to the direct left or right of the driver's seat may not be coated with any color spray or other colored or reflective material that substantially obscures the interior of the motor vehicle when viewed from outside the motor vehicle.

Telematics: No person may drive a motor vehicle that is equipped with a television set, any part of which is located forward of the back of the driver's seat, or that is visible to the driver while he or she is operating the vehicle.

- No person may drive a motor vehicle in which a television set is being operated forward of the back of the driver's seat, or that is visible to the driver while he or she is operating the motor vehicle.

- The prohibition on television sets does not apply where the set is being used only: (1) as an aid for the safe and efficient operation of a motor vehicle; or (2) in carrying out a service or conducting a business where the use does not involve recreation or entertainment and does not affect the safe operation of the motor vehicle.

Windshield Stickers: No person may drive a motor vehicle on a highway with any sign, poster or other non-transparent material or object placed on the windshield or on any window of the vehicle in a manner that will obstruct the driver's view of the highway or any intersecting highway.

Motorcycles & Motor-Assisted Bicycles

Equipment: When on a highway at any time every motorcycle must have 2 lighted lamps, 1 white lamp on the front of the vehicle, and 1 red lamp on the rear of the vehicle.

- A motorcycle with a side car must have at all times a lighted lamp on each side of the front of the vehicle.
- Motorcycles manufactured prior to 1970 are required only to have lighted lamps at nighttime and other periods of poor visibility.
- No person may ride on or operate a motorcycle or motor-assisted bicycle on a highway unless all riders are wearing a helmet that complies with the regulations and the chin strap of the helmet is securely fastened under the chin.

Licenses: The holder of a Class M1 license must ride under the following conditions: (1) with a BAC of zero; (2) only during daylight hours; (3) not on highways with speed limits of more than 80 km/h except for specified highways; and (4) not carrying passengers.

- Applicants for a Class M1 license must pass a knowledge test. The license is valid for 60 to 90 days. An M1 licensee who successfully completes an approved motorcycle safety course can skip the MTO's M1 road test and move to a Class M2 license after 60 days. The M2 licensee can obtain a Class M license after 22 months. That time is reduced to 18 months if the licensee completed a safety course while they held either an M1 or M2 license.
- The holder of a Class M2 license must have a BAC of zero while operating the motorcycle.

Noise Limits: Every motor vehicle or motor-assisted bicycle must be equipped with a muffler in good working order and in constant operation to prevent excessive or unusual noise and excessive smoke. No person may use a muffler cut-out, straight exhaust, gutted muffler, hollywood muffler, by-pass, or similar device on a motor vehicle or motor-assisted bicycle.

Mopeds: At night and during periods of poor visibility, every motor-assisted bicycle must have a lighted white lamp on the front, a lighted red light on the rear, white reflective material on the front forks, and red reflective material on the rear.

- No person driving a motor-assisted bicycle may carry any other person on the vehicle.

Passenger Car Trailers

Brakes: Every trailer having a gross weight of 1,360 kg or more must be equipped with brakes adequate to stop and hold the vehicle.

- A combination of a motor vehicle and a trailer where the trailer has an RGW of 3,000 lbs. or less must have brakes adequate to stop within 40 feet while being operated at a speed of 20 mph on a dry, smooth, hard-paved surface free from loose material and having not more than 1% gradient.
- A combination of a motor vehicle and a trailer where the trailer has an RGW of more than 3,000 lbs. must have brakes adequate to stop within 50 feet while being operated at a speed of 20 mph on a dry, smooth, hard-paved surface free from loose material and having not more than 1% gradient.
- A combination of a motor vehicle and a mobile home must have brakes adequate to stop within 50 feet while being operated at a speed of 20 mph on a dry, smooth, hard-paved surface free from loose material and having not more than 1% gradient.

Dimensions: No combination of vehicles, including load, coupled together may exceed the total length of 23 meters while on a highway.

- A city council may prohibit the operation of a combination of vehicles having a total length, including load, in excess of 15.25 meters.

Hitch: Two separate means of attachments required; so constructed and attached that the failure of 1 such means will not permit the motor vehicle, trailer, object, or device being drawn to become detached.

Lighting: When on a highway at night or during periods of poor visibility, every trailer must display 1 lighted red lamp which is clearly discernible from a distance of 150 meters or less.

Speed Limits: Same as passenger cars.

Towing: No driver of a motor vehicle to which a house trailer or boat trailer is attached may operate the motor vehicle on a highway if the trailer is occupied by any persons.

Miscellaneous Provisions

Border Inspections: American visitors crossing the border, either way, may be asked to verify their citizenship with a passport or birth certificate. Naturalized U.S. citizens should carry a naturalization certificate, and permanent U.S. residents who are not citizens should carry their Alien Registration Receipt Card.

- Children under 18 years of age should have their birth certificate, and if the parents are separated or divorced, the parent crossing the border should have proof of custody or a letter from the other parent. Persons under 18 years of age who are not accompanied by a parent should bring a letter from their parent or guardian giving them permission to cross the border.
- A visitor is permitted to bring a reasonable amount of personal effects, a reasonable supply of food, and a full tank of gas. Reasonable means enough for personal use during the length of stay in Canada. Any unreasonable amounts are subject to duty.
- A visitor must have a rabies vaccination certificate signed by a licensed veterinarian to bring dogs or cats into Canada.

Liability Laws: Every motor vehicle liability policy must provide coverage of at least C$200,000 against liability resulting from bodily injury to or the death of 1 or more persons and loss of or damage to property. Claims against the insured arising out of bodily injury or death have priority to the extent of C$190,000 over claims arising out of loss of or damage to property. Claims arising out of loss of or damage to property have priority to the extent of C$10,000 over claims arising out of bodily injury or death.

Weigh Stations: All commercial vehicles must stop.

Fees & Taxes

Table 1: Vehicle Registration Fees (Canadian Dollars)

Vehicle Type	Registration Fee
Motor Vehicle or Trailer Permit	$10.00
Motor Vehicle Permit and Number Plate(s)	$20.00
Trailer Permit and Plate	$35.00
Passenger Vehicles and Motorized Mobile Homes	
Southern Ontario	$74.00*
Northern Ontario	$37.00*
Historical Vehicles	$18.00*
Motorcycles	
Southern Ontario	$42.00*
Northern Ontario	$21.00*

*Additional Fee for Validation if purchased through a Service Ontario Kiosk: $1.00

Table 2: License Fees (Canadian Dollars)

License Class	Fee Amount
G1 License-Includes Knowledge Test, G1 Road Test and 5-Year License Fee	$125.00
Knowledge Test	$10.00
90-Day M1 License	$7.50
5-Year License (Renewal)	$75.00
Class G1 or M1 Road Test	$40.00
Class G2 or M2 Road Test	$75.00
Replacement Driver's License	$10.00
2 to 8 Character Personalized Plates	$239.35
2 to 6 Character Graphic Plates	$319.60
Convert a Regular Series Plate to a Personalized Plate	$239.35
Personalized Motorcycle Plates (2 to 5 Characters)	$239.35
Add a Graphic to a Regular Series Plate	$78.85
Plates Bearing Amateur Radio Operator Call Sign	$30.00
Additional Fee if Purchased through a Service Ontario Kiosk	$1.00

Table 3: Vehicle Taxes and Fees in Lieu of Taxes (Canadian Dollars)

Tax	Rate
Personal Property Tax	Ontario does not have a personal property tax.
Provincial Sales Tax	8%
Federal Goods and Services Tax	7%
Gasoline Tax (Diesel)	$0.147/gallon ($0.143/gallon)

ON

Table 4: Miscellaneous Fees (Canadian Dollars)

Fee	Amount
License Plate Replacement	$20.00*
Graphic Plate Replacement	$30.70*
Personalized Plate Replacement	$30.70*
Personalized Graphic Plate Replacement	$30.70*
Replacement Validation Sticker	$7.00
Replacement Vehicle Permit	$10.00*

*Plus any outstanding amounts registered against the plate owner.

PRINCE EDWARD ISLAND

Contact Information

Motor Vehicle Registrar and Licensing Department
33 Riverside Drive
P.O. Box 2000
Charlottetown, PE C1A 7N8

(902) 368-5220
http://www.gov.pe.ca/

Vehicle Registration

Application: Unless the law grants an exemption, every motor vehicle in Prince Edward Island must be registered with the Department.

- The application for a certificate of registration must be on a form prescribed by the Department. This form must contain the following information: (1) the name and mailing address of the vehicle owner; (2) the make of the vehicle, the vehicle's serial number, any distinguishing marks on the vehicle, and whether it is new or used; and (3) any other information the Department requires.
- When a vehicle is registered, the Department will issue the owner a permit, which contains the vehicles, registration number, the name and address of the owner, a description of the registered vehicle, and anything else the Department determines is necessary.

Non-Residents: Any private passenger motor vehicle that is properly registered in another jurisdiction and owned by a non-resident who is enrolled in a Prince Edward college or university, does not have to be registered in Prince Edward.

- A non-resident who resides in Prince Edward for more than 120 consecutive days in any year must register his or her vehicle with the Department.
- A non-resident must have his or her vehicle registered within 10 days of becoming employed in Prince Edward.

Registration Type: Every registration permit and license plate issued expires at midnight on the birthday of the registered owner.

Safety Inspection: An annual safety inspection is required on all motor vehicles and trailers.

License Plates

Disbursement: One license plate will be disbursed for all vehicles. The license plates for motor vehicles must be attached to the front. A license plate for a truck must be attached to the rear of the truck.

Transfer of Plates: When a vehicle is transferred, the seller must detach and keep the license plate. The plate may be used on another vehicle registered in his or her name. When a person purchases a vehicle, he or she can attach any valid license plate issued to him or her and may operate the vehicle with this plate for a period of up to 7 days pending the registration of the transfer of ownership of the vehicle.

Driver's Licenses

Examination: A written or oral exam, a driving test, and a vision test are required for an original license.

- The road test is waived if the applicant has a license from another North American jurisdiction that has not been expired over 1 year; the vision test is required if the license has been expired for more than 1 year.
- Written, vision, and driving tests are required if the applicant's out-of-province license has been expired over 1 year.

Graduated Drivers Licensing: Province has some form of graduated licensing for teen drivers. At 15 1/2, teens are eligible for a learner's permit if enrolled in a driver education program.

- A holder of a learner's permit can only drive if he or she meets the following criteria: (1) must be accompanied by a licensed driver who has held a license for 4 years; (2) the licensed driver must sit in the passenger seat; and (3) only members of the immediate family of the licensed operator can be in the vehicle, or the permit holder can be accompanied by a licensed instructor and no more than 4 persons, not including the instructor.
- A learner's permit holder must hold the permit for 6 months before being eligible for a regular driver's license.
- At 16, teens are eligible for a regular license. However, a driver of a motor vehicle who has held a driver's license for less than 1 year may only be accompanied by 3 passengers who are immediate family of the driver, or the immediate family of the driver and one other passenger.
- The number of passengers allowed in the vehicle must not exceed the number of passengers that can be accommodated in seating positions that have seat belts.
- When the driver of a motor vehicle has held a valid driver's license for more than 1 year but less than 2 years, the driver may not transport more passengers than seat belts.
- The minimum age for an unrestricted license is 17.

Issuance/Application: The application for a driver's license must contain the name, address, and mailing address of the applicant, and any other information the Department requires to enable it to determine whether a driver's license should be issued to the applicant and the class of the license that should be issued.

Renewal: Licenses are valid for 3 years and expire on the licensee's birthday. Regular driver's license renewal must be done in person.

PE

Types of Licenses: Driver's license classes include: Class 1 – any tractor-trailer or truck-trailer combination; Class 2 – buses, taxis, and ambulances over 24 passengers; Class 3 – straight truck over 4,600 kg, over 14,000 kg if trailer is less than 4,500 kg; Class 4 – buses under 24 passengers; Class 5 – passenger cars and light trucks, not exceeding 14,000 kg; Class 6 – motorcycles; Class 7 – learner's permit; Class 8 – mopeds; and Class 9 – farm tractor permit.

Traffic Rules

Alcohol Laws: Open containers are not permitted.
- Illegal per se BAC is .08. For minors, presumptive level is zero tolerance.
- The legal drinking age is 19.

Barefoot Driving: Barefoot driving is permitted.

Headsets: Wearing radio headsets while driving is permitted.

Left Foot Braking: Left foot braking is permitted.

Occupant Restraints: The driver and passengers of a motor vehicle must wear a seat belt.
- Children under 16 years and 18 kg or more are required to be in a child restraint or seat belt.
- Child restraints are required for all children under 18 kg.
- The owner of a motor vehicle must make sure that all seat belts are in good working condition.

School Buses: The driver of a vehicle meeting or overtaking a school bus on a highway when the flashing red lights are displayed must bring the vehicle to a stop at least 6 meters from the school bus, and must not pass the school bus until the flashing red lights are no longer displayed.
- The driver of a vehicle meeting or overtaking a school bus on a highway when the flashing amber lights are displayed on the school bus must reduce speed and proceed with caution, and may only pass the school bus with caution.

Vehicle Equipment & Rules

Bumper Height: Modification of original bumper height is illegal.

Glass/Window Tinting: It is illegal to install transparent, opaque, or translucent material on a front or side window, unless the material is a replacement glazing installed by the manufacturer, or the material is a clear untinted frost shield.
- It is illegal to install transparent, opaque, or translucent material on the rear windshield, unless the motor vehicle is equipped with outside rear view mirrors on the left and right of the motor vehicle, and unless the material is a replacement glazing installed by the manufacturer, or the material is a clear untinted frost shield.
- A person must not place or install any material on or in place of any window glazing that casts a glare on other vehicles on the highway because of sunlight or headlights.

Telematics: A person must not drive on a highway a motor vehicle equipped with a television set, and a person must not drive a vehicle carrying a television set while the set is in operation.

Windshield Stickers: Windshield stickers are permissible as long as they do not impair the safe operation of the motor vehicle.

Motorcycles & Mopeds

Equipment: Every motorcycle must be equipped with at least 1 and not more than 2 headlamps.

- Every headlamp must be located at a height of not more than 1,400 mm nor less than 600 mm.
- Every headlamp must be of sufficient intensity to reveal a person or a vehicle at a distance of not less than 30 meters when the motorcycle is driven less than 40 km/h, 60 meters when the motorcycle is operated at a speed of 40 km/h, and at a distance of not less than 90 meters when the motorcycle is operated at a speed of 60 km/h or more.
- If a motorcycle is equipped with a single-beam headlamp or headlamps, the lamp or lamps must be aimed so that the high-intensity portion of the light does not project higher than the level of the center of the lamp at a distance of 10 meters.
- The headlamps of a motorcycle must not be covered with any material to color or tint the lamp if this coloring or tint reduces the intensity of the light.
- Every motorcycle must have rear red taillamps that become illuminated when the driver applies pressure to the brakes.
- Every motorcycle must be equipped with brakes on at least 2 wheels.
- All motorcycle riders must wear helmets approved by the Canadian Department of Transportation.

Licenses: Class 6 motorcycle license required. Fee, $45 for 3 years of Class 6 endorsement to regular license. Expires on birthday.

- License plates required. Fee, $5; valid for one year. Registration fee, $30.

Mopeds: A permit holder can operate a moped with either a Class 8 license or a Class 6 license.

- Registration is required.
- Minimum age to ride a moped is 16 with parental consent.
- The following safety equipment is required: helmet, head- and taillamp, reflectors, and brakes.

Passenger Car Trailers

Brakes: Every trailer or semitrailer weighing 1,500 kg or more must be equipped with brakes that can control the movement of and stop and hold the towing vehicle, and the vehicles being towed.

- These brakes must also be designed so that when the driver of the towing vehicles presses on the brakes, he or she stops and holds the towing vehicle and the vehicles being towed.
- The brakes must be designed and connected so that the brakes are automatically applied if 1 of the vehicles being towed breaks away.
- Every trailer or semitrailer weighing 1,500 kg or more must be equipped with service brakes on all the wheels.
- Any trailer or semitrailer weighing less than 1,500 kg is not required to be equipped with service brakes on the wheels.

- A trailer equipped with brakes must be designed so that when the brakes on the towing vehicle are applied, the trailer brakes stop the trailer, and there must be a mechanical connection that is capable of holding the vehicle, or combination of vehicles under any condition upon which it is operated.
- Every motor vehicle and combination of motor-drawn vehicles must be capable of being stopped on a dry, smooth, level road free from loose material, within the distances specified: vehicles or a combination of vehicles having brakes on all wheels going 30 km/h must stop within 9.15 meters; and vehicles or a combination of vehicles not having brakes on all wheels must stop within 12.20 meters.

Dimensions: Total length: 25 meters; trailer length: 16.2 meters; width: 2.6 meters; height: 4.5 meters.

Hitch: When 1 vehicle is towing another with a drabber, ball hitch, or other type of utility trailer hitch, the connection must be of sufficient strength to pull all the weight being towed. Also, the combination of vehicles must be connected with at least 2 safety chains of equal length, and each chain must be of sufficient strength to hold the vehicles together in case the connection between the vehicles breaks or is accidentally disconnected.

Lighting: Every semitrailer or trailer must be equipped with at least 2 rear red taillamps, one on each side of the vehicle. These rear taillamps must emit a light visible from a distance of 150 meters.

- Every taillamp and reflector must be located at a height between 500 mm and 1,520 mm.
- Every vehicle must have a light on the rear of the vehicle that illuminates the license plate for 15 meters.
- Every motor vehicle must have rear red brake lights.
- Every trailer or semitrailer that is 2 meters or more in overall length must meet the following requirements: on the front as high as possible, have 2 amber clearance lamps mounted at the same height; on the rear and as high as practicable, have 2 red clearance lamps mounted at the same height; on the front and each side at or near the midpoint, have an amber reflector, all reflectors being mounted not less than 375 mm or more than 1,500 mm when measured from the ground; and have 3 red indicator lamps in a horizontal row close to the top with the center lamp on center line and others mounted an equal distance from the center lamp, not less than 150 mm or more than 300 mm.

Mirrors: Every motor vehicle, other than a farm tractor, must be equipped with a mirror located and adjusted to give the driver an unobstructed rear view for at least 60 meters to the rear of the vehicle.

- The operator of a towing vehicle which has an exterior accessory rearview mirror which extends beyond the length of a fixed standard mirror, or more than 10 inches beyond the body of the towing vehicle, must remove or fix the exterior accessory rearview mirror so that it is 250 mm or less beyond the body of the towing vehicle when the equipment being towed is disconnected.

Speed Limits: 80 km/h unless posted otherwise.

Miscellaneous Provisions

Border Inspections: American visitors crossing the border, either way, may be asked to verify their citizenship with a passport or birth certificate. Naturalized U.S. citizens

should carry a naturalization certificate, and permanent U.S. residents who are not citizens should carry their Alien Registration Receipt Card.
- Children under 18 years of age should have their birth certificate, and if the parents are separated or divorced, the parent crossing the border should have proof of custody or a letter from the other parent. Persons under 18 years of age who are not accompanied by a parent should bring a letter from their parent or guardian giving them permission to cross the border.
- A visitor is permitted to bring a reasonable amount of personal effects, a reasonable supply of food, and a full tank of gas. Reasonable means enough for personal use during the length of stay in Canada. Any unreasonable amounts are subject to duty.
- A visitor must have a rabies vaccination certificate signed by a licensed veterinarian to bring dogs or cats into Canada.

Liability Laws: All motor vehicle operators must have at least C$200,000, exclusive of interest and cost against liability resulting from bodily injury to, or the death of, or damage to property for one accident.
- Compulsory 3rd party insurance for limits of C$200,000.
- Judgment recover (PEI) Ltd. available for judgments up to C$200,000 for bodily injury or death of any person or for property damage. Such payment not required to non-residents unless they reside in a jurisdiction where recourse of substantial similar type is afforded to residents of Prince Edward Island. Proof of insurance is required. Penalty, for noncompliance: minimum C$600; maximum C$2,000.

Weigh Stations: Agricultural vehicles and trucks over 3,000 kg GVW must stop.

Fees & Taxes

Table 1: Registration Fees (Canadian Dollars)

Vehicle Type	Registration Fee
Private Passenger Vehicles, Taxicabs, and Trucks less than 3.859 kg	$80.00 per year
Passenger Car Trailer Registration	depends on the size of the trailer
Non-Compliance Renewal Registration Fee	between $25.00 and $100.00
Motorcycles	$30.00 per year
Mopeds	$20.00 per year

Table 2: License Fees (Canadian Dollars)

License Class	Fee	Driving Test Fees
Class 1, Class 2, Class 3, Class 4, Class 5, Class 8	$50.00 every 3 years	duplicate $10.00
Class 7 (Learner's Permit Fee)	$5.00	$20.00
Class 6 (Motorcycle Endorsement)	$30.00 every 3 years	

Table 3: Vehicle Taxes (Canadian Dollars)

Tax	Rate
Use Tax	12.5%
Province Sales Tax	12.5%
Gasoline Tax	$0.13 per liter

PE

Table 4: Miscellaneous Fees (Canadian Dollars)

Fee	Amount	Payable Upon
Safety Inspection Fee for Passenger Cars	$12.00	before inspection
Safety Inspection Fee for All Other Motor Vehicles	$9.00 - $20.00	before inspection
Replacement License Plate	$5.00	request
License Plate Fee	$5.00	request
Motorcycle License Plate Fee	$5.00	request
Moped License Plate Fee	$5.00	request
Title Transfer Fee	$10.00	request

QUEBEC

Contact Information

Société de l'Assurance Automobile du Québec (SAAQ)
Case postale 19600, Succursale Terminus   Québec (418) 643-7620
333, boulevard Jean-Lesage   Montréal (514) 873-7620
Québec G1K 8J6   Other areas in the province (800) 361-7620

Sûreté du Québec
(General Headquarters Highway Patrol)
1701 rue Parthenais
Montréal, Québec H2L 4K7

Vehicle Registration

Application: Every road vehicle must be registered except vehicles specifically exempted.

- Every owner of a road vehicle must apply to the SAAQ for its registration upon taking possession of it.
- An owner may obtain a 10-day temporary registration for a vehicle sold by a dealer.
- A vehicle owner who establishes residence in Québec must apply to the SAAQ for the vehicle's registration within 90 days.
- A vehicle's registration expires when the owner ceases to own the vehicle.
- A trailer leased for a period not exceeding 12 months is exempt from registration if: (1) the leasing contract is entered into outside Québec; (2) its owner is not required to hold a leasing permit from the Commission des Transports du Québec; (3) it is in the possession of the lessee; and (4) its net mass is 900 kg or less.
- The owner of a vehicle must pay the registration fees and the insurance contribution fee prior to obtaining registration and the right to use the vehicle on a public highway or on private land open to public traffic.
- An applicant must supply the applicant's name, address, birth date, status, vehicle description, net weight, name of the lessor if applicable, category of the vehicle, use of the vehicle, professional activity or legal personality of the owner if applicable, and the territory where the vehicle is used. The "status" of the owner includes whether the owner is the sole owner, joint owner, or a partner; whether there is a lease for a period of at least 1 year; and whether the person is the guardian of a minor owning the vehicle.

- The owner of a vehicle must notify the SAAQ within 30 days of any changes to the information concerning the registration certificate. In Québec, no yearly stickers are put on plates.
- The person driving or having the care or control of a road vehicle must have with him or her the registration certificate of the vehicle and the certificate of insurance or of financial responsibility. If the vehicle is leased for less than 1 year or if it has been lent by a dealer, the person must also have with him or her a copy of the lease or a document evidencing the loan.
- The owner of a passenger vehicle or a motor home with a net weight of 3,000 kg or less must pay registration-related fees sometime during a designated 3-month period based on the first letter of the owner's surname.
- The owner of a motor home with a net weight of more than 3,000 kg or of a motorcycle or moped must pay the registration-related fees between the 1st day of February and the last day of April.
- Four-day temporary registration certificates are available for: (1) vehicles acquired in Québec by non-residents; (2) vehicles owned in Québec; (3) vehicles recently acquired outside of Québec by a non-resident; (4) vehicles registered outside of Québec; and (5) trailers.

Non-Residents: The passenger vehicle or trailer of a non-resident is exempt from registration for a period of 6 consecutive months if: (1) the vehicle is registered as required by the law of the main place of residence or the business establishment of its owner; (2) the vehicle carries a valid registration plate of that jurisdiction; and (3) the driver furnishes proof of that registration at the request of the SAAQ or of a peace officer.

- A road vehicle acquired outside Québec by a foreign student, coopérant, or trainee staying in Québec is exempt from registration for the duration of his or her studies or training if: (1) the vehicle is registered as required by the law of the main place of residence of its owner or the place where he or she established residence; (2) the vehicle carries a valid registration plate of that place; (3) the student, coopérant, or trainee furnishes proof of that registration at the request of the SAAQ or of a peace officer; and the same right is granted to students, coopérants, or trainees from Québec staying in the place of domicile of that student, coopérant, or trainee.

Transfer of Ownership: Where the right of ownership of a road vehicle is transferred between parties neither of whom is a dealer, the transferor or seller must endorse the registration certificate and return the registration certificate to the SAAQ. The new owner must apply for a new registration.

- Where road vehicles are exchanged between parties neither of whom is a dealer, each owner must return to the SAAQ the endorsed registration certificate issued for his or her vehicle and apply for a new registration.
- Where the right of ownership of a road vehicle is transferred to a dealer, the transferor must remit the registration certificate of the vehicle to the dealer after endorsing it. If the transferor is not purchasing a new vehicle, then a person may keep the plate for further use. If the transferor is purchasing a new vehicle, the transferor can use the registration plate and apply for a new registration certificate.
- The lessee of a road vehicle leased for a term of one year or more must, at the end of the lease, return the registration certificate and registration plate of the leased vehicle to the SAAQ.

- A person who becomes the owner of a road vehicle as a result of a death, a gift, a partition, a winding-up, a bankruptcy, a repossession, the complete transfer of a business, or a judicial sale must return the registration certificate to the SAAQ and apply for a new registration for the vehicle.

Safety Inspection: Mandatory inspections for taxis, emergency vehicles, driving school cars or motorcycles, trucks and trailers over 3,000 kg net weight, buses, and minibuses. Spot checks are conducted on highways.

License Plates

Disbursement: The owner of a road vehicle must place the temporary registration certificate issued to him or her in the upper left-hand part of the rear window of the vehicle.

- Where it is impossible to affix a temporary registration certificate in the upper left portion of a vehicle's rear window, the temporary registration must be affixed in the upper left portion of the windshield.
- When the registration plate is issued, the owner must firmly attach the plate to the rear of the vehicle.
- Where a vehicle is essentially designed to tow a trailer, the license plate must be affixed to the front of the vehicle.
- No registration plate may bear any inscription other than those determined by the SAAQ. The registration plate must be free of any object or matter that could impair its legibility. If the plate is attached to the rear of the vehicle, it must be sufficiently lighted.
- No plate that may be confused with a registration plate issued by the SAAQ or by any other competent administrative authority may be attached to a road vehicle or affixed to a plate, except in the case of a plate required by another law in force in Québec.

Driver's Licenses

Examination: Driving knowledge test, vision test, and road test are required for original permit.

Graduated Drivers Licensing: Province has graduated licensing for new drivers. Before they may apply for any type of license (see below) except for a motorcycle or moped or a farm tractor, they must obtain, at least, a learner's license. The rules to obtain a motorcycle license differ from those for a passenger vehicle. They are explained further:

- **Passenger vehicle:** New drivers are eligible for a learner's permit from the age of 16. They can obtain it after passing the driving knowledge test and the vision test. The holder of a learner's permit must, when driving a passenger vehicle, be assisted by a person who has held, for at least 2 years, a valid driver's license for that class of vehicle. The person must be seated beside the holder of the learner's license, and be in position to give him or her assistance and advice.
- New drivers must hold the learner's permit for at least 12 months (8 with driver education) before being eligible for a probationary driving license if they are less than 25 years of age, or a regular driving license if they are 25 years of age or older. The appropriate license is obtained after passing the road test. It is valid for 24 months or until the age of 25, whichever comes first. Drivers then qualify for a regular driver's license.

- **Motorcycle:** New drivers are eligible for a learner's permit from the age of 16. All prospective motorcycle operators must first pass a visual test and a knowledge test in order to get a class 6R learner's license, valid for use only within a driving school's course or for the Société's test on a closed circuit. After having held a class 6R license for at least 1 month, learners must successfully complete a driving school's course for operating a motorcycle and a closed circuit test. Only then are prospective motorcycle operators issued a class 6A learner's license, which must be held for at least 7 months.
- The holder of a learner's license must, when driving a motorcycle, be accompanied by a person on a separate motorcycle who has held, for at least 2 years, a valid driver's license authorizing the driving of a motorcycle of the appropriate class (6A, 6B, or 6C) and who is able to provide assistance and advice.
- The last step is a road test, which prospective operators must pass in order to obtain a probationary or regular license for a motorcycle.
- A person who is less than 25 years of age and has never held a probationary license, other than a moped or a farm tractor, must hold a probationary license for 24 months or until the age of 25, whichever comes first, before obtaining a class 6A, 6B, or 6C license.
- A person who is 25 of age or older, or who has already held a driver's license, other than for a moped or farm tractor, may obtain a class 6A, 6B, or 6C license after passing the road test.
- **Moped:** A person applying for a class 6D license must be 14 years of age or older and must attest that he or she has completed independent learning activities comprising the following elements: (1) pre-driving procedures; (2) basic controls; (3) communication; (4) observation; (5) use of the road; (6) maintaining a safe distance; (7) controlling speed; (8) intersections; and (9) learning exercises.

Issuance/Application: No person may drive a vehicle on a public highway or on private property open to public traffic unless he or she holds a driver's license of the appropriate class for the vehicle.

- No person may hold more than 1 valid driver's license.
- A person wishing to obtain a driver's license must: (1) submit a document proving his or her identity, in particular, name (first and last), birth date, and where applicable a French or English translation of the document; (2) indicate his or her eye color, height, and sex; (3) provide his or her principal address; (4) submit the declaration of illness or functional impairment; and (5) a written consent of his or her father, mother, or legal guardian, if he or she is a minor.
- A learner's license is issued in paper form without a photograph. The probationary and driver's license are issued in plastic form with a photograph.
- Learner's and probationary license holders are subject to ceiling of 4 demerit points and zero tolerance for alcohol use when driving. Each breach of one of these conditions results in license suspension for 3 months that are added to the required holding period of the license.
- A person holding a valid driver's license issued by another administration authority must obtain a driver's license issued by the SAAQ within 90 days of settling in Québec.
- A person holding a valid non-commercial driver's license issued by another Canadian or U.S. jurisdiction may exchange that license for a driver's license issued by the SAAQ without an examination.

Renewal:

- A plastic license is valid from the date on which it is issued until the end of the holder's birthday occurring during the year determined by adding multiples of 4 to the holder's year of birth until the year thus obtained is that immediately following the year in which the license is issued.
- The holder of a driver's license must pay biennial duties, fees, and a biennial automobile insurance contribution during a 3-month period ending with his birthday every other year.

Types of Licenses: The SAAQ issues learner's licenses, probationary licenses, driver's licenses, and restricted licenses.

- Class 1, 2, 3, 4A, 4B, and 4C driver's licenses are commercial driver's licenses. Class 1, 2, and 3 are more specifically for heavy vehicles (including buses), class 4A for emergency vehicles, class 4B for minibuses (24 passengers or less), and class 4C for taxis.
- Class 5 authorizes the holder to drive a motor vehicle having 2 axles and a net mass of less than 4,500 kg, a motor vehicle permanently converted into a dwelling, an equipment vehicle, a service vehicle, a moped, and a farm tractor. The holder may also drive a covered vehicle hauling a trailer.
- Class 6A authorizes the holder to drive any motorcycle or moped.
- Class 6B authorizes the holder to drive any motorcycle with an engine size of not more than 400 cc or a moped.
- Class 6C authorizes the holder to drive any motorcycle with an engine size of not more than 125 cc or a moped.
- Class 6D authorizes the holder to drive a moped. No person may ride a motorcycle or moped equipped with a 125 cc or less engine on a limited access highway or on an entrance or exit ramp.
- Class 8 authorizes the holder to drive a farm tractor.

Traffic Rules

Alcohol Laws: Open containers are not permitted.

- A person may not operate a motor vehicle or have the care or control of a motor vehicle, whether it is in motion or not, while the person's ability to operate the vehicle is impaired by alcohol, a drug, or if the person's blood alcohol content exceeds .08%.
- The legal drinking age is 18.

Barefoot Driving: Barefoot driving is permitted.

Emergency Radio/Cellular: Citizen band radio channel 9 is not monitored for emergency calls. The emergency cellular number is *4141.

Headsets: In no case may the driver of a road vehicle or person riding a bicycle use headphones or earphones unless the device is used in conversational exchanges among its users to the extent that the device allows surrounding traffic noises to be heard.

Left Foot Braking: Left foot braking is permitted.

Occupant Restraints: Every person, while in a moving road vehicle, must wear, properly fastened, the seat belt with which his or her seat is equipped unless: (1) the person is driving in reverse; (2) the person is a taxi driver performing his or her functions on a numbered highway with a speed limit set by a municipality or on an unnumbered highway; or (3) the person has been issued a medical exemption certificate by the SAAQ.

- Children whose seated height is less than 63 cm are required to be in a child restraint.
- In no case may the driver of a vehicle allow more passengers in his or her vehicle than there are places available for them to sit.
- No person may drive a vehicle if the front seat is occupied by more than 3 persons or more than 2 persons if the front of the vehicle is equipped with chair seats.
- Riding in pickup truck beds is not permitted.

Railroad Crossing: At a railroad crossing, the driver of a road vehicle or any person riding a bicycle must stop his or her vehicle not less than 5 meters from the railway where a sign, signal, lowered gate, or railway employee signals an approaching rail vehicle, or where the driver or cyclist sees or hears a rail vehicle approaching the railroad crossing.

- Even if so authorized by traffic lights, no driver of a road vehicle may enter a railroad crossing if there is not sufficient space ahead of the vehicle to allow him or her to cross the level crossing.

School Buses: The driver of a road vehicle who is approaching a school bus with flashing lights turned on or whose compulsory stop signal has been activated, must stop his or her vehicle more than 5 meters from the bus and must not proceed in either direction until the flashing lights are turned off and the compulsory stop signal has been retracted, and he or she ascertains that he or she can do so in safety. A driver is not required to stop upon meeting a school bus on an adjacent roadway separated by a median strip or any other raised physical separation.

Vehicle Equipment & Rules

Bumper Height: Modification of original vehicle bumper height is illegal.

Glass/Window Tinting: No person may coat the windshield or the front side windows of a road vehicle or cause them to be coated with a substance having the effect of reducing or preventing good visibility from inside or outside the vehicle.

Telematics: No person may drive a road vehicle in which a television set or a display screen is so placed that the image broadcast on the screen is directly or indirectly visible to the driver, except in the case of a closed circuit system used by the driver to operate the vehicle, or a system used by a peace officer or ambulance driver in the performance of their duties.

Windshield Stickers: Windshields and other windows of a motor vehicle must be free of any material that might reduce visibility from inside or outside the vehicle.

Motorcycles & Mopeds

Equipment: Every motorcycle or moped must carry at least: (1) 1 headlight; (2) 1 red taillight; (3) 2 white or amber turn-signal lights on the front and 2 red or amber turn-

signal lights at the rear; and (4) 1 red stop light at the rear.
- When a motorcycle is equipped with a sidecar, the sidecar must carry a red taillight, which must be as near as practicable to the right extremity of the sidecar.
- Every motorcycle or moped must be equipped with 2 rearview mirrors, 1 solidly attached to each side of the vehicle.
- No driver of a motorcycle or moped may carry any other person unless his or her vehicle is equipped with permanently fixed seats designed for that purpose and with footrests fixed on each side of the vehicle.
- The driver of a motorcycle or moped must keep the headlight of his or her vehicle on at all times.
- Every person riding on a motorcycle or moped or in a sidecar must wear a protective helmet.

Licenses: Class 6A authorizes the holder to drive any motorcycle or moped.
- Class 6B authorizes the holder to drive any motorcycle with an engine size of not more than 400 cc or moped.
- Class 6C authorizes the holder to drive any motorcycle with an engine size of not more than 125 cc or moped.
- Class 6D authorizes the holder to drive a moped.
- The holder of a learner's license must, when driving a motorcycle, be accompanied by a person on a separate motorcycle, who has held for at least 2 years, a valid driver's license authorizing the driving of a motorcycle and who is able to provide assistance and advice.
- A person applying for a Class 6D license must attest that he or she has completed independent learning activities comprising the following elements: (1) pre-driving procedures; (2) basic controls; (3) communication; (4) observation; (5) use of the road; (6) maintaining a safe distance; (7) controlling speed; (8) intersections; and (9) learning exercises.
- A person who is less than 25 years of age who has never held a probationary license, other than for a moped or farm tractor, must hold a probationary license for at least 2 years before obtaining a Class 6A, 6B, or 6C license.
- A person who is 25 years of age or older or who has already held a driver's license, other than for a moped or farm tractor, may obtain a Class 6A, 6B, or 6C license after holding a Class 6A learner's license for at least 7 months.

Mopeds: No person may ride a motorcycle or moped equipped with a 125 cc or less engine on a limited access highway or on an entrance or exit ramp.

Passenger Car Trailers

QC

Brakes: Every road vehicle must be equipped with at least 1 service system allowing sufficient braking force to be applied on each weight-bearing wheel to stop the vehicle quickly in case of emergency.
- Every trailer that is part of a combination of road vehicles and that has a mass, once loaded, of 1,300 kg or more or that has a mass, once loaded, of over half the net mass of the motor vehicle by which it is being towed, must be equipped with an independent braking system allowing application of a braking force on each weight-bearing wheel. The towing vehicle must carry the necessary equipment for operating the braking system of any trailer being towed.

Dimensions: The maximum length for any combination consisting of a towing vehicle and a single or double trailer is 19 meters. Under certain conditions the maximum length could be 23 meters.

- The maximum width of any trailer, load included, is 2.60 meters.
- The maximum height of any trailer, load included, is 4.15 meters.

Hitch: Every trailer operated without an independent brake system adequate to stop the vehicle if the trailer becomes separated from the towing vehicle must be equipped with chains, cables, or any other safety device that is sufficiently solid and installed to ensure that the trailer and towing vehicle remain attached in the event of a failure in the attachment devices. The towing vehicle must carry the necessary equipment for attaching the chains, cables, or safety device of any trailer being towed.

- No person may pull a trailer without using an adequate coupling device. The lights, braking system, chains, cables, and any other safety device on the trailer must be connected to the towing vehicle and in proper working condition.

Mirrors: Where the motor vehicle pulls a trailer, rearview mirrors must be attached so as to enable the driver to have a clear view to the back of the combination of vehicles: (1) 1 rearview mirror attached to the exterior of the motor vehicle on the left side if the existing rearview mirror cannot be used; and (2) another rearview mirror attached to the exterior of the motor vehicle on the right side if the existing interior or exterior rearview mirror on the right side cannot be used.

Speed Limits: 100 km/h on highways.

Towing: No person may occupy a trailer in motion or tolerate such practice. Where a trailer is specially designed and equipped for the transportation of persons, it may be used for that purpose in parades or other popular events provided the highway used is closed to all other traffic.

- No person may use a road vehicle for pulling another road vehicle the wheels of which remain on the ground, unless the vehicle is firmly held by a bar.

Miscellaneous Provisions

Border Inspections: American visitors crossing the border, either way, may be asked to prove their citizenship with a passport or birth certificate. Naturalized U.S. citizens should carry a naturalization certificate, and permanent U.S. residents who are not citizens should carry their Alien Registration Receipt Card.

- Children under 18 years of age should have their birth certificate, and if the parents are separated or divorced, the parent crossing the border should have proof of custody or a letter from the other parent. Persons under 18 years of age who are not accompanied by a parent should bring a letter from their parent or guardian giving them permission to cross the border.
- A visitor is permitted to bring a reasonable amount of personal effects, a reasonable supply of food, and a full tank of gas. Reasonable means enough for personal use during the length of stay in Canada. Any unreasonable amounts are subject to duty.
- A visitor must have a rabies vaccination certificate signed by a licensed veterinarian to bring dogs or cats into Canada.

Liability Laws: The owner of any automobile operating in Québec must have a liability insurance contract. The insurance contract must cover property damage caused in an accident in Canada or the United States and bodily injury or death caused by the automobile outside Québec, elsewhere in Canada, and in the United States. The minimum coverage required for an individual owner is C$50,000, and the minimum coverage required for a commercial operator is C$1,000,000.

- Québec has an automobile insurance fund administered by the SAAQ that compensates bodily injury and death as a result of automobile accidents. Residents of Québec are covered inside and outside of Québec. Non-residents are covered for accidents occurring in Québec to the extent that they were not responsible for the accident.
- A person registering a vehicle in Québec or obtaining a Québec driver's license must make payments into the fund.
- Residents: All Quebecers, victims of automobile accidents in or outside Quebec, shall be compensated by the Société regardless of fault.
- Non-residents: Non-resident victim of an accident in Quebec shall be compensated to the extent he or she is not responsible for the accident unless a different agreement between the Société and the jurisdiction where he or she resides. In case of disagreement between the victim and the Société concerning his or her responsibility, the victim may have recourse to the law court. He or she will be entirely compensated if he or she is the owner, driver, or passenger of a vehicle registered in Quebec. Benefits include: Indemnity for loss of income: 90% of net income (maximum gross income considered is C$56,000 (CDN/yearly). Reimbursement of medical, hospital, and rehabilitation expenses (disfigurement, dismemberment, pain, and suffering). The maximum lump sum awarded for permanent impairment was C$197,012 for 2005. Death benefits depend on the age and marital status of the deceased. For 2005, a lump sum of C$4,212 was forwarded to cover funeral expenses.
- Financing: Each owner of vehicle registered in Quebec contributes to the financing of the plan depending on the class of his or her vehicle. In 2005, passenger car, C$117; trailer, C$13 including a 9% insurance tax. Once every 2 years, a contribution is also payable on the driver's permit dependent upon number of demerit points: 0-3, C$50; 4-7, C$100; 8-11, C$174; 12-14, C$286; and 15 or more, C$398.

Weigh Stations: An owner of a road vehicle must, at the request of the SAAQ or a peace officer, furnish the weighing certificate within 10 days of the request to establish the net mass of the vehicle.

Fees & Taxes

Table 1: Annual vehicle registration fee and insurance contribution (Canadian Dollars)

Vehicle Type	Registration Fee	Insurance Contribution	Total
Passenger vehicle or motor home with net weight of 3,000 kg or less owned by an individual * depend on owner's principal residence region	$52.00-$134.00*	$117.00	$169.00-$251.00*
Motor home with net weight of 3,000 kg or less owned by a business or organization	$182.00	$134.00	$316.00
Motor home with a net weight of more than 3,000 kg but not exceeding 8,000 kg	$327.00	$134.00	$461.00
Motor home with a net weight of more than 8,000 kg but not exceeding 10,000 kg	$435.00	$134.00	$569.00
Motor home with net weight of more than 10,000 kg	$570.00	$134.00	$704.00
Trailer (one time cost for the same owner)	$44.00	$13.00	$57.00
Motorcycle	$40.00	Cylinder size of 50 cc or less: $81.00	$121.00
		Cylinder size 51 cc to 125 cc: $131.00	$171.00
		Cylinder size 126 cc to 400 cc: $206.00	$246.00
		Cylinder size 401 cc and over $276.00	$316.00
Moped	$12.00	$50.00	$62.00
Snowmobile	$69.00	N/A	$69.00
Snowmobile with net weight of more than 450 kg	$44.00	$37.00	$81.00
Vehicle more than 25 years old	$44.00	$37.00	$81.00
Antique vehicle (more than 30 years old)	$44.00	$37.00	$81.00
4-day temporary registration	$2.00	$2.00	$4.00
10-day temporary registration for a vehicle sold by a dealer	$2.00	$2.00	$4.00

Table 2: Annual license fee and insurance contribution (Canadian Dollars)

Class or Permit	License Fee	Insurance Contribution	Total
1-2-3-4a-4b-4c-5-6a-6b-6c	$16.00	$25.00	$41.00
6D	$21.00	N/A	$21.00
8	$21.00	$11.00	$32.00
Learner	$8.00	$11.00	$19.00

Table 3: Vehicle Taxes and Fees (Canadian Dollars)

Tax	Rate
Luxury Duty on Vehicles 7 Years Old or Less with a Value Exceeding $40,000	1% of the value of the vehicle in excess of $40,000
Federal Goods and Services Tax	7%
Provincial Tax	7.5%

QC

Table 4: Miscellaneous Fees (Canadian Dollars)

Contribution to Public Transit	$30.00/year (only if person has access to that service, when available)

SASKATCHEWAN

Contact Information

Saskatchewan Government Insurance
Licensing and Registration Services Department (Department)
2260 11th Avenue (306) 775-6900 Customer Service Center
Regina, SK S4P 0J9 1-800-667-9868 North American Customer Service Line
www.sgi.sk.ca

Vehicle Registration

Application: If an owner of a vehicle applies on a form provided by the Department and pays the prescribed fees, the Department may register the vehicle and issue the owner a certificate of registration and license plates.

- The Department may refuse to issue a certificate if, in the opinion of the Department the person is unfit to operate a vehicle, the applicant is unfit according to the law, the vehicle is unsafe, the vehicle is ineligible for registration, the applicant has failed to provide all information requested by the Department, or the applicant has made any false statement on the registration application.

Non-Residents: A non-resident temporarily residing in Saskatchewan while attending an educational institution as a student, or a student participating in an exchange program, does not have to apply for a certificate of registration while he or she is a student, provided that he or she is in compliance with the laws of his or her jurisdiction, has a valid certificate of registration and license plate from that jurisdiction, and can provide proof of financial responsibility.

Registration Type: Every certificate of registration and registration permit expires on the date shown on the certificate of registration or registration permit.

Safety Inspection: All passenger motor vehicles must pass a safety inspection before they are registered in Saskatchewan.

License Plates

Disbursement: When a vehicle is registered, 1 license plate will be disbursed to the vehicle's owner, for motor vehicles.

Transfer of Plates: A person who intends to transfer license plates, from 1 vehicle to another without changing the name in which the certificate of registration is issued, must apply on a form provided by the Department and pay the appropriate fee. After the fee is paid, the Department will issue a receipt. Once the receipt is issued, the license plates can be transferred.

Driver's Licenses

Examination: A written or oral exam, a driving test, a vision test, and driver education are required for the original license. If a license holder is moving from a jurisdiction outside of Canada, the United States, Switzerland, Germany, Austria, or Great Britian, he or she will have to take a written, vision, and a driving examination.

- If an applicant is moving from another Canadian jurisdiction, the United States, Switzerland, Germany, Austria, or Great Britian and he or she holds a valid driver's license, the applicant can apply for a Saskatchewan Class 5 and motorcycle driver's license by surrendering his or her out-of-state driver's license and by paying the appropriate fees; the applicant will not have to take any examination, unless the Department determines that any tests are needed.

Graduated Drivers Licensing: Province has a probationary licensing program. At 15, teens are eligible for a Class 7 license, if they complete the high school driver education program (otherwise 16 years).

- Class 7 license holders under the age of 16 may not operate a motor vehicle unless accompanied and supervised by either an approved instructor or by a parent or guardian or by a person authorized by the Department.
- This person must occupy the front passenger's seat, be conscious and capable of lawfully assuming operation of the vehicle, and hold or have held a license that permits him or her to operate the vehicle being operated by the driver, for at least 1 year.
- All first time drivers must hold the Class 7 license for at least 9 months.
- At 16 years, teens who have a driver education certificate are eligible for a Class 5 - Novice 1 license. They are probationary for 6 months and are subject to monitoring and zero blood alcohol content and restricted to 1 passenger only who is not a family member. All passengers must wear seat belts.
- At 16 years and 6 months, teens are eligible for a Class 5 - Novice 2 license. Teens must hold this license for 12 months (crash conviction-free) to get an unrestricted license.

Issuance/Application: An applicant for a Class 7 driver's license must meet the following criteria: (1) be at least 16 years of age, or 15 years of age and enrolled in a government-sanctioned high school driver training program, unless he or she previously held a driver's license and submits proof of this to the Department; (2) except where he or she previously held a driver's license, submits evidence of his or her name and age; (3) passes the vision, sign, road, and written oral tests for the class of license for which he or she is applying; and (4) has held a Class 7 license for at least 6 months.

- The driver's license of a new driver is a probationary license for 2 years.

Renewal: A probationary driver's license is valid for 2 years. New drivers are on probation for 2 years and are monitored for convictions and accidents. A new driver is someone who has not held a valid Class 6 or higher driver's license in Canada, the United States, or another country that has a signed reciprocity agreement with Saskatchewan, within the last 5 years or who has less than 2 years of driving experience in those jurisdictions.

- Driver's licenses can be renewed by mail. If the driver's license of a Saskatchewan resident has lapsed for more than 5 years, then a written, vision, and a driving test are required.

New Residents: New residents who wish to drive in Saskatchewan must obtain a Saskatchewan driver's license within 90 days of moving to the province, or upon expiry of their out-of-province license, whichever is earliest.

Types of Licenses: Class 1 motor vehicles are power unit[1] and semitrailer combinations, trucks when towing a vehicle, or vehicles the Combined Gross Weight (CGW) of which exceeds 4,600 kg, and buses when towing a vehicle or vehicles, the CGW of which exceeds 4,600 kg (minimum age 18).

- Class 2 motor vehicles are buses that have a seating capacity of more than 24 passengers.
- Class 3 motor vehicles are trucks with more than 2 axles, trucks when towing a vehicle, or vehicles the CGW of which does not exceed 4,600 kg, and power units with more than 2 axles when not towing a trailer.
- Class 4 motor vehicles are buses that have a seating capacity of not more than 24 passengers, public service vehicles used in the operation of a taxi service when being used for hire, ambulances when being used for hire.
- Class 5 motor vehicles are vehicles with no more than 2 axles, other than motorcycles, vehicles with 2 axles when towing a vehicle or vehicles whose CGW does not exceed 4,600 kg, buses when not carrying passengers, motor homes with 3 axles, public service vehicles used in the operation of a taxi service when not being used for hire, law enforcement vehicles, and any vehicle registered as a school bus, without passengers.
- Class 6 motor vehicles are motorcycles (minimum age 16 with parental approval).
- A Class 7 license allows the holder to drive Class 5 motor vehicles as a learner.
- Any person age 16 or over can obtain an endorsement to his or her regular driver's license by passing a vision, sign, road, and written or oral test for the endorsement that he or she is trying to obtain and by filing any appropriate medical report requested by the Department.

Traffic Rules

Alcohol Laws: Open containers are not permitted. The legal drinking age is 19.

- The maximum blood alcohol content is 80 mg of alcohol in 100 milliliters of blood, or .08% for criminal sanctions.
- A new driver with a probationary license (2 years) and a Class 7 license holder cannot have any alcohol in his or her system when driving a motor vehicle, or roadside administrative suspensions are applied.
- Experienced drivers are subject to roadside administrative suspensions for a blood alcohol content between .04% and .08%.

Barefoot Driving: Barefoot driving is permitted.

Headsets: Wearing radio headsets is permitted.

Left Foot Braking: Left foot braking is permitted.

Occupant Restraints: The driver of a motor vehicle must wear a seat belt that is properly adjusted and securely fastened. All passengers over age 16 that are in a seat with a seat belt must wear the seat belt. The above provisions do not apply to specific industries that require the driver to re-enter the vehicle at intermittant spots of 100 meters or less and the person is driving at 40 km/h or less.

---

[1] A power unit is defined as a vehicle designed and used for towing a semitrailer on a highway with a substantial part of the weight of the semitrailer and its load carried by the power unit.

- A person must not drive a motor vehicle on a highway with a passenger under the age of 16 years who weighs more than 18 kg unless the passenger occupies a seat that is equipped with a seat belt, and the passenger must wear the seat belt.
- If a passenger under 16 years weighs less than 18 kg that passenger must be placed in an age and weight appropriate child or infant restraint system. This child or infant restraint system must be properly adjusted and securely fastened in the manner recommended by the manufacturer.
- Passengers should not ride in pickup truck beds.

Railroad Crossing: The driver of a vehicle must bring the vehicle to a stop when approaching a railway crossing when a signal person or an automatic signal indicates an approaching train.

School Buses: The driver of a vehicle proceeding in the same direction on a highway as a school bus that has its safety lights in operation must not pass the school bus.

- The driver of a vehicle proceeding in the same direction on a highway as a school bus that is stopped and that has its safety lights and stop arm in operation must stop at least 5 meters from the rear of the school bus. The vehicle must not proceed until the operation of the safety lights and stop arm has been discontinued.
- When a school bus is stopped and has its safety lights and stop arm in operation, the driver of a vehicle that is approaching the school bus from the opposite direction on a highway, other than a divided highway, must stop at least 5 meters from the front of the school bus and must not proceed until the operation of the safety lights and stop arm has been discontinued.

Vehicle Equipment & Rules

Bumper Height: On passenger motor vehicles, the center part of the bumper must be between 380 mm and 560 mm above the ground when the vehicle is unloaded on level ground and the tires are inflated within the range specified by the tire manufacturer.

Glass/Window Tinting: The windshield and front side windows must not have a coating of sunscreen or reflective material other than that applied by the glass manufacturer.

Telematics: An image displayed on a television set, video screen or computer screen may be located so that it is visible to the driver if the image only displays information that is solely designed to assist the driver in the safe operation of the vehicle, or in ensuring the safety and security of its load or its passengers or to navigate. The equipment must be secure and located so that it does not obstruct the view of the driver.

Windshield Stickers: Windshield stickers are allowed as long as they are less than 51.20 mm in diameter in the area swept by the windshield wipers.

Motorcycles & Mopeds

SK

Equipment: All motorcycle operators must wear helmets.

- If a motorcycle is not equipped with a windshield, the driver and any passengers must wear protective eye goggles.
- All motorcycles must have at least 1 brake system. If the motorcycle has 1 brake system, the application of the brakes must be to both the front and the rear wheels.

- If the motorcycle has 2 brake systems, each brake system must have a separate means of application; 1 brake system must be effective on the front wheels and 1 brake system must be effective on the rear wheels.
- The brake system or systems must stop the vehicle in an upright position, from a speed of 30 km/h within a distance of 8 meters on a dry, smooth, level, paved surface without deviating by more than 300 mm from a straight line.
- All motorcycles must have handlebars that have grips that are no higher than the shoulder of the seated driver; a speedometer that is in good working condition; horn that can be heard under normal conditions from a distance of 60 meters and is within reach of the driver's seat.
- All lamps, except for headlamps, must emit a light that is visible from a distance of 200 meters on a clear night.
- All motorcycles must have 1 or more headlamps that have a high and low beam.
- The headlamps must, while on high beams or low beams, emit a white light visible from a distance of 500 meters on a clear night.
- The headlamp must be automatically activated when any forward gear is engaged while the engine is running.
- A motorcycle must have red taillamps that emit a red light that is visible from any point along a 180 horizontal arc. This lamp must be activated by a headlamp control.
- A motorcycle must have a rear brake lamp that emits a red light and is activated by the application of brakes on any wheel.
- A motorcycle must have reflectors or reflective tape that is located at the rear and on each side at the front and rear; emits a red reflection from the rear and rear side reflectors and an amber reflection from the front side reflectors; and is visible from a distance of 60 meters when illuminated on a clear night.
- When a passenger is being transported on the motorcycle, the motorcycle must be fitted with foot pegs. These foot pegs must fold rearward and upward when not in use.
- A motorcycle must not carry a passenger unless the seat is designed to carry an additional passenger.
- The vehicle must have a mirror that has an effective area of at least 5,500 mm and also provide the driver with a clear view of the road.

Licenses: A person cannot operate a motorcycle as a learner at night, when accompanied by a passenger, or on a public highway that has a maximum allowable speed greater than 80 km/h.

- A Class 7 driver's license may only be endorsed for the operation of a Class 6 motor vehicle if the holder of the Class 7 driver's license is at least 16 years old.
- A person is not eligible for a Class 6 driver's license except under the following conditions: (1) he or she is at least 16 years of age, except where he or she previously held a driver's license and submits evidence satisfactory to the Department confirming this; (2) if he or she is under 18 years of age and has not previously held a driver's license, he or she must submit to the Department the written consent of 1 of his or her parents or guardians; (3) he or she submits a medical report if required by the Department; and (5) he or she has passed the vision, sign, and written or oral tests for motorcycles.

Noise Limits: A motorcycle must have 1 or more mufflers that ensure exhaust gases are cooled, and that effectively reduce combustion noise.

Passenger Car Trailers

Registration: All trailer and semitrailers must be registered with the Department.

Brakes: A trailer or semitrailer that has a Gross Vehicle Weight Rating (GVWR) of more than 1,360 kg or has a GVWR that exceeds the GVWR of the towing vehicle by more than 50% must have the following type of brake system: (1) if the vehicle was manufactured before 1985, the brakes are applied on wheels on opposite ends of at least 1 axle; and (2) if the vehicle was manufactured in or after 1985, the brakes are applied on opposite ends of all axles.

- The brake system must automatically activate the brakes in the case of a breakaway from the towing vehicle without affecting the brakes of the towing vehicle.
- The service brakes must be adjusted so that they apply braking as nearly as equal on the wheels on the opposite ends of the same axle.
- The weight of a trailer and its load or a combination of trailers and their loads must not exceed the following: (1) in the case of a trailer or semitrailer with a gooseneck hitch (not equipped with air brakes), a 5th-wheel hitch or a weight distributing hitch, 2 times the GVWR of the towing vehicle; or (2) in the case of a ball hitch, the GVWR of the towing vehicle.
- The maximum width for a house trailer that is being moved between sunrise and sunset is 3.05 meters.
- The maximum length for any combination of vehicles is 23 meters.

Hitch: Must be connected by a safe clevis or catch; ball hitch mounted on bumper permitted up to 1400 kg; safety chain required. Hitch must be rated for the combined weight of trailer(s) and contents. Two safety chains must cross under the hitch.

Lighting: Brake, tail, and signal lights required.

Speed Limits: 80 km/h unless posted otherwise.

Miscellaneous Provisions

Border Inspections: American visitors crossing the border, either way, may be asked to verify their citizenship with a passport or birth certificate. Naturalized U.S. citizens should carry a naturalization certificate, and permanent U.S. residents who are not citizens should carry their Alien Registration Receipt Card.

- Children under 18 years of age should have their birth certificate, and if the parents are separated or divorced, the parent crossing the border should have proof of custody or a letter from the other parent. Persons under 18 years of age who are not accompanied by a parent should bring a letter from their parent or guardian giving them permission to cross the border.
- A visitor is permitted to bring a reasonable amount of personal effects, a reasonable supply of food, and a full tank of gas. Reasonable means enough for personal use during the length of stay in Canada. Any unreasonable amounts are subject to duty.
- A visitor must have a rabies vaccination certificate signed by a licensed veterinarian to bring dogs or cats into Canada.

Liability Laws: Province has future-proof law applicable for failure to satisfy judgment for death, bodily injury, or property damage exceeding C$1,000 due to traffic accident. Minimum financial responsibility limits: C$200,000 inclusive.

- The Automobile Accident Insurance Act provides limited compensation, regardless

SK

of fault, for accident victims.

Weigh Stations: All trucks over 10 metric tons must stop, except 2- and 3-axle Saskatchewan registered farm trucks.

Fees & Taxes

Table 1: Title & Registration Fees (Canadian Dollars)

Vehicle Type	Registration Fee
Vehicles with the Body Style of a Car that are less than 5,000 kg	$68.00
Passenger Vehicles 5,000 kg – 15,001 kg	$112.00 – $258.00
Motorcycles with an Engine Capacity of 50 cubic centimeters or less	$34.00
Motorcycles with an engine capacity of more than 50 cubic centimeters	$50.00
Any Motor Vehicle of a Model Year of 1941 or earlier	$5.00

Table 2: Driver License Test Fees (Canadian Dollars)

License Class	Road Test Fee	Written Test Fees
Class 1, 2, or 3	$40.00	written examination $10.00
Class 4, 5, or 7	$22.00	written examination $10.00
Issuance of a School Bus Endorsement Requiring a Road Test	$20.00	written examination $10.00
Issuance of an Air Brake Endorsement Requiring a Practical Test	$15.00	written examination $10.00
Issuance of a Motorcycle Endorsement Requiring a Road Test	$22.00	written examination $10.00

Table 3: Driver License Fee (Canadian Dollars)

License	Fee
Annual Driver's License	$25.00

Table 4: Vehicle Taxes (Canadian Dollars)

Tax	Rate
Provincial Sales Tax	7% tax on the sale of used vehicles. Taxable value on dealer sales is calculated on the cash difference, which is the purchase price less the trade-in value. There is a $3,000 reduction from the value for tax purposes for private sales. On private sales, the taxpayer is allowed the greater of the $3,000 deduction or the trade-in value, but not both. At the time of registration the $3,000 deduction is recognized but not the trade-in value. If the trade-in value exceeds the $3,000 deduction, the purchaser must request a tax adjustment for the trade from the Department of Finance. The provincial sales tax does not apply to gifts of motor vehicles between first-degree relatives (i.e. spouse, parent, child, etc.)
Motor Vehicle Insurance Premium Tax Fee	1% of gross motor vehicle insurance premiums
Gasoline Tax	$0.15 per liter

Table 5: Miscellaneous Fees (Canadian Dollars)

Fee	Amount	Payable Upon
Photo Identification Card Without an Endorsement	$10.00	request
Personalized License Plates	$75.00	request
Replacement License Plates	$20.00	request
Transfer or Exchange of a Certificate of Registration	$10.00	request
Registration Search by Name	$10.00	request
Registration Search by License	$10.00	request
Registration Search by Vehicle Identification Number	$10.00	request
Certified Copy of a Driver's Record	$10.00	request

YUKON TERRITORY

Contact Information

Motor Vehicles Community Services
Government of Yukon
P.O. Box 2703
Whitehorse, YT Y1A 2C6

Department of Community and Transportation Services (CTS)
Transport Services Branch
Motor Vehicles Section
1st Floor, Lynn Building,
308 Steele Street P.O. Box 2703   (867) 667-5315; (800) 661-0408 (within the Yukon)
Whitehorse, YT Y1A 2C6   www.cts.gov.yk.ca/motor_vehicles.asp

Royal Canadian Mounted Police
Division Headquarters
4100 4th Avenue   (867) 633-8611
Whitehorse, YT Y1A 1H5

Vehicle Registration

Application: A certificate of registration or permit issued by the CTS is required to operate a motor vehicle or trailer on a highway unless otherwise exempted.

- A motor vehicle or trailer must be registered in the Yukon within 7 days of being brought into the territory for the first time in the previous 12 months unless otherwise exempted.
- The owner of a motor vehicle must provide proof of insurance and a bill of sale signed by the seller to register the motor vehicle. If the vehicle is new, the owner must also provide a New Vehicle Information Statement (NVIS) form or the original factory invoice if the NVIS is not available.
- The vehicle must be registered for a period of between 3 months and 15 months unless the vehicle is a commercial vehicle that weighs 4,500 kg or more, in which case the vehicle must be registered for a period of between 6 and 18 months.

Non-Residents: Non-residents are not required to register their vehicles in the Yukon if: (1) the vehicle is registered in another jurisdiction; (2) the registration plates or other identification issued by the other jurisdiction is displayed on the vehicle; (3) the vehicle has not been in the Yukon for a continuous period of more than 60 days in the preceding 12 months; (4) the person in whose name the vehicle is registered is not a resident of the Yukon; (5) the vehicle is not rented; (6) and the vehicle is not leased for a period of more than 30 days to a person who is a resident of the Yukon.

- A person is deemed to be a resident of the Yukon when: (1) he or she makes his or her home in the Yukon and is ordinarily present in the Yukon; (2) he or she earns income from employment in the Yukon; or (3) he or she carries on a business in the Yukon.

Registration Type: A temporary operation permit may be issued to the purchaser of a vehicle who is unable to register the vehicle, or for the temporary operation of the vehicle for a period not to exceed 10 days from date of issue.

- Vehicle registrations are renewed on a staggered basis depending on the first letter of the owner's surname or the first letter of a corporation's name if a corporation owns the vehicle.
- Registration may be renewed, and the license plates or validation tabs may be issued for the renewal, during the period that begins 2 months before the month for renewal and ends with the last day of the month for renewal, and the renewal may be for a period between 3 months and 15 months, unless the vehicle is a commercial vehicle that weighs 4,500 kg or more.

Transfer of Ownership: When the ownership of a registered vehicle passes from the registered owner to any other person, whether by an act of the owner or by operation of law, the registration of the vehicle expires at the time of transfer.

Safety Inspection: An officer may require the owner or operator of a vehicle that is being operated on a highway to submit the vehicle to examination and tests to ensure that the motor vehicle can be operated in compliance with the law.

License Plates

Disbursement: License plates are issued by the CTS at the same time the certificate of registration is issued.

- No person may attach to a motor vehicle or trailer or operate a motor vehicle or trailer to which is attached a license plate other than a license plate authorized for use on that motor vehicle or trailer.
- No person may operate or park a motor vehicle or trailer unless each license plate required is attached to the vehicle in the proper location and manner.
- The operator of a motor vehicle or trailer must at all times keep any license plate required to be attached to the vehicle secured in a manner and maintained in a condition so as to be clearly visible and readable and unobscured.
- Only 1 license plate is issued per vehicle, except that 2 personalized plates may be issued.
- Except for truck tractors and dump trucks, the plate must be attached to the rear of the vehicle so that the bottom of the plate is at least as high off the ground as the rear axle. A second plate may be attached to the front of the vehicle so that the bottom of the plate is at least as high off the ground as the front axle.

Transfer of Plates: When the ownership of a registered vehicle passes from the registered owner to any other person, whether by an act of the owner or by operation of law, the registered owner of the vehicle must remove the license plates from the vehicle and retain them in his or her possession. If the registered owner fails to remove

the license plates, the new owner must remove the plates and return them to the CTS.
- At any time during the registration year for which license plates are issued, the person to whom they are issued may apply to the CTS to use the plates on another vehicle registered in his or her name, and if the application is made within 14 days after acquiring ownership of the other vehicle, that person may display the plates on the newly acquired vehicle during that 14-day period.

Driver's Licenses

Examination: To receive a license each applicant for each class of driver's license must (1) take a basic written and sign recognition test and receive a score of at least 80%; (2) take a supplementary written test and receive a score of at least 80%; (3) meet the vision standards; and (4) pass a road test.

- Road tests may be waived for Classes 1, 2, 3, 4, and 5 where the applicant has successfully competed tests conducted by the applicant's employer or an approved training school.
- The CTS may require an applicant to take a medical examination.
- An applicant must pass a written and eye examination to obtain a Class 7 GDL learner's license.
- A person must hold a learner's license for at least 6 months and pass a road test before obtaining a novice license.

Graduated Drivers Licensing: Territory has some form of graduated licensing.

- A learner's licensee may operate a motor vehicle while accompanied by a person who holds a subsisting license for the operation of the vehicle being used, who has held such license for a period of at least 2 years, and who is seated immediately beside the licensee. In addition the person accompanying the learner licensee must not have any alcohol in his or her blood, and his or her ability to operate a motor vehicle must not be impaired by drugs or any other substance.
- A novice licensee may drive without a co-driver except between the hours of midnight and 5:00 a.m.
- Except in the case of a learner's license, a driver's license is not issued to anyone under the age of 16 years.
- The application of a person under 18 years of age must be signed by the person's parent or legal guardian unless the applicant can prove that he or she is self-supporting and unable to obtain the consent of a parent or guardian, or that he or she is married. The minimum age for an unrestricted license is 17 years and 6 months.

Issuance/Application: No person may operate a vehicle on a highway unless he is the holder of a driver's license authorizing him or her to operate that class of vehicle.

- An application for a driver's license is made to the CTS.
- A non-resident is not required to hold a driver's license if he or she does not remain in the Yukon for more than 120 consecutive days in any year, and if he or she is authorized by the laws of his or her place of residence to operate a motor vehicle of the type or class being operated by him or her.
- A non-resident student is not required to hold a driver's license if he or she holds a valid license issued by his place of residence.
- Every person who holds a license issued outside the Yukon authorizing him or her to operate a motor vehicle must surrender that license when issued a Yukon driver's license unless the CTS waives the surrender on grounds that the person is not able to surrender the license.

- No person may attempt to obtain a driver's license during a period when his or her license is canceled or suspended in any province or in any state, territory, or the District of Columbia in the United States.
- Learner's and novice's licenses are available from a Territorial Agent or Territorial Office.
- A person may apply for a full privilege driver's license at any motor vehicle office.
- The CTS must suspend the license of a person under 18 years of age if a parent withdraws consent.
- An applicant must provide his or her surname, given names, postal address, date of birth, height, weight, and sex.
- An applicant must provide a primary and secondary form of identification when obtaining a Yukon driver's license for the first time. Photocopies are not acceptable. Primary forms of identification include a birth certificate, proof of Canadian citizenship, a foreign passport, a driver's license issued by another jurisdiction, and a Canadian Armed Forces ID or discharge papers. Secondary forms of identification include a baptismal certificate showing date of birth, social insurance card, health care card, certificate of Indian status, liquor ID, landed immigrant papers, and a Canadian or U.S. passport.
- A licensee must sign the license in the space provided or the license is not valid.
- A licensee must notify the CTS of every change of address or change of name.
- An applicant must disclose to the CTS any disease or disability that may interfere with the safe operation of a motor vehicle.
- A person holding a driver's license from another jurisdiction has 120 days to obtain a Yukon driver's license upon taking up residency or employment in the territory. However, if the person has an air-brake endorsement, the person must exchange their license within 30 days.
- The holder of a driver's license from another jurisdiction must surrender the license from the other jurisdiction, provide 1 piece of secondary identification, and provide a medical report if the person is applying for a Class 1, 2, 3, or 4 license or if the person is 70 years of age or older.
- A duplicate license and a security keyword are required to obtain a duplicate license. If the previous license is found, it must be returned immediately to the CTS. It is an offense to hold more than 1 driver's license at any 1 time.
- Every driver of a motor vehicle must carry his or her driver's license with him or her at all times while driving a motor vehicle and must produce it for inspection upon demand by any peace officer.
- The CTS may issue a temporary license effective for 90 days.

Renewal: A driver's license is valid, unless otherwise suspended or revoked, for a period of 5 years.

- Any license that is not renewed within 6 months from the expiration date will be considered a first application.
- A driver's license may be renewed by mail or in person.
- If a person is 70 years of age or older, he or she must file a medical examination certificate signed by a licensed physician and submit to a vision examination.

Types of Licenses: Class 1, 2, 3, and 4 licenses are for the operation of large commercial vehicles. An applicant must be 18 years of age or older.

- A Class 5 license permits the operation of a single motor vehicle up to 11,000 kg

(24,000 lbs.) Gross Vehicle Weight (GVW), vehicle-trailer combinations up to 11,000 kg GVW where the trailer does not exceed 4,550 kg (10,000 lbs.) and learners being instructed on vehicles in Class 1, 2, 3, or 4.
- Class 6 permits the operation of motorcycles and mopeds. An applicant must be 16 years of age or older.
- Class 7 is a learner's permit for the operation of all Class 5 and 6 vehicles.
- A person who is 15 years of age or older may obtain a Class 7 learner's license for the operation of passenger vehicles and motorcycles.
- A novice license is available for a person who is at least 16 years of age.
- A person may obtain a full privilege driver's license at the age of 18 years of age if the person has met all of the conditions of the learner's and novice stages.

Traffic Rules

Alcohol Laws: Open containers are not permitted. The legal drinking age is 19.
- A person may not operate a motor vehicle or have the care or control of a motor vehicle, whether it is in motion or not, while the person's ability to operate the vehicle is impaired by alcohol or a drug or if the person's BAC exceeds .08%.

Barefoot Driving: Barefoot driving is permitted.

Emergency Radio/Cellular: Citizen band radio channel 9 may be monitored for emergency calls. Emergency number is 911 in Whitehorse only.

Headsets: Wearing of radio headsets while operating a motor vehicle is permitted.

Left Foot Braking: Left foot braking is permitted.

Occupant Restraints: Every person who drives on a highway a motor vehicle in which a seat belt is installed for the driver must be properly secured in a seat belt unless the person is doing work that requires him or her to get out of and re-enter the motor vehicle at frequent intervals and who, while doing that work, does not drive the motor vehicle faster than 30 km/h, does not drive through an intersection, and does not drive more than 250 meters without stopping.

- Every person over 7 years of age who is a passenger in a motor vehicle that is being operated on a highway must wear a seat belt if a seat belt is installed for the seat the passenger occupies, or if there is an unoccupied seat with a seat belt.
- Children under 7 years of age and under 22 kg. must be secured in a child restraint system. A child weighing less than 9 kg. must be secured in an infant restraint system. A child weighing 9 to 22 kg. must be secured in a child restraint system. Children weighing over 18 kg. may use a booster cushion. Children weighing over 22 kg. may use a standard seat belt.
- The following vehicles are exempted from the passenger restraint requirements: taxis, school buses, transit buses, motor coaches, emergency vehicles, rental vehicles, vehicles not licensed in the Yukon, and motor homes.
- Riding in the bed of a truck is permitted.

Railroad Crossing: At a railway crossing at any time when (1) a clearly visible electrical or mechanical signal device gives warning of the approach of a railway train, (2) a crossing gate is lowered or a flagman is giving a signal of the approach or passage of a train, (3) a train within approximately 500 meters of the crossing is approaching the crossing and either sounds an audible signal or is visible, or (4) a train is visible and

YT

approaching the crossing and by reason of its speed or nearness is an immediate hazard, a driver approaching the crossing must not proceed until the train has passed or come to a stop and the driver can proceed safely.

- No person may drive through, around, or under a crossing gate or barrier at a railway crossing while the gate or barrier is closed or is being opened or closed.
- Where a stop sign is erected at a railway crossing, a driver approaching the railway crossing must stop his or her vehicle no closer than 5 meters and no further than 15 meters from the nearest rail of the railway and must proceed until he can do so safely.
- When a driver has stopped at a railway crossing, he or she must cross the railway tracks in a gear that he or she will not need to change while crossing the tracks and must not shift gears while crossing.

School Buses: When a school bus has stopped on a highway to receive or discharge passengers or while the vehicle is displaying alternately flashing red lights, a driver approaching the school bus from the rear, if the highway is physically divided by a median strip into 2 separate roadways, or from either direction, if the highway is not so divided, must stop before reaching the school bus.

- A person who is required to stop before reaching the school bus must not proceed to pass the school bus (1) until the school bus resumes motion, (2) until the driver of the school bus indicates by a signal that he may proceed, or (3) where the school bus is displaying alternately flashing red lights, until the lights stop flashing.

Vehicle Equipment & Rules

Bumper Height: Modification of original vehicle bumper height is permitted within regulated limits.

Glass/Window Tinting: Application of after-market vehicle glass-darkening material is permitted on all windows except windshield. Tinting permitted on rear window cannot obstruct driver's view.

Telematics: No person may drive on a highway a vehicle that is equipped with a television set unless the television set is located and operated so that the driver cannot by any means see the screen of the television while the vehicle is in motion.

Tires: No restrictions on studded tires.

Windshield Stickers: No person may drive a vehicle on a highway if the view through the windshield or windows is so obscured by mud, frost, steam, or any other thing as to make the driving of the vehicle hazardous or dangerous.

Motorcycles, Mopeds & Snowmobiles

Equipment: Any person operating or riding as a passenger on a motorcycle, moped, or snowmobile is required to wear an approved helmet.

- Every motorcycle, moped, and snowmobile must be equipped with at least 1 headlamp but not more than 2 headlamps, and at least 1 taillamp mounted at the rear of the vehicle.
- No motorcycle may be in motion on a highway at any time unless the lamp or lamps with which it is equipped are alight.
- A person who is operating a motorcycle, moped, or snowmobile on a highway: (1) must keep both hands on the handlebars, except when making a signal; (2) must keep both feet on the pedals or footrests; (3) must not ride other than upon or

astride the regular seat, and must not use the vehicle to carry more people at 1 time than the number for which it is designed or equipped.
- A person who is riding as a passenger on a motorcycle, moped, or snowmobile must not ride other than upon a regular seat of the vehicle intended for a passenger, and must keep both feet on the footrests provided for the use of a passenger riding on the seat.
- Every motorcycle, moped, and snowmobile must be equipped with at least 1 brake light.

Licenses: Class 6 permits the operation of motorcycles and mopeds.
- A Class 7 learner's permit may be issued for the purpose of operating a motorcycle.
- The holder of any class of driver's license is not entitled to operate a motorcycle, except for the purpose of learning, unless the operator has successfully passed the applicable examination and has the number 6 included in the Class as provided on the driver's license.
- No person under the age of 16 years may operate a motorcycle, moped, or snowmobile on a highway.
- A person who is operating a motorcycle, moped, or snowmobile on a highway must ride as near as practicable to the right-hand curb or edge of the roadway and must not operate the vehicle on a roadway where signs prohibit its use.

Noise Limits: No person may create or cause the emission of any loud and unnecessary noise from the motor vehicle, any part thereof, or anything or substance that the motor vehicle or part of the motor vehicle comes into contact with.
- No person may operate a vehicle on a residential street within a municipality between the hours of 10:00 p.m. and 7:00 a.m. so as to disturb residents of that street unduly.
- Every motor vehicle propelled by an internal combustion engine must be equipped with a properly functioning muffler.

Mopeds: Same requirements as motorcycles.

Passenger Car Trailers

Brakes: Independent braking system required if gross weight exceeds 910 kg or one-half licensed weight of towing vehicle.

Dimensions: Total length of trailer and vehicle: 22 meters; width: 2.5 meters; height: 4.2 meters.

Hitch: Hitch must be secured to frame. Safety chain is required.

License Plates: The registered owner of a trailer may transfer a trailer license plate from 1 to another of his or her own trailers upon completion of the forms supplied by the CTS and payment of a transfer fee, but trailer license plates must not be transferred from 1 owner to another.
- A trailer license plate or temporary operation permit must be placed at the rear of the trailer, in such a position that the lower edge of the plate or permit is not lower than the rear axle of the trailer.

Lighting: No trailer, whether in motion or stationary, may be on a highway unless it has at least 1 light visible at a distance of 30 meters or more from the rear of the vehicle, or 2 reflectors that will reflect the light from a vehicle approaching from the rear.
- No trailer pulled by or attached to a motor vehicle and having a width at any part, including any load, in excess of 205 cm, may be on any highway unless it has affixed in conspicuous positions, at its widest point and as near the top as practical, at

least 1 lighted amber clearance light on each side of the front and at least 1 lighted red clearance light on each side of the rear.

Mirrors: Where the driver's view of the roadway to the rear of the vehicle is obstructed or interfered with in any manner, a side rear vision mirror must be attached to each side of the motor vehicle and must be placed in such a position as to afford the driver a clear view of the roadway to the rear and to each side of the motor vehicle.

Speed Limits: Same as for passenger cars.

Towing: No person may occupy or permit any other person to occupy a house trailer while it is being moved on a highway.

Miscellaneous Provisions

Border Inspections: American visitors crossing the border, either way, may be asked to verify their citizenship with a passport or birth certificate. Naturalized U.S. citizens should carry a naturalization certificate, and permanent U.S. residents who are not citizens should carry their Alien Registration Receipt Card.

- Children under 18 years of age should have their birth certificate, and if the parents are separated or divorced, the parent crossing the border should have proof of custody or a letter from the other parent. Persons under 18 years of age who are not accompanied by a parent should bring a letter from their parent or guardian giving them permission to cross the border.
- A visitor is permitted to bring a reasonable amount of personal effects, a reasonable supply of food, and a full tank of gas. Reasonable means enough for personal use during the length of stay in Canada. Any unreasonable amounts are subject to duty.
- A visitor must have a rabies vaccination certificate signed by a licensed veterinarian to bring dogs or cats into Canada.

Liability Laws: Province has compulsory third-party liability insurance on all vehicles with C$200,000 minimum personal injury or property damage. Proof is required at all times. Driving without such proof is C$400 fine.

- Every person who owns and operates a motor vehicle on a highway must maintain an insurance policy that provides liability coverage, in respect of any 1 accident, to the limit of not less than C$200,000, exclusive of interest and costs, against liability resulting from bodily injury to or the death of 1 or more persons, and loss of or damage to property.
- Claims arising out of bodily injury or death must have priority to the extent of C$190,000 over claims arising out of loss of damage to property, and claims arising out of loss of or damage to property must have priority to the extent of C$10,000 over claims arising out of bodily injury or death.

Weigh Stations: All vehicles over 9,000 kg must stop.

Fees & Taxes

Table 1: Vehicle Registration Fees (Canadian Dollars)

Vehicle Type	Registration Fee (per month)
Private Vehicles: Cars with up to 300 cm Wheel Base	$3.00
Private Vehicles: Cars with 301 cm and over Wheel Base	$4.00
Private Vehicles: Trucks (Including Motor Homes) up to 2,999 kg GVW	$3.00
Private Vehicles: Trucks (Including Motor Homes) 3,000 - 4,999 kg GVW	$4.00
Private Vehicles: Trucks (Including Motor Homes) 5,000 - 11,999 kg GVW	$6.00
Passenger Bus with a Seating Capacity of 15 or Less	$11.00
Passenger Bus with a Seating Capacity Exceeding 15	$12.00
Moped, Motorcycle, or Snowmobile	$1.00
Trailer	$1.00

Table 2: License Fees (Canadian Dollars)

License Class	Fee
Special or Personalized License Plate	$100.00
Learner's License Written Test	$20.00
Class 7 GDL Learner's License	$10.00
5-Year License	$50.00
License for Issued for Less than 5 Years	$3.00 per year
Duplicate Driver's License	$3.00

Table 3: Vehicle Taxes and Fees in Lieu of Taxes (Canadian Dollars)

Tax	Rate
Personal Property Tax	none
Provincial Sales Tax	none
Federal Goods and Services Tax	7%
Gasoline Tax; (Diesel)	$0.042/liter; ($0.052/liter)

Table 4: Miscellaneous Fees (Canadian Dollars)

Replacement of Defective Registration Certificate or License Plate	no fee
Replacement of Lost, Stolen, or Damaged License Plate	$5.00
Replacement of Lost, Stolen, or Damaged Personalized Plate or Set of 2 Plates	$25.00
Replacement or Transfer of a Registration Certificate	$6.00
Sample Plate	$5.00
Non-Commercial In-Transit Permit	$5.00
Non-Commercial Temporary Permit	$5.00

YT

APPENDIX

General Information

Vehicle Title and Registration

Information is presented relating to requirements for passenger vehicle registration, renewal, and transfer. Grace periods are sometimes granted beyond dates noted in the Digest. Law enforcement officers are advised to ascertain whether or not the official expiration date has been extended by a period of grace before making arrests for display of "dead tags." Information is also included on emissions and safety inspection, where applicable.

It is general practice among the states to permit non-resident drivers to use the highways of the state for a specified period without requiring them to register their vehicles in the state. This privilege is reciprocal among the states. All states require, under certain circumstances, a non-resident to register his/her vehicle and obtain a driver's license before being allowed to continue driving in the state.

Generally a non-resident must obtain a driver's license and register his or her car after a certain period of time within the state, or if at any time he or she obtains employment in the state or places his or her children in school within the state. State laws invariably require a person to register his or her motor vehicle and obtain a local driver's license when he or she becomes a resident of a state. Establishment of legal residency (domicile) in a state requires one's physical presence in a state plus an intention on that person's part to make that state his or her home permanently or for a considerable period of time.

Vehicle Registration

Onboard Diagnostics (OBD): OBD is a computer-based system utilized in model year 1996 and newer vehicles that monitors various operating systems, including emissions. The Clean Air Act requires inspection and maintenance programs to incorporate onboard diagnostic testing as part of the vehicle emissions inspection. In the past few years, a number of states have begun to implement OBD as part of the emissions inspection.

Driver's License

Reference is made in the Digest to written and oral examinations in connection with applications for driver's licenses. These tests cover knowledge of traffic laws and signs, safety rules, various motorists' liability laws, and driving courtesy. It is common to require eyesight examinations and driving demonstrations. Information on license issuance/application, renewal, and types of licenses is also contained in this section.

Graduated Drivers Licensing: Fifty states and the District of Columbia have some form of graduated licensing for teen drivers. States with mandatory holding periods for learner's permits prohibit teens from driving unless accompanied by a supervisory driver. In most states the supervisory driver is a parent or guardian. However, in many states accommodations are made for driver instructors and/or licensed drivers 21 and older.

States with night driving provisions restrict teens from driving unsupervised during certain hours. However, most states make exceptions for driving to and from work, school, or church activities.

Traffic Rules

Alcohol Laws: All 50 states and the District of Columbia prohibit the operation of a motor vehicle while under the influence of intoxicating liquors. Those states having chemical test laws establish certain standards of measurement for degree of intoxication as determined by chemical analysis of the percentage of alcohol found in the defendant's blood, breath, urine, or other body substance. Such measurements are generally admissible as evidence. Canada has a federal chemical test law with implied consent applicable in all provinces.

Every state's chemical test law has "an implied consent" provision providing that any person operating a motor vehicle on a public highway, who is suspected of driving while intoxicated, implies consent to a chemical test to determine if he or she is inebriated. Failure to submit or pass such a test may cause the driver's license to be suspended or revoked regardless of any court action finding the person innocent of the charge. As of July 2005, 41 states and the District of Columbia have enacted Administrative License Suspension Laws.

Cellular Phones and Distracted Driving: Properly used, cellular phones enhance driver safety and provide a mobile alert network for the community. AAA's distracted driving campaign, Stay-Focused: Keep Your Mind on the Road, is designed to teach motorists about the significant safety risks associated with all distractions in the vehicle and to help them manage those distractions. Please contact your local club for campaign materials.

In every state persons are able to call 911 from their cellular phone to report emergencies. Most states have another number that can be used to report non-emergencies from their cellular phone. You will find this information under each jurisdiction's Traffic Rules section. Emergency number 1-800-525-5555 will route your phone call directly to the state police/patrol of the state from which you are calling.

Laws exist in 35 states and the District of Columbia that regulate the use of cell phones in motor vehicles. For more information please see the Distracted Driving Law chart.

Child Restraints: All 50 states and the District of Columbia have enacted mandatory child restraint usage laws. These laws are primary or standard in all states and the District of Columbia – meaning that police may stop vehicles solely for violations of these laws. They are described under each jurisdiction's, Traffic Rules section and in the corresponding Occupant Protection chart.

School Buses: Special attention is given to the identification of school buses since state laws requiring traffic to stop for loading and unloading of school children are strictly enforced. When a school bus is loading or unloading children, motorists must stop and remain stopped until the bus driver turns off the stop lights and the bus resumes movement.

Motorcycles and Mopeds

In general, motorcycles registered for use on public highways must meet the equipment requirements in the state in which they are registered. This is in addition to compliance with Federal Motor Vehicle Safety Standards.

Federal regulations require all mopeds sold in the United States to be equipped with a headlamp, a taillamp, a stop light, a network of reflectors, a rearview mirror, a strong brake system, and an extra switch to shut down the engine. These are mandated by the U.S. Department of Transportation. Additional requirements are outlined in each jurisdiction.

Passenger Car Trailers

Information of interest to the passenger car operator who tows a camping, baggage, boat trailer, or other passenger vehicle is provided in each state summary and in the Towing table. The reader should note, however, that this information may not be complete. Heavier trailers and house trailers frequently necessitate higher registration fees, more stringent equipment requirements, and sometimes lower permissible operating speeds.

Miscellaneous Section and Tables

Arrest Bond Certificates

Most states and the District of Columbia accept AAA Guaranteed Arrest Bond Certificates in lieu of cash or surety bonds for traffic violations.

The member posts his AAA membership card and Arrest Bond Certificate with the court. He may then leave the jurisdiction. If he appears for trial, his card and certificate are returned to him or his club. If, however, he elects to forfeit his bond and does not appear for trial, the court notifies the AAA club of the forfeiture, and the club arranges for payment of the forfeiture and obtains the member's card from the court. The motorist-member then reimburses the club for the amount spent on his or her behalf, and his or her membership card is returned by the club.

Most states accepting certificates allow for amounts ranging from $200 to $1,000. In states that do not have mandatory acceptance of AAA Guaranteed Arrest Bond Certificates, acceptance is at the discretion of the magistrate who sets bail.

Liability Laws

There are 5 types of liability laws.

1. "Financial Responsibility" law of which there are 2 types. Minimum requirements of financial responsibility are shown in terms of amounts applicable to death or injury of one person, death or injury of more than one person, and property damage. For example: $25,000/$50,000/$10,000. The "Security-Type" laws require that, following report of an accident, each driver or owner of the vehicles involved show his or her ability to pay any damages which may be charged to him or her in subsequent litigation of negotiation arising out of the accident. The "Future-Proof Type" law requires a similar showing of financial responsibility be made by persons who have been convicted of certain serious traffic offenses or who have failed to pay a judgment against them for damages arising out of an accident.
2. "Compulsory Insurance" requires that motorists file proof of financial responsibility prior to annual vehicle registration as a condition of vehicle registration.
3. Under the "No-Fault" automobile insurance statute, the owner of the vehicle looks to his own insurance company for reimbursement for damage sustained in an accident, rather than having to go to court and prove that the other party caused the accident. Usually compulsory, most no-fault laws cover only bodily injury and not vehicle damage. Those insured under no-fault receive prompt payment from their own insurance company but have their right to sue for general damages restricted. Some plans specify a dollar "threshold" below which tort suits for general damages are barred. Once the "threshold" amount is reached in terms of the damages suffered, the motorist is permitted to institute a suit to recover general damages. Few states have "verbal thresholds," while others have only "add-on" no-fault laws. These latter statutes do not limit the right to sue; rather, they merely "add-on" no-

fault benefits, usually consisting of first party medical coverage. Motorists traveling in states having no-fault laws are urged to consult with their insurance agent to determine if their policy covers them in such states. Most insurance companies automatically extended their policy provisions to cover no-fault states. Motorists are reminded that enactment of no-fault type insurance laws in no way eliminates the requirements for the filing of timely and accurate accident reports with the proper officials.

4. A number of states have experimented with a fourth type of liability law, the so-called "Unsatisfied Judgment Funds." The state-operated funds are commonly financed with fees from motorists who are unable to provide evidence of insurance when they register their vehicles, or from assessments levied on auto insurance companies. While the need for this type of fund is not as great with no-fault insurance, it has been necessary to establish a similar fund to cover pedestrians and others who do not have no-fault insurance. These funds are generally referred to as assigned claims plans.

5. The fifth type of law, "Uninsured Motorist Laws," has been enacted in many states. These laws generally require insurance companies to offer, as part of their basic policy, coverage against potential damage by motorists who are not insured.

Guest suit laws also exist in several states. These laws limit the amount of damages that can be collected from the driver or owner of a vehicle by a victim riding as a gratuitous guest at the time of injury. They generally require a showing of gross negligence by the driver or owner before damages can be collected. Substitute Service: Nonresidents who leave a state where they have been involved in an accident may legally be made parties to lawsuits arising out of such accidents.

It is now general practice to provide for service of process on nonresidents by mailing a copy of the process to their last known address and leaving a copy with some designated official in the state where the accident occurred. Thereafter, such nonresident's liability may be determined even though he or she never appears in court.

Nonresident Violator Compact

The Nonresident Violator Compact of 1977 assures nonresident motorists receiving citations for minor traffic violations in a party state the same treatment accorded resident motorists. A procedure is established whereby a nonresident receiving a traffic citation in a party state must fulfill the terms of that citation or face the possibility of license suspension in the motorist's home state until the terms of the citation are met. Safeguards are built into the compact so that a nonresident driver receiving a citation has due process protection. At present, 46 states and the District of Columbia are members of the compact with legislation pending in other states providing for membership in the compact. As of 2005 the following states do not belong to the compact: Alaska, California, Michigan, and Wisconsin.

The National Driver License Compact (NDLC) is an agreement among the states to control problem drivers. It provides for the exchange of information to keep unsafe drivers from accumulating violations in many states and escaping control action; it implements the "one license" concept. Forty-five states and the District of Columbia are members of the NDLC. States that are not members are Georgia, Massachusetts, Michigan, Tennessee, and Wisconsin.

Taxes

Several types of taxes are mentioned in addition to fees charged for issuance of registration cards, driver's licenses, and Certificates of Title.

- *Personal Property Tax:* A general tax levied annually on owners of personal property. Rates are based on a percentage of the value of all such property, including motor vehicles.
- *Sales Tax:* A tax levied on proceeds of retail sales of tangible personal property, including automobiles. Rates are based on percentage of total sale price.
- *Use Tax:* A tax levied on the right to operate vehicles within a state, usually at the same rate as the sales tax.
- *Gasoline Tax:* A tax levied upon purchases of gasoline. Rates based on the flat fee per gallon (or liter) of fuel purchased or a percentage of the wholesale price.

Other excise taxes are levied on sales of lubricating oil, tires and tubes, and automotive accessories by both state and federal government.

Foreign Driver's Licenses and Foreign License Plates/ Registration Tags Recognized in the United States

Foreign motorists from any of the countries on the following list who visit the United States as bona fide tourists can drive legally using their valid domestic driver's license for a period not to exceed one year from date of arrival. This arrangement applies to driving either personal or rental cars. Bona fide tourists from countries on this same list can also legally drive their own private cars bearing valid license plates/registration tags issued in their native country for a period not to exceed one year from date of arrival.

This privilege is made possible as a result of the United Nations Convention on Road Traffic (Geneva, 1949), and the Convention on the Regulation of Inter-American Motor Vehicle Traffic (Washington, D.C. 1943), both of which have been ratified by the United States. In the event the foreign tourist's country is not listed below, he or she may be required to obtain a driver's license and secure license plates/registration tags upon arrival in the United States.

If the visiting tourist accepts a job or attends school in the United States, he or she then loses tourist status and may be required to obtain a state driver's license and plates in accordance with the regulations in effect in the state where residence is chosen. Motorists from countries on the following list, with the exception of those from Canada and Mexico, are required to exhibit the International Distinguishing Sign on the rear exterior of their private vehicle. This standardized sign, oval in shape, is composed of one to three black capital letters on a white background, and indicates where the vehicle is registered. This sign must be obtained in the motorist's home country.

The following countries are party to the above-mentioned 1943 or 1949 Conventions:

Afghanistan*	Belize	Cape Verde Islands*	Cuba
Albania	Benin		Curacao
Algeria	Bhutan*	Cayman Islands*	Cyprus
Andorra	Bolivia*/***	Central African Republic	Czech Rep.
Angola*	Bostwana		Denmark
Antigua*	Brazil (Inter-American Driving Permit Only)	Chad*	Djibouti*
Argentina***		Chile***	Dominica*/**
Armenia*	Brunei*	Colombia*/***	Dominican Republic***
Australia	Bulgaria	Comoros*	
Austria	Burkina Faso* (was Upper Volta)	Congo, Rep. of (Brazzaville)	Ecuador***
Bahamas		Congo, Dem. Rep. of (Kinshasa)	Egypt
Bahrain*	Cambodia (was Kampuchea)		El Salvador*/***
Bangladesh		Costa Rica*/***	Equatorial Guinea*
Barbados**	Cameroon	Côte d'Ivoire	Estonia*
Belgium	Canada	Croatia*	Fiji

Finland
France (including French overseas territories)
French Polynesia
Gabon*
Gambia
Georgia
Germany*
Ghana
Gibraltar
Greece
Grenada
Guadeloupe
Guatemala***
Guernsey
Guinea*
Guinea-Bissau*
Guyana
Haiti***
Honduras*/***
Hong Kong
Hungary
Iceland
India
Indonesia*
Iran*
Ireland
Isle of Man
Israel
Italy
Jamaica
Japan
Jersey

Jordan
Kazakhstan*
Kenya*
Korea, Rep. of
Kuwait*
Kyrgyzstan
Laos
Latvia
Lebanon
Lesotho
Liberia*
Libya*
Liechtenstein*
Lithuania*
Luxembourg
Macao*
Macedonia
Madagascar
Malawi
Malaysia
Mali
Malta
Martinique
Mauritania*
Mauritius
Mexico*/***
Monaco
Morocco
Mozambique*
Myanmar*
Namibia
Nepal*
Netherlands
New Caledonia

New Zealand
Nicaragua*/***
Niger
Norway
Oman*
Pakistan*
Panama*
Papua New Guinea
Paraguay***
Peru***
Philippines
Poland
Portugal
Qatar*
Romania
Russia
Rwanda
St. Kitts
Nevis & Anguilla*/**
St. Lucia
St. Vincent & The Grenadines
San Marino
Sâo Tomé & Principe*
Saudi Arabia*
Senegal
Seychelles
Sierra Leone
Singapore
Slovakia
Slovenia*
South Africa
Spain

Sri Lanka
Sudan*
Suriname
Swaziland
Sweden
Switzerland
Syria
Taiwan
Tajikistan*
Tanzania
Thailand
Togo
Trinidad & Tobago***
Tunisia
Turkey
Turkmenistan*
Uganda
Ukraine
United Arab Emirates*
United Kingdom
Uruguay (Inter-American Driving Permit Only)
Vatican City (Holy See)
Venezuela***
Vietnam*
Western Samoa
Windward Islands
Yemen*
Yugoslavia
Zambia
Zimbabwe

In addition to having a valid foreign driver's license, visitors are advised to carry an International Driving Permit, as authorized by the 1943/1949 or 1968 Conventions, or attach an English translation to their national driving license. The International Driving Permit is translated into the 9 official languages of the United Nations, including English, and serves as a translation to be used in conjunction with the visitor's valid driver's license. It can be useful in emergencies such as traffic violations or auto accidents, particularly when a foreign language is involved.

Visitors from foreign countries must obtain their International Driving Permit in their native country, prior to arrival in the United States.

*Not party to 1949 Convention - International Driving Permit honored.

** U.S. driver's license and IDP recognized on presentation to local police and payment of special registration fee upon arrival.

*** Geographical areas which honor Inter-American Driving Permits (Convention on Regulation of Inter-American Motor Vehicle Traffic, Organization of American States, Washington, D.C., 1943) as of June 1996.

These countries also made the convention applicable to their territorial possessions.

State Insurance Commission Offices

Alabama
201 Monroe Street
Suite 1700
Montgomery, AL 36104
(334) 269-3550
(334) 241-4192 FAX

Alaska
3601 C Street
Suite 1324
Anchorage, AK 99503-5948
(907) 269-7900
(907) 269-7912 FAX

Arizona
2910 North 44th Street
Suite 210
Phoenix, AZ 85018-7256
(602) 912-8400
(602) 912-8452 FAX

Arkansas
1200 West 3rd Street
Little Rock, AR 72201-1904
(501) 371-2600
(501) 371-2629 FAX

California
300 Capitol Mall
Suite 1500
Sacramento, CA 95814
(916) 492-3500
(916) 445-5280 FAX

Colorado
1560 Broadway
Suite 850
Denver, CO 80202
(303) 894-7499
(303) 894-7455 FAX

Connecticut
P.O. Box 816
Hartford, CT 06142-0816
(860) 297-3800
(860) 566-7410 FAX

Delaware
The Rodney Building
841 Silver Lake Boulevard
Dover, DE 19904
(302) 739-4251
(302) 739-5280 FAX

District of Columbia
810 First Street, N.E.
Suite 701
Washington, DC 20002
(202) 727-3800, x 3018
(202) 535-1196 FAX

Florida
State Capitol
Plaza Level Eleven
Tallahassee, FL 32399-0300
(850) 413-2804
(850) 413-2950 FAX

Georgia
2 Martin Luther King Jr. Drive
Floyd Memorial Building
704 W. Tower
Atlanta, GA 30334
(404) 656-2056
(404) 657-7493 FAX

Hawaii
250 South King Street
5th Floor
Honolulu, HI 96813
(808) 586-2790
(808) 586-2806 FAX

Idaho
700 West State Street
3rd Floor
Boise, ID 83720-0043
(208) 334-4250
(208) 334-4398 FAX

Illinois
320 West Washington Street
4th Floor
Springfield, IL 62767-0001
(217) 782-4515
(217) 524-6500 FAX

Indiana
311 West Washington Street
Suite 300
Indianapolis, IN 46204-2787
(317) 232-2385
(317) 232-5251 FAX

Iowa
330 East Maple Street
Des Moines, IA 50319
(515) 281-5705
(515) 281-3059 FAX

Kansas
420 S.W. 9th Street
Topeka, KS 66612-1678
(785) 296-7801
(785) 296-2283 FAX

Kentucky
P.O. Box 517
215 West Main Street
Frankfort, KY 40602-0517
(502) 564-6027
(502) 564-1453 FAX

Louisiana
950 North 5th Street
Baton Rouge, LA 70802
(225) 342-5423
(225) 342-8622 FAX

Maine
State Office Building
Station 34
Augusta, ME 04333-0034
(207) 624-8475
(207) 624-8599 FAX

Maryland
525 St. Paul Place
Baltimore, MD 21202-2272
(410) 468-2090
(410) 468-2020 FAX

Massachusetts
One South Station
4th Floor
Boston, MA 02110
(617) 521-7301
(617) 521-7758 FAX

Michigan
611 West Ottawa Street
2nd Floor - North
Lansing, MI 48933-1020
(517) 335-3167
(517) 373-4870 FAX

Minnesota
85 7th Place East
Suite 500
St. Paul, MN 55101-2198
(651) 296-6025
(651) 282-2568 FAX

Mississippi
501 N. West Street
Woolfolk State Office Building, 10th Floor
Jackson, MS 39201
(601) 359-3569
(601) 359-2474 FAX

Missouri
301 West High Street
Suite 530
Jefferson City, MO 65101
(573) 751-4126
(573) 751-1165 FAX

Montana
840 Helena Avenue
Helena, MT 59601
(406) 444-2040
(406) 444-3497

Nebraska
Terminal Building
941 'O' Street
Suite 400
Lincoln, NE 68508
(402) 471-2201
(402) 471-4610 FAX

Nevada
788 Fairview Drive
Suite 300
Carson City, NV 89701-5753
(775) 687-4270
(775) 687-3937 FAX

New Hampshire
56 Old Suncook Road
Concord, NH 03301
(603) 271-2261
(603) 271-1406 FAX

New Jersey
20 West State Street
CN325
Trenton, NJ 08625
(609) 292-5360
(609) 984-5273 FAX

New Mexico
P.O. Drawer 1269
Santa Fe, NM 87504-1269
(505) 827-4601
(505) 476-0326 FAX

New York
25 Beaver Street
New York, NY 10004-2319
(212) 480-2292
(212) 480-2310 FAX

North Carolina
P.O. Box 26387
Raleigh, NC 27611
(919) 733-3058
(919) 733-6495 FAX

North Dakota
600 East Boulevard
Bismarck, ND 58505-0320
(701) 328-2440
(701) 328-4880 FAX

Ohio
2100 Stella Court
Columbus, OH 43215-1067
(614) 644-2658
(614) 644-3743 FAX

Oklahoma
2401 NW 23rd Street
Suite 28
Oklahoma City, OK 73107
(405) 521-2828
(405) 521-6635 FAX

Oregon
350 Winter Street, NE
Room 440
Salem, OR 97310-3883
(503) 947-7980
(503) 378-4351 FAX

Pennsylvania
1326 Strawberry Square
13th Floor
Harrisburg, PA 17120
(717) 783-0442
(717) 772-1969 FAX

Rhode Island
233 Richmond Street
Suite 233
Providence, RI 02903-4233
(401) 222-2223
(401) 222-5475 FAX

South Carolina
300 Lake Arbor Drive
Suite 1200
Columbia, SC 29201
(803) 737-6212
(803) 737-6229 FAX

South Dakota
445 East Capitol Avenue
Pierre, SD 57501-2000
(605) 773-3563
(605) 773-5369 FAX

Tennessee
Davy Crockett Tower
5th Floor
500 James Robertson
Parkway
Nashville, TN 37243-0565
(615) 741-2241
(615) 532-6934 FAX

Texas
333 Guadalupe Street
Austin, TX 78701
(512) 463-6464
(512) 475-2005 FAX

Utah
3110 State Office
Building
Salt Lake City, UT 84114-1201
(801) 538-3800
(801) 538-3829 FAX

Vermont
89 Main Street
Drawer 20
Montpelier, VT 05620-3101
(802) 828-3301
(802) 828-3306 FAX

Virginia
P.O. Box 1157
Richmond, VA 23218
(804) 371-9694
(804) 371-9873 FAX

Washington
14th Avenue & Water
Streets
P.O. Box 40255
Olympia, WA 98504-0255
(360) 664-8137
(360) 586-3535 FAX

West Virginia
P.O. Box 50540
Charleston, WV 25305-0540
(304) 558-3354
(304) 558-0412 FAX

Wisconsin
121 East Wilson Street
Madison, WI 53702
(608) 267-1233
(608) 261-8579 FAX

Wyoming
Herschler Building
122 West 25th Street
3rd Floor - East
Cheyenne, WY 82002-0440
(307) 777-7401
(307) 777-5895 FAX

Accident Report Filing

In addition to reporting accidents to local police agencies at the time of a crash, some states require a written report be filed with a state agency. Should you be requested or required to file an additional report, you may contact:

Alabama
Department of Public Safety
Safety Responsibility Bureau
P.O. Box 1471
Montgomery, AL 36102-1471

Alaska
Division of Motor Vehicles
P.O. Box 20020
Juneau, AK 99802-0020

Arizona
Arizona Department of Public Safety
Department of Records Unit
P.O. Box 6638
Phoenix, AZ 85005

Arkansas
Department of Finance and Administration
Office of Driver Services
Safety Responsibility Section
P.O. Box 1272
Little Rock, AR 72203

California
Department of Motor Vehicles
Financial Responsibility Unit MS J237
P.O. Box 942884
Sacramento, CA 94284-0884

Colorado
Driver Control
1881 Pierce Street
Lakewood, CO 80214

Connecticut
Connecticut Department of Transportation
Division of Highway Safety
2800 Berlin Turnpike
Newington, CT 06131-7546

Delaware
Copies of accident reports can be obtained from:
Delaware State Police
Traffic Section
P.O. Box 430
Dover, DE 19903

District of Columbia
Government of the District of Columbia
Dept. of Motor Vehicles
65 K Street NE
Room 200
Washington, DC 20002

Florida
Traffic Accident Records and Forms Management
Department of Highway Safety and Motor Vehicles
Neil Kirkman Building,
Tallahassee, FL 32399-0575

Georgia
No accident report is required.

Hawaii
State Department of Transportation
Motor Vehicle Safety Office
1505 Dillingham Boulevard
Suite 214
Honolulu, HI 96817

Idaho
Idaho Transportation Department
Highway Safety-Accident Records
P.O. Box 7129
Boise, ID 83707

Illinois
Department of Transportation
Safety Responsibility Section
Springfield, IL 62766

Indiana
Indiana State Police
Indiana Government Center North
Vehicle Crash Records Section
Indianapolis, IN 46204-2259

Iowa
Department of Transportation
Park Fair Mall
100 Euclid
P.O. Box 9204
Des Moines, IA 50306-9204

Kansas
Required only if local law enforcement officer's report is incomplete.

Kentucky
Kentucky State Police
919 Versailles Road
Frankfort, KY 40601

Louisiana
Office of Motor Vehicles
Department of Public Safety
P.O. Box 64886
Baton Rouge, LA 70896

Maine
Secretary of State
Bureau of Motor Vehicles
29 State House Station
Augusta, ME 04333-0029

Maryland
Motor Vehicle Administration
Financial Responsibility Division
6601 Ritchie Highway, NE
Glen Burnie, MD 21062

Massachusetts
Registrar of Motor Vehicles
P.O. Box 19100
Boston, MA 02119-9100

Michigan
Michigan State Police
Support Services Bureau
Traffic Accident Records Section
711 South Harrison Road
East Lansing, MI 48823

Minnesota
Department of Public Safety
Driver and Vehicle Services
445 Minnesota Street
St. Paul, MN 55101

Mississippi
Department of Public Safety
Safety Responsibility Branch
P.O. Box 958
Jackson, MS 39205-0958

Missouri
Drivers and Vehicle Services Bureau
Motor Vehicle Accident Processing Section
P.O. Box 200
Jefferson City, MO 65105-0200

Montana
Montana Highway Patrol
2550 Prospect
P.O. Box 201419
Helena, MT 59620-1419

Nebraska
Department of Roads
Accident Records Bureau
P.O. Box 94669
Lincoln, NE 68509-4669

Nevada
Department of Public Safety
Highway Patrol Office
555 Wright Way
Carson City, NV 89711-0400

New Hampshire
New Hampshire Department of Safety
Division of Motor Vehicles
10 Hazen Drive
Concord, NH 03305

New Jersey
Division of Motor Vehicles
Accident Reporting
CN-050
Trenton, NJ 08666-0050

New Mexico
Transportation Department
P.O. Box 1149
Santa Fe, NM 87504-1149

New York
New York State Department of Motor Vehicles
Accident Records Bureau
P.O. Box 2925
Albany, NY 12220-0925

North Carolina
Division of Motor Vehicles
Collision Report Section
1100 New Bern Avenue
Raleigh, NC 27697

North Dakota
Reported by law enforcement officer.

Ohio
Bureau of Motor Vehicles
Attn: Accident Reports
P.O. Box 16583
Columbus, OH 43216-6583

Oklahoma
Financial Responsibility
Division
Oklahoma Department of
Public Safety
P.O. Box 11415
Oklahoma City, OK 73136

Oregon
Department of
Transportation
Driver and Motor Vehicle
Services
1905 Lana Avenue, NE
Salem, OR 97314

Pennsylvania
Reports Section
Bureau of Highway Safety
and Traffic Engineering
Room 212
P.O. Box 2047
Harrisburg, PA 17105-2047

Rhode Island
Department of
Administration
Division of Motor
Vehicles
Office of Safety
Responsibility
286 Main Street
Pawtucket, RI 02860

South Carolina
Department of Public
Safety
Financial Responsibility
Office
P.O. Box 1498
Columbia, SC 29216-0040

South Dakota
Copies of accident
reports can be
obtained from:
Department of
Public Safety
Accident Records
118 West Capitol Avenue
Pierre, SD 57501-2586

Tennessee
Department of Safety
1150 Foster Avenue
Nashville, TN 32710

Texas
Attn: Financial
Responsibilities
Records Section
Accident Records
Texas Department of
Public Safety
P.O. Box 4087
Austin, TX 78773-0001

Utah
Department of Public
Safety
Driver License Division
Box 30560
Salt Lake City, UT 84130-0560

Vermont
Department of Motor
Vehicles
Driver Improvement
Division
Records Unit
120 State Street
Montpelier, VT 05630

Virginia
Department of Motor
Vehicles
Accident Processing
Room 307
P.O. Box 27412
Richmond, VA 23269

Washington
Washington State Patrol
Accident Records
P.O. Box 42628
4242 Martin Way
Olympia, WA 98504

West Virginia
Division of Highways
Traffic Engineering
Section, Room A550
Building 5 - Capitol
Complex
Charleston, WV 25305

Wisconsin
Wisconsin Department of
Transportation
Traffic Accident Section
P.O. Box 7919
Madison, WI 53707-7919

Wyoming
Wyoming Department
of Transportation
Driver Services
5300 Bishop Blvd
Cheyenne, WY 82009-3340

Alcohol Laws Chart

State	Administrative Per Se Law/BAC Level	Mandatory Suspension/Revocation Administrative Per Se 1st	2nd	3rd	Preliminary Breath Tests	Mandatory Administrative Suspension/Revocation BAC Test Refusal* 1st	2nd
Alabama	•/.08%	S-90 Days	S-1 Yr.	S-3 Yrs.	○	S-90 Days	S-1 Yr.
Alaska	•/.08%	R-30 Days	R-1 Yr.	R-3 Yrs.	•	R-90 Days	R-1 Yr.
Arizona	•/.08%	S-30 Days	S-90 Days	S-90 Days	•	S-12 Mos.	S-24 Mos.
Arkansas	•/.08%	See[2]	S-24 Mos.[3]	S-30 Mos.[3]	○	S-180 Days[3]	S-2 Yrs.
California	•/.08%[5]	S-30 Days[5]	S-1 Yr.[5]	S-1 Yr.[5]	•	S-1 Yr.[6]	R-2 Yrs.
Colorado	•/.10%	R-3 Mos.[8]	R-1 Yr.[8]	R-1 Yr.[8]	•	R-1 Yr.[8]	R-2 Yrs.[8]
Connecticut	•/.10%	S-90 Days[9]	S-9 Mos.	S-2 Yrs.	○	S-90 Days	S-9 Mos.
Delaware	•/.10%[11]	R-3 Mos.	R-1 Yr.	R-18 Mos.	•	R-6 Mos.	R-18 Mos.
D.C.	•/.05%[12]	-	-	-	•	S-12 Mos.	S-12 Mos.
Florida	•/.08%	S-30 Days	S-1 Yr.[13]	S-1 Yr.[13]	•	S-90 Days	S-18 Mos.
Georgia	•/.08%	-	S-12 Mos.	S-18 Mos.	○	S-1 Yr.	S-1 Yr.
Hawaii	•/.08%	R-1 Yr.	R-1 Yr.	R-2 Yrs.	○	R-1 Yr.	R-2 Yrs.
Idaho	•/.08%	S-30 Days	S-1 Yr.	S-1 Yr.	○	S-180 Days	S-1 Yr.
Illinois	•/.08%	-	S-1 Yr.	S-1 Yr.	•	-	S-2 Yrs.
Indiana	•/.08%	S-180 Days[16]	S-180 Days[16]	S-180 Days[16]	•[46]	S-1 Yr.	S-1 Yr.
Iowa	•/.10%	R-30 Days	R-1 Yr.	R-1 Yr.	•	R-90 Days	R-1 Yr.
Kansas	•/.08%	S-30 Days	S-1 Yr.	S-1 Yr.	•	S-1 Yr.	S-2 Yrs.
Kentucky	○	-	-	-	•	_[17]	_[17]

Alcohol Laws Chart

Illegal Per Se BAC Level	BAC Test Required For Traffic Fatalities or Serious Injuries	Lower BAC for Youth	Drug Alcohol License Postponement	Open Container Law	Anti-Consumption Law	"Happy Hours" Prohibition	Dram Shop
.08%	•	.02%	○	•	○	•	✗
.08%	•	0%	•	○	•[1]	•	✗
.08%	○	0%	•	•	•	•	✗
.08%	•	.02%	•	○	•	○	▲[4]
.08%	•	.01%	•	•	•	○	✗[7]
.08%	•[1]	.02%	○	○	•	○	✗
.08%	○	.02%	•	○	○	○	✗[10]
.08%	•[2]	.02%	•	○	•[1]	○	✓
.08%	•	0%	○	•	•	○	▲
.08%	•	.02%	•	•	•	○	✗[14]
.08%	•	.02%	•	•	•[1]	○[1]	✗
.08%	•	.02%	•	•	•	•	▲
.08%	○	.02%	○	•	•	○	✗
.08%	•	0%	•	•	•[15]	•	✗[10]
.08%	•	.02%	•	•	•[1]	•	✗
.08%	•[8]	.02%	•	•	•	○	✗
.08%	○	.02%	•	•	•	•	✓
.08%	•	.02%	•	•	•	○	✗

Alcohol Laws Chart

State	Administrative Per Se Law/BAC Level	Mandatory Suspension/ Revocation Administrative Per Se 1st	2nd	3rd	Preliminary Breath Tests	Mandatory Administrative Suspension/Revocation BAC Test Refusal* 1st	2nd
Louisiana	•/.10%	-[18]	-[18]	-[18]	o	-[18]	-[18]
Maine	•/.08%	-	S-18. Mos.	S-4 Yrs.	o	S-275 Days	S-18 Mos.
Maryland	•/.08%	-	S-90 Days[20]	S-90 Days[20]	•	S-120 Days[20]	S-1 Yr.[20]
Massachusetts	•/.08%	S-90 Days or less[21]	S-90 Days or less[21]	S-90 Days or more[21]	o	S-120 Days[22]	S-120 Days[22]
Michigan	o	-	-	-	•	-	S-1 Yr.
Minnesota	•/.10%	R-15 Days[23]	R-90 Days[23]	R-90 Days[23]	•	R-15 Days	R-180 Days
Mississippi	•/.10%[24]	-	-	-	•	S-90 Days[25]	S-90 Days[25]
Missouri	•/.08%	S-30 Days	R-1 Yr.	R-1 Yr.	•	R-90 Days	R-1 Yr.
Montana	o	S-6 Mos.	R-1 Yr.	R-1 Yr.	•	S-6 Mos.	R-1 Yr.
Nebraska	•/.08%	R-30 Days	R-1 Yr.	R-1 Yr.	•	R-1 Yr.[28]	R-1 Yr.[28]
Nevada	•/.10%	R-90 Days[29]	R-90 Days[29]	R-90 Days[29]	•	n/a[30]	n/a[30]
New Hampshire	•/.08%	S-6 Mos.	S-2 Yrs.	S-2 Yrs.	•	S-180 Days	S-2 Yrs.
New Jersey	o[45]	-	-	-	o	R-6 Mos.	R-2 Yrs.
New Mexico	•/.08%	-	R-1 Yr.	R-1 Yr.	o	R-1 Yr.	R-1 Yr.
New York	o	-	-	-	•	R-6 Mos.	R-1 Yr.
North Carolina	•/.08%	R-10 Days	R-10 Days	R-10 Days	•	R-10 Days	R-12 Mos.[32]
North Dakota	•/.08%	S-30 Days	S-365 Days	S-2 Yrs.	•	R-1 Yr.	R-2 Yrs.
Ohio	•/.08%	S-90 Days	S-1 Yr.[34]	S-2 Yrs.[35]	o	S-1 Yr.	S-2 Yrs.
Oklahoma	•/.08%	R-1 Yr.	R-1 Yr.	R-1 Yr.	o	-	-
Oregon	•/.08%	S-30 Days	S-1 Yr.	S-1 Yr.	o	S-1 Yr.	S-3 Yrs.

Alcohol Laws Chart

Illegal Per Se BAC Level	BAC Test Required For Traffic Fatalities or Serious Injuries	Lower BAC for Youth	Drug Alcohol License Postponement	Open Container Law	Anti-Con-sumption Law	"Happy Hours" Prohibition	Dram Shop
.08%	•	.02%	•	○	•[1]	•	✗[19]
.08%	•	0%	•	•	•	•	✗[10]
.08%	•	.02%	•	•	•[1]	○	✓
.08%	○	.02%	•	•	○	•	▲
.08%	•	.02%	•	•	•	•	✗
.08%	•[1]	0%	•	•	•	○	✗
.08%	•[3]	.02%	•	○	○	○	✗
.08%	○	.02%	•	○	•[1]	○	✗[26]
.08%	•	.02%	○	•	○[27]	○	✗
.08%	•[4]	.02%	○	•	•	•	✓
.08%	•	.02%	•	•	•[1]	○	✓
.08%	•	.02%	•	•	○[31]	○	✗
.08%	•[5]	.01%	•	•	•	•	✗
.08%	•	.02%	○	•	•	○	✗
.08%	•	.02%	•	•	•	○	✗
.08%	○	0%	•	•	•	•	✗[10,33]
.08%	•[3]	.02%	•	•	•	○	✗
.08%	•[3]	.02%	•	•	•	•	✗
.08%	•[7]	0%	•	•	•[1]	•	▲
.08%	○	0%	•	•	•	○	✗

Alcohol Laws Chart

State	Administrative Per Se Law/BAC Level	Mandatory Suspension/ Revocation Administrative Per Se 1st	2nd	3rd	Preliminary Breath Tests	Mandatory Administrative Suspension/Revocation BAC Test Refusal* 1st	2nd
Pennsylvania	o	-	-	-	•	S-12 Mos.	S-12 Mos.
Rhode Island	o	-	-	-	•	S-3 Mos.	S-1 Yr.
South Carolina	•/.15%	-	-	-	o	-	-
South Dakota	o	-	-	-	•	-	-
Tennessee	o	-	-	-	o	-	-
Texas	•/.08%	-	S-90 Days	S-90 Days	o	-38	S-90 Days[38]
Utah	•/.08%	S-90 Days	S-1 Yr.	S-1 Yr.	o	R-18 Mos.	R-24 Mos.
Vermont	•/.08%	S-90 Days	S-18 Mos.	S-2 Yrs.	•	S-6 Mos.	S-18 Mos.
Virginia	•/.08%	S-7 Days	S-7 Days	S-7 Days	•	S-1 Yr.	S-1 Yr.
Washington	•/.08%	S-30 Days	R-2 Yrs.	R-2 Yrs.	o	R-1 Yr.	R-2 Yrs.
West Virginia	•/.10%[41]	R-30 Days[42]	R-1 Yr.[42]	R-1 Yr.[42]	•	R-90 Days[42]	R-1 Yr.[42]
Wisconsin	•/.08%[43]	-	-	-	•	R-30 Days	R-90 Days
Wyoming	•/.10%	-	S-90 Days	S-90 Days	o	S-6 Mos.	S-18 Mos.

LEGEND

•=Yes o=No

The following columns from the chart are based on 2000 NHTSA Digest of State-Alcohol-Highway Safety Related Legislation: Administrative Per Se Law/BAC Level, Mandatory Suspension/Revocation Administrative Per Se, Mandatory Administrative Suspension/Revocation BAC Test Refusal (*=BAC test refusal resulting in revocation or suspension based on number of offenses), Anti-Consumption Law and Dram Shop:

[1]=Applies only to drivers.
[2]=A restricted hardship license may be issued for a 1st violation.
[3]=If an offender is allowed to operate motor vehicles that are equipped with an ignition interlock device, the mandatory license suspension period is one year.
[4]=Case law has been modified by statute
[5]=Applies only to persons ≥21 years old.
[6]=90 days if the person pleads guilty to a DWI charge at the time of first arraignment with counsel.
[7]=Applies only to the actions of intoxicated minors.
[8]=Refusal: The mandatory revocation periods for 1st and 2nd refusals may be reduced to respectively 3 months and 6 months if the driver participates in the ignition interlock program. Admin. Per Se: The mandatory revocation periods for 1st and subsequent administrative per se violations may be reduced respectively to 1 month and 3 months if the driver participates in the ignition interlock program.
[9]=A person may receive a "special permit" based on a showing of "extreme hardship." Under proposed regulations dated 9/13/93, there would be a 30-day mandatory suspension.

Alcohol Laws Chart

Illegal Per Se BAC Level	BAC Test Required For Traffic Fatalities or Serious Injuries	Lower BAC for Youth	Drug Alcohol License Postponement	Open Container Law	Anti-Consumption Law	"Happy Hours" Prohibition	Dram Shop
.08%	○	.02%	•	•	•	○	✗
.08%	○	.02%	○	•	○	•	✗
.08%	○	.02%	•	•	•	•	▲36,37
.08%	•6	.02%	•	•	•	○	✓
.08%	•1	.02%	•	○	•1	○	✗
.08%	•	0%	•	•	•1	•	✗39
.08%	•	0%	•	•	•	•	✗10
.08%	○	.02%	○	•	•1	○	✗
.08%	○	.02%	•	○	•1	•	✓
.08%	•	.02%	•	•	•	○	▲40
.08%	○	.02%	•	○	•	•	▲
.08%	•	0%	•	•	•	○	▲7
.08%	•1	.02%	○	○	•1	○	✗44

[10]=This state has a statute that places a monetary limit on the amount of damages that can be awarded in dram shop liability actions.
[11]=Based on probable cause of DWI. A BAC ≥ 0.10 is conclusive evidence of a DWI offense for the purposes of an administrative per se law violation.
[12]=An administrative per se violation is based on driving while under the influence of intoxicating liquor or drugs. A BAC ≥ 0.05 is *prima facie* evidence of driving while under the influence of intoxicating liquor.
[13]=This 1-year suspension only applies if there have been two or more drunk driving offense convictions. The "actual" suspension period appears to be only 11 months.
[14]=Applies only to the actions of intoxicated minors or persons known to be habitually addicted to alcohol.
[15]=Limited application.
[16]=Suspension up to 180 days or until the DWI charges have been disposed of, whichever occurs first.
[17]=Licensing action for a refusal only occurs if the offender is not convicted of the related DWI offense.
[18]=There is no mandatory licensing action if the violator is allowed to participate in the ignition interlock program.
[19]=The statute appears to have limited actions to those committed by minors.
[20]=A suspension may be modified or a restricted license may be issued if an offender participates in the "ignition interlock" program for at least 1 year.
[21]=Suspension for 180 days if the driver has had a previous drunk driving offense conviction. Suspension for 1 year if the driver has had two or more previous drunk driving offense convictions.
[22]=Suspension until the drunk driving charges are disposed of but not more than 90 days.

Alcohol Laws Chart

23=If the BAC was ≥ 0.20, the mandatory license revocation is double that given.

24=License suspension for 1 year if the driver has a prior DWI offense conviction.

25=Special/provisions/procedures.

26=The law provides that a cause of action for damages under the dram shop act may only be brought against a liquor by the drink licensee.

27=The Open Container/Anti-Consumption law appears to be limited to persons who are operating "common carriers."

28= This revocation is based on administrative action.

29= A DWI conviction following an administrative revocation cancels the administrative revocation action. Thereafter, the licensing sanctions for a DWI offense apply; this includes the right to obtain restricted driving privileges.

30= According to MADD, Nevada is the only state in which you cannot refuse the test. Officers have the right to hold you down and draw your blood.

31=However, the law does prohibit drivers and passengers from possessing alcoholic beverages within the passenger area of any motor vehicle. This prohibition does not apply to persons transporting, carrying, possessing such beverages in a chartered bus, taxi, limousine for hire, or a section of a motor vehicle designed for overnight accommodations.

32= If a person does not have previous conviction for a drunk driving offense, he/she may only be subject to a 10-day mandatory license revocation.

33=The statute applies specifically to the actions of intoxicated minors, but the law does not foreclose developing case law as to other types of dram shop actions.

34=Applies only if there was a prior DWI offense conviction.

35=Applies only if there were 2 prior DWI offense convictions.

36=Possible case law.

37=*Prima facie* evidence of impairment.

38=Mandatory 90-day suspension if the person has either a previous refusal or a prior administrative per se violation. Mandatory 180-day suspension if the person has a drunk/drug driving offense conviction.

39=Statutory law has limited dram shop actions.

40=Applies only to the actions of (1) intoxicated minors or (2) adults who have lost their will to stop drinking.

41=Or under the influence of alcohol.

Alcohol Laws Chart

[42]=Provided the person participates in the ignition interlock program.
[43]=For a 1st, 2nd, and 3rd offense, an alcohol concentration ≥0.08 and, for a 4th or subsequent offense, an alcohol concentration ≥0.02.
[44]=Liability limited only to the actions of persons who are under 21 years old.
[45]=For New Jersey, the Ignition Interlock Device became law as an additional penalty for driving while intoxicated.
[46]=Only applies to drunken driving offenses that are related to either death or injury.

BAC Test Required for Traffic Fatalities or Serious Injuries:

[1]=A driver, based on probable cause for DWI, may be required to submit to a chemical test for drunk driving law violation regardless of whether there was a death or serious injury.
[2]=A driver may be required to submit to a chemical test if he/she is involved in a DWI-related crash regardless of whether there has been a death or injury.
[3]=Only in fatal crashes.
[4]=BAC test taken on all drivers, survivor and/or non-survivor, involved in fatality traffic accident for statistical purposes.
[5]=A test for any DWI offense; also, a BAC test shall be made on an automobile driver who has survived a traffic crash fatal to another.
[6]=Possible.
[7]=A chemical test is required for persons who have been arrested for a third DWI offense regardless of whether it is injury or death related.
[8]=Iowa per se law/level now includes the presence of a controlled substance (same penalties in effect as .10% per se law).

NOTE: A third DWI offense is a felony.

Dram shop: ✗=Statute ▲=Case (Common) Law ✔=No law
"Happy hours" prohibition information courtesy of Mothers Against Drunk Driving (MADD)
[1]=For Georgia, while there is currently no state law regarding happy hour prohibition, there may be local ordinances in effect in some communities.

Automated Enforcement Chart

State	Location	Violations	Citation Issued to Whom	Liability
Alabama	No automated enforcement in this state.			
Alaska	No automated enforcement in this state.			
Arizona	No specific statute; red light and speed cameras in use in Phoenix, Tempe, and Chandler. Traditional enforcement penalties include a maximum fine of $250 and 2 points on the driver's record.			
Arkansas[5]	Prohibits use of photo-radar by a county government or department of state government except at school zones and railroad crossings. An officer must be present and the citation must be issued at the time of the offense.			
California[5]	Statewide	Red light;[1] rail crossing	Registered owner	Driver or owner if owner does not identify driver
Colorado[5]	Statewide	Any traffic violation[2]	Registered owner	Driver
Connecticut	No automated enforcement in this state.			
Delaware[5]	Statewide	Red light	Registered owner	Owner
D.C.[5]	Entire jurisdiction	Moving infractions	Registered owner	Owner
Florida	No automated enforcement in this state.			
Georgia[5]	Statewide	Red light	Registered owner	Owner
Hawaii	No automated enforcement in this state.			

Automated Enforcement Chart

Image	Traditional Enforcement Penalties	Records/Points/ Penalties	Defenses	Privacy
Plate and driver	$100 fine/ 1 point	Penalty same as for traditional citation	Driver not owner if owner identifies driver	Photo may be used only for purposes of the Act; available only to owner and alleged driver
Plate and driver	$39 fine (including surcharge) /4 points	Points and report to DMV prohibited; maximum $40 fine[3] for speeding (doubled in school zones); $75 for red light running	Driver not owner	Not addressed
Two or more images of the vehicle	$75-$230 fine	Not a conviction; not recorded; not to be used for insurance purposes; maximum fine $50 plus costs	Owners of commercial vehicles must identify driver or be held responsible	Not addressed
Not addressed	$75 fine/ 2 points	Penalty same as for traditional citation	Driver not owner supported by affidavit; driver yielding to emergency vehicle; funeral procession or responding to officer direction	Not addressed
License plate, intersection, and light	$1000 max. fine/3 points	No points assessed; not part of record; not moving violation; not criminal conviction; not used for insurance purposes; $70 maximum fine	Owner not driver	Images and information are not part of the public record

605

Automated Enforcement Chart

State	Location	Violations	Citation Issued to Whom	Liability
Idaho	No automated enforcement in this state.			
Illinois[5]	Municipalities with 1,000,000 or more	Red light violations resulting in crash, leaving scene of crash, or reckless driving resulting in bodily injury	Not addressed	Not addressed
	Chicago (by home rule ordinance)	Red light	Registered Owner	Owner
Indiana	No automated enforcement in this state.			
Iowa	No automated enforcement in this state.			
Kansas	No automated enforcement in this state.			
Kentucky	No automated enforcement in this state.			
Louisiana	No automated enforcement in this state.			
Maine	No automated enforcement in this state.			
Maryland[5]	Statewide	Red light	Registered Owner	Owner
Massachusetts	No automated enforcement in this state.			
Michigan	No automated enforcement in this state.			
Minnesota	No automated enforcement in this state.			
Mississippi	No automated enforcement in this state.			
Missouri	No automated enforcement in this state.			
Montana	No automated enforcement in this state.			
Nebraska	No automated enforcement in this state.			
Nevada[5]	Prohibits use of photographic, video, or digital equipment unless it is hand held by an officer or installed within a vehicle or facility of a law enforcement agency. Traditional enforcement penalties include a maximum fine of $1000 and 4 points on the driver's record.			
New Hampshire	No automated enforcement in this state.			
New Jersey[5]	Photo-radar enforcement is prohibited in this state.			
New Mexico	No automated enforcement in this state.			

Automated Enforcement Chart

Image	Traditional Enforcement Penalties	Records/Points/ Penalties	Defenses	Privacy
Photograph of vehicle and tag	$500 max. fine	Penalty same as for traditional citation	Not addressed	Not addressed
Photograph of vehicle and tag	$500 max. fine	$90 fine	Light violation occurred as part of a funeral procession; vehicle or plates were stolen	Not addressed
Rear of vehicle and tag; two or more: photos; micro-photos; electronic images; videotape; any other medium	$500 max. fine/2 points	Not a moving violation; no points; no record; treated as parking violation; may not be considered by insurers; maximum $100 civil penalty	Light violation occurred in order to yield to an emergency vehicle or as part of a funeral procession; vehicle or plates were stolen; light not properly positioned or visible; owner not operator by providing name of operator and address	Not addressed

Automated Enforcement Chart

State	Location	Violations	Citation Issued to Whom	Liability
New York[5]	Cities with a population of 1,000,000 or more limited to 50 intersections within each city	Red light	Owner	Owner
North Carolina[5]	Albemarle, Charlotte, Chapel Hill, Cornelius, Durham, Fayetteville, Greensboro, Greenville, High Point, Huntersville, Lumberton, Matthews, Nags Head, Newton, Pineville, Rocky Mount, Spring Lake, Wilmington	Red light	Owner	Owner
North Dakota	No automated enforcement in this state.			
Ohio	No specific statute. Red light cameras authorized by ordinance in Dayton and Toledo; owner is liable, not criminal conviction, not on operating record, no points; in Toledo, $75 maximum; in Dayton, $250 maximum. Traditional enforcement penalties include a maximum fine of $100 and 2 points on the driver's record.			
Oklahoma	No automated enforcement in this state.			
Oregon[5]	Cities with 30,000 or more people; in cities with 30,000 to 300,000 limited to 8 intersections per city; in cities with more than 300,000 limited to 12 intersections per city	Red light (photo radar authorized by a separate provision, 4 hours per day §810.438)	Registered owner or driver, if identifiable	Registered owner
Pennsylvania[5]	Philadelphia[4]	Red light	Registered owner	Owner

Automated Enforcement Chart

Image	Traditional Enforcement Penalties	Records/Points/ Penalties	Defenses	Privacy
Photographs, micro-photographs, videotape, other recorded images, requires 2 or more images	$100 max. fine/3 points	$50 with a possible $25 fine for failure to respond to a notice of liability. Imposition of liability is not the equivalent of a conviction; not part of driver record; may not be used for insurance purposes	Vehicle stolen; vehicle leased or rented by another; owner responsible even if not driving but may seek indemnification by driver, driver already convicted	Not addressed
Photo, video, electronic	$100 max. fine/3 points	Non-criminal violation; no points; $50 civil penalty or if not paid $100	Owner not operator but must furnish name and address of operator; vehicle stolen	Not addressed
Photographs; digital images	$300 max. fine	Penalty same as for traditional citation	Owner may submit a "certificate of innocence"; owner employer, business, rental agency may certify that the vehicle was being operated by employee or lessee and must provide name and address and driver license number of operator	Not addressed
Photographs	$25 fine/ 3 points	$100 maximum; not on operating record	Owner not driver; vehicle stolen; did not own vehicle at time of violation	Images and information are not part of public record

Automated Enforcement Chart

State	Location	Violations	Citation Issued to Whom	Liability
Rhode Island	Statewide	Red light	Registered owner	Driver
South Carolina	No automated enforcement in this state.			
South Dakota	No specific statute; red light cameras authorized by ordinance in Sioux Falls; owner is liable; not on record; $86 fine.			
Tennessee	No specific statute; red light cameras authorized by ordinance in Germantown; owner is liable unless produces driver's name and address or signs an affidavit stating that the person driving did not have the owner's permission to use the vehicle; not criminal conviction; not on operating record; no points; $50 maximum. Traditional enforcement penalties include a maximum fine of $50 and/or up to 2 days in jail and points may be assessed on the driver's record.			
Texas	No specific statute; red light cameras authorized by ordinance in Garland; owner is liable unless produces driver's name and address; not criminal conviction; not on operating record; no points; $75 fine. Traditional enforcement penalties include a maximum fine of $100.			
Utah[5]	Statewide	Speed; prohibits use except in school zone or in areas with speeds posted at 30 mph or less and there is a local ordinance and an officer is present		Not addressed
Vermont	No automated enforcement in this state.			
Virginia	No automated enforcement in this state.			
Washington[5]	Cities and counties statewide.	Red light violations at two-arterial intersections; rail crossing, school speed zone violations	Registered owner	Registered owner
West Virginia	No automated enforcement in this state.			
Wisconsin[5]	Photo-radar enforcement is prohibited in this state.			
Wyoming	No automated enforcement in this state.			

Automated Enforcement Chart

Image	Traditional Enforcement Penalties	Records/Points/ Penalties	Defenses	Privacy
At least 2 micro-photographs, photographs, or other recorded images of the vehicle and license plates	$75 fine	$75 fine. Not a criminal offense; not a moving violation; not included on driving record; not to be considered for insurance purposes until there is a final adjudication of the violation	Same that apply to citations issued through traditional enforcement	Images not a public record; images not identifying a violation to be destroyed within 90 days; those revealing a violation within 1 year of disposition; privacy of records to be protected
Photograph	$1000 max. fine/50 points	Not reportable; no points may be assessed	Not addressed	Not addressed
Vehicle, license plate	$250 max. fine	Not on record; no points; fine limited to the maximum fine for parking violations in the jurisdiction.	Affidavit or testimony in court that owner not operator; vehicle stolen	No photo may be taken in the absence of a violation; photo may not reveal driver or passenger's face.

Automated Enforcement Chart

[1] System must be identified with signs visible to traffic approaching from any direction or signs must be posted at all major entrances to the city. The intersections where a red light camera is present must have a minimum yellow light change interval established in accordance with the Traffic Manual of the Department of Transportation. Warning notices required for first 30 days after implementation. Public announcement required at least 30 days prior to implementation.

[2] Photo radar may only be used in school zones, residential neighborhoods, or along a street bordering a municipal park. If first photo radar offense and traveling 10 mph or less over the posted limit, only a warning may be issued.

[3] Fine may not be used to compensate vendor or lessor for equipment. Cost must be based on the value of the equipment, not the number of citations issued or revenue generated.

[4] Red light cameras are only permitted to be installed at the following intersections: U.S. Route 1 at Grant

Automated Enforcement Chart

Avenue; U.S. Route 1 at Red Lion Road; U.S. Route 1 at Cottman Street; Kensington Avenue at Clearfield Street; Richmond Street at Allegheny Avenue; Richmond Street at Castor Avenue; Aramingo Avenue at New York Street; Thompson Street at Lehigh Avenue; and Broad Street at Washington Avenue.

[5] The code citation for the statutes are as follows: Cal. Vehicle Code §§210, 21455.5, 21455.6, 40518 - 40521 (West 2000); Colo. Rev. Stat. Ann. §42-4-110.5 (West 1997); Del. Code Ann. tit. 21, §4101(d) (1995); D.C. Code Ann. §40-751 (1998); Ga. Code Ann. §40-6-20 (2001); 625 Ill. Comp. Stat. Ann. 5/11-306(c)(5), 5/1-105.5 (West 1993); Md. Ann. Code art. 21 §202.1, 207 (2000); Nev. Rev. Stat. Ann. 484.910 (Michie 1998); N.J. Stat. Ann. §39:4-103.1 (West 1990); N.Y. Vehicle and Traffic Law §1111-a (Consol. 1992); N.C. Gen. Stat. §160A-300.1 (1997); 1999 Oregon Laws 1999, 851 § 1-3; 75 Pa. Cons. Stat. Ann. 3166; Utah Code Ann. §41-6-52.5 (2001); RCW 46.63. §, 2005 WA. S. Bill 5060, eff. 7/21/05; Wis. Stat. Ann. §349.02 (West 1999).

Distracted Driving Chart

State	Statewide Hand-held Cell Phone Ban	Teen Driver Cell Phone Ban	Distracted/ Negligent Driving
Alabama	○	○	○
Alaska	○	○	○
Arizona	○	○	○
Arkansas	○	○	○
California[1]	○	○	○
Colorado	○	●[2]	○
Connecticut	●	●	●
Delaware	○	●	○
D.C.	●	●	●
Florida[3]	○	○	○
Georgia	○	○	○
Hawaii	○	○	○
Idaho	○	○	○
Illinois[4]	○	●	○
Indiana	○	○	○
Iowa	○	○	○
Kansas	○	○	○
Kentucky	○	○	○
Louisiana	○	○	○
Maine	○	●	○
Maryland	○	●[2]	○
Massachusetts[5]	○	○	○
Michigan	○	○	○
Minnesota	○	●	○
Mississippi	○	○	○
Missouri	○	○	○
Montana	○	○	○
Nebraska	○	○	○
Nevada	○	○	○
New Hampshire	○	○	●[6]
New Jersey	●[7]	●	○
New Mexico[8]	○	○	○
New York	●	○	○
North Carolina	○	○	○
North Dakota	○	○	○
Ohio[9]	○	○	○
Oklahoma	○	○	○
Oregon	○	○	○
Pennsylvania	○	○	○
Rhode Island	○	○	○
South Carolina	○	○	○
South Dakota	○	○	○

Distracted Driving Chart

	Laws	
Study/Data Collection	State Preemption on Cell Phones	School Bus Driver Cell Phone Ban
○	○	○
○	○	○
○	○	●
○	○	●
●	○	●
○	○	○
●	○	●
●	○	●
●	○	●
●	●	○
○	○	○
●	○	○
○	○	○
○	○	●
○	○	○
●	○	○
○	○	○
○	●	○
●	●	○
○	○	○
●	○	○
●	○	●
●	○	○
●	○	○
○	●	○
○	○	○
●	○	○
●	○	○
●	○	○
●	●	○
○	○	○
●	●	●
○	○	○
●	●	○
●	○	○
○	○	○
○	○	○
●	●	○
●	●	○
○	○	●
○	○	○
○	○	○

Distracted Driving Chart

State	Statewide Hand-held Cell Phone Ban	Teen Driver Cell Phone Ban	Distracted/ Negligent Driving
Tennessee	o	•	o
Texas	o	•	o
Utah[10]	o	o	o
Vermont	o	o	o
Virginia	o	o	o
Washington	o	o	o
West Virginia	o	o	o
Wisconsin	o	o	o
Wyoming	o	o	o

LEGEND

•=Yes o=No

Distracted Driving Laws:

[1] In California, rental cars must be equipped with safe operating instructions for cell phones.
[2] In Colorado and Maryland, the teen driver cell phone ban is secondarily enforced.
[3] In Florida, cell phone use is permitted as long as it provides sounds to only one ear and allows surrounding sound to be heard with the other ear.
[4] In Chicago, Illinois, drivers are banned from using hand-held cell phones.
[5] In Massachusetts, cell phone use is permitted as long as it does not interfere with the operation of the motor vehicle. The driver must also keep one hand on the steering wheel at all times; first-time fines for violating these laws range from $30 to $100.
[6] In New Hampshire, drivers are accountable for distractions that contribute to a crash -- motorists can be fined $250 to $1000 for engaging in a distracting activity.
[7] In New Jersey, the hand-held cell phone ban for drivers is secondarily enforced.
[8] In Santa Fe, New Mexico, drivers are banned from using hand-held cell phones.
[9] In Brooklyn, North Olmstead and Walton Hills, Ohio, drivers are banned from using hand-held cell phones.
[10] In Sandy, Utah, drivers can be fined up to $300 for engaging in a distracting activity that causes an accident or violation.

Distracted Driving Chart

Study/Data Collection	Laws State Preemption on Cell Phones	School Bus Driver Cell Phone Ban
●	○	●
●	○	●
●	○	○
○	○	○
○	○	○
●	○	○
○	○	○
○	○	○
○	○	○

Driver's License Laws Chart

State	Graduated Licensing	Night Restrictions	Passenger Restrictions	Hours Behind the Wheel (at night in parentheses)	Can the Holder of a Permit From Another State Drive in Your State?*
Alabama	●	●	●	30[1]	●
Alaska	●	●	●	40 (10)	●
Arizona	●[1]	○	○	25 (5)[1]	●
Arkansas	●[1]	○	○	None	●
California	●	●	●	50 (10)	●
Colorado	●	●	●	50 (10)	●
Connecticut	●	●	●	20	●
Delaware	●	●	●	None	●
D.C.	●	●	●	50 in learner's stage (10 hours at night in intermediate stage)	●
Florida	●	●	○	50 (10)	●
Georgia	●	●	●	40 (6)	●
Hawaii	●	●	●	None	○
Idaho	●	●	○	50 (10)	●
Illinois	●	●	●	25	●
Indiana	●	●	●	None	●
Iowa	●	●	○	30 (4)	●

Driver's License Laws Chart

Older Drivers		Vision Requirements	Social Security	Duration in Years/	Non-resident
Accelerated Renewal	Other Provisions	Visual Acuity	Number On License	Expiration Date	Violator Compact
○	○	20/40	○	4/DOB	●
○	●[1]**	20/40[1]	○	5/DOB	○
●[1]	●[2]	20/40 (in at least one eye)	Optional	Valid until 65th Birthday: Renewable thereafter for successive 5 year periods	●
○	○	20/40[1]	○	4/DOB	●
○	●[3]*	20/40 (may not be worse than 20/200 with corrective lenses)	○	5/DOB	○
●[2]	●[4]**	20/40	Optional	5/DOB	●
●[3]	●[5]	20/40[2]	○	4 or 6, 16-64 2 or 4/if 65 or older, DOB	●
○	○	20/40[3] 20/50[4]	Optional	5/DOB	●
○	●[6]	20/40[5]	Optional	5/DOB	●
○	●[7]***	20/40[1]	○	4 or 6/DOB	●
○	●[8]	20/60[1,15]	Optional	4/DOB	●
●[4]	○	20/40[1]	○	4, 15-17 6, 18-71/DOB 2, 72 or older	●
●[5]	○	20/40[1]	○	4/DOB or 8/DOB if 21-62 years	●
●[6]	●[9]	20/40	○	4/DOB	●
●[7]	○	20/40[1]	Optional	4, 18-74; 3, over 75/DOB	●
●[8]	○	20/40[6]	Optional	2 or 4, 17-70; 2, others; DOB	●

619

Driver's License Laws Chart

State	Graduated Licensing	Night Restrictions	Passenger Restrictions	Hours Behind the Wheel (at night in parentheses)	Can the Holder of a Permit From Another State Drive in Your State?*
Kansas	●[1]	○	○	50 (10)	●
Kentucky	●[1]	○	○	None	●
Louisiana	●	●	○	None	●
Maine	●	●	●	35 (5)	●
Maryland	●	●	●	60 (10)	●
Massachusetts	●	●	●	12	●
Michigan	●	●	○	50 (10)	●
Minnesota	●[1]	○	○	40 (10)	●
Mississippi	●	●	○	None	●
Missouri	●	●	○	20	○[1]
Montana	●	●	●	50 (10)	●
Nebraska	●[2]	●	○	50[1]	●
Nevada	●	●	●	50 (10)	●
New Hampshire	●	●	●	20	●
New Jersey	●	●	●	None	●
New Mexico	●	●	●	50 (10)	●
New York	●	●	●	20	●
North Carolina	●	●	●	None	●
North Dakota	●[1]	○	○	None	●
Ohio	●	●	○	50 (10)	○
Oklahoma	●	●	●	40 (10)	●

Driver's License Laws Chart

Older Drivers		Vision Requirements	Social Security	Duration in Years/	Non-resident
Accelerated Renewal	Other Provisions	Visual Acuity	Number On License	Expiration Date	Violator Compact
•9	o	20/40 in one eye at exam station or 20/60 from an ophthalmologist or optometrist exam[1]	o	4, under 21 and over 65 6, 21-65/DOB	•
o	o	20/40	o	4/Last Day Birth Mo.	•
o	•10**	20/40	Optional	4/DOB	•
•9	•11	20/40	Optional	6, 16-64 4, 65 and older/DOB	•
o	•12,13	20/40[7]	o	5/DOB	•
o	•13	20/40	Optional	5/DOB	•
o	o	20/40[1]	o	4/DOB	o
o	•13	20/40[1]	o	4/DOB	•
o	o	20/40[8]	Optional	4, 18 and above 1, under 18/DOB	•
•10	o	20/40	Optional	3, 18-20** 3 or 6, 21-69** 3, 70 and above	•
•11	•**	20/40[1]	Optional	8, 21-67*** 6, 68-74 4, other DOB	•
o	o	20/40[1]	o	5/DOB	•
o	•14	20/40[9]	•	4/DOB	•
o	•9	20/40 (for both eyes or 20/30 if there is vision only in one eye unless special consideration is granted by DMV)[1]	o	5/DOB and Youth Operator valid for 1 yr.	•
o	o	20/50[10]	o	4/Month of Issue	•
•12	o	20/40[9]	Optional	4 or 8/DOB	•
o	o	20/40[9,11]	o	8/DOB	•
o	•15	20/40	•	4/DOB	•
o	o	20/40[12]	o	4/DOB	•
o	o	20/40[1]	Optional	4/DOB	•
o	o	20/60 or better in both eyes; or 20/50 or better in at least one eye	Optional	4/Last Day Issue Mo.	•

Driver's License Laws Chart

State	Graduated Licensing	Night Restrictions	Passenger Restrictions	Hours Behind the Wheel (at night in parentheses)	Can the Holder of a Permit From Another State Drive in Your State?*
Oregon	•	•	•	50[2]	•
Pennsylvania	•	•	○	50	○
Rhode Island	•	•	•	50 (10)	•
South Carolina	•	•	•	40 (10)	•
South Dakota	•	•	○	None	○
Tennessee	•	•	•	50 (10)	•
Texas	•	•	•	None	•
Utah	•[2]	•	•	40 (10)	•
Vermont	•	○	•	40 (10)	○
Virginia	•	•	•	40 (10)	•
Washington	•	•	•	50 (10)	•
West Virginia	•	•	•	30[1]	•
Wisconsin	•	•	•	30 (10)	•
Wyoming	•[2]	•	•	50 (10)	•

LEGEND •=Yes ○=No

Graduated Driver Licensing:

1=Mandatory learner's permit.
2=Nebraska and Utah have intermediate licenses, but no mandatory learner's permit. The holding period for Wyoming's law is 10 days.

Behind the Wheel:

1=None with driver education.
2=100 hours without driver education.

Older Driver Laws:

Accelerated renewal

1=5 years for people 65 and older.
2=5 years for people 61 and older.
3=65 and older may choose 2-year or 6-year renewal. A personal appearance at renewal is required. Upon a showing of hardship, people 65 and older may renew by mail.
4=2 years for people 72 and older.
5=Drivers 21-62 have the choice of a 4- or 8-year license; drivers 63 and older will receive a 4-year license.
6=2 years for drivers 81-86; 1 year for drivers 87 and older.
7=3 years for drivers 75 and older.
8=2 years for drivers 70 and older.
9=4 years for drivers 65 and older.
10=3 years for people 70 and older and 21 and younger.
11=4 years for drivers 75 and older.
12=4 years for drivers who would turn 75 in the last half of an 8-year renewal cycle.

Driver's License Laws Chart

Older Drivers — Accelerated Renewal	Older Drivers — Other Provisions	Vision Requirements Visual Acuity	Social Security Number On License	Duration in Years/ Expiration Date	Non-resident Violator Compact
○	•16	20/70 in both eyes; if 20/40 or worse in best eye, then restricted to daytime hours	○	8, (in person)	•
○	○	20/40[9]	○	4*, Last Day Birth Mo.	•
•8	○	20/40	○	5, under 70 2, 70 or older/DOB	•
•1	•8,17	20/40[13]	○	5/DOB	•
○	○	20/40[1]	Optional	5/DOB or 30 days after 21st birthday	•
○	•18	20/40, each eye separately and both eyes together	Optional	5/DOB	•
○	○	20/40	○	6/DOB	•
○	•8	20/40[10,14]	Optional	5/DOB	•
○	○	20/40	○	4/DOB	•
○	•19	20/40[1]	○	5/Last Day Birth Mo.	•
○	○	20/40[1]	○	5/DOB	•
○	○	20/40 (20/60 if doctor certifies driver can safely operate the vehicle)	○	5/DOB	•
○	○	20/40	○	8/DOB	○
○	○	20/40[1]	Optional	4/DOB	•

Other Provisions:

1=Mail renewal not available to people 69 and older.
2=Mail renewal not available to people 70 and older. Any person 65 years and older who is renewing by mail must submit a vision test verification form, provided by the department, or verification of an examination of the applicant's eyesight. The vision test must be conducted not more than 3 months before.
3=At age 70, mail renewal is prohibited.
4=Mail or electronic renewal not available to people 61 and older.
5=65 and older may choose 2-year or 6-year renewal. A personal appearance at renewal is required. Upon a showing of hardship, people 65 and older may renew by mail.
6=At age 70, or nearest renewal date thereafter, a vision test is required and a reaction test may be required. Applicant must provide a statement from a practicing physician certifying the applicant to be physically and mentally competent to drive. At 75 years, or nearest renewal date thereafter, and on each subsequent renewal date, the applicant may be required to also complete the written and road tests.
7=Renewal applicants over 79 must pass a vision test administered at any driver's license office or, if applying for an extension by mail, must pass a vision test administered by a licensed physician or optometrist.
8=Vision test required for people 65 and older.
9=Renewal applicants 75 and older must take a road test.

Driver's License Laws Chart

10=Mail renewal not available to people 70 and older and to people whose prior renewal was by mail.
11=Vision test required at first renewal after 40th birthday and at every second renewal until age 62; thereafter, at every renewal.
12=Vision test required at age 40 and older for every renewal. Applicants for an initial license age 70 and older must provide proof of previous satisfactory operation of a vehicle or physician's certificate of fitness.
13=Age alone is not grounds for re-examination of drivers.
14=Age alone is not grounds for re-examination of drivers; applicants for mail renewal age 70 and older must include a medical report.
15=60 and older not required to parallel park during road test.
16=Vision screening required every 8 years for drivers 50 and over.
17=Beginning October 1, 2008, every licensee will be required to submit to a vision test every 5 years.
18=Licenses issued to people 65 and older do not expire.
19=Applicants 80 years and older must undergo vision examinations either in person or provide a report of the examination.

*=No more than two sequential mail renewals are permitted, regardless of age.
**=Mail renewal not available to people whose prior renewal was electronic or by mail.
***=Only two successive renewals may be made electronically or by mail, regardless of age.

Duration and Expiration Date:

*=New drivers ages 16-20 – 3 year driver license issued that will expire on the applicant's date of birth in the third year after date of issuance. Drivers who are between the ages of 16-18 will be issued an intermediate license that will expire two years from the date issued. 21-69 – 6-year license issued that will expire on the applicant's date of birth in the sixth year after date of issuance. 70 and over – Driver license will expire on the applicant's date of birth in the third year after date of issuance.

Renewal drivers ages 16-20 - 3 year driver license issued that will expire on the applicant's date of birth in the third year after date of issuance. 21-69 - During phase-in period, applicant's with an odd number year of birth get a 3-year license, even number year get a 6-year license. Beginning in July 2003, all licenses in this age group will expire on the applicant's date of birth on the sixth year after date of issuance. 70 and over – Driver license will expire on the applicant's date of birth in the third year after date of issuance.

**= New drivers ages 16-20 – 3 year driver license issued that will expire on the applicant's date of birth in the third year after date of issuance. Drivers who are between the ages of 16-18 will be issued an intermediate license that will expire two years from the date issued. 21-69 – 6-year license issued that will expire on the applicant's date of birth in the sixth year after date of issuance. 70 and over – Driver license will expire on the applicant's date of birth in the third year after date of issuance.

Renewal drivers ages 18-20 - 3 year driver license issued that will expire on the applicant's date of birth in the third year after date of issuance. 21-69 - During phase-in period, applicant's with an odd number year of birth get a 3-year license, even number year get a 6-year license. Beginning in July 2003, all licenses in this age group will expire on the applicant's date of birth on the sixth year after date of issuance. 70 and over – Driver license will expire on the applicant's date of birth in the third year after date of issuance.

***=Stipulation states that except for a license renewed by mail, a license expires on the anniversary of the licensee's birthday eight years or less after the date of issue or on the licensee's 75th birthday, whichever comes first.

Driver's License Laws Chart

Visual Acuity:

1=Required to take and pass eye exam with every renewal.
2=Must pass eye exam at 1st renewal and then every other one.
3=20/40 Full Privileges
4=Daylight Driving
5=20/40 One eye, with 20/70 in other eye
6=Must take and pass eye exam or have a vision report signed by a licensed vision specialist at every renewal.
7=For unrestricted license: minimum vision of 20/40 in each eye and continuous field of vision of 140 degrees; For restricted license: minimum vision of 20/40 in at least one eye and a continuous field of vision of 110 degrees with at least 35 degrees lateral to the midline of each side: For restricted license for daylight driving: minimum vision of 20/70 in one eye and a continuous field of vision of 110 degrees with at least 35 degrees lateral to the midline of each side.
8=Peripheral vision must be at least 55 degrees in either right or left eye with Y or T-restriction (outside rearview mirror required).
9=May require to take and pass vision test with every renewal.
10=Every licensed driver is required to pass a vision test successfully once every 10 years as a condition of driver license renewal.
11=Required minimum visual acuity is 20/40, either corrected or uncorrected, in either or both eyes. If an individual has a visual acuity of less than 20/40 but not less than 20/70 and a horizontal field of vision of 140 degrees or has a visual acuity of 20/40 with telescopic lenses and a corrected visual activity through carrier lenses of 20/100 and a horizontal field of vision no less than 140 degrees with the telescopic lenses in place without the use of field of vision expanders, only a statement from a physician, ophthalmologist or optometrist will be accepted. This statement must also contain a statement as to whether the person's vision condition is deteriorating and recommendations of any driving restrictions.
12=All applications for renewal of a driver's license must be accompanied by a certificate from either the driver licensing or examining authorities or a physician or optometrist stating the corrected or uncorrected vision of the applicant.
13=Vision test must be taken and passed for all renewals but may be waived if license holder submits a certificate from a person authorized by law to examine eyes.
14=Required to have 20/40 vision and peripheral fields (side vision) of 120 degrees in each eye.
15=Required to have 20/60 visual acuity, corrected or uncorrected, in at least one eye or better and a horizontal field of vision with both eyes open of at least 140 degrees or, in the event that one eye only has usable vision, horizontal field must be at least 70 degrees temporally and 50 degrees nasally.

Permits:

*Permit holders are subject to the driving laws and restrictions of both states.
1=Unless 16 years of age.

Electric Personal Assistive Mobility Devices

State	Permitted on Sidewalks/Bicycle Paths	Permitted on Roads
Alabama	Sidewalks and bicycle paths	Yes[1]
Alaska	Sidewalks and bicycle paths	Yes
Arizona	Sidewalks	Yes, if no sidewalk available
Arkansas	--	--
California	Sidewalks and bicycle paths[1]	Yes[1]
Colorado	--	--
Connecticut	Sidewalks[2]	No[3]
Delaware	Sidewalks and bicycle paths	Yes, on highways with speed limits up to 30 mph[4]
D.C.	Sidewalks	--
Florida	Sidewalks and bicycle paths[1]	Yes, on streets with speed limits up to 25 mph[1]
Georgia	Sidewalks	Yes, on streets with speed limits up to 35 mph
Hawaii	Sidewalks and bicycle paths	--
Idaho	Sidewalks	--
Illinois	Sidewalks[1]	Yes
Indiana	Bicycle paths	Yes
Iowa	Sidewalks and bicycle paths	No
Kansas	Sidewalks	Yes
Kentucky	--	--
Louisiana	Sidewalks and bicycle paths	Yes, on streets with speed limits up to 35 mph[1]
Maine	Sidewalks and bicycle paths[1]	Yes, on streets with speed limits up to 35 mph if no sidewalk or bicycle path available[1]
Maryland	Sidewalks	Yes, on streets with speed limits up to 30 mph if no sidewalk available[1]
Massachusetts	--	--
Michigan	Sidewalks[5]	Yes, on streets with speed limits up to 25 mph[1]
Minnesota	Sidewalks and bicycle paths	Yes, on streets with speed limits up to 35 mph[6] if no sidewalk available
Mississippi	Sidewalks and bicycle paths	Yes, on streets where bicycles are permitted
Missouri	Sidewalks and bicycle paths	Yes, on streets with speed limits up to 45 mph[1]
Montana	--	--
Nebraska	Sidewalks and bicycle paths[3]	Yes, except freeways and the interstate highway system[3]

Electric Personal Assistive Mobility Devices

Helmets Required	Minimum Age	Pedestrian Laws Apply
--	--	--
No	--	--
No	16	Yes
--	--	--
No	--	Yes
--	--	--
No	16	--
Younger than 16	--	--
No	16	--
Younger than 16	--	--
Younger than 16	16 on highways	Yes
--	16	--
No	--	Yes
No	--	Yes
No	--	--
No	16	--
No	--	Yes
--	--	--
--	--	--
No	--	--
Younger than 16	--	--
--	--	--
No	--	--
No	--	Yes
No	--	--
No	16[7]	Yes
--	--	--
No	--	--

Electric Personal Assistive Mobility Devices

State	Permitted on Sidewalks/Bicycle Paths	Permitted on Roads
Nevada	Sidewalks and bicycle paths	--
New Hampshire	Sidewalks	Yes
New Jersey	Sidewalks and bicycle paths	Yes[1]
New Mexico	Sidewalks and bicycle paths	Yes
New York	--	--
North Carolina	Sidewalks and bicycle paths[1]	Yes, on streets with speed limits up to 25 mph[1]
North Dakota	--	--
Ohio	Sidewalks, unless marked for the exclusive use of pedestrians and bicycle paths[1]	Yes, on streets with speed limits up to 55 mph[1]
Oklahoma	Sidewalks and bicycle paths	Yes, on municipal streets[9]
Oregon	Sidewalks, bicycle lanes and paths[1]	Yes, on streets with speed limits up to 35 mph[1]
Pennsylvania	Sidewalks, unless prohibited by local jurisdiction	Yes, but not on a freeway
Rhode Island	Sidewalks and bicycle paths	Yes, unless highway prohibits bicycles
South Carolina	Sidewalks	Yes, if no sidewalk available
South Dakota	Sidewalks[1]	--
Tennessee	Sidewalks and bicycle paths	Yes
Texas	Sidewalks and bicycle paths	Yes, on streets with speed limits up to 30 mph and if no sidewalk available
Utah	Sidewalks	Yes, on streets with speed limits up to 35 mph and less than 4 lanes
Vermont	Sidewalks and bicycle paths	No
Virginia	Sidewalks, unless prohibited by local jurisdiction	Yes, on streets with speed limits up to 25 mph and if no sidewalk available
Washington	Sidewalks and bicycle paths[1]	Yes, but not on controlled highways[12]
West Virginia	Sidewalks	Yes
Wisconsin	Sidewalks, unless prohibited by local jurisdiction[13]	Yes, however the department or the locality may prohibit them by rule on certain streets or on streets with speed limits over 25 mph
Wyoming	--	--

Electric Personal Assistive Mobility Devices

Helmets Required	Minimum Age	Pedestrian Laws Apply
No	--	Yes
No	--	--
Yes	16[7]	--
No	--	Yes
--	--	--
No	--	Yes
--	--	--
Younger than 18	14[8]	--
No	--	--
No	16	Yes
Younger than 12	--	--
No	16	--
No	--	--
No	--	Yes
No	--	--
--	--	--
Younger than 18	16[10]	--
No	16	Yes
Younger than 15 if by local ordinance	14[11]	--
No	--	--
No	--	Yes
No	--	No
--	--	--

Electric Personal Assistive Mobility Devices

[1] EPAMD use may be restricted by local ordinance. San Francisco has banned the use of EPAMDs on all sidewalks in the city and county as well as in public transit stations and vehicles. Municipalities in Alabama may prohibit EPAMDs on roads where the speed limit is greater than 25 mph.

[2] Only a person with a disability who was been issued a disability placard may use an EPAMD on a sidewalk or highway.

[3] EPAMDs are only allowed on highways to cross; EPAMDs may not be ridden along highways.

[4] EPAMDs are only allowed on highways with a speed limit of more than 30 mph to cross.

[5] EPAMDs may be required by local ordinance to use bicycle paths located adjacent to a roadway.

If a rider is less than 16 years of age and not accompanied by an adult, they must use a bikepath if located adjacent to a roadway.

Electric Personal Assistive Mobility Devices

[6] Local jurisdictions may allow EPAMDs on roads with speed limits higher than 35 mph.

[7] Persons younger than 16 years of age may operate an EPMAD if the person has a mobility related disability.

[8] Persons 14 through 15 may only operate an EPAMD if under the supervision of a person 18 years old or older who is responsible for the immediate care of the operator.

[9] EPAMDs may be prohibited by municipality from operating on streets with speed limits higher than 25 mph.

[10] A person under 16 may operate an EPAMD if accompanied by the person's parent or guardian.

[11] Persons younger than 14 may operate an EPAMD if under the supervision of a person 18 years old or older.

[12] EPAMDs can locally be restricted to streets with speed limits up to 25 mph.

[13] EPAMDs cannot be operated on trails in state parks or forests unless specifically allowed by posted sign.

Gas Tax Chart

State	Tax: gas; (diesel)
Alabama	$0.18/gallon; ($0.19/gallon)
Alaska	$0.08/gallon; ($0.08/gallon)
Arizona	$0.18/gallon; ($0.18/gallon)
Arkansas	$0.215/gallon; ($0.225/gallon)
California	$0.18/gallon; ($0.18/gallon); + 7-8% sales tax
Colorado	$0.22/gallon; ($0.205/gallon)
Connecticut	$0.25/gallon; ($0.26/gallon)
Delaware	$0.23/gallon; ($0.22/gallon)
D.C.	$0.20/gallon; ($0.20/gallon)
Florida	$0.141/gallon; ($0.267/gallon)
Georgia	$0.075/gallon; ($0.075/gallon) + 4% sales tax
Hawaii	$0.16/gallon; ($0.16/gallon)
Idaho	$0.25/gallon; ($0.25/gallon)
Illinois	$0.19/gallon; ($0.215/gallon)
Indiana	$0.18/gallon; ($0.16/gallon)
Iowa	$0.203/gallon; ($0.225/gallon)
Kansas	$0.24/gallon; ($0.26/gallon)
Kentucky	$0.15/gallon; ($0.12/gallon + $0.14 environmental fee for diesel)
Louisiana	$0.20/gallon; ($0.20/gallon)
Maine	$0.246/gallon; ($0.257/gallon)
Maryland	$0.235/gallon; ($0.243/gallon)
Massachusetts	$0.21/gallon; ($0.21/gallon); + $0.025 UST fund tax
Michigan	$0.19/gallon; ($0.15/gallon)
Minnesota	$0.20/gallon; ($0.20/gallon)
Mississippi	$0.18/gallon; ($0.18/gallon)
Missouri	$0.17/gallon; ($0.17/gallon)
Montana	$0.278/gallon; ($0.285/gallon)
Nebraska	Changes every 3 months
Nevada	$0.24/gallon; ($0.27/gallon)
New Hampshire	$0.18/gallon; ($0.18/gallon)
New Jersey	$0.145/gallon; ($0.175/gallon)
New Mexico	$0.19/gallon; ($0.21/gallon)
New York	$0.327/gallon; ($0.305/gallon)
North Carolina	$0.175/gallon; ($0.175/gallon) + either $0.035/gallon or 7% avg. wholesale price, whichever is greater
North Dakota	$0.23/gallon; ($0.23/gallon)
Ohio	$0.24/gallon; ($0.24/gallon)
Oklahoma	$0.16/gallon; ($0.13/gallon)
Oregon	$0.26/gallon; ($0.24/gallon)
Pennsylvania	$0.311/gallon; ($0.351/gallon)

Gas Tax Chart

State	Tax: gas; (diesel)
Rhode Island	$0.31/gallon; ($0.31/gallon)
South Carolina	$0.16/gallon; ($0.16/gallon)
South Dakota	$0.22/gallon; ($0.22/gallon)
Tennessee	$0.20/gallon; ($0.18/gallon + $0.04/gallon for environmental assurance fee)
Texas	$0.20/gallon; ($0.20/gallon)
Utah	$0.245/gallon; ($0.245/gallon)
Vermont	$0.20/gallon; ($0.26/gallon)
Virginia	$0.175/gallon; ($0.16/gallon) + 2% in Northern VA Metro Area
Washington	$0.375/gallon; ($0.375/gallon)
West Virginia	$0.257/gallon; ($0.257/gallon)
Wisconsin	$0.285/gallon; ($0.285/gallon) (annually indexed in April to the rate of inflation, $0.03 for petroleum inspection fee)
Wyoming	$0.14/gallon; ($0.14/gallon)

Motor Vehicle Registration Chart

State	City	Official Name of Department	Head of Department	Period of Grace for Securing New Tag to Midnight
Alabama	Montgomery	Dept. of Revenue Motor Vehicle Division	Terry Lane Director	10 Days
Alaska	Anchorage	Dept. of Administration Motor Vehicle Division	Mary Marshburn Director	None
Arizona	Phoenix	Dept. of Transportation Motor Vehicle Division	Stacey K. Stanton Division Director	None
Arkansas	Little Rock	Dept. of Finance & Administration Office of Motor Vehicles Revenue Division	Fred Porter Administrator	None
California	Sacramento	Dept. of Motor Vehicles	Steven Gourley Director	None
Colorado	Lakewood	Dept. of Revenue Motor Vehicle Division	Aurora Ruiz-Hernandez Director	30 Days (a)
Connecticut	Waterbury	Dept. of Motor Vehicles	Gary DeFilippo Commissioner	None
Delaware	Dover	Dept. of Public Safety Motor Vehicles Division	Michael D. Shahan Director	None
D.C.	Washington	Dept. of Motor Vehicles	Sherryl Hobbs Newman Director	None
Florida	Tallahassee	Department of Highway Safety and Motor Vehicles	Fred O. Dickinson, III Executive Director	None
Georgia	Conyers	Dept. of Motor Vehicle Safety	Tim Burgess Commissioner	None
Hawaii	See[1]	See[1]	See[1]	None
Idaho	Boise	Dept. of Transportation Division of Motor Vehicles	Pamela Lowe Administrator	None
Illinois	Springfield	Office of the Secretary of State Vehicle Services	Edmund Michalowski Director	None
Indiana	Indianapolis	Bureau of Motor Vehicles	Mary L. De Prez Commissioner	None
Iowa	Des Moines	Dept. of Transportation Motor Vehicle Division	Shirley Andre Director	30 Days (a)
Kansas	Topeka	Dept. of Revenue Motor Vehicle Division	Sheila Walker Director	None

Motor Vehicle Registration Chart

Minimum Financial Responsibility (in thousands) of dollars	No-Fault Insurance Law	Transfer of Plates to Another Owner	Color Scheme for License Plates	Vehicle Inspection
20/40/10	No	No Special-Yes	Red and Blue (1)a*	o
50/100/25	No*	Yes Special-No	Blue on Yellow/Gold or Black on Blue Sky with White Mountains and Trail Climbers for Gold Rush Centennial (2)a*	•*8 E, S
15/30/10	No	Yes	Blue/White with Grand Canyon Background (1)a*	•*3 E, S
25/50/25	Yes*	No	Red & Blue on White (1)a*	• S
15/30/5	No	Yes Special-No	Blue on White (2)a* or Yellow on Black or Blue (2)a and Blue on White (2)a*	•** E
25/50/15	Yes*	No	White and Green (2)a or Green on White	•* E, S
20/40/10	No*	No	White on Blue (2)a*	•*1,2 E, S
15/30/10	Yes*	Yes	Gold on Blue (1)a*	•* E, S
25/50/10	No*	No	Red & Blue on White (2)a*	•** E, S
10/20/10	Yes*	No	Green on White or Orange on White (1)a*	• S
15/30/10	No*	No	Black & White w/ Peach Emblem (1)a*	•* E, S
20/40/10	No	Yes	Rainbow Design (2)a	• S
25/50/15	No*	No	Blue on Red, White and Blue (2)a*	•*1,3 E
20/40/15	No	No	Blue on White (2)a* with Red Letters	•**6 E, S
25/50/10	No	No	White, Green, Blue & Black with Farmhouse Scene	•*8 E, S
20/40/15	No	No	Blue on White Scenic Background (2)a	o
25/50/10	Yes*	No	Gold & Blue on White (1)a*	o

635

Motor Vehicle Registration Chart

State	City	Official Name of Department	Head of Department	Period of Grace for Securing New Tag to Midnight
Kentucky	Frankfort	Transportation Cabinet Vehicle Regulation Department	Ed Logsdon Commissioner	None
Louisiana	Baton Rouge	Public Safety Services	Col. Terry Landry Deputy Secretary	None
Maine	Augusta	Office of the Secratary of State Bureau of Motor Vehicles	Peter C. Brazier Deputy Secretary of State	30 Days (a)
Maryland	Glen Burnie	Dept. of Transportation Motor Vehicle Administration	Anne S. Ferro Administrator	None
Massachusetts	Boston	Registry of Motor Vehicles	Daniel A. Grabauskas Registrar	None
Michigan	Lansing	Dept. of State	Terry Lynn Land Secretary of State	None
Minnesota	St. Paul	Dept. of Public Safety	Charles R. Weaver, Jr. Commissioner	10 days passenger vehicles
Mississippi	Jackson	Dept. of Public Safety	Lt. Colonel Ron Ford Director	None
Missouri	Jefferson City	Dept. of Revenue	Carol Russell Fischer Director	None
Montana	Helena	Motor Vehicle Division Dept. of Justice	Dean Roberts Administrator	Last day of month (a)
Nebraska	Lincoln	Dept. of Motor Vehicles	Beverly Neth Director	30 Days
Nevada	Carson City	Dept. of Motor Vehicles	Ginny Lewis Director	None
New Hampshire	Concord	Dept. of Safety Div. of Motor Vehicles	Virginia Beecher Director	None
New Jersey	Trenton	Dept. of Transportation N.J. Motor Vehicle Commission	Sharon Harrington Chief Administrator	None
New Mexico	Santa Fe	Taxation and Revenue Dept. Division of Motor Vehicles	Larry Kehoe Director	None
New York	Albany	Dept. of Motor Vehicles	Raymond Martinez Commissioner	None
North Carolina	Raleigh	Dept. of Transportation Div. of Motor Vehicles	Carol Howard Commissioner (Acting)	15 days (a)
North Dakota	Bismarck	Dept. of Transportation Driver & Vehicle Services Div.	Keith Magnusson Director	None

Motor Vehicle Registration Chart

Minimum Financial Responsibility (in thousands) of dollars	No-Fault Insurance Law	Transfer of Plates to Another Owner	Color Scheme for License Plates	Vehicle Inspection
25/50/10	Yes*	Yes	Blue on Scenic Background (1)a*	•*8 E
10/20/10	No*	No	Blue on White (1)a*	•* E, S
	No*	No	Blue & Red Chikadee Plate (2)a	•* E, S
20/40/15	No*	No	Black on White (2)a	•*5 E, S
20/40/5	Yes*	No	Red & Blue on White (2)a Green on White (1)a	•** E, S
20/40/10	Yes*	No	White on Blue (1)a	o
30/60/10	Yes*	Yes Special-No	Blue on White (2)a*	o
25/50/25	No	No	Yellow on Green (1)a*	• S
25/50/10	No	No	Blue & Green on White (2)a*	•* E, S
25/50/10	No*	No	Blue Color Graphis (2)a*	o
25/50/25	No*	No	Black on Yellow (2)a*	o
15/30/10	No*	No	Blue on Sunset (2)a*	•* E, S
25/50/25	No	No	Green on White (2)a*	•** E, S
15/30/5	Yes*	No	Black on Goldfinch & Pale Yellow (2)a	•* E, S
25/50/10	No*	No	Red on Yellow (1)a*	•**8 E
25/50/10	Yes*	No	Red & Blue on White (2)b* or Blue on White	•** E, S
30/60/25	No*	No	Red & Blue on White (1)a*	•* E, S
25/50/25	Yes*	No	Black on Blue and Gold (2)a*	o

Motor Vehicle Registration Chart

State	City	Official Name of Department	Head of Department	Period of Grace for Securing New Tag to Midnight
Ohio	Columbus	Dept. of Public Safety Bureau of Motor Vehicles	Franklin R. Caltrider Registrar	None
Oklahoma	Oklahoma City	Oklahoma Tax Commission Motor Vehicle Division	Curt Byers Director	30 Days (a)
Oregon	Salem	Dept. of Transportation Driver & Motor Vehicle Services Division	Lorna Youngs Deputy Director	None
Pennsylvania	Harrisburg	Dept. of Transportation Safety Administration	Betty L. Serian Deputy Secretary	None
Rhode Island	Pawtucket	Dept. of Administration Division of Motor Vehicles	Charles Dolan Administrator	None
South Carolina	Columbia	Dept. of Public Safety Div. of Motor Vehicles	David Burgis Deputy Director	45 Days
South Dakota	Pierre	Dept. of Revenue Div. of Motor Vehicles	Debra Hillmer Director	None
Tennessee	Nashville	Dept. of Safety Div. of Title & Registration	Martha Irwin Director	None
Texas	Austin	Texas Dept. of Transportation Vehicle Titles & Registration Division	Jerry L. Dike Director	5 working days (a)
Utah	Salt Lake City	State Tax Commission Motor Vehicle Division	Viola Bodrero Director	None
Vermont	Montpelier	Transportation Agency Dept. of Motor Vehicles	Bonnie L. Rutledge Commissioner	None
Virginia	Richmond	Transportation Secretariat Dept. of Motor Vehicles	Asbury Quillian Commissioner	None
Washington	Olympia	Dept. of Licensing	Fred Stephens Director	None
West Virginia	Charleston	Dept. of Transportation Div. of Motor Vehicles	F. Douglas Stump Commissioner	None
Wisconsin	Madison	Dept. of Transportation Div. of Motor Vehicles	Roger D. Cross Administrator	2 business days
Wyoming	Cheyenne	Dept. of Transportation Motor Vehicle Services	Sleeter Dover Administrator	None
Alberta	Edmonton	Alberta Municipal Affairs Registries	Laurie Beveridge Registrar	None

Motor Vehicle Registration Chart

Minimum Financial Responsibility (in thousands) of dollars	No-Fault Insurance Law	Transfer of Plates to Another Owner	Color Scheme for License Plates	Vehicle Inspection
12.5/25/7.5	No*	No	Red with Sunburst in Background, White and Blue (2)a*	•**8 E, S
25/50/25	No*	Yes	Green on White (1)a*	•8 E
25/50/10	Yes*	No	Graphic Background (2)a*	•* E
15/30/5	No*	No	Blue Fading into White Fading into Yellow with Blue Letters and Numbers (1)a	•** E, S
25/50/25	No*	No	Grey-Blue on Off White (2)a*	•* E, S
15/30/10	No*	No	Blue & Green Mtn. Background Yellow & Brown-White (1)a*	o
25/50/25	No*	No^	Red, White & Blue on White Background (2)a*	o
25/50/10	No	No	Black on White (1)a*	•*8 E
20/40/15	No	Yes	Red & Blue on White (2)b*	•* E, S
25/50/15	Yes*	No	Blue on Orange & Blue (2)a* Blue on White (2)a*	•* E, S
25/50/10	No	No	White on Green (1 or 2)a*	•* E, S
25/50/20	No	No	Blue on White (2)a*	•** E, S
25/50/10	No*	Yes Special Only	Red & Blue on White (2)a	•*3 E
20/40/10	No*	No	Blue and Gold on White (1)a	• E, S
25/50/10	No	No	Blue on White (2)a* Red on White (2)a* Black on White	•*8 E
25/50/20	No*	No	Dark Blue on Light Blue Graphic Background (2)a*	o
N/A	No*	No	Red & Blue on White (1)a	•

639

Motor Vehicle Registration Chart

State	City	Official Name of Department	Head of Department	Period of Grace for Securing New Tag to Midnight
British Columbia	North Vancouver	Insurance Corporation British Columbia	Rod Davey Registrar	None
Manitoba	Winnipeg	Dept. of Highways	A.T. Horosko Deputy Minister	None
New Brunswick	Fredericton	Dept. of Transportation	David Johnstone Deputy Minister	None
Newfoundland	St. John's	Government Services & Lands	G.M. Husey Registrar	None
NW Territories	Yellowknife	Motor Vehicle Div.	Richard MacDonald Registrar	None
Nova Scotia	Halifax	Registry of Motor Vehicles Dept. of Business & Consumer Services	Marie Mullally Registrar	None
Ontario	Toronto	Ministry of Transportation	Jan Rush Deputy Minister	None
Prince Edward Island	Alberton	Motor Vehicle Registrar and Licensing Dept.	John MacDonald Registrar	None
Quebec	Quebec	Societe de L'assurance Automobile	Louise Guimond Vice Presidente	None
Saskatchewan	Regina	Saskatchewan Government Insurance Auto Fund Div.	Alan Cockman	None
Yukon Territory	Whitehorse	Transport Services Branch Motor Vehicles Section	Fred Jensen Deputy Minister	None

LEGEND •=Yes o=No

Certificate of Title:
Required in all states although in Alabama and Maine required only on 75 and subsequent models; required in Guam and the Virgin Islands but not in Puerto Rico; required in two Canadian Provinces: Nova Scotia and Prince Edward Island.

Tag Expiration:
Is staggered in all states and provinces except: Michigan (Birthdate), Manitoba (4 months after Birthdate), and Ontario (Birthdate). *Staggered in certain counties in Georgia.

Period of Grace:
(a) Some states provide a further grace period by administrative order. These periods can vary considerably from year to year. Grace periods set forth in this chart are primarily statutory grace periods.

New Tag Displayed:
When issued in all states except: Georgia (Jan. 1), Maine (1st day/month of expiration), Ohio (90 days before expiration).

Transfer of Plates:
^=For South Dakota, plates stay with vehicle unless organizational license plates obtained.

Minimum Financial Responsibility:
Minimum financial requirements of financial resposibility are shown in terms of amounts applicable to death or injury of 1 person, death or injury of more than 1 person, and property damage.

No-Fault Insurance Law:
*Indicates purchase of insurance is compulsory whether no-fault or other.

Motor Vehicle Registration Chart

Minimum Financial Responsibility (in thousands) of dollars	No-Fault Insurance Law	Transfer of Plates to Another Owner	Color Scheme for License Plates	Vehicle Inspection
N/A	No	No	Blue on White (2)a	•
$200,000	Yes	No	Blue on Graphic (2)a*	o
N/A	No	Yes	Maroon & Green on White (2)*	•
N/A	No	Yes	Red on White (2)a or (1)a	•4
N/A	No*	No	Blue on White (1)a	o
N/A	No	No	Blue on White (1)a*	•
N/A	Yes	No	Blue on White (2)a*	o
N/A	No	No	Green on White (1)a*	•
$50,000	Yes	No	Blue on White (1)*	•3,6
N/A	No	No	Green on White (2)a*	•6
N/A	No*	No	Black on White and Blue (1)a	•7

Color Scheme of License Plates:
(1) One plate used. (2) Two plates used. (1 or 2) One or two plates used.
a. Plates revalidated by tab or sticker.
b. Plates revalidated by windshield sticker.
*Indicates plates are reflectorized.

[1]=Various Counties Have Different Directors:
Honolulu, Licensing Administrator, Dennis Kamimura
Hawaii, Treasurer, Frank Manalili
Hawaii, Acting Lieutenant, Randy Apele
Maui, Motor Vehicle and Licensing Manager, Carmelito Vila
Kauai, Treasurer, David Spanski
Kauai, Chief License Examiner and Inspector, Matthew Ruiz

Vehicle Inspection:
(1) Used motor vehicle being registered from out of state.
(2) Cars 10 years old or older upon transfer or being sold.
(3) When registering a vehicle previously registered in another jurisdiction.
(4) Required before vehicle is registered.
(5) Used vehicles upon resale or transfer.
(6) All commercial vehicles.
(7) Cars sold by dealer.
(8) In certain cities and counties.
*OBD is utilized as part of the state emissions inspection process.
**States scheduled to implement OBD in 2004.
E = Emissions inspection required   S = Safety inspection required

Occupant Protection Chart

State	Child Restraint Required ≤ 4 years and/or 40 lbs.	Booster Seat Required[1]	Back Seat Provision
Alabama	•**	○	○
Alaska	•**	○	○
Arizona	•**	○	○
Arkansas	•**	•	○
California	•**	•	•
Colorado	•**	•	○
Connecticut	•	•	○
Delaware	•**	•	•
D.C.	•**	•	○
Florida	•**	○	○
Georgia	•**	•	•
Hawaii	•**	○	○
Idaho	•**	•	○
Illinois	•**	•	○
Indiana	•**	•	○
Iowa	•**	•	○
Kansas	•	○	○
Kentucky	○[2]**	○	○
Louisiana	•**	•	•
Maine	•**	•	•
Maryland	•**	•	○
Massachusetts	•**	○	○
Michigan	•**	○	○
Minnesota	•**	○	○
Mississippi	•**	○	○
Missouri	•	○	○
Montana	•**	•	○
Nebraska	•	•	○
Nevada	•**	•	○
New Hampshire	•**	•	○
New Jersey	•**	•	•
New Mexico	•**	•	•
New York	•	•	○
North Carolina	•**	•	•
North Dakota	•**	•	○
Ohio	•**	○	○
Oklahoma	•	•	○
Oregon	•	•	○
Pennsylvania	•**	•	○
Rhode Island	•**	•	•
South Carolina	•**	•	•
South Dakota	•**	○	○

Occupant Protection Chart

Child Passenger Safety Laws		Seat Belt Law	Standard Enforcement
Primary Enforcement for Children up to 18	Prohibit ≤ 18 from Riding in a Pick-up Truck Bed		
•	○	•	•
○	○	•	○
○	○	•	○
○	•	•	○
•	•	•	•
○	•	•	○
•	○	•	•
•	○	•	•
•	•	•	•
•	•	•	○
•	•	•	•
•	•	•	•
○	○	•	○
•	○	•	•
•	○	•	•
•	○	•	•
○	○	•	○
○	○	•	○
•	○	•	•
•	•	•	○
•	○	•	•
○	○	•	○
•	•	•	•
○	○	•	○
○	○	•	○
○	•	•	○
○	○	•	○
•	•	•	○
○	•	•	○
•	○	No Law	N/A
•	•	•	•
•	•	•	•
•	•	•	•
•	○	•	•
•	○	•	○
○	○	•	○
•	○	•	•
•	•	•	•
○	•	•	○
•	○	•	○
•	○	•	•
•	○	•	○

Occupant Protection Chart

State	Child Restraint Required ≤ 4 years and/or 40 lbs.	Booster Seat Required[1]	Back Seat Provision
Tennessee	•	•	•
Texas	•**	o	o
Utah	•**	o	o
Vermont	•**	o	o
Virginia	•**	o	o
Washington	•**	•	•
West Virginia	•**	o	o
Wisconsin	•**	o	o
Wyoming	•**	•	•

LEGEND

•=Yes o=No

Child Passenger Safety Laws:
[1]All child restraint laws are primary; however, Colorado's and Pennsylvania's booster seat laws are secondary, and Nebraska's law is secondary for those who may be in safety belts and primary for those in a child restraint device.
[2]In Kentucky, children must be in a child restraint until they are over 40 inches in height.
**All of these laws indicate that a child must be properly secured/restrained, which means that the seat must be used in accordance with manufacturer's instructions.

Occupant Protection Chart

Child Passenger Safety Laws		Seat Belt Law	Standard Enforcement
Primary Enforcement for Children up to 18	Prohibit ≤ 18 from Riding in a Pick-up Truck Bed		
●	○	●	●
●	●	●	●
●	●	●	○
○	○	●	○
○	○	●	○
●	○	●	●
○	○	●	○
○	●	●	○
○	○	●	○

Other Traffic Laws Chart

State	Headlight Use	Studded Tires
Alabama	1,2	Permitted, only for rubber studs. Metal studs are permitted only during bad weather.
Alaska	3,4	Permitted, only for rubber studs, September 15 to May 1 north of 60 degrees N; September 30 to April 15, south of 60 degrees N
Arizona	2	Permitted, October 1 to May 1
Arkansas	1,2	Permitted, November 15 to April 15
California	4	Permitted, November 1 to April 30
Colorado	4	Permitted
Connecticut	4,5	Permitted, November 15 to April 30
Delaware	1,4	Permitted, October 15 to April 15
D.C.	2	Permitted, October 15 to March 15
Florida	4,5	Permitted, only for rubber studs
Georgia	2,5	Not permitted, except for snow and ice driving conditions
Hawaii	8	Not permitted
Idaho	2	Permitted, October 1 to April 30[1]
Illinois	1,4	Not permitted
Indiana	2	Permitted, October 1 to May 1
Iowa	2,5	Permitted, November 1 to April 1
Kansas	4	Permitted, November 1 to April 15
Kentucky	6	Permitted
Louisiana	1	Not permitted
Maine	1,4,5	Permitted, October 2 to April 30
Maryland	1,4	Not permitted, except in Western counties from November 1 to March 31[2]
Massachusetts	1	Permitted, November 2 to April 30 unless otherwise authorized by registrar
Michigan	2	Permitted, only for rubber studs
Minnesota	5	Not permitted, except for nonresidents, who may use them for 30 days.[3] Rural mail carriers may use studded tires under certain conditions between November 1 and April 15.
Mississippi	2	Not permitted
Missouri	2	Permitted, November 2 to March 31
Montana	2,5	Permitted, October 1 to May 31
Nebraska	2	Permitted, November 1 to April 1
Nevada	4	Permitted, October 1 to April 30
New Hampshire	4,5	Permitted
New Jersey	1,2,5	Permitted, November 15 to April 1
New Mexico	2	No regulation

Other Traffic Laws Chart

Hazard Light Usage	Tire Chains[1]	Accident Report Filing Requirements Property Damage in Excess of	Days to File Report	Radar Detectors*
P	●	$250.00	30	●1
NP	●	$501.00	10	●
NP(1)	●	$500.00	See[1]	●
NP(2)	●	$1000.00	30	●
NP(2)	●	$500.00	10	●
NP(3)	●	$0	10	●1
P	●	$1000.00	5	●
NP(2)	●	$1400.00	See[1]	●
P	●	$250.00	5	○
NP	●	$500.00	10	●
P	●	$500.00	See[1]	●
NP	○	$3000.00	1	●
NP	●	$750.00	See[1]	●1
NP	●	$500.00	10	●1
NP(1)	●	$750.00	10	●
NP(2)	●	$1000.00	3	●
NP	●	$500.00	1	●1
P	●	$500.00	10	●
NP	●	$500.00	10	●
NP(2)	●	$1000.00	2	●
NP(1)	●	No Limit	15	●1
NP	●	$1000.00	5	●
P	●	$1000.00	1	●
NP(2)	●	$1000.00	10	●
P	●	$1000.00	10	●
P	●	$500.00	5	●1
NP(2)	●	$500.00	1	●1
P	●	$500.00	10	●1
NP	●	$750.00	10	●
P	●	$1000.00	15	●
NP	●	$500.00	10	●
NP	●	$500.00	5	●

Other Traffic Laws Chart

State	Headlight Use	Studded Tires
New York	1,4,5	Permitted, October 16 to April 30
North Carolina	1,7	Permitted
North Dakota	4,5	Permitted, October 15 to April 15. School buses may use studded tires anytime during the year.
Ohio	4	Permitted, November 1 to April 15
Oklahoma	2,5	Permitted, November 1 to April 1
Oregon	4	Permitted, November 1 to April 1
Pennsylvania	4,5	Permitted, November 1 to April 15
Rhode Island	1,2,5	Permitted, November 15 to April 1
South Carolina	1	Permitted, if do not project more than 1/16 inch when compressed.
South Dakota	8	Permitted, October 1 to April 30. School buses and municipal fire vehicles permitted to use studs anytime.
Tennessee	5,8	Permitted, October 1 through April 15
Texas	4	Permitted, as long as the studs do not damage highway and are rubber.
Utah	4,5	Permitted, October 15 to March 31
Vermont	5,9	Permitted
Virginia	1,2	Permitted, October 15 to April 15
Washington	4	Permited, November 1 to April 1
West Virginia	2,5	Permited, November 1 to April 15
Wisconsin	6	Not permitted, except for authorized emergency vehicles, vehicles used to deliver mail, and automobiles with out-of-state registration.[4] Also permitted for school buses from November 15 to April 1.
Wyoming	4,5	Permitted. Chains required in snow emergencies.

LEGEND

•=Yes o=No

Headlight Use
1=Wipers in use.
2=Visibility less than 500 feet.
3=When speed exceeds 45 mph on designated highways.
4=Visibility less than 1000 feet.
5=Insufficient light/adverse weather.
6=Must use low beams at 100 feet and high beams at 350 feet or greater.
7=Insufficient light at a distance of at least 400 feet.
8=Visibility less than 200 feet.
9=Visibility less than 150 feet.

Studded Tires:
1=Fire departments and firefighting agencies are exempt. Other exemptions may be granted by the Idaho Transportation Board.
2=These counties are Allegany, Carroll, Frederick, Garrett, and Washington.
3=Full-time non-resident students and nonresidents employed within Minnesota are not permitted use of studded tires regardless of vehicle registry.
4=Out-of-state vehicles are permitted only if such vehicle is in the course of passing through the state for a period of not more than 30 days.

Radar Detectors:
1=Prohibited for use by commercial vehicles and in New York, all commercial vehicles weighing more than 10,000 pounds, and all vehicles weighing more than 18,000 pounds.
2=In Oklahoma, it is not illegal by code of law to use a radar detector but there is a DOT regulation which can be used to cite use of a detector as a traffic violation.
*Radar detectors are prohibited in Canada.

Other Traffic Laws Chart

Hazard Light Usage	Tire Chains[1]	Accident Report Filing Requirements		Radar Detectors*
		Property Damage in Excess of	Days to File Report	
P	•	$1000.00	10	•1
P	•	$1000.00	1	•
P	•	$1000.00	10	•1
NP(5)	•	$400.00	30	•1
NP(1,2)	•	See[1]	10	•1,2
P	•	$1500.00	3	•1
P	•	No Limit	5	•
NP	•	$500.00	21	•
NP	•	$1000.00	15	•
P	•	$1000.00	1	•
NP(1)	•	$400.00	20	•1
P	•	$1000.00	10	•1
P	•	$1000.00	10	•1
P	•	$1000.00	3	•
NP(4)	•	$1000.00	1	o
NP(2)	•	$700.00	4	•1
NP(1)	•	$500.00	See[1]	•
NP(2,6)	•	$1000.00	1	•1
P	•	$1000.00	10	•1

Hazard Light Usage:
NP= Not permitted
P= Permitted unless otherwise posted.
(1) Except in emergency situation.
(2) Except to indicate a traffic hazard.
(3) Except if vehicle speed is 25 mph or less.
(4) Restricted to use by vehicles stopped on the traveled or paved portion of the highway, and when traveling 30 mph or less.
(5) Except when hazardous condition is present.
(6) School buses.

Accident Report Filing Requirements:
Property Damage in Excess of:
1=A written accident report must be completed by a law enforcement officer if the accident results in an injury to or the death of a person, or total property damage exceeds $500.00. A written accident report is required by the operator of a motor vehicle whenever an accident results in the bodily injury to or death of a person, or if it is apparent that property damage is in excess of $300.00, if the settlement of the accident has not been reached within six months of the accident.

Days to File Report
1=Must immediately and by the quickest method report accident to the authorities.

Tire Chains:
1=Tire chain usage is for hazardous weather or other related incidents only and they must not damage the highway surface.

State Safety Chart

State	Aggressive Driving	Riding Between Lanes on a Motorcycle	Speed Limits* Rural Interstates	Speed Limits* Urban Interstates	Speed Limits* Other Limited Access Roads	Speed Limits* Other Roads
Alabama	o	o	Cars: 70	Cars: 65	Cars: 65	Cars: 65
Alaska	o	o	Cars: 65	Cars: 55	Cars: 65	Cars: 55
Arizona	•	o	Cars: 75	Cars: 55	Cars: 55	Cars: 55
Arkansas	o	o	Cars: 70; Trucks: 65	Cars: 55	Cars: 60	Cars: 55
California	o	•[1]	Cars: 70; Trucks: 55	Cars: 65	Cars: 70	Cars: 55
Colorado	o	o	Cars: 75	Cars: 65	Cars: 65	Cars: 65
Connecticut	o	o	Cars: 65	Cars: 55	Cars: 65	Cars: 55
Delaware	•	o	Cars: 65	Cars: 55	Cars: 65	Cars: 55
D.C.	o	o	n/a	Cars: 55	n/a	Cars: 25
Florida	•	o	Cars: 70	Cars: 65	Cars: 70	Cars: 65
Georgia	•	o	Cars: 70	Cars: 65	Cars: 65	Cars: 65
Hawaii	o	o	Cars: 60	Cars: 50	Cars: 45	Cars: 45
Idaho	o	o	Cars: 75; Trucks: 65	Cars: 75	Cars: 65	Cars: 65
Illinois	o	o	Cars: 65; Trucks: 55	Cars: 55	Cars: 65	Cars: 55
Indiana	o	o	Cars: 70; Trucks: 60	Cars: 55	Cars: 55	Cars: 55
Iowa	o	o	Cars: 70	Cars: 55	Cars: 65	Cars: 55
Kansas	o	o	Cars: 70	Cars: 70	Cars: 70	Cars: 65
Kentucky	o	o	Cars: 65	Cars: 65	Cars: 65	Cars: 55
Louisiana	o	o	Cars: 70	Cars: 70	Cars: 70	Cars: 65

State Safety Chart

Left Foot Braking	Left Lane Restriction	Turning Right on Red	Turning Left on Red	Helmets Bicycles	Helmets Motorcycles
●	○	●	●	●[1]	●[1]
●	○	●	●	○	●[2,3]
●	○	●	●	○	●[3]
●	●	●	●	○	●[4]
●	●	●	●	●[2]	●[1]
●	●	●	●	○	○
●	●	●	○	●[1]	●[3]
●	○	●	●	●[1]	●[5]
●	○	●	●	●[1]	●[1]
●	○	●	●	●[1]	●[4,6]
●	○	●	●	●[1]	●[1]
●	●	●	●	●[1]	●[3]
●	●	●	●	○	●[3]
●	●	●	●	○	○
●	●	●	●	○	●[3]
●	○	●	●	○	○
●	○	●	●	○	●[3]
●	●	●	●	○	●[4,7]
●	○	●	●	●[3]	●[1]

State Safety Chart

State	Aggressive Driving	Riding Between Lanes on a Motorcycle	Speed Limits* Rural Interstates	Urban Interstates	Other Limited Access Roads	Other Roads
Maine	○	○	Cars: 65	Cars: 65	Cars: 65	Cars: 60
Maryland	●	○	Cars: 65	Cars: 65	Cars: 65	Cars: 55
Massachusetts	○	○	Cars: 65	Cars: 65	Cars: 65	Cars: 55
Michigan	○	○	Cars: 70; Trucks: 55	Cars: 65	Cars: 70	Cars: 55
Minnesota	○	○	Cars: 70	Cars: 65	Cars: 65	Cars: 55
Mississippi	○	○	Cars: 70	Cars: 70	Cars: 70	Cars: 65
Missouri	○	○	Cars: 70	Cars: 60	Cars: 70	Cars: 65
Montana	○	○	Cars: 75; Trucks: 65	Cars: 65	Day: 70 Night: 65	Day: 70 Night: 65
Nebraska	○	○	Cars: 75	Cars: 65	Cars: 65	Cars: 60
Nevada	●	○	Cars: 75	Cars: 65	Cars: 70	Cars: 70
New Hampshire	○	○	Cars: 65	Cars: 65	Cars: 55	Cars: 55
New Jersey	○	○	Cars: 65	Cars: 55	Cars: 65	Cars: 55
New Mexico	○	○	Cars: 75	Cars: 75	Cars: 65	Cars: 55
New York	○	○	Cars: 65	Cars: 65	Cars: 65	Cars: 55
North Carolina	●	○	Cars: 70	Cars: 70	Cars: 70	Cars: 55
North Dakota	○	○	Cars: 75	Cars: 75	Cars: 70	Cars: 65
Ohio	○	○	Cars: 65; Trucks: 55	Cars: 65	Cars: 55	Cars: 55
Oklahoma	○	○	Cars: 75	Cars: 70	Cars: 70	Cars: 70
Oregon	○	○	Cars: 65; Trucks: 55	Cars: 55	Cars: 55	Cars: 55

State Safety Chart

Left Foot Braking	Left Lane Restriction	Turning - Right on Red	Turning - Left on Red	Helmets - Bicycles	Helmets - Motorcycles
●	●	●	●	●[1]	●[7,8,9]
●	○	●	●	●[1]	●[1]
●	●	●	●	●[4*]	●[1]
●	●	●	●	○	●[1]
●	○	●	●	○	●[3,7]
●	●	●	●	○	●[1]
●	●	●	○	○	●[1]
●	○	●	●	○	●[3]
●	●	●	●	○	●[1]
●	●	●	●	○	●[1]
●	●	●	●	●[1]	●[3]
●	●	●	○	●[4]	●[1]
●	○	●	●	○	●[3]
●	○	●[1]	●[1]	●[5*]	●[1]
●	○	●	○	●[1]	●[1]
●	○	●	●	○	●[3,9]
●	○	●	●	○	●[3,7,9]
●	●	●	●	○	●[3]
●	●	●	●	●[1]	●[1]

State Safety Chart

State	Aggressive Driving	Riding Between Lanes on a Motorcycle	Speed Limits* Rural Interstates	Speed Limits* Urban Interstates	Speed Limits* Other Limited Access Roads	Speed Limits* Other Roads
Pennsylvania	o	o	Cars: 65	Cars: 55	Cars: 65	Cars: 55
Rhode Island	•	o	Cars: 65	Cars: 55	Cars: 55	Cars: 55
South Carolina	o	o	Cars: 70	Cars: 70	Cars: 60	Cars: 55
South Dakota	o	o	Cars: 75	Cars: 75	Cars: 65	Cars: 65
Tennessee	o	o	Cars: 70	Cars: 70	Cars: 70	Cars: 65
Texas	o	o	Day: 75 Night: 65 Trucks: 65	Day: 70 Night: 65	Day: 75 Night: 65 Trucks: 65	Day: 60 Night: 55
Utah	•	o	Cars: 75	Cars: 65	Cars: 75	Cars: 65
Vermont	o	o	Cars: 65	Cars: 55	Cars: 50	Cars: 50
Virginia	•	o	Cars: 65	Cars: 65	Cars: 65	Cars: 55
Washington	o	o	Cars: 70; Trucks: 60	Cars: 60	Cars: 60	Cars: 60
West Virginia	o	o	Cars: 70	Cars: 55	Cars: 65	Cars: 55
Wisconsin	o	o	Cars: 65	Cars: 65	Cars: 65	Cars: 55
Wyoming	o	o	Cars: 75	Cars: 60	Cars: 65	Cars: 65

LEGEND

•=Yes o=No

Riding Between Lanes on a Motorcycle:
1=It is legal to ride between lanes on a motorcycle, so long as it is being done in a safe manner.

Interstate Speed Limits:
*=Limited access highways are multiple-lane roads with restricted access using exit and entrance ramps rather than intersections. Interstate highways are part of the national system of limited access highways that connect the nation's principal metropolitan areas and industrial centers. The distinction between urban and rural areas is based on population density figures from the U.S. Census and adjusted by state and local governments to reflect planning and other issues. Urban sections are within a census area with an urban population of 5,000 to 49,999 or within a designated urbanized area with a population of 50,000 or greater. Unless otherwise listed, speeds are for both cars and commercial vehicles.

Left Lane Restriction:
Requires that vehicles may only use the left-hand lane to pass slower vehicles in the right-hand lane.

Turning:
1=Right and left turn on red not permitted in New York City.

Helmets:
Bicycles:
1=Riders under 16.

State Safety Chart

Left Foot Braking	Left Lane Restriction	Turning Right on Red	Turning Left on Red	Helmets Bicycles	Helmets Motorcycles
●	●	●	●	●3	●4,10
●	●	●	○	●1	●4,7,11
●	●	●	●	○	●4
●	○	●	●	○	●3
●	●	●	●	●1	●1
●	●	●	●	○	●4,12
●	●	●	○	○	●3
●	○	●	○	○	●1
●	●	●	●	○	●1
●	●	●	●	○	●1
●	●	●	●	●6	●1
●	○	●	●	○	●3,7
●	●	●	●	○	●5

2=Riders under 18.
3=Riders under 12.
4=Riders under 17.
5=Riders under 14.
6=Riders under 15.
*=Prohibits transportation of children under 1 on a bicycle.

Motorcycles:
1=All riders.
2=Passengers of all ages and drivers with learner's or instructional permits.
3=Under 18.
4=Under 21.
5=Under 19.
6=Permits riders 21 and older to ride without a helmet if they can provide proof of medical insurance policy.
7=Covers all drivers in the first year of licensure, or drivers with learner's or instructional permits.
8=Drivers and passengers under 15.
9=Passengers traveling with drivers who are covered by the law.
10=Drivers over 21 years of age are exempt if the motorcyclist completed a motorcycle safety course or has had a motorcycle license for more than 2 years. Passengers 21 years of age or older are also exempt.
11=All passengers.
12=Permits riders 21 and older to ride without a helmet if they can provide proof of medical insurance policy or completion of a motorcycle training and safety course.

Title & Registration Fees Chart

State	Automobile Title Fee	Automobile Registration Fee	Motorcycle Title Fee	Motorcycle Registration Fee
Alabama	$18.00	$23.00 + issuance fee (may differ by county)	$18.00	$23.00 + issuance fee
Alaska	$5.00	$100.00 - once every 2 years	$5.00 - once every 2 years	$38.00 - once every 2 years
Arizona	$4.00	$8.00; $8.25 in Metro Phoenix and Tucson	$4.00	$9.00
Arkansas	$5.00	$17.00 for less than 3,000 lbs. $25.00 between 3,001 and 4,500 lbs.; $30.00 for greater than 4,500 lbs.	$5.00	$3.25 for 0-250cc; $6.50 for 251cc+
California	n/a	$31.00	n/a	$31.00[1]
Colorado	$7.20	$10.00 for less than 2,000 + $0.20 extra per 100 lbs. up to 4,500; $17.50 + $0.60 each extra 100 lbs greater than 4,500 lbs.	$6.50	$2.25
Connecticut	$25.00	$70.00 every 2 years + $4.00 renewal fee	$25.00	$36.00 every 2 yrs. + $4.00 renewal fee
Delaware	If no lien: $15.00 With lien: $25.00	6 months: $11.00 1-5 yrs: $20.00/yr.	If no lien: $15.00 With lien: $25.00	$10.00/yr.
D.C.	$26.00	Below 3,500 lbs: $72.00; 3,500 or above: $115.00	$26.00	$26.00
Florida	New, never previously titled: $31.25; Previously titled in Florida: $29.25; Previously titled in another state: $33.25	Initial registration: $100.00; Vehicle under 2,500 lbs: $27.60; Vehicle between 2,500-3,499: $35.60; Vehicle 3,500 or more: $45.60	n/a	$24.10
Georgia	$18.00	$20.00	$18.00	$20.00
Hawaii	n/a	$25.00[2]	n/a	$20.00[2]

Title & Registration Fees Chart

Plate Fee	Duplicates Registration Fee	License Fee	Title Fee	Special Plates
$2.00	$3.00	$15.00	n/a	$50.00
$5.00	$2.00	$15.00	$5.00	$50.00-$150.00
$5.00	$4.00	$4.00	$4.00	$25.00
n/a	$4.00	$5.00	$4.00	$5.00-$25.00
$7.00	$7.00	$12.00	n/a	$10.00-$50.00 depending on type
$5.00	$2.20	$5.00 for the 1st; $10.00 for 2 or more	$7.50	varies
$11.00	$5.00	$30.00	$25.00	$50.00-$70.00 one time fee
$6.00 plain plate $10.00 special plate	$2.00 for card $1.00 for sticker	$5.00	$15.00	Title: $35.00-$50.00
$5.00	$5.00	$10.00	$20.00	$25.00
$10.00	$2.50	$29.25	$10.00	$15.00-$25.00
$8.00	$1.00	$5.00	$8.00	$25.00
See[3]	See[4]	See[5]	n/a	$25.00

657

Title & Registration Fees Chart

State	Automobile Title Fee	Automobile Registration Fee	Motorcycle Title Fee	Motorcycle Registration Fee
Idaho	$8.00	$35.00 to $60.00[6]	$8.00	$15.25 (except Ada County, where the fee is $19.25)
Illinois	$65.00	$78.00	$65.00	$38.00 (year) $19.00 (half-year)
Indiana	$15.00	$20.75	$15.00	n/a
Iowa	$15.00	See[7]	$15.00	5 years old or newer: $20.00; more than 5 years old: $10.00
Kansas	$10.00	$30.00 to $40.00	$10.00	$16.00
Kentucky	$6.00	$11.50	$6.00	$9.00
Louisiana	$18.50	See[8]	$18.50	$12.00
Maine	$23.00	$25.00	$23.00	$21.00
Maryland	$23.00	$128.00 for vehicles 3,700 lbs. or less; $180.00 for vehicles over 3,700 lbs.[9] ($51.00 for historic motor vehicle)	$23.00	$97.00[9]
Massachusetts	$50.00 + 5% sales tax	$30.00 (biennial)	$50.00	$20.00; $70.00-vanity
Michigan	$15.00	See[10]	$10.50	$23.00
Minnesota	$4.00	See[11]	$2.00	$10.00
Mississippi	$4.00	$13.00	$2.50	$11.00

Title & Registration Fees Chart

Plate Fee	Duplicates Registration Fee	License Fee	Title Fee	Special Plates
$3.00	$4.00 (additional title fee)	$11.50	$25.00-$35.00 initial fee; $15.00-$25.00 renewal	$25.00 initial fee; $15.00 renewal
$6.00 (one) $9.00 (two)	$3.00 (cards); $5.00 (stickers)	$10.00	$65.00	$78.00-$91.00 (auto); $50.00 (motorcycle)
$9.00	$6.00	$10.00	n/a	Fees vary
$5.00	$3.00	$3.00	$16.00	$25.00
$2.00	$1.00	$8.00	$16.00	n/a
$6.00	$3.00	$12.00	$4.00	$25.00
$4.00	$4.00	$5.00*	$18.50	$25.00-$250.00
$5.00	Card: $2.00 Stickers: $0.50 each	$5.00	$23.00	$15.00
$20.00	$5.00	$20.00	$20.00	$27.00 to $184.00 plus an $11.00 surcharge for emergency medical services
$10.00 per plate	$15.00	$15.00	$25.00	$8.00-$35.00
$5.00	no fee	$9.00	n/a	$30.00-$35.00
n/a	$1.00	$8.00	$4.00	$14.00-$40.00
$10.00	$1.00	$8.00 for 2nd and subsequent request	$4.00 for motor vehicles	$30.00 + regular cost of tags

* = $8.00 handling fee added to all transactions. A Parish fee not to exceed $3.00 is asked in certain Parishes.

Title & Registration Fees Chart

State	Automobile Title Fee	Automobile Registration Fee	Motorcycle Title Fee	Motorcycle Registration Fee
Missouri	$8.50	See[12]	$8.50	$8.50
Montana	One ton or less =$7.00; More than 1 ton: $5.00	Less than 2,850 lbs.= $13.75: 2,850 lbs. or more= $18.75[13]	$5.00	$9.75
Nebraska	$10.00	$20.00	$10.00	$20.00
Nevada	$20.00	$33.00 each for the first four cars; $16.50 for 5-6 cars; $12.00 for 7-8 cars; and $8.00 for 9 or more cars	$20.00	$33.00 + $6.00 for motorcycle safety course
New Hampshire	$25.00	$25.20 to $49.20	$25.00	$13.00
New Jersey	$20.00 without lien	$32.50 to $81.00	$20.00 without lien	$28.50
New Mexico	$3.50	$27.00 to $63.00 (1 yr) and $52.00 to $124.00 (2 yr)	$3.50	$15.00
New York	$5.00 plus $5.00 security interest fee	See[14]	$5.00	$14.00
North Carolina	$35.00	$20.00 + $1.00 if renewing by mail	$35.00	$12.00 for 1 passenger capacity and $19.00 for more than 1 person or for property
North Dakota	$5.00	$49.00 to $247.00[15]	$5.00	$28.00

Title & Registration Fees Chart

Plate Fee	Duplicates Registration Fee	License Fee	Title Fee	Special Plates
$8.50	$8.50; $5.00 more to have it processed fast	Intermediate license: $5.00; Driver's License: $7.50; Commercial driver's license: $20.00; Motorcycle: $7.50	$8.50	$15.00
$2.00	$2.00	$5.00	n/a	$25.00
$9.10	$6.00	$11.25	$14.00	$30.00-$70.00
$10.00	$5.00	$14.00 ($19.00 for commercial)	$20.00	$25.00-$35.00
$4.00 per plate $6.00 to $11.00	$10.00 $5.00	$10.00 $11.00	$25.00 $25.00	$25.00-$30.00 $50.00 for new; $10.00 for renewal; $100.00 personalized specialty
$15.00	$3.50	$10.00	n/a	$15.00-$40.00
$8.50	$3.00	$8.00	$10.00	n/a
$10.00	$10.00	$10.00	$10.00	$20.00-$30.00
$5.00	Not to exceed $5.00	$8.00 if lost, mutilated or destroyed; $3.00 for a name or address or erroneous information change	No fee if the DOT is satisfied the original was not received	$25.00-$100.00

661

Title & Registration Fees Chart

State	Automobile Title Fee	Automobile Registration Fee	Motorcycle Title Fee	Motorcycle Registration Fee
Ohio	$5.00 + $1.00 to notarize signatures	$34.50-$54.50	$5.00 + $1.00 to notarize signatures	$21.00 base fee, $4.00 motorcycle fee and county fees
Oklahoma	$11.00	$85.00 for the 1st - 4th years; $75.00 for the 5th - 8th years; $55.00 for the 9th - 12th years; $35.00 for the 13th - 16th years; $15.00 for 17+ years. All vehicles are also subject to an additional $5.00 in other fees and $2.00 to be paid to the Oklahoma Tax Commission for every vehicle registered	$11.00	n/a
Oregon	$55.00	$54.00 - 2 year[16] $105.00 - 4 year[16]	$55.00	$30.00 - 2 years[16] $60.00 - 4 years[16]
Pennsylvania	$22.50	$36.00	$22.50	$18.00
Rhode Island	$25.00	$30.00	$25.00	$13.00
South Carolina	$10.00	For persons 65 years or older or handicapped, the fee is $20.00; if under age 65, then $24.00	$10.00	$10.00
South Dakota	$5.00	For vehicles less than 2,000 lbs. and less than 5 yrs. old: $30.00; less than 2,000 lbs. and 5 yrs. or older: $21.00; 2,001-4,000 and less than 5 yrs. old: $42.00; 2,001-4,000 and 5 yrs. or older: $29.40; 4,001-6,000 and less than 5 yrs old: $55.00; 4,001-6,000 and 5 yrs. or older: $38.50; 6,001-10,000 and less than 5 yrs. old: $65.00; 6,001-10,000 and 5 yrs. or older: $45.50	$5.00	Less than 350cc and 0-4 years old: $9.50; less than 350cc and 5 years or older: $6.65; 350cc or more and 0-4 years old: $12.00; 350cc or more and 5 years or older: $8.40 (plus a $7.00 motorcycle education fee)

Title & Registration Fees Chart

Plate Fee	Duplicates Registration Fee	License Fee	Title Fee	Special Plates
Regular: $6.00; Special: $8.40	$4.50	$6.75	$5.00	$10.00-$35.00 plus registration fee
$9.00	n/a	$5.00	$11.00	Ranges from $5.00 - $25.00, plus regular registration fees
$13.00 for 1 $15.00 for 2	$5.00	$21.00	$55.00	See state file
$7.50	$1.50 at original registration, transfer, or renewal; replacement registration card: $4.50	$9.00	$22.50	n/a
$5.00	$1.00		$25.00	$30.00 or $50.00
n/a	$1.00	$3.00	$10.00	$30.00 + registration fee (for personalized); other plate fees vary by speciality
$10.00	$2.00	$6.00	$10.00 (Duplicate)	$10.00 for historical plates

663

Title & Registration Fees Chart

State	Automobile Title Fee	Automobile Registration Fee	Motorcycle Title Fee	Motorcycle Registration Fee
Tennessee	$8.00	$25.00 ($24.00 in Shelby County)	$8.00 - $25.00	$11.75
Texas	$13.00	For vehicles 6,000 lbs. or less and more than 6 yrs. old: $40.50; For vehicles 6,000 lbs. or less and between 4-6 yrs. old: $50.50; For vehicles 6,000 lbs. or less and younger than 4 yrs. old: $58.50; For vehicles greater than 6,000 lbs.:$25.00 + $0.60 for each 100 lbs.	$13.00	$30.00
Utah	$6.00	For vehicles under 12,000 lbs.: $21.00; Between 12,000-14,000 lbs.: $49.50; $18.50 for each 2,000 lbs over 14,000 lbs.	$6.00	$22.50
Vermont	$15.00	$52.00 (1 yr) and $92.00 (2 yr.)	$15.00	$30.50 - $53.50
Virginia	$10.00	$30.50 to $35.50	$10.00	$28.50
Washington	$5.00 ($15.00 additional fee for vehicles previously titled in another state or country)	$30.00	$5.25 + $6.50 Emergency Medical Services Fee	$30.00

Title & Registration Fees Chart

Plate Fee	Duplicates Registration Fee	License Fee	Title Fee	Special Plates
$10.00	n/a	$8.00 for initial duplicate, $12.00 for every subsequent one thereafter	n/a	$25.00
n/a	$2.00	$10.00	$2.00	$40.00
$5.00	$4.00	$13.00	$6.00	Up to $50.00
$7.00 per plate	$7.00	$10.00	$10.00	$15.00 - $30.00
n/a	$2.00	$10.00	$10.00	$10.00 - $25.00 (one time fee)
$3.00 per plate ($2.00 for motorcycle)	$1.25	$15.00	$5.00	$30.00 - $40.00 (in addition to regular plate fee); renewal of plates is $10.00

Title & Registration Fees Chart

	Automobile		Motorcycle	
State	Title Fee	Registration Fee	Title Fee	Registration Fee
West Virginia	$10.00	For vehicles weighing under 8,000 lbs.: $30.00	$10.00	$16.00
Wisconsin	$35.00	$55.00	$25.00	$23.00 (biennial fee)
Wyoming	$9.00	$15.00	$6.00	$12.00

[1]= Includes $1 supplement payable on original registration only.
[2]= State Registration fees are $25.00 for all motor vehicles plus an applicable weight tax. 0.75¢ per pound for every vehicle up to 4,000 pounds net weight; 1¢ per pound for every vehicle between 4,000 and 7,000 pounds; 1.25¢ per pound for every vehicle between 7,000 and 10,000 pounds; and $150 flat rate for every vehicle over 10,000 pounds. The various counties have varied rate fees as well: Honolulu City and County-$10.00 + 1.25¢ per pound; Maui County-$6.00 + 0.75¢ per pound; Hawaii County-$4.00 + 0.50¢ per pound; Kauai County-1.25¢ per pound.
[3]= For Honolulu and Kauai Counties: $5.00; Hawaii and Maui Counties: $3.50.
[4]= For Honolulu City and County: no fee; Maui County: $10.00; Hawaii County: $2.00; Kauai County: $3.00.
[5]= For Kauai County: $6.00; all other counties: $5.00.
[6]= Depends on vehicle age and county of residence.
[7]= Vehicle registration fee is based on the number of model years and then subsequently the formula is based on a percentage of the vehicle's value as decided by the Dept of Motor Vehicles plus $.40 for each 100 lbs or fraction thereof the vehicle's weight (i.e., motor vehicle not more than 5 model years old has a fee of 1% of the value plus $.40 for each 100 lbs or fraction thereof).
[8]= Based on the selling price of the vehicle. The current rate is .1% of the value of the vehicle per year, with a minimum base of $10,000. The license plates are sold in 2-year increments, therefore the minimum price is $20.00.
[9]= Registration fee is a 2-year fee plus $13.50 annual emergency medical services surcharge.
[10]= If vehicle model is earlier than 1983, then fee depends on weight. If vehicle model is 1983 or later, the fee depends on the list price of the vehicle. Range is from $33.00-$148.00 for vehicles priced from $0-$30,000 for the first registration. Registration fee declines by 10% each year until the 5th renewal.

Title & Registration Fees Chart

	Duplicates			Special
Plate Fee	Registration Fee	License Fee	Title Fee	Plates
$5.50	$5.00	$5.00	n/a	$15.00 - $55.00
$2.00 for each plate $5.00 for personalized $6.00 for special	$2.00	$4.00	$8.00	$15.00 for initial year and $15.00 for renewals
$8.00	$4.00	$15.00	$9.00	$30.00

[11] = Registration tax system for passenger class vehicles. This means that the tax is determined in part upon the base value of the vehicle as provided by the manufacturer when the vehicle was new, and the age of the vehicle. The first registration renewal of a vehicle will cost no more than $189.00. The second and subsequent renewals will have a cap of $99.00.

[12] = Registration fee based on horsepower: Between 9 and less than 12: $18.00; 12 and less than 24: $21.00; 24 and less than 36: $24.00; 36 and less than 48: $33.00; 48 and less than 60: $39.00; 60 and less than 72: $45.00; 72 and higher: $51.00.

[13] = Permanent registration fee for all light vehicles 11 years or older: $50.00. In addition, there is an additional fee for all vehicles except permanently registered vehicles, travel trailers, and recreational vehicles: 25¢. Also, for collector's vehicles more than 30 years old: $5.00 if vehicle is 2,850 lbs. or less; $10.00 if vehicle is more than 2,850 lbs.

[14] = Varies based on weight.

[15] = Annual fee varies based on weight and 1st year of registration.

[16] = Plate fee included.

Towing Chart

State	Towing Requirements
Alabama	Connection between vehicles must not exceed 15 feet in length; bill of sale required.[1]
Alaska	Vehicle towed upon a street or highway must be coupled by means of a safety chain, chains, cable, or other equivalent device, in addition to the regular hitch or coupling; the additional connecting safety devices must be connected to prevent the device from dropping to the ground. Drawbar permitted if car being towed is not occupied. Brake hookup required if over 3,000 lbs.[2]
Arizona	Towed vehicle must be currently registered. Devices used for towing shall not exceed 15 feet from 1 vehicle to the other. If a chain, rope, or cable is being used, a white flag at least 12 inches square must be displayed on the device.[2,3]
Arkansas	Special permit required if towed vehicle not registered. Proof of ownership is required. Drawbar required (maximum length 15 feet). Connection must be sufficiently strong to pull all weight towed; in addition, a safety chain and 12 inch flag required on all connections consisting only of chains, ropes, or cables.[2,3]
California	No passenger vehicle or any other vehicle under 4,000 lbs. unladen may tow more than 1 vehicle in combination unless an auxiliary or tow dolly may be used with towed vehicle; no vehicle under 4,000 lbs. unladen may tow a vehicle more than 6,000 lbs.; the raised end of the motor vehicle being towed by another vehicle using tow dolly must be secured by 2 separate chains, cables, or equivalent devices; drawbar connection between 1 vehicle towing another may not exceed 15 feet. Max speed for any vehicle towing another is 55 mph. Advisable to carry bill of sale. Lights of towed vehicle must be operational. Brake lights and signal lamps must be operational. Brakes must be sufficient to stop within a specified distance, according to vehicle weight, at 20 mph.
Colorado	Proof of ownership required. White cloth must be hung from towing device, if towing device is a chain, rope or cable. Maximum length of device is 15 feet. Lights must be mounted and displayed on the rear of the towed vehicle. Lights must be actuated by the driver of the towing vehicle.[2,3]
Connecticut	Rigid towbar required when traveling on a highway (maximum length 20 feet). Every camp trailer is required to be attached by a hitch, and shall be occupied to the frame of the towing vehicle by means of a safety chain, chains, cables, or equivalent device which shall be of sufficient strength to control the trailer in the event of failure of the regular hitch or coupling.[2,3]

Towing Chart

State	Towing Requirements
Delaware	Permit required if towed vehicle not registered. No vehicle shall be driven upon any highway pulling more than 1 other vehicle; drawbar or other connection between any vehicle and the vehicle it is towing shall not exceed 15 feet in length; if there is a connection between 2 vehicles, 1 towing the other, consists of a chain, rope or cable, there shall be a red flag or other cloth 12 inches square attached to the connection. If towed vehicle over 4,000 lbs., brakes must be connected to those of towing vehicle.[2,3]
D.C.	When towing is done by chain, rope or cable, driver is required in each vehicle and there should be a white flag or cloth connected to the chain, rope, or cable.[2]
Florida	When 1 vehicle is towing another, the drawbar or other connection shall be of sufficient strength to pull all weight towed; drawbar connection shall not exceed 15 feet from 1 vehicle to the other. When 1 vehicle is towing another and connection consists of chain, rope, or cable, there shall be displayed a white flag or cloth not less than 12 inches square. If dolly is used, tow bar is not required. If weight of towed vehicle exceeds 3,000 lbs., a brake hookup is required as well as breakaway system.[2]
Georgia	Towbar is required.[2]
Hawaii	Registration not required for towed vehicle if car is being towed between storage places. Brake hookup required. A 12-inch square white flag (required when using chain, cable, strap, or rope as a towing connection) must be hung from towing device.[2,3]
Idaho	Must stop at any weigh station. Bill of sale or other proof of ownership required, if not registered. Drawbar/towbar required.[2]
Illinois	Drawbar or other connection shall be of sufficient strength to pull all the weight towed and shall not exceed 15 feet in length. Outside a business, residential or suburban district, or highway, no vehicle shall be towed on a roadway except by a drawbar and each such vehicle so towed shall, in addition, be coupled with 2 safety chains or cables to the towing vehicle. Chains or cables shall be of sufficient size and strength to prevent towed vehicle parting from towing vehicle in case drawbar should break or become disengaged. Special permit required if combination exceeds size limit. Brake hookup required if vehicle towed is over 3,000 lbs.
Indiana	Maximum length of 2 or more vehicles together, including any cargo, is 60 feet. Maximum load size in length is 3 feet beyond front and 4 feet beyond rear. Drawbar/towbar required (maximum length 15 feet).[2,3]

Towing Chart

State	Towing Requirements
Iowa	Drawbar or other connection must not exceed 15 feet. Drawbar must be of sufficient strength to pull all weight towed and must be fastened to the frame of the towing vehicle in such manner as to prevent side sway. In addition to the principal connection, there must be a safety chain which must be fastened as to be capable of holding towed vehicle should the principal connection fail for any reason. Registration required. Towing for hire outside incorporated city or town prohibited, except for disabled vehicles or while using a dealer or transporter plate.[2,3]
Kansas	Drawbar, towbar, or other connection must be of sufficient strength to pull, stop, and hold all weight towed. When towing connection consists of rope, chain, or cable, a white flag or cloth 12 inches square shall be displayed on the towing connection. Also, not more than 2 vehicles shall be connected by a towbar.[2]
Kentucky	No vehicle may haul with a towline more than 1 other vehicle and the towline may not exceed 15 feet in length and must have a white cloth fastened at or near the center of the towline. No vehicle may haul more than 2 vehicles connected in such a manner as to keep them evenly spaced, at any 1 time.[2,3]
Louisiana	Connection must be of sufficient strength to pull all weight towed. Connection must not exceed 15 feet. When connection between a vehicle and a towed vehicle is a chain, rope, or cable, a red flag or cloth at least 1-foot square must be displayed on the connection and a red light visible for a distance of at least 500 feet must be visible on the connection between sunrise and sunset. Bill of sale required. Brake hookup and light connection must be connected to primary towing vehicle lights. Speed limit is 45 mph.[2,3]
Maine	Special permit required if car not registered. Available from state police. Towbar and safety chains required; tow dolly acceptable. Taillights, brake, and turn signals of towed vehicle must be visible. Additional lights required: red light in center rear or left rear of car being towed, visible from 100 feet; white light illuminating rear license plate visible from 50 feet, not to exceed combined length of 65 feet. Vehicle being towed must be by tow truck or use of tow bar and safety chain.
Maryland	Drawbar required; tow dolly acceptable. Towbar or connection used shall be strong enough to pull the weight towed and shall not exceed 15 feet in length. When 1 vehicle is towing another and the connection is a chain, rope, or cable, a white, red, or orange-fluorescent flag or cloth at 18 inches square shall be displayed on the connection.
Massachusetts	Every trailer, except a semitrailer, shall, in addition to a regular hitch, be fastened by safety chains to prevent it from breaking away from the towing vehicle.[2,3]

Towing Chart

State	Towing Requirements
Michigan	Registration of towed vehicle not required if car inoperable. Bill of sale required. Drawbar or other connection between 2 vehicles, 1 of which is towing or pulling the other on a highway, shall not exceed 15 feet in length. If connection consists of a chain, rope, or cable, there shall be displayed upon the connection a red flag or other signal or cloth 12 inches square. A passenger vehicle or pickup truck shall not be driven upon a highway pulling or having attached to the passenger vehicle or pickup truck more than 1 vehicle or trailer. The hitch cannot exceed 15 feet in length from 1 vehicle to the other and may not allow either vehicle to deviate more than 3 inches from the other. If the connection consists of a chain, rope, or cable, there shall be displayed upon the connection a red flag or other signal or cloth not less than 12 inches square.[2,3]
Minnesota	Drawbar or other connection between the 2 vehicles must not be more than 15 feet. When connection is a chain, rope or cable, the connection must display a white, red, yellow or orange flag that is at least 12 square inches. Every trailer or semitrailer must be hitched to the towing device approved by the Department. Every trailer and semitrailer must be equipped with safety chains or cables permanently attached to the trailer except in cases where the coupling device is a regulation 5th wheel and kingpin assembly approved by the Department. In towing, the chains or cables must be attached to the vehicles near the points of bumper attachments to the chassis of each vehicle, and must be of sufficient strength to control the trailer in the event of failure of the towing device. The length of chain or cable must be no more than necessary to permit free turning of the vehicles. Brake hookup required except where brakes on towing vehicle are adequate to stop both vehicles within distance required by law.[4,5]
Mississippi	Drawbar or other connection shall be of sufficient strength to pull all weight towed and shall not exceed 15 feet, except for a connection between 2 vehicles carrying poles, pipes, machinery, or other objects of a structural nature which cannot be dismembered. When connection consists of a rope, chain, or cable, there shall be displayed upon such connection a 12-inch-square white flag or cloth. Not more than 3 vehicles in combination shall be towed by saddle-mounts, provided the overall length of the towing and towed vehicles shall not exceed 75 feet in length. Not more than 1 vehicle shall be towed by a towbar. Every trailer which shall be towed on public highways at a speed greater than 20 mph shall be coupled to the towing vehicle by means of a safety chain, chains, cables, or equivalent devices in addition to the regular trailer hitch or coupling. The safety chains, cables, or equivalent device shall be so connected to the towed and towing vehicles and to the drawbar to prevent the drawbar from dropping to the ground if the drawbar fails, and shall be of sufficient strength to control the trailer in the event of failure of the regular trailer hitch or coupling.[2]

Towing Chart

State	Towing Requirements
Missouri	Connecting device shall not exceed 15 feet. Every towed vehicle shall be coupled to the towed vehicle by a safety chain, cable, or equivalent device in addition to the primary coupling device, except that such secondary coupling device shall not be necessary if the connecting device is connected to the towing vehicle by a center-locking ball located over or nearly over the rear axle and not supported by the rear bumper of the towing vehicle. Also, such secondary safety connecting devices shall be strong enough to control the towed vehicle in the event of failure of the primary coupling device. Also, during the time that lights are required, both vehicles shall display the required lights. Safety chains or an equivalent device are required in addition to the primary coupling device, except for 5th-wheel or gooseneck-type vehicles. Maximum length is 65 feet on interstate highways; 55 feet on others.[2]
Montana	Trailer or pole trailer with a GVW of 3,000 lbs. must be equipped with a steel safety chain or cable with a minimum diameter of 1/4 of an inch must be securely fastened to the towing unit. The safety chain or cable may not be connected to the ball but must be connected to the hitch or other frame member of the towing vehicle to prevent the drawbar from dropping to the ground if the ball, socket, or coupler fails.[2,3]
Nebraska	Drawbar or other connection shall not exceed 15 feet in length. The connecting device between any 2 vehicles, 1 towing the other, shall have displayed at the halfway point between the towing vehicle and the towed vehicle a red flag or other signal or cloth not less than 12 inches square. Whenever the load on any vehicle extends more than 4 feet beyond the rear of the bed or body, there shall be displayed at the end of such a load a red flag not less than 12 inches square. Whenever the load on any vehicle extends more than 4 feet beyond the rear of the bed or body and is being operated between sunset and sunrise, there shall be displayed a red light plainly visible under normal weather conditions at least 200 feet from the rear of the vehicle. 20,000 lbs. per axle weight limit. The total length may not exceed 130 feet if the wrecker or tow truck is towing a combination of disabled vehicles.[2]
Nevada	Drawbar advised, but not required. Light connections must be connected to towing vehicle. Maximum length 70 feet. Braking system required when gross weight exceeds 3,000 lbs.; 1,500 lbs. if 1975 or newer model.[6]

Towing Chart

State	Towing Requirements
New Hampshire	Every trailer or semitrailer shall have, in addition to the towbar or coupling device, a safety chain or cable to prevent breakaway from the towing vehicle. Each chain or cable shall have an ultimate strength at least equal to the gross weight of the trailer and the load being towed. Chains or cables shall be connected to the towed and towing vehicle to prevent the towbar from dropping to the ground in the event the towbar fails. Except for duly registered wrecking vehicles and transporters or motor vehicles towing with a chain or cable for no more than 1 mile another vehicle which is disabled and unable to proceed under its own power, no motor vehicle shall be used to tow another vehicle on any road unless the 2 vehicles are connected by a towbar of sufficient strength to control the movements of the vehicle being towed without manual steering of the towed vehicle. No vehicle may tow on any road more than 1 vehicle, trailer or semitrailer, except 1 used exclusively for agricultural purposes or authorized by the DMV. Registration not required for towed vehicle. When vehicle is towed between 1/2 hour after sundown and 1/2 hour before sunrise, it must display at least 1 lighted tail lamp or auxiliary rear light to the extreme left of the rear axle.[2,3]
New Jersey	Registration of towed vehicles required if required by home state. Bill of sale required. Brake hookup required. Trailers shall be connected to the towing vehicle by at least 1 chain or cable, in addition to the hitch bar, of sufficient strength to hold the trailer on the hill if the hitching bar becomes disconnected, or be provided with an adequate device to prevent its rolling backward.[2]
New Mexico	When connection consists of a chain, rope, or cable, a white flag or cloth not less than 12 inches square must be displayed. When a combination of vehicles are engaged in transporting poles, pipe, machinery, or other objects of structural nature which cannot readily be dismembered, the load shall be distributed so as to equalize the weights on the axle of each vehicle insofar as possible. Special permit required, available at ports of entry for $5. Bill of sale, title or ownership document required. Brake hookups required.[7]
New York	State Highways: Registration of towed auto not required. Safety chains required if towbar connection was purchased after November 1, 1972. No vehicle shall be towed by a rope or other non-rigid connection which is longer than 16 feet. A motor vehicle being towed by a rope or other non-rigid connection must have a licensed driver in such motor vehicle who shall steer it when it is being towed. Parkways: Automobile towing is prohibited. N.Y.S. Thruway: Registration and plates required for towed automobile, which must be in operable condition. Towing with rope or non-rigid connection prohibited. It is unlawful to operate any open truck or trailer transporting loose materials, unless the truck or trailer has a cover, tarpaulin, or other device that covers the opening on the truck or trailer to prevent the falling of any material; however, if the load is arranged so that no loose material can fall from or blow out of the truck or trailer, the covering is not necessary.

Towing Chart

State	Towing Requirements
North Carolina	Towbar or other rigid connection required.[2,3]
North Dakota	None.[2,8]
Ohio	Drawbar or other connection may not exceed 15 feet. When the connection consists only of a chain, rope, or cable, there shall be displayed upon such connection a white flag or cloth not less than 12 inches square. In addition to a drawbar or other connection, each trailer and each semitrailer which is not connected to a commercial tractor by means of a 5th wheel shall be coupled with stay chains or cables to the vehicle by which it is being drawn. Every trailer or semitrailer shall be equipped with a coupling device, which shall be so designed and constructed that the trailer will follow substantially in the path of the vehicle drawing it, without whipping or swerving from side to side. Brake lights and turn signals must be connected between vehicles.[2,3]
Oklahoma	Every trailer, semitrailer, or manufactured home shall be equipped with a coupling device designed and constructed so that the trailer will follow in substantially the same path as the vehicle towing it without whipping or swerving from side to side. Special permit not required unless towed car is for resale. Bill of sale required. Two tail lights, 2 reflectors, brake lights if the vehicle obscures the brake lights of the towing vehicle, turn signals if the length of the 2 vehicles is more than 14 feet from the center of the steering wheel of the towing vehicle to the rear of the towed vehicle, and fenders or mud flaps on the rear wheels of the towed vehicle are required.[2,3]
Oregon	Unlawful to operate more than 2 vehicles in combination. If any vehicle is towing another and the connection between the 2 is a rope, chain, cable, or any flexible material, a red flag or cloth not less than 12 inches square must be displayed upon the connection. Any vehicle being towed must be equipped with safety chains or cables. It is unlawful for a person to be a passenger in any towed vehicle; this provision does not apply to a 5th-wheel trailer if the trailer is equipped with safety glazing materials on the windows and doors, an auditory or visual signaling device that may be used to contact the driver, and at least 1 unobstructed exit capable of being opened from both the interior and exterior. Special certificate required if vehicle is being towed for compensation. A trip permit is also required if the towed vehicle is not currently registered and is being towed by other than a licensed tower.[2,9]

Towing Chart

State	Towing Requirements
Pennsylvania	Connection must be of sufficient strength to pull all of the weight towed and the distance between the 2 vehicles must be not more than 15 feet. If the distance between the vehicles is more than 5 feet, a red cloth or flag at least 12 inches square must be displayed on the connection. This flag must be centered between the 2 vehicles and light must shine on the flag. Every trailer must be attached to the towing vehicle so that the path of the trailer's wheels is no more than 6 inches from the path of the towing vehicle's wheels. Whenever 2 vehicles are connected by a ball-and-socket-type hitch or pintle hook without a locking device, they must also be connected by 2 safety chains of equal length, each safety chain having an ultimate strength at least equal to the gross weight of the towed vehicles. The safety chains must be crossed and connected to the towed and towing vehicle and to the towbar to prevent the towbar from dropping to the ground in the event the towbar fails or becomes disconnected. Safety chains (cross chains) required.[10,11]
Rhode Island	Drawbar or other connection must be of sufficient strength to pull the weight towed, and must not exceed 15 feet in its span from 1 vehicle to the other. A tow truck or any vehicle towing another, except when designed to be in combination, when on any public highway divided into multiple lanes for travel in the same direction, may travel only in the right lane of a 2-lane highway, or the right 2 lanes of a 3 or more lane highway.[2,3]
South Carolina	Drawbar or other connection must be of sufficient strength to pull all weight towed and the must not exceed 15 feet. When a vehicle is towing another vehicle on a public road or highway, the towing vehicle must be attached to the towed vehicle by a safety chain, cable, or equivalent device in addition to the regular drawbar, tongue, trailer hitch, or other connection. The safety connection or attachments must be of sufficient strength to maintain connection of the towed vehicle to the pulling vehicle under all conditions while the towed vehicle is being pulled by the towed vehicle. The provisions of this section do not apply to vehicles using a hitch known as a 5th-wheel and kingpin assembly.[2]
South Dakota	For passenger car trailers, in addition to the regular trailer hitch or coupling device, every trailer that is towed on the public highways at a speed of more than 20 mph must be coupled to the towing vehicle with a safety chain, chains, cables, or an equivalent device. This requirement does not apply to a semitrailer having a connecting device composed of a 5th-wheel and kingpin assembly that meets the requirements of the interstate commerce commission. Valid license required on towed vehicle except implements of husbandry. Safety cables required. Drawbar required. Brakes, turn signals, and rear lights required. Towed vehicle cannot exceed 53 feet.[2,3]

Towing Chart

State	Towing Requirements
Tennessee	Safety chains required. Maximum length cannot exceed 48 feet. Lights, turn signals, and brakes must be connected. Registration of towed vehicle required plus owner's identification card, if home state issues one. Brake hookups required.[2,3]
Texas	Vehicle with unloaded weight of less than 2,500 lbs. may not be coupled with more than 1 other vehicle or towing device at 1 time. A motor vehicle, including a passenger car that has an unloaded weight of 2,500 lbs. or more, may be coupled with a towing device and 1 other vehicle. For passenger car trailers, the drawbar or other connection between a vehicle towing another vehicle and the towed vehicle must be strong enough to pull all the weight towed and must not exceed 15 feet except for the connection between 2 vehicles transporting poles, pipe machinery, or other objects of a structural nature that cannot be readily dismembered. A driver towing another vehicle and using a chain, rope, or cable to connect the vehicles must display on the connection a white flag or cloth not less than 12 inches square. A driver of a passenger car or light truck may not tow a trailer, semitrailer, house trailer, or another motor vehicle unless safety chains of a type approved by the DPS are attached in an approved manner from the trailer, semitrailer, house trailer, or towed motor vehicle to the towing vehicle. Political subdivisions cannot regulate or restrict the use of lighting equipment more than the extent allowed by state and federal law. Requires non-consent towers to maintain at least $50,000 of on-hook cargo insurance per truck.[2]
Utah	Towed vehicle shall be coupled by means of a safety chain, cable or equivalent device, in addition to the regular trailer hitch or coupling. The safety chain or cable shall be securely connected with the chassis of the towing vehicle, the towed vehicle, and the drawbar. The safety chain or cable shall be attached to the trailer drawbar so as to prevent it from dropping to the ground and to ensure that the towed vehicle follows in the course of the towing vehicle in case the vehicles become separated. The requirement for chains or a cable does not apply to a semitrailer having a connecting device composed of a 5th wheel and kingpin assembly, nor to a pole trailer. Whenever the load upon any vehicle extends to the rear 4 feet or more beyond the bed or body of the vehicle there shall be displayed at the extreme rear end of the load, between 1/2 hour after sunset and 1/2 hour before sunrise, 2 red lamps and 2 red reflectors located so as to indicate maximum width and maximum overhang. At all other times, there shall be displayed red flags 12 inches square. A person may not occupy a trailer or semitrailer while it is being drawn by a motor vehicle on a public highway; this does not apply to livestock trailers, a trailer used in a parade, or a trailer or semitrailer used in an agricultural operation. Registration or proof of ownership of towed vehicle required. [2]

Towing Chart

State	Towing Requirements
Vermont	Rigid connection is required. Maximum length is 65 feet.[3,12]
Virginia	Connection between any 2 vehicles must consist of a 5th-wheel drawbar, or other similar device not to exceed 15 feet in length. A safety chain/cable is required. Taillights and brake lights required. Exempts tow trucks towing vehicles by means of a wheel lift apparatus from requirement to have a drawbar and safety chain.[2,13]
Washington	No vehicle towing a trailer may be driven in the left-hand lane of a limited access roadway having 3 or more lanes for traffic moving in 1 direction except when preparing for a left-hand turn. No person may occupy any trailer while it is being moved on a highway, except a person occupying a proper position for steering a trailer to be steered from a rear-end position. A vehicle towing a trailer must use safety chains. The drawbar or other connection between the vehicles in combination must be of sufficient strength to hold the weight of the towed vehicle on any grade where operated. No trailer may whip, weave, or oscillate or fail to follow substantially in the course of the towing vehicle. Special permit required if towed vehicle is not registered. Proof of ownership is required. Towbar required. White flag in the center of a towing chain if chain is over 15 feet long. Not required otherwise. Light hookup required. 20,000 lbs. limit per axle.[2]
West Virginia	Vehicles used in the business of towing must carry a safety chain at all times. The operator of a towing vehicle must not tow a wrecked or disabled vehicle unless a safety chain secures the towed vehicle to the towing vehicle. A drawbar or connection must be of sufficient strength to pull the weight towed and must not exceed 15 feet except when transporting poles, pipe machinery, or other objects of a structural nature that cannot be dismembered. When a vehicle is towing another, and the connection consists of a chain, rope, or cable, a white flag or cloth 12 inches square must be displayed. Bill of sale required. Rear lights and brake lights required.[2]

Towing Chart

State	Towing Requirements
Wisconsin	No vehicle with a load or fixture which extends more than 4 feet beyond the rear of the bed or body of the vehicle may be operated during the hours of darkness unless a red light or lantern, visible from a distance of 500 feet, is displayed on the extreme rear of the load or fixture. A motor vehicle may be towed without being equipped with brakes if the GVW of the towed vehicle is not more than 40% of the GVW of the towing vehicle and the towing vehicle has brakes adequate enough to stop the combination of vehicles. It is unlawful for a single vehicle to tow more than 1 vehicle unless the vehicles are being towed by the drive-away method in saddlemount combination and their overall length does not exceed 65 feet. For passenger car trailers, it is unlawful for any person to operate a motor vehicle towing any mobile home or boat on a trailer when any person is in such mobile home or boat. It is unlawful for any person to operate a motor vehicle towing a 5th-wheel mobile home when any person under the age of 12 is in the 5th-wheel mobile home, unless that person is accompanied by at least 1 person who is at least 16 years old. It is unlawful to operate a motor vehicle towing a 5th-wheel mobile home while passengers are in the 5th-wheel mobile home unless there is a 2-way communication device capable of providing voice communications between the operator of the motor vehicle and the occupants of the mobile home. The drawbar or other connection between the 2 vehicles may not exceed 12 feet in length. In addition to the hitch, every towed vehicle must be coupled to the towing vehicle by means of safety chains, leveling bars, or cables. This provision does not apply to a vehicle equipped with a 5th-wheel and kingpin assembly.[2,3]
Wyoming	None.[14]
Canada	
Alberta	Registration of towed vehicle required; proof of ownership required; drawbar required.[2,15]
British Columbia	Towbar or other connection: maximum length 5 meters. Brake hook-up not required when trailer weight less than 1,400 kg. When the in-tow vehicle weighs more that 4,200 lbs., the unit must have a functional safety breakaway brake on the attachment.[2]
Manitoba	Towed vehicles must have a driver or be equipped with an adequate towing device (tow dolly, drawbar, lift arm) which compels it to remain in the course of the towing vehicle. Distance shall not exceed 5 meters. Towed vehicle must have functional brakes when not connected to towbar.[2]
New Brunswick	Drawbar required (maximum length 4.5 meters). Where connection consists of chain, rope, or cable, white flag 30 meters square must be displayed.[2]
Newfoundland	Special permit required if towed vehicle not registered.[2]
Northwest Territories	None.[2]

Towing Chart

State	Towing Requirements
Nova Scotia	Drawbar/towbar not required, but where used maximum length of 4.6 meters. Where connection consists of chain, rope, or cable, safety chains are required. All lights must function on rear of towed vehicles. Tow dollies require trailer plates unless towed by vehicle plated in jurisdiction exempting dollies from registration.
Ontario	None.
Prince Edward Island	Registration of towed vehicle not required. Safety chains required. Towbar required (maximum length 3.66 meters or 12 feet). Light hookup is required. Towing behind pickup camper/motor home is permitted.
Quebec	Drawbar or other connections required towing not recommended.[16]
Saskatchewan	Drawbar, towbar, safety chains not required. Registration not required.[2]
Yukon Territory	Must be secured in a manner that if tow hitch breaks, chains must keep towed vehicle tracking. Towbar and safety chains required. Length must not exceed Highway Regulation Limits. Brake lights and turn signals required. Brakes required if GVW exceeds 9,100 kgs.

[1] = Tow dollies/lift arms permitted with license plate.
[2] = Tow dollies/lift arms permitted.
[3] = Reciprocity granted.
[4] = Tow dollies/lift arms permitted, but must comply with trailer requirements.
[5] = Reciprocity granted for registration purposes only.
[6] = Tow dollies/lift arms permitted. Lift arms must have rigid connection.
[7] = Tow dollies/lift arms permitted; drawbar or other connection required.
[8] = Reciprocity granted with Minnesota and Canada.
[9] = Reciprocity granted on trip permits to border states.
[10] = Tow dollies/lift arms permitted provided the combination meets the safety requirements established under Section 4905 of the vehicle code.
[11] = Reciprocity granted except for size limits.
[12] = Tow dollies/lift arms permitted, but registration required.
[13] = Reciprocity granted, except as to towbar, chain, and cable regulations.
[14] = Tow dollies/lift arms permitted. Lights required.
[15] = Reciprocity granted, if motor vehicle insurance is required by the home state.
[16] = Tow dollies/lift arm permitted if meeting regulations and is registered.

Notes

Notes

ASHLAND COMMUNITY COLLEGE

3 3631 1115407 Z

WITHDRAWN